The World Treasury of Love Stories

The World Treasury of
Love Stories

SELECTED AND WITH AN INTRODUCTION BY

Lucy Rosenthal

WITH A FOREWORD BY

Clifton Fadiman

GENERAL EDITOR

Oxford   New York
OXFORD UNIVERSITY PRESS
1995

Oxford University Press

Oxford   New York   Athens   Auckland
Bangkok   Bombay   Calcutta   Cape Town
Dar es Salaam   Delhi   Florence   Hong Kong
Istanbul   Karachi   Kuala Lumpur   Madras
Madrid   Melbourne   Mexico City   Nairobi
Paris   Singapore   Taipei   Tokyo   Toronto

Copyright © 1995 by Lucy Rosenthal

Published by Oxford University Press, Inc.
200 Madison Avenue, New York, New York 10016

Oxford is a registered trademark of Oxford University Press

Library of Congress Cataloging-in-Publication Data

The world treasury of love stories /
selected and with an introduction by Lucy Rosenthal ;
with a foreword by Clifton Fadiman, general editor
p. cm.   Includes index.
ISBN 0-19-509361-5
1. Love—Literary collections.
I. Rosenthal, Lucy.
II. Fadiman, Clifton, 1904–   .
PN6071.L7W67   1995   808.83′85—dc20   94-34849

2 4 6 8 9 7 5 3 1

Printed in the United States of America
on acid-free paper

To Rachel
who was loved

Foreword

THIS VOLUME FORMS ONE of a continuing series of World Treasuries published in cooperation with Book-of-the-Month Club, of which the following have already been published: *The World Treasury of Physics, Astronomy and Mathematics*, edited by Timothy Ferris; *The World Treasury of Modern Religious Thought*; edited by Jaroslav Pelikan; *The World Treasury of Science Fiction*; edited by David Hartwell; and *The World Treasury of Children's Literature*, edited by Clifton Fadiman. Each of these treasuries gathers, from as many literatures as possible, previously published, higher-order writing of our time. Each covers a specific field or genre of general interest to the intelligent reader. Each has been constructed and edited by a recognized authority in the field.

The underlying purpose of the series is to meet the expectations of the thoughtful modern reader, one conscious of the striking change that has taken place in our view of the world. That change has run counter to parochialism. It recognizes the contribution made by thinkers and prose artists of the Orient as well as the Occident, of those who use languages other than English. Hence *World* Treasuries.

Clifton Fadiman
General Editor

August's more than half over;
dove, it's time for peace,
Time to taste the round mountains, the white and green,
and the dusk rose of relationship again,
for the first time, it's time to take off our clothes,
and the fortresses around our eyes, to touch our first fingers,
you and I, like God, across everything.

—Jean Valentine
from "The Summer Was Not Long Enough"

Contents

Contents

Epilogue

Introduction

"WHAT IS THIS THING CALLED LOVE?" the song inquires. The experience of working on this volume—from identifying "love stories" to establishing the criteria for their inclusion—suggests that the area of disagreement is vast. These love stories are as various as lovers themselves—as, in fact, are *people*—and as diverse as the tastes and values driving individual lovers toward each other.

The conversations that occurred in the course of my assembling this collection elicited sometimes fiercely diverging opinions about what a love story is or is not. We, lovers of stories all, seemed to be having our own mini-versions of lovers' quarrels and reconciliations, sparked in some telling way by the stories themselves.

Like their subject matter, the stories cut deep. Touching often uninsulated nerves (of readers as well as characters), the emotions depicted in these stories both plumb depths and scale heights. Rationality often vies with irrationality, and it seems to be up to the lovers themselves, along with whatever forces or influences have molded them, to determine which will give ground. The stories have the capability, moreover, of exposing core values, or in some instances, the absence or inversion of those values. The codes of conduct societies devise to regulate behavior can either dovetail or clash with the instincts ruling individual lovers. These stories, accordingly, vary from a celebration of love as domestic order, friendship, and familial devotion to its exposure as anarchic, an agent of illicit and disruptive passions.

This anthology, whose stories range over cultures and a couple of centuries, was conceived to provide a wonderful selection of love stories showing love in diverse cultural and psychological contexts. The collection's purpose was not to represent the entire tradition of the love story, but to focus on those that seem to speak most directly, in idiom, form, and theme, to our own time, where the language becomes more colloquial, the narrative techniques more flexible (a reflection in part of the growth of the novel as a literary form), and where psychological and social realism provides a predominating frame of reference. These stories exhibit also the contemporary focus on the individual and his or her interior life. They contrast with the decidedly more patterned and ritualized storytelling modes of earlier times, medieval epics, for instance, where the emphasis was largely on the uninterpreted narration of external action and events. Romance, a form that originated in the late middle ages, presents a somewhat different case. As a literary genre, Romance, in its many permutations, was vastly influential in making early narratives more nuanced by explaining the significance of the action and elucidating the motives of the characters. The influence was far-reaching; these early manifestations of narrative, invested with meaning and analysis, made Romance, in fact, a kind of literary forebear of the novel. Even so, the line of descent was long, and literary convention, however varied, still tended to dictate predetermined paths and fixed roles for men and women—accounts of courtly love, including the Arthurian tales of gallant knights and fair ladies, being notable examples.

For the most part, the period covered here is the nineteenth century to the present. But I wanted as well to include two examples of stories central to the literature of love, *The Book of Ruth* from the Hebrew Scriptures and Dante's story of Francesca and Paolo from *The Divine Comedy*, the one a paradigm of filial devotion and the bond between women, the other of adulterous passion.

Most of the stories are by writers of the English-speaking world—for example, the United States, Britain, Ireland, South Africa—with the balance drawn from Latin America, Europe, and Asia.

While the majority of the selections deal with romantic love, the collection is not confined to it. *The Book of Ruth* and Raymond Carver's "Fever," for instance, highlight the love between parents and children. Jewelle Gomez's "Don't Explain" illuminates love as friendship, glowing with the comfort of a figurative hearth—the place where someone waits up for you and where romance may wait in the wings. In Honoré de Balzac's "A Passion in the Desert," the hearth is situated in a desert, the scene of infatuation between a man and a panther, illustrating among other things love's power to domesticate even the most incongruously matched pair. The setting seems also a metaphor for the emotional desert—the quicksand of loneliness—where lovers stumble before finding the oasis (real? or mirage?) of a partner. In José Donoso's "The Walk," a woman who has faded into the loveless woodwork of her family begins to blossom when a small dog enters her life and effects a liberation as mysterious as it is astonishing.

Love's moods vary from the sweep and ferocity of Giovanni Verga's "The Wolf" to the lyric realism of Anton Chekhov's "Lady with the Pet Dog." Yasunari Kawabata's delicately traced *Moon on the Water* seems rarefied next to Gail Godwin's earthy and ironic "My Lover, His Summer Vacation," though both grapple with the theme of lost or unattainable love. The protagonist of Alice Adams's "Sintra" keeps love alive by remembering almost deliberately the acuteness of its torment, while the young couple in Colette's "April," notwithstanding a wrong turn inadvertently taken, remains innocent of such pain.

Among the disparities, strong parallels emerge: Yukio Mishima's "Patriotism" and Isaac Bashevis Singer's "Short Friday" offer similarly powerful treatments of marital fidelity, at the same time that their different approaches—Mishima's depiction of Japanese tradition on the one hand and Singer's account of the European *shtetl*'s rituals on the other—are precisely traceable to the two widely divergent cultures. Isak Dinesen's "The Immortal Story" and Myra Goldberg's "Whistling" shed light, among other things, on love's ripple effect via the technique of telling a story within a story. Along with words and voice, lovers beguile by looks: The cosmetic preoccupation of Nathaniel Hawthorne's "The Birthmark" finds, if not its complement, an echo in V. S. Pritchett's "Blind Love," where the wish to conceal or cure imperfection reveals not only the characters of the lovers but also the stuff, durable or other, each love is made on. In the excerpt from Dante, where Francesca and Paolo "read of Lancelot—how love had overcome him," literature itself becomes implicated in the sparks struck between lovers. Similarly, Gail Godwin's contemporary protagonist in "My Lover, His Summer Vacation," finding literary precedent for her plight in a previous century's novel, conveys her rueful observations in a letter to its author. It's as if love stories themselves serve as love letters, forging links between writers across regions and centuries.

The circumstances of love in these stories encompass such competing emotions, often co-existing within a given relationship, as friendship and enmity, constancy and betrayal, generosity and greed, modesty and arrogance, candor and chicanery. Love's sacrificial qualities, taking the form in some cases of a lover's quixotic willingness to set the other free (Carver), are in other instances matched by the relentless drive for control and conquest (Verga). Courage and cowardice, attributes frequently aroused in the pursuit of love, are etched with particular sharpness in two stories—one Italian, one French—featuring soldiers: Italo Calvino's "Adventure of a Soldier" and Balzac's "A Passion in the Desert." Calvino's young soldier, finding himself in unknown territory, must gather the courage either to advance on his quarry or retreat; similarly, Balzac's soldier must decide whether the wild animal lying beside him is friend or foe. Another battle waged is the one between love and sex—with a happy synthesis sometimes the outcome. And when it isn't, as in the case of Doris Lessing's "One off the Short List," love's absence from the story's equation conjures, paradoxically, its presence, as if love and loathing were mirror images of one another.

As a matter both of theme and craft, the emotions love generates often extend well beyond the private sphere. In John Cheever's "The Country Husband," for example, personal betrayal has its echo in a remembered vignette involving betrayal of country. The narrator of Sandra Cisneros's "Eyes of Zapata," lying beside her lover, reflects how Zapata, so singular in his devotion to the cause of the Mexican Revolution, has betrayed her many times over. In Mishima's "Patriotism," the lovers' fierce sense of duty to their nation becomes virtually interchangeable with their passion for each other. The lovers in Milan Kundera's "The Hitchhiking Game" dissemble in ways that may mirror the dodges and deceits made necessary in the climate of Czechoslovakia as a police state during the Cold War.

The course of love (true or otherwise) in these stories does not, as the saying goes, run smooth; it is an obstacle course. Lovers must clear hurdles to realize their ideal of love, just as they must labor to come to terms with its failure. In John Updike's "Separation," the devoutly wished-for consummation seems to be the split-up itself. In the contemporary stories, the obstacles to love tend to be internal, spun by lovers themselves from their own psyches. In Kundera's "The Hitchhiking Game," for example, role-playing also serves as a method the lovers devise to put distance between themselves and intimacy. In Pritchett's "Blind Love," the barrier seemingly presented by a cosmetic flaw may be a way to avoid exposing deeper scars of the spirit.

However magical, allegorical, or mystical these stories' methods may be, their portrayal of love is, almost without exception, realistic. The characters may idealize love, but their authors are far more knowing. The expertise here has to do with each writer's unique insight into a confounding human emotion, and the memorable rendering of it on the page.

At the same time, the stories show that in the face of love's unpredictability, the likelihood is that we are, none of us, experts. We are all, in the true sense of the word, amateurs.

But one thing seems overridingly clear. A love story isn't just a story. It's the whole story.

The World Treasury of Love Stories

ALICE ADAMS
(1926–)

ALICE ADAMS, born in Fredericksburg, Virginia, has lived for more than forty years in San Francisco; the Bay Area is one of the chief settings of her work. Her numerous awards, over a writing career spanning more than twenty-five years, include a National Endowment for the Arts fiction grant in 1976 and a Guggenheim Fellowship in 1978–79. Among her story collections are *Beautiful Girl* (1979), *To See You Again* (1982), and *Return Trips* (1985). Her novels include *Careless Love* (1966), *Families and Survivors* (1975), *Listening to Billie* (1978), and *Superior Women* (1984).

Her work—the short stories in particular—characteristically mixes irony with compassion. The emotion underlying her tales may seem banked, initially, by an ironic edge and an ostensibly reportorial style. This surface, however, is supported by an emotional fullness infused with the author's intelligence, accuracy of observation, and unsentimental empathy for her characters.

In "Sintra" (1984), Arden, accompanied by her current lover, Gregor, visits Portugal, the native country of an earlier lover, Luiz. "Theirs," she recalls, "was an adversary passion, almost fatal." At the same time, we're told, Luiz may be dying, may already be dead. The crosscurrents of her indelible feelings for Luiz begin to supersede her feelings for Gregor. A drive to Sintra in a violent storm tears the underpinnings from what Arden and Gregor, together and separately, call love. In exposing what Arden has called the adversariness of passion, the story as it unfolds may be sounding notes of the death of love itself.

Sintra

In Lisbon, Portugal, on a brilliant October Sunday morning, an American woman, a tourist, experiences a sudden rush of happiness, as clear and pure as the sunshine that warms the small flowers near her feet. She is standing in the garden of the Castel San Jorgio, and the view before her includes a great spread of the city: the river and its estuary, the shining new bridge; she can see for miles!

Her name is Arden Kinnell, and she is a journalist, a political-literary critic, sometimes writing on films; she survives somewhat precariously, although recently she has begun to enjoy a small success. Tall and thin, Arden is a little awkward,

3

shy, and her short blond hair is flimsy, rather childlike. Her face is odd, but striking in its oddity: such wide-spaced, staring, yellow-green eyes, such a wide, clearly sensual mouth. And now she is smiling, out of sheer pleasure at this moment.

Arden and her lover-companion—Gregor, the slightly rumpled young man at her side—arrived the night before from Paris, and they slept long and well, after only a little too much wine at their hotel. Healthy Californians, they both liked the long, rather steep walk up those winding, cobbled streets, through the picturesquely crumbling, red-tile roofed old quarter, the Alfama, up to this castle, this view of everything. Arden is especially struck by the sight of the distant, lovely bridge, which she has read was dedicated to the revolution of April 1974, the so-called Generals' Revolution that ended fascism in Portugal.

The air is so good, so fresh and clear! Breathing in, Arden thinks, Ah, Lisbon, how beautiful it is. She thinks, I must tell Luiz how much I like his city.

Madness: in that demented instant she has forgotten that at a recent party in San Francisco a woman told her that Luiz was dying (was "terminal," as she put it). Here in Lisbon. Now.

And even stranger than that friendly thought of Luiz, whom she once loved wildly, desperately, entirely—dear God, friends is the last thing they were; theirs was an adversary passion, almost fatal—stranger than the friendly impulse is the fact that it persists, in Arden, generally a most disciplined woman; her mind is—usually—strong and clear, her habits of work exemplary. However, *insanely*, there in Lisbon, that morning, as she continues to admire and to enjoy the marvelous sweep of city roofs, the graceful bridge above the shining water, she even feels the presence of Luiz, and happily; that is the incredible part. Luiz, with whom she experienced the wildest reaches of joy, but never the daily, sunny warmth of happiness.

Can Luiz possibly just that day have died? Can this lively blue Portuguese air be giving her that message, and thus causing her to rejoice? Quickly she decides against this: Luiz is not dead, he cannot be—although a long time ago she surely wished him dead, believing as she then did that only his death could release her from the brutal pain of his absence in her life.

Or, could the woman at the San Francisco party (a woman whom she did not like at all, Arden now remembers—so small and tautly chic), could that woman have been mistaken? Some other Luiz V. was dying in Lisbon? But that was unlikely; the woman clearly meant the person that Arden knew, or had known—the rich and well-connected, good but not very famous painter. The portraitist.

Then, possibly Luiz was ill but has recovered? A remission, or possibly a misdiagnosis in the first place? Everyone knows that doctors make such mistakes; they are often wrong.

Arden decides that Luiz indeed is well; he is well and somewhere relatively nearby, in some house or apartment that she can at least distantly see from where she is standing, near the crenellated battlements of the castle, on the sun-warmed yellow gravel. She looks back down into the Alfama, where Luiz might be.

Gregor, the young lover—only five years younger than Arden, actually—Gregor, a photographer, "knows" about Luiz. Friends before they became lovers (a change in status that more than once has struck Arden as an error), in those days Arden and Gregor exchanged life stories, finding that they shared a propensity for romantic disaster—along with their similarly precarious free-lance professions. (And surely there is some connection? Both she and Gregor take romantic as well as economic risks?)

"Can you imagine a woman dumb enough to believe that a Portuguese Catholic would leave his wife and children just for her?" Arden asked, in the wry mode that had become a useful second nature to her. "Oh, how stupid I was!" she lamentingly laughed. And Gregor countered with his own sad love adventure; she was a model, Lisa. "Well, can you imagine a photographer who wouldn't know not to take up with a model?" This was when Gregor, just out of art school, was trying to get a start in New York; Lisa, though younger than he, was already doing quite well. But Lisa's enchanting liveliness, and her wit, as well as her lovely thin body, turned out to be coke-maintained. "No one then was doing anything but plain old dope and a little acid," was Gregor's comment. "I have to hand it to her, she was really ahead of her time. But *crazy*."

Gregor too can be wry, or does he imitate Arden? She sometimes has an alarmed sense that he sounds like her, or tries to. But he is fun to talk to, still, and often funny. And he is smart, and sexy. Tall and light-haired, he is not handsome but very attractive, with his huge pale Russian eyes, his big confident body. A good photographer; in fact, he is excellent.

At moments, though, Arden feels a cold enmity from Gregor, which is when she wishes that they were still "just friends." And is he an alcoholic, really? He drinks too much, too often. And does he love her?

Oh, *love*, Arden thinks. How can I even use that word.

Gregor and Arden do not in fact live together, and although she sometimes tells friends that she considers this an ideal arrangement, often she actually does not. Her own house in Larkspur is small, but hardly too small for two, and it is pleasantly situated on a wooded knoll, no other houses in sight. There is a pool, and what Arden considers her recreational garden, an eccentric plot all crowded with squash and nasturtiums and various lettuces. Gregor spends much of his time there with her—he likes to swim, although gardening does not interest him—but he also keeps a small place of his own on a rather bleak street near Twin Peaks, in San Francisco, high up in the fog and winds. And his apartment itself is bleak: three small rooms, monastically clean and plain and white. There is also a darkroom, of course, where he often works late at night. No personal traces anywhere, no comfortable mess. Forbidding. Arden has been there only twice. Even when they are in the city it always seems better to drive on back to Larkspur, after the movie or concert, whatever. But Arden thinks of him there, in those rooms, on the nights that he stays in town, and her thoughts are uneasy. Not only the existence of that apartment, an alternative to her house, as well as to herself, but its character is threatening to Arden, reminding her of aspects of Gregor himself: a sensed interior coldness, an implacable emptiness. When she thinks of Gregor's house she could be imagining an enemy.

She has never seen any food around, for instance: does he only drink there, alone, in his white, white rooms? She does not imagine that he sees other women, but certainly he could. He could go out to bars, bring women home. This, though, seems less likely, and therefore possibly less threatening than just drinking alone, so grimly.

At the end of Arden's love affair with Luiz there were hints in local gossip columns that he had a "somewhat less than professional relationship" with a few of the subjects of his portraits, and the pain of this information (explaining so much! so plausible!) was a further unbearable thrust to Arden.

In any case, since Gregor knows about Luiz, including the fact of Lisbon, home of Luiz (but not the possible mortal illness; Arden has not been able or perhaps not seen fit to mention this), does Gregor think it strange that so far in Lisbon Arden has not mentioned Luiz, whom she used sometimes to talk about? Here she has not once said his name, in any context. She herself does not quite know why she has not.

Still, just now she is happy, looking down to small balconies of flowers, of vines that climb up on intricate iron grillwork. She wonders: Possibly, is that where Luiz lives, that especially handsome, long-windowed apartment? With the dark gray drapery?

Arden is happy and well and suddenly very hungry. She says to Gregor, "Isn't that a restaurant over there? Shouldn't we try it? It looks nice, and I can't bear to leave this view."

"Well, sure." Gregor's look in Arden's direction is slightly puzzled—as well it might be, Arden thinks. She too is puzzled, very. She loves Lisbon, though, and her blood races dizzily.

They go into the restaurant; they are quickly seated at a white-clothed table, with the glorious Lisbon view.

"Had you ever, uh, heard about this place before?" asks Gregor, once their wine has come. This is his closest—if oblique—reference to Luiz, who surely might have mentioned to Arden a favorite restaurant, with its marvelous view. But as though realizing what he has done Gregor then covers up. "Or did you read about it somewhere? a restaurant guide?"

"No, actually not. It just looked good. The doors—" The front door is of heavy glass, crossed with pitted, old-looking iron bars. "An interesting use of glass, don't you think?"

"Yes," says Gregor.

They regard one another suspiciously.

Remembering Luiz, Arden sees flat smooth black hair, that shines, in bedside lamplight. She watches him as he dresses, while she lies there spent and languid; she watches everything shining, his hair and his bright black eyes, their dark glitter. He comes over to kiss her good-bye, for that day, and then he cannot, does not leave.

"This is an illness, this endless craving that I have for you. A mania—" Luiz more than once remarked, with an accuracy that Arden could not then admit to herself. She did not feel ill, only that all her nerves had been touched, involved.

Luiz is (or was) an excellent portraitist. His paintings were both elegant and penetrating, often less than flattering; on the other hand, on occasion, very flattering indeed. He was at his best with women (well, of course he was, Arden has thought). Once she went to an exhibit of his paintings at a Sutter Street gallery— though not, naturally, to the opening, a social event much reported in the papers.

In fact they first met at a gallery opening. From across the room Luiz found Arden (that is how he put it, "I *found* you there"), coming over to talk to her intently for a while (about what? later she could never remember). He called the next day; he called and called, he would not be put off.

This was in the early sixties. Arden, then much involved in the peace movement, saw his assault on her life as an incursion, an invasion. He attacked with superior weapons, and with the violence of his passion for her. And he won. "I think that you have fallen in love with my love for you," he once (again accurately) remarked.

Out of her depth, and dismayed by everything about Luiz—the wife and family at home in Portugal, a Fascist country—Arden found some small comfort in the fact that all his favorite writers seemed to be of the left: Silone, Camus—and that his favorite movie director was Pasolini.

She pointed this out, rather shyly—the shyness of an essentially defeated person.

"My darling, I have a horror of the right, of *fascisme*." (But in much the same tone he also said, "I have a horror of *fat*," as he stroked her thin thigh, then cupped the sharp crest with his wise and skillful hand.)

You could simply look at his eyes, or his mouth, Arden thinks now, and know that Luiz was remarkable.

She remembers his walk. The marvelous confidence in that stride. During all the weeks of suffering so acutely from his absence in her life (classically, Luiz did not get the promised divorce, nor did he defect from the Fascist government he railed against; he went back to Lisbon, to his wife, to that regime)—during all that time of suffering, it was the thought of his walk that caused Arden the most piercing pain: that singular, energetic motion of his body, its course through the world, without her.

After lunch, much more slowly than earlier they had climbed the streets, Arden and Gregor start down. The day is still glorious; at one point they stop at a small terrace where there are rounded cypresses, very small, and a lovely wall of soft blue tiles, in an intricate, fanciful design—and a large and most beautiful view of sky and majestic, glossy white clouds, above the shimmering water of the sea. From this distance the commemorative suspension bridge is a graceful sculpture; catching the sunlight, it shines.

Arden is experiencing some exceptional, acute alertness; as though layers of skin had peeled away, all her senses are opened wide. She sees, in a way that she never has before. She feels all the gorgeous day, the air, and the city spread below her.

She hardly thinks of Gregor, at her side, and this is something of a relief; too often he is a worrying preoccupation for her.

Their plan for the afternoon has been to go back to their hotel, where they have left a rental car, and to drive north to Cascais, Estoril, and Sintra. And that is what they now proceed to do, not bothering to go into the hotel but just taking their car, a small white Ford Escort, and heading north.

As they reach the outskirts of the city, a strange area of new condominiums, old shacks, and some lovely, untouched woods—just then, more quickly than seemed possible, the billowing clouds turn black, a strong wind comes up, and in another minute a violent rainstorm has begun, rains lashing at the windshield, water sweeping across the highway.

Arden and Gregor exchange excited grins: an adventure. She thinks, Oh, good, we are getting along, after all.

"Maybe we should just go to Sintra, though," he says, a little later. "Not too much point in looking at beach resorts?"

Yielding to wisdom, Arden still feels a certain regret. *Cascais*. She can hear Luiz saying the word, and *Estoril*, with the sibilant Portuguese s's. But she can also hear him saying *Sintra*, and she says it over to herself, in his voice.

A little later, looking over at her, Gregor asks, "Are you okay? You look sort of funny."

"How, funny?"

"*Odd*. You look odd. And your nose. It's so, uh, pink."

Surprising them both, and especially herself, Arden laughs. "Noses are supposed to be pink," she tells him.

Normally, what Arden thinks of as Gregor's lenslike observations make her nervous; they make her feel unattractive, and unloved. But today—here in Portugal!—her strange happiness separates her like a wall, or a moat, from possible slights, and she thinks, How queer that Gregor should even notice the color of my nose, in a driving rainstorm—here, north of Lisbon, near Sintra. As, in her mind, she hears the deep, familiar, never-forgotten voice of Luiz saying, "I adore your face! Do you *know* how I adore it? How lovely you are?" She hears Luiz, she sees him.

Then quite suddenly, as suddenly as it began the storm is over. The sky is brilliantly blue again, and the clouds are white, as Arden thinks, No wonder Luiz is more than a little erratic—it's the weather. And she smiles to herself. Suppose she sent him a postcard from Lisbon? *Ego absolvo te.* Love, Arden.

Would he laugh and think fondly of her, for a moment? *Is* he dying?

In Sintra they drive past a small town square, with a huge, rather forbidding municipal building, some small stores. The wet stone pavement is strewn with fallen wet yellow leaves. They start up a narrow road, past gates and driveways that lead to just-not-visible mansions, small towered castles. (The sort of places that Luiz might visit, or own, for weekends, elegant parties.) As they climb up and up in the small white car, on either side of the road the woods become thicker, wilder, more densely and violently green—everything green, every shape and shade of green, all rain-wet, all urgently growing. And giant rocks, great dead trees lying beside them. Ferns, enormously sprouting. Arden is holding her breath, forgetting to breathe. It is crazy with green, she thinks, crazy growth, so old and strong, ancient, endless and wild, ferocious. Like Luiz. Like Portugal, dying.

Gregor is making some odd maneuver with the car; is he turning around, midroad? Trying to park, among so many giant rocks, heavy trees, and brilliant, dripping leaves?

In any case he has stopped the car. On a near hill Arden can see the broken ruins of a castle, jagged black fragments of stone, and in the sky big clouds are blackening again.

Willing calm (though still having trouble with her breath), Arden says, "I think it's going to rain again."

Huge-eyed, pale, Gregor is staring across at her. He says, "You cut me out—all the way! You might as well be here alone!"

He is right, of course; she is doing just that, pretending he is not there. So unfair—but his staring eyes are so light, so *blue*. Arden says, "I'm sorry, really—" but she can feel her voice getting away from her, can feel tears.

Gregor shouts, "I don't know why we came here! Why Portugal? What did you expect? You could have just come by yourself!"

But Arden can hardly hear him. The rain has indeed begun again; it is pelting like bullets against the glass, and wind is bending down all the trees, flattening leaves.

And suddenly in those moments Arden has understood that Luiz is dead—and that she will never again feel for anyone what she felt for him. Which, even though she does not want to—she would never choose to feel so much again—still, it seems a considerable loss.

In fact, though, at that particular time, the hour of that passionate October storm (while Arden quarreled with Gregor), Luiz is still alive, although probably "terminal." And she learns of his death only the following spring, and then more or less by accident: she is in Washington, D.C., for some meetings having to do with grants for small magazines and presses, and in a hasty scanning of the *Post* she happens to glance at a column headed "Deaths Elsewhere."

Luiz— —V. (There were two intervening names that Arden has not known about.) Luiz V. had died a few days earlier in Lisbon, the cause of death not reported. Famous portraitist, known for satire, and also (this is quite as surprising to Arden as the unfamiliar names)—"one of the leading intellectuals in Lisbon to voice strong public support for the armed forces coup in April 1974 that ended half a century of right-wing dictatorship."

Curiously—years back she would not have believed this possible, ever—that day Arden is too busy with her meetings to think about this fact: Luiz dead. No longer someone she might possibly see again, by accident in an airport, or somewhere. No longer someone possibly to send a postcard to.

That day she is simply too busy, too harried, really, with so many people to see, and with getting back and forth from her hotel to her meetings, through the strange, unseasonable snow that has just begun, relentlessly, to fall. She thinks of the death of Luiz, but she does not absorb it.

That quarrel with Gregor in Sintra, which prolonged itself over the stormy drive back to Lisbon, and arose, refueled, over dinner and too much wine—that quarrel was not final between them, although Arden has sometimes thought that it should have been. They continue to see each other, Arden and Gregor, in California, but considerably less often than they used to. They do not quarrel; it is as though they were no longer sufficiently intimate to fight, as though they both knew that any altercation would indeed be final.

Arden rather thinks, or suspects, that Gregor sees other women, during some of their increasing times apart. She imagines that he is more or less actively looking for her replacement. Which, curiously, she is content to let him do.

She herself has not been looking. In fact lately Arden has been uncharacteristically wary in her dealings with men. In her work she is closely allied with a lot of men, who often become good friends, her colleagues and companions. However, recently she has rather forcibly discouraged any shifts in these connections; she has chosen to ignore or to put down any possible romantic overtones. She spends time with women friends, goes out to dinner with women, takes small trips. She is quite good at friendship, has been Arden's conclusion, or one of them. Her judgment as to lovers seems rather poor. And come to think of it her own behavior in that area is not always very good. Certainly her strangeness, her removal in Lisbon, in Sintra, was quite enough to provoke a sensitive man, which Gregor undoubtedly is.

On that night, the night of reading the news item (Deaths Elsewhere) containing the death of Luiz—that night Arden is supposed to meet a group of friends in a Georgetown restaurant. At eight. In character, she gets there a little early, and is told that she will be seated as soon as her friends arrive; would she like to wait in the bar?

She would not, especially, but she does so anyway, going into a dark, paneled room, of surpassing anonymity, and seating herself in a shadowed corner from which new arrivals in the restaurant are visible. She orders a Scotch, and then wonders why; it is not her usual drink, she has not drunk Scotch for years.

By eight-ten she has begun to wonder if perhaps she confused the name of the restaurant. It was she who made the reservation, and her friends could have gone to some other place, with a similar French name. These friends like herself are always reliably on time, even in snow, strange weather.

The problem of what to do next seems almost intolerable, suddenly—and ridiculously: Arden has surely coped with more serious emergencies. But: should she try to get a cab, which at this crowded dinner hour, in the snow, would be difficult? And if she did where would she go?

In the meantime, at eight-twenty, she orders another drink, and she begins to think about the item in the paper. About Luiz.

Odd, she casually thinks, at first, that she should have "adored" a man—have planned to marry a man whose full name she did not know. And much more odd, she thinks, that he should have publicly favored the '74 revolution, the end of dictatorship. Opportunism, possibly, Arden first thinks. On the other hand, is she being unfair, unnecessarily harsh? He did always describe himself as anti-Fascist. And perhaps that was true?

Perhaps everything he said to her was true?

Arden has finished her second drink. It is clear that her friends will not come; they have gone somewhere else by mistake, and she must decide what to do. But still she sits there, as though transfixed, and she is transfixed, by a sudden nameless pain. Nameless, but linked to loss: loss of Luiz, even, imminently, of Gregor. Perhaps of love itself.

Understanding some of this, in a hurried, determined way Arden gets to her feet and summons the bill from her waiter. She has decided that she will go back to her hotel and order a sandwich in her room. Strange that she didn't think of that before. Of course she will eventually get a cab, even in the steadily falling, unpredicted snow.

HONORÉ DE BALZAC
(1799–1850)

HONORÉ DE BALZAC was born in Tours, France, and attended a grammar school there; later, he went to a boarding school at Vendôme. In 1816 he began the study of law at the Sorbonne but, after receiving his degree in 1819, decided to pursue literature rather than the law. His literary career began with formula novels published pseudonymously. His first successful novel, *Les Chouans,* was published in 1829; in 1831 he published *Le Peau de Chagrin.* Between 1827 and 1847 he produced the work for which he is most celebrated, a series of 91 stories and novels with the overall title "La Comédie humaine." It was the product of scrupulous research, intended to give a precise account of the full range of French life at the turn of the century, and cutting across all classes and professions. The major novels of "La Comédie humaine" are *Louis Lambert* (1832,), *Eugénie Grandet* (1833), *La Recherche de l'absolu* (1834), *Le Père Goriot* (1835), *Les Illusions perdues* (1837), *César Birotteau* (1837), *La Cousine Bette* (1847), and *Le Cousin Pons* (1847). Balzac's dedication to accuracy notwithstanding, exaggeration of effects and extreme situations was characteristic of his portraits. Along with the novels, his short stories—which often transcend realism as well—are viewed as masterly. In his *From a Writer's Notebook* (Dutton: New York, 1958, p. 15), Van Wyck Brooks wrote of Balzac: "One has to be interested in England to enjoy Trollope, but to enjoy Balzac all one needs is to be interested in life."

"A Passion in the Desert" (1832) is a parable of love's taming. A Frenchman from Provence, taken prisoner in the desert, manages to escape only to find himself alone in the desert's infinite, shimmering expanse. The need to break his solitude is so profound that he "threw his arms around the trunk of one of the palm trees, as though it were the body of a friend." After many days he awakens to find a panther, its muzzle bloodied with a meal just consumed, sleeping beside him. The beast and the fear it engenders is emblematic of love's wildness and ferocity—its undertow, perhaps, of betrayal. The unfolding passion between man and beast seems to encompass love's ecstatic play of sense and spirit, along with its potential for tragedy. Thus the story, apparently an account of an idiosyncratic love, illuminates much more universal experience.

A Passion in the Desert

"The whole show is dreadful," she cried, coming out of the menagerie of M. Martin. She had just been looking at that daring speculator "working with his hyena"—to speak in the style of the program.

"By what means," she continued, "can he have tamed these animals to such a point as to be certain of their affection for—."

"What seems to you a problem," said I, interrupting, "is really quite natural."

"Oh!" she cried, letting an incredulous smile wander over her lips.

"You think that beasts are wholly without passions?" I asked her. "Quite the reverse; we can communicate to them all the vices arising in our own state of civilization."

She looked at me with an air of astonishment.

"Nevertheless," I continued, "the first time I saw M. Martin, I admit, like you, I did give vent to an exclamation of surprise. I found myself next to an old soldier with the right leg amputated, who had come in with me. His face had struck me. He had one of those intrepid heads, stamped with the seal of warfare, and on which the battles of Napoleon are written. Besides, he had that frank good-humored expression which always impresses me favorably. He was without doubt one of those troopers who are surprised at nothing, who find matter for laughter in the contortions of a dying comrade, who bury or plunder him quite light-heartedly, who stand intrepidly in the way of bullets; in fact, one of those men who waste no time in deliberation, and would not hesitate to make friends with the devil himself. After looking very attentively at the proprietor of the menagerie getting out of his box, my companion pursed up his lips with an air of mockery and contempt, with that peculiar and expressive twist which superior people assume to show they are not taken in. Then when I was expiating on the courage of M. Martin, he smiled, shook his head knowingly, and said, 'Well known.'

"How 'well known'?" I said. "If you would only explain to me the mystery I should be vastly obliged."

"After a few minutes, during which we made acquaintance, we went to dine at the first *restaurateur's* whose shop caught our eye. At dessert a bottle of champagne completely refreshed and brightened up the memories of this odd old soldier. He told me his story, and I said he had every reason to exclaim, 'Well known.' "

When she got home, she teased me to that extent and made so many promises, that I consented to communicate to her the old soldier's confidences. Next day she received the following episode of an epic which one might call "The Frenchman in Egypt."

During the expedition in Upper Egypt under General Desaix, a Provençal soldier fell into the hands of the Mangrabins, and was taken by these Arabs into the deserts beyond the falls of the Nile.

In order to place a sufficient distance between themselves and the French army, the Mangrabins made forced marches, and only rested during the night. They camped round a well overshadowed by palm trees under which they had previously concealed a store of provisions. Not surmising that the notion of flight would occur to their prisoner, they contented themselves with binding his hands, and after eating a few dates, and giving provender to their horses, went to sleep.

When the brave Provençal saw that his enemies were no longer watching him, he made use of his teeth to steal a scimitar, fixed the blade between his knees, and cut the cords which prevented using his hands; in a moment he was free. He at once seized a rifle and dagger, then taking the precaution to provide himself with a sack of dried dates, oats, and powder and shot, and to fasten a scimitar to his waist he leaped onto a horse, and spurred on vigorously in the direction where he thought to find the French army. So impatient was he to see a bivouac again that he pressed on the already tired courser at such speed that its flanks were lacerated with his spurs, and at last the poor animal died, leaving the Frenchman alone in the desert. After walking some time in the sand with all the courage of an escaped convict, the soldier was obliged to stop, as the day had already ended. In spite of the beauty of an oriental sky at night, he felt he had not strength enough to go on. Fortunately he had been able to find a small hill, on the summit of which a few palm trees shot up into the air; it was their verdure seen from afar which had brought hope and consolation to his heart. His fatigue was so great that he lay down upon a rock of granite, capriciously cut out like a camp-bed; there he fell asleep without taking any precaution to defend himself while he slept. He had made the sacrifice of his life. His last thought was one of regret. He repented having left the Mangrabins, whose nomad life seemed to smile on him now that he was afar from them and without help. He was awakened by the sun, whose pitiless rays fell with all their force on the granite and produced an intolerable heat—for he had had the stupidity to place himself inversely to the shadow thrown by the verdant majestic heads of the palm trees. He looked at the solitary trees and shuddered—they reminded him of the graceful shafts crowned with foliage which characterize the Saracen columns in the cathedral of Arles.

But when, after counting the palm trees, he cast his eye around him, the most horrible despair was infused into his soul. Before him stretched an ocean without limit. The dark sand of the desert spread farther than sight could reach in every direction, and glittered like steel struck with a bright light. It might have been a sea of looking-glass, or lakes melted together in a mirror. A fiery vapor carried up in streaks made a perpetual whirlwind over the quivering land. The sky was lit with an oriental splendor of insupportable purity, leaving naught for the imagination to desire. Heaven and earth were on fire.

The silence was awful in its wild and terrible majesty. Infinity, immensity, closed in upon the soul from every side. Not a cloud in the sky, not a breath in the air, not a flaw on the bosom of the sand, ever moving in diminutive waves; the horizon ended as at sea on a clear day, with one line of light, definite as the cut of a sword.

The Provençal threw his arms around the trunk of one of the palm trees, as though it were the body of a friend, and then in the shelter of the thin straight shadow that the palm cast upon the granite, he wept. Then sitting down he remained as he was, contemplating with profound sadness the implacable scene, which was all he had to look upon. He cried aloud, to measure the solitude. His voice, lost in the hollows of the hill, sounded faintly, and aroused no echo—the echo was in his own heart. The Provençal was twenty-two years old;—he loaded his carbine.

"There'll be time enough," he said to himself, laying on the ground the weapon which alone could bring him deliverance.

Looking by turns at the black expanse and the blue expanse, the soldier dreamed of France—he smelt with delight the gutters of Paris—he remembered the towns through which he had passed, the faces of his fellow-soldiers, the most minute details of his life. His southern fancy soon showed him the stones of his beloved Provence, in the play of the heat which waved over the spread sheet of the desert. Fearing the danger of this cruel mirage, he went down the opposite side of the hill to that by which he had come up the day before. The remains of a rug showed that this place of refuge had at one time been inhabited; at a short distance he saw some palm trees full of dates. Then the instinct which binds us to life awoke again in his heart. He hoped to live long enough to await the passing of some Arabs, or perhaps he might hear the sound of cannon; for at this time Bonaparte was traversing Egypt.

This thought gave him new life. The palm tree seemed to bend with the weight of the ripe fruit. He shook some of it down. When he tasted this unhoped-for manna, he felt sure that the palms had been cultivated by a former inhabitant—the savory, fresh meat of the dates was proof of the care of his predecessor. He passed suddenly from dark despair to an almost insane joy. He went up again to the top of the hill, and spent the rest of the day in cutting down one of the sterile palm trees, which the night before had served him for shelter. A vague memory made him think of the animals of the desert; and in case they might come to drink at the spring, visible from the base of the rocks but lost farther down, he resolved to guard himself from their visits by placing a barrier at the entrance of his hermitage.

In spite of his diligence, and the strength which the fear of being devoured asleep gave him, he was unable to cut the palm in pieces, though he succeeded in cutting it down. At eventide the king of the desert fell; the sound of its fall resounded far and wide, like a sign in the solitude; the soldier shuddered as though he had heard some voice predicting woe.

But like an heir who does not long bewail a deceased parent, he tore off from this beautiful tree the tall broad green leaves which are its poetic adornment, and used them to mend the mat on which he was to sleep.

Fatigued by the heat and his work, he fell asleep under the red curtains of his wet cave.

In the middle of the night his sleep was troubled by an extraordinary noise; he sat up, and the deep silence around him allowed him to distinguish the alternative accents of a respiration whose savage energy could not belong to a human creature.

A profound terror, increased still further by the darkness, the silence, and his waking images, froze his heart within him. He almost felt his hair stand on end, when by straining his eyes to their utmost he perceived through the shadows two faint yellow lights. At first he attributed these lights to the reflection of his own pupils, but soon the vivid brilliance of the night aided him gradually to distinguish the objects around him in the cave, and he beheld a huge animal lying but two steps from him. Was it a lion, a tiger, or a crocodile?

The Provençal was not educated enough to know under what species his enemy ought to be classed; but his fright was all the greater, as his ignorance led him to imagine all terrors at once; he endured a cruel torture, noting every variation of the breathing close to him without daring to make the slightest movement. An odor, pungent like that of a fox, but more penetrating, profounder—so to speak—filled the cave, and when the Provençal became sensible of this, his terror reached its height, for he could not longer doubt the proximity of a terrible companion, whose royal dwelling served him for shelter.

Presently the reflection of the moon, descending on the horizon, lit up the den, rendering gradually visible and resplendent the spotted skin of a panther.

This lion of Egypt slept, curled up like a big dog, the peaceful possessor of a sumptuous niche at the gate of an hotel; its eyes opened for a moment and closed again; its face was turned toward the man. A thousand confused thoughts passed through the Frenchman's mind; first he thought of killing it with a bullet from his gun, but he saw there was not enough distance between them for him to take proper aim—the shot would miss the mark. And if it were to wake!—the thought made his limbs rigid. He listened to his own heart beating in the midst of the silence, and cursed the too violent pulsations which the flow of blood brought on, fearing to disturb that sleep which allowed him time to think of some means of escape.

Twice he placed his hand on his scimitar, intending to cut off the head of his enemy; but the difficulty of cutting the stiff, short hair compelled him to abandon this daring project. To miss would be to die for *certain*, he thought; he preferred the chances of fair fight, and made up his mind to wait till morning; the morning did not leave him long to wait.

He could now examine the panther at ease; its muzzle was smeared with blood.

"She's had a good dinner," he thought, without troubling himself as to whether her feast might have been on human flesh. "She won't be hungry when she gets up."

It was a female. The fur on her belly and flanks was glistening white; many small marks like velvet formed beautiful bracelets round her feet; her sinuous tail was also white, ending with black rings; the overpart of her dress, yellow like unburnished gold, very lissom and soft, had the characteristic blotches in the form of rosettes, which distinguish the panther from every other feline species.

This tranquil and formidable hostess snored in an attitude as graceful as that of a cat lying on a cushion. Her blood-stained paws, nervous and well-armed, were stretched out before her face, which rested upon them, and from which radiated her straight, slender whiskers, like threads of silver.

If she had been like that in a cage, the Provençal would doubtless have admired the grace of the animal, and the vigorous contrasts of vivid color which gave her robe an imperial splendor; but just then his sight was troubled by her sinister appearance.

The presence of the panther, even asleep, could not fail to produce the effect which the magnetic eyes of the serpent are said to have on the nightingale.

For a moment the courage of the soldier began to fail before this danger, though no doubt it would have risen at the mouth of a cannon charged with shell. Nevertheless, a bold thought brought daylight to his soul and sealed up the source of the cold sweat which sprang forth on his brow. Like men driven to bay who defy death and offer their body to the smiter, so he, seeing in this merely a tragic episode, resolved to play his part with honor to the last.

"The day before yesterday the Arabs would have killed me perhaps," he said; so considering himself as good as dead already, he waited bravely, with excited curiosity, his enemy's awakening.

When the sun appeared, the panther suddenly opened her eyes; then she put out her paws with energy, as if to stretch them and get rid of cramp. At last she yawned, showing the formidable apparatus of her teeth and pointed tongue, rough as a file.

"A regular *petite maitresse*," thought the Frenchman, seeing her roll herself about so softly and coquettishly. She licked off the blood which stained her paws and muzzle, and scratched her head with reiterated gestures full of prettiness. "All right, make a little toilet," the Frenchman said to himself, beginning to recover his gaiety with his courage; "we'll say good morning to each other presently," and he seized the small, short dagger which he had taken from the Mangrabins. At this moment the panther turned her head toward the man and looked at him fixedly without moving.

The rigidity of her metallic eyes and their insupportable luster made him shudder, especially when the animal walked toward him. But he looked at her caressingly, staring into her eyes in order to magnetize her, and let her come quite close to him; then with a movement both gentle and amorous, as though he were caressing the most beautiful of women, he passed his hand over her whole body, from the head to the tail, scratching the flexible vertebrae which divided the panther's yellow back. The animal waved her tail voluptuously, and her eyes grew gentle; and when for the third time the Frenchman accomplished this interesting flattery, she gave forth one of those purrings by which our cats express their pleasure; but this murmur issued from a throat so powerful and so deep, that it resounded through the cave like the last vibrations of an organ in a church. The man, understanding the importance of his caresses, redoubled them in such a way as to surprise and stupefy his imperious courtesan. When he felt sure of having extinguished the ferocity of his capricious companion, whose hunger had so fortunately been satisfied the day before, he got up to go out of the cave; the panther let him go out, but when he had reached the summit of the hill she sprang with the lightness of a sparrow hopping from twig to twig, and rubbed herself against his legs, putting up her back after the manner of all the race of cats. Then regarding her guest with eyes whose glare had softened a little, she gave vent to that wild cry which naturalists compare to the grating of a saw.

"She is exacting," said the Frenchman, smilingly.

He was bold enough to play with her ears; he caressed her belly and scratched her head as hard as he could.

When he saw that he was successful, he tickled her skull with the point of his dagger, watching for the right moment to kill her, but the hardness of her bones made him tremble for his success.

The sultana of the desert showed herself gracious to her slave; she lifted her head, stretched out her neck, and manifested her delight by the tranquillity of her attitude. It suddenly occurred to the soldier that to kill this savage princess with one blow he must poignard her in the throat.

He raised the blade, when the panther, satisfied no doubt, laid herself gracefully at his feet, and cast up at him glances in which, in spite of their natural fierceness, was mingled confusedly a kind of good-will. The poor Provençal ate his dates, leaning against one of the palm trees, and casting his eyes alternately on the desert in quest of some liberator and on his terrible companion to watch her uncertain clemency.

The panther looked at the place where the date stones fell, and every time that he threw one down her eyes expressed an incredible mistrust.

She examined the man with an almost commercial prudence. However, this examination was favorable to him, for when he had finished his meager meal she licked his boots with her powerful rough tongue, brushing off with marvellous skill the dust gathered in the creases.

"Ah, but when she's really hungry!" thought the Frenchman. In spite of the shudder this thought caused him, the soldier began to measure curiously the proportions of the panther, certainly one of the most splendid specimens of its race. She was three feet high and four feet long without counting her tail; this powerful weapon, rounded like a cudgel, was nearly three feet long. The head, large as that of a lioness, was distinguished by a rare expression of refinement. The cold cruelty of a tiger was dominant, it was true, but there was also a vague resemblance to the face of a sensual woman. Indeed, the face of this solitary queen had something of the gaiety of a drunken Nero: she had satiated herself with blood, and she wanted to play.

The soldier tried if he might walk up and down, and the panther left him free, contenting herself with following him with her eyes, less like a faithful dog than a big Angora cat, observing everything, and every movement of her master.

When he looked around, he saw, by the spring, the remains of his horse; the panther had dragged the carcass all that way; about two-thirds of it had been devoured already. The sight reassured him.

It was easy to explain the panther's absence, and the respect she had had for him while he slept. The first piece of good luck emboldened him to tempt the future, and he conceived the wild hope of continuing on good terms with the panther during the entire day, neglecting no means of taming her, and remaining in her good graces.

He returned to her, and had the unspeakable joy of seeing her wag her tail with an almost imperceptible movement at his approach. He sat down then, without fear, by her side, and they began to play together; he took her paws and muzzle, pulled her ears, rolled her over on her back, stroked her warm, delicate flanks. She let him do whatever he liked, and when he began to stroke the hair on her feet she drew her claws in carefully.

The man, keeping the dagger in one hand, thought to plunge it into the belly of the too-confiding panther, but he was afraid that he would be immediately strangled in her last conclusive struggle; besides, he felt in his heart a sort of remorse which bid him respect a creature that had done him no harm. He seemed to have found a friend, in a boundless desert; half unconsciously he thought of his first sweetheart, whom he had nicknamed "Mignonne" by way of contrast, because she was so atrociously jealous that all the time of their love he was in fear of the knife with which she had always threatened him.

This memory of his early days suggested to him the idea of making the young panther answer to this name, now that he began to admire with less terror her swiftness, suppleness, and softness. Toward the end of the day he had familiarized himself with his perilous position; he now almost liked the painfulness of it. At last his companion had got into the habit of looking up at him whenever he cried in a falsetto voice, "Mignonne."

At the setting of the sun Mignonne gave, several times running, a profound melancholy cry. "She's been well brought up," said the light-hearted soldier; "she says her prayers." But this mental joke only occurred to him when he noticed what a pacific attitude his companion remained in. "Come, *ma petite blonde*, I'll let you go to bed first," he said to her, counting on the activity of his own legs to run away as quickly as possible, directly she was asleep, and seek another shelter for the night.

The soldier waited with impatience the hour of his flight, and when it had arrived he walked vigorously in the direction of the Nile; but hardly had he made a quarter of a league in the sand when he heard the panther bounding after him, crying with that saw-like cry more dreadful even than the sound of her leaping.

"Ah!" he said, "then she's taken a fancy to me; she has never met any one before, and it is really quite flattering to have her first love." That instant the man fell into one of those movable quicksands so terrible to travellers and from which it is impossible to save oneself. Feeling himself caught, he gave a shriek of alarm; the panther seized him with her teeth by the collar, and, springing vigorously backward, drew him as if by magic out of the whirling sand.

"Ah, Mignonne!" cried the soldier, caressing her enthusiastically; "we're bound together for life and death—but no jokes, mind!" and he retraced his steps.

From that time the desert seemed inhabited. It contained a being to whom the man could talk, and whose ferocity was rendered gentle by him, though he could not explain to himself the reason for their strange friendship. Great as was the soldier's desire to stay upon guard, he slept.

On awakening he could not find Mignonne; he mounted the hill, and in the distance saw her springing toward him after the habit of these animals, who cannot run on account of the extreme flexibility of the vertebral column. Mignonne arrived, her jaws covered with blood; she received the wonted caress of her companion, showing with much purring how happy it made her. Her eyes, full of languor, turned still more gently than the day before toward the Provençal, who talked to her as one would to a tame animal.

"Ah! Mademoiselle, you are a nice girl, aren't you? Just look at that! so we like to be made much of, don't we? Aren't you ashamed of yourself? So you have been eating some Arab or other, have you? that doesn't matter. They're animals just the same as you are; but don't you take to eating Frenchmen, or I shan't like you any longer."

She played like a dog with its master, letting herself be rolled over, knocked about, and stroked, alternately; sometimes she herself would provoke the soldier, putting up her paw with a soliciting gesture.

Some days passed in this manner. This companionship permitted the Provençal to appreciate the sublime beauty of the desert; now that he had a living thing to think about, alternations of fear and quiet, and plenty to eat, his mind became filled with contrast and his life began to be diversified.

Solitude revealed to him all her secrets, and enveloped him in her delights. He discovered in the rising and setting of the sun sights unknown to the world. He knew what it was to tremble when he heard over his head the hiss of a bird's wing, so rarely did they pass, or when he saw the clouds, changing and many-colored travellers, melt one into another. He studied in the night time the effect of the moon upon the ocean of sand, where the simoon made waves swift of movement and rapid in their change. He lived the life of the Eastern day, marvelling at its wonderful pomp; then, after having revelled in the sight of a hurricane over the plain where the whirling sands made red, dry mists and death-bearing clouds, he would welcome the night with joy, for then fell the healthful freshness of the stars, and he listened to imaginary music in the skies. Then solitude taught him to unroll the treasures of dreams. He passed whole hours in remembering mere nothings, and comparing his present life with his past.

At last he grew passionately fond of the panther; for some sort of affection was a necessity.

Whether it was that his will powerfully projected had modified the character of his companion, or whether, because she found abundant food in her predatory excursions in the deserts, she respected the man's life, he began to fear for it no longer, seeing her so well tamed.

He devoted the greater part of his time to sleep, but he was obliged to watch like a spider in its web that the moment of his deliverance might not escape him, if any one should pass the line marked by the horizon. He had sacrificed his shirt to make a flag with, which he hung at the top of a palm tree, whose foliage he had torn off. Taught by necessity, he found the means of keeping it spread out, by fastening it with little sticks; for the wind might not be blowing at the moment when the passing traveller was looking through the desert.

It was during the long hours, when he had abandoned hope, that he amused himself with the panther. He had come to learn the different inflections of her voice, the expressions of her eyes; he had studied the capricious patterns of all the rosettes which marked the gold of her robe. Mignonne was not even angry when he took hold of the tuft at the end of her tail to count the rings, those graceful ornaments which glittered in the sun like jewelry. It gave him pleasure to contemplate the supple, fine outlines of her form, the whiteness of her belly, the graceful pose of her head. But it was especially when she was playing that he felt most pleasure in looking at her; the agility and youthful lightness of her movements were a continual surprise to him; he wondered at the supple way in which she jumped and climbed, washed herself and arranged her fur, crouched down and prepared to spring. However rapid her spring might be, however slippery the stone she was on, she would always stop short at the word "Mignonne."

One day, in a bright mid-day sun, an enormous bird coursed through the air. The man left his panther to look at this new guest; but after waiting a moment the deserted sultana growled deeply.

"My goodness! I do believe she's jealous," he cried, seeing her eyes become hard again; "the soul of Virginie has passed into her body; that's certain."

The eagle disappeared into the air, while the soldier admired the curved contour of the panther.

But there was such youth and grace in her form! she was beautiful as a woman! the blond fur of her robe mingled well with the delicate tints of faint white which marked her flanks.

The profuse light cast down by the sun made this living gold, these russet markings, to burn in a way to give them an indefinable attraction.

The man and the panther looked at one another with a look full of meaning;

21

the coquette quivered when she felt her friend stroke her head; her eyes flashed like lightning—then she shut them tightly.

"She has a soul," he said, looking at the stillness of this queen of the sands, golden like them, white like them, solitary and burning like them.

"Well," she said, "I have read your plea in favor of beasts; but how did two so well adapted to understand each other end?"

"Ah, well! you see, they ended as all great passions do end—by a misunderstanding. For some reason *one* suspects the other of treason; they don't come to an explanation through pride, and quarrel and part from sheer obstinacy."

"Yet sometimes at the best moments a single word or a look is enough—but anyhow go on with your story."

"It's horribly difficult, but you will understand, after what the old villain told me over his champagne.

"He said—'I don't know if I hurt her, but she turned round, as if enraged, and with her sharp teeth caught hold of my leg—gently, I daresay; but I, thinking she would devour me, plunged my dagger into her throat. She rolled over, giving a cry that froze my heart; and I saw her dying, still looking at me without anger. I would have given all the world—my cross even, which I had not got then—to have brought her to life again. It was as though I had murdered a real person; and the soldiers who had seen my flag, and were come to my assistance, found me in tears.'

" 'Well sir,' he said, after a moment of silence, 'since then I have been in war in Germany, in Spain, in Russia, in France; I've certainly carried my carcass about a good deal, but never have I seen anything like the desert. Ah! yes, it is very beautiful!'

" 'What did you feel there?' I asked him.

" 'Oh! that can't be described, young man. Besides, I am not always regretting my palm trees and my panther. I should have to be very melancholy for that. In the desert, you see, there is everything, and nothing.'

" 'Yes, but explain—'

" 'Well,' he said, with an impatient gesture, 'it is God without mankind.' "

THE BOOK OF RUTH

Biblical scholars think that the events recounted in the BOOK OF RUTH in the Hebrew Scriptures may have taken place around 1100 B. C., when Israel, before it became a kingdom, was ruled by judges. However, the story itself is thought to have been written later, after the Babylonian exile of 586 B.C.

The tale is of a loving bond between two women—the chosen love of Ruth for her mother-in-law, Naomi. The story's dimensions are so large, the work has become archetypal. Ruth, a Moabite, pledges to forsake her own country, people, and religion for Naomi's country, its people, and their monotheistic beliefs. The two women are widowed when their bond is forged. Just as Ruth elects to remain with Naomi, the other widowed daughter-in-law, Orpah, kisses her mother-in-law good-bye. Naomi's womanly realism guides them as she and Ruth join forces. At length they arrive in Bethlehem, where they encounter Boaz, a wealthy kinsman of Ruth's late husband. Boaz's duty as a kinsman requires him to marry Ruth, but when he fails to come forward, the two women—working together—trick him. Their benevolent conspiracy results not only in the marriage of Ruth and Boaz but also in a child whom Naomi cares for, Obed, the father of Jesse, who becomes in turn the father of David, Israel's great king. The story is launched with Ruth's expression of unwavering fidelity. In its most-celebrated passage, we are shown Ruth's all-encompassing commitment to Naomi: "Where you go, I will go, and where you stay, I will stay. Your people shall be my people, and your God my God."

Naomi and Ruth

1

Long ago, in the time of the judges, there was a famine in the land, and a man from Bethlehem in Judah went to live in the Moabite country with his wife and his two sons. The man's name was Elimelech, his wife's name was Naomi, and the names of his two sons Mahlon and Chilion. They were Ephrathites from Bethlehem in Judah. They arrived in the Moabite country and there they stayed.

Elimelech Naomi's husband died, so that she was left with her two sons. These sons married Moabite women, one of whom was called Orpah and the other Ruth. They had lived there about ten years, when both Mahlon and Chilion died, so that the woman was bereaved of her two sons as well as of her husband. Thereupon she set out with her two daughters-in-law to return home, because she had heard while still in the Moabite country that the LORD had cared for his people and given them food. So with her two daughters-in-law she left the place where she had been living, and took the road home to Judah. Then Naomi said to her two daughters-in-law, 'Go back, both of you, to your mothers' homes. May the LORD keep faith with you, as you have kept faith with the dead and with me; and may he grant each of you security in the home of a new husband.' She kissed them and they wept aloud. Then they said to her, 'We will return with you to your own people.' But Naomi said, 'Go back, my daughters. Why should you go with me? Am I likely to bear any more sons to be husbands for you? Go back, my daughters, go. I am too old to marry again. But even if I could say that I had hope of a child, if I were to marry this night and if I were to bear sons, would you then wait until they grew up? Would you then refrain from marrying? No, no, my daughters, my lot is more bitter than yours, because the LORD has been against me.' At this they wept again. Then Orpah kissed her mother-in-law and returned to her people, but Ruth clung to her.

'You see,' said Naomi, 'your sister-in-law has gone back to her people and her gods, go back with her.' 'Do not urge me to go back and desert you,' Ruth answered. 'Where you go, I will go, and where you stay, I will stay. Your people shall be my people, and your God my God. Where you die, I will die, and there I will be buried. I swear a solemn oath before the LORD your God: nothing but death shall divide us.' When Naomi saw that Ruth was determined to go with her, she said no more, and the two of them went on until they came to Bethlehem. When they arrived in Bethlehem, the whole town was in great excitement about them, and the women said, 'Can this be Naomi?' 'Do not call me Naomi,' she said, 'call me Mara, for it is a bitter lot that the Almighty has sent me. I went away full, and the LORD has brought me back empty. Why do you call me Naomi? The LORD has pronounced against me; the Almighty has brought disaster on me.' This is how Naomi's daughter-in-law, Ruth the Moabitess, returned with her from the Moabite country. The barley harvest was beginning when they arrived in Bethlehem.

Ruth and Boaz

2

Now Naomi had a kinsman on her husband's side, a well-to-do man of the family of Elimelech; his name was Boaz. Ruth the Moabitess said to Naomi, 'May I go out to the cornfields and glean behind anyone who will grant me that favour?' 'Yes, go, my daughter', she replied. So Ruth went gleaning in the fields behind the reapers. As it happened, she was in that strip of the fields which belonged to Boaz of Elimelech's family, and there was Boaz coming out from Bethlehem. He greeted the reapers, saying, 'The LORD be with you'; and they replied, 'The LORD bless you.' Then he asked his servant in charge of the reapers, 'Whose girl is this?' 'She is a Moabite girl,' the servant answered, 'who has just come back with Naomi from the Moabite country. She asked if she might glean and gather among the swathes behind the reapers. She came and has been on her feet with hardly a moment's rest from daybreak till now.' Then Boaz said to Ruth, 'Listen to me, my daughter: do not go and glean in any other field, and do not look any further, but keep close to my girls. Watch where the mean reap, and follow the gleaners; I have given them orders not to molest you. If you are thirsty, go and drink from the jars the men have filled.' She fell prostrate before him and said, 'Why are you so kind as to take notice of me when I am only a foreigner?' Boaz answered, 'They have told me all that you have done for your mother-in-law since your husband's death, how you left your father and mother and the land of your birth, and came to a people you did not know before. The LORD reward your deed; may the LORD the God of Israel, under whose wings you have come to take refuge, give you all that you deserve.' 'Indeed, sir,' she said, 'you have eased my mind and spoken kindly to me; may I ask you as a favour not to treat me only as one of your slave-girls?' When meal-time came round, Boaz said to her, 'Come here and have something to eat, and dip your bread into the sour wine.' So she sat beside the reapers, and he passed her some roasted grain. She ate all she wanted and still had some left over. When she got up to glean, Boaz gave the men orders. 'She', he said, 'may glean even among the sheaves; do not scold her. Or you may even pull out some corn from the bundles and leave it for her to glean, without reproving her.'

So Ruth gleaned in the field till evening, and when she beat out what she had gleaned, it came to about a bushel of barley. She took it up and went into the town, and her mother-in-law saw how much she had gleaned. Then Ruth brought out what she had saved from her meal and gave it to her. Her mother-in-law asked her, 'Where did you glean today? Which way did you go? Blessings on the man who kindly took notice of you.' So she told her mother-in-law whom she had been working with. 'The man with whom I worked today', she said, 'is called Boaz.' 'Blessings on him from the LORD', said Naomi. 'The LORD has kept faith with the living and the dead. For this man is related to us and is our next-of-kin.' 'And what is more,' said Ruth the Moabitess, 'he told me to stay close to his men until they had finished all his harvest.' 'It is best for you, my daughter,' Naomi answered, 'to go out with his girls; let no one catch you in another field.' So she kept close to his girls, gleaning with them till the end of both barley and wheat harvests; but she lived with her mother-in-law.

3

One day Ruth's mother-in-law Naomi said to her, 'My daughter, I want to see you happily settled. Now there is our kinsman Boaz; you were with his girls.

Tonight he is winnowing barley at his threshing-floor. Wash and anoint yourself, put on your cloak and go down to the threshing-floor, but do not make yourself known to the man until he has finished eating and drinking. But when he lies down, take note of the place where he lies. Then go in, turn back the covering at his feet and lie down. He will tell you what to do.' 'I will do whatever you tell me', Ruth answered. So she went down to the threshing-floor and did exactly as her mother-in-law had told her. When Boaz had eaten and drunk, he felt at peace with the world and went to lie down at the far end of the heap of grain. She came in quietly, turned back the covering at his feet and lay down. About midnight something disturbed the man as he slept; he turned over and, lo and behold, there was a woman lying at his feet. 'Who are you?' he asked. 'I am your servant, Ruth', she replied. 'Now spread your skirt over your servant, because you are my next-of-kin.' He said, 'The LORD has blessed you, my daughter. This last proof of your loyalty is greater than the first; you have not sought after any young man, rich or poor. Set your mind at rest, my daughter. I will do whatever you ask; for, as the whole neighbourhood knows, you are a capable woman. Are you sure that I am the next-of-kin? There is a kinsman even closer than I. Spend the night here and then in the morning, if he is willing to act as your next-of-kin, well and good; but if he is not willing, I will do so; I swear it by the LORD. Now lie down till morning.' So she lay at his feet till morning, but rose before one man could recognize another; and he said, 'It must not be known that a woman has been to the threshing-floor.' Then he said, 'Bring me the cloak you have on, and hold it out.' So she held it out, and he put in six measures of barley and lifted it on her back, and she went to the town. When she came to her mother-in-law, Naomi asked, 'How did things go with you, my daughter?' Ruth told her all that the man had done for her. 'He gave me these six measures of barley,' she said; 'he would not let me come home to my mother-in-law empty-handed.' Naomi answered, 'Wait, my daughter, until you see what will come of it. He will not rest until he has settled the matter today.'

4

Now Boaz had gone up to the city gate, and was sitting there; and, after a time, the next-of-kin of whom he had spoken passed by. 'Here,' he cried, calling him by name, 'come and sit down.' He came and sat down. Then Boaz stopped ten elders of the town, and asked them to sit there, and they did so. Then he said to the next-of-kin, 'You will remember the strip of field that belonged to our brother Elimelech. Naomi has returned from the Moabite country and is selling it. I promised to open the matter with you, to ask you to acquire it in the presence of those who sit here, in the presence of the elders of my people. If you are going to do your duty as next-of-kin, then do so, but if not, someone must do it. So tell me, and then I shall know; for I come after you as next-of-kin.' He answered, 'I will act as next-of-kin.' Then Boaz said, 'On the day when you acquire the field from Naomi, you also acquire Ruth the Moabitess, the dead man's wife, so as to perpetuate the name of the dead man with his patrimony.' Thereupon the next-of-kin said, 'I cannot act myself, for I should risk losing my own patrimony. You must therefore do my duty as next-of-kin. I cannot act.'

Now in those old days, when property was redeemed or exchanged, it was the custom for a man to pull off his sandal and give it to the other party. This was the form of attestation in Israel. So the next-of-kin said to Boaz, 'Acquire it for yourself,' and pulled off his sandal. Then Boaz declared to the elders and all the people, 'You are witnesses today that I have acquired from Naomi all that belonged to Elimelech and all that belonged to Mahlon and Chilion; and, further, that I have myself acquired Ruth the Moabitess, wife of Mahlon, to be my wife, to perpetuate the name of the deceased with his patrimony, so that his name may not be missing among his kindred and at the gate of his native place. You are witnesses this day.' Then the elders and all who were at the gate said, 'We are witnesses. May the LORD make this woman, who has come to your home, like Rachel and Leah, the two who built up the house of Israel. May you do great things in Ephrathah and keep a name alive in Bethlehem. May your house be like the house of Perez, whom Tamar bore to Judah, through the offspring the LORD will give you by this girl.'

So Boaz took Ruth and made her his wife. When they came together, the LORD caused her to conceive and she bore Boaz a son. Then the women said to Naomi, 'Blessed be the LORD today, for he has not left you without a next-of-kin. May the dead man's name be kept alive in Israel. The child will give you new life and cherish you in your old age; for your daughter-in-law who loves you, who has proved better to you than seven sons, has borne him.' Naomi took the child and laid him in her lap and became his nurse. Her neighbours gave him a name: 'Naomi has a son,' they said; 'we will call him Obed.' He was the father of Jesse, the father of David.

THIS IS THE GENEALOGY of Perez: Perez was the father of Hezron, Hezron of Ram, Ram of Amminadab, Amminadab of Nahshon, Nahshon of Salmon, Salmon of Boaz, Boaz of Obed, Obed of Jesse, and Jesse of David.

ITALO CALVINO

(1923–1985)

ITALO CALVINO was born in Santiago de Las Vegas, Cuba, and grew up in San Remo, Italy. During World War II he was a member of the Italian Resistance. He graduated from the University of Turin in 1947; in 1964 he married Chichita Singer, with whom he had a daughter. In the years following, he spent winters in Rome and summers in Siena. He died after a cerebral hemorrhage, in 1985.

Among his principal works are some seventeen novels and stories, spanning the years 1947–85. They include the novels *The Path to the Nest of Spiders* (tr. 1956), *The Non-Existent Knight,* published in *The Non-Existent Knight and The Cloven Viscount* (tr. 1962), *If on a Winter's Night a Traveler* (tr. 1981), and *Mr. Palomar* (tr. 1985); the novella *The Argentine Ant,* collected in *Adam, One Afternoon and Other Stories* (tr. 1957); and the stories *Marcovaldo: The Seasons in the City* (tr. 1983), *Cosmicomics* (tr. 1968), and *Difficult Loves* (tr. 1984).

Calvino was the recipient of numerous awards, both in Europe and the United States. In 1975 he was admitted as an honorary member to the American Academy and Institute of Arts and Letters, and in 1984 was awarded an honorary degree from Mount Holyoke College.

Calvino's early work, principally *The Path to the Nest of Spiders,* which dealt with Italian resistance to fascism, was in the Italian neorealistic vein. Subsequent work reflected the influence of the Latin American magical realists, notably Jorge Luis Borges. Calvino's work became increasingly innovative, allegorical, and lighthearted, though some individual pieces—those dealing with the war, for example—were somber.

In *The Non-Existent Knight,* a historical fantasy, Calvino engages the materials of Renaissance chivalric epics. A variation on this theme may be discerned in "The Adventure of a Soldier," which embraces as well the precision of realism.

One Easter Sunday, Private Tomagra is on his first leave. He is sitting in a train compartment beside a widow who is dressed in black silk, her body "in full bloom." In the seated ballet that follows, Tomagra, a desirous and fearful soldier-knight, makes furtive advances. Unable to read the widow, he proceeds, giddy with uncertainty as to whether a drastic rebuff, or something much sweeter, awaits him.

The Adventure of a Soldier

In the compartment, a lady came and sat down, tall and buxom, next to Private Tomagra. She must have been a widow from the provinces, to judge by her dress and her veil: the dress was black silk, appropriate for prolonged mourning, but with useless frills and furbelows; and the veil went all around her face, falling from the brim of a massive, old-fashioned hat. Other places were free, there in the compartment, Private Tomagra noticed, and he had assumed the widow would surely choose one of them. But, on the contrary, despite the vicinity of a coarse soldier like himself, she came and sat right there—no doubt for some reason connected with travel, the soldier quickly decided, a draft, or the direction of the train.

Her body was in full bloom, solid, indeed a bit square. If its upper curves had not been tempered by a matronly softness, you would have said she was no more than thirty; but when you looked at her face, at the complexion both marmoreal and relaxed, the unattainable gaze beneath the heavy eyelids and the thick black brows, at the sternly sealed lips, hastily colored with a jarring red, she seemed, instead, past forty.

Tomagra, a young infantryman on his first leave (it was Easter), huddled down in his seat for fear that the lady, so ample and shapely, might not fit; immediately he found himself in the aura of her perfume, a popular and perhaps cheap scent, but now, out of long wear, blended with natural human odors.

The lady sat down with a composed demeanor, revealing, there beside him, less majestic proportions than he had imagined when he had seen her standing. Her hands were plump, with tight, dark rings; she kept them folded in her lap, over a shiny purse and a jacket she had taken off to expose round, white arms. At her first movement Tomagra had shifted to make space for a broad maneuvering of her arms; but she had remained almost motionless, slipping out of the sleeves with a few brief twitches of her shoulders and torso.

The railroad seat was therefore fairly comfortable for two, and Tomagra could feel the lady's extreme closeness, though without any fear of offending her by his contact. All the same, Tomagra reasoned, lady though she was, she had surely not shown any sign of repugnance toward him, toward his rough uniform; otherwise she would have sat farther away. And at these thoughts his muscles, till now contracted and tensed, relaxed freely, serenely; indeed, without his moving, they tried to expand to their greatest extension, and his leg—its tendons taut, at first detached even from the cloth of his trousers—settled more broadly, tightening the material that covered it, and the wool grazed the widow's black silk. And now, through this wool and that silk, the soldier's leg was adhering to her leg with a soft, fleeting motion, like one shark grazing another, and sending waves through its veins to those other veins.

It was still a very light contact, which every jolt of the train could break off

29

and re-create; the lady had strong, fat knees, and Tomagra's bones could sense at every jerk the lazy bump of the kneecap. The calf had raised a silken cheek that, with an imperceptible thrust, had to be made to coincide with his own. This meeting of calves was precious, but it came at a price, a loss: in fact, the body's weight was shifted and the reciprocal support of the hips no longer occurred with the same docile abandon. In order to achieve a natural and satisfied position, it was necessary to move slightly on the seat, with the aid of a curve in the track, and also of the comprehensible need to shift position every so often.

The lady was impassive beneath her matronly hat, her gaze fixed, lidded, and her hands steady on the purse in her lap. And yet her body, for a very long stretch, rested against that stretch of man: hadn't she realized this yet? Or was she preparing to flee? To rebel?

Tomagra decided to transmit, somehow, a message to her: he contracted the muscle of his calf into a kind of hard, square fist, and then with this calf-fist, as if a hand inside it wanted to open, he quickly knocked at the calf of the widow. To be sure, this was a very rapid movement, barely long enough for a flicker of the tendons; but in any case, she didn't draw back—at least not so far as he could tell, because immediately, needing to justify that covert movement, Tomagra extended his leg as if to get a kink out of it.

Now he had to begin all over again; that patient and prudently established contact had been lost. Tomagra decided to be more courageous; as if looking for something, he stuck his hand in his pocket, the pocket toward the woman, and then, as if absently, he left it there. It had been a rapid action, Tomagra didn't know whether he had touched her or not, an inconsequential gesture; yet he now realized what an important step forward he had made, and in what a risky game he was now involved. Against the back of his hand, the hip of the lady in black was now pressing; he felt it weighing on every finger, every knuckle; now any movement of his hand would have been an act of incredible intimacy toward the widow. Holding his breath, Tomagra turned his hand inside his pocket; in other words, he set the palm toward the lady, open against her, though still in that pocket. It was an impossible position, the wrist twisted. And yet at this point he might just as well attempt a decisive action: and so he ventured to move the fingers of that contorted hand. There could no longer be any possible doubt: the widow couldn't have helped noticing his maneuvering, and if she didn't draw back, but pretended to be impassive and absent, it meant that she wasn't rejecting his advances. When Tomagra thought about it, however, her paying no attention to his mobile right hand might mean that she really believed he was hunting for something in that pocket: a railroad ticket, a match. . . . There: and if now the soldier's fingertips, the pads, seemingly endowed with a sudden clairvoyance, could sense through those different stuffs the hems of subterranean garments and even the very minute roughness of skin, pores, and moles—if, as I said, his fingertips arrived at this, perhaps her flesh, marmoreal and lazy, was hardly aware that these were, in fact, fingertips, and not, for example, nails or knuckles.

Then, with furtive steps, the hand emerged from the pocket, paused there undecided, and, with sudden haste to adjust the trouser along the side seam, proceeded all the way down to the knee. More precisely, it cleared a path: to go forward, it had to dig in between himself and the woman, a route that, even in its speed, was rich in anxieties and sweet emotions.

It must be said that Tomagra had thrown his head back against the seat, so one might also have thought he was sleeping: this was not so much an alibi for himself as it was a way of offering the lady, in the event that his insistence didn't irritate her, a reason to feel at ease, knowing that his actions were divorced from his consciousness, barely surfacing from the depths of sleep. And there, from this alert semblance of sleep, Tomagra's hand, clutching his knee, detached one finger, and sent it out to reconnoiter. The finger slid along her knee, which remained still and docile; Tomagra could perform diligent figures with the little finger on the silk of the stocking, which, through his half-closed eyes, he could barely glimpse, light and curving. But he realized that the risk of this game was without reward, because the little finger, scant of surface and awkward in movement, transmitted only partial hints of sensations and was incapable of conceiving the form and substance of what it was touching.

Then he reattached the little finger to the rest of the hand, not withdrawing it, but adding to it the ring finger, the middle finger, the forefinger: now his whole hand rested inert on that female knee, and the train cradled it in a rocking caress.

It was then that Tomagra thought of the others: if the lady, whether out of compliance or out of a mysterious intangibility, didn't react to his boldness, facing them were still seated other persons who might be scandalized by that non-soldierly behavior of his, and by that possible silent complicity on the woman's part. Chiefly to spare the lady such suspicion, Tomagra withdrew his hand, or rather, he hid it, as if it were the only guilty party. But hiding it, he later thought, was only a hypocritical pretext: in abandoning it there on the seat he intended simply to move it closer to the lady, who occupied, in fact, such a large part of the space.

Indeed, the hand groped around. There: like a butterfly's lighting, the fingers already sensed her presence; and there: it was enough merely to thrust the whole palm forward gently, and the widow's gaze beneath the veil was impenetrable, the bosom only faintly stirred by her respiration. But no! Tomagra had already withdrawn his hand, like a mouse scurrying off.

She didn't move; he thought: Maybe she wants this. But he also thought: Another moment and it will be too late. Or maybe she's sitting there studying me, preparing to make a scene.

Then, for no reason except prudent verification, Tomagra slid his hand along the back of the seat and waited until the train's jolts, imperceptibly, made the lady slide over his fingers. To say he waited is not correct: actually, with the tips of his fingers wedgelike between the seat and her, he made an invisible push, which could also have been the effect of the train's speeding. If he stopped at a certain point, it wasn't because the lady had given any indication of disapproval, but, on the contrary, because Tomagra thought that if she did accept, it would be easy for her, with a half rotation of the muscles, to meet him halfway, to fall, as it were, on that expectant hand. To suggest to her the friendly nature of his attention, Tomagra, in that position beneath the lady, attempted a discreet wiggle of the fingers; the lady was looking out of the window, and her hand was idly toying with the purse clasp, opening and closing it. Was this a signal to him to stop? Was it a final concession she was granting him, a warning that her patience could be tried no longer? Was it this?—Tomagra asked himself—Was it this?

He noticed that his hand, like a stubby octopus, was clasping her flesh. Now all was decided: he could no longer draw back, not Tomagra. But what about her? She was a sphinx.

With a crab's oblique scuttle, the soldier's hand now descended her thigh. Was it out in the open, before the eyes of the others? No, now the lady was adjusting the jacket she held folded on her lap, allowing it to spill to one side. To offer him cover, or to block his path? There: now the hand moved freely and unseen, it clasped her, it opened in fleeting caresses like brief puffs of wind. But the widow's face was still turned away, distant; Tomagra stared at a part of her, a zone of naked skin between the ear and the curve of her full chignon. And in that dimple beneath the ear a vein throbbed: this was the answer she was giving him, clear, heart-rending, and fleeting. She turned her face all of a sudden, proud, and marmoreal; the veil hanging below the hat stirred like a curtain; the gaze was lost beneath the heavy lids. But that gaze had gone past him, Tomagra, perhaps had not even grazed him; she was looking beyond him, at something, or nothing, the pretext of some thought, but anyway something more important than he. This he decided later, because earlier, when he had barely seen that move- ment of hers, he had immediately thrown himself back and shut his eyes tight, as if he were asleep, trying to quell the flush spreading over his face, and thus per- haps losing the opportunity to catch in the first glint of her eyes an answer to his own extreme doubts.

His hand, hidden under the black jacket, had remained as if detached from him, numb, the fingers drawn back toward the wrist: no longer a real hand, now without sensitivity beyond that arboreal sensitivity of the bones. But as the truce the widow had granted to her own impassivity with that vague glance around soon ended, blood and courage flowed back into the hand. And it was then that, re- suming contact with that soft saddle of leg, he realized he had reached a limit: the fingers were running along the hem of the skirt, beyond which there was the leap to the knee, and the void.

It was the end, Private Tomagra thought, of this secret spree. Thinking back, he found it truly a poor thing in his memory, though he had greedily blown it up while experiencing it: a clumsy feel of a silk dress, something that could in no way have been denied him simply because of his miserable position as a soldier, and something that the lady had discreetly condescended, without any show, to concede.

He was interrupted, however, in his desolate intention of withdrawing his hand when he noticed the way she was holding her jacket on her knees: no longer folded (though it had seemed so to him before), but flung carelessly, so that one edge fell in front of her legs. His hand was thus in a sealed den—perhaps a final proof of the trust the lady was giving him, confident that the disparity between her station and the soldier's was so great that he surely wouldn't take advantage of the opportunity. And the soldier recalled, with effort, what had happened so far between the widow and himself as he tried to discover something in her behavior that hinted at further condescension; now he considered whether his own actions had been insignificant and trivial, casual grazings and strokings, or, on the other hand, of a decisive intimacy, committing him not to withdraw again.

His hand surely agreed with this second consideration, because before he could reflect on the irreparable nature of the act, he was already passing the frontier. And the lady? She was asleep. She had rested her head, with the pompous hat, against a corner of the seat, and she was keeping her eyes closed. Should he, Tomagra, respect this sleep, genuine or false as it might be, and retire? Or was it a consenting woman's device, which he should already know, for which he should somehow indicate gratitude? The point he had now reached admitted no hesitation: he could only advance.

Private Tomagra's hand was small and plump, and its hard parts and calluses had become so blended with the muscle that it was uniform, flexible; the bones could not be felt, and its movement was made more with nerves, though gently, than with joints. And this little hand had constant and general and minuscule movements, to maintain the completeness of the contact alive and burning. But when, finally, a first stirring ran through the widow's softness, like the motion of distant marine currents through secret underwater channels, the soldier was so surprised by it that, as if he really supposed the widow had noticed nothing till then, had really been asleep, he drew his hand away in fright.

Now he sat there with his hands on his own knees, huddled in his seat as he had been when she came in. He was behaving absurdly; he realized that. With a scraping of heels, a stretching of hips, he seemed eager to re-establish the contacts, but this prudence of his was absurd, too, as if he wanted to start his extremely patient operation again from the beginning, as if he were not sure now of the deep goals already gained. But had he really gained them? Or had it been only a dream?

A tunnel fell upon them. The darkness became denser and denser, and Tomagra, first with timid gestures, occasionally drawing back as if he were really at the first advances and amazed at his own temerity, then trying more and more to convince himself of the profound intimacy he had already reached with that woman, extended one hand, shy as a pullet, toward her bosom, large and somewhat abandoned to its own gravity, and with an eager groping he tried to explain to her the misery and the unbearable happiness of his condition, and his need of nothing else but for her to emerge from her reserve.

The widow did react, but with a sudden gesture of shielding herself and rejecting him. It was enough to send Tomagra crouching in his corner, wringing his hands. But it was, probably, a false alarm caused by a passing light in the corridor, which had made the widow fear the tunnel was suddenly going to end. Perhaps; or had he gone too far, had he committed some horrible rudeness toward her, who had already been so generous toward him? No, by now there could be nothing forbidden between them; and her action, on the contrary, was a sign that this was all real, that she accepted, participated. Tomagra approached again. To be sure, in these reflections a great deal of time had been wasted; the tunnel wouldn't last much longer, and it wasn't wise to allow oneself to be caught by the sudden light. Tomagra was already expecting the first grayness there on the wall; the more he expected it, the riskier it was to attempt anything. Of course, this was a long tunnel; he remembered it from other journeys as very, very long. And if he took advantage immediately, he would have a lot of time ahead of him. Now it was best to wait for the end, but it never ended, and so this had perhaps been his last chance. There: now the darkness was being dispelled, it was ending.

They were at the last stations of a provincial line. The train was emptying; some passengers in the compartment had already got out, and now the last ones were taking down their bags, leaving. Finally they were alone in the compartment, the soldier and the widow, very close and detached, their arms folded, silent, eyes staring into space. Tomagra still had to think: Now that all the seats are free, if she wanted to be nice and comfortable, if she were fed up with me, she would move. . . .

Something restrained him and frightened him still, perhaps the presence of a group of smokers in the passage, or a light that had come on because it was evening. Then he thought to draw the curtains on the passage, like somebody wanting to get some sleep. He stood up with elephantine steps; with slow, meticulous care he began to unfasten the curtains, draw them, fasten them again. When he turned, he found her stretched out. As if she wanted to sleep: even though she had her eyes open and staring, she had slipped down, maintaining her matronly composure intact, with the majestic hat still on her head, which was resting on the seat arm.

Tomagra was standing over her. Still, to protect this image of sleep, he chose also to darken the outside window; and he stretched over her, to undo the curtain. But it was only a way of shifting his clumsy actions above the impassive widow. Then he stopped tormenting that curtain's snap and understood he had to do something else; show her all his own, compelling condition of desire, if only to explain to her the misunderstanding into which she had certainly fallen, as if to say to her: You see, you were kind to me because you believe we have a remote need for affection, we poor lonely soldiers, but here is what I really am, this is how I received your courtesy, this is the degree of impossible ambition I have reached, you see, here.

And since it was now evident that nothing could manage to surprise the lady, and indeed everything seemed somehow to have been foreseen by her, Private Tomagra could only make sure that no further doubts were possible; and finally the urgency of his madness managed also to grasp its mute object: her.

When Tomagra stood up and, beneath him, the widow remained with her clear, stern gaze (she had blue eyes), with her hat and veil still squarely on her head, and the train never stopped its shrill whistling through the fields, and outside those endless rows of grapevines went on, and the rain that throughout the journey had tirelessly streaked the panes now resumed with new violence, he had again a brief spurt of fear, thinking how he, Private Tomagra, had been so daring.

RAYMOND CARVER

(1938–1988)

RAYMOND CARVER was born in Clatskanie, Oregon. He married his first wife in 1957 and had two children. The couple were divorced in 1982. In 1988, shortly before his death, Carver married Tess Gallagher, the poet. He received a B.A. from Humboldt State College in 1963. The colleges and universities at which he taught include the University of California at Santa Cruz and at Berkeley; the University of Texas at El Paso, where during 1978–79 he was the "visiting distinguished writer"; the University of Iowa Writers' Workshop, where he was a guest lecturer in 1973–74; and Syracuse University. In his twenties Carver worked as a manual laborer, and later as an editor, lecturer, writer, and teacher. His books include four volumes of poetry (*Near Klamath*, 1968; *Winter Insomnia*, 1970; *At Night the Salmon Move*, 1976; and *Where Water Comes Together with Other Water*, 1985) as well as six collections of stories (*Put Yourself in My Shoes*, 1974; *Will You Please Be Quiet, Please?*, 1976; *Furious Seasons*, 1977; *What We Talk about When We Talk about Love*, 1981; and *Cathedral*, 1983). He contributed extensively to literary magazines and other journals. Among his awards were two National Endowment of the Arts grants (poetry, 1971; fiction, 1980); a Guggenheim Fellowship (1979–80); the Strauss Living Award, American Academy and Institute of Arts and Letters (1983); and a Wallace Stegner Fellowship (1972–73). At his untimely death from lung cancer, Carver's reputation as one of the exemplary practitioners of the short story was secure; since his death that reputation has grown, along with his influence. He began writing in a mode that was called, loosely, minimalist. His spare style and plain and truthful language, however, were distilled from a rich understanding of how people cope with lives that are inevitably hard. His characters—waitresses, workers, and, as in "Fever," high-school teachers— are drawn from ordinary life. Their extraordinariness is revealed through Carver's keen vision.

"Fever" (1981) traces the tortuous path of family love. When his wife Eileen leaves him for one of his friends, Carlyle, the protagonist, becomes the sole parent to his children. His frustrating search for a responsible baby-sitter comes to stand for all of his despair—at Eileen's abandonment of him and their children, at the inexplicable end of love. Though he does his best to protect his children, he feels as orphaned as they. The solution is found, oddly, through the long-distance efforts of Eileen. Carver seems to imply love is a chain. It has a life of its own, the power of which persists even after a lover defaults.

Fever

Carlyle was in a spot. He'd been in a spot all summer, since early June when his wife had left him. But up until a little while ago, just a few days before he had to start meeting his classes at the high school, Carlyle hadn't needed a sitter. He'd been the sitter. Every day and every night he'd attended to the children. Their mother, he told them, was away on a long trip.

Debbie, the first sitter he contacted, was a fat girl, nineteen years old, who told Carlyle she came from a big family. Kids loved her, she said. She offered a couple of names for reference. She penciled them on a piece of notebook paper. Carlyle took the names, folded the piece of paper, and put it in his shirt pocket. He told her he had meetings the next day. He said she could start to work for him the next morning. She said, "Okay."

He understood that his life was entering a new period. Eileen had left while Carlyle was still filling out his grade reports. She'd said she was going to Southern California to begin a new life for herself there. She'd gone with Richard Hoopes, one of Carlyle's colleagues at the high school. Hoopes was a drama teacher and glass-blowing instructor who'd apparently turned his grades in on time, taken his things, and left town in a hurry with Eileen. Now, the long and painful summer nearly behind him, and his classes about to resume, Carlyle had finally turned his attention to this matter of finding a baby-sitter. His first efforts had not been successful. In his desperation to find someone—anyone—he'd taken Debbie on.

In the beginning, he was grateful to have this girl turn up in response to his call. He'd yielded up the house and children to her as if she were a relative. So he had no one to blame but himself, his own carelessness, he was convinced, when he came home early from school one day that first week and pulled into the drive next to a car that had a big pair of flannel dice hanging from the rearview mirror. To his astonishment, he saw his children in the front yard, their clothes filthy, playing with a dog big enough to bite off their hands. His son, Keith, had the hiccups and had been crying. Sarah, his daughter, began to cry when she saw him get out of the car. They were sitting on the grass, and the dog was licking their hands and faces. The dog growled at him and then moved off a little as Carlyle made for his children. He picked up Keith and then he picked up Sarah. One child under each arm, he made for his front door. Inside the house, the phonograph was turned up so high the front windows vibrated.

In the living room, three teenaged boys jumped to their feet from where they'd been sitting around the coffee table. Beer bottles stood on the table and cigarettes burned in the ashtray. Rod Stewart screamed from the stereo. On the sofa, Debbie, the fat girl, sat with another teenaged boy. She stared at Carlyle with dumb disbelief as he entered the living room. The fat girl's blouse was unbuttoned. She had her legs drawn under her, and she was smoking a cigarette. The living room was filled with smoke and music. The fat girl and her friend got off the sofa in a hurry.

"Mr. Carlyle, wait a minute," Debbie said. "I can explain."

"Don't explain," Carlyle said. "Get the hell out of here. All of you. Before I throw you out." He tightened his grip on the children.

"You owe me for four days," the fat girl said, as she tried to button her blouse. She still had the cigarette between her fingers. Ashes fell from the cigarette as she tried to button up. "Forget today. You don't owe me for today. Mr. Carlyle, it's not what it looks like. They dropped by to listen to this record."

"I understand, Debbie," he said. He let the children down onto the carpet. But they stayed close to his legs and watched the people in the living room. Debbie looked at them and shook her head slowly, as if she'd never laid eyes on them before. "Goddamn it, get out!" Carlyle said. "Now. Get going. All of you."

He went over and opened the front door. The boys acted as if they were in no real hurry. They picked up their beer and started slowly for the door. The Rod Stewart record was still playing. One of them said, "That's my record."

"Get it," Carlyle said. He took a step toward the boy and then stopped.

"Don't touch me, okay? Just don't touch me," the boy said. He went over to the phonograph, picked up the arm, swung it back, and took his record off while the turntable was still spinning.

Carlyle's hands were shaking. "If that car's not out of the drive in one minute—one minute—I'm calling the police." He felt sick and dizzy with his anger. He saw, really saw, spots dance in front of his eyes.

"Hey, listen, we're on our way, all right? We're going," the boy said.

They filed out of the house. Outside, the fat girl stumbled a little. She weaved as she moved toward the car. Carlyle saw her stop and bring her hands up to her face. She stood like that in the drive for a minute. Then one of the boys pushed her from behind and said her name. She dropped her hands and got into the back seat of the car.

"Daddy will get you into some clean clothes," Carlyle told his children, trying to keep his voice steady. "I'll give you a bath, and put you into some clean clothes. Then we'll go out for some pizza. How does pizza sound to you?"

"Where's Debbie?" Sarah asked him.

"She's gone," Carlyle said.

That evening, after he'd put the children to bed, he called Carol, the woman from school he'd been seeing for the past month. He told her what had happened with his sitter.

"My kids were out in the yard with this big dog," he said. "The dog was as big as a wolf. The baby-sitter was in the house with a bunch of her hoodlum boyfriends. They had Rod Stewart going full blast, and they were tying one on while my kids were outside playing with this strange dog." He brought his fingers to his temples and held them there while he talked.

"My God," Carol said. "Poor sweetie, I'm so sorry." Her voice sounded indistinct. He pictured her letting the receiver slide down to her chin, as she was in the habit of doing while talking on the phone. He'd seen her do it before. It was a habit of hers he found vaguely irritating. Did he want her to come over to his place? she asked. She would. She thought maybe she'd better do that. She'd call her sitter. Then she'd drive to his place. She wanted to. He shouldn't be afraid to say when he needed affection, she said. Carol was one of the secretaries in the principal's office at the high school where Carlyle taught art classes. She was divorced and had one child, a neurotic ten-year-old the father had named Dodge, after his automobile.

"No, that's all right," Carlyle said. "But thanks. *Thanks*, Carol. The kids are in bed, but I think I'd feel a little funny, you know, having company tonight."

She didn't offer again. "Sweetie, I'm sorry about what happened. But I understand your wanting to be alone tonight. I respect that. I'll see you at school tomorrow."

He could hear her waiting for him to say something else. "That's two baby-sitters in less than a week," he said. "I'm going out of my tree with this."

"Honey, don't let it get you down," she said. "Something will turn up. I'll help you find somebody this weekend. It'll be all right, you'll see."

"Thanks again for being there when I need you," he said. "You're one in a million, you know."

" 'Night, Carlyle," she said.

After he'd hung up, he wished he could have thought of something else to say to her instead of what he'd just said. He'd never talked that way before in his life. They weren't having a love affair, he wouldn't call it that, but he liked her. She knew it was a hard time for him, and she didn't make demands.

After Eileen had left for California, Carlyle had spent every waking minute for the first month with his children. He supposed the shock of her going had caused this, but he didn't want to let the children out of his sight. He'd certainly not been interested in seeing other women, and for a time he didn't think he ever would be. He felt as if he were in mourning. His days and nights were passed in the company of his children. He cooked for them—he had no appetite himself— washed and ironed their clothes, drove them into the country, where they picked flowers and ate sandwiches wrapped up in waxed paper. He took them to the supermarket and let them pick out what they liked. And every few days they went to the park, or else to the library, or the zoo. They took old bread to the zoo so they could feed the ducks. At night, before tucking them in, Carlyle read to them—Aesop, Hans Christian Andersen, the Brothers Grimm.

"When is Mama coming back?" one of them might ask him in the middle of a fairy tale.

"Soon," he'd say. "One of these days. Now listen to this." Then he'd read the tale to its conclusion, kiss them, and turn off the light.

And while they'd slept, he had wandered the rooms of his house with a glass in his hand, telling himself that, yes, sooner or later, Eileen would come back. In the next breath, he would say, "I never want to see your face again. I'll never forgive you for this, you crazy bitch." Then, a minute later, "Come back, sweetheart, please. I love you and need you. The kids need you, too." Some nights that summer he fell asleep in front of the TV and woke up with the set still going and the screen filled with snow. This was the period when he didn't think he would be seeing any women for a long time, if ever. At night, sitting in front of the TV with an unopened book or magazine next to him on the sofa, he often thought of Eileen. When he did, he might remember her sweet laugh, or else her hand rubbing his neck if he complained of a soreness there. It was at these times that he thought he could weep. He thought, You hear about stuff like this happening to other people.

Just before the incident with Debbie, when some of the shock and grief had worn off, he'd phoned an employment service to tell them something of his predicament and his requirements. Someone took down the information and said they would get back to him. Not many people wanted to do housework *and* baby-sit, they said, but they'd find somebody. A few days before he had to be at the high school for meetings and registration, he called again and was told there'd be somebody at his house first thing the next morning.

That person was a thirty-five-year-old woman with hairy arms and run-over shoes. She shook hands with him and listened to him talk without asking a single question about the children—not even their names. When he took her into the back of the house where the children were playing, she simply stared at them for a minute without saying anything. When she finally smiled, Carlyle noticed for the first time that she had a tooth missing. Sarah left her crayons and got up to come over and stand next to him. She took Carlyle's hand and stared at the woman. Keith stared at her, too. Then he went back to his coloring. Carlyle thanked the woman for her time and said he would be in touch.

That afternoon he took down a number from an index card tacked to the bulletin board at the supermarket. Someone was offering baby-sitting services. References furnished on request. Carlyle called the number and got Debbie, the fat girl.

Over the summer, Eileen had sent a few cards, letters, and photographs of herself to the children, and some pen-and-ink drawings of her own that she'd done since she'd gone away. She also sent Carlyle long, rambling letters in which she asked for his understanding in this matter—*this matter*—but told him that she was happy. Happy. As if, Carlyle thought, happiness was all there was to life. She told him that if he really loved her, as he said he did, and as she really believed—

she loved him, too, don't forget—then he would understand and accept things as they were. She wrote, "That which is truly bonded can never become unbonded." Carlyle didn't know if she was talking about their own relationship or her way of life out in California. He hated the word *bonded*. What did it have to do with the two of them? Did she think they were a corporation? He thought Eileen must be losing her mind to talk like that. He read that part again and then crumpled the letter.

But a few hours later he retrieved the letter from the trash can where he'd thrown it, and put it with her other cards and letters in a box on the shelf in his closet. In one of the envelopes, there was a photograph of her in a big, floppy hat, wearing a bathing suit. And there was a pencil drawing on heavy paper of a woman on a riverbank in a filmy gown, her hands covering her eyes, her shoulders slumped. It was, Carlyle assumed, Eileen showing her heartbreak over the situation. In college, she had majored in art, and even though she'd agreed to marry him, she said she intended to do something with her talent. Carlyle said he wouldn't have it any other way. She owed it to herself, he said. She owed it to both of them. They had loved each other in those days. He knew they had. He couldn't imagine ever loving anyone again the way he'd loved her. And he'd felt loved, too. Then, after eight years of being married to him, Eileen had pulled out. She was, she said in her letter, "going for it."

After talking to Carol, he looked in on the children, who were asleep. Then he went into the kitchen and made himself a drink. He thought of calling Eileen to talk to her about the baby-sitting crisis, but decided against it. He had her phone number and her address out there, of course. But he'd only called once and, so far, had not written a letter. This was partly out of a feeling of bewilderment with the situation, partly out of anger and humiliation. Once, earlier in the summer, after a few drinks, he'd chanced humiliation and called. Richard Hoopes answered the phone. Richard had said, "Hey, Carlyle," as if he were still Carlyle's friend. And then, as if remembering something, he said, "Just a minute, all right?"

Eileen had come on the line and said, "Carlyle, how are you? How are the kids? Tell me about yourself." He told her the kids were fine. But before he could say anything else, she interrupted him to say, "I know *they're* fine. What about *you?*" Then she went on to tell him that her head was in the right place for the first time in a long time. Next she wanted to talk about his head and his karma. She'd looked into his karma. It was going to improve any time now, she said. Carlyle listened, hardly able to believe his ears. Then he said, "I have to go now, Eileen." And he hung up. The phone rang a minute or so later, but he let it ring. When it stopped ringing, he took the phone off the hook and left it off until he was ready for bed.

He wanted to call her now, but he was afraid to call. He still missed her and wanted to confide in her. He longed to hear her voice—sweet, steady, not manic as it had been for months now—but if he dialed her number, Richard Hoopes might answer the telephone. Carlyle knew he didn't want to hear that man's voice again. Richard had been a colleague for three years and, Carlyle supposed, a kind of friend. At least he was someone Carlyle ate lunch with in the faculty dining room, someone who talked about Tennessee Williams and the photographs of Ansel Adams. But even if Eileen answered the telephone, she might launch into something about his karma.

While he was sitting there with the glass in his hand, trying to remember what it had felt like to be married and intimate with someone, the phone rang. He picked up the receiver, heard a trace of static on the line, and knew, even before she'd said his name, that it was Eileen.

"I was just thinking about you," Carlyle said, and at once regretted saying it.

"See! I knew I was on your mind, Carlyle. Well, I was thinking about you, too. That's why I called." He drew a breath. She *was* losing her mind. That much was clear to him. She kept talking. "Now listen," she said. "The big reason I called is that I know things are in kind of a mess out there right now. Don't ask me how, but I know. I'm sorry, Carlyle. But here's the thing. You're still in need of a good housekeeper and sitter combined, right? Well, she's practically right there in the neighborhood! Oh, you may have found someone already, and that's good, if that's the case. If so, it's supposed to be that way. But see, just in case you're having trouble in that area, there's this woman who used to work for Richard's mother. I told Richard about the potential problem, and he put himself to work on it. You want to know what he did? Are you listening? He called his mother, who used to have this woman who kept house for her. The woman's name is Mrs. Webster. She looked after things for Richard's mother before his aunt and her daughter moved in there. Richard was able to get a number through his mother. He talked to Mrs. Webster today. Richard did. Mrs. Webster is going to call you tonight. Or else maybe she'll call you in the morning. One or the other. Anyway, she's going to volunteer her services, if you need her. You might, you never can tell. Even if your situation is okay right now, which I hope it is. But some time or another you might need her. You know what I'm saying? If not this minute, some other time. Okay? How are the kids? What are they up to?"

"The children are fine, Eileen. They're asleep now," he said. Maybe he should tell her they cried themselves to sleep every night. He wondered if he should tell her the truth—that they hadn't asked about her even once in the last couple of weeks. He decided not to say anything.

"I called earlier, but the line was busy. I told Richard you were probably talking to your girlfriend," Eileen said and laughed. "Think positive thoughts. You sound depressed," she said.

"I have to go, Eileen." He started to hang up, and he took the receiver from his ear. But she was still talking.

"Tell Keith and Sarah I love them. Tell them I'm sending some more pictures. Tell them that. I don't want them to forget their mother is an artist. Maybe not a great artist yet, that's not important. But, you know, an artist. It's important they shouldn't forget that."

Carlyle said, "I'll tell them."

"Richard says hello."

Carlyle didn't say anything. He said the word to himself—*hello*. What could the man possibly mean by this? Then he said, "Thanks for calling. Thanks for talking to that woman."

"Mrs. Webster!"

"Yes. I'd better get off the phone now. I don't want to run up your nickel."

Eileen laughed. "It's only money. Money's not important except as a necessary medium of exchange. There are more important things than money. But then you already know that."

He held the receiver out in front of him. He looked at the instrument from which her voice was issuing.

"Carlyle, things are going to get better for you. I *know* they are. You may think I'm crazy or something," she said. "But just remember."

Remember what? Carlyle wondered in alarm, thinking he must have missed something she'd said. He brought the receiver in close. "Eileen, thanks for calling," he said.

"We have to stay in touch," Eileen said. "We have to keep all lines of communication open. I think the worst is over. For both of us. I've suffered, too. But we're going to get what we're supposed to get out of this life, both of us, and we're going to be made *stronger* for it in the long run."

"Goodnight," he said. He put the receiver back. Then he looked at the phone. He waited. It didn't ring again. But an hour later it did ring. He answered it.

"Mr. Carlyle." It was an old woman's voice. "You don't know me, but my name is Mrs. Jim Webster. I was supposed to get in touch."

"Mrs. Webster. Yes," he said. Eileen's mention of the woman came back to him. "Mrs. Webster, can you come to my house in the morning? Early. Say seven o'clock?"

"I can do that easily," the old woman said. "Seven o'clock. Give me your address."

"I'd like to be able to count on you," Carlyle said.

"You can count on me," she said.

"I can't tell you how important it is," Carlyle said.

"Don't you worry," the old woman said.

The next morning, when the alarm went off, he wanted to keep his eyes closed and keep on with the dream he was having. Something about a farmhouse. And there was a waterfall in there, too. Someone, he didn't know who, was walking along the road carrying something. Maybe it was a picnic hamper. He was not made uneasy by the dream. In the dream, there seemed to exist a sense of well-being.

Finally, he rolled over and pushed something to stop the buzzing. He lay in bed awhile longer. Then he got up, put his feet into his slippers, and went out to the kitchen to start the coffee.

He shaved and dressed for the day. Then he sat down at the kitchen table with coffee and a cigarette. The children were still in bed. But in five minutes or so he planned to put boxes of cereal on the table and lay out bowls and spoons, then go in to wake them for breakfast. He really couldn't believe that the old woman who'd phoned him last night would show up this morning, as she'd said she would. He decided he'd wait until five minutes after seven o'clock, and then he'd call in, take the day off, and make every effort in the book to locate someone reliable. He brought the cup of coffee to his lips.

It was then that he heard a rumbling sound out in the street. He left his cup and got up from the table to look out the window. A pickup truck had pulled over to the curb in front of his house. The pickup cab shook as the engine idled. Carlyle went to the front door, opened it, and waved. An old woman waved back and then let herself out of the vehicle. Carlyle saw the driver lean over and disappear under the dash. The truck gasped, shook itself once more, and fell still.

"Mr. Carlyle?" the old woman said, as she came slowly up his walk carrying a large purse.

"Mrs. Webster," he said. "Come on inside. Is that your husband? Ask him in. I just made coffee."

"It's okay," she said. "He has his thermos."

Carlyle shrugged. He held the door for her. She stepped inside and they shook hands. Mrs. Webster smiled. Carlyle nodded. They moved out to the kitchen. "Did you want me today, then?" she asked.

"Let me get the children up," he said. "I'd like them to meet you before I leave for school."

"That'd be good," she said. She looked around his kitchen. She put her purse on the drainboard.

"Why don't I get the children?" he said. "I'll just be a minute or two."

In a little while, he brought the children out and introduced them. They were still in their pajamas. Sarah was rubbing her eyes. Keith was wide awake. "This is Keith," Carlyle said. "And this one here, this is my Sarah." He held on to Sarah's hand and turned to Mrs. Webster. "They need someone, you see. We need someone we can count on. I guess that's our problem."

Mrs. Webster moved over to the children. She fastened the top button of Keith's pajamas. She moved the hair away from Sarah's face. They let her do it. "Don't you kids worry, now," she said to them. "Mr. Carlyle, it'll be all right. We're going to be fine. Give us a day or two to get to know each other, that's all. But if I'm going to stay, why don't you give Mr. Webster the all-clear sign? Just wave at him through the window," she said, and then she gave her attention back to the children.

Carlyle stepped to the bay window and drew the curtain. An old man was watching the house from the cab of the truck. He was just bringing a thermos cup to his lips. Carlyle waved to him, and with his free hand the man waved back. Carlyle watched him roll down the truck window and throw out what was left in his cup. Then he bent down under the dash again—Carlyle imagined him touching some wires together—and in a minute the truck started and began to shake. The old man put the truck in gear and pulled away from the curb.

Carlyle turned from the window. "Mrs. Webster," he said. "I'm glad you're here."

"Likewise, Mr. Carlyle," she said. "Now you go on about your business before you're late. Don't worry about anything. We're going to be fine. Aren't we, kids?"

The children nodded their heads. Keith held on to her dress with one hand. He put the thumb of his other hand into his mouth.

"Thank you," Carlyle said. "I feel, I really feel a hundred percent better." He shook his head and grinned. He felt a welling in his chest as he kissed each of his children goodbye. He told Mrs. Webster what time she could expect him home, put on his coat, said goodbye once more, and went out of the house. For the first time in months, it seemed, he felt his burden had lifted a little. Driving to school, he listened to some music on the radio.

During first-period art-history class, he lingered over slides of Byzantine paintings. He patiently explained the nuances of detail and motif. He pointed out the emotional power and fitness of the work. But he took so long trying to place the anonymous artists in their social milieu that some of his students began to scrape their shoes on the floor, or else clear their throats. They covered only a third of the lesson plan that day. He was still talking when the bell rang.

In his next class, watercolor painting, he felt unusually calm and insightful. "Like this, like this," he said, guiding their hands. "Delicately. Like a breath of air on the paper. Just a touch. Like so. See?" he'd say and felt on the edge of discovery himself. "*Suggestion* is what it's all about," he said, holding lightly to Sue Colvin's fingers as he guided her brush. "You've got to work with your mistakes until they look intended. Understand?"

As he moved down the lunch line in the faculty dining room, he saw Carol a few places ahead of him. She paid for her food. He waited impatiently while his own bill was being rung up. Carol was halfway across the room by the time he caught up with her. He slipped his hand under her elbow and guided her to an empty table near the window.

"God, Carlyle," she said after they'd seated themselves. She picked up her glass of iced tea. Her face was flushed. "Did you see the look Mrs. Storr gave us? What's wrong with you? Everybody will know." She sipped from her iced tea and put the glass down.

"The hell with Mrs. Storr," Carlyle said. "Hey, let me tell you something. Honey, I feel light-years better than I did this time yesterday. Jesus," he said.

"What's happened?" Carol said. "Carlyle, tell me." She moved her fruit cup to one side of her tray and shook cheese over her spaghetti. But she didn't eat anything. She waited for him to go on. "Tell me what it is."

He told her about Mrs. Webster. He even told her about Mr. Webster. How the man'd had to hot-wire the truck in order to start it. Carlyle ate his tapioca while he talked. Then he ate the garlic bread. He drank Carol's iced tea down before he realized he was doing it.

"You're nuts, Carlyle," she said, nodding at the spaghetti in his plate that he hadn't touched.

He shook his head. "My God, Carol. God, I feel good, you know? I feel better than I have all summer." He lowered his voice. "Come over tonight, will you?"

He reached under the table and put his hand on her knee. She turned red again. She raised her eyes and looked around the dining room. But no one was paying any attention to them. She nodded quickly. Then she reached under the table and touched his hand.

That afternoon he arrived home to find his house neat and orderly and his children in clean clothes. In the kitchen, Keith and Sarah stood on chairs, helping Mrs. Webster with gingerbread cookies. Sarah's hair was out of her face and held back with a barrette.

"Daddy!" his children cried, happy, when they saw him.

"Keith, Sarah," he said. "Mrs. Webster, I—" But she didn't let him finish.

"We've had a fine day, Mr. Carlyle," Mrs. Webster said quickly. She wiped her fingers on the apron she was wearing. It was an old apron with blue windmills on it and it had belonged to Eileen. "Such beautiful children. They're a treasure. Just a treasure."

"I don't know what to say." Carlyle stood by the drainboard and watched Sarah press out some dough. He could smell the spice. He took off his coat and sat down at the kitchen table. He loosened his tie.

"Today was a get-acquainted day," Mrs. Webster said. "Tomorrow we have some other plans. I thought we'd walk to the park. We ought to take advantage of this good weather."

"That's a fine idea," Carlyle said. "That's just fine. Good. Good for you, Mrs. Webster."

"I'll finish putting these cookies in the oven, and by that time Mr. Webster should be here. You said four o'clock? I told him to come at four."

Carlyle nodded, his heart full.

"You had a call today," she said as she went over to the sink with the mixing bowl. "Mrs. Carlyle called."

"Mrs. Carlyle," he said. He waited for whatever it was Mrs. Webster might say next.

"Yes. I identified myself, but she didn't seem surprised to find me here. She said a few words to each of the children."

Carlyle glanced at Keith and Sarah, but they weren't paying any attention. They were lining up cookies on another baking sheet.

Mrs. Webster continued. "She left a message. Let me see, I wrote it down, but I think I can remember it. She said, 'Tell him'—that is, tell you—'what goes around, comes around.' I think that's right. She said you'd understand."

Carlyle stared at her. He heard Mr. Webster's truck outside.

"That's Mr. Webster," she said and took off the apron.

Carlyle nodded.

"Seven o'clock in the morning?" she asked.

"That will be fine," he said. "And thank you again."

That evening he bathed each of the children, got them into their pajamas, and then read to them. He listened to their prayers, tucked in their covers, and turned out the light. It was nearly nine o'clock. He made himself a drink and watched something on TV until he heard Carol's car pull into the drive.

Around ten, while they were in bed together, the phone rang. He swore, but he didn't get up to answer it. It kept ringing.

"It might be important," Carol said, sitting up. "It might be my sitter. She has this number."

"It's my wife," Carlyle said. "I know it's her. She's losing her mind. She's going crazy. I'm not going to answer it."

"I have to go pretty soon anyway," Carol said. "It was real sweet tonight, honey." She touched his face.

It was the middle of the fall term. Mrs. Webster had been with him for nearly six weeks. During this time, Carlyle's life had undergone a number of changes. For one thing, he was becoming reconciled to the fact that Eileen was gone and, as far as he could understand it, had no intention of coming back. He had stopped imagining that this might change. It was only late at night, on the nights he was not with Carol, that he wished for an end to the love he still had for Eileen and felt tormented as to why all of this had happened. But for the most part he and the children were happy; they thrived under Mrs. Webster's attentions. Lately, she'd gotten into the routine of making their dinner and keeping it in the oven, warming, until his arrival home from school. He'd walk in the door to the smell of something good coming from the kitchen and find Keith and Sarah helping to set the dining-room table. Now and again he asked Mrs. Webster if she would care for overtime work on Saturdays. She agreed, as long as it wouldn't entail her being at his house before noon. Saturday mornings, she said, she had things to do for Mr. Webster and herself. On these days, Carol would leave Dodge with Carlyle's children, all of them under Mrs. Webster's care, and Carol and he would drive to a restaurant out in the country for dinner. He believed his life was beginning again. Though he hadn't heard from Eileen since that call six weeks ago, he found himself able to think about her now without either being angry or else feeling close to tears.

At school, they were just leaving the medieval period and about to enter the Gothic. The Renaissance was still some time off, at least not until after the Christmas recess. It was during this time that Carlyle got sick. Overnight, it seemed, his chest tightened and his head began to hurt. The joints of his body became stiff. He felt dizzy when he moved around. The headache got worse. He woke up with it on a Sunday and thought of calling Mrs. Webster to ask her to come and take the children somewhere. They'd been sweet to him, bringing him glasses of juice and some soda pop. But he couldn't take care of them. On the second morning of his illness, he was just able to get to the phone to call in sick. He gave his name, his school, department, and the nature of his illness to the person who answered the number. Then he recommended Mel Fisher as his substitute. Fisher was a man who painted abstract oils three or four days a week, sixteen hours a day, but who didn't sell or even show his work. He was a friend of Carlyle's. "Get Mel Fisher," Carlyle told the woman on the other end of the line. "Fisher," he whispered.

He made it back to his bed, got under the covers, and went to sleep. In his sleep, he heard the pickup engine running outside, and then the backfire it made as the engine was turned off. Sometime later he heard Mrs. Webster's voice outside the bedroom door.

"Mr. Carlyle?"

"Yes, Mrs. Webster." His voice sounded strange to him. He kept his eyes shut. "I'm sick today. I called the school. I'm going to stay in bed today."

"I see. Don't worry, then," she said. "I'll look after things at this end."

He shut his eyes. Directly, still in a state between sleeping and waking, he thought he heard his front door open and close. He listened. Out in the kitchen, he heard a man say something in a low voice, and a chair being pulled away from the table. Pretty soon he heard the voices of the children. Sometime later—he wasn't sure how much time had passed—he heard Mrs. Webster outside his door.

"Mr. Carlyle, should I call the doctor?"

"No, that's all right," he said. "I think it's just a bad cold. But I feel hot all over. I think I have too many covers. And it's too warm in the house. Maybe you'll turn down the furnace." Then he felt himself drift back into sleep.

In a little while, he heard the children talking to Mrs. Webster in the living room. Were they coming inside or going out? Carlyle wondered. Could it be the next day already?

He went back to sleep. But then he was aware of his door opening. Mrs. Webster appeared beside his bed. She put her hand on his forehead.

"You're burning up," she said. "You have a fever."

"I'll be all right," Carlyle said. "I just need to sleep a little longer. And maybe you could turn the furnace down. Please, I'd appreciate it if you could get me some aspirin. I have an awful headache."

Mrs. Webster left the room. But his door stood open. Carlyle could hear the TV going out there. "Keep it down, Jim," he heard her say, and the volume was lowered at once. Carlyle fell asleep again.

But he couldn't have slept more than a minute, because Mrs. Webster was suddenly back in his room with a tray. She sat down on the side of his bed. He roused himself and tried to sit up. She put a pillow behind his back.

"Take these," she said and gave him some tablets. "Drink this." She held a glass of juice for him. "I also brought you some Cream of Wheat. I want you to eat it. It'll be good for you."

He took the aspirin and drank the juice. He nodded. But he shut his eyes once more. He was going back to sleep.

"Mr. Carlyle," she said.

He opened his eyes. "I'm awake," he said. "I'm sorry." He sat up a little. "I'm too warm, that's all. What time is it? Is it eight-thirty yet?"

"It's a little after nine-thirty," she said.

"Nine-thirty," he said.

"Now I'm going to feed this cereal to you. And you're going to open up and eat it. Six bites, that's all. Here, here's the first bite. Open," she said. "You're going to feel better after you eat this. Then I'll let you go back to sleep. You eat this, and then you can sleep all you want."

He ate the cereal she spooned to him and asked for more juice. He drank the juice, and then he pulled down in the bed again. Just as he was going off to sleep, he felt her covering him with another blanket.

The next time he awoke, it was afternoon. He could tell it was afternoon by the pale light that came through his window. He reached up and pulled the curtain back. He could see that it was overcast outside; the wintry sun was behind the clouds. He got out of bed slowly, found his slippers, and put on his robe. He went into the bathroom and looked at himself in the mirror. Then he washed his face and took some more aspirin. He used the towel and then went out to the living room.

On the dining-room table, Mrs. Webster had spread some newspaper, and she and the children were pinching clay figures together. They had already made some things that had long necks and bulging eyes, things that resembled giraffes, or else dinosaurs. Mrs. Webster looked up as he walked by the table.

"How are you feeling?" Mrs. Webster asked him as he settled onto the sofa. He could see into the dining-room area, where Mrs. Webster and the children sat at the table.

"Better, thanks. A little better," he said. "I still have a headache, and I feel a little warm." He brought the back of his hand up to his forehead. "But I'm better. Yes, I'm better. Thanks for your help this morning."

"Can I get you anything now?" Mrs. Webster said. "Some more juice or some tea? I don't think coffee would hurt, but I think tea would be better. Some juice would be best of all."

"No, no thanks," he said. "I'll just sit here for a while. It's good to be out of bed. I feel a little weak is all. Mrs. Webster?"

She looked at him and waited.

"Did I hear Mr. Webster in the house this morning? It's fine, of course. I'm just sorry I didn't get a chance to meet him and say hello."

"It was him," she said. "He wanted to meet you, too. I asked him to come in. He just picked the wrong morning, what with you being sick and all. I'd wanted to tell you something about our plans, Mr. Webster's and mine, but this morning wasn't a good time for it."

"Tell me what?" he said, alert, fear plucking at his heart.

She shook her head. "It's all right," she said. "It can wait."

"Tell him what?" Sarah said. "Tell him what?"

"What, what?" Keith picked it up. The children stopped what they were doing.

"Just a minute, you two," Mrs. Webster said as she got to her feet.

"Mrs. Webster, Mrs. Webster!" Keith cried.

"Now see here, little man," Mrs. Webster said. "I need to talk to your father. Your father is sick today. You just take it easy. You go on and play with your clay. If you don't watch it, your sister is going to get ahead of you with these creatures."

Just as she began to move toward the living room, the phone rang. Carlyle reached over to the end table and picked up the receiver.

As before, he heard faint singing in the wire and knew that it was Eileen. "Yes," he said. "What is it?"

"Carlyle," his wife said, "I know, don't ask me how, that things are not going so well right now. You're sick, aren't you? Richard's been sick, too. It's something going around. He can't keep anything on his stomach. He's already missed a week of rehearsal for this play he's doing. I've had to go down myself and help block out scenes with his assistant. But I didn't call to tell you that. Tell me how things are out there."

"Nothing to tell," Carlyle said. "I'm sick, that's all. A touch of the flu. But I'm getting better."

"Are you still writing in your journal?" she asked. It caught him by surprise. Several years before, he'd told her that he was keeping a journal. Not a diary, he'd said, a journal—as if that explained something. But he'd never shown it to her, and he hadn't written in it for over a year. He'd forgotten about it.

"Because," she said, "you ought to write something in the journal during this period. How you feel and what you're thinking. You know, where your head is at during this period of sickness. Remember, sickness is a message about your health and your well-being. It's telling you things. Keep a record. You know what I mean? When you're well, you can look back and see what the message was. You can read it later, after the fact. Colette did that," Eileen said. "When she had a fever this one time."

"Who?" Carlyle said. "What did you say?"

"Colette," Eileen answered. "The French writer. You know who I'm talking about. We had a book of hers around the house. *Gigi* or something. I didn't read *that* book, but I've been reading her since I've been out here. Richard turned me on to her. She wrote a little book about what it was like, about what she was thinking and feeling the whole time she had this fever. Sometimes her temperature was a hundred and two. Sometimes it was lower. Maybe it went higher than a hundred and two. But a hundred and two was the highest she ever took her temperature and wrote, too, when she had the fever. Anyway, she wrote about it."

That's what I'm saying. Try writing about what it's like. Something might come of it," Eileen said and, inexplicably, it seemed to Carlyle, she laughed. "At least later on you'd have an hour-by-hour account of your sickness. To look back at. At least you'd have that to show for it. Right now you've just got this discomfort. You've got to translate that into something usable."

He pressed his fingertips against his temple and shut his eyes. But she was still on the line, waiting for him to say something. What could he say? It was clear to him that she was insane.

"Jesus," he said. "Jesus, Eileen. I don't know what to say to that. I really don't. I have to go now. Thanks for calling," he said.

"It's all right," she said. "We have to be able to communicate. Kiss the kids for me. Tell them I love them. And Richard sends his hellos to you. Even though he's flat on his back."

"Goodbye," Carlyle said and hung up. Then he brought his hands to his face. He remembered, for some reason, seeing the fat girl make the same gesture that time as she moved toward the car. He lowered his hands and looked at Mrs. Webster, who was watching him.

"Not bad news, I hope," she said. The old woman had moved a chair near to where he sat on the sofa.

Carlyle shook his head.

"Good," Mrs. Webster said. "That's good. Now, Mr. Carlyle, this may not be the best time in the world to talk about this." She glanced out to the dining room. At the table, the children had their heads bent over the clay. "But since it has to be talked about sometime soon, and since it concerns you and the children, and you're up now, I have something to tell you. Jim and I, we're getting on. The thing is, we need something more than we have at the present. Do you know what I'm saying? This is hard for me," she said and shook her head. Carlyle nodded slowly. He knew that she was going to tell him she had to leave. He wiped his face on his sleeve. "Jim's son by a former marriage, Bob—the man is forty years old—called yesterday to invite us to go out to Oregon and help him with his mink ranch. Jim would be doing whatever they do with minks, and I'd cook, buy the groceries, clean house, and do anything else that needed doing. It's a chance for both of us. And it's board and room and then some. Jim and I won't have to worry anymore about what's going to happen to us. You know what I'm saying. Right now, Jim doesn't have anything," she said. "He was sixty-two last week. He hasn't had anything for some time. He came in this morning to tell you about it himself, because I was going to have to give notice, you see. We thought—I thought—it would help if Jim was here when I told you." She waited for Carlyle to say something. When he didn't, she went on. "I'll finish out the week, and I could stay on a couple of days next week, if need be. But then, you know, for sure, we really have to leave, and you'll have to wish us luck. I mean, can you imagine—all the way out there to Oregon in that old rattletrap of ours? But I'm going to miss these little kids. They're so precious."

After a time, when he still hadn't moved to answer her, she got up from her chair and went to sit on the cushion next to his. She touched the sleeve of his robe. "Mr. Carlyle?"

"I understand," he said. "I want you to know your being here has made a big difference to me and the children." His head ached so much that he had to squint his eyes. "This headache," he said. "This headache is killing me."

Mrs. Webster reached over and laid the back of her hand against his forehead. "You still have some fever," she told him. "I'll get more aspirin. That'll help bring it down. I'm still on the case here," she said. "I'm still the doctor."

"My wife thinks I should write down what this feels like," Carlyle said. "She thinks it might be a good idea to describe what the fever is like. So I can look back later and get the message." He laughed. Some tears came to his eyes. He wiped them away with the heel of his hand.

"I think I'll get your aspirin and juice and then go out there with the kids," Mrs. Webster said. "Looks to me like they've about worn out their interest with that clay."

Carlyle was afraid she'd move into the other room and leave him alone. He wanted to talk to her. He cleared his throat. "Mrs. Webster, there's something I want you to know. For a long time, my wife and I loved each other more than anything or anybody in the world. And that includes those children. We thought, well, we *knew* that we'd grow old together. And we knew we'd do all the things in the world that we wanted to do, and do them together." He shook his head. That seemed the saddest thing of all to him now—that whatever they did from now on, each would do it without the other.

"There, it's all right," Mrs. Webster said. She patted his hand. He sat forward and began to talk again. After a time, the children came out to the living room. Mrs. Webster caught their attention and held a finger to her lips. Carlyle looked at them and went on talking. Let them listen, he thought. It concerns them, too. The children seemed to understand they had to remain quiet, even pretend some interest, so they sat down next to Mrs. Webster's legs. Then they got down on their stomachs on the carpet and started to giggle. But Mrs. Webster looked sternly in their direction, and that stopped it.

Carlyle went on talking. At first, his head still ached, and he felt awkward to be in his pajamas on the sofa with this old woman beside him, waiting patiently for him to go on to the next thing. But then his headache went away. And soon he stopped feeling awkward and forgot how he was supposed to feel. He had begun his story somewhere in the middle, after the children were born. But then he backed up and started at the beginning, back when Eileen was eighteen and he was nineteen, a boy and girl in love, burning with it.

He stopped to wipe his forehead. He moistened his lips.

"Go on," Mrs. Webster said. "I know what you're saying. You just keep talking, Mr. Carlyle. Sometimes it's good to talk about it. Sometimes it has to be talked about. Besides, I want to hear it. And you're going to feel better afterwards.

Something just like it happened to me once, something like what you're describing. Love. That's what it is."

The children fell asleep on the carpet. Keith had his thumb in his mouth. Carlyle was still talking when Mr. Webster came to the door, knocked, and then stepped inside to collect Mrs. Webster.

"Sit down, Jim," Mrs. Webster said. "There's no hurry. Go on with what you were saying, Mr. Carlyle."

Carlyle nodded at the old man, and the old man nodded back, then got himself one of the dining-room chairs and carried it into the living room. He brought the chair close to the sofa and sat down on it with a sigh. Then he took off his cap and wearily lifted one leg over the other. When Carlyle began talking again, the old man put both feet on the floor. The children woke up. They sat up on the carpet and rolled their heads back and forth. But by then Carlyle had said all he knew to say, so he stopped talking.

"Good. Good for you," Mrs. Webster said when she saw he had finished. "You're made out of good stuff. And so is she—so is Mrs. Carlyle. And don't you forget it. You're both going to be okay after this is over." She got up and took off the apron she'd been wearing. Mr. Webster got up, too, and put his cap back on.

At the door, Carlyle shook hands with both of the Websters.

"So long," Jim Webster said. He touched the bill of his cap.

"Good luck to you," Carlyle said.

Mrs. Webster said she'd see him in the morning then, bright and early as always.

As if something important had been settled, Carlyle said, "Right!"

The old couple went carefully along the walk and got into their truck. Jim Webster bent down under the dashboard. Mrs. Webster looked at Carlyle and waved. It was then, as he stood at the window, that he felt something come to an end. It had to do with Eileen and the life before this. Had he ever waved at her? He must have, of course, he knew he had, yet he could not remember just now. But he understood it was over, and he felt able to let her go. He was sure their life together had happened in the way he said it had. But it was something that had passed. And that passing—though it had seemed impossible and he'd fought against it—would become a part of him now, too, as surely as anything else he'd left behind.

As the pickup lurched forward, he lifted his arm once more. He saw the old couple lean toward him briefly as they drove away. Then he brought his arm down and turned to his children.

JOHN CHEEVER
(1912–1982)

JOHN CHEEVER was born in Quincy, Massachusetts, and attended Thayer Academy. In 1941 he married Mary Winternitz; their three children are Susan (a novelist and memoirist), Benjamin (editor of *The Letters of John Cheever* and a novelist himself), and Federico. His adult years were spent largely in New York, the last twenty or so in an old Dutch farmhouse in Ossining, New York.

Cheever published five novels in all: *The Wapshot Chronicle* (1957), *The Wapshot Scandal* (1964), *Bullet Park* (1969), *Falconer* (1977), and *Oh What a Paradise It Seems* (1982). The *Wapshot* novels draw their setting and exuberant comic life from their author's Massachusetts family lore and background. After that, the principal locale of his work, notably his short stories, is the New York suburb (often dubbed Shady Hill); these and other plots often involve excursions into the city. His story collections, published between 1953 and 1978, include *The Way Some People Live* (1943), *The Enormous Radio* (1953), *The Housebreaker of Shady Hill* (1958), *Some People, Places, and Things That Will Not Appear in My Next Novel* (1961), *The Brigadier and the Golf Widow* (1964), *The World of Apples* (1973), and *The Stories of John Cheever* (1978). The crowning achievement of a luminous career, *Stories* received the National Book Critics Circle Award, the American Book Award, and the 1979 Pulitzer Prize for fiction. Included among Cheever's other awards are the 1958 National Book Award for *The Wapshot Chronicle,* the 1965 Howells Medal of the American Academy of Arts and Letters for *The Wapshot Scandal,* two Guggenheim Fellowships, and memberships in the National Institute and the American Academy of Arts and Letters. Shortly before his death, in his acceptance remarks for the 1982 National Medal for Literature, he said, "A page of good prose seems to me the most serious dialogue that well-informed and intelligent men and women carry on today in their endeavor to make sure that the fires of this planet burn peaceably." In Cheever's stories an off-tilt situation is often righted by the leap of language itself to realms of magic or myth. His own prose, threaded with irony and compassion, made of gossamer and steel, ranks with the best there is.

"The Country Husband" (1964) is a subtly layered story, with the theme of betrayal filtered through seriocomic incident and the poetic density of the language. Francis Weed, whose family life is rich in small disappointments, escapes a plane crash, only to discover when he arrives home that no one is paying any attention. The story's large events are upstaged by the small ones, as Weed dives headlong into love and the regions of his own faithlessness.

The Country Husband

To begin at the beginning, the airplane from Minneapolis in which Francis Weed was traveling East ran into heavy weather. The sky had been a hazy blue, with the clouds below the plane lying so close together that nothing could be seen of the earth. Then mist began to form outside the windows, and they flew into a white cloud of such density that it reflected the exhaust fires. The color of the cloud darkened to gray, and the plane began to rock. Francis had been in heavy weather before, but he had never been shaken up so much. The man in the seat beside him pulled a flask out of his pocket and took a drink. Francis smiled at his neighbor, but the man looked away; he wasn't sharing his pain killer with anyone. The plane began to drop and flounder wildly. A child was crying. The air in the cabin was overheated and stale, and Francis' left foot went to sleep. He read a little from a paper book that he had bought at the airport, but the violence of the storm divided his attention. It was black outside the ports. The exhaust fires blazed and shed sparks in the dark, and, inside, the shaded lights, the stuffiness, and the window curtains gave the cabin an atmosphere of intense and misplaced domesticity. Then the lights flickered and went out. "You know what I've always wanted to do?" the man beside Francis said suddenly. "I've always wanted to buy a farm in New Hampshire and raise beef cattle." The stewardess announced that they were going to make an emergency landing. All but the children saw in their minds the spreading wings of the Angel of Death. The pilot could be heard singing faintly, "I've got sixpence, jolly, jolly sixpence. I've got sixpence to last me all my life . . ." There was no other sound.

The loud groaning of the hydraulic valves swallowed up the pilot's song, and there was a shrieking high in the air, like automobile brakes, and the plane hit flat on its belly in a cornfield and shook them so violently that an old man up forward howled, "Me kidneys! Me kidneys!" The stewardess flung open the door, and someone opened an emergency door at the back, letting in the sweet noise of their continuing mortality—the idle splash and smell of a heavy rain. Anxious for their lives, they filed out of the doors and scattered over the cornfield in all directions, praying that the thread would hold. It did. Nothing happened. When it was clear that the plane would not burn or explode, the crew and the stewardess gathered the passengers together and led them to the shelter of a barn. They were not far from Philadelphia, and in a little while a string of taxis took them into the city. "It's just like the Marne," someone said, but there was surprisingly little relaxation of that suspiciousness with which many Americans regard their fellow travelers.

In Philadelphia, Francis Weed got a train to New York. At the end of that journey, he crossed the city and caught just as it was about to pull out the commuting train that he took five nights a week to his home in Shady Hill.

He sat with Trace Bearden. "You know, I was in that plane that just crashed outside Philadelphia," he said. "We came down in a field . . ." He had traveled faster than the newspapers or the rain, and the weather in New York was sunny and mild. It was a day in late September, as fragrant and shapely as an apple. Trace listened to the story, but how could he get excited? Francis had no powers that would let him re-create a brush with death—particularly in the atmosphere of a commuting train, journeying through a sunny countryside where already, in the slum gardens, there were signs of harvest. Trace picked up his newspaper, and Francis was left alone with his thoughts. He said good night to Trace on the platform at Shady Hill and drove in his secondhand Volkswagen up to the Blenhollow neighborhood, where he lived.

The Weeds' Dutch Colonial house was larger than it appeared to be from the driveway. The living room was spacious and divided like Gaul into three parts. Around an ell to the left as one entered from the vestibule was the long table, laid for six, with candles and a bowl of fruit in the center. The sounds and smells that came from the open kitchen door were appetizing, for Julia Weed was a good cook. The largest part of the living room centered on a fireplace. On the right were some bookshelves and a piano. The room was polished and tranquil, and from the windows that opened to the west there was some late-summer sunlight, brilliant and as clear as water. Nothing here was neglected; nothing had not been burnished. It was not the kind of household where, after prying open a stuck cigarette box, you would find an old shirt button and a tarnished nickel. The hearth was swept, the roses on the piano were reflected in the polish of the broad top, and there was an album of Schubert waltzes on the rack. Louisa Weed, a pretty girl of nine, was looking out the western windows. Her younger brother Henry was standing beside her. Her still younger brother, Toby, was studying the figures of some tonsured monks drinking beer on the polished brass of the woodbox. Francis, taking off his hat and putting down his paper, was not consciously pleased with the scene; he was not that reflective. It was his element, his creation, and he returned to it with that sense of lightness and strength with which any creature returns to his home. "Hi, everybody," he said. "The plane from Minneapolis . . ."

Nine times out of ten, Francis would be greeted with affection, but tonight the children are absorbed in their own antagonisms. Francis had not finished his sentence about the plane crash before Henry plants a kick in Louisa's behind. Louisa swings around, saying, "*Damn* you!" Francis makes the mistake of scolding Louisa for bad language before he punishes Henry. Now Louisa turns on her father and accuses him of favoritism. Henry is always right; she is persecuted and lonely; her lot is hopeless. Francis turns to his son, but the boy has justification for the kick—she hit him first; she hit him on the ear, which is dangerous. Louisa agrees with this passionately. She hit him on the ear, and she *meant* to hit him on the ear, because he messed up her china collection. Henry says that this is a lie. Little Toby turns away from the woodbox to throw in some evidence for Louisa. Henry claps his hand over little Toby's mouth. Francis separates the two boys but accidentally pushes Toby into the woodbox. Toby begins to cry. Louisa is already crying. Just then, Julia Weed comes into that part of the room where the table is laid. She is a pretty, intelligent woman, and the white in her hair is premature. She does not seem to notice the fracas. "Hello, darling," she says serenely to Francis. "Wash your hands, everyone. Dinner is ready." She strikes a match and lights the six candles in this vale of tears.

This simple announcement, like the war cries of the Scottish chieftains, only refreshes the ferocity of the combatants. Louisa gives Henry a blow on the shoulder. Henry, although he seldom cries, has pitched nine innings and is tired. He bursts into tears. Little Toby discovers a splinter in his hand and begins to howl. Francis says loudly that he has been in a plane crash and that he is tired. Julia appears again from the kitchen and, still ignoring the chaos, asks Francis to go upstairs and tell Helen that everything is ready. Francis is happy to go; it is like getting back to headquarters company. He is planning to tell his oldest daughter about the airplane crash, but Helen is lying on her bed reading a *True Romance* magazine, and the first thing Francis does is to take the magazine from her hand and remind Helen that he has forbidden her to buy it. She did not buy it, Helen replies. It was given to her by her best friend, Bessie Black. Everybody reads *True Romance*. Bessie Black's father reads *True Romance*. There isn't a girl in Helen's class who doesn't read *True Romance*. Francis expresses his detestation of the magazine and then tells her that dinner is ready—although from the sounds downstairs it doesn't seem so. Helen follows him down the stairs. Julia has seated herself in the candlelight and spread a napkin over her lap. Neither Louisa nor Henry has come to the table. Little Toby is still howling, lying face down on the floor. Francis speaks to him gently: "Daddy was in a plane crash this afternoon, Toby. Don't you want to hear about it?" Toby goes on crying. "If you don't come to the table now, Toby," Francis says, "I'll have to send you to bed without any supper." The little boy rises, gives him a cutting look, flies up the stairs to his bedroom, and slams the door. "Oh dear," Julia says, and starts to go after him. Francis says that she will spoil him. Julia says that Toby is ten pounds underweight and has to be encouraged to eat. Winter is coming, and he will spend the cold months in bed unless he has his dinner. Julia goes upstairs. Francis sits down at the table with Helen. Helen is suffering from the dismal feeling of having read too intently on a fine day, and she gives her father and the room a jaded look. She doesn't understand about the plane crash, because there wasn't a drop of rain in Shady Hill.

Julia returns with Toby, and they all sit down and are served. "Do I have to look at that big, fat slob?" Henry says, of Louisa. Everybody but Toby enters into this skirmish, and it rages up and down the table for five minutes. Toward the end, Henry puts his napkin over his head and, trying to eat that way, spills spinach all over his shirt. Francis asks Julia if the children couldn't have their dinner earlier. Julia's guns are loaded for this. She can't cook two dinners and lay two tables. She paints with lightning strokes that panorama of drudgery in which her youth, her beauty, and her wit have been lost. Francis says that he must be understood; he was nearly killed in an airplane crash, and he doesn't like to come home every night to a battlefield. Now Julia is deeply concerned. Her voice trembles. He doesn't come home every night to a battlefield. The accusation is stupid and mean. Everything was tranquil until he arrived. She stops speaking, puts down her knife and fork, and looks into her plate as if it is a gulf. She begins to cry. "Poor Mummy!" Toby says, and when Julia gets up from the table, drying her tears with a napkin, Toby goes to her side. "Poor Mummy," he says. "Poor Mummy!" And they climb the stairs together. The other children drift away from the battlefield, and Francis goes into the back garden for a cigarette and some air.

It was a pleasant garden, with walks and flower beds and places to sit. The sunset had nearly burned out, but there was still plenty of light. Put into a thoughtful mood by the crash and the battle, Francis listened to the evening sounds of Shady Hill. "Varmints! Rascals!" old Mr. Nixon shouted to the squirrels in his bird-feeding station. "Avaunt and quit my sight!" A door slammed. Someone was cutting grass. Then Donald Goslin, who lived at the corner, began to play the "Moonlight Sonata." He did this nearly every night. He threw the tempo out the window and played it *rubato* from beginning to end, like an outpouring of tearful petulance, lonesomeness, and self-pity—of everything it was Beethoven's greatness not to know. The music rang up and down the street beneath the trees like an appeal for love, for tenderness, aimed at some lovely housemaid—some fresh-faced, homesick girl from Galway, looking at old snapshots in her third-floor room. "Here, Jupiter, here, Jupiter," Francis called to the Mercers' retriever. Jupiter crashed through the tomato vines with the remains of a felt hat in his mouth.

Jupiter was an anomaly. His retrieving instincts and his high spirits were out of place in Shady Hill. He was as black as coal, with a long, alert, intelligent, rakehell face. His eyes gleamed with mischief, and he held his head high. It was the fierce, heavily collared dog's head that appears in heraldry, in tapestry, and that used to appear on umbrella handles and walking sticks. Jupiter went where he pleased, ransacking wastebaskets, clotheslines, garbage pails, and shoe bags. He broke up garden parties and tennis matches, and got mixed up in the processional at Christ Church on Sunday, barking at the men in red dresses. He crashed through old Mr. Nixon's rose garden two or three times a day, cutting a wide swath through the Condesa de Sastagos, and as soon as Donald Goslin lighted his barbecue fire on Thursday nights, Jupiter would get the scent. Nothing the Goslins did could drive him away. Sticks and stones and rude commands only moved him to the edge of the terrace, where he remained, with his gallant and heraldic muzzle, waiting for Donald Goslin to turn his back and reach for the salt. Then he would spring onto the terrace, lift the steak lightly off the fire, and run away with the Goslins' dinner. Jupiter's days were numbered. The Wrightsons' German gardener or the Farquarsons' cook would soon poison him. Even old Mr. Nixon might put some arsenic in the garbage that Jupiter loved. "Here, Jupiter, Jupiter!" Francis called, but the dog pranced off, shaking the hat in his white teeth. Looking at the windows of his house, Francis saw that Julia had come down and was blowing out the candles.

Julia and Francis Weed went out a great deal. Julia was well liked and gregarious, and her love of parties sprang from a most natural dread of chaos and loneliness. She went through her morning mail with real anxiety, looking for invitations, and she usually found some, but she was insatiable, and if she had gone out seven nights a week, it would not have cured her of a reflective look—the look of someone who hears distant music—for she would always suppose that there was a more brilliant party somewhere else. Francis limited her to two weeknight parties, putting a flexible interpretation on Friday, and rode through the weekend like a dory in a gale. The day after the airplane crash, the Weeds were to have dinner with the Farquarsons.

Francis got home late from town, and Julia got the sitter while he dressed, and then hurried him out of the house. The party was small and pleasant, and Francis settled down to enjoy himself. A new maid passed the drinks. Her hair was dark, and her face was round and pale and seemed familiar to Francis. He had not developed his memory as a sentimental faculty. Wood smoke, lilac, and other such perfumes did not stir him, and his memory was something like his appendix—a vestigial repository. It was not his limitation at all to be unable to escape the past; it was perhaps his limitation that he had escaped it so successfully. He might have seen the maid at other parties, he might have seen her taking a walk on Sunday afternoons, but in either case he would not be searching his memory now. Her face was, in a wonderful way, a moon face—Norman or Irish—but it was not beautiful enough to account for his feeling that he had seen her before, in circumstances that he ought to be able to remember. He asked Nellie Farquarson who she was. Nellie said that the maid had come through an agency, and that her home was Trenon, in Normandy—a small place with a church and a restaurant that Nellie had once visited. While Nellie talked on about her travels abroad, Francis realized where he had seen the woman before. It had been at the end of the war. He had left a replacement depot with some other men and taken a three-day pass in Trenon. On their second day, they had walked out to a crossroads to see the public chastisement of a young woman who had lived with the German commandant during the Occupation.

It was a cool morning in the fall. The sky was overcast, and poured down onto the dirt crossroads a very discouraging light. They were on high land and could see how like one another the shapes of the clouds and the hills were as they stretched off toward the sea. The prisoner arrived sitting on a three-legged stool in a farm cart. She stood by the cart while the Mayor read the accusation and the sentence. Her head was bent and her face was set in that empty half smile behind which the whipped soul is suspended. When the Mayor was finished, she undid her hair and let it fall across her back. A little man with a gray mustache cut off her hair with shears and dropped it on the ground. Then, with a bowl of soapy water and a straight razor, he shaved her skull clean. A woman approached and began to undo the fastenings of her clothes, but the prisoner pushed her aside and undressed herself. When she pulled her chemise over her head and threw it on the ground, she was naked. The women jeered; the men were still. There was no change in the falseness or the plaintiveness of the prisoner's smile. The cold wind made her white skin rough and hardened the nipples of her breasts. The jeering ended gradually, put down by the recognition of their common humanity. One woman spat on her, but some inviolable grandeur in her nakedness lasted through the ordeal. When the crowd was quiet, she turned—she had begun to cry—and, with nothing on but a pair of worn black shoes and stockings, walked down the dirt road alone away from the village. The round white face had aged a little, but there was no question but that the maid who passed his cocktails and later served Francis his dinner was the woman who had been punished at the crossroads.

The war seemed now so distant and that world where the cost of partisanship had been death or torture so long ago. Francis had lost track of the men who had been with him in Vesey. He could not count on Julia's discretion. He could not tell anyone. And if he had told the story now, at the dinner table, it would have been a social as well as a human error. The people in the Farquarsons' living room seemed united in their tacit claim that there had been no past, no war—that there was no danger or trouble in the world. In the recorded history of human arrangements, this extraordinary meeting would have fallen into place, but the atmosphere of Shady Hill made the memory unseemly and impolite. The prisoner withdrew after passing the coffee, but the encounter left Francis feeling languid; it had opened his memory and his senses, and left them dilated. Julia went into the house. Francis stayed in the car to take the sitter home.

Expecting to see Mrs. Henlein, the old lady who usually stayed with the children, he was surprised when a young girl opened the door and came out onto the lighted stoop. She stayed in the light to count her textbooks. She was frowning and beautiful. Now, the world is full of beautiful young girls, but Francis saw here the difference between beauty and perfection. All those endearing flaws, moles, birthmarks; and healed wounds were missing, and he experienced in his consciousness that moment when music breaks glass, and felt a pang of recognition as strange, deep, and wonderful as anything in his life. It hung from her frown, from an impalpable darkness in her face—a look that impressed him as a direct appeal for love. When she had counted her books, she came down the steps and opened the car door. In the light, he saw that her cheeks were wet. She got in and shut the door.

"You're new," Francis said.

"Yes. Mrs. Henlein is sick. I'm Anne Murchison."

"Did the children give you any trouble?"

"Oh, no, no." She turned and smiled at him unhappily in the dim dashboard light. Her light hair caught on the collar of her jacket, and she shook her head to set it loose.

"You've been crying."

"Yes."

"I hope it was nothing that happened in our house."

"No, no, it was nothing that happened in your house." Her voice was bleak. "It's no secret. Everybody in the village knows. Daddy's an alcoholic, and he just called me from some saloon and gave me a piece of his mind. He thinks I'm immoral. He called just before Mrs. Weed came back."

"I'm sorry."

"Oh, *Lord!*" She gasped and began to cry. She turned toward Francis, and he took her in his arms and let her cry on his shoulder. She shook in his embrace, and this movement accentuated his sense of the fineness of her flesh and bone. The layers of their clothing felt thin, and when her shuddering began to diminish, it was so much like a paroxysm of love that Francis lost his head and pulled her roughly against him. She drew away. "I live on Belleview Avenue," she said. "You go down Lansing Street to the railroad bridge."

"All right." He started the car.

"You turn left at that traffic light. . . . Now you turn right here and go straight on toward the tracks."

The road Francis took brought him out of his own neighborhood, across the tracks, and toward the river, to a street where the near-poor lived, in houses whose peaked gables and trimmings of wooden lace conveyed the purest feelings of pride and romance, although the houses themselves could not have offered much privacy or comfort, they were all so small. The street was dark, and, stirred by the grace and beauty of the troubled girl, he seemed, in turning into it, to have come into the deepest part of some submerged memory. In the distance, he saw a porch light burning. It was the only one, and she said that the house with the light was where she lived. When he stopped the car, he could see beyond the porch light into a dimly lighted hallway with an old-fashioned clothes tree. "Well, here we are," he said, conscious that a young man would have said something different.

She did not move her hands from the books, where they were folded, and she turned and faced him. There were tears of lust in his eyes. Determinedly—not sadly—he opened the door on his side and walked around to open hers. He took her free hand, letting his fingers in between hers, climbed at her side the two concrete steps, and went up a narrow walk through a front garden where dahlias, marigolds, and roses—things that had withstood the light frosts—still bloomed, and made a bittersweet smell in the night air. At the steps, she freed her hand and then turned and kissed him swiftly. Then she crossed the porch and shut the door. The porch light went out, then the light in the hall. A second later, a light went on upstairs at the side of the house, shining into a tree that was still covered with leaves. It took her only a few minutes to undress and get into bed, and then the house was dark.

Julia was asleep when Francis got home. He opened a second window and got into bed to shut his eyes on that night, but as soon as they were shut—as soon as he had dropped off to sleep—the girl entered his mind, moving with perfect freedom through its shut doors and filling chamber after chamber with her light, her perfume, and the music of her voice. He was crossing the Atlantic with her on the old *Mauretania* and, later, living with her in Paris. When he woke from his dream, he got up and smoked a cigarette at the open window. Getting back into bed, he cast around in his mind for something he desired to do that would injure no one, and he thought of skiing. Up through the dimness in his mind rose the image of a mountain deep in snow. It was late in the day. Wherever his eyes looked, he saw broad and heartening things. Over his shoulder, there was a snow-filled valley, rising into wooded hills where the trees dimmed the whiteness like a sparse coat of hair. The cold deadened all sound but the loud, iron clanking of the lift machinery. The light on the trails was blue, and it was harder than it had been a minute or two earlier to pick the turns, harder to judge—now that the snow was all deep blue—the crust, the ice, the bare spots, and the deep piles of dry powder. Down the mountain he swung, matching his speed against the contours of a slope that had been formed in the first ice age, seeking with ardor some simplicity of feeling and circumstance. Night fell then, and he drank a Martini with some old friend in a dirty country bar.

In the morning, Francis' snow-covered mountain was gone, and he was left with his vivid memories of Paris and the *Mauretania*. He had been bitten gravely. He washed his body, shaved his jaws, drank his coffee, and missed the seven-thirty-one. The train pulled out just as he brought his car to the station, and the longing he felt for the coaches as they drew stubbornly away from him reminded him of the humors of love. He waited for the eight-two, on what was now an empty platform. It was a clear morning; the morning seemed thrown like a gleaming bridge of light over his mixed affairs. His spirits were feverish and high. The image of the girl seemed to put him into a relationship to the world that was mysterious and enthralling. Cars were beginning to fill up the parking lot, and he noticed that those that had driven down from the high land above Shady Hill were white with hoarfrost. This first clear sign of autumn thrilled him. An express train—a night train from Buffalo or Albany—came down the tracks between the platforms, and he saw that the roofs of the foremost cars were covered with a skin of ice. Struck by the miraculous physicalness of everything, he smiled at the passengers in the dining car, who could be seen eating eggs and wiping their mouths with napkins as they traveled. The sleeping-car compartments, with their soiled bed linen, trailed through the fresh morning like a string of rooming-house windows. Then he saw an extraordinary thing; at one of the bedroom windows sat an unclothed woman of exceptional beauty, combing her golden hair. She passed like an apparition through Shady Hill, combing and combing her hair, and Francis followed her with his eyes until she was out of sight. Then old Mrs. Wrightson joined him on the platform and began to talk.

"Well, I guess you must be surprised to see me here the third morning in a row," she said, "but because of my window curtains I'm becoming a regular commuter. The curtains I bought on Monday I returned on Tuesday, and the curtains I bought Tuesday I'm returning today. On Monday, I got exactly what I wanted— it's a wool tapestry with roses and birds—but when I got them home, I found they were the wrong length. Well, I exchanged them yesterday, and when I got them home, I found they were still the wrong length. Now I'm praying to high heaven that the decorator will have them in the right length, because you know my house, you *know* my living-room windows, and you can imagine what a problem they present. I don't know what to do with them."

"I know what to do with them," Francis said.

"What?"

"Paint them black on the inside, and shut up."

There was a gasp from Mrs. Wrightson, and Francis looked down at her to be sure that she knew he meant to be rude. She turned and walked away from him, so damaged in spirit that she limped. A wonderful feeling enveloped him, as if light were being shaken about him, and he thought again of Venus combing and combing her hair as she drifted through the Bronx. The realization of how many years had passed since he had enjoyed being deliberately impolite sobered him. Among his friends and neighbors, there were brilliant and gifted people—he saw that—but many of them, also, were bores and fools, and he had made the mistake of listening to them all with equal attention. He had confused a lack of discrimination with Christian love, and the confusion seemed general and destructive. He was grateful to the girl for this bracing sensation of independence. Birds were singing—cardinals and the last of the robins. The sky shone like enamel. Even the smell of ink from his morning paper honed his appetite for life, and the world that was spread out around him was plainly a paradise.

If Francis had believed in some hierarchy of love—in spirits armed with hunting bows, in the capriciousness of Venus and Eros—or even in magical potions, philters, and stews, in scapulae and quarters of the moon, it might have explained his susceptibility and his feverish high spirits. The autumnal loves of middle age are well publicized, and he guessed that he was face to face with one of these, but there was not a trace of autumn in what he felt. He wanted to sport in the green woods, scratch where he itched, and drink from the same cup.

His secretary, Miss Rainey, was late that morning—she went to a psychiatrist three mornings a week—and when she came in, Francis wondered what advice a psychiatrist would have for him. But the girl promised to bring back into his life something like the sound of music. The realization that this music might lead him straight to a trial for statutory rape at the county courthouse collapsed his happiness. The photograph of his four children laughing into the camera on the beach at Gay Head reproached him. On the letterhead of his firm there was a drawing of the Laocoön, and the figure of the priest and his sons in the coils of the snake appeared to him to have the deepest meaning.

He had lunch with Pinky Trabert. At a conversational level, the mores of his friends were robust and elastic, but he knew that the moral card house would come down on them all—on Julia and the children as well—if he got caught taking advantage of a baby-sitter. Looking back over the recent history of Shady Hill for some precedent, he found there was none. There was no turpitude; there had not been a divorce since he lived there; there had not even been a breath of scandal. Things seemed arranged with more propriety even than in the Kingdom of Heaven. After leaving Pinky, Francis went to a jeweler's and bought the girl a bracelet. How happy this clandestine purchase made him, how stuffy and comical the jeweler's clerks seemed, how sweet the women who passed at his back smelled! On Fifth Avenue, passing Atlas with his shoulders bent under the weight of the world, Francis thought of the strenuousness of containing his physicalness within the patterns he had chosen.

He did not know when he would see the girl next. He had the bracelet in his inside pocket when he got home. Opening the door of his house, he found her in the hall. Her back was to him, and she turned when she heard the door close. Her smile was open and loving. Her perfection stunned him like a fine day—a day after a thunderstorm. He seized her and covered her lips with his, and she struggled but she did not have to struggle for long, because just then little Gertrude Flannery appeared from somewhere and said, "Oh, Mr. Weed . . ."

Gertrude was a stray. She had been born with a taste for exploration, and she did not have it in her to center her life with her affectionate parents. People who did not know the Flannerys concluded from Gertrude's behavior that she was the child of a bitterly divided family, where drunken quarrels were the rule. This was not true. The fact that little Gertrude's clothing was ragged and thin was her own triumph over her mother's struggle to dress her warmly and neatly. Garrulous, skinny, and unwashed, she drifted from house to house around the Blenhollow neighborhood, forming and breaking alliances based on an attachment to babies, animals, children her own age, adolescents, and sometimes adults. Opening your front door in the morning, you would find Gertrude sitting on your stoop. Going into the bathroom to shave, you would find Gertrude using the toilet. Looking into your son's crib, you would find it empty, and, looking further, you would find that Gertrude had pushed him in his baby carriage into the next village. She was helpful, pervasive, honest, hungry, and loyal. She never went home of her own choice. When the time to go arrived, she was indifferent to all its signs. "Go home, Gertrude," people could be heard saying in one house or another, night after night. "Go home, Gertrude. It's time for you to go home now, Gertrude." "You had better go home and get your supper, Gertrude." "I told you to go home twenty minutes ago, Gertrude." "Your mother will be worrying about you, Gertrude." "Go home, Gertrude, go home."

There are times when the lines around the human eye seem like shelves of eroded stone and when the staring eye itself strikes us with such a wilderness of animal feeling that we are at a loss. The look Francis gave the little girl was ugly and queer, and it frightened her. He reached into his pockets—his hands were shaking—and took out a quarter. "Go home, Gertrude, go home, and don't tell anyone, Gertrude. Don't—" He choked and ran into the living room as Julia called down to him from upstairs to hurry and dress.

The thought that he would drive Anne Murchison home later that night ran like a golden thread through the events of the party that Francis and Julia went to, and he laughed uproariously at dull jokes, dried a tear when Mabel Mercer told him about the death of her kitten, and stretched, yawned, sighed, and grunted like any other man with a rendezvous at the back of his mind. The bracelet was in his pocket. As he sat talking, the smell of grass was in his nose, and he was wondering where he would park the car. Nobody lived in the old Parker mansion, and the driveway was used as a lovers' lane. Townsend Street was a dead end, and he could park there, beyond the last house. The old lane that used to connect Elm Street to the riverbanks was overgrown, but he had walked there with his children, and he could drive his car deep enough into the brushwoods to be concealed.

The Weeds were the last to leave the party, and their host and hostess spoke of their own married happiness while they all four stood in the hallway saying good night. "She's my girl," their host said, squeezing his wife. "She's my blue sky. After sixteen years, I still bite her shoulders. She makes me feel like Hannibal crossing the Alps."

The Weeds drove home in silence. Francis brought the car up the driveway and sat still, with the motor running. "You can put the car in the garage," Julia said as she got out. "I told the Murchison girl she could leave at eleven. Someone drove her home." She shut the door, and Francis sat in the dark. He would be spared nothing then, it seemed, that a fool was not spared: ravening lewdness, jealousy, this hurt to his feelings that put tears in his eyes, even scorn—for he could see clearly the image he now presented, his arms spread over the steering wheel and his head buried in them for love.

Francis had been a dedicated Boy Scout when he was young, and, remembering the precepts of his youth, he left his office early the next afternoon and played some round-robin squash, but, with his body toned up by exercise and a shower, he realized that he might better have stayed at his desk. It was a frosty night when he got home. The air smelled sharply of change. When he stepped into the house, he sensed an unusual stir. The children were in their best clothes, and when Julia came down, she was wearing a lavender dress and her diamond sunburst. She explained the stir: Mr. Hubber was coming at seven to take their photograph for the Christmas card. She had put out Francis' blue suit and a tie with some color in it, because the picture was going to be in color this year. Julia was lighthearted at the thought of being photographed for Christmas. It was the kind of ceremony she enjoyed.

Francis went upstairs to change his clothes. He was tired from the day's work and tired with longing, and sitting on the edge of the bed had the effect of deepening his weariness. He thought of Anne Murchison, and the physical need to express himself, instead of being restrained by the pink lamps of Julia's dressing table, engulfed him. He went to Julia's desk, took a piece of writing paper, and began to write on it. "Dear Anne, I love you, I love you, I love you . . ." No one would see the letter, and he used no restraint. He used phrases like "heavenly bliss," and "love nest." He salivated, sighed, and trembled. When Julia called him to come down, the abyss between his fantasy and the practical world opened so wide that he felt it affected the muscles of his heart.

Julia and the children were on the stoop, and the photographer and his assistant had set up a double battery of floodlights to show the family and the architectural beauty of the entrance to their house. People who had come home on a late train slowed their cars to see the Weeds being photographed for their Christmas card. A few waved and called to the family. It took half an hour of smiling and wetting their lips before Mr. Hubber was satisfied. The heat of the lights made an unfresh smell in the frosty air, and when they were turned off, they lingered on the retina of Francis' eyes.

Later that night, while Francis and Julia were drinking their coffee in the living room, the doorbell rang. Julia answered the door and let in Clayton Thomas. He had come to pay for some theatre tickets that she had given his mother some time ago, and that Helen Thomas had scrupulously insisted on paying for, though Julia had asked her not to. Julia invited him in to have a cup of coffee. "I won't have any coffee," Clayton said, "but I will come in for a minute." He followed her into the living room, said good evening to Francis, and sat awkwardly in a chair.

Clayton's father had been killed in the war, and the young man's fatherlessness surrounded him like an element. This may have been conspicuous in Shady Hill because the Thomases were the only family that lacked a piece; all the other marriages were intact and productive. Clayton was in his second or third year of college, and he and his mother lived alone in a large house, which she hoped to sell. Clayton had once made some trouble. Years ago, he had stolen some money and run away; he had got to California before they caught up with him. He was tall and homely, wore horn-rimmed glasses, and spoke in a deep voice.

"When do you go back to college, Clayton?" Francis asked.

"I'm not going back," Clayton said. "Mother doesn't have the money, and there's no sense in all this pretense. I'm going to get a job, and if we sell the house, we'll take an apartment in New York."

"Won't you miss Shady Hill?" Julia asked.

"No," Clayton said. "I don't like it."

"Why not?" Francis asked.

"Well, there's a lot here I don't approve of," Clayton said gravely. "Things like the club dances. Last Saturday night, I looked in toward the end and saw Mr. Granner trying to put Mrs. Minot into the trophy case. They were both drunk. I disapprove of so much drinking."

"It was Saturday night," Francis said.

"And all the dovecotes are phony," Clayton said. "And the way people clutter up their lives. I've thought about it a lot, and what seems to me to be really wrong with Shady Hill is that it doesn't have any future. So much energy is spent in perpetuating the place—in keeping out undesirables, and so forth—that the only idea of the future anyone has is just more and more commuting trains and more parties. I don't think that's healthy. I think people ought to be able to dream big dreams about the future. I think people ought to be able to dream great dreams."

"It's too bad you couldn't continue with college," Julia said.

"I wanted to go to divinity school," Clayton said.

"What's your church?" Francis asked.

"Unitarian, Theosophist, Transcendentalist, Humanist," Clayton said.

"Wasn't Emerson a transcendentalist?" Julia asked.

"I mean the English transcendentalists," Clayton said. "All the American transcendentalists were goops."

"What kind of job do you expect to get?" Francis asked.

"Well, I'd like to work for a publisher," Clayton said, "but everyone tells me there's nothing doing. But it's the kind of thing I'm interested in. I'm writing a long verse play about good and evil. Uncle Charlie might get me into a bank, and that would be good for me. I need the discipline. I have a long way to go in forming my character. I have some terrible habits. I talk too much. I think I ought to take vows of silence. I ought to try not to speak for a week, and discipline myself. I've thought of making a retreat at one of the Episcopalian monasteries, but I don't like Trinitarianism."

"Do you have any girl friends?" Francis asked.

"I'm engaged to be married," Clayton said. "Of course, I'm not old enough or rich enough to have my engagement observed or respected or anything, but I bought a simulated emerald for Anne Murchison with the money I made cutting lawns this summer. We're going to be married as soon as she finishes school."

Francis recoiled at the mention of the girl's name. Then a dingy light seemed to emanate from his spirit, showing everything—Julia, the boy, the chairs—in their true colorlessness. It was like a bitter turn of the weather.

"We're going to have a large family," Clayton said. "Her father's a terrible rummy, and I've had my hard times, and we want to have lots of children. Oh, she's wonderful, Mr. and Mrs. Weed, and we have so much in common. We like all the same things. We sent out the same Christmas card last year without planning it, and we both have an allergy to tomatoes, and our eyebrows grow together in the middle. Well, goodnight."

Julia went to the door with him. When she returned, Francis said that Clayton was lazy, irresponsible, affected, and smelly. Julia said that Francis seemed to be getting intolerant; the Thomas boy was young and should be given a chance. Julia had noticed other cases where Francis had been short-tempered. "Mrs. Wrightson has asked everyone in Shady Hill to her anniversary party but us," she said.

"I'm sorry, Julia."

"Do you know why they didn't ask us?"

"Why?"

"Because you insulted Mrs. Wrightson."

"Then you know about it?"

"June Masterson told me. She was standing behind you."

Julia walked in front of the sofa with a small step that expressed, Francis knew, a feeling of anger.

"I did insult Mrs. Wrightson, Julia, and I meant to. I've never liked her parties, and I'm glad she's dropped us."

"What about Helen?"

"How does Helen come into this?"

"Mrs. Wrightson's the one who decides who goes to the assemblies."

"You mean she can keep Helen from going to the dances?"

"Yes."

"I hadn't thought of that."

"Oh. I knew you hadn't thought of it," Julia cried, thrusting hilt-deep into this chink of his armor. "And it makes me furious to see this kind of stupid thoughtlessness wreck everyone's happiness."

"I don't think I've wrecked anyone's happiness."

"Mrs. Wrightson runs Shady Hill and has run it for the last forty years. I don't know what makes you think that in a community like this you can indulge every impulse you have to be insulting, vulgar, and offensive."

"I have very good manners," Francis said, trying to give the evening a turn toward the light.

"Damn you, Francis Weed!" Julia cried, and the spit of her words struck him in the face. "I've worked hard for the social position we enjoy in this place, and I won't stand by and see you wreck it. You must have understood when you settled here that you couldn't expect to live like a bear in a cave."

"I've got to express my likes and dislikes."

"You can conceal your dislikes. You don't have to meet everything head on, like a child. Unless you're anxious to be a social leper. It's no accident that we get asked out a great deal! It's no accident that Helen has so many friends. How would you like to spend your Saturday nights at the movies? How would you like to spend your Sundays raking up dead leaves? How would you like it if your daughter spent the assembly nights sitting at her window, listening to the music from the club? How would you like it—" He did something then that was, after all, not so unaccountable, since her words seemed to raise up between them a wall so deadening that he gagged. He struck her full in the face. She staggered and then, a moment later, seemed composed. She went up the stairs to their room. She didn't slam the door. When Francis followed, a few minutes later, he found her packing a suitcase.

"Julia, I'm very sorry."

"It doesn't matter," she said. She was crying.

"Where do you think you're going?"

"I don't know. I just looked at a timetable. There's an eleven-sixteen into New York. I'll take that."

"You can't go, Julia."

"I can't stay. I know that."

"I'm sorry about Mrs. Wrightson, Julia, and I'm—"

"It doesn't matter about Mrs. Wrightson. That isn't the trouble."

"What is the trouble?"

"You don't love me."

"I do love you, Julia."

"No, you don't."

"Julia, I do love you, and I would like to be as we were—sweet and bawdy and dark—but now there are so many people."

"You hate me."

"I don't hate you, Julia."

"You have no idea of how much you hate me. I think it's subconscious. You don't realize the cruel things you've done."

"What cruel things, Julia?"

"The cruel acts your subconscious drives you to in order to express your hatred of me."

"What, Julia?"

"I've never complained."

"Tell me."

"You don't know what you're doing."

"Tell me."

"Your clothes."

"What do you mean?"

"I mean the way you leave your dirty clothes around in order to express your subconscious hatred of me."

"I don't understand."

"I mean your dirty socks and your dirty pajamas and your dirty underwear and your dirty shirts!" She rose from kneeling by the suitcase and faced him, her eyes blazing and her voice ringing with emotion. "I'm talking about the fact that you've never learned to hang up anything. You just leave your clothes all over the floor where they drop, in order to humiliate me. You do it on purpose!" She fell on the bed, sobbing.

"Julia, darling!" he said, but when she felt his hand on her shoulder she got up.

"Leave me alone," she said. "I have to go." She brushed past him to the closet and came back with a dress. "I'm not taking any of the things you've given me," she said. "I'm leaving my pearls and the fur jacket."

"Oh, Julia!" Her figure, so helpless in its self-deceptions, bent over the suitcase made him nearly sick with pity. She did not understand how desolate her life would be without him. She didn't understand the hours that working women have to keep. She didn't understand that most of her friendships existed within the framework of their marriage, and that without this she would find herself alone. She didn't understand about travel, about hotels, about money. "Julia, I can't let you go! What you don't understand, Julia, is that you've come to be dependent on me."

She tossed her head back and covered her face with her hands. "Did you say that *I* was dependent on *you?*" she asked. "Is that what you said? And who is it that tells you what time to get up in the morning and when to go to bed at night? Who is it that prepares your meals and picks up your dirty clothes and invites your friends to dinner? If it weren't for me, your neckties would be greasy and your clothing would be full of moth holes. You were alone when I met you, Francis Weed, and you'll be alone when I leave. When Mother asked you for a list to send out invitations to our wedding, how many names did you have to give her? Fourteen!"

"Cleveland wasn't my home, Julia."

"And how many of your friends came to the church? Two!"

"Cleveland wasn't my home, Julia."

"Since I'm not taking the fur jacket," she said quietly, "you'd better put it back into storage. There's an insurance policy on the pearls that comes due in January. The name of the laundry and the maid's telephone number—all those things are in my desk. I hope you won't drink too much, Francis. I hope that nothing bad will happen to you. If you do get into serious trouble, you can call me."

"Oh, my darling, I can't let you go!" Francis said. "I can't let you go, Julia!" He took her in his arms.

"I guess I'd better stay and take care of you for a little while longer," she said.

Riding to work in the morning, Francis saw the girl walk down the aisle of the coach. He was surprised; he hadn't realized that the school she went to was in the city, but she was carrying books, she seemed to be going to school. His surprise delayed his reaction, but then he got up clumsily and stepped into the aisle. Several people had come between them, but he could see her ahead of him, waiting for someone to open the car door, and then, as the train swerved, putting out her hand to support herself as she crossed the platform into the next car. He followed her through that car and halfway through another before calling her name—"Anne! Anne!"—but she didn't turn. He followed her into still another car, and she sat down in an aisle seat. Coming up to her, all his feelings warm and bent in her direction, he put his hand on the back of her seat—even this touch warmed him—and leaning down to speak to her, he saw that it was not Anne. It was an older woman wearing glasses. He went on deliberately into another car, his face red with embarrassment and the much deeper feeling of having his good sense challenged; for if he couldn't tell one person from another, what evidence was there that his life with Julia and the children had as much reality as his dreams of iniquity in Paris or the litter, the grass smell, and the cave-shaped trees in Lovers' Lane.

Late that afternoon, Julia called to remind Francis that they were going out for dinner. A few minutes later, Trace Bearden called. "Look, fellar," Trace said. "I'm calling for Mrs. Thomas. You know? Clayton, that boy of hers, doesn't seem able to get a job, and I wondered if you could help. If you'd call Charlie Bell—I know he's indebted to you—and say a good word for the kid, I think Charlie would—"

"Trace, I hate to say this," Francis said, "but I don't feel that I can do anything for that boy. The kid's worthless. I know it's a harsh thing to say, but it's a fact. Any kindness done for him would backfire in everybody's face. He's just a worthless kid, Trace, and there's nothing to be done about it. Even if we got him a job, he wouldn't be able to keep it for a week. I know that to be a fact. It's an awful thing, Trace, and I know it is, but instead of recommending that kid, I'd feel obligated to warn people against him—people who knew his father and would naturally want to step in and do something. I'd feel obliged to warn them. He's a thief . . ."

The moment this conversation was finished, Miss Rainey came in and stood by his desk. "I'm not going to be able to work for you any more, Mr. Weed," she said. "I can stay until the seventeenth if you need me, but I've been offered a whirlwind of a job, and I'd like to leave as soon as possible."

She went out, leaving him to face alone the wickedness of what he had done to the Thomas boy. His children in their photograph laughed and laughed, glazed with all the bright colors of summer, and he remembered that they had met a bagpiper on the beach that day and he had paid the piper a dollar to play them a battle song of the Black Watch. The girl would be at the house when he got home. He would spend another evening among his kind neighbors, picking and choosing dead-end streets, cart tracks, and the driveways of abandoned houses. There was nothing to mitigate his feeling—nothing that laughter or a game of softball with the children would change—and, thinking back over the plane crash, the Farquarsons' new maid, and Anne Murchison's difficulties with her drunken father, he wondered how he could have avoided arriving at just where he was. He was in trouble. He had been lost once in his life, coming back from a trout stream in the north woods, and he had now the same bleak realization that no amount of cheerfulness or hopefulness or valor or perseverance could help him find, in the gathering dark, the path that he'd lost. He smelled the forest. The feeling of bleakness was intolerable, and he saw clearly that he had reached the point where he would have to make a choice.

He could go to a psychiatrist, like Miss Rainey; he could go to church and confess his lusts; he could go to a Danish massage parlor in the West Seventies that had been recommended by a salesman; he could rape the girl or trust that he would somehow be prevented from doing this; or he could get drunk. It was his life, his boat, and, like every other man, he was made to be the father of thousands, and what harm could there be in a tryst that would make them both feel more kindly toward the world? This was the wrong train of thought, and he came back to the first, the psychiatrist. He had the telephone number of Miss Rainey's doctor, and he called and asked for an immediate appointment. He was insistent with the doctor's secretary—it was his manner in business—and when she said that the doctor's schedule was full for the next few weeks, Francis demanded an appointment that day and was told to come at five.

The psychiatrist's office was in a building that was used mostly by doctors and dentists, and the hallways were filled with the candy smell of mouthwash and memories of pain. Francis' character had been formed upon a series of private resolves—resolves about cleanliness, about going off the high diving board or repeating any other feat that challenged his courage, about punctuality, honesty, and virtue. To abdicate the perfect loneliness in which he had made his most vital decisions shattered his concept of character and left him now in a condition that felt like shock. He was stupefied. The scene for his *miserere mei Deus* was, like the waiting room of so many doctor's offices, a crude token gesture toward the sweets of domestic bliss: a place arranged with antiques, coffee tables, potted plants, and etchings of snow-covered bridges and geese in flight, although there were no children, no marriage bed, no stove, even, in this travesty of a house, where no one had ever spent the night and where the curtained windows looked straight onto a dark air shaft. Francis gave his name and address to a secretary and then saw, at the side of the room, a policeman moving toward him. "Hold it, hold it," the policeman said. "Don't move. Keep your hands where they are."

"I think it's all right, Officer," the secretary began. "I think it will be—"

"Let's make sure," the policeman said, and he began to slap Francis' clothes, looking for what—pistols, knives, an icepick? Finding nothing, he went off and the secretary began a nervous apology: "When you called on the telephone, Mr. Weed, you seemed very excited, and one of the doctor's patients has been threatening his life, and we have to be careful. If you want to go in now?" Francis pushed open a door connected to an electrical chime, and in the doctor's lair sat down heavily, blew his nose into a handkerchief, searched in his pockets for cigarettes, for matches, for something, and said hoarsely, with tears in his eyes, "I'm in love, Dr. Herzog."

It is a week or ten days later in Shady Hill. The seven-fourteen has come and gone, and here and there dinner is finished and the dishes are in the dish-washing machine. The village hangs, morally and economically, from a thread; but it hangs by its thread in the evening light. Donald Goslin has begun to worry the "Moonlight Sonata" again. *Marcato ma sempre pianissimo!* He seems to be wringing out a wet bath towel, but the housemaid does not heed him. She is writing a letter to Arthur Godfrey. In the cellar of his house, Francis Weed is building a coffee table. Dr. Herzog recommends woodwork as a therapy, and Francis finds some true consolation in the simple arithmetic involved and in the holy smell of new wood. Francis is happy. Upstairs, little Toby is crying, because he is tired. He puts off his cowboy hat, gloves, and fringed jacket, unbuckles the belt studded with gold and rubies, the silver bullets and holsters, slips off his suspenders, his checked shirt, and Levi's, and sits on the edge of his bed to pull off his high boots. Leaving this equipment in a heap, he goes to the closet and takes his space suit off a nail. It is a struggle for him to get into the long tights, but he succeeds. He loops the magic cape over his shoulders and, climbing onto the footboard of his bed, he spreads his arms and flies the short distance to the floor, landing with a thump that is audible to everyone in the house but himself.

"Go home, Gertrude, go home," Mrs. Masterson says. "I told you to go home an hour ago, Gertrude. It's way past your suppertime, and your mother will be worried. Go home!" A door on the Babcocks' terrace flies open, and out comes Mrs. Babcock without any clothes on, pursued by a naked husband. (Their children are away at boarding school, and their terrace is screened by a hedge.) Over the terrace they go and in at the kitchen door, as passionate and handsome a nymph and satyr as you will find on any wall in Venice. Cutting the last of the roses in her garden, Julia hears old Mr. Nixon shouting at the squirrels in his bird-feeding station. "Rapscallions! Varmints! Avaunt and quit my sight!" A miserable cat wanders into the garden, sunk in spiritual and physical discomfort. Tied to its head is a small straw hat—a doll's hat—and it is securely buttoned into a doll's dress, from the skirts of which protrudes its long, hairy tail. As it walks, it shakes its feet, as if it had fallen into water.

"Here, pussy, pussy, pussy!" Julia calls.

"Here, pussy, here, poor pussy!" But the cat gives her a skeptical look and stumbles away in its skirts. The last to come is Jupiter. He prances through the tomato vines, holding in his generous mouth the remains of an evening slipper. Then it is dark; it is a night where kings in golden suits ride elephants over the mountains.

ANTON CHEKHOV

(1860–1904)

ANTON CHEKHOV was born in Taganrog, a port on the Sea of Azov in southern Russia. His grandfather and father were serfs; when Alexander II freed the serfs in 1861, Chekhov's father became a grocer. The proceeds from this small business enabled the family to send Chekhov to Moscow, where he entered medical school at the University of Moscow; he graduated in 1884. During his medical studies he began to publish short stories, pseudonymously at first. The hundreds of stories he wrote won him not only early critical acclaim, but an enduring place at the summit of literary achievement. His plays are masterpieces as well, innovative in their focus on the internal drama of the characters; they include *The Seagull* (1898), *Uncle Vanya* (1899), *The Three Sisters* (1901), and *The Cherry Orchard* (1904). His publications included *Motley Stories* (1886), *At Twilight* (stories, 1887), and *Stories* (1888; "The Steppe," from this collection, won the Pushkin Prize), and *The Island of Sakhalin* (1890), a study that examines the conditions of convicts there, and that led to social reform. In both his life and his work Chekhov's compassion was his hallmark. His short stories are noted for their distribution of sympathy among characters, simplicity of style, and fluent shifts between the serious and comic modes.

The last three years of Chekhov's life were marked by both his happy marriage to the Moscow Art Theater actress Olga Knipper and by his ongoing suffering from tuberculosis, which he had contracted at medical school; it caused his death at age forty-four. His illness necessitated frequent separations from his wife; while she worked at the Moscow Art Theater, frequently acting in her husband's plays, he lived in the warmer climate of Yalta, a resort city on the Black Sea, where the opening of the story "The Lady with the Pet Dog" is set. Published in 1899, the work ranks with the best of his artistically evolved final stories.

Dmitry Gorov, vacationing from Moscow and his loveless marriage, from a distance spots Anna Sergeyevna, accompanied by her small, white Pomeranian dog. Even as a philanderer, Gorov's nervous exasperation with women, masking dependency, is hard to shake. Their flirtation, for him, begins frivolously. She too is married; but her impulse to flee from her new lover is matched by the depth of her longing and her passion for him. In charting the journey of these two people toward their real selves and each other, Chekhov gives us a love story of singular truth and wisdom.

The Lady with the Pet Dog

I

A new person, it was said, had appeared on the esplanade: a lady with a pet dog. Dmitry Dmitrich Gurov, who had spent a fortnight at Yalta and had got used to the place, had also begun to take an interest in new arrivals. As he sat in Vernet's confectionery shop, he saw, walking on the esplanade, a fair-haired young woman of medium height, wearing a beret; a white Pomeranian was trotting behind her.

And afterwards he met her in the public garden and in the square several times a day. She walked alone, always wearing the same beret and always with the white dog; no one knew who she was and everyone called her simply "the lady with the pet dog."

"If she is here alone without husband or friends," Gurov reflected, "it wouldn't be a bad thing to make her acquaintance."

He was under forty, but he already had a daughter twelve years old, and two sons at school. They had found a wife for him when he was very young, a student in his second year, and by now she seemed half as old again as he. She was a tall, erect woman with dark eyebrows, stately and dignified and, as she said of herself, intellectual. She read a great deal, used simplified spelling in her letters, called her husband, not Dmitry, but Dimitry, while he privately considered her of limited intelligence, narrow-minded, dowdy, was afraid of her, and did not like to be at home. He had begun being unfaithful to her long ago—had been unfaithful to her often and, probably for that reason, almost always spoke ill of women, and when they were talked of in his presence used to call them "the inferior race."

It seemed to him that he had been sufficiently tutored by bitter experience to call them what he pleased, and yet he could not have lived without "the inferior race" for two days together. In the company of men he was bored and ill at ease, he was chilly and uncommunicative with them; but when he was among women he felt free, and knew what to speak to them about and how to comport himself; and even to be silent with them was no strain on him. In his appearance, in his character, in his whole make-up there was something attractive and elusive that disposed women in his favor and allured them. He knew that, and some force seemed to draw him to them, too.

Oft-repeated and really bitter experience had taught him long ago that with decent people—particularly Moscow people—who are irresolute and slow to move, every affair which at first seems a light and charming adventure inevitably grows into a whole problem of extreme complexity, and in the end a painful situation is created. But at every new meeting with an interesting woman this lesson of experience seemed to slip from his memory, and he was eager for life, and everything seemed so simple and diverting.

One evening while he was dining in the public garden the lady in the beret walked up without haste to take the next table. Her expression, her gait, her dress, and the way she did her hair told him that she belonged to the upper class, that she was married, that she was in Yalta for the first time and alone, and that she was bored there. The stories told of the immorality in Yalta are to a great extent untrue; he despised them, and knew that such stories were made up for the most part by persons who would have been glad to sin themselves if they had had the chance; but when the lady sat down at the next table three paces from him, he recalled these stories of easy conquests, of trips to the mountains, and the tempting thought of a swift, fleeting liaison, a romance with an unknown woman of whose very name he was ignorant suddenly took hold of him.

He beckoned invitingly to the Pomeranian, and when the dog approached him, shook his finger at it. The Pomeranian growled; Gurov threatened it again.

The lady glanced at him and at once dropped her eyes.

"He doesn't bite," she said and blushed.

"May I give him a bone?" he asked; and when she nodded he inquired affably, "Have you been in Yalta long?"

"About five days."

"And I am dragging out the second week here."

There was a short silence.

"Time passes quickly, and yet it is so dull here!" she said, not looking at him.

"It's only the fashion to say it's dull here. A provincial will live in Belyov or Zhizdra and not be bored, but when he comes here it's 'Oh, the dullness! Oh, the dust!' One would think he came from Granada."

She laughed. Then both continued eating in silence, like strangers, but after dinner they walked together and there sprang up between them the light banter of people who are free and contented, to whom it does not matter where they go or what they talk about. They walked and talked of the strange light on the sea: the water was a soft, warm, lilac color, and there was a golden band of moonlight upon it. They talked of how sultry it was after a hot day. Gurov told her that he was a native of Moscow, that he had studied languages and literature at the university, but had a post in a bank; that at one time he had trained to become an opera singer but had given it up, that he owned two houses in Moscow. And he learned from her that she had grown up in Petersburg, but had lived in S——— since her marriage two years previously, that she was going to stay in Yalta for about another month, and that her husband, who needed a rest, too, might perhaps come to fetch her. She was not certain whether her husband was a member of a Government Board or served on a Zemstvo Council, and this amused her. And Gurov learned too that her name was Anna Sergeyevna.

Afterwards in his room at the hotel he thought about her—and was certain that he would meet her the next day. It was bound to happen. Getting into bed he recalled that she had been a schoolgirl only recently, doing lessons like his own daughter; he thought how much timidity and angularity there was still in her laugh and her manner of talking with a stranger. It must have been the first time in her life that she was alone in a setting in which she was followed, looked at, and spoken to for one secret purpose alone, which she could hardly fail to guess. He thought of her slim, delicate throat, her lovely gray eyes.

"There's something pathetic about her, though," he thought, and dropped off.

II

A week had passed since they had struck up an acquaintance. It was a holiday. It was close indoors, while in the street the wind whirled the dust about and blew people's hats off. One was thirsty all day, and Gurov often went into the restaurant and offered Anna Sergeyevna a soft drink or ice cream. One did not know what to do with oneself.

In the evening when the wind had abated they went out on the pier to watch the steamer come in. There were a great many people walking about the dock; they had come to welcome someone and they were carrying bunches of flowers. And two peculiarities of a festive Yalta crowd stood out: the elderly ladies were dressed like young ones and there were many generals.

Owing to the choppy sea, the steamer arrived late, after sunset, and it was a long time tacking about before it put in at the pier. Anna Sergeyevna peered at the steamer and the passengers through her lorgnette as though looking for acquaintances, and whenever she turned to Gurov her eyes were shining. She talked a great deal and asked questions jerkily, forgetting the next moment what she had asked; then she lost her lorgnette in the crush.

The festive crowd began to disperse; it was now too dark to see people's faces; there was no wind any more, but Gurov and Anna Sergeyevna still stood as though waiting to see someone else come off the steamer. Anna Sergeyevna was silent now, and sniffed her flowers without looking at Gurov.

"The weather has improved this evening," he said. "Where shall we go now? Shall we drive somewhere?"

She did not reply.

Then he looked at her intently, and suddenly embraced her and kissed her on the lips, and the moist fragrance of her flowers enveloped him; and at once he looked round him anxiously, wondering if anyone had seen them.

"Let us go to your place," he said softly. And they walked off together rapidly.

The air in her room was close and there was the smell of the perfume she had bought at the Japanese shop. Looking at her, Gurov thought: "What encounters life offers!" From the past he preserved the memory of carefree, good-natured women whom love made gay and who were grateful to him for the happiness he gave them, however brief it might be; and of women like his wife who loved without sincerity, with too many words, affectedly, hysterically, with an expression that it was not love or passion that engaged them but something more significant; and of two or three others, very beautiful, frigid women, across whose faces would suddenly flit a rapacious expression—an obstinate desire to take from life more than it could give, and these were women no longer young, capricious, unreflecting, domineering, unintelligent, and when Gurov grew cold to them their beauty aroused his hatred, and the lace on their lingerie seemed to him to resemble scales.

But here there was the timidity, the angularity of inexperienced youth, a feeling of awkwardness; and there was a sense of embarrassment, as though someone had suddenly knocked at the door. Anna Sergeyevna, "the lady with the pet dog," treated what had happened in a peculiar way, very seriously, as though it were her fall—so it seemed, and this was odd and inappropriate. Her features drooped and faded, and her long hair hung down sadly on either side of her face; she grew pensive and her dejected pose was that of a Magdalene in a picture by an old master.

"It's not right," she said. "You don't respect me now, you first of all."

There was a watermelon on the table. Gurov cut himself a slice and began eating it without haste. They were silent for at least half an hour.

There was something touching about Anna Sergeyevna; she had the purity of a well-bred, naive woman who has seen little of life. The single candle burning on the table barely illumined her face, yet it was clear that she was unhappy.

"Why should I stop respecting you, darling?" asked Gurov. "You don't know what you're saying."

"God forgive me," she said, and her eyes filled with tears. "It's terrible."

"It's as though you were trying to exonerate yourself."

"How can I exonerate myself? No. I am a bad, low woman; I despise myself and I have no thought of exonerating myself. It's not my husband but myself I have deceived. And not only just now; I have been deceiving myself for a long time. My husband may be a good, honest man, but he is a flunkey! I don't know what he does, what his work is, but I know he is a flunkey! I was twenty when I married him. I was tormented by curiosity; I wanted something better. 'There must be a different sort of life,' I said to myself. I wanted to live! To live, to live! Curiosity kept eating at me—you don't understand it, but I swear to God I could no longer control myself; something was going on in me; I could not be held back. I told my husband I was ill, and came here. And here I have been walking about as though in a daze, as though I were mad; and now I have become a vulgar, vile woman whom anyone may despise."

Gurov was already bored with her; he was irritated by her naive tone, by her repentance, so unexpected and so out of place, but for the tears in her eyes he might have thought she was joking or play-acting.

"I don't understand, my dear," he said softly. "What do you want?"

She hid her face on his breast and pressed close to him.

"Believe me, believe me, I beg you," she said, "I love honesty and purity, and sin is loathsome to me; I don't know what I'm doing. Simple people say, 'The Evil One has led me astray.' And I may say of myself now that the Evil One has led me astray."

"Quiet, quiet," he murmured.

He looked into her fixed, frightened eyes, kissed her, spoke to her softly and affectionately, and by degrees she calmed down, and her gaiety returned; both began laughing.

Afterwards when they went out there was not a soul on the esplanade. The town with its cypresses looked quite dead, but the sea was still sounding as it broke upon the beach; a single launch was rocking on the waves and on it a lantern was blinking sleepily.

They found a cab and drove to Oreanda.

"I found out your surname in the hall just now: it was written on the board— von Dideritz," said Gurov. "Is your husband German?"

"No; I believe his grandfather was German, but he is Greek Orthodox himself."

At Oreanda they sat on a bench not far from the church, looked down at the sea, and were silent. Yalta was barely visible through the morning mist; white clouds rested motionlessly on the mountaintops. The leaves did not stir on the trees, cicadas twanged, and the monotonous muffled sound of the sea that rose from below spoke of the peace, the eternal sleep awaiting us. So it rumbled below when there was no Yalta, no Oreanda here; so it rumbles now, and it will rumble as indifferently and as hollowly when we are no more. And in this constancy, in this complete indifference to the life and death of each of us, there lies, perhaps, a pledge of our eternal salvation, of the unceasing advance of life upon earth, of unceasing movement towards perfection. Sitting beside a young woman who in the dawn seemed so lovely, Gurov, soothed and spellbound by these magical surroundings—the sea, the mountains, the clouds, the wide sky—thought how everything is really beautiful in this world when one reflects: everything except what we think or do ourselves when we forget the higher aims of life and our own human dignity.

A man strolled up to them—probably a guard—looked at them and walked away. And this detail, too, seemed so mysterious and beautiful. They saw a steamer arrive from Feodosia, its lights extinguished in the glow of dawn.

"There is dew on the grass," said Anna Sergeyevna, after a silence.

"Yes, it's time to go home."

They returned to the city.

Then they met every day at twelve o'clock on the esplanade, lunched and dined together, took walks, admired the sea. She complained that she slept badly, that she had palpitations, asked the same questions, troubled now by jealousy and now by the fear that he did not respect her sufficiently. And often in the square or the public garden, when there was no one near them, he suddenly drew her to him and kissed her passionately. Complete idleness, these kisses in broad daylight exchanged furtively in dread of someone's seeing them, the heat, the smell of the sea, and the continual flitting before his eyes of idle, well-dressed, well-fed people, worked a complete change in him; he kept telling Anna Sergeyevna how beautiful she was, how seductive, was urgently passionate; he would not move a step away from her, while she was often pensive and continually pressed him to confess that he did not respect her, did not love her in the least, and saw in her nothing but a common woman. Almost every evening rather late they drove somewhere out of town, to Oreanda or to the waterfall; and the excursion was always a success, the scenery invariably impressed them as beautiful and magnificent.

They were expecting her husband, but a letter came from him saying that he had eye-trouble, and begging his wife to return home as soon as possible. Anna Sergeyevna made haste to go.

"It's a good thing I am leaving," she said to Gurov. "It's the hand of Fate!"

She took a carriage to the railway station, and he went with her. They were driving the whole day. When she had taken her place in the express, and when the second bell had rung, she said, "Let me look at you once more—let me look at you again. Like this."

She was not crying but was so sad that she seemed ill and her face was quivering.

"I shall be thinking of you—remembering you," she said. "God bless you; be happy. Don't remember evil against me. We are parting forever—it has to be, for we ought never to have met. Well, God bless you."

The train moved off rapidly, its lights soon vanished, and a minute later there was no sound of it, as though everything had conspired to end as quickly as possible that sweet trance, that madness. Left alone on the platform, and gazing into the dark distance, Gurov listened to the twang of the grasshoppers and the hum of the telegraph wires, feeling as though he had just waked up. And he reflected, musing, that there had now been another episode or adventure in his life, and it, too, was at an end, and nothing was left of it but a memory. He was moved, sad, and slightly remorseful: this young woman whom he would never meet again had not been happy with him; he had been warm and affectionate with her, but yet in his manner, his tone, and his caresses there had been a shade of light irony, the slightly coarse arrogance of a happy male who was, besides, almost twice her age. She had constantly called him kind, exceptional, high-minded; obviously he had seemed to her different from what he really was, so he had involuntarily deceived her.

Here at the station there was already a scent of autumn in the air; it was a chilly evening.

"It is time for me to go north, too," thought Gurov as he left the platform. "High time!"

III

At home in Moscow the winter routine was already established; the stoves were heated, and in the morning it was still dark when the children were having breakfast and getting ready for school, and the nurse would light the lamp for a short time. There were frosts already. When the first snow falls, on the first day the sleighs are out, it is pleasant to see the white earth, the white roofs; one draws easy, delicious breaths, and the season brings back the days of one's youth. The old limes and birches, white with hoar-frost, have a good-natured look; they are closer to one's heart than cypresses and palms, and near them one no longer wants to think of mountains and the sea.

Gurov, a native of Moscow, arrived there on a fine frosty day, and when he put on his fur coat and warm gloves and took a walk along Petrovka, and when on Saturday night he heard the bells ringing, his recent trip and the places he had visited lost all charm for him. Little by little he became immersed in Moscow life, greedily read three newspapers a day, and declared that he did not read the Moscow papers on principle. He already felt a longing for restaurants, clubs, formal dinners, anniversary celebrations, and it flattered him to entertain distinguished lawyers and actors, and to play cards with a professor at the physicians' club. He could eat a whole portion of meat stewed with pickled cabbage and served in a pan, Moscow style.

A month or so would pass and the image of Anna Sergeyevna, it seemed to him, would become misty in his memory, and only from time to time he would dream of her with her touching smile as he dreamed of others. But more than a month went by, winter came into its own, and everything was still clear in his memory as though he had parted from Anna Sergeyevna only yesterday. And his memories glowed more and more vividly. When in the evening stillness the voices of his children preparing their lessons reached his study, or when he listened to a song or to an organ playing in a restaurant, or when the storm howled in the chimney, suddenly everything would rise up in his memory; what had happened on the pier and the early morning with the mist on the mountains, and the steamer coming from Feodosia, and the kisses. He would pace about his room a long time, remembering and smiling; then his memories passed into reveries, and in his imagination the past would mingle with what was to come. He did not dream of Anna Sergeyevna, but she followed him about everywhere and watched him. When he shut his eyes he saw her before him as though she were there in the flesh, and she seemed to him lovelier, younger, tenderer than she had been, and he imagined himself a finer man than he had been in Yalta. Of evenings she peered out at him from the bookcase, from the fireplace, from the corner—he heard her breathing, the caressing rustle of her clothes. In the street he followed the women with his eyes, looking for someone who resembled her.

Already he was tormented by a strong desire to share his memories with someone. But in his home it was impossible to talk of his love, and he had no one to talk to outside; certainly he could not confide in his tenants or in anyone at the bank. And what was there to talk about? He hadn't loved her then, had he? Had there been anything beautiful, poetical, edifying, or simply interesting in his relations with Anna Sergeyevna? And he was forced to talk vaguely of love, of women, and no one guessed what he meant; only his wife would twitch her black eyebrows and say, "The part of a philanderer does not suit you at all, Dimitry."

One evening, coming out of the physicians' club with an official with whom he had been playing cards, he could not resist saying:

"If you only knew what a fascinating woman I became acquainted with at Yalta!"

The official got into his sledge and was driving away, but turned suddenly and shouted:

"Dmitry Dmitrich!"

"What is it?"

"You were right this evening: the sturgeon was a bit high."

These words, so commonplace, for some reason moved Gurov to indignation, and struck him as degrading and unclean. What savage manners, what mugs! What stupid nights, what dull, humdrum days! Frenzied gambling, gluttony, drunkenness, continual talk always about the same thing! Futile pursuits and conversations always about the same topics take up the better part of one's time, the better part of one's strength, and in the end there is left a life clipped and wingless, an absurd mess, and there is no escaping or getting away from it—just as though one were in a madhouse or a prison.

Gurov, boiling with indignation, did not sleep all night. And he had a headache all the next day. And the following nights too he slept badly; he sat up in bed, thinking, or paced up and down his room. He was fed up with his children, fed up with the bank; he had no desire to go anywhere or to talk of anything.

In December during the holidays he prepared to take a trip and told his wife he was going to Petersburg to do what he could for a young friend—and he set off for S——. What for? He did not know, himself. He wanted to see Anna Sergeyevna and talk with her, to arrange a rendezvous if possible.

He arrived at S—— in the morning, and at the hotel took the best room, in which the floor was covered with gray army cloth, and on the table there was an inkstand, gray with dust and topped by a figure on horseback, its hat in its raised hand and its head broken off. The porter gave him the necessary information: von Dideritz lived in a house of his own on Staro-Goncharnaya Street, not far from the hotel: he was rich and lived well and kept his own horses; everyone in the town knew him. The porter pronounced the name: "Dridiritz."

Without haste Gurov made his way to Staro-Goncharnaya Street and found the house. Directly opposite the house stretched a long gray fence studded with nails.

"A fence like that would make one run away," thought Gurov, looking now at the fence, now at the windows of the house.

He reflected: this was a holiday, and the husband was apt to be at home. And in any case, it would be tactless to go into the house and disturb her. If he were to send her a note, it might fall into her husband's hands, and that might spoil everything. The best thing was to rely on chance. And he kept walking up and down the street and along the fence, waiting for the chance. He saw a beggar go in at the gate and heard the dogs attack him; then an hour later he heard a piano, and the sound came to him faintly and indistinctly. Probably it was Anna Sergeyevna playing. The front door opened suddenly, and an old woman came out, followed by the familiar white Pomeranian. Gurov was on the point of calling to the dog, but his heart began beating violently, and in his excitement he could not remember the Pomeranian's name.

He kept walking up and down, and hated the gray fence more and more, and by now he thought irritably that Anna Sergeyevna had forgotten him, and was perhaps already diverting herself with another man, and that that was very natural in a young woman who from morning till night had to look at that damn fence. He went back to his hotel room and sat on the couch for a long while, not knowing what to do, then he had dinner and a long nap.

"How stupid and annoying all this is!" he thought when he woke and looked at the dark windows: it was already evening. "Here I've had a good sleep for some reason. What am I going to do at night?"

He sat on the bed, which was covered with a cheap gray blanket of the kind seen in hospitals, and he twitted himself in his vexation:

"So there's your lady with the pet dog. There's your adventure. A nice place to cool your heels in."

That morning at the station a playbill in large letters had caught his eye. *The Geisha* was to be given for the first time. He thought of this and drove to the theater.

"It's quite possible that she goes to first nights," he thought.

The theater was full. As in all provincial theaters, there was a haze above the chandelier, the gallery was noisy and restless; in the front row, before the beginning of the performance the local dandies were standing with their hands clasped behind their backs; in the Governor's box the Governor's daughter, wearing a boa, occupied the front seat, while the Governor himself hid modestly behind the portiere and only his hands were visible; the curtain swayed; the orchestra was a long time tuning up. While the audience was coming in and taking their seats, Gurov scanned the faces eagerly.

Anna Sergeyevna, too, came in. She sat down in the third row, and when Gurov looked at her his heart contracted, and he understood clearly that in the whole world there was no human being so near, so precious, and so important to him; she, this little, undistinguished woman, lost in a provincial crowd, with a vulgar lorgnette in her hand, filled his whole life now, was his sorrow and his joy, the only happiness that he now desired for himself, and to the sounds of the bad orchestra, of the miserable local violins, he thought how lovely she was. He thought and dreamed.

A young man with small side-whiskers, very tall and stooped, came in with Anna Sergeyevna and sat down beside her; he nodded his head at every step and seemed to be bowing continually. Probably this was the husband whom at Yalta, in an access of bitter feeling, she had called a flunkey. And there really was in his lanky figure, his side-whiskers, his small bald patch, something of a flunkey's retiring manner; his smile was mawkish, and in his buttonhole there was an academic badge like a waiter's number.

During the first intermission the husband went out to have a smoke; she remained in her seat. Gurov, who was also sitting in the orchestra, went up to her and said in a shaky voice, with a forced smile:

"Good evening!"

She glanced at him and turned pale, then looked at him again in horror, unable to believe her eyes, and gripped the fan and the lorgnette tightly together in her hands, evidently trying to keep herself from fainting. Both were silent. She was sitting, he was standing, frightened by her distress and not daring to take a seat beside her. The violins and the flute that were being tuned up sang out. He suddenly felt frightened: it seemed as if all the people in the boxes were looking at them. She got up and went hurriedly to the exit; he followed her, and both of them walked blindly along the corridors and up and down stairs, and figures in the uniforms prescribed for magistrates, teachers, and officials of the Department of Crown Lands, all wearing badges, flitted before their eyes, as did also ladies, and fur coats on hangers; they were conscious of drafts and the smell of stale tobacco. And Gurov, whose heart was beating violently, thought:

"Oh, Lord! Why are these people here and this orchestra!"

And at that instant he suddenly recalled how when he had seen Anna Sergeyevna off at the station he had said to himself that all was over between them and that they would never meet again. But how distant the end still was!

On the narrow, gloomy staircase over which it said "To the Amphitheatre," she stopped.

"How you frightened me!" she said, breathing hard, still pale and stunned. "Oh, how you frightened me! I am barely alive. Why did you come? Why?"

"But do understand, Anna, do understand—" he said hurriedly, under his breath. "I implore you, do understand—"

She looked at him with fear, with entreaty, with love; she looked at him intently, to keep his features more distinctly in her memory.

"I suffer so," she went on, not listening to him. "All this time I have been thinking of nothing but you; I live only by the thought of you. And I wanted to forget, to forget; but why, oh, why have you come?"

On the landing above them two high school boys were looking down and smoking, but it was all the same to Gurov; he drew Anna Sergeyevna to him and began kissing her face and hands.

"What are you doing, what are you doing!" she was saying in horror, pushing him away. "We have lost our senses. Go away today; go away at once—I conjure you by all that is sacred, I implore you—People are coming this way!"

Someone was walking up the stairs.

"You must leave," Anna Sergeyevna went on in a whisper. "Do you hear, Dmitry Dmitrich? I will come and see you in Moscow. I have never been happy; I am unhappy now, and I never, never shall be happy, never! So don't make me suffer still more! I swear I'll come to Moscow. But now let us part. My dear, good, precious one, let us part!"

She pressed his hand and walked rapidly downstairs, turning to look round at him, and from her eyes he could see that she really was unhappy. Gurov stood for a while, listening, then when all grew quiet, he found his coat and left the theater.

IV

And Anna Sergeyevna began coming to see him in Moscow. Once every two or three months she left S——telling her husband that she was going to consult a doctor about a woman's ailment from which she was suffering—and her husband did and did not believe her. When she arrived in Moscow she would stop at the Slavyansky Bazar Hotel, and at once send a man in a red cap to Gurov. Gurov came to see her, and no one in Moscow knew of it.

Once he was going to see her in this way on a winter morning (the messenger had come the evening before and not found him in). With him walked his daughter, whom he wanted to take to school; it was on the way. Snow was coming down in big wet flakes.

"It's three degrees above zero, and yet it's snowing," Gurov was saying to his daughter. "But this temperature prevails only on the surface of the earth; in the upper layers of the atmosphere there is quite a different temperature."

"And why doesn't it thunder in winter, papa?"

He explained that, too. He talked, thinking all the while that he was on his way to a rendezvous, and no living soul knew of it, and probably no one would ever know. He had two lives, an open one, seen and known by all who needed to know it, full of conventional truth and conventional falsehood, exactly like the lives of his friends and acquaintances; and another life that went on in secret. And through some strange, perhaps accidental, combination of circumstances, everything that was of interest and importance to him, everything that was essential to him, everything about which he felt sincerely and did not deceive himself, everything that constituted the core of his life, was going on concealed from others; while all that was false, the shell in which he hid to cover the truth—his work at the bank, for instance, his discussions at the club, his references to the "inferior race," his appearances at anniversary celebrations with his wife—all that went on in the open. Judging others by himself, he did not believe what he saw, and always fancied that every man led his real, most interesting life under cover of secrecy as under cover of night. The personal life of every individual is based on secrecy, and perhaps it is partly for that reason that civilized man is so nervously anxious that personal privacy should be respected.

Having taken his daughter to school, Gurov went on to the Slavyansky Bazar Hotel. He took off his fur coat in the lobby, went upstairs, and knocked gently at the door. Anna Sergeyevna, wearing his favorite gray dress, exhausted by the journey and by waiting, had been expecting him since the previous evening. She was pale, and looked at him without a smile, and he had hardly entered when she flung herself on his breast. That kiss was a long, lingering one, as though they had not seen one another for two years.

"Well, darling, how are you getting on there?" he asked. "What news?"

"Wait; I'll tell you in a moment—I can't speak."

She could not speak; she was crying. She turned away from him, and pressed her handkerchief to her eyes.

"Let her have her cry; meanwhile I'll sit down," he thought, and he seated himself in an armchair.

Then he rang and ordered tea, and while he was having his tea she remained standing at the window with her back to him. She was crying out of sheer agitation, in the sorrowful consciousness that their life was so sad; that they could only see each other in secret and had to hide from people like thieves! Was it not a broken life?

"Come, stop now, dear!" he said.

It was plain to him that this love of theirs would not be over soon, that the end of it was not in sight. Anna Sergeyevna was growing more and more attached to him. She adored him, and it was unthinkable to tell her that their love was bound to come to an end some day; besides, she would not have believed it!

He went up to her and took her by the shoulders, to fondle her and say something diverting, and at that moment he caught sight of himself in the mirror.

His hair was already beginning to turn gray. And it seemed odd to him that he had grown so much older in the last few years, and lost his looks. The shoulders on which his hands rested were warm and heaving. He felt compassion for this life, still so warm and lovely, but probably already about to begin to fade and wither like his own. Why did she love him so much? He always seemed to women different from what he was, and they loved in him not himself, but the man whom their imagination created and whom they had been eagerly seeking all their lives; and afterwards, when they saw their mistake, they loved him nevertheless. And not one of them had been happy with him. In the past he had met women, come together with them, parted from them, but he had never once loved; it was anything you please, but not love. And only now when his head was gray he had fallen in love, really, truly—for the first time in his life.

Anna Sergeyevna and he loved each other as people do who are very close and intimate, like man and wife, like tender friends; it seemed to them that Fate itself had meant them for one another, and they could not understand why he had a wife and she a husband; and it was as though they were a pair of migratory birds, male and female, caught and forced to live in different cages. They forgave each other what they were ashamed of in their past, they forgave everything in the present, and felt that this love of theirs had altered them both.

Formerly in moments of sadness he had soothed himself with whatever logical arguments came into his head, but now he no longer cared for logic; he felt profound compassion, he wanted to be sincere and tender.

"Give it up now, my darling," he said. "You've had your cry; that's enough. Let us have a talk now, we'll think up something."

Then they spent a long time taking counsel together, they talked of how to avoid the necessity for secrecy, for deception, for living in different cities, and not seeing one another for long stretches of time. How could they free themselves from these intolerable fetters?

"How? How?" he asked, clutching his head. "How?"

And it seemed as though in a little while the solution would be found, and then a new and glorious life would begin; and it was clear to both of them that the end was still far off, and that what was to be most complicated and difficult for them was only just beginning.

SANDRA CISNEROS

(1954–)

SANDRA CISNEROS was born in Chicago, the daughter of a Mexican father and a Mexican-American mother. She is the only daughter in a family with six sons. Educated in Chicago Catholic schools, Cisneros says in an interview (*Library Journal,* January 1992) that most of her learning came from the books she borrowed from the public library.

She began writing in earnest at the University of Iowa Writers' Workshop. Her works include *Bad Boys* (poems, 1980); *The House on Mango Street* (fiction, 1983), for which she won the Before Columbus Foundation's American Book Award; *The Rodrigo Poems* (1985); and *Woman Hollering Creek and Other Stories* (1991), including "Eyes of Zapata" (1991), a collection that *Library Journal* cited as one of the best books of the year. Her other awards include a National Endowment for the Arts Fellowship in fiction. Cisneros has worked as a poet-in-the-schools, a teacher of high-school dropouts, a college recruiter, and an arts administrator. She has also taught as a visiting writer in various universities, including California State University in Chico.

"Eyes of Zapata" is narrated by Inés Alfaro, a Mexican peasant woman, who as a young girl falls in love with the Mexican revolutionary Emiliano Zapata and bears him two children. His eyes and wide-ranging glance represent hope to her and to his followers as well. The hope is betrayed, however. General Zapata comes and goes as he pleases. There are other women, but his main mistress is really the Mexican Revolution—war and politics. Inés's hopes both for herself and for an end to the exploitation of women recede, even as her memories of love and longing continue unabated. The story is lush, the telling associative, the voice layered: poetic, indignant, sensual.

Eyes of Zapata

I put my nose to your eyelashes. The skin of the eyelids as soft as the skin of the penis, the collarbone with its fluted wings, the purple knot of the nipple, the dark, blue-black color of your sex, the thin legs and long thin feet. For a moment I don't want to think of your past nor your future. For now you are here, you are mine.

Would it be right to tell you what I do each night you sleep here? After your cognac and cigar, after I'm certain you're asleep, I examine at my leisure your black trousers with the silver buttons—fifty-six pairs on each side; I've counted them—your embroidered sombrero with its horsehair tassel, the lovely Dutch linen shirt, the fine braid stitching on the border of your *charro* jacket, the handsome black boots, your tooled gun belt and silver spurs. Are you my general? Or only that boy I met at the country fair in San Lázaro?

Hands too pretty for a man. Elegant hands, graceful hands, fingers smelling sweet as your Havanas. I had pretty hands once, remember? You used to say I had the prettiest hands of any woman in Cuautla. *Exquisitas* you called them, as if they were something to eat. It still makes me laugh remembering that.

Ay, but now look. Nicked and split and callused—how is it the hands get old first? The skin as coarse as the wattle of a hen. It's from the planting in the *tlacolol*, from the hard man's work I do clearing the field with the hoe and the machete, dirty work that leaves the clothes filthy, work no woman would do before the war.

But I'm not afraid of hard work or of being alone in the hills. I'm not afraid of dying or jail. I'm not afraid of the night like other women who run to the sacristy at the first call of *el gobierno*. I'm not other women.

Look at you. Snoring already? *Pobrecito. Sleep, papacito.* There, there. It's only me—Inés. *Duerme, mi trigueño, mi chulito, mi bebito. Ya, ya, ya.*

You say you can't sleep anywhere like you sleep here. So tired of always having to be *el gran general* Emiliano Zapata. The nervous fingers flinch, the long elegant bones shiver and twitch. Always waiting for the assassin's bullet.

Everyone is capable of becoming a traitor, and traitors must be broken, you say. A horse to be broken. A new saddle that needs breaking in. To break a spirit. Something to whip and lasso like you did in the *jaripeos* years ago.

Everything bothers you these days. Any noise, any light, even the sun. You say nothing for hours, and then when you do speak, it's an outburst, a fury. Everyone afraid of you, even your men. You hide yourself in the dark. You go days without sleep. You don't laugh anymore.

I don't need to ask; I've seen for myself. The war is not going well. I see it in your face. How it's changed over the years, Miliano. From so much watching, the face grows that way. These wrinkles new, this furrow, the jaw clenched tight. Eyes creased from learning to see in the night.

They say the widows of sailors have eyes like that, from squinting into the line where the sky and sea dissolve. It's the same with us from all this war. We're all widows. The men as well as the women, even the children. All *clinging to the tail of the horse of our* jefe *Zapata*. All of us scarred from these nine years of *aguantando*—enduring.

Yes, it's in your face. It's always been there. Since before the war. Since before I knew you. Since your birth in Anenecuilco and even before then. Something hard and tender all at once in those eyes. You knew before any of us, didn't you?

This morning the messenger arrived with the news you'd be arriving before

89

nightfall, but I was already boiling the corn for your supper tortillas. I saw you riding in on the road from Villa de Ayala. Just as I saw you that day in Anenecuilco when the revolution had just begun and the government was everywhere looking for you. You were worried about the land titles, went back to dig them up from where you'd hidden them eighteen months earlier, under the altar in the village church—am I right?—reminding Chico Franco to keep them safe. *I'm bound to die*, you said, *someday. But our titles stand to be guaranteed.*

I wish I could rub the grief from you as if it were a smudge on the cheek. I want to gather you up in my arms as if you were Nicolás or Malena, run up to the hills. I know every cave and crevice, every back road and ravine, but I don't know where I could hide you from yourself. You're tired. You're sick and lonely with this war, and I don't want any of those things to ever touch you again, Miliano. It's enough for now you are here. For now. Under my roof again.

Sleep, *papacito*. It's only Inés circling above you, wide-eyed all night. The sound of my wings like the sound of a velvet cape crumpling. A warm breeze against your skin, the wide expanse of moon-white feathers as if I could touch all the walls of the house at one sweep. A rustling, then weightlessness, light scattered out the window until it's the moist night wind beneath my owl wings. Whorl of stars like the filigree earrings you gave me. Your tired horse still as tin, there, where you tied it to a guamuchil tree. River singing louder than ever since the time of the rains.

I scout the hillsides, the mountains. My blue shadow over the high grass and slash of *barrancas*, over the ghosts of haciendas silent under the blue night. From this height, the village looks the same as before the war. As if the roofs were still intact, the walls still whitewashed, the cobbled streets swept of rubble and weeds. Nothing blistered and burnt. Our lives smooth and whole.

Round and round the blue countryside, over the scorched fields, giddy wind barely ruffling my stiff, white feathers, above the two soldiers you left guarding our door, one asleep, the other dull from a day of hard riding. But I'm awake, I'm always awake when you are here. Nothing escapes me. No coyote in the mountains, or scorpion in the sand. Everything clear. The trail you rode here. The night jasmine with its frothy scent of sweet milk. The makeshift roof of cane leaves on our adobe house. Our youngest child of five summers asleep in her hammock—*What a little woman you are now, Malenita*. The laughing sound of the river and canals, and the high, melancholy voice of the wind in the branches of the tall pine.

I slow-circle and glide into the house, bringing the night-wind smell with me, fold myself back into my body. I haven't left you. I don't leave you, not ever. Do you know why? Because when you are gone I re-create you from memory. The scent of your skin, the mole above the broom of your mustache, how you fit in my palms. Your skin dark and rich as *piloncillo*. This face in my hands. I miss you. I miss you even now as you lie next to me.

To look at you as you sleep, the color of your skin. How in the half-light of moon you cast your own light, as if you are all made of amber, Miliano. As if you are a little lantern, and everything in the house is golden too.

You used to be *tan chistoso. Muy bonachón, muy bromista.* Joking and singing off-key when you had your little drinks. *Tres vicios tengo y los tengo muy arraigados; de ser borracho, jugador, y enamorado . . .* Ay, my life, remember? Always *muy enamorado,* no? Are you still that boy I met at the San Lázaro country fair? Am I still that girl you kissed under the little avocado tree? It seems so far away from those days, Miliano.

We drag these bodies around with us, these bodies that have nothing at all to do with you, with me, with who we really are, these bodies that give us pleasure and pain. Though I've learned how to abandon mine at will, it seems to me we never free ourselves completely until we love, when we lose ourselves inside each other. Then we see a little of what is called heaven. When we can be that close that we no longer are Inés and Emiliano, but something bigger than our lives. And we can forgive, finally.

You and I, we've never been much for talking, have we? Poor thing, you don't know how to talk. Instead of talking with your lips, you put one leg around me when we sleep, to let me know it's all right. And we fall asleep like that, with one arm or a leg or one of those long monkey feet of yours touching mine. Your foot inside the hollow of my foot.

Does it surprise you I don't let go little things like that? There are so many things I don't forget even if I would do well to.

Inés, for the love I have for you. When my father pleaded, you can't imagine how I felt. How a pain entered my heart like a current of cold water and in that current were the days to come. But I said nothing.

Well then, my father said, *God help you. You've turned out just like the* perra *that bore you.* Then he turned around and I had no father.

I never felt so alone as that night. I gathered my things in my *rebozo* and ran out into the darkness to wait for you by the jacaranda tree. For a moment, all my courage left me. I wanted to turn around, call out, *'apá,* beg his forgiveness, and go back to sleeping on my *petate* against the cane-rush wall, waking before dawn to prepare the corn for the day's tortillas.

Perra. That word, the way my father spat it, as if in that one word I were betraying all the love he had given me all those years, as if he were closing all the doors to his heart.

Where could I hide from my father's anger? I could put out the eyes and stop the mouths of all the saints that wagged their tongues at me, but I could not stop my heart from hearing that word—*perra.* My father, my love, who would have nothing to do with me.

You don't like me to talk about my father, do you? I know, you and he never, well . . . Remember that thick scar across his left eyebrow? Kicked by a mule when he was a boy. Yes, that's how it happened. Tía Chucha said it was the reason he sometimes acted like a mule—but you're as stubborn as he was, aren't you, and no mule kicked you.

It's true, he never liked you. Since the days you started buying and selling livestock all through the *rancheritos*. By the time you were working the stables in Mexico City there was no mentioning your name. Because you'd never slept under a thatch roof, he said. Because you were a *charro*, and didn't wear the cotton whites of the *campesino*. Then he'd mutter, loud enough for me to hear, *That one doesn't know what it is to smell his own shit.*

I always thought you and he made such perfect enemies because you were so much alike. Except, unlike you, he was useless as a soldier. I never told you how the government forced him to enlist. Up in Guanajuato is where they sent him when you were busy with the Carrancistas, and Pancho Villa's boys were giving everyone a rough time up north. My father, who'd never been farther than Amecameca, gray-haired and broken as he was, they took him. It was during the time the dead were piled up on the street corners like stones, when it wasn't safe for anyone, man or woman, to go out into the streets.

There was nothing to eat, Tía Chucha sick with the fever, and me taking care of us all. My father said better he should go to his brother Fulgencio's in Tenexcapán and see if they had corn there. *Take Malenita,* I said. *With a child they won't bother you.*

And so my father went out toward Tenexcapán dragging Malenita by the hand. But when night began to fall and they hadn't come back, well, imagine. It was the widow Elpidia who knocked on our door with Malenita howling and with the story they'd taken the men to the railroad station. *South to the work camps, or north to fight?* Tía Chucha asked. *If God wishes,* I said, *he'll be safe.*

That night Tía Chucha and I dreamt this dream. My father and my Tío Fulgencio standing against the back wall of the rice mill. *Who lives?* But they don't answer, afraid to give the wrong *viva. Shoot them; discuss politics later.*

At the moment the soldiers are about to fire, an officer, an acquaintance of my father's from before the war, rides by and orders them set free.

Then they took my father and my Tío Fulgencio to the train station, shuttled them into box cars with others, and didn't let them go until they reached Guanajuato where they were each given guns and orders to shoot at the Villistas.

With the fright of the firing squad and all, my father was never the same. In Guanajuato, he had to be sent to the military hospital, where he suffered a collapsed lung. They removed three of his ribs to cure him, and when he was finally well enough to travel, they sent him back to us.

All through the dry season my father lived on like that, with a hole in the back of his chest from which he breathed. Those days I had to swab him with a sticky pitch pine and wrap him each morning in clean bandages. The opening oozed a spittle like the juice of the prickly pear, sticky and clear and with a smell both sweet and terrible like magnolia flowers rotting on the branch.

We did the best we could to nurse him, my Tía Chucha and I. Then one morning a *chachalaca* flew inside the house and battered against the ceiling. It took both of us with blankets and the broom to get it out. We didn't say anything but we thought about it for a long time.

Before the next new moon, I had a dream I was in church praying a rosary. But what I held between my hands wasn't my rosary with the glass beads, but one of human teeth. I let it drop, and the teeth bounced across the flagstones like pearls from a necklace. The dream and the bird were sign enough.

When my father called my mother's name one last time and died, the syllables came out sucked and coughed from that other mouth, like a drowned man's, and he expired finally in one last breath from that opening that killed him.

We buried him like that, with his three missing ribs wrapped in a handkerchief my mother had embroidered with his initials and with the hoofmark of the mule under his left eyebrow.

For eight days people arrived to pray the rosary. All the priests had long since fled, we had to pay a *rezandero* to say the last rites. Tía Chucha laid the cross of lime and sand, and set out flowers and a votive lamp, and on the ninth day, my *tía* raised the cross and called out my father's name—Remigio Alfaro—and my father's spirit flew away and left us.

But suppose he won't give us his permission.

That old goat, we'll be dead by the time he gives his permission. Better we just run off. He can't be angry forever.

Not even on his deathbed did he forgive you. I suppose you've never forgiven him either for calling in the authorities. I'm sure he only meant for them to scare you a little, to remind you of your obligations to me since I was expecting your child. Who could imagine they would force you to join the cavalry.

I can't make apologies on my father's behalf, but, well, what were we to think, Miliano? Those months you were gone, hiding out in Puebla because of the protest signatures, the political organizing, the work in the village defense. Me as big as a boat, Nicolás waiting to be born at any moment, and you nowhere to be found, and no money sent, and not a word. I was so young, I didn't know what else to do but abandon our house of stone and adobe and go back to my father's. Was I wrong to do that? You tell me.

I could endure my father's anger, but I was afraid for the child. I placed my hand on my belly and whispered—Child, be born when the moon is tender; even a tree must be pruned under the full moon so it will grow strong. And at the next full moon, I gave light, Tía Chucha holding up our handsome, strong-lunged boy.

Two planting seasons came and went, and we were preparing for the third when you came back from the cavalry and met your son for the first time. I thought you'd forgotten all about politics, and we could go on with our lives. But by the end of the year you were already behind the campaign to elect Patricio Leyva governor, as if all the troubles with the government, with my father, had meant nothing.

You gave me a pair of gold earrings as a wedding gift, remember? *I never said I'd marry you, Inés. Never.* Two filagree hoops with tiny flowers and fringe. I buried them when the government came, and went back for them later. But even these I had to sell when there was nothing to eat but boiled corn silk. They were the last things I sold.

Never. It made me feel a little crazy when you hurled that at me. That word with all its force.

But, Miliano, I thought . . .

You were foolish to have thought then.

That was years ago. We're all guilty of saying things we don't mean. *I never said . . .* I know. You don't want to hear it.

What am I to you now, Miliano? When you leave me? When you hesitate? Hover? The last time you gave a sigh that would fit into a spoon. What did you mean by that?

If I complain about these woman concerns of mine, I know you'll tell me—Inés, these aren't times for that—wait until later. But, Miliano, I'm tired of being told to wait.

Ay, you don't understand. Even if you had the words, you could never tell me. You don't know your own heart, men. Even when you are speaking with it in your hand.

I have my livestock, a little money my father left me. I'll set up a house for us in Cuautla of stone and adobe. We can live together, and later we'll see.

Nicolás is crazy about his two cows, La Fortuna y La Paloma. Because he's a man now, you said, when you gave him his birthday present. When you were thirteen, you were already buying and reselling animals throughout the ranches. To see if a beast is a good worker, you must tickle it on the back, no? If it can't bother itself to move, well then, it's lazy and won't be of any use. See, I've learned that much from you.

Remember the horse you found in Cuernavaca? Someone had hidden it in an upstairs bedroom, wild and spirited from being penned so long. She had poked her head from between the gold fringe of velvet drapery just as you rode by, just at that moment. A beauty like that making her appearance from a balcony like a woman waiting for her serenade. You laughed and joked about that and named her La Coquetona, remember? La Coquetona, yes.

When I met you at the country fair in San Lázaro, everyone knew you were the best man with horses in the state of Morelos. All the hacienda owners wanted you to work for them. Even as far as Mexico City. A *charro* among *charros*. The livestock, the horses bought and sold. Planting a bit when things were slow. Your brother Eufemio borrowing time and time again because he'd squandered every peso of his inheritance, but you've always prided yourself in being independent, no? You once confessed one of the happiest days of your life was the watermelon harvest that produced the 600 pesos.

And *my* happiest memory? The night I came to live with you, of course. I remember how your skin smelled sweet as the rind of a watermelon, like the fields after it has rained. I wanted my life to begin there, at that moment when I balanced that thin boy's body of yours on mine, as if you were made of balsa, as if you were boat and I river. The days to come, I thought, erasing the bitter sting of my father's good-bye.

There's been too much suffering, too much of our hearts hardening and drying like corpses. We've survived, eaten grass and corn cobs and rotten vegetables. And the epidemics have been as dangerous as the *federales*, the deserters, the bandits. Nine years.

In Cuautla it stank from so many dead. Nicolás would go out to play with the bullet shells he'd collected, or to watch the dead being buried in trenches. Once five federal corpses were piled up in the *zócalo*. We went through their pockets for money, jewelry, anything we could sell. When they burned the bodies, the fat ran off them in streams, and they jumped and wiggled as if they were trying to sit up. Nicolás had terrible dreams after that. I was too ashamed to tell him I did, too.

At first we couldn't bear to look at the bodies hanging in the trees. But after many months, you get used to them, curling and drying into leather in the sun day after day, dangling like earrings, so that they no longer terrify, they no longer mean anything. Perhaps that is worst of all.

Your sister tells me Nicolás takes after you these days, nervous and quick with words, like a sudden dust storm or shower of sparks. When you were away with the Seventh Cavalry, Tía Chucha and I would put smoke in Nicolás's mouth, so he would learn to talk early. All the other babies his age babbling like monkeys, but Nicolás always silent, always following us with those eyes all your kin have. Those are not Alfaro eyes, I remember my father saying.

The year you came back from the cavalry, you sent for us, me and the boy, and we lived in the house of stone and adobe. From your silences, I understood I was not to question our marriage. It was what it was. Nothing more. Wondering where you were the weeks I didn't see you, and why it was you arrived only for a few slender nights, always after nightfall and leaving before dawn. Our lives ran along as they had before. What good is it to have a husband and not have him? I thought.

When you began involving yourself with the Patricio Leyva campaign, we didn't see you for months at a time. Sometimes the boy and I would return to my father's house where I felt less alone. *Just for a few nights*, I said, unrolling a *petate* in my old corner against the cane-rush wall in the kitchen. *Until my husband returns*. But a few nights grew into weeks, and the weeks into months, until I spent more time under my father's thatch roof than in our house with the roof of tiles.

That's how the weeks and months passed. Your election to the town council. Your work defending the land titles. Then the parceling of the land when your name began to run all along the villages, up and down the Cuautla River. Zapata this and Zapata that. I couldn't go anywhere without hearing it. And each time, a kind of fear entered my heart like a cloud crossing the sun.

I spent the days chewing on this poison as I was grinding the corn, pretending to ignore what the other women washing at the river said. That you had several *pastimes*. That there was a certain María Josefa in Villa de Ayala. Then they would just laugh. It was worse for me those nights you did arrive and lay asleep next to me. I lay awake watching and watching you.

In the day, I could support the grief, wake up before dawn to prepare the day's tortillas, busy myself with the chores, the turkey hens, the planting and collecting of herbs. The boy already wearing his first pair of trousers and getting into all kinds of trouble when he wasn't being watched. There was enough to distract me in the day. But at night, you can't imagine.

Tía Chucha made me drink heart-flower tea—*yoloxochitl*, flower from the magnolia tree—petals soft and seamless as a tongue. *Yoloxochitl, flor de corazón*, with its breath of vanilla and honey. She prepared a tonic with the dried blossoms and applied a salve, mixed with the white of an egg, to the tender skin above my heart.

It was the season of rain. *Plum . . . plum plum*. All night I listened to that broken string of pearls, bead upon bead upon bead rolling across the waxy leaves of my heart.

I lived with that heartsickness inside me, Miliano, as if the days to come did not exist. And when it seemed the grief would not let me go, I wrapped one of your handkerchiefs around a dried hummingbird, went to the river, whispered, *Virgencita, ayúdame*, kissed it, then tossed the bundle into the waters where it disappeared for a moment before floating downstream in a dizzy swirl of foam.

That night, my heart circled and fluttered against my chest, and something beneath my eyelids palpitated so furiously, it wouldn't let me sleep. When I felt myself whirling against the beams of the house, I opened my eyes. I could see perfectly in the darkness. Beneath me—all of us asleep. Myself, there, in my *petate* against the kitchen wall, the boy asleep beside me. My father and my Tía Chucha sleeping in their corner of the house. Then I felt the room circle once, twice, until I found myself under the stars flying above the little avocado tree, above the house and the corral.

I passed the night in a delirious circle of sadness, of joy, reeling round and round above our roof of dried sugarcane leaves, the world as clear as if the noon sun shone. And when dawn arrived I flew back to my body that waited patiently for me where I'd left it, on the *petate* beside our Nicolás.

Each evening I flew a wider circle. And in the day, I withdrew further and further into myself, living only for those night flights. My father whispered to my Tía Chucha, *Ojos que no ven, corazón que no siente*. But my eyes did see and my heart suffered.

One night over *milpas* and beyond the *tlacolol*, over *barrancas* and thorny scrub forests, past the thatch roofs of the *jacales* and the stream where the women do the wash, beyond bright bougainvillea, high above canyons and across fields of rice and corn, I flew. The gawky stalks of banana trees swayed beneath me. I saw rivers of cold water and a river of water so bitter they say it flows from the sea. I didn't stop until I reached a grove of high laurels rustling in the center of a town square where all the whitewashed houses shone blue as abalone under the full moon. And I remember my wings were blue and soundless as the wings of a *tecolote*.

And when I alighted on the branch of a tamarind tree outside a window, I saw you asleep next to that woman from Villa de Ayala, that woman who is your wife sleeping beside you. And her skin shone blue in the moonlight and you were blue as well.

She wasn't at all like I'd imagined. I came up close and studied her hair. Nothing but an ordinary woman with her ordinary woman smell. She opened her mouth and gave a moan. And you pulled her close to you, Miliano. Then I felt a terrible grief inside me. The two of you asleep like that, your leg warm against hers, your foot inside the hollow of her foot.

They say I am the one who caused her children to die. From jealousy, from envy. What do you say? Her boy and girl both dead before they stopped sucking teat. She won't bear you any more children. But my boy, my girl are alive.

When a customer walks away after you've named your price, and then he comes back, that's when you raise your price. When you know you have what he wants. Something I learned from your horse-trading years.

You married her, that woman from Villa de Ayala, true. But see, you came back to me. You always come back. In between and beyond the others. That's my magic. You come back to me.

You visited me again Thursday last. I yanked you from the bed of that other one. I dreamt you, and when I awoke I was sure your spirit had just fluttered from the room. I have yanked you from your sleep before into the dream I was dreaming. Twisted you like a spiral of hair around a finger. Love, you arrived with your heart full of birds. And when you would not do my bidding and come when I commanded, I turned into the soul of a *tecolote* and kept vigil in the branches of a purple jacaranda outside your door to make sure no one would do my Miliano harm while he slept.

You sent a letter by messenger how many months afterward? On paper thin and crinkled as if it had been made with tears.

I burned copal in a clay bowl. Inhaled the smoke. Said a prayer in *mexicano* to the old gods, an Ave María in Spanish to La Virgen, and gave thanks. You were on your way home to us. The house of stone and adobe aired and swept clean, the night sweet with the scent of candles that had been burning continually since I saw you in the dream. Sometime after Nicolás had fallen asleep, the hoofbeats.

A silence between us like a language. When I held you, you trembled, a tree in rain. Ay, Miliano, I remember that, and it helps the days pass without bitterness.

What did you tell her about me? *That was before I knew you, Josefa. That chapter of my life with Inés Alfaro is finished.* But I'm a story that never ends. Pull one string and the whole cloth unravels.

Just before you came for Nicolás, he fell ill with the symptoms of the jealousy sickness, big boy that he was. But it was true, I was with child again. Malena was born without making a sound, because she remembered how she had been conceived—nights tangled around each other like smoke.

You and Villa were marching triumphantly down the streets of Mexico City, your hat filled with flowers the pretty girls tossed at you. The brim sagging under the weight like a basket.

I named our daughter after my mother. María Elena. Against my father's wishes.

You have your *pastimes*. That's how it's said, no? Your many *pastimes*. I know you take to your bed women half my age. Women the age of our Nicolás. You've left many mothers crying, as they say.

They say you have three women in Jojutla, all under one roof. And that your women treat each other with *a most extraordinary harmony, sisters in a cause who believe in the greater good of the revolution.* I say they can all go to hell, those newspaper journalists and the mothers who bore them. Did they ever ask me?

These stupid country girls, how can they resist you? The magnificent Zapata in his elegant *charro* costume, riding a splendid horse. Your wide sombrero a halo around your face. You're not a man for them; you're a legend, a myth, a god. But you are as well my husband. Albeit only sometimes.

How can a woman be happy in love? To love like this, to love as strong as we hate. That is how we are, the women of my family. We never forget a wrong. We know how to love and we know how to hate.

I've seen your other children in the dreams. María from that Gregoria Zúñiga in Quilamula after her twin sister Luz died on you childless. Diego born in Tlatizapán of that woman who calls herself *Missus* Jorge Piñeiro. Ana María in Cuautla from that she-goat Petra Torres. Mateo, son of that nobody, Jesusa Pérez of Temilpa. All your children born with those eyes of Zapata.

I know what I know. How you sleep cradled in my arms, how you love me with a pleasure close to sobbing, how I still the trembling in your chest and hold you, hold you, until those eyes look into mine.

Your eyes. Ay! Your eyes. Eyes with teeth. Terrible as obsidian. The days to come in those eyes, *el porvenir*, the days gone by. And beneath that fierceness, something ancient and tender as rain.

Miliano, Milianito. And I sing you that song I sang Nicolás and Malenita when they were little and would not sleep.

Seasons of war, a little half-peace now and then, and then war and war again. Running up to the hills when the *federales* come, coming back down when they've gone.

Before the war, it was the *caciques* who were after the young girls and the married women. They had their hands on everything it seems—the land, law, women. Remember when they found that *desgraciado* Policarpo Cisneros in the arms of the Quintero girl? ¡*Virgen purísima!* She was only a little thing of twelve years. And he, what? At least eighty, I imagine.

Desgraciados. All members of one army against us, no? The *federales,* the *caciques,* one as bad as the other, stealing our hens, stealing the women at night. What long sharp howls the women would let go when they carried them off. The next morning the women would be back, and we would say *Buenos días,* as if nothing had happened.

Since the war began, we've gotten used to sleeping in the corral. Or in the hills, in trees, in caves with the spiders and scorpions. We hide ourselves as best we can when the *federales* arrive, behind rocks or in *barrancas,* or in the pine and tall grass when there is nothing else to hide behind. Sometimes I build a shelter for us with cane branches in the mountains. Sometimes the people of the cold lands give us boiled water sweetened with cane sugar, and we stay until we can gather a little strength, until the sun has warmed our bones and it is safe to come back down.

Before the war, when Tía Chucha was alive, we passed the days selling at all the town markets—chickens, turkey hens, cloth, coffee, the herbs we collected in the hills or grew in the garden. That's how our weeks and months came and went.

I sold bread and candles. I planted corn and beans back then and harvested coffee at times too. I've sold all kinds of things. I even know how to buy and resell animals. And now I know how to work the *tlacolol,* which is the worst of all—your hands and feet split and swollen from the machete and hoe.

Sometimes I find sweet potatoes in the abandoned fields, or squash, or corn. And this we eat raw, too tired, too hungry to cook anything. We've eaten like the birds, what we could pluck from the trees—guava, mango, tamarind, almond when in season. We've gone without corn for the tortillas, made do when there were no kernels to be had, eaten the cobs as well as the flower.

My *metate,* my good shawl, my fancy *huipil,* my filigree earrings, anything I could sell, I've sold. The corn sells for one peso and a half a *cuartillo* when one can find a handful. I soak and boil and grind it without even letting it cool, a few tortillas to feed Malenita, who is always hungry, and if there is anything left, I feed myself.

Tía Chucha caught the sickness of the wind in the hot country. I used all her remedies and my own, *guacamaya* feathers, eggs, cocoa beans, chamomile oil, rosemary, but there was no help for her. I thought I would finish myself crying, all my mother's people gone from me, but there was the girl to think about. Nothing to do but go on, *aguantar*, until I could let go that grief. Ay, how terrible those times.

I go on surviving, hiding, searching if only for Malenita's sake. Our little plantings, that's how we get along. The government run off with the *maíz*, the chickens, my prize turkey hens and rabbits. Everyone has had his turn to do us harm.

Now I'm going to tell you about when they burned the house, the one you bought for us. I was sick with the fever. Headache and a terrible pain in the back of my calves. Fleas, babies crying, gunshots in the distance, someone crying out *el gobierno*, a gallop of horses in my head, and the shouting of those going off to join troops and of those staying. I could barely manage to drag myself up the hills. Malenita was suffering one of her *corajes* and refused to walk, sucking the collar of her blouse and crying. I had to carry her on my back with her little feet kicking me all the way until I gave her half of a hard tortilla to eat and she forgot about her anger and fell asleep. By the time the sun was strong and we were far away enough to feel safe, I was weak. I slept without dreaming, holding Malenita's cool body against my burning. When I woke the world was filled with stars, and the stars carried me back to the village and showed me.

It was like this. The village did not look like our village. The trees, the mountains against the sky, the land, yes, that was still as we remembered it, but the village was no longer a village. Everything pocked and in ruins. Our house with its roof tiles gone. The walls blistered and black. Pots, pans, jugs, dishes axed into shards, our shawls and blankets torn and trampled. The seed we had left, what we'd saved and stored that year, scattered, the birds enjoying it.

Hens, cows, pigs, goats, rabbits, all slaughtered. Not even the dogs were spared and were strung from the trees. The Carrancistas destroyed everything, because, as they say, *Even the stones here are Zapatistas.* And what was not destroyed was carried off by their women, who descended behind them like a plague of vultures to pick us clean.

It's *her* fault, the villagers said when they returned. *Nagual. Bruja.* Then I understood how alone I was.

Miliano, what I'm about to say to you now, only to you do I tell it, to no one else have I confessed it. It's necessary I say it; I won't rest until I undo it from my heart.

They say when I was a child I caused a hailstorm that ruined the new corn. When I was so young I don't even remember. In Tetelcingo that's what they say.

That's why the years the harvest was bad and the times especially hard, they wanted to burn me with green wood. It was my mother they killed instead, but not with green wood. When they delivered her to our door, I cried until I finished myself crying. I was sick, sick, for several days, and they say I vomited worms, but I don't remember that. Only the terrible dreams I suffered during the fever.

My Tía Chucha cured me with branches from the pepper tree and with the broom. And for a long time afterward, my legs felt as if they were stuffed with rags, and I kept seeing little purple stars winking and whirling just out of reach.

It wasn't until I was well enough to go outside again that I noticed the crosses of pressed *pericón* flowers on all the village doorways and in the *milpa* too. From then on the villagers avoided me, as if they meant to punish me by not talking, just as they'd punished my mother with those words that thumped and thudded like the hail that killed the corn.

That's why we had to move the seven kilometers from Tetelcingo to Cuautla, as if we were from that village and not the other, and that's how it was we came to live with my Tía Chucha, little by little taking my mother's place as my teacher, and later as my father's wife.

My Tía Chucha, she was the one who taught me to use my sight, just as her mother had taught her. The women in my family, we've always had the power to see with more than our eyes. My mother, my Tía Chucha, me. Our Malenita as well.

It's only now when they murmur *bruja, nagual*, behind my back, just as they hurled those words at my mother, that I realize how alike my mother and I are. How words can hold their own magic. How a word can charm, and how a word can kill. This I've understood.

Mujeriego. I dislike the word. Why not *hombreriega?* Why not? The word loses its luster. *Hombreriega*. Is that what I am? My mother? But in the mouth of men, the word is flint-edged and heavy, makes a drum of the body, something to maim and bruise, and sometimes kill.

What is it I am to you? Sometime wife? Lover? Whore? Which? To be one is not so terrible as being all.

I've needed to hear it from you. To verify what I've always thought I knew. You'll say I've grown crazy from living on dried grass and corn silk. But I swear I've never seen more clearly than these days.

Ay, Miliano, don't you see? The wars begin here, in our hearts and in our beds. You have a daughter. How do you want her treated? Like you treated me?

All I've wanted was words, that magic to soothe me a little, what you could not give me.

The months I disappeared, I don't think you understood my reasons. I assumed I made no difference to you. Only Nicolás mattered. And that's when you took him from me.

When Nicolás lost his last milk tooth, you sent for him, left him in your sister's care. He's lived like deer in the mountains, sometimes following you, sometimes meeting you ahead of your campaigns, always within reach. I know. I let him go. I agreed, yes, because a boy should be with his father, I said. But the truth is I wanted a part of me always hovering near you. How hard it must be for you to keep letting Nicolás go. And yet, he is always yours. Always.

When the *federales* captured Nicolás and took him to Tepaltzingo, you arrived with him asleep in your arms after your brother and Chico Franco rescued him. If anything happens to this child, you said, if anything . . . and started to cry. I didn't say anything, Miliano, but you can't imagine how in that instant, I wanted to be small and fit inside your heart, I wanted to belong to you like the boy, and know you loved me.

If I am a witch, then so be it, I said. And I took to eating black things— *huitlacoche*, the corn mushroom, coffee, dark chiles, the bruised part of fruit, the darkest, blackest things to make me hard and strong.

You rarely talk. Your voice, Miliano, thin and light as a woman's, almost delicate. Your way of talking is sudden, quick, like water leaping. And yet I know what that voice of yours is capable of.

I remember after the massacre of Tlatizapán, 286 men and women and children slaughtered by the Carrancistas. Your thin figure, haggard and drawn, your face small and dark under your wide sombrero. I remember even your horse looked half-starved and wild that dusty, hot June day.

It was as if misery laughed at us. Even the sky was sad, the light leaden and dull, the air sticky and everything covered with flies. Women filled the streets searching among the corpses for their dead.

Everyone was tired, exhausted from running from the Carrancistas. The government had chased us almost as far as Jojutla. But you spoke in *mexicano*, you spoke to us in our language, with your heart in your hand, Miliano, which is why we listened to you. The people were tired, but they listened. Tired of surviving, of living, of enduring. Many were deserting and going back to their villages. *If you don't want to fight anymore*, you said, *we'll all go to the devil. What do you mean you are tired? When you elected me, I said I would represent you if you backed me. But now you must back me, I've kept my word. You wanted a man who wore pants, and I've been that man. And now, if you don't mean to fight, well then, there's nothing I can do.*

We were filthy, exhausted, hungry, but we followed you.

Under the little avocado tree behind my father's house is where you first kissed me. A crooked kiss, all wrong, on the side of the mouth. *You belong to me now,* you said, and I did.

The way you rode in the morning of the San Lázaro fair on a pretty horse as dark as your eyes. The sky was sorrel-colored, remember? Everything swelled and smelled of rain. A cool shadow fell across the village. You were dressed all in black as is your custom. A graceful, elegant man, thin and tall.

You wore a short black linen *charro* jacket, black trousers of cashmere adorned with silver buttons, and a lavender shirt knotted at the collar with a blue silk neckerchief. Your sombrero had a horsehair braid and tassel and a border of carnations embroidered along the wide brim in gold and silver threads. You wore the sombrero set forward—not at the back of the head as others do—so it would shade those eyes of yours, those eyes that watched and waited. Even then I knew it was an animal to match mine.

Suppose my father won't let me?
  We'll run off, he can't be angry for always.
  Wait until the end of the harvest.
  You pulled me toward you under the little avocado tree and kissed me. A kiss tasting of warm beer and whiskers. *You belong to me now.*

It was during the plum season we met. I saw you at the country fair at San Lázaro. I wore my braids up away from the neck with bright ribbons. My hair freshly washed and combed with oil prepared with the ground bone of the mamey. And the neckline of my *huipil*, a white one, I remember, showed off my neck and collarbones.

You were riding a fine horse, silver-saddled with a fringe of red and black silk tassels, and your hands, beautiful hands, long and sensitive, rested lightly on the reins. I was afraid of you at first, but I didn't show it. How pretty you made your horse prance.

You circled when I tried to cross the *zócalo*, I remember. I pretended not to see you until you rode your horse in my path, and I tried to dodge one way, then the other, like a calf in a *jaripeo*. I could hear the laughter of your friends from under the shadows of the arcades. And when it was clear there was no avoiding you, I looked up at you and said, *With your permission.* You did not insist, you touched the brim of your hat, and let me go, and I heard your friend Francisco Franco, the one I would later know as Chico, say, *Small, but bigger than you, Miliano.*

So is it yes? I didn't know what to say, I was still so little, just laughed, and you kissed me like that, on my teeth.

Yes? and pressed me against the avocado tree. *No, is it?* And I said yes, then I said no, and yes, your kisses arriving in between.

Love? We don't say that word. For you it has to do with stroking with your eyes what catches your fancy, then lassoing and harnessing and corraling. Yanking home what is easy to take.

But not for me. Not from the start. You were handsome, yes, but I didn't like handsome men, thinking they could have whomever they wanted. I wanted to be, then, the one you could not have. I didn't lower my eyes like the other girls when I felt you looking at me.

I'll set up a house for us. We can live together, and later we'll see.
  But suppose one day you leave me.

Never.
Wait at least until the end of the harvest.

I remember how your skin burned to the touch. How you smelled of lemongrass and smoke. I balanced that thin boy's body of yours on mine.

Something undid itself—gently, like a braid of hair unraveling. And I said, Ay, *mi chulito, mi chulito, mi chulito,* over and over.

Mornings and nights I think your scent is still in the blankets, wake remembering you are tangled somewhere between the sleeping and the waking. The scent of your skin, the mole above the broom of your thick mustache, how you fit in my hands.

Would it be right to tell you, each night you sleep here, after your cognac and cigar, when I'm certain you are finally sleeping, I sniff your skin. Your fingers sweet with the scent of tobacco. The fluted collarbones, the purple knot of the nipple, the deep, plum color of your sex, the thin legs and long, thin feet.

I examine at my leisure your black trousers with the silver buttons, the lovely shirt, the embroidered sombrero, the fine braid stitching on the border of your *charro* jacket, admire the workmanship, the spurs, leggings, the handsome black boots.

And when you are gone, I re-create you from memory. Rub warmth into your fingertips. Take that dimpled chin of yours between my teeth. All the parts are there except your belly. I want to rub my face in its color, say no, no, no. Ay. Feel its warmth from my left cheek to the right. Run my tongue from the hollow in your throat, between the smooth stones of your chest, across the trail of down below the navel, lose myself in the dark scent of your sex. To look at you as you sleep, the color of your skin. How in the half-light of moon you cast your own light, as if you are a man made of amber.

Are you my general? Or only my Milianito? I think, I don't know what you say, you don't belong to me nor to that woman from Villa de Ayala. You don't belong to anyone, no? Except the land. *La madre tierra que nos mantiene y cuida.* Every one of us.

I rise high and higher, the house shutting itself like an eye. I fly farther than I've ever flown before, farther than the clouds, farther than our Lord Sun, husband of the moon. Till all at once I look beneath me and see our lives, clear and still, far away and near.

And I see our future and our past, Miliano, one single thread already lived and nothing to be done about it. And I see the face of the man who will betray you. The place and the hour. The gift of a horse the color of gold dust. A breakfast of warm beer swirling in your belly. The hacienda gates opening. The pretty bugles doing the honors. *TirriLEE tirREE.* Bullets like a sudden shower of stones.

And in that instant, a feeling of relief almost. And loneliness, just like that other loneliness of being born.

And I see my clean *huipil* and my silk Sunday shawl. My rosary placed between my hands and a palm cross that has been blessed. Eight days people arriving to pray. And on the ninth day, the cross of lime and sand raised, and my name called out—Inés Alfaro. The twisted neck of a rooster. Pork tamales wrapped in corn leaves. The masqueraders dancing, the men dressed as women, the women as men. Violins, guitars, one loud drum.

And I see other faces and other lives. My mother in a field of cempoaxúchitl flowers with a man who is not my father. Her *rebozo de bolita* spread beneath them. The smell of crushed grass and garlic. How, at a signal from her lover, the others descend. The clouds scurrying away. A machete-sharp cane stake greased with lard and driven into the earth. How the men gather my mother like a bundle of corn. Her sharp cry against the infinity of sky when the cane stake pierces her. How each waiting his turn grunts words like hail that splits open the skin, just as before they'd whispered words of love.

The star of her sex open to the sky. Clouds moving soundlessly, and the sky changing colors. Hours. Eyes still fixed on the clouds the morning they find her—braids undone, a man's sombrero tipped on her head, a cigar in her mouth, as if to say, this is what we do to women who try to act like men.

The small black bundle that is my mother delivered to my father's door. My father without a "who" or "how." He knows as well as everyone.

How the sky let go a storm of stones. The corn harvest ruined. And how we move from Tetelcingo to my Tía Chucha's in Cuautla.

And I see our children. Malenita with her twins, who will never marry, two brave *solteronas* living out their lives selling herbs in La Merced in Mexico City.

And our Nicolás, a grown man, the grief and shame Nicolás will bring to the Zapata name when he kicks up a fuss about the parcel of land the government gives him, how it isn't enough, how it's never enough, how the son of a great man should not live like a peasant. The older Anenecuilcans shaking their heads when he sells the Zapata name to the PRI campaign.

And I see the ancient land titles the smoky morning they are drawn up in Náhuatl and recorded on tree-bark paper—*conceded to our pueblo the 25th of September of 1607 by the Viceroy of New Spain*—the land grants that prove the land has always been our land.

And I see that dappled afternoon in Anenecuilco when the government has begun to look for you. And I see you unearth the strong box buried under the main altar of the village church, and hand it to Chico Franco—*If you lose this, I'll have you dangling from the tallest tree,* compadre. *Not before they fill me with bullets,* Chico said and laughed.

And the evening, already as an old man, in the Canyon of the Wolves, Chico Franco running and running, old wolf, old cunning, the government men Nicolás sent shouting behind him, his sons Vírulo and Julián, young, crumpled on the cool courtyard tiles like bougainvillea blossoms, and how useless it all is, because the deeds are buried under the floorboards of a *pulquería* named La Providencia, and no one knowing where they are after the bullets pierce Chico's body. Nothing better or worse than before, and nothing the same or different.

And I see rivers of stars and the wide sea with its sad voice, and emerald fish fluttering on the sea bottom, glad to be themselves. And bell towers and blue forests, and a store window filled with hats. A burnt foot like the inside of a plum. A lice comb with two nits. The lace hem of a woman's dress. The violet smoke from a cigarette. A boy urinating into a tin. The milky eyes of a blind man. The chipped finger of a San Isidro statue. The tawny bellies of dark women giving life.

And more lives and more blood, those being born as well as those dying, the ones who ask questions and the ones who keep quiet, the days of grief and all the flower colors of joy.

Ay papacito, cielito de mi corazón, now the burros are complaining. The rooster beginning his cries. Morning already? Wait, I want to remember everything before you leave me.

How you looked at me in the San Lázaro plaza. How you kissed me under my father's avocado tree. Nights you loved me with a pleasure close to sobbing, how I stilled the trembling in your chest and held you, held you. Miliano, Milianito.

My sky, my life, my eyes. Let me look at you. Before you open those eyes of yours. The days to come, the days gone by. Before we go back to what we'll always be.

COLETTE
(1873–1954)

COLETTE was born Sidonie Gabrielle Colette in a town in Burgundy, France. Her early novels, the *Claudine* series (*Claudine à l'école,* 1900; *Claudine à Paris,* 1901; *Claudine en ménage,* 1902; *Claudine s'en va,* 1903), were published by her first husband, Henry Gautier Villars, under his pen name, Willy. She was, in fact, published under the name Colette Willy until 1921, when she dropped the Willy and became simply Colette. Following her divorce from Villars in 1906, Colette worked until 1914 on the music-hall stage as a dancer and mime. This experience served as a source for her works *La Vagabonde* (1910), *L'Envers du music-hall* (1913), and *Mitsou* (1919). A second marriage to Henri de Juvenal also ended in divorce; her final marriage, to Maurice Goudeket, was, by all accounts, happy. Colette's other works, story collections largely, include *Cheri* (1920), *La Fin de Cheri* (1926), *Douze dialogues de bêtes* (1930), *Bella Vista* (1937), *Paris de ma fenêtre* (1944), *L'Etoile Vesper* (1946), and *Le Fanal Bleu* (1949).

Assessments of Colette's work have focused on the sensuousness and lyricism of her prose and her ability to convey atmosphere, notably of feminine romantic and sexual experience. Recent reassessments, however, such as that by Robert Phelps in his introduction to the *Collected Stories,* (1983) make the point that her "basic subject matter was not the world she described so reverently but the drama of her personal relation to the world" (p. xii). The unflinching perceptiveness and toughmindedness of Colette's art (neither one sacrificing her tenderness of language) are qualities perhaps more easily discernible by the contemporary reader, who is conditioned by the life and literature of our time to look for them.

"April" (1949) gives a lyrically compressed account of young love that appears to be moving toward a fuller flowering.

April

"Count again," ordered Vinca. "That makes nine. You made a mistake."

Phil sighed, and then raised his lustrous eyebrows in weariness.

"The two Viénots, Maria and her brother, La Folle and her little dog . . ."

Vinca chewed on her pencil anxiously, turning her blue eyes up toward the denser blue of a spring storm which was raining down a soft and ephemeral snow of plum blossoms and hazelnut-tree caterpillars, blown down from an invisible garden in Auteuil.

"Will the dog follow along?"

"No, he doesn't follow. She puts him in a strawberry basket attached to the handlebars, nestled in a Basque beret and slipped into the sleeve of an old sweater. He loves it."

"Well, it's fine with me . . . We said six, including us, the three Lapins-Géants-des-Flandres, nine. That's all."

"Worse than a wedding," said Phil scornfully.

"The hard-boiled eggs, the pâté, the roast beef, and the ham . . ."

". . . Thirteen," said Philippe. "Miscount."

Vinca burst out laughing, once again behaving like the fifteen-year-old girl she was, and Phil deigned to smile. He dark, she blond and rosy, they looked vaguely alike from having lived near one another since they were born and having loved one another in the aggressive way of adolescents.

"Viénot Henri says he's bringing some Calvados and some . . . kümmel."

Phil raised his head from the back of the wicker chair.

"Oh, yeah? Viénot Henri can do whatever he wants. We're not touching any liquor, if you don't mind! Viénot Henri has the manners of a boor!"

Vinca blushed and did not reply. With Philippe, she would accept authority and rebelled only when teased. She raised her generous face toward him, the face of a blossoming young girl with glowing cheeks. She had glistening, decidedly blue eyes, straight blond hair, and between her slightly chapped lips, teeth that were strong, white, and rounded at the edges.

"You know, Phil, I have a rack on my bike. I can take whatever might get in your way."

"Nothing'll get in my way," said Phil roguishly. "Nothing except our caravan, all the others . . . I'd like for us to go by car, you and me . . ."

"Yes, but since we don't have a car, Phil . . ."

He felt ashamed of himself, as he did whenever Vinca accepted her situation as a young girl without means and without money, taught to ride a bike as well as do the laundry, adept at beating and folding an omelette, at shampooing her little sister Lisette's hair and ironing her father's pants. Tall for her age, long-legged and lanky, she was nonetheless exactly like a woman and often anxious.

"Phil, does your mother know about the roast beef? Tell her she should only get enough for six, meat is so overpriced . . ."

She broke off to listen to the pearly rippling of a hailstorm and Phil snickered, pointing to the low sky.

"A week from today . . ." said Vinca hopefully.

And already her eyes were the color of clear blue skies.

And so it was that the weather did in fact change.

The next day, around the church in Auteuil, Palm Sunday gave forth its odor of tomcat and flowers. Vinca opened the window facing the street, one of the last village streets left in Auteuil, to watch for Philippe and his parents, who were coming for lunch. She leaned out to wonder at the spent lilacs and the mahonia with leaves the color of reddish iron, squeezed in between the gate and the front of the house.

"When we're married, this is where I'll wait for Philippe . . ."

She belonged to that sweet, tenacious, hardy race, oblivious to progress, with no desire either to change or to perish.

Nine bicycles passed through the gate of the park of St.-Cloud in the early-morning sun of Holy Saturday. Pedaling hard up the wide road leading toward Marnes, the nine bicyclists registered without a word the complete image of the motorists who passed them by, and pricked up their ears to the muffled *putt-putt-putt* of the new motorcycles. None of them was satisfied with his lot, or his age, and none had any burning desire to exchange secrets with the others. Only Philippe and Vinca the Periwinkle shared a past as old as their own sixteen years, rich in tender fraternity and silence.

Most of the nine bicyclists were the children of poor, small-scale Parisian business, cut off from costly pleasures, accustomed to curbing and nourishing their longings in secret. All they lacked was a little simplicity in their way of being poor. So one of the boys, upon reaching Marnes, deliberately tore a hole in the elbow of his threadbare pullover, made one of his socks fall down around his ankle, and gathered magpie feathers, which he stuck in his hair. But his ragamuffin getup did not make anyone laugh. La Folle with the big eyes sped through Marnes, letting out her war cry, and was first to arrive at the woods of Fausses-Reposes, where her tiny dog decided to make a hygienic stop. Out of courtesy, her eight companions dismounted and stood off to the side of the road, in a clearing where the peacefulness of the morning retook possession of the woods with the steady, strong murmuring of the breeze and the birds and the little leaves. Philippe stroked the satiny trunk of a wild-cherry tree; looking up, he saw that the tree bore all its flowers in full bloom. Whenever he felt happy, he appealed, with words and gestures, to Vinca. She tilted back her head to gaze up at the tree and her blue eyes filled with splendor. Nothing more was needed for them to feel bound to each other and withdrawn into that secret place where their tenderness regained its strength and self-awareness.

Back on the road, they took over the lead, wheel to wheel. The steep hill, leading out of Versailles, seemed long to them. The boys stripped; one took off his sweater, one the jacket of his ready-made plus fours. All of them already had wind-whipped cheeks, red eyes, and the happy expression of comforted children with tear-stained faces. They did not even glance at the romantic pond at Voisins-Bretonncux, but at long intervals they shouted out startling truths about temperature, perspiration, and speed. The bitter northwest wind and the biting April sun made them shout out without thinking from time to time, and from the top of its strawberry basket the tiny little dog would respond.

"Peach trees in bloom! . . . Wild daffodils! I saw some daffodils! I'm stopping!" yelped Maria, dark and curly-haired.

"Quiet!" ordered her twin brother, curly-haired and dark. "We can get them on the way back."

"There won't be any left for us! I'm stopping!"

She jumped to the ground, twisted her ankle, and screamed. One of the Viénots yelled out a nasty remark, sharply picked up on by the twin, and La Folle, turning back so as not to miss out on any of the altercation, blocked a car from getting by.

Philippe lost his patience, any desire to wait for his comrades; and the sound of their voices, their choice of insults, made the blood rise in his cheeks.

"C'mon," he said to Vinca. "They'll catch up soon enough. Because of all this it's already eleven-thirty."

The two set off again, relieved, enjoying their solitude and their reawakened good mood. Spring still bathed in the translucent yellow which precedes the universal green. The yellow primroses in the meadows, the honeyed catkins of the willows, the leaves of the poplars which are born pink and golden, enchanted Vinca and Phil only from the moment they felt themselves alone. On the thorny blackthorn hedges, the belated flowering held up round pearls white as hail.

Before passing though Dampierre, the two friends slackened their pace at the Seventeen Turns.

"I only count fourteen," said Vinca at the bottom of the hill.

"What a child you are," said Phil indulgently.

But he too had counted, and he could not keep from breaking into a fit of laughter, which brought tears to his eyes. Winded, sweating, his forehead hot beneath his hair, and his ears cold, he breathed in large gulps, prey to a somewhat exhausted, drained, and contented sense of well-being, as if he had just thrown up some indigestible food.

"Ah!" he sighed as he got off his bike, "that's better . . ."

Under the noonday sun, they climbed the last hill before Les Vaux, between the sparse woods starred with wild anemones.

"Come on, Vinca, let's take a rest."

She was already following him, guiding her bicycle onto a narrow path between low oaks and delicately leaved birch trees.

"Listen . . ." said Vinca. "That's a cuckoo. When the cuckoo sings, it means the wild violets have lost their fragrance."

Philippe had stopped short, his shoulder against Vinca's shoulder. Closer than the two notes of the cuckoo he could hear Vinca breathing. Her eyes, raised toward the tops of the copse, were sparkling with a blue which he believed he had discovered, flecked with slate, speckled with mauve . . . She held her red chapped lips half open, and Philippe suddenly shivered, imagining the coldness of the strong, beautiful teeth.

"Come on, Vinca . . ."

"Where?"

"There . . . over there . . ."

He pointed to a spot that was unfamiliar to him, off the path, a place he imagined as mossy, or blanketed with white sand, or grassy like a June meadow. He came upon it as in a dream. White with sand, green with finely spiked forest grass, mossy at the foot of a beech tree, and frighteningly narrow . . . At the same moment, he nearly stumbled over what he had neither imagined nor seen: a couple, lying spent and motionless on the ground, who did not move under their gaze. The outstretched woman merely closed her eyes and pressed closer to the man.

Turning his bike around, Philippe almost knocked Vinca down. She stumbled and did not say a word.

"Go on, turn around, we made a mistake," he said in a loud, forced voice.

He pushed her inconsiderately toward the road. "Move it, go on, move it! You have lead in your legs today?"

He wished she had not seen the couple lying there. He wanted her, having seen them, to run away, embarrassed and revolted.

"Move, little girl, move . . ."

"It's a bramble, Phil . . . It's caught in my spokes . . ."

He did not help her, and left her to pull free from the fierce old brambles herself, giving her a hard look. She did not ask him for either help or an explanation, and once back on the road she was content to lick her stinging hand.

"Back it up, Vinca . . . Your wheel's sticking out . . . a little farther and that maniac would have mowed you down."

"Yes . . ."

"Twelve-twenty! . . . If they're not here in two minutes, we're leaving."

"Whatever you say . . ."

"You have to say one thing for her, she does what she's told," he thought. "What if, back there in the woods, I'd told her to . . ."

From down in the little valley came shouts and the shrill barking of the little dog. Philippe raised his arms and called back, "Hey, up here!" in a loud voice. When the main body of riders reached the rise, he jumped onto his bicycle and, with a kind of thankfulness, mingled in among his companions.

DANTE ALIGHIERI
(1265–1321)

DANTE ALIGHIERI was born in Florence, where classical and Christian literature were part of his early education. At the age of twelve he was betrothed to Gemma Donati, whom he later married. In his early youth he fell in love with the girl he called Beatrice, who inspired the *Divina commedia* and *La vita nuova* (c. 1292). As a member of a Guelph family, Dante was frequently involved in both political and military struggles with the rival Ghibelline party. In 1289 he was a member of the Florentine cavalry, which, after a series of raging battles, defeated the Ghibellines. Far from resolving Florentine conflicts, however, this struggle gave way to an internecine fight among Guelph factions, leading to Dante's permanent banishment from Florence (1302); death by fire would be the penalty if he returned. He went into exile unaccompanied by his wife and three children, and spent most of the last part of his life in Verona and Ravenna. Eventually, he came to support the Holy Roman Emperor Henry VII and the concept of a united Italy.

Dante's greatest work is the *Divina commedia*, a magisterial depiction of the Christian cosmos peopled with figures from myth and history. He began it sometime between 1307 and 1314, and completed it shortly before his death. The *Commedia* consists of three parts: the *Inferno*, in which the poet Virgil guides Dante through a hell where sinners are assigned to one of a series of descending circles, according to the category of their sin; the *Purgatorio*, in which Dante ascends a mountain past groups of repentant sinners; and the *Paradiso*, in which Beatrice guides him to paradise. For this work, Dante abandoned the customary literary language of Latin for his native Tuscan, using as his poetic form terza rima, a complex triadic rhyme scheme.

In this selection from the *Inferno* (Canto V, 34–142), those who commit the sin of lust, among them Francesca and Paolo, are found in the second circle of Hell, blown and buffeted by an unceasing wind: "So does that blast bear on the guilty spirits: / now here, now there, now down, now up, it drives them. / There is no hope that ever comforts them—/ no hope for rest and none for lesser pain." Dido, Helen, Achilles, and Cleopatra are among the tormented shades the poet recognizes before Francesca and Paolo arrest his attention. He asks to meet and speak with them, and hears their heartrending story of illicit love, as told by Francesca. Now the wind batters them both; they are joined not by their love but by their agony, which is augmented for each by the presence of the other. Francesca tells Dante how it began, over a book recounting Lancelot's surrender to his passion for Guinevere. She concludes, "That day, we read no more." The poet, in his pity for them, falls into a swoon.

🦂

Francesca and Paolo

When they come up against the ruined slope,
then there are cries and wailing and lament,
and there they curse the force of the divine.

I learned that those who undergo this torment
are damned because they sinned within the flesh,
subjecting reason to the rule of lust.

And as, in the cold season, starlings' wings
bear them along in broad and crowded ranks,
so does that blast bear on the guilty spirits:

now here, now there, now down, now up, it drives them.
There is no hope that ever comforts them—
no hope for rest and none for lesser pain.

And just as cranes in flight will chant their lays,
arraying their long file across the air,
so did the shades I saw approaching, borne

by that assailing wind, lament and moan;
so that I asked him: "Master, who are those
who suffer punishment in this dark air?"

"The first of those about whose history
you want to know," my master then told me,
"once ruled as empress over many nations.

Her vice of lust became so customary
that she made license licit in her laws
to free her from the scandal she had caused.

She is Semíramis, of whom we read
that she was Ninus' wife and his successor:
she held the land the Sultan now commands.

That other spirit killed herself for love,
and she betrayed the ashes of Sychaeus;
the wanton Cleopatra follows next.

See Helen, for whose sake so many years
of evil had to pass; see great Achilles,
who finally met love—in his last battle.

See Paris, Tristan . . ."—and he pointed out
and named to me more than a thousand shades

113

departed from our life because of love.
    No sooner had I heard my teacher name
the ancient ladies and the knights, than pity
seized me, and I was like a man astray.
    My first words: "Poet, I should willingly
speak with those two who go together there
and seem so lightly carried by the wind."
    And he to me: "You'll see when they draw closer
to us, and then you may appeal to them
by that love which impels them. They will come."
    No sooner had the wind bent them toward us
than I urged on my voice: "O battered souls,
if One does not forbid it, speak with us."
    Even as doves when summoned by desire,
borne forward by their will, move through the air
with wings uplifted, still, to their sweet nest,
    those spirits left the ranks where Dido suffers,
approaching us through the malignant air;
so powerful had been my loving cry.
    "O living being, gracious and benign,
who through the darkened air have come to visit
our souls that stained the world with blood, if He
    who rules the universe were friend to us,
then we should pray to Him to give you peace,
for you have pitied our atrocious state.
    Whatever pleases you to hear and speak
will please us, too, to hear and speak with you,
now while the wind is silent, in this place.
    The land where I was born lies on that shore
to which the Po together with the waters
that follow it descends to final rest.
    Love, that can quickly seize the gentle heart,
took hold of him because of the fair body
taken from me—how that was done still wounds me.
    Love, that releases no beloved from loving,
took hold of me so strongly through his beauty
that, as you see, it has not left me yet.
    Love led the two of us unto one death.
Caïna waits for him who took our life."
These words were borne across from them to us.
    When I had listened to those injured souls,
I bent my head and held it low until

the poet asked of me: "What are you thinking?"
    When I replied, my words began: "Alas,
how many gentle thoughts, how deep a longing,
had led them to the agonizing pass!"
    Then I addressed my speech again to them,
and I began: "Francesca, your afflictions
move me to tears of sorrow and of pity.
    But tell me, in the time of gentle sighs,
with what and in what way did Love allow you
to recognize your still uncertain longings?"
    And she to me: "There is no greater sorrow
than thinking back upon a happy time
in misery—and this your teacher knows.
    Yet if you long so much to understand
the first root of our love, then I shall tell
my tale to you as one who weeps and speaks.
    One day, to pass the time away, we read
of Lancelot—how love had overcome him.
We were alone, and we suspected nothing.
    And time and time again that reading led
our eyes to meet, and made our faces pale,
and yet one point alone defeated us.
    When we had read how the desired smile
was kissed by one who was so true a lover,
this one, who never shall be parted from me,
    while all his body trembled, kissed my mouth.
A Gallehault indeed, that book and he
who wrote it, too; that day we read no more."
    And while one spirit said these words to me,
the other wept, so that—because of pity—
I fainted, as if I had met my death.
    And then I fell as a dead body falls.

ISAK DINESEN
(1885–1962)

ISAK DINESEN was born Karen Christence Dinesen in Denmark. In her childhood she wrote sketches, plays, and stories, and as a young woman, she studied painting, first in Copenhagen and later in Paris and Rome. In 1914 she married her cousin, Baron Bror Blixen, and accompanied him to British East Africa (now Kenya), where they ran a large coffee plantation her family had purchased for them. After their divorce in 1921, Dinesen managed the farm on her own. When coffee prices dropped in 1931, Dinesen had to give up the farm, and she returned to Denmark to live. Her first important work, *Seven Gothic Tales,* was published three years later, followed in 1937 by *Out of Africa. Winter's Tales* was published in 1942; *The Angelic Avengers,* a novel about the Nazi invaders of Denmark, was published in 1946 under the name Pierre Andrezel; and *Last Tales* appeared in 1957, followed in 1958 by *Anecdotes of Destiny* (from which "The Immortal Story" is taken) and *Shadows on the Grass* in 1961. *Ehrengard* was published in 1963, a year after her death.

For Dinesen, the story itself was a paramount force in life, and storytelling an essential transforming instrument in any culture.

"The Immortal Story," set in nineteenth-century Canton, spins stories within stories. Mr. Clay, a cynical and misanthropic tea trader of immense wealth, goes over his accounts with his young bookkeeper, Elishama, a Polish Jew whose family had died in the pogroms of 1848. When Clay asks Elishama if he's ever heard of another kind of book, Elishama produces fragments from the Book of Isaiah handed over to him during his escape from Poland. For his part, Mr. Clay tells a story—believing it to be fact—of an elderly man of wealth offering a sailor on shore leave a gold five-guinea piece to sleep with his young wife. This tale, Elishama informs him, is *not* fact, "but a story all sailors tell." Clay then decides he will use his power and wealth to make this piece of make-believe real, assembling the cast of characters and having the story enacted in his own home. When the sailor and the woman are brought together for the night, a love that abides only by its own rules is set in motion.

The Immortal Story

I. Mr Clay

In the 'sixties of last century there lived in Canton an immensely rich tea-trader, whose name was Mr Clay.

He was a tall, dry and close old man. He had a magnificent house and a splendid equipage, and he sat in the midst of both, erect, silent and alone.

Amongst the other Europeans of Canton Mr Clay had the name of an iron-hard man and a miser. People kept away from him. His looks, voice and manner, more than anything actually known against him, had gained him this reputation. All the same two or three stories about him, many times repeated, seemed to bear out the general opinion of the man. One of the stories ran as follows:

Fifteen years ago a French merchant, who at one time had been Mr Clay's partner but later, after a quarrel between them, had started on his own, was ruined by unlucky speculations. As a last chance he tried to get a consignment of tea on board the clipper *Thermopylae*, which lay in the harbour ready to go under weigh. But he owed Mr Clay the sum of three hundred guineas, and his creditor laid hands on the tea, got his own shipment of tea off with the *Thermopylae*, and by this move finally ruined his rival. The Frenchman lost all, his house was sold, and he was thrown upon the streets with his family. When he saw no way out of his misfortune he committed suicide.

The French merchant had been a talented, genial man, he had had a lovely wife and a big family. Now that, in the eyes of his friends, he was contrasted with the stony figure of Mr Clay, he began to shine with a halo of gay and gentle rays, and they started a collection of money for his widow. But owing to the rivalry between the French and English communities of Canton it did not come to much, and after a short time the French lady and her children disappeared from the horizon of their acquaintances.

Mr Clay took over the dead man's house, a big beautiful villa with a large garden in which peacocks strutted on the lawns. He was living in it today.

In the course of time this story had taken the character of a myth. Monsieur Dupont, it was told, on the last day of his life had called together his pretty, gentle wife and his bright young children. Since all their misery, he declared, had risen from the moment when he first set eyes on the face of Mr Clay, he now bound them by a solemn vow never, in any place or under any circumstances, to look into that face again. It was also told that when he had been about to leave his house, of which he was very proud, he had burnt or smashed up every object of art in it, asserting that no thing made for the embellishment of life would ever consent to live with the new master of the house. But he had left in all the rooms the tall gilt-framed looking-glasses brought out from France, which till now had reflected only gay and affectionate scenes, with the words that it

117

should be his murderer's punishment to meet, wherever he went, a portrait of the hangman.

Mr Clay settled in the house, and sat down to dine in solitude, face to face with his portrait. It is doubtful whether he was ever aware of the lack of friendliness in his surroundings, for the idea of friendliness had never entered into his scheme of life. If things had been left entirely to himself, he would have arranged them in the same way, it was only natural that he should believe them to be as they were because he had willed them to be so. Slowly, in his career as a Nabob, Mr Clay had come to have faith in his own omnipotence. Other great merchants of Canton held the same faith in regard to themselves and, like Mr Clay, kept it up by ignoring that part of the world which lay outside the sphere of their power.

When Mr Clay was seventy years old he fell ill with the gout, and for a long time was almost paralysed. The pain was so severe that he could not sleep at nights, and his nights then seemed infinitely long.

Late one night it happened that one of Mr Clay's young clerks came to his house with a pile of accounts that he had been revising. The old man in his bed heard him talk to the servants, he sent for him and made him go through the account-books with him. When the morning came he found that this night had passed less slowly than the others. So the next evening he again sent for the young clerk, and again made him read out his books to him.

From this time it became an established rule that the young man should make his appearance in the huge, grandly furnished bedroom by nine o'clock, to sit by his employer's bedside and read out, by the light of a candle, the bills, contracts and estimates of Mr Clay's business. He had a sonorous voice, but towards morning it would grow a little hoarse. This vexed Mr Clay, who in his young days had had sharp ears, but was now getting hard of hearing. He told his clerk that he was paying him to do this work and that, if he could not do it well, he would dismiss him and take on another reader.

When the two had come to the end of the books now in use at the office, the old man sighed and turned his head on the pillow. The clerk thought the matter over, he went to the lockers and took out books five, ten and fifteen years old, and these he read out, word for word, during the hours of the night. Mr Clay listened attentively, the reading brought back to him schemes and triumphs of the past. But the nights were long, in the course of time the reader ran short even of such old books and had to read the same things over again.

One morning when the young man had for the third time gone through a deal of twenty years ago, and was about to go home to bed himself, Mr Clay held him back, and seemed to have something on his mind. The workings of his master's mind were always of great moment to the clerk, he stayed on a little to give the old man time to find words for what he wanted.

After a while Mr Clay asked him, reluctantly and as if himself uneasy and doubtful, whether he had not heard of other kinds of books. The clerk answered no, he had no knowledge of other kinds of books, but he would find them if Mr

Clay would explain to him what he meant. Mr Clay in the same hesitating manner told him that he had in mind books and accounts, not of deals or bargains, but of other things which people at times had put down, and which other people did at times read. The clerk reflected upon the matter and repeated, no, he had never heard of such books. Here the talk ended, and the clerk took his leave. On his way home the young man turned Mr Clay's question over in his mind. He felt that it had been uttered out of some deep need, half against the speaker's own will, with bashfulness and even with shame. If the clerk had himself had any sense of shame in his nature he might have left his old employer at that, and have wiped his one slip from dignity off his memory. But since he had nothing of this quality in him he began to ponder the matter. The demand, surely, was a symptom of weakness in the old man, it might even be a foreboding of death. What would be, he reflected, the consequence to him himself of such a state of things?

II. Elishama

The young clerk who had been reading to Mr Clay was known to the other accountants of the office as Ellis Lewis, but this was not his real name. He was named Elishama Levinsky. He had given himself a new name, not—like some other people in those days emigrating to China—in order to cover up any trespass or crime of his own, he had done it to obliterate crimes committed against himself, and a past of hard trials.

He was a Jew and had been born in Poland. His people had all been killed in the big Pogrom of 1848, at a time when he himself had been, he believed, six years old. Other Polish Jews, who had happened to escape, had happened to carry him with them among other sad and ragged bundles. Since that time, like some little parcel of goods in small demand, he had been carried and dropped, set against a wall and forgotten, and after a while once more flung about.

A lost and lonely child, wholly in the hands of chance, he had gone through strange sufferings in Frankfurt, Amsterdam, London and Lisbon. Things not to be recounted and hardly to be recalled still moved, like big deep-water fish, in the depths of his dark mind. In London chance had put him in the hands of an ingenious old Italian book-keeper, who had taught him to read and write, and who had, before he died, in one year implanted in him as much knowledge of book-keeping by double entry as other people will acquire in ten years. Later the boy was lifted up and shifted eastward, where in the end he was set down in Mr Clay's office in Canton. Here he sat by his desk like a tool grinded upon the grindstone of life to an exceedingly sharp edge, with eyes and ears like a lynx, and without any illusions whatever of the world or of humanity.

With this equipment Elishama might have made a career for himself, and might have been a highly dangerous person to meet and deal with. But it was not so, and the reason for the apparently illogical state of things was the total lack of ambition in the boy's own soul. Desire, in any form, had been washed, bleached and burnt out of him before he had learnt to read. To look at he was a fairly ordinary young man, small, slim and very dark, with veiled brown eyes, and might have passed as a citizen of any nation. Mentally he had nothing of a youth, but all of a precocious child or a very old man. He had no softness or fullness in him, no yearning for love or adventure, no sense of competition, no fear and no wish to fight. Outwardly and inwardly he was like some kind of insect, an ant hard to crush even to the heel of a boot.

One passion he had, if passion it may be called—a fanatical craving for security and for being left alone. In its nature this feeling was akin to homesickness or to the instinct of the homing pigeon. His soul was concentrated upon this one request: that he might enter his closet and shut his door, with the certainty that here no one could possibly follow or disturb him.

The closet which he entered, and to which he shut the door, was a modest place, a small dark room in a narrow street. Here he slept on an old sofa rented from his landlady. But in the room there were a few objects which did really belong to him—a painted, ink-stained table, two chairs and a chest. These objects to their owner were of great significance. Sometimes in the night he would light a small candle to lie and gaze at them, as if they proved to him that the world was still fairly safe. He would also, at night, draw comfort from the idea of the numeral series. He went over its figures—10, 20, 7,000. They were all there, and he went to sleep.

Elishama, who despised the goods of this world, passed his time from morning till night amongst greedy and covetous people, and had done so all his life. This to him was as it should be. He understood to a nicety the feelings of his surroundings and he approved of them. For out of those feelings came, in the end, his closet with the door to it. If the world's desperate struggle for gold and power were ever to cease, it was not certain that this room or this door would remain. So he used his talents to fan and stir up the fire of ambition and greed in people round him. He particularly fanned the fire of Mr Clay's ambition and greed, and watched it with an attentive eye.

Even before the time of their nocturnal readings there had existed between Mr Clay and Elishama a kind of relation, a rare thing to both of them. It had first begun when Elishama had drawn Mr Clay's attention to the fact that he was being cheated by the people who bought his horses for him. Some unknown ancestor of Elishama's had been a horse-dealer to Polish Princes and Magnates, and the young book-keeper in Canton had all this old Jew's knowledge of horses in his blood. He would not for anything in the world have been the owner of a horse himself, but he encouraged Mr Clay's vanity about his carriage and pair, from which, in the end, his own security might benefit. Mr Clay on his side had been struck by the young man's insight and judgement, he had left the superintendence of his stable to him and never been disappointed. They had had no other direct dealings, but Mr Clay had become aware of Elishama's existence, as Elishama had for a long time been aware of Mr Clay's.

The relationship showed itself in a particular way. It might have been observed that neither of the two ever spoke about the other to anybody else. In both the old and the young man this was a breach of habit. For Mr Clay constantly fretted over his young staff to his overseers, and Elishama had such a sharp tongue that his remarks about the great and small merchants of Canton had become proverbial in the storehouses and the offices. In this way the master and the servant seemed to be standing back to back, facing the rest of the world, and did indeed, unknowingly, behave exactly as they would have behaved had they been father and son.

In his own room Elishama now thought of Mr Clay, and put him down as a greater fool than he had held him to be. But after a time he rose to make a cup of tea—a luxury which he permitted himself when he came back from his nightly readings—and while he drank it, his mind began to move in a different way. He took up Mr Clay's question for serious consideration. It was possible, he reflected, that such books as Mr Clay had asked about did really exist. He was accustomed to getting Mr Clay the things he wanted. If these books existed, he must look out for them, and even if they were rare he would find them in the end.

Elishama sat for a long time with his chin in his hand, then stood up and went to the chest in the corner of the room. Out of it he took a smaller, red-painted box which, when he first came to Canton, had contained all that he owned in the world. He looked it through carefully and came upon an old yellow piece of paper folded up and preserved in a small silk bag. He read it by the candle on the table.

III. The Prophecy of Isaiah

In the party of Jews who in their flight from Poland had taken Elishama with them, there had been a very old man who had died on the way. Before he died he gave the child the piece of paper in the red bag. Elishama tied it round his neck and managed to keep it there for many years, mainly because during this time he rarely undressed. He could not read, and did not know what was written on it.

But when in London he learned to read and was told that people set a value on written matter, he took his paper out and found it to be written in letters different to those he had been taught. His master from time to time sent him on an errand to a dark and dirty little pawnshop, the owner of which was an unfrocked clergyman. Elishama took the paper to this man and asked him if it meant anything. When he was informed that it was written in Hebrew he suggested that the pawnbroker should translate it to him for a fee of three pence. The old man read the paper through and recognised its contents, he looked them up in their own place, copied them out in English and gravely accepted the three pence. The boy from now kept both the original and the translation in his small red bag.

In order to help Mr Clay, Elishama now took the bag from his box. Under other circumstances he would not have done so, for it brought with it notions of darkness and horror and the dim picture of a friend. Elishama did not want friends any more than Mr Clay did. They were, to him, people who suffered and per-ished—the word itself meant separation and loss, tears and blood dripped from it.

Thus it came about that a few nights later, when Elishama had finished read-ing the accounts to Mr Clay, and the old man growled and prepared to send him off, the clerk took from his pocket a small dirty sheet of paper and said: 'Here, Mr Clay, is something that I shall read to you.' Mr Clay turned his pale eyes to the reader's face. Elishama read out:

'The wilderness and the solitary places shall be glad for them. And the desert shall rejoice and blossom as the rose. It shall blossom abundantly. And sing even with joy and singing. The glory of Lebanon shall be given to it . . .'

'What is that?' Mr Clay asked angrily.

Elishama laid down his paper. 'That, Mr Clay,' he said, 'is what you have asked for. Something besides the account-books, which people have put together and written down.' He continued:

'The excellency of Carmel and Sharon. They shall see the glory of the Lord. And the excellency of our God. Strengthen ye the weak hands. And confirm the feeble knees. Say to them . . .'

'What is it? Where have you got it?' Mr Clay again asked.

Elishama held up his hand to impose silence, and read:

'Say to them that are of a fearful heart: be strong, fear not. Behold, your God will come with a vengeance. Even God with a recompense. He will come and save you. Then the eyes of the blind shall be opened and the ears of the deaf shall be un-stopped. Then shall the lame man leap as a hart, and the tongue of the dumb sing. For in the wilderness shall waters break out. And streams in the desert. And the parched ground shall become a pool, and the thirsty land springs of water, and the habitation of dragons, where each lay, shall be grass with reeds and rushes.'

When Elishama had got so far, he laid down his paper and looked straight in front of him.

Mr Clay drew in his breath asthmatically. 'What was all that?' he asked.

'I have told you, Mr Clay,' said Elishama. 'You have heard it. This is a thing which a man has put together and written down.'

'Has it happened?' asked Mr Clay.

'No,' answered Elishama with deep scorn.

'Is it happening now?' said Mr Clay.

'No,' said Elishama in the same way.

After a moment Mr Clay asked: 'Who on earth has put it together?'

Elishama looked at Mr Clay and said: 'The Prophet Isaiah.'

'Who was that?' Mr Clay asked sharply. 'The Prophet—pooh! What is a Prophet?'

Elishama said: 'A man who foretells things.'

'Then all these things should come to happen!' Mr Clay remarked disdainfully.

Elishama did not want to disavow the Prophet Isaiah, he said: 'Yes. But not now.'

After a while Mr Clay ordered: 'Read again that of the lame man.'

Elishama read: 'Then the lame man shall leap as a hart.'

Again after a moment Mr Clay ordered: 'And that of the feeble knees.'

'And confirm the feeble knees,' Elishama read.

'And of the deaf,' said Mr Clay.

'And the ears of the deaf,' said Elishama, 'shall be unstopped.'

There was a long pause. 'Is anybody doing anything to make these things happen?' asked Mr Clay.

'No,' said Elishama with even deeper contempt than before.

When after another pause Mr Clay took up the matter, Elishama by the tone of his voice realised that he was now wide awake.

'Read the whole thing over again,' he commanded.

Elishama did as he was told. When he had finished, Mr Clay asked: 'When did the prophet Isaiah live?'

'I do not know, Mr Clay,' said Elishama. 'I think that it will have been about a thousand years ago.'

Mr Clay's knees were at this moment hurting badly, and he was painfully aware of his lameness and infirmity.

'It is a foolish thing,' he declared, 'to foretell things which do not begin to take place within a thousand years. People,' he added slowly, 'should record things which have already happened.'

'Do you want me,' Elishama asked, 'to take out the books of accounts once more?'

There was a very long pause.

'No,' Mr Clay said. 'No. People can record things which have already happened, outside of account-books. I know what such a record is called. A story. I once heard a story myself. Do not disturb me, and I shall remember it.'

'When I was twenty years old,' he said after a long silence, 'I sailed from England to China. And I heard this story on the night before we touched the Cape of Good Hope. Now I remember it all well. It was a warm night, the sea was calm, and there was a full moon. I had been sitting for some time by myself on the afterbody, when three sailors came up and sat down on the deck. They were so close to me that I could hear all that they said, but they did not see me. One of the sailors told the others a story. He recorded to them things which had happened to him himself. I heard the story from the beginning to the end, I shall tell it to you.'

IV. The Story

'The sailor,' Mr Clay began, 'had once come ashore in a big town. I do not remember which, but it does not matter. He was walking by himself in a street near the harbour, when a fine costly carriage drove up to him, and an old gentleman descended from it. This gentleman said to the sailor: "You are a fine-looking sailor. Do you want to earn five guineas tonight?" '

Mr Clay was so completely unaccustomed to telling a story, that it is doubtful whether he could have gone on with this one except in the dark. He continued with an effort and repeated: 'Do you want to earn five guineas tonight?'

Elishama, here, put the prophecy of Isaiah back into its bag and into his pocket.

'The sailor,' Mr Clay related, 'naturally answered yes. The rich gentleman then told him to come with him, and drove him in his carriage to a big and splendid house just outside the town. Within the house everything was equally grand and sumptuous. The sailor had never believed that such riches existed in the world, for how would a poor boy like him ever have come inside a really great man's house? The gentleman gave him a fine meal and expensive wine, and the sailor recounted all that he had had to eat and drink, but I have forgotten the names of the courses and the wines. When they had finished this meal, the master of the house said to the sailor: 'I am, as you see, a very rich man, the richest man in this town. But I am old. I have not got many years left, and I dislike and distrust the people who will inherit what I have collected and saved up in life. Three years ago I married a young wife. But she has been no good to me, for I have got no child.'

Here Mr Clay made a pause to collect his thoughts.

'With your permission,' said Elishama, 'I, too, can tell that story.'

'What is that?' exclaimed Mr Clay, very angry at the interruption.

'I shall tell you the rest of that story, with your permission, if you will listen, Mr Clay,' said Elishama.

Mr Clay did not find a word to say, and Elishama went on.

'The old gentleman,' he recounted, 'led the sailor to a bedroom which was lighted by candlesticks of pure gold, five on the right side and five on the left. Was it not so, Mr Clay? On the walls were carved pictures of palm trees. In the room there was a bed, and a partition was made by chains of gold before the bed, and in the bed lay a lady. The old man said to this lady: "You know my wish. Now do your best to have it carried out." Then from his purse he took a piece of gold—a five-guinea piece, Mr Clay—and handed it to the sailor, and after that he left the room. The sailor stayed with the lady all night. But when the day began to spring, the door of the house was opened to him by the old man's servant, and he left the house and went back to his ship. Was it not so, Mr Clay?'

Mr Clay for a minute stared at Elishama, then asked: 'How do you come to know this story? Have you too met the sailor from my ship near the Cape of Good

Hope? He will be an old man by now, and these things happened to him many years ago.'

'That story, Mr Clay,' said Elishama, 'which you believe to have happened to the sailor on your ship, has never happened to anyone. All sailors know it. All sailors tell it, and each of them, because he wishes that it had happened to him himself, tells it as if it were so. But it is not so. All sailors, when they listen to the story, like to have it told in that way, and expect to have it told in that way. The sailor who tells it may vary it a little, and add a few things of his own, as when he explains how the lady was made, and how in the night he made love to her. But otherwise the story is always the same.'

The old man in the bed at first did not say a word, then in a voice hoarse with anger and disappointment he asked: 'How do you know?'

'I shall tell you, Mr Clay,' said Elishama. 'You have travelled on one ship only, out here to China, so you have heard this story only once. But I have sailed with many ships. First I sailed from Gravesend to Lisbon, and on the ship a sailor told the story which tonight you have told me. I was very young then, so I almost believed it, but not quite. Then I sailed from Lisbon to the Cape of Good Hope, and on the ship there was a sailor who told it. Then I sailed to Singapore, and on my way I heard a sailor tell the story. It is the story of all sailors in the world. Even the phrases and the words are the same. But all sailors are pleased when, once more, one of them begins to tell it.'

'Why should they tell it,' said Mr Clay, 'if it were not true?'

Elishama thought the question over. 'I shall explain that to you,' he said, 'if you will listen. All people, Mr Clay, in one respect are the same.

'When a new financial scheme is offered for subscription, it is proved on paper that the shareholders will make on it a hundred per cent, or two hundred per cent, as the case may be. Such a profit is never made, and everybody knows that it is never made, still people must see these figures on paper in the issue of stocks, or they will have nothing to do with the scheme.

'It is the same, Mr Clay with the prophecy which I have read it to you. The Prophet Isaiah, who told it, will, I believe, have been living in a country where it rained too little. Therefore he tells you that the parched ground becomes a pool. In England, where the ground is almost always a pool, people do not care to write it down or to read about it.

'The sailors who tell this story, Mr Clay, are poor men and lead a lonely life on the sea. That is why they tell about that rich house and that beautiful lady. But the story which they tell has never happened.'

Mr Clay said: 'The sailor told the others that he held a five-guinea piece on his hand, and that he felt the weight and the cold of gold upon it.'

'Yes, Mr Clay,' said Elishama, 'and do you know why he told them so? It was because he knew, and because the other sailors knew, that such a thing could never happen. If they had believed that it could ever happen, they would not have told it. A sailor goes ashore from his ship, and pays a woman in the street to let him come with her. Sometimes he pays her ten shillings, sometimes five, and sometimes only two, and none of these women is young, or beautiful, or rich. It might possibly happen—although I myself doubt it—that a woman would let a sailor come with her for nothing, but if she did so, Mr Clay, the sailor would never tell. Here a sailor will tell you that a young, beautiful and rich lady—such a lady as he may have seen at a distance, but has never spoken to—has been paying him, for the same thing, five guineas. In the story, Mr Clay, it is always five guineas. That is contrary to the law of demand and supply, Mr Clay, and it never has happened, and it never will happen, and that is why it is told.'

Mr Clay at this moment was so upset, puzzled and angry that he could not speak. He was angry with Elishama, because he felt that his clerk was taking advantage of his weakness, and was defying his authority. But he was upset and puzzled by the prophet Isaiah, who was about to annihilate his whole world, and him himself with it. The two of them, he felt, were holding together against him. After a while he spoke.

His voice was harsh and grating, but as firm as when he was giving an order in his office.

'If this story,' he said, 'has never happened before, I shall make it happen now. I do not like pretence, I do not like prophecies. It is insane and immoral to occupy oneself with unreal things. I like facts. I shall turn this piece of make-believe into solid fact.'

The old man when he had spoken was a little easier at heart. He felt that he was getting the better of Elishama and the Prophet Isaiah. He was still going to prove to them his omnipotence.

'The story shall become reality,' he said slowly. 'One sailor in the world shall tell it, from beginning to end with everything that is in it, as it has actually, from beginning to end, happened to him.'

When Elishama walked home in the morning he said to himself: 'Either this old man is going mad, and nearing his end. Or otherwise he will tomorrow be ashamed of his project of tonight, he will want to forget it, and it will be the safest thing not to mention it to him again.'

V. The Mission of Elishama

Mr Clay, however, was not ashamed. His project of the night had seized hold of him, the matter had become a trial of strength between him and the insurgents. Next midnight, as the clock struck, he took up the theme and said to Elishama: 'Do you think that I can no longer do what I want to do?'

This time Elishama did not contradict Mr Clay with a word, he answered: 'No, Mr Clay. I think you can do whatever you want.'

Mr Clay said: 'I want the story which I told you last night to happen in real life, to real people.'

'I shall see to it, Mr Clay,' said Elishama. 'Where do you want it to happen?'

'I want it to happen here,' said Mr Clay, and proudly looked round his big, richly furnished bedroom. 'In my house. I want to be present myself, and to see it all with my own eyes. I want to pick up the sailor myself, in the street by the harbour. I want to dine with him myself, in my dining room.'

'Yes, Mr Clay,' said Elishama. 'And when do you want the story to happen, to real people?'

'It ought to be done quickly,' said Mr Clay after a pause. 'It will have to be done quickly. But I am feeling better tonight, in a week's time I shall be strong enough.'

'Then,' Elishama said, 'I shall have everything ready within a week.'

After a while Mr Clay said: 'It will involve expenses. I do not mind what the expenses may come to.'

These words gave Elishama such an impression of cold and loneliness in the old man, that it was as if they had been spoken from the grave. But since he himself did feel at home in the grave, he and his employer were at this moment brought closer together.

'Yes,' he said, 'it is going to cost us some money. For you will remember that there is a young woman in the story.'

'Yes, a woman,' said Mr Clay. 'The world is full of women. A young woman one can always buy, and that will be the cheapest thing in the story.'

'No, Mr Clay,' said Elishama, 'it will not be the cheapest thing in this story. For if I bring you a woman of the town, the sailor will know her for what she is. And he will lose his faith in the story.'

Mr Clay growled a little.

'And a young Miss I shall not be able to get you,' said Elishama.

'I am paying you to do this work,' said Mr Clay. 'It will be part of your work to find me a woman.'

'I shall have to think it over,' said Elishama.

But he had already, while they talked together, been thinking it over.

Elishama, as has been told, was well versed in book-keeping by double entry. He saw Mr Clay with the eyes of the world, and to the eyes of the world—had the world known of his scheme—the old man was undoubtedly mad. At the same time he saw Mr Clay with his own eyes, and to his own eyes his employer, with his colleagues in the tea-trade and in other trades, had always been mad. And indeed he was not sure whether, to a man with one foot in the grave, the pursuit of a story was not a sounder undertaking than the pursuit of profit. Elishama at any time would side with the individual against the world, since, however mad the individual might be, the world in general was sure to be still more hopelessly and wickedly idiotic. As, once more, he walked away from Mr Clay's house, he realised that from this moment he was indispensible to his master, and could get out of him whatever he wanted. He did not intend to derive any advantage from the circumstance, but the idea pleased him.

In Mr Clay's office there was a young accountant whose name was Charley Simpson. He was an ambitious young man and had resolved to become, in his own time, a millionaire and Nabob like Mr Clay himself. The big ruddy young gentleman considered himself to be Elishama's only friend, treated him with pa-tronising joviality, and had lately honoured him with his confidence.

Charley kept a mistress in town, her name was Virginie. She was, he told his protégé, a Frenchwoman of very good family, but she had been ruined by her amorous temperament and now lived only for passion. Virginie wanted a French shawl. Her lover meant to make her a present of one, but he was afraid to go into a shop to buy it, as somebody might spot him there and report to his father in England. If Elishama would take a collection of shawls to Virginie's house, Char-ley would show his gratitude by introducing him to the lady herself.

The lovers had had a row immediately before Elishama's arrival with the shawls. But the sight of these somewhat appeased Virginie. She draped one shawl after another round her fine figure before the looking-glass, as if the men had not been in the room, and even lifted her skirts neatly over her knee and made a couple of *pas-de-basque's*. Over her shoulder she told her lover that he must now, surely, be able to see for himself that her real calling was the theatre. If she could only raise the money, the wisest thing she could do was to go back to France. There the comedy, the drama and the tragedy still existed, and the great actresses were the idols of a nation!

Elishama was not familiar with the words comedy, drama or tragedy. But an instinct now told him that there was a connection between these phenomena and Mr Clay's story. The day after his last conversation with Mr Clay he turned his steps towards Virginie's house.

Elishama within his nature had a trait which few people would have expected to find there. He felt a deep innate sympathy or compassion towards all women of this world, and particularly towards all young women.

Although, as has already been told, he did not himself want a horse, he could fix to a penny the price of any horse shown him. And although he did not himself in the least want a woman he could view a woman with the eyes of other young men, and accurately determine her value. Only in the latter case he considered the eyes of other young men to be shortsighted or blind, the price to be erroneous, and the article itself in some sad way underestimated and wronged.

Mysteriously, he felt the same sympathy and compassion towards birds. The quadrupeds all left him indifferent, and horses—in spite of his knowledge and understanding of them—he disliked. But he would take a roundabout way to his office in order to pass the Chinese bird-sellers' shops, and to stand for a long time in front of their piled-up birdcages, and he knew the individual birds within them and followed their fate with concern.

Walking along to Virginie's house he might well feel a twofold sympathy. For she was a young woman who reminded him of a bird. As in his thoughts he compared her to the other young women of Canton she there took on the aspect of a golden pheasant or a peacock within a poultry yard. She was bigger than her sisters, nobler and more pompous of gait and feather, strutting somewhat lonely amongst the smaller domestic fowl. At their one meeting she had been a little downcast and fretful, like a golden pheasant in the moulting season. But she was always a golden pheasant.

VI. The Heroine of the Story

Virginie lived in a small neat Chinese house with a little garden to it and green shutters to the windows. The old Chinese woman, who owned the house, kept it in order and cooked for her tenant, was out today. Elishama found the door open and went straight in.

Virginie was playing a patience on her table by the window. She looked up and said: 'God, is it you? What are you bringing? Shawls?'

'No, Miss Virginie, I am bringing nothing today,' said he.

'What is the use of you then?' she asked. 'Sit down and keep me company, in God's name, now that you are here.'

Upon this invitation he sat down.

Virginie, in spite of her venturesome past, was still young and fresh, with a flowerlike quality in her, as if there had been a large rose in water in the room. She was dressed in a white muslin negligée with flounces and a train to it, but had not yet done up her rich brown hair, which floated down to the pink sash round her waist. The golden afternoon sun fell between the shutters into her lap.

She went on with her patience, but spoke the while. 'Are you still with the old devil?' she asked.

Elishama said: 'He is ill and cannot go out.'

'Good,' said Virginie, 'is he going to die?'

'No, Miss Virginie,' said Elishama. 'He is even strong enough to make up new schemes. With your permission, I am now going to tell you one of them. I shall begin at the beginning.'

'Well, so long as he is too ill to go out, I can stand hearing about him,' said Virginie.

'Mr Clay,' said Elishama, 'has heard a story told. Fifty years ago—on a ship, one night off the Cape—he heard a story told. Now that he is ill and cannot sleep at night, he has been pondering this story. He dislikes pretence, he dislikes prophecies, he likes facts. He has made up his mind to have the story happen in real life, to real people. I have been in his service for seven years—who would he get to carry out his wish if not me? He is the richest man in Canton, Miss Virginie, he must have what he wants. Now I shall tell you the story.

'There was a sailor,' he began, 'who went ashore from his ship in the harbour of a big town. As he was walking by himself in a street near the harbour, a carriage with two fine, well-paired bay horses drove up to him, and an old gentleman stepped out of the carriage and said to him: "You are a fine-looking sailor. Do you want to earn five guineas tonight?" When the sailor said yes, the old gentleman drove him to his house and gave him food and wine. He then, Miss Virginie, said to him: "I am a merchant of immense wealth, as you will have seen for yourself, but I am all alone in the world. The people who, when I die, are to inherit my fortune are all silly people, continually disturbing and distressing me. I have taken to myself a young wife, but . . ." '

Here Virginie cut short Elishama's tale. 'I know that story,' she said. 'It happened in Singapore to an English merchant-captain, a friend of mine. Has he been telling it to you as well?'

'No, Miss Virginie,' said Elishama. 'He has not told it to me, but other sailors have told it. This is a story that lives on the ships, all sailors have heard it, and all sailors have told it. It might have been left on sea and never come ashore, if it had not been that Mr Clay cannot sleep. He is now going to make it happen here in Canton, in order that one sailor in the world may be able to tell it from beginning to end, exactly as, from beginning to end, it has happened to him.'

'He was sure to go mad in the end, with his sins,' said Virginie. 'If now he wants to play a comedy with the Devil, it is a matter between the two of them.'

'Yes, a comedy,' said Elishama. 'I had forgotten the word. People play in comedies and make money by it, they become the idols of nations. Now there are three people in Mr Clay's comedy. The old gentleman he will play himself, and the young sailor he will himself find in the street by the harbour, where sailors come ashore from their ships. But if an English merchant-captain has told you this story, Miss Virginie, he will have told you that beside these two there is also a beautiful young lady in it. On Mr Clay's behalf I am now looking for this beautiful young lady. If she will come into this story, and finish it for him, Mr Clay will pay her one hundred guineas.'

Virginie, in her chair, turned her rich young torso all round towards Elishama, folded her arms upon her bosom and laughed to his face. 'What is all this?' she inquired.

'It is a comedy, Miss Virginie,' said he. 'A dream or a tragedy. It is a story.'

'The old man has got strange ideas of a comedy,' said Virginie. 'In a comedy the actors pretend to do things, to kill one another or to die, or to go to bed with their lovers. But they do not really do any of these things. Indeed your master is like the Emperor Nero of Rome, who, to amuse himself, had people eaten up by lions. But since then it has not been done, and that is a long time ago.'

'Was the Emperor Nero very rich?' asked Elishama.

'Oh, he owned all the world,' said Virginie.

'And were his comedies good?' he again asked.

'He liked them himself, I suppose,' said Virginie. 'But who would he nowadays get to play in them?'

'If he owned all the world, he would get people to play in them,' said he.

Virginie looked hard at Elishama, her dark eyes shining. 'I suppose that nobody could insult *you*, even if they tried hard?'

Elishama thought her remark over. 'No,' he said, 'they could not. Why should I let them?'

'And if I told you,' she said, 'to go out of my house, you would just go?'

'Yes, I should go,' he said. 'It is your house. But when I had gone you would sit and think of the things for which you had turned me out. It is when people are told their own thoughts that they think they are being insulted. But why should not their own thoughts be good enough for other people to tell them?'

Virginie kept looking at him. Early that same day she had been so furious with her destiny that she had been planning to throw herself into the harbour. The patience had calmed her a little. Now she suddenly felt that she and Elishama were alone in the house and that he had not got it in him to repeat their conversation to anybody. Under the circumstances she might go on with it.

'What does Mr Clay pay you for coming here and proposing this thing to me?' she asked. '*Trente pièces d'argent, n'est-ce pas? C'est le prix!*' When Virginie's mind moved in high spheres she thought, and expressed herself, in French.

Elishama, who spoke French well, did not recognise her quotation, but imagined that she was mocking him for being poorly paid in Mr Clay's service. 'No,' he said. 'I am not being paid for this. I am in Mr Clay's employ, I cannot take on work anywhere but with him. But you, Miss Virginie, you can go wherever you like.'

'Yes, I presume so,' said Virginie.

'Yes, you presume so,' said Elishama, 'and you have been able to go wherever you liked all your life. And you have gone here, Miss Virginie, to this house.'

Virginie blushed deeply with anger, but at the same time she once more felt, and more deeply than before, that the two were alone in the house, with the rest of the world shut out.

VII. Virginie

Virginie's father had been a merchant in Canton. His motto in life, engraved in his signet ring, had been '*Pourquoi pas?*' All through his twenty years in China his heart had still been in France, and the great things going on there had filled and moved it.

At the time of his death Virginie had been twelve years old. She was his eldest child and his favourite. As a little girl she was as lovely as an angel, the proud father amused himself taking her round and showing her off to his friends, and in a few years she had seen and learned much. She had a talent for mimicry, at home she gave pretty little performances imitating the scenes she had witnessed, and repeating the remarks and the gay songs she had listened to. Her mother, who came from an old seafaring family of Brittany and was well aware that a wife ought to bear with her man's exuberant spirit, would still at times gently reprove her husband for spoiling his pretty daughter. She would get but a kiss in return, and the laughing comment: '*Ah, Virginie est fine! Elle s'y comprend, en ironie!*'

In his young days the handsome and winning gentleman had travelled much. In Spain he had done business with, and been on friendly terms with a very great lady, the Countess de Montijo. When later, out in China, he learned that this lady's daughter had married the Emperor Napoleon III and become Empress of the French, he was as proud and pleased as if he himself had arranged the match. With him Virginie had for many years lived in the grand world of the French Court, in the vast radiant ballrooms of the Tuileries, among receptions of foreign Majesties, Court cabals, romantic love-affairs, duels and the waltzes of Strauss.

After her father's death, during long years of poverty and hardship, and while she herself lost the angelic grace of her childhood and grew up too big, Virginie had secretly turned to this glorious world for consolation. She still walked up marble stairs lighted by a thousand candles, herself all sparkling with diamonds, to dance with Princes and Dukes—and her companions of a lonely, monotonous existence in dreary rooms wondered at the girl's pluck. In the end, however, the Tuileries themselves had faded and vanished round her.

Even when the father had endeavoured to engraft moral principles in the daughter's young mind he had illustrated them with little anecdotes from the Imperial Court. One of them had impressed itself deeply in the little girl's heart. The lovely Mademoiselle de Montijo had informed the Emperor Napoleon that the only way to her bedroom ran through the Cathedral of Notre Dame. Virginie was familiar with the Cathedral of Notre Dame, a big engraving of it hung in her parents' drawing-room. She had pictured to herself a bedroom of corresponding dimensions, and in the middle of it the lovely Mademoiselle Virginie, all in lace. The vision many times had warmed and cheered her heart.

Alas, the way to her bedroom had not run through the Cathedral of Notre Dame! It had not even run through the little grey French Church of Canton. Lately it had run, without much of a detour, from the offices and counting-houses of the town. For this reason Virginie despised the men that had come by it.

One triumph she had had in her career of disappointments, but nobody but herself knew of it.

Her first lover had been an English merchant-captain, who had made her run away with him to Japan, just then opened to foreign trade. On the couple's very first night in Japan there was an earthquake. All round their little hotel houses cracked and tumbled down and more than a hundred people were killed. Virginie that night had experienced something beside terror—she had lived through the great moment of her life. The thundering roar from heaven was directed against her personally, the earth shook and trembled at the loss of her innocence, the mighty breakers of the sea bewailed Virginie's fall! Frivolous human beings only— her lover with them—within this hour ignored the law of cause and effect and failed to realise the extent of her ruin.

Virginie had a good deal of kindness in her nature. In her present sad situation, after she had definitely come down from the Tuileries, she would have liked her lovers better had they left her free to love them in her own way, as poor pitiful people in need of sympathy. She might have put up with her present lover, Elishama's friend, if she could have made him see their liaison such as she herself saw it—as two lonely people's attempt to make, in an unpretentious bourgeois way and by means of a little mutual gentleness, the best of a sorry world. But

Charley was an ambitious young man who liked to see himself as a man of fashion and his mistress as a great Demimondaine. His mistress, who knew the real meaning of the word, in their daily life together was tried hard by this vanity of his, and it lay at the root of most of their quarrels.

Now she sat and listened to Elishama, with her arms folded, and her lustrous eyes half closed, like a cat watching a mouse. If at this moment he had wanted to run away she would not have let him go.

'Mr Clay,' said the young man, 'is prepared to pay you a hundred guineas if, on a night appointed by him, you will come to his house. This, Miss Virginie . . .'

'To his house!' cried Virginie and looked up quite bewildered.

'Yes,' said he. 'To his house. And this, Miss Virginie . . .'

Virginie rose from her chair so violently that it tumbled over, and struck Elishama in the face with all her might.

'Jesus!' she cried. 'His house! Do you know what house that is? It is my father's house! I played in it when I was a little girl!'

She had a ring on her finger, when she struck him it scratched Elishama's face. He wiped off a drop of blood and looked at his fingers. The sight of blood shed by her hand put Virginie into a fury beyond words, she walked to and fro in the room so that her white gown swished on the floor, and Elishama got an idea of the drama. She sat down on a chair, got up, and sat down on another.

VIII. Virginie and Elishama

'That house,' she said at last, 'was the only thing left me from the time when I was a rich, pretty and innocent girl. Every time that I have since then walked past it I have dreamt of how I were to enter it once more!' She caught at her breath as she spoke, white spots sprang out on her face.

'So you are to enter it now, Miss Virginie,' said Elishama. 'So is, Miss Virginie, the young lady of Mr Clay's story rich, pretty and innocent.'

Virginie stared at him as if she did not see him at all, or as if she sat gazing at a doll.

'God,' she said. 'My God! Yes—"*Virginie est fine, elle s'y comprend, en ironie!*" ' She looked away, then back at him. 'You may hear it all now,' she said. 'My father said that to me!'

She stopped her ears with her fingers for a moment, again let her hands drop and turned straight towards him.

'You can have it all now,' she cried, 'you can have it all!' My father and I used to talk—in that house—of great, splendid, noble things! The Empress Eugenie of France wore her white satin shoes one single time only, then made a present of them to the convent schools for the little girls there to wear at their first communion! I was to have done the same thing—for Papa was proud of my small feet!' She lifted her skirt a little and looked down at her feet, in a pair of old slippers. 'The Empress of France made a great unexampled career for herself, and I was to have done the same. And the way to her bedroom—you can have it all now, you can have it all—the way to her bedroom ran through the Cathedral of Notre Dame! *Virginie,*' she added slowly, '*s'y comprend, en ironie!*'

Now there was a long silence.

'Listen, Miss Virginie,' said Elishama. 'In the shawls . . .'

'Shawls?' she repeated, amazed.

'Yes, in the shawls that I brought you,' he continued, 'there was a pattern. You told your friend Mr Simpson that you liked one pattern better than another. But there was a pattern in all of them.'

Virginie had a taste for patterns, one of the things for which she despised the English was that to her mind they had no pattern in their lives. She frowned a little, but let Elishama go on.

'Only,' he went on, 'sometimes the lines of a pattern will run the other way of what you expect. As in a looking-glass.'

'As in a looking-glass,' she repeated slowly.

'Yes,' he said. 'But for all that it is still a pattern.'

This time she looked at him in silence.

'You told me,' he said, 'that the Emperor of Rome owned all the world. So does Mr Clay own Canton and all the people of Canton'—all except myself, he thought—'Mr Clay, and other rich merchants like him, own it. If you look out into the street you will see many hundred people going north and south, east and west. How many of them would be going at all, if they had not been told to do so by other people? And the people who have told them, Miss Virginie, are Mr Clay and other rich merchants like him. Now he has told you to go to his house, and you will have to go.'

'No,' said Virginie.

Elishama waited a moment, but as Virginie said no more he went on.

'What Mr Clay tells people to do,' he said, 'that is what matters. You struck me a little while ago, you tremble now, because of what he told you to do. It matters very little in comparison whether you do go or not.'

'It was you who told me,' she said.

'Yes, because he has told me to do so,' said Elishama.

There was another pause.

'Let down your hair over your face, Miss Virginie,' said he. 'If one must sit in darkness, one should sit in one's own darkness. I can wait for as long as you like.'

Virginie, in her very refusal to do as he advised her, furiously shook her head. Her long hair from which, when she rushed up and down the room, the ribbon had fallen, floated round her like a dark cloud, and as she let her head drop, it tumbled forward and hid her face. She sat for a while immovable in this chiaroscuro.

'That road of which you spoke,' said Elishama, 'which ran through the Cathedral of Notre Dame—it is in this pattern. Only in this pattern it is reversed.'

From behind her veil of hair Virginie said. 'Reversed?'

'Yes,' said Elishama. 'Reversed. In this pattern the road runs the other way. And runs on.'

The strange sweetness of his voice, against her own will, caught Virginie's ear.

'You will make a career for yourself, Miss Virginie,' said Elishama, 'no less than the Empress of France. Only it runs the other way. And why not, Miss Virginie?'

Virginie, after a minute, asked: 'Did you know my father?'

'No, I did not know him,' said Elishama.

'Then,' she asked again, 'from where do you know that the pattern of which you speak does run in my family, and that there it is called a tradition?'

Elishama did not answer her, because he did not know the meaning of the word.

After another minute she said very slowly: 'And *pourquoi pas?*'

She flung back her hair, raised her head, and sat behind her table like a saleswoman behind her desk. To Elishama her face looked broader and flatter than before, as if a roller had passed over it.

'Tell Mr Clay from me,' she said, 'that I will not come for the price which he has offered me. But that I shall come for the price of three hundred guineas. That, if you like, is a pattern. Or—in such terms as Mr Clay will understand—it is an old debt.'

'Is that your last word, Miss Virginie?' he asked.

'Yes,' said Virginie.

'Your very last word?' he asked again.

'Yes,' she said.

'Then, if it is so,' he said, 'I shall now hand you over three hundred guineas.' He took up his wallet and laid the notes on the table.

'Do you want a receipt?' she asked.

'No,' he said, reflecting that this bargain would be safer without a receipt.

Virginie swept the notes and the playing-cards, all together, into the drawer of the table. She was not going to play any more patience today.

'How do you know,' she said and looked Elishama in the face, 'that I shall not set fire to the house in the morning, before I leave it again, and burn your master in it?'

Elishama had been about to go, now he stood still.

'I shall tell you one thing before I go,' said he. 'This story is the end of Mr Clay.'

'Do you believe that he is going to die with malice?' asked Virginie.

'No,' said he. 'No, I cannot tell. But one way or another, it will be the end of him. No man in the world, not the richest man within it, can take a story, which people have invented and told, and make it happen.'

'How do you know?' she asked.

He waited a moment. 'If you add up a column of figures,' he said slowly so as to make the matter clear to her, 'you begin from your right-hand side, with the lowest figure, and move left, to the tens, the hundreds, the thousands and the ten thousands. But if a man took into his head to add up a column the other way, from the left, what would he find? He would find that his total would come out wrong, and that his account-books would be worth nothing. Mr Clay's total will come out wrong, and his books will be worth nothing. And what will Mr Clay do without his books? It is not a good thing to me myself, Miss Virginie, I have been in his employ for seven years, and I shall now lose my situation. But there is no getting away from it.' This was the first time that Elishama did ever speak confidentially about his master to a third party.

'Where are you going now?' Virginie asked him.

'Me?' he said, surprised that anybody should take an interest in his movements. 'I am going home now to my room.'

'I wonder,' said she with a kind of awe in her voice, 'where that will be. And what it will be like. Had you a home when you were a child?'

'No,' said he.

'Had you brothers and sisters?' she asked again.

'No,' said he.

'No, I thought so,' said Virginie. 'For I see now who you are. When you came in, I thought that you were a small rat, out of Mr Clay's storehouses. *Mais toi—tu es le Juif Errant!*'

Elishama gave her a quick deep glance from his veiled eyes and walked away.

IX. The Hero of the Story

On the night which Mr Clay had destined for his story to materialise, the full moon shone down upon the city of Canton and the Chinese Sea. It was an April night, the air was warm and sweet, and already innumerable bats were soundlessly swishing to and fro in it. The oleander bushes in Mr Clay's garden looked almost colourless in the moonlight, the wheels of his Victoria made but low whisper on the gravel of his drive.

Mr Clay with much trouble had been dressed and got into his carriage. Now he sat in it gravely, erect against the silk upholstering, in a black cloak and with a London top-hat on his head. On the smaller seat opposite to him Elishama, cutting a less magnificent figure, silently watched his master's face. This dying man was driving out to manifest his omnipotence, and to do the thing that could not be done.

They passed from the rich quarters of the town, with its villas and gardens, down into the streets by the harbour, where many people were about and the air was filled with noises and smells. At this time of day nobody was in a hurry, people walked about leisurely or stood still and talked together, the carriage had to drive along slowly. Here and there lamps in many colours were hung out from the houses, like bright jewels in the pale evening air.

Mr Clay from his seat looked sharply at the men on the pavement. He had never before watched the faces of men in the street, the situation was new to him and would not be repeated.

A lonely sailor came walking up the street, gazing about him, and Mr Clay ordered Elishama to stop the carriage and accost him. So the clerk got out and under his master's eye addressed the stranger.

'Good evening,' he said. 'My master, in this carriage, requests me to tell you that you are a fine-looking sailor. He asks you whether you would like to earn five guineas tonight.'

'What is that?' said the sailor. Elishama repeated his phrase.

The sailor took a step towards the carriage to have a better look at the old man in it, then turned to Elishama. 'Say that again, will you?' he said.

As Elishama spoke the words for the third time, the sailor's mouth fell open. Suddenly he turned round and walked off as fast as he could, he took the first turning into a side-street and disappeared.

Upon a sign from Mr Clay Elishama got back into the carriage, and ordered the coachman to drive on.

A little further on, a square-built young man with the look of a seaman was about to cross the street, and had to stop before the carriage, he and Mr Clay looked one another in the face even before it halted. Elishama once more got out, and spoke to him in the same words as to the first sailor. This young man obviously came from a public-house, and was somewhat unsteady on his legs. He too made the clerk repeat the sentence to him, but before Elishama had finished it the second time he burst out laughing and beat his thigh.

'Why, God help me!' he cried out. 'This, I know, is what happens to a good-looking sailor when he visits the landlubbers. You need not say any more! I am coming with you, old Master, and you have hit on the right man, too. Jesus Christ!'

He vaulted into the carriage by Mr. Clay's side, stared at him, at Elishama and at the coachman, and let his hand run along the seat.

'All silk!' he cried out laughing. 'All silk and softness! And more to come!'

As they drove on he began to whistle, then took off his cap to cool his head. All at once he clapped both hands to his face and sat like that for a moment, then without a word jumped out of the carriage, began to run, and disappeared into a side-street just as the first sailor had done.

Mr Clay made the carriage turn and go back along the same street, then turn once more and drive back slowly. But he did not stop it again. He said nothing during the drive, and Elishama, who now kept his eyes off him, began to wonder if they were to drive like this all night. Then suddenly Mr Clay ordered the coachman to return to the house.

They had already got out of the narrow streets near the harbour and on to the road leading to Mr. Clay's house, when three young sailors came straight towards them, arm in arm. As the carriage approached, the two at the sides let go their hold of the one in the middle and ran on leaving the last one in front of it.

Mr Clay stopped the carriage and held up his hand to Elishama.

'I will get out myself this time,' he said.

Slowly and laboriously he descended upon the arm of his clerk, took a step towards the sailor, stood still before him as straight as a pillar, and poked his stick at him. When he spoke, his voice was hard and cracked, with a little deadly note to it.

'Good evening,' he said. 'You are a fine-looking sailor. Do you want to earn five guineas tonight?'

The young sailor was tall, broad and large-limbed, with very big hands. His hair was so fair and stood out so long and thick round his head, that at first Elishama believed him to have on a white fur cap. He did not speak or move, but looked at Mr Clay quietly and dully, somewhat in the manner of a young bull. In his right hand he carried a big bundle, he now shifted it over to the left and began to rub his free hand up and down his thigh as if at the next moment he meant to strike out a blow. But instead he reached out and took hold of Mr Clay's hand.

The old man swallowed, and repeated his proposal. 'You are a fine-looking sailor, my young friend,' he said. 'Do you want to earn five guineas tonight?'

The boy for a moment thought the question over. 'Yes,' he said. 'I want to earn five guineas. I was thinking about it just now, in what way I was to earn five guineas. I shall come with you, old gentleman.'

He spoke slowly, with a stop between each of his phrases and with a quaint, strong accent.

'Then,' said Mr Clay, 'you will get into my carriage. And when we arrive at my house I shall tell you more.'

The sailor set down his bundle on the bottom of the carriage, but did not get in himself. 'No,' he said, 'your carriage is too fine. My clothes are all dirty and tarred. I shall run beside, and I can go as fast as you.'

He placed his big hand on the mudguard, and as the carriage started he began to run. He kept pace with the two tall English horses all the way, and when they stopped at the front door of Mr Clay's house he did not seem to be much out of breath.

Mr Clay's servants came out to receive their master and to help him out of his carriage and his cloak, and the butler of the house, a fat and bald Chinaman all dressed in green silk, appeared on the veranda and held up a lantern on a long pole. In the golden light of the lamp Elishama took a look at the host and the guest.

Mr Clay had strangely come to life. It was as if the young runner by his carriage had made his own old blood run freer, he even had a faint pink in his cheeks, like that of a painted woman. He was satisfied with his catch out of the harbour of Canton. And very likely there was not another fish of just that kind to be caught there.

The sailor was little more than a boy. He had a broad tanned face and clear light blue eyes. He was so very lean, his big bones showing wherever his clothes did not cover him, and his young face was so grave, that there was something uncanny about him, as about a man come from a dungeon. He was poorly dressed, in a blue shirt and a pair of canvas trousers, with bare feet in his old shoes. He lifted his bundle from the carriage and slowly followed the butler with the lantern into Mr Clay's house.

X. The Supper of the Story

The lighted candles upon the dinner-table, in heavy silver candlesticks, were manifoldly reflected in the gilt-framed glasses on the walls, so that the whole long room glittered with a hundred little bright flames. The table was laid, the food ready and the bottles drawn.

To Elishama, who had come into the room last and had sat down silently on a chair at one end of it, the two diners and the servants going to and fro noiselessly, waiting on them, all looked like human figures in a picture seen at a great distance.

Mr Clay had been helped into his pillow-filled armchair by the table, and here sat as erect as in the carriage. But the young sailor slowly gazed round him, afraid to touch anything in the room, and had to be invited two or three times to sit down before he did so.

The old man by a movement of his hand told his butler to pour out wine for his companion, watched him as he drank, and all through the meal had his glass refilled. To keep him company he did even, against his habit, sip a little wine himself.

The first glass of wine had a quick and strong effect on the boy. As he put down the empty glass he suddenly blushed so deeply that his eyes seemed to water with the heat from his burning cheeks.

Mr Clay in his armchair drew one profound sigh and coughed twice. When he began to speak his voice was low and a little hoarse, while he spoke it became shriller and stronger. But all the time he spoke very slowly.

'Now, my young friend,' he said, 'I am going to tell why I have fetched you, a poor sailor-boy, from a street by the harbour I am going to tell you why I have brought you to this house of mine, into which few people, even amongst the richest merchants of Canton, are ever allowed. Wait, and you shall hear all. For I have got many things to tell you.'

He paused a little, drew in his breath, and continued:

'I am a rich man, I am the richest man in Canton. Some of the wealth which in the course of a long life I have made, is here in my house, more is in my storehouses, and more even is on the rivers and on the sea. My name in China is worth more money than you have ever heard of. When, in China or in England, they name me, they name a million pounds.'

Again he made a short pause.

Elishama reflected that so far Mr Clay had recorded only such facts as had been long stored up in his mind, and he wondered how he would get on when he should have to move from the world of reality into that of imagination. For the old man, who in his long life had heard one story told, in his long life had never himself told a story, and had never pretended or dissimulated to anybody. When, however, Mr Clay again took up his recount, the clerk understood that he had on his mind more things of which he meant to clear it. Deep down within it there were ideas, perceptions, emotions even, of which he had never spoken and of which he could never have spoken, to any human being except to the nameless, barefooted boy before him. Elishama began to realise the value of what is named a comedy, in which a man may at last speak the truth.

'A million pounds,' Mr Clay repeated. 'That million pounds is me myself. It is my days and my years, it is my brain and my heart, it is my life. I am alone with it in this house, I have been alone with it for many years, and I have been happy that it should be so. For the human beings whom in my life I have met and dealt with I have always disliked and despised. I have allowed few of them to touch my hand, I have allowed none of them to touch my money.

'And I have never,' he added thoughtfully, 'like other rich merchants, dreaded that my fortune should not last as long as myself. For I have always known how to keep it tight, and how to make it multiply.

'But then lately,' he went on, 'I have comprehended that I myself shall not last as long as my fortune. The moment will come, it is approaching, when we two shall have to part, when one half of me must go and the other half live on. Where and with whom, then, will it live on? Am I to let it fall into the hands which till now I have managed to keep off it, to be fingered and meddled with by those greedy and offensive hands? I would as soon let my body be fingered and meddled with by them. When at night I think of it I cannot sleep.

'I have not troubled,' he said, 'to look for a hand into which I might like to deliver my possessions, for I know that no such hand exists in the world. But it has, in the end, occurred to me that it might give me pleasure to leave them in a hand which I myself had caused to exist.

'Had caused to exist,' he repeated slowly. 'Caused to exist, and called forth. As I have begotten my fortune, my million pounds.

'For it was not my limbs that ached in the tea-fields, in the mist of morning and the burning heat of midday. It was not my hand that was scorched on the hot iron-plates upon which the tea-leaves are dried. Not my hands that were torn in hauling taut the braces of the clipper, pressing her to her utmost speed. The starving coolies in the tea-fields, the dog-tired seamen on the middle watch never knew that they were contributing to the making of a million pounds. To them the minutes only, the pain in their hands, the hail-showers in their faces, and the poor copper coins of their wages had real existence. It was in my brain and by my will that this multitude of little things were combined and set to co-operate to make up one single thing: a million pounds. Have I not, then, legally begotten it?

'Thus, in combining the things of life and by making them co-operate according to my will, I may legally beget the hand into which I can with some pleasure leave my fortune, the lasting part of me.'

He was silent for a long time. Then he dipped his own old, skinny hand deep into his pocket, drew it out and looked at it. 'Have you ever seen gold?' he asked the sailor.

'No,' said the boy. 'I have heard of it from Captains and Super-cargoes, who have seen it. But I have not seen it myself.'

'Hold out your hand,' said Mr Clay.

The boy held out his big hand. On the back of it a cross, a heart and an anchor were tattooed.

'This,' said Mr Clay, 'is a five-guinea piece. The five guineas which you are to earn. It is gold.'

The sailor kept the coin on the flat of his hand, and for a while both looked at it concernedly. When Mr Clay took his eyes off it he drank a little wine.

'I myself,' he said, 'am hard, I am dry. I have always been so, and I would not have it otherwise. I have a distaste for the juices of the body. I do not like the sight of blood, I cannot drink milk, sweat is offensive to me, tears disgust me. In such things a man's bones are dissolved. And in those relationships between people which they name fellowship, friendship or love, a man's bones are likewise dissolved. I did away with a partner of mine because I would not allow him to become my friend and dissolve my bones. But gold, my young sailor, is solid. It is hard, it is proof against dissolution. Gold,' he repeated, a shadow of a smile passing over his face, 'is solvency.'

'You,' he went on after a pause, 'are full of the juices of life. You have blood in you, you have, I suppose, tears. You long and yearn for the things which dissolve people, for friendship and fellowship, for love. Gold you have tonight seen for the first time. I can use you.

'To you, tonight, the minutes only, the pleasure of your body and the five guineas in your pocket will have real existence. You will not be aware that you are contributing to a worthy piece of work of mine. To the fine bafflement of my relations in England, who were once pleased to get rid of me, but who have now for twenty years been on the look-out for the legacy from China. May they sleep well on that.'

The sailor stuck the piece of gold into his pocket. He was by now flushed with food and wine. Big and bony, with his shaggy hair and shining eyes, he looked as strong, greedy and lusty as a bear just out of his winter lair.

'Say no more, old master,' he broke out. 'I know what you are going to tell me. I have, before now, heard it told on the ships, every word. This, I know, is what happens to a sailor when he comes ashore. And you, old gentleman, are in luck tonight. If you want a strong, hearty sailor, you are in luck. You will find none stronger on any ship. Who stood by the pumps in the blizzard off Lofoten for eleven hours? It is hard on you being so old and dry. As for me, I shall know well enough what I am doing.'

141

Once more the boy suddenly and violently blushed crimson. He broke off his bragging and was silent for a minute.

'I am not,' he said, 'in the habit of talking to rich old people. To tell you the truth, old master, I am not just now in the habit of talking to anybody at all. I shall tell you the whole story. A fortnight ago, when the schooner *Barracuda* picked me up and took me on board, I had not spoken a word for a whole year. For a year ago, by the middle of March, my own ship, the bark *Amelia Scott*, went down in a storm, and of all her crew I alone was cast ashore on an island. There was nobody but me there. It is not, tonight, more than three weeks since I walked there, on the beach of my island. There were many sounds on my island, but no one ever spoke. I myself sang a song there sometimes—you may sing to yourself. But I never spoke.'

XI. The Boat

The unexpected strain of adventure in his sailor, and in his story, came agreeable to Mr Clay. He turned his half-closed eyes to the boy's face and for a moment let them rest there with approval, almost with kindness.

'Ah,' he said, 'so you have starved, slept on the ground, and dressed in rags, for a year?' He looked proudly round the rich room. 'Then all this must be a change to you?'

The sailor looked round too. 'Yes,' he said. 'This house is very different from my island.' As he looked back at the old man, he stuck his hand into his hair. 'And that is why my hair is so long,' he said. 'I meant to have it cut tonight. The other two promised to take me to a barber's shop, but they changed their mind and were going to take me to the girls instead. It was good luck to me that I did not get there, for then I should not have met you. I shall soon get used to talking to people again. I have talked before, I am not such a fool as I look.'

'A pleasant thing,' said Mr Clay, as if to himself. 'A highly pleasant thing, I should say, to be all by yourself on an island, where nobody can possibly intrude upon you.'

'It was good in many ways,' said the boy gravely. 'There were birds' eggs on the beach, and I fished there too. I had my knife with me, a good knife, I cut a mark with it in the bark of a big tree each time that I saw a new moon. I had cut nine marks, then I forgot about it, and there were two or three more new moons before the *Barracuda* came along.'

'You are young,' said Mr Clay. 'I presume that you were pleased when the ship came and took you back to people.'

'I was pleased,' said the sailor, 'for one reason. But I had got used to the island, I had come to think that I were to remain there all my life. I told you there were sounds on the island. All night I heard the waves, and when the wind rose I would hear it round me to all sides. I heard when the sea-birds woke in the morning. One time it rained for a whole month and another time for a fortnight. Both times there were great thunderstorms. The rain came from the sky like a song, and the thunder like a man's voice, like my old Captain's voice. I was surprised. I had not heard a voice for many months.'

'Were the nights long?' asked Mr Clay.

'They were as long as the days,' answered the sailor. 'The day came, then the night, then the day. The one was as long as the other. Not like in my country, where the nights are short in summer and long in winter.'

'What did you think of at night?' asked Mr Clay.

'I thought mostly of one thing,' said the sailor. 'I thought of a boat. Many times I also dreamed that I had got her, that I launched her and steered her. She was to be a good strong, seaworthy boat. But she need not be big, not more than five lastages. A sloop would be the thing for me, with tall bulwarks. The stern should be blue, and I should carve stars round the cabin windows. My own home is in Marstal in Denmark. The old shipbuilder Lars Jensen Bager was a friend of my father's, he might help me to build the boat. I should make her trade with corn from Bandholm and Skelskor to Copenhagen. I did not want to die before I had got my boat. When I was taken up by the *Barracuda*, I thought that this was the first bit of my way to her, and that was the reason why I was pleased, then. And when I met you, old gentleman, and you asked me if I would earn five guineas, I knew that I had been right to come away from the island. And that was why I went with you.'

'You are young,' said Mr Clay again. 'Surely on the island you also thought about women?'

The boy sat silent for a long time and looked straight in front of him, as if he had in reality forgotten to speak.

'Yes,' he said. 'On the *Amelia Scott*, and on the *Barracuda* too, the others talked about their girls. I know, I know very well what you are paying me to do tonight. I am as good as any sailor. You will have no reason to complain of me, Master. Your lady here, waiting for me, will have no reason to complain of me.'

Suddenly, for a third time, the blood rushed to his face—it sank back, mounted again and kept glowing darkly through the tan of his cheeks. He stood up from his chair, tall and broad and very grave.

'All the same,' he said in a new, deep voice, 'I may as well now go back to my ship. And you, my old gentleman, will take on another sailor for your job.' He stuck his hand into his pocket.

The faint rosy tinge disappeared from Mr Clay's cheeks. 'No,' he said. 'No, I do not want you to go back to your ship. You have been cast on a desert island, you have not spoken to a human being for a year. I like to think of that. I can use you. I shall take on no other sailor for my job.'

Mr Clay's guest took one step forward and there looked so big that the old man suddenly clenched the arms of the chair with his hands. He had before now been threatened by desperate men, and had beaten them off by the weight of his wealth, or by the force of his cool sharp brain. But the irate creature before him was too simple to give in to any of those arguments. He might have stuck his hand in his pocket to draw out the good knife of which he had just spoken. Was it, then, a matter of life and death to make a story come true?

The sailor took from his pocket the gold coin which Mr Clay had given him, and held it towards the old man.

'You had better not try to hold me back,' he said. 'You are very old, you have but little strength to stand up against me. Thank you, old Master, for the food and the wine. I shall now go back to my ship. Good night, old Gentleman.'

Mr Clay in his state of surprise and alarm could speak only lowly and hoarsely, but he spoke.

'And your boat, my fine young seaman,' he said. 'The boat which is to be all your own? The seaworthy smack of five lastages, which is to trade with corn from your own place to Copenhagen? What will she be, now that you are paying back your five guineas and going away? A story only, which you have been telling me—which will never come to be launched, which will never come to sail!'

After a moment the boy put the coin back in his pocket.

XII. The Speech of the Old Gentleman in the Story

While the Nabob and the sailor-boy were entertaining one another in the brilliantly lighted dining-room, Virginie in the bedroom, where tonight all candles had been softly shaded by rose-coloured screens, was preparing herself for her own part, the heroine's part, in Mr Clay's story.

She had sent away the little Chinese maid, who had helped her to arrange the room and adorn it with such objects as would make it appear like an elegant lady's bedroom. Two or three times she had suddenly stopped the work and informed the girl that they were both immediately going to leave the house. Now that she was alone she no longer thought of leaving.

The room in which she found herself had been her parents' bedroom, where on Sunday mornings the children were let in to play in the big bed. Her father and mother, who for a long time had seemed far away, were with her tonight, she had entered their old house with their consent. To them as to her, this night would bring about the final judgment of their old deadly enemy, the disgrace and humiliation of their daughter provided the conclusive evidence against him. The daughter, according to her vow of long ago, would not see his face at the verdict, but the dead father and mother were there to watch it.

The ornaments with which Virginie had embellished her bedroom of one night—the figurines, Chinese fans and Maquart bouquets—were all similar to those she remembered from her childhood, and which had been so sadly burnt or smashed up by her father before Mr Clay ever entered the house. A few bibelots had come from her own house. In this way Virginie had joined her gloomy existence of the last ten years with her gay and guiltless past of long ago, and had had it recognised by Monsieur and Madame Dupont.

She set to dress and adorn her own person. She started on the task solemnly and darkly, such as Judith in the tent of the Babylonions adorned her face and body for the meeting with Holofernes. But she immediately and inevitably became absorbed in the process—such as, very likely, Judith herself did.

Virginie was an honest person in money matters, out of Mr Clay's three hundred guineas she had conscientiously and generously purchased everything belonging to her role. She had a weakness for lace, and was at this moment floating in a cloud of Valenciennes, with a coral necklace round her throat, pearls in her ears and a pair of pink satin slippers on her feet. She powdered and rouged her face, blackened her eyebrows and painted her full lips, she let down her hair in rich silky ringlets over her smooth shoulders, and scented her neck, arms and bosom. When all was done, she gravely went up to one after another of the long looking-glasses in the room.

These glasses had reflected her figure as a little girl, and had told her, then, that she was pretty and graceful. As she looked into them she remembered how, at the age of twelve, she had entreated them to show her what she would be like in years to come, as a lady. The child, she felt, could never have hoped to be shown, in a sweeter or rosier light, a lovelier, a more elegant and bewitching lady. Virginie's love of the dramatic art, inherited from her father and encouraged by him, came to her aid in the hour of need. If she was not what she appeared to be, neither had her father's business-transactions always been quite what they appeared to be.

During these reflections she had stepped out of her small silk slippers and stretched her fair, slim, strong body between the smooth sheets rich with lace, her dark silken tresses spread over the pillow-case.

She had been engrossed in the thought of her enemy, and she had become engrossed in the vision of herself. It was not till she heard steps in the corridor outside that she gave any thought to the third party in the story, her unknown guest of the night. Then for a second a little cold draught of contempt for Mr Clay's hired and bribed puppet ran through her mind.

When the doorknob turned she cast down her eyes, and till the door was once more opened and shut she kept her glance fixed upon the sheet. But in this withdrawal there was as much energy and vigour as in any direct glance of deadly, uncompromising enmity.

Mr Clay, in his long dressing-gown of heavy Chinese silk, came into the room leaning on his stick. Two respectful steps behind him a big, blurred shadow slowly crossed the threshold.

The one glass of wine he had taken with his guest had acted upon the invalid of many sleepless nights. He had also, a few minutes ago, been frightened a little, and although in the course of his life he had frightened many people, fear to himself was a rare experience and might well stir his blood in a new way. But the old man was drunk with a still stronger liquor. For tonight he was moving in a world created by his will and at his word.

His triumph had aged him, in a few hours his hair seemed to have grown whiter. But at the same time it had strangely rejuvenated him. He was at this hour conquering and subjugating, he was indeed, in absorbing them into his own being, annihilating the forces which unexpectedly had bid defiance to him. He was materialising a fantasy and changing a fable into fact. Dimly he felt that he was about to triumph over the person who had attempted to upset his own idea of the world—the Prophet Isaiah.

He smiled a little, he was a little bit unsteady on his legs. For the first time in his life he was impressed by a woman's beauty. He gazed almost happily at the girl in the bed, whom his command had called to life—and for a second the vague picture of a child, long ago shown to him by a proud father, appeared before him, and disappeared. He nodded his head in approval. His dolls were behaving well. The heroine of his story was pink and white, and her downcast eyes bore witness to alarmed modesty. The story was fetching headway.

This was the moment, Mr Clay knew, for the speech of the old gentleman in the story. He remembered it, word for word, from the night fifty years ago. But the consciousness of his power was somehow going to the head of the Nabob of Canton. The Prophet Isaiah is crafty, behind a pious mien he has knowledge of many ways and measures. Mr Clay had been a child only a very short time, until he had learned to speak and to understand the speech of other people. Now, as he was about to enter the heaven of his omnipotence, the Prophet laid his hand on his head and turned him into a child—in other words, the old stoneman was quietly entering his second childhood. He began to play with his story, he could not let go the theme of the dinner-table.

'You,' he began, poking his forefinger at the girl in the bed, 'and you'—without looking at him he poked it at the boy, 'are young. You are in fine health, your limbs do not ache, you sleep at night. And because you can walk and move without pain, you believe that you are walking and moving according to your own will. But it is not so. You walk and move at my bidding. You are, in reality, two young, strong and lusty jumping-jacks within this old hand of mine.'

He paused, the little hard smile still on his face.

'So,' he went on, 'so are, as I have told you, all people jumping-jacks in a hand stronger than their own. So are, as I have told you, the poor jumping-jacks in the hands of the rich, the fools of this earth in the hands of the shrewd. They dance and drop as these hands pull the strings.

'When I am gone,' he finished, 'and when you two are left to yourselves, and believe that you are following the command of your own young blood only, you will still be doing nothing, nothing at all, but what I have willed you to do. You will be conforming to the plot of my story. For tonight this room, this bed, you yourselves with this same young hot blood in you—it is all nothing but a story turned, at my word, into reality.'

It came hard on him to tear himself from the room. He remained standing by the end of the bed for another minute, hung on his stick. Then with fine dignity he turned his back on the small actors upon the stage of his omnipotence.

As he opened the door Virginie raised her eyes.

She looked straight at the figure of her father's murderer, and saw a withdrawing and disappearing figure. Mr Clay's long Chinese dressing-gown trailed on the floor, and as he closed the door behind him it was caught in it, he had to open and close the door a second time.

XIII. The Meeting

The room remained without a sound or a stir till, in the very same instant, the boy took two long steps forward and Virginie, in the bed, turned her head and looked at him.

At that she was so mortally frightened that she forgot her high mission, and for a moment wished herself back in her own house, and even under the patronage, such as it was, of Charley Simpson. For the figure by the end of the bed was not a casual sailor out of the streets of Canton. It was a huge wild animal brought in to crush her beneath him.

The boy stared at her, immovable except for his broad chest slowly going up and down with his deep regular breath. At last he said: 'I believe that you are the most beautiful girl in the world.' Virginie then saw that she had to do with a child.

He asked her. 'How old are you?'

She could not find a word to say. Was it possible, now, that her great dark tragedy was to be turned into a comedy?

The boy waited for an answer, then asked her again: 'Are you seventeen?'

'Yes,' said Virginie. And as she heard her own voice pronounce the word her face, turned towards him, softened a little.

'Then you and I are the same age,' said the boy.

He took another slow step and sat down on the bed.

'What is your name?' he asked.

'Virginie,' she answered.

He repeated the name twice and sat for some time looking at her. Then he lay down gently beside her on top of the quilt. In spite of his size he was light and easy in all his movements. She heard his deep breathing quicken, break off, and start again with a faint moan, as if something was giving way within him. They lay like this for a while.

'I have got something to tell you,' he suddenly broke out in a low voice. 'I have never till tonight slept with a girl. I have thought of it, often. I have meant to do it, many times. But I have never done it.'

He was silent once more, waiting to hear what she would say to this. As she said nothing he went on.

'It was not all my own fault,' he said. 'I have been away for a long time, in a place a long way off, where there were no girls.'

Again he stopped, and again spoke. 'I have never told the others on the boat,' he said. 'Nor my friends with whom I came ashore tonight. But I thought that I had better tell you.'

Against her will Virginie turned her face towards him. His own face, quite close to hers, was all aglow.

'When I was in the place, far away from here, that I told you about,' he went on, 'I sometimes fancied that I had a girl with me, who was mine. I brought her bird's eggs and fish, and some big sweet fruits that grew there, but of which I do not know the name, and she was kind to me. We slept together in a cave that I found when I had been in the place for three months. When the full moon rose it shone into it. But I could not think of a name for her. I did not remember any girl's name—Virginie,' he added very slowly. 'Virginie.' And one more: 'Virginie.'

All at once he lifted the quilt and the sheet, and slid in beneath them. Although he still kept a little away from her she sensed his body there, big, supple, and very young. After a time he stretched out his hand and touched her. Her lace nightgown had slipped up on her leg, as now slowly the boy put out his hand it met her round naked knee. He started a little, let his fingers run gently over it, then withdrew his hand and felt his own lean and hard knee over.

A moment later Virginie cried out in fear of her life. 'God!' she screamed. 'For God's sake! Get up, we must get up. There is an earthquake—do you not feel the earthquake!'

'No,' the boy panted lowly into her face. 'No. It is not an earthquake. It is me.'

XIV. The Parting

When at last he fell asleep he held her close to him as in a vice, with his face bored into her shoulder, breathing deeply and peacefully.

Virginie, who had lately thought of so many things, lay awake but could think of nothing in the world. She had never in her life met with such strength. It would be useless and hopeless for her, here, to try to act on her own. She felt his mighty grip round her as a hitherto unknown kind of reality, which made everything else seem hollow and falsified.

In the middle of the night she suddenly remembered things which her mother had told her about her own people, the seafaring men of Brittany. Old French songs of the sailor's dangers, and of his homecoming, came back to her as on their own. In the end, from far away, came the sailor-wife's cradlesong.

When in the course of the night the boy woke up, he behaved with the girl in his bed like a bear with a honeycomb, growling over her in a wild state of greed and ecstasy. A couple of times they talked together.

'On the ships,' he said, 'I sometimes made a song.'

'What were your songs about?' she asked.

'About the sea,' he answered. 'And the life of the sailors. And their death.'

'Say a little of them to me,' said she.

After a moment he slowly recited:

> As I was keeping the middle watch,
> and the night was cold,

three swans flew across the moon,
over her round face of gold.

'Gold,' he repeated, somewhat uneasily. And after a pause: 'A five-guinea piece is like the moon. And then not at all like her.'

'Did you make other songs?' asked Virginie, who did not understand what he meant, but somehow did not want him to be worried.

'Yes, I made other songs,' he said. 'About my boat.'

'Say a little of them to me, then,' she again asked.

Again he recited slowly:

When the sky is brown,
and the sea yawns, three thousand fathoms down,
and the boat runs downward like a whale,
still Povl Velling will not turn pale.

'Is your name Paul, then?' she asked.

'Yes, Povl,' he answered. 'It is not a bad name. My father was named Povl, and his father too. It is the name of good seamen, faithful to their ship. My father was drowned six months before I was born. He is down there, in the sea.'

'But you are not going to drown, Paul?' she said.

'No,' said he. 'Maybe not. But I have many times wondered what my father thought of, when the sea took him at last, altogether.'

'Do you like to think of that sort of thing?' she asked, somewhat alarmed.

He thought her question over. 'Yes,' he said. 'It is good to think of the storms and the high sea. It is not bad to think of death.'

A little while after he called out, in a sudden, low cry: 'I shall have to go back to my ship as soon as it grows light. She sails in the morning.'

At these words a long, sad pain ran through Virginie's whole body. But the next moment it was again swallowed up in his strength. Soon after they both fell asleep in one another's arms.

Virginie woke up when the morning showed in grey stripes between the window curtains. The boy had loosened his grasp of her, but was still, in his deep sleep, holding on to her hand.

The moment she woke she was gripped, as in a strangle-hold, by one single thought. Never before had one thought filled her so entirely, to the exclusion of everything else. 'When he sees my face in the daylight,' she reflected, 'it will be old, powdered and rouged. An aged, wicked woman's face!'

She watched the light growing stronger. She had got ten minutes yet, she had got five minutes yet, she thought—her heart heavy, heavy in her breast. Time was up, and she called his name twice.

When he woke she told him that he must get up in order to be back on his ship before she sailed. He did not answer her, but clung to her hand, and in a while pressed it to his face, moaning.

149

She heard a bird singing in the garden and said: 'Listen, Paul, there is a bird singing. The candles are burnt out, the night is over.'

Suddenly, without a sound, like an animal springing, he flung himself out of the bed, seized her, and lifted her up with him.

'Come!' he cried, 'Come with me, away from here!'

His voice was like a song, like a storm, it lifted her higher than his arms.

'I shall take you with me!' he cried again, 'to my ship. I shall hide you there, in the hold. I shall take you home with me!'

She thrust her hands against his chest to get away from him, and felt it going up and down like a pair of bellows, but she only made him, and herself within his embrace, sway a little, like a tree in the wind. He tightened his hold of her, raising her as if to throw her over his shoulder.

'I am not going to leave you!' he sang out. 'I am not going to let anybody in the world part us—What! Now that you are mine! Never! Never! Never!'

Virginie at this moment caught sight of their two dim figures in one of the looking-glasses. She could not have asked for a more dramatic scene. The boy looked super-humanly big, formidable now, like an enraged bear, risen on his hindlegs, and swinging his right forelimb in the air—and she herself, with her long hair hanging down, was the limp, defenceless prey in his left arm. Writhing, she managed to get one foot to the ground. The boy felt her tremble, he let her down, but still held her close.

'What are you afraid of?' he asked, forcing her face up towards his own. 'You do not believe that I shall let anybody take you away from me!—You are coming home with me. You will not be afraid of the storms, or the blizzards, or the big waves, when I am with you. You will never be afraid in Denmark. There we shall sleep together every night. Like tonight. Like tonight!'

Virginie's deadly terror had nothing to do with storms, blizzards or big waves—she did not even, at this moment, dread death. She dreaded that he should see her face in the light of day. At first she dared not speak, for she did not feel sure of herself, and might say anything. But when she had stood on both feet for a minute she collected her whole being to find a way of escape.

'You can not do that,' she said, 'he has paid you.'

'What?' he cried out bewildered.

'That old man has paid you!' she repeated. 'He has paid you to go away at dawn. You have taken his money!'

When he grasped the meaning of her words his face grew white and he let go his hold of her so suddenly that she swayed on her feet.

'Yes,' he said slowly. 'He has paid me. And I took his money.—But at that time' he cried, 'I did not know!'

He stared into the air before him, above her head. 'I have promised him!' he said heavily. Letting his head drop upon her shoulders he buried his face in her hair and her flesh. 'Oh! oh! oh!' he wailed.

He lifted her, carried her back on to the bed and sat down on it beside her, his eyes closed. Time after time he raised her and pressed her body to his own, then laid her down again. Virginie was calmer as long as he kept his eyes closed. She looked back over their short acquaintance to find a word to say to him.

'You will have your boat,' she said at last.

After a long silence he said: 'Yes, I shall have the boat.' And again after a while: 'Was that what you said: that I shall have the boat?'

Once more he lifted her and held her for a long time in his arms. 'But you!' he said.

'But you?' he repeated, slowly, after a moment. 'What is going to happen to you, my girl?'

Virginie did not say a word.

'Then I must go,' he said, 'I must go back to my ship.' He listened and added: 'There is a bird singing. The candles are burnt out. The night is over. I must go.' But he did not go till a little later.

'Good-bye, Virginie,' he said. 'That is your name—Virginie. I shall name the boat after you. I shall give her both our names—"Povl and Virginie." She will sail with both our names on her, up through the Storstroem and the Bay of Koege.'

'Will you remember me?' Virginie asked.

'Yes,' the sailor said. 'Always, all my life.' He rose.

'I shall think of you all my life,' he said. 'How would I not think of you in my boat? I shall think of you when I hoist the sails and when I weigh anchor. And when I cast anchor. I shall think of you in the mornings when I hear the birds singing. Of your body, of your smell. I shall never think of any other girl, of any girl at all. Because you are the most beautiful girl in the world.'

She followed him to the door and put her arms round his neck. Here, away from the window, the room was still dark. Here she suddenly heard herself weeping. 'But I have got one minute more,' she thought, as she held him in her arms and they kissed.

'Look at me,' she begged him. 'Look at me, Paul.'

Gravely, he looked her in the face.

'Remember my face,' she said. 'Look at my face well, and remember it. Remember that I am seventeen. Remember that I have never loved anybody till I met you.'

'I shall remember it all,' he said, 'I shall never forget your face.'

Clinging to him, her wet face lifted, she felt that he was freeing himself of her arms.

'Now you must go,' she said.

XV. The Shell

By the light of that same dawn Elishama walked up Mr Clay's gravelled drive and entered the house, in order to be, in his quiet way, the full stop, or the epilogue, to the story.

In the long dining-room the table was still laid, and there was still a little wine in the glasses. The candles were burnt out, only one last flame flickered on its candlestick.

Mr Clay, too, was still there, propped up with cushions in his deep armchair, his feet on a stool. He had been sitting up, waiting for the morning, to drink off at sunrise the cup of his triumph. But the cup of triumph had been too strong for him.

Elishama stood for a long time, immovable as the old man himself, looking at him. He had never till now seen his master asleep and from his complaints and laments had concluded that he should never see him so. Well, he thought, Mr Clay had been right, he had struck on the one effective remedy against his suffering. The realisation of a story was the thing to set a man at rest.

The old man's eyes were slightly open—pale like pebbles—but his thin lips were closed in a little wry smile. His face was grey like the bony hands upon his knees. His dressing-gown hung in such deep folds that there hardly seemed to be a body in it to connect this face and head with these hands. The whole proud and rigid figure, envied and feared by thousands, this morning looked like a jumping-jack when the hand which has pulled the strings has suddenly let them go.

His servant and confidant sat down on a chair, listening for the usual whining and snarling in the old man's chest. But there was not a sound in the room. Elishama repeated to himself the words of his Prophet:

'And sorrow and sighing shall flee away.'

For a long time Mr Clay's clerk sat with him, meditating upon the events of the night, and upon human conditions in general. What had happened, he asked himself, to the three people who, each of them, had had his or her role in Mr Clay's story? Could they not have done without it? It was hard, he reflected as he had often done before, it was very hard on people who wanted things so badly that they could not do without them. If they could not get these things it was hard, and when they did get them, surely it was very hard.

After a while he wondered whether he were to touch the sunken, immovable body before him, to demonstrate, in a gesture, his intention to wake up Mr Clay to the triumphal end of his story. But again he made up his mind to wait a little and to watch this end himself first. He silently left the silent room.

He went to the bedroom door, and as he waited outside it he heard voices. Two people were talking at the same time. What had happened to those two in the night, and what was happening to them now? Could they not have done without it? Someone was weeping inside the room, the voice came to the listener's ear broken, stifled by tears. Again Elishama quoted to himself the words of Isaiah:

'In the wilderness shall waters break out, and streams in the desert. And the parched ground shall become a pool.'

152

A little later the door was opened, two figures were embracing and clinging to one another in the doorway. Then they severed, the one sliding back and disappearing, the other advancing and closing the door behind him. The sailor of last night for a few seconds stood still outside the door and gazed round him, then moved on.

Elishama took a step forward. He was loyal to his master and felt that he ought to get the attestation of Mr Clay's victory from the boy's own lips.

The sailor looked at him gravely and said: 'I am going away. I am going back to my ship. You will tell the old man that I have gone.'

Elishama now saw that he had been mistaken the evening before, the boy was not so young as he had taken him to be. It made but little difference—it was still a long time till he would be as old as Mr Clay, peacefully at rest in his armchair. For a long time yet he would be unsafe, in the hands of the elements, and of his own wants.

The clerk took upon himself to settle and balance up his master's concern.

'Now you can tell the story,' he said to the boy.

'What story?' the boy asked.

'The whole story,' Elishama answered. 'When you tell what has happened to you, what you have seen and done, from yesterday evening till now, you will be telling the whole story. You are the one sailor in the world who can tell it truthfully, from beginning to end, with everything that is in it, as it has actually, from beginning to end, happened to you.'

The boy looked at Elishama for a long time.

'What has happened to me?' he said at last. 'What I have seen and done from yesterday evening till now?' And again after a while: 'Why do you call it a story?'

'Because,' said Elishama, 'you yourself have heard it told as a story. About a sailor who comes ashore from his ship in a big town. And he is walking by himself in a street near the harbour, when a carriage drives up, and an old gentleman steps out of it and says to him: "You are a fine-looking sailor, do you want to earn five guineas tonight?" '

The boy did not move. But he had a curious capacity of collecting, suddenly and imperceptibly, his great strength, and of turning it towards the person with whom he spoke, like some threatening, like some formidable weight, which might well make the other feel in danger of his life. So he had puzzled Mr Clay at their first meeting in the street, and had downright scared him later in the evening, in the dining-room. Elishama, who had no fear in him, for a second was moved and stirred—so that he even drew back a little from the gigantic creature before him—not, however, with fright, but with the same strange kind of sympathy and compassion as all his life he had felt towards women and birds.

But the gigantic creature before him proved to be a peaceful beast. He waited a moment, then very quietly stated: 'But that story is not in the least like what happened to me.'

Again he waited a little.

'Tell it?' he said lowly. 'To whom would I tell it? Who in the world would believe it if I told it?'

He laid his collected, concentrated strength and weight into a last sentence:

'I would not tell it,' he said, 'for a hundred times five guineas.'

Elishama opened the door of the house to its guest of the night. Outside, the trees and flowers of Mr Clay's garden were wet with dew, in the morning light they looked new and fresh, as if they had just this hour been created. The sky was red as a rose and there was not a cloud in it. One of Mr Clay's peacocks screeched on the lawn—dragging its tail after it, it made a dark stripe in the silvery grass. From far away came the faint noises of the awakening town.

The sailor's eyes fell upon the bundle which last night he had left on a lacquered table in the verandah. He took it up to carry it away with him, then thought better of it, laid it down again and undid the knots.

'Will you remember to do something for me?' he asked Elishama.

'Yes, I shall remember,' answered Elishama.

'A long time ago,' said the boy, 'I was on an island where there were many thousand shells along the shore. Some of them were beautiful, perhaps they were rare, perhaps they were only to be found on that same island. I picked up a few every day, in the morning. I took some of them, the most beautiful of them, with me. I meant to take them home to Denmark. They are the only things I have got, to take home with me.'

He spread his collections of shells over the table, looked them over thoughtfully, and in the end picked out one big shining pink shell. He handed it to Elishama.

'I shall not give her them all,' he said. 'She has got so many fine things, she would not care to have a lot of shells lying about. But this one is rare, I think. I think that perhaps there is not another one just like it in all the world.'

He slowly felt the shell over with his fingers. 'It is as smooth and silky as a knee,' he said. 'And when you hold it to your ear there is a sound in it, a song. Will you give it to her from me? And will you tell her to hold it to her ear?'

He held it to his own ear, and immediately his face took on an attentive, peaceful look. Elishama reflected that after all he had been right last night, and that the boy was very young.

'Yes,' he said. 'I shall remember to give it to her.'

'And will you remember to tell her to hold it to her ear?' asked the boy.

'Yes,' said Elishama.

'Thank you. And good-bye,' said the sailor, and gave Elishama his big hand.

He went down the verandah steps and along the drive with the bundle in his hand, and disappeared.

Elishama stood and looked after him. When the big young figure was no longer in sight, he himself lifted the shell to his ear. There was a deep, low surge in it, like the distant roar of great breakers. Elishama's face took on exactly the same expression as the sailor's face a few moments ago. He had a strange, gentle, profound shock, from the sound of a new voice in the house, and in the story. 'I have heard it before,' he thought, 'long ago. Long, long ago. But where?'

He let his hand sink.

JOSÉ DONOSO

(1924–)

JOSÉ DONOSO was born into a family of lawyers and physicians in Santiago, Chile. He attended the Instituto Pedagógico at the University of Chile, and then Princeton University, where he received an A.B. degree. In 1961 he married Maria del Pilar Serrano; they have a daughter. In Chile as well as the United States, he has worked as a journalist and teacher; among his other positions, Donoso taught at the University of Iowa Writers' Workshop in 1966–67. Before attending college, he tended sheep in Patagonia; he disliked being a shepherd. ("Sheep," he confided in a talk at New York University, "are very terrible people.") He is the author of several novels, as well as essays, novellas, and numerous short stories, including "The Walk" (which in some collections is given the title of the Spanish original, "Paseo," translated loosely as "Promenade"). For *Coronation* (tr. 1965), the first of his novels to be published in the United States, he was awarded the 1962 William Faulkner Foundation Prize for Chile. In Donoso's writing, the veins of both magic and realism are well mined. At times one predominates; at other times they are in balance. Like *Coronation, This Sunday* (tr. 1967) gives an essentially realistic account of life within and surrounding families, but the magical-mysterious is also present. The terrain of *The Obscene Bird of Night* (tr. 1973) is surrealistic and hallucinatory. What begins as a family story in *A House in the Country* (tr. 1984) becomes chilling political allegory. After living for many years in Europe, Donoso returned with his wife and daughter to Pinochet's Chile, where *Curfew's* (tr. 1988) account of political oppression is set. *The Garden Next Door* (tr. 1992) tells of the upheaval in the life a Chilean writer dwelling with his wife in exile in Madrid.

Donoso is a writer whose power to transform experience is informed by wisdom and driven by passion. "The Walk" (1977) tells, from the point of view of a motherless boy, how Aunt Matilde, entering the household to care both for him and her adult brothers, regulates everything in it—including love. Affection, the boy explains, is channeled obscurely, deployed largely as a habit among the adults: "Love was retained within each separate being, never leaping over the boundaries to express itself and unite us. . . . Respect alone remained, as a point of contact among four silent, isolated relatives who moved through the halls of the deep house which, like a book, revealed only its narrow spine to the street." From the street, in fact, comes a small, white, stray dog who insinuates its way into the household. "The Walk" tells how an unorthodox liberation is achieved via the love the dog compels.

Narrating the story matter-of-factly, the boy nonetheless transmits the sense of awe and alarm inhering in these complex events. Does the dog, as surrogate, draw a love intended for others? For the boy? Is the stray dog also emblematic of the boy himself, who will not be alone among those indelibly marked by this story?

The Walk

1

It happened when I was very small, when my Aunt Matilde and Uncle Gustavo and Uncle Armando, my father's unmarried sister and brothers, and my father himself, were still alive. Now they are all dead. That is, I'd rather think they are all dead, because it's easier, and it's too late now to be tortured with questions that were certainly not asked at the opportune moment. They weren't asked because the events seemed to paralyze the three brothers, leaving them shaken and horrified. Afterwards, they erected a wall of forgetfulness or indifference in front of it all so they could keep their silence and avoid tormenting themselves with futile conjectures. Maybe it wasn't that way; it could be that my imagination and my memory play me false. After all, I was only a boy at the time, and they weren't required to include me in their anguished speculations, if there ever were any, or keep me informed of the outcome of their conversations.

What was I to think? Sometimes I heard the brothers talking in the library in low voices, lingeringly, as was their custom; but the thick door screened the meaning of the words, allowing me to hear only the deep, deliberate counterpoint of their voices. What were they saying? I wanted them to be talking in there about what was really important; to abandon the respectful coldness with which they addressed one another, to open up their doubts and anxieties and let them bleed. But I had so little faith that would happen; while I loitered in the high-walled vestibule near the library door, the certainty was engraved on my mind that they had chosen to forget, and had come together only to discuss, as always, the cases that fell within their bailiwick, maritime law. Now I think perhaps they were right to want to erase it all, for why should they live with the useless terror of having to accept that the streets of a city can swallow a human being, annul it, leave it without life or death, suspended in a dimension more threatening than any dimension with a name?

And yet . . .

One day, months after the incident, I surprised my father looking down at the street from the second-floor sitting room. The sky was narrow, dense, and the humid air weighed on the big limp leaves of the ailanthus trees. I went over to my father, anxious for some minimal explanation

'What are you doing here, father?' I whispered.

When he answered, something closed suddenly over the desperation on his face, like a shutter slamming on an unmentionable scene.

'Can't you see? I'm smoking,' he answered.

And he lit a cigarette.

It wasn't true. I knew why he was looking up and down the street, with his eyes saddened, once in a while bringing his hand up to his soft brown goatee: it was in hopes of seeing her reappear, come back just like that, under the trees along the sidewalk, with the white dog trotting at her heels. Was he waiting there to gain some certainty?

Little by little I realized that not only my father but both his brothers, as if hiding from one another and without admitting even to themselves what they were doing, hovered around the windows of the house, and if a passerby chanced to look up from the sidewalk across the street, he might spot the shadow of one of them posted beside a curtain, or a face aged by suffering in wait behind the window panes.

2

Yesterday I passed the house we lived in then. It's been years since I was last there. In those days the street under the leafy ailanthus trees was paved with quebracho wood, and from time to time a noisy streetcar would go by. Now there aren't any wooden pavements, or streetcars, or trees along the sidewalk. But our house is still standing, narrow and vertical as a book slipped in between the thick shapes of the new buildings; it has stores on the ground floor and a loud sign advertising knit undershirts stretched across the two second-floor balconies.

When we lived there, most of the houses were tall and slender like ours. The block was always cheerful, with children playing games in the splashes of sunlight on the sidewalks, and servants from the prosperous homes gossiping as they came back from shopping. But our house wasn't happy. I say 'wasn't happy' as opposed to 'was sad,' because that's exactly what I mean. The word 'sad' wouldn't be correct because it has connotations that are too clearly defined; it has a weight and dimensions of its own. And what went on in our house was exactly the opposite: an absence, a lack, which, because it was unknown, was irremediable, something that had no weight, yet weighed because it didn't exist.

When my mother died, before I turned four, they thought I needed to have a woman around to care for me. Because Aunt Matilde was the only woman in the family and lived with my uncles Gustavo and Armando, the three of them came to our house, which was big and empty.

Aunt Matilde carried out her duties toward me with the punctiliousness characteristic of everything she did. I didn't doubt that she cared for me, but I never experienced that affection as something palpable that united us. There was something rigid about her feelings, as there was about those of the men in the family, and love was retained within each separate being, never leaping over the boundaries to express itself and unite us. Their idea of expressing affection consisted of carrying out their duties toward one another perfectly, and above all, of never upsetting one another. Perhaps to express affection otherwise was no longer necessary to them, since they shared so many anecdotes and events in which, possibly, affection had already been expressed to the saturation point, and all this conjectural past of tenderness was now stylized in the form of precise actions, useful symbols that did not require further explanation. Respect alone remained, as a point of contact among four silent, isolated relatives who moved through the halls of that deep house which, like a book, revealed only its narrow spine to the street.

I, of course, had no anecdotes in common with Aunt Matilde. How could I, since I was a boy and only half understood the austere motives of grown-ups? I desperately wanted this contained affection to overflow, to express itself differently, in enthusiasm, for example, or a joke. But she could not guess this desire of mine because her attention wasn't focused on me. I was only a peripheral person in her life, never central. And I wasn't central because the center of her whole being was filled with my father and my uncles Gustavo and Armando. Aunt Matilde was the only girl—an ugly girl at that—in a family of handsome men, and realizing she was unlikely to find a husband, she dedicated herself to the comfort of those men: keeping house for them, taking care of their clothes, preparing their favorite dishes. She carried out these functions without the slightest servility, proud of her role because she had never once doubted her brothers' excellence and dignity. In addition, like all women, she possessed in great measure that mysterious faith in physical well-being, thinking that if it is not the main thing, it is certainly the first, and that not to be hungry or cold or uncomfortable is the prerequisite of any good of another order. It wasn't that she suffered if defects of that nature arose, but rather that they made her impatient, and seeing poverty or weakness around her, she took immediate steps to remedy what she did not doubt were mere errors in a world that ought to be—no, *had* to be—perfect. On another plane, this was intolerance of shirts that weren't ironed exquisitely, of meat that wasn't a prime cut, of dampness leaking into the humidor through someone's carelessness. Therein lay Aunt Matilde's undisputed strength, and through it she nourished the roots of her brothers' grandness and accepted their protection because they were men, stronger and wiser than she.

Every night after dinner, following what must have been an ancient family ritual, Aunt Matilde went upstairs to the bedrooms and turned down the covers on each one of her brothers' beds, folding up the bedspreads with her bony hands. For him who was sensitive to the cold, she would lay a blanket at the foot of the bed; for him who read before going to sleep, she would prop a feather pillow against the headboard. Then, leaving the lamps lit on the night tables beside their vast beds, she went downstairs to the billiard room to join the men, to have coffee with them and play a few caroms before they retired, as if by her command, to fill the empty effigies of the pajamas laid out on the neatly turned-down white sheets.

But Aunt Matilde never opened my bed. Whenever I went up to my room I held my breath, hoping to find my bed turned down with the recognizable expertise of her hands, but I always had to settle for the style, so much less pure, of the servant who did it. She never conceded me this sign of importance because I was not one of her brothers. And not to be 'one of my brothers' was a shortcoming shared by so many people . . .

Sometimes Aunt Matilde would call me in to her room, and sewing near the high window she would talk to me without ever asking me to reply, taking it for granted that all my feelings, tastes, and thoughts were the result of what she was saying, certain that nothing stood in the way of my receiving her words intact. I listened to her carefully. She impressed on me what a privilege it was to have been born the son of one of her brothers, which made it possible to have contact with all of them. She spoke of their absolute integrity and genius as lawyers in the most intricate of maritime cases, informing me of her enthusiasm regarding their prosperity and distinction, which I would undoubtedly continue. She explained the case of an embargo on a copper shipment, another about damages resulting from a collision with an insignificant tugboat, and another having to do with the disastrous effects of the overlong stay of a foreign ship. But in speaking to me of ships, her words did not evoke the magic of those hoarse foghorns I heard on summer nights when, kept awake by the heat, I would climb up to the attic and watch from a roundel the distant lights floating, and those darkened blocks of the recumbent city to which I had no access because my life was, and always would be, perfectly organized. Aunt Matilde did not evoke that magic for me because she was ignorant of it; it had no place in her life, since it could not have a place in the life of people destined to die with dignity and then establish themselves in complete comfort in heaven, a heaven that would be identical to our house. Mute, I listened to her words, my eyes fixed on the length of light-colored thread which, rising against the black of her blouse, seemed to catch all the light from the window. I had a melancholy feeling of frustration, hearing those foghorns in the night and seeing that dark and starry city so much like the heaven in which Aunt Matilde saw no mystery at all. But I rejoiced at the world of security her words sketched out for me, that magnificent rectilinear road which ended in a death not feared, exactly like this life, lacking the fortuitous and unexpected. For death was not terrible. It was the final cutoff, clean and definite, nothing more. Hell existed, of course, though not for us, but rather to punish the rest of the city's inhabitants, or those nameless sailors who caused the damages that, after the struggle in the courts was over, always filled the family bank accounts.

Any notion of the unexpected, of any kind of fear, was so alien to Aunt Matilde that, because I believe fear and love to be closely related, I am overcome by the temptation to think that she didn't love anybody, not at that time. But perhaps I am wrong. In her own rigid, isolated way, it is possible that she was tied to her brothers by some kind of love. At night, after dinner, when they gathered in the billiard room for coffee and a few rounds, I went with them. There, faced with this circle of confined loves which did not include me, I suffered, perceiving that they were no longer tied together by their affection. It's strange that my imagination, remembering that house, doesn't allow more than grays, shadows, shades; but when I evoke that hour, the strident green of the felt, the red and white of the billiard balls, and the tiny cube of blue chalk begin to swell in my memory, illuminated by the hanging lamp that condemned the rest of the room to darkness. Following one of the many family rituals, Aunt Matilde's refined voice would rescue each of her brothers from the darkness as his turn came up: 'Your shot, Gustavo . . .'

And cue in hand, Uncle Gustavo would lean over the green of the table, his face lit up, fragile as paper, the nobility of it strangely contradicted by his small, close-set eyes. When his turn was over, he retreated into the shadows, where he puffed on a cigar whose smoke floated lackadaisically off, dissolved by the darkness of the ceiling. Then their sister would say: 'Your shot, Armando . . .'

And Uncle Armando's soft, timid face, his great blue eyes shielded by gold-framed glasses, would descend into the light. His game was generally bad, because he was the 'baby,' as Aunt Matilde sometimes called him. After the comments elicited by his game, he would take refuge behind the newspaper and Aunt Matilde would say: 'Pedro, your shot . . .'

I held my breath watching my father lean over to shoot; I held it seeing him succumb to his sister's command, and, my heart in a knot, I prayed he would rebel against the established order. Of course, I couldn't know that that rigid order was in itself a kind of rebellion invented by them against the chaotic, so that the terrible hand of what cannot be explained or solved would never touch them. Then my father would lean over the green felt, his soft glance measuring the distances and positions of the balls. He would make his play and afterwards heave a sigh, his moustache and goatee fluttering a little around his half-open mouth. Then he would hand me his cue to chalk with the little blue cube. By assigning me this small role, he let me touch at least the periphery of the circle that tied him to his brothers and sister, without letting me become more than tangential to it.

Afterwards Aunt Matilde played. She was the best shot. Seeing her ugly face, built up it seemed out of the defects of her brothers' faces, descend into the light, I knew she would win; she had to win. And yet . . . didn't I see a spark of joy in those tiny eyes in the middle of that face, as irregular as a suddenly clenched fist, when by accident one of the men managed to defeat her? That drop of joy was because, although she might want to, she could never have *let* them win. That would have been to introduce the mysterious element of love into a game which should not include it, because affection had to remain in its place, without overflowing to warp the precise reality of a carom.

3

I never liked dogs. Perhaps I had been frightened by one as a baby, I don't remember, but they have always annoyed me. In any case, at that time my dislike of animals was irrelevant since we didn't have any dogs in the house; I didn't go out very often, so there were few opportunities for them to molest me. For my uncles and father, dogs, as well as the rest of the animal kingdom, did not exist. Cows, of course, supplied the cream that enriched our Sunday dessert brought in on a silver tray; and birds chirped pleasantly at dusk in the elm tree, the only inhabitant of the garden behind our house. The animal kingdom existed only to the extent that it contributed to the comfort of their persons. It is needless to say, then, that the existence of dogs, especially our ragged city strays, never even grazed their imaginations.

It's true that occasionally, coming home from Mass on Sunday, a dog might cross our path, but it was easy to ignore it. Aunt Matilde, who always walked ahead with me, simply chose not to see it, and some steps behind us, my father and uncles strolled discussing problems too important to allow their attention to be drawn by anything so banal as a stray dog.

Sometimes Aunt Matilde and I went early to Mass to take communion. I was almost never able to concentrate on receiving the sacrament, because generally the idea that she was watching me without actually looking at me occupied the first plane of my mind. Although her eyes were directed toward the altar or her head bowed before the Almighty, any movement I made attracted her attention, so that coming out of church, she would tell me with hidden reproach that doubt-less some flea trapped in the pews had prevented my concentrating on the thought that we shall all meet death in the end and on praying for it not to be too painful, for that was the purpose of Mass, prayer, and communion.

It was one of those mornings.

A fine mist was threatening to transform itself into a storm, and the quebracho paving extended its neat glistening fan shapes from sidewalk to sidewalk, bisected by the streetcar rails. I was cold and wanted to get home, so I hurried the pace under Aunt Matilde's black umbrella. Few people were out because it was early. A colored gentleman greeted us without tipping his hat. My aunt then proceeded to explain her dislike of persons of mixed race, but suddenly, near where we were walking, a streetcar I didn't hear coming braked loudly, bringing her monologue to an end. The conductor put his head out the window: 'Stupid dog!' he shouted.

We stopped to look. A small white bitch escaped from under the wheels, and, limping painfully with its tail between its legs, took refuge in a doorway. The streetcar rolled off.

'These dogs, it's the limit the way they let them run loose . . .' protested Aunt Matilde.

Continuing on our way, we passed the dog cowering in the doorway. It was small and white, with legs too short for its body and an ugly pointed nose that revealed a whole genealogy of alleyway misalliances, the product of different races running around the city for generations looking for food in garbage cans and harbor refuse. It was soaking wet, weak, shivering with the cold or a fever. Passing in front of it, I witnessed a strange sight: my aunt's and the dog's eyes met. I couldn't see the expression on my aunt's face. I only saw the dog look at her, taking possession of her glance, whatever it contained, merely because she was looking at it.

We headed home. A few paces further on, when I had almost forgotten the dog, my aunt startled me by turning abruptly around and exclaiming: 'Shoo, now! Get along with you!'

She had turned around completely certain of finding it following us and I trembled with the unspoken question prompted by my surprise: 'How did she know?' She couldn't have heard it because the dog was following us at some distance. But she didn't doubt it. Did the glance that passed between them, of which I had only seen the mechanical part—the dog's head slightly raised toward Aunt Matilde, Aunt Matilde's head slightly turned toward it—did it contain some secret agreement, some promise of loyalty I hadn't perceived? I don't know. In any case, when she turned to shoo the dog, her voice seemed to contain an impotent desire to put off a destiny that had already been accomplished. Probably I say all this in hindsight, my imagination imbuing something trivial with special meaning. Nevertheless, I certainly felt surprise, almost fear, at the sight of my aunt suddenly losing her composure and condescending to turn around, thereby conceding rank to a sick, dirty dog following us for reasons that could not have any importance.

We arrived home. We climbed the steps and the animal stayed down below, watching us through the torrential rain that had just begun. We went inside, and the delectable smell of a post-communion breakfast erased the dog from my mind. I had never felt the protectiveness of our house so deeply as I did that morning; the security of those walls delimiting my world had never been so delightful to me.

What did I do the rest of the day? I don't remember, but I suppose I did the usual thing: read magazines, did homework, wandered up and down the stairs, went to the kitchen to ask what was for dinner.

On one of my tours through the empty rooms—my uncles got up late on rainy Sundays, excusing themselves from church—I pulled a curtain back to see if the rain was letting up. The storm went on. Standing at the foot of the steps, still shivering and watching the house, I saw the white dog again. I let go of the curtain to avoid seeing it there, soaking wet and apparently mesmerized. Suddenly, behind me, from the dark part of the sitting room, Aunt Matilde's quiet voice reached me, as she leaned over to touch a match to the wood piled in the fireplace: 'Is she still there?'

'Who?'

I knew perfectly well who.

'The white dog.'

I answered that it was. But my voice was uncertain in forming the syllables, as if somehow my aunt's question was pulling down the walls around us, letting the rain and the inclement wind enter and take over the house.

4

That must have been the last of the winter storms, because I remember quite vividly that in the following days the weather cleared and the nights got warmer.

The white dog remained posted at our door, ever trembling, watching the window as though looking for somebody. In the morning, as I left for school, I would try to scare it away, but as soon as I got on the bus, I saw it peep timidly around the corner or from behind a lamppost. The servants tried to drive it away too, but their attempts were just as futile as my own, because the dog always came back, as if to stay near our house was a temptation it had to obey, no matter how dangerous.

One night we were all saying good night to one another at the foot of the stairs. Uncle Gustavo, who always took charge of turning off the lights, had taken care of all of them except that of the staircase, leaving the great dark space of the vestibule populated with darker clots of furniture. Aunt Matilde, who was telling Uncle Armando to open his window to let some air in, suddenly fell silent, leaving her good nights unfinished. The rest of us, who had begun to climb the stairs, stopped cold.

'What's the matter?' asked my father, coming down a step.

'Go upstairs,' murmured Aunt Matilde, turning to gaze into the shadows of the vestibule.

But we didn't go upstairs.

The silence of the sitting room, generally so spacious, filled up with the secret voice of each object—a grain of dirt slipping down between the old wallpaper and the wall, wood creaking, a loose window pane rattling—and those brief seconds were flooded with sounds. Someone else was in the room with us. A small white shape stood out in the shadows near the service door. It was the dog, who limped slowly across the vestibule in the direction of Aunt Matilde, and without even looking at her lay down at her feet.

It was as if the dog's stillness made movement possible for us as we watched the scene. My father came down two steps, Uncle Gustavo turned on the lights, Uncle Armando heavily climbed the stairs and shut himself into his room.

'What is this?' my father asked.

Aunt Matilde remained motionless.

'How could she have got in?' she asked herself suddenly.

Her question seemed to imply a feat: in this lamentable condition, the dog had leaped over walls, or climbed through a broken window in the basement, or evaded the servants' vigilance by slipping through a door left open by accident.

'Matilde, call for somebody to get it out of here,' my father said, and went upstairs followed by Uncle Gustavo.

The two of us stood looking at the dog.

'She's filthy,' she said in a low voice. 'And she has a fever. Look, she's hurt . . .'

She called one of the servants to take her away, ordering her to give the dog food and call the veterinarian the next day.

'Is it going to stay in the house?' I asked.

'How can she go outside like that?' Aunt Matilde murmured. 'She has to get better before we can put her out. And she'll have to get better quickly, because I don't want any animals in the house.' Then she added: 'Get upstairs to bed.'

She followed the servant who was taking the dog away.

I recognized Aunt Matilde's usual need to make sure everything around her went well, the strength and deftness that made her the undoubted queen of things immediate, so secure inside her limitations that for her the only necessary thing was to correct flaws, mistakes not of intention or motive, but of state of being. The white dog, therefore, was going to get well. She herself would take charge of that, because the dog had come within her sphere of power. The veterinarian would bandage the dog's foot under her watchful eyes, and, protected by gloves and a towel, she herself would undertake to clean its sores with disinfectants that would make it whimper. Aunt Matilde remained deaf to those whimpers, certain, absolutely certain, that what she was doing was for the dog's good.

And so it was.

The dog stayed in the house. It wasn't that I could see it, but I knew the balance between the people who lived there, and the presence of any stranger, even if in the basement, would establish a difference in the order of things. Something, something informed me of its presence under the same roof as myself. Perhaps that something was not so very imponderable. Sometimes I saw Aunt Matilde with rubber gloves in her hand, carrying a vial full of red liquid. I found scraps of meat on a dish in a basement passageway when I went down to look at a bicycle I had recently been given. Sometimes, the suspicion of a bark would reach my ears faintly, absorbed by floors and walls.

One afternoon I went down to the kitchen and the white dog came in, painted like a clown with the red disinfectant. The servants threw it out unceremoniously. But I could see it wasn't limping anymore, and its once droopy tail now curled up like a plume, leaving its hindquarters shamelessly exposed.

That afternoon I said to Aunt Matilde: 'When are you going to get rid of it?'

'What?' she asked.

She knew perfectly well what I meant.

'The white dog.'

'She's not well yet,' she answered.

Later on, I was about to bring up the subject again, to tell her that even if the dog wasn't completely well yet, there was nothing to prevent it from standing on its hind legs and rooting around in the garbage pails for food. But I never did, because I think that was the night Aunt Matilde, after losing the first round of billiards, decided she didn't feel like playing anymore. Her brothers went on playing and she, sunk in the big leather sofa, reminded them of their turns. After a while she made a mistake in the shooting order. Everybody was disconcerted for a moment, but the correct order was soon restored by the men, who rejected chance if it was not favorable. But I had seen.

It was as if Aunt Matilde was not there. She breathed at my side as always. The deep, muffling rug sank as usual under her feet. Her hands, crossed calmly on her lap—perhaps more calmly than on other evenings—weighed on her skirt. How is it that one feels a person's absence so clearly when that person's heart is in another place? Only her heart was absent, but the voice she used to call her brothers contained new meanings because it came from that other place.

The next nights were also marred by this almost invisible smudge of her absence. She stopped playing billiards and calling out turns altogether. The men seemed not to notice. But perhaps they did, because the matches became shorter, and I noted that the deference with which they treated her grew infinitesimally.

One night, as we came out of the dining room, the dog made its appearance in the vestibule and joined the family. The men, as usual, waited at the library door for their sister to lead the way into the billiard room, this time gracefully followed by the dog. They made no comment, as if they hadn't seen it, and began their match as on other nights.

The dog sat at Aunt Matilde's feet, very quiet, its lively eyes examining the room and watching the players' maneuvers, as if it was greatly amused. It was plump now, and its coat, its whole body glowed, from its quivering nose to its tail, always ready to wag. How long had the dog been in the house? A month? Longer, perhaps. But in that month Aunt Matilde had made it get well, caring for it without displays of emotion, but with the great wisdom of her bony hands dedicated to repairing what was damaged. Implacable in the face of its pain and whimpers, she had cured its wounds. Its foot was healed. She had disinfected it, fed it, bathed it, and now the white dog was whole again.

And yet none of this seemed to unite her to the dog. Perhaps she accepted it in the same way that my uncles that night had accepted its presence: to reject it would have given it more importance than it could have for them. I saw Aunt Matilde tranquil, collected, full of a new feeling that did not quite overflow to touch its object, and now we were six beings separated by a distance vaster than stretches of rug and air.

It happened during one of Uncle Armando's shots, when he dropped the little cube of blue chalk. Instantly, obeying a reflex that linked it to its picaresque past in the streets, the dog scampered to the chalk, yanked it away from Uncle Armando who had leaned over to pick it up, and held it in its mouth. Then a surprising thing happened. Aunt Matilde, suddenly coming apart, burst out in uncontrollable guffaws that shook her whole body for a few seconds. We were paralyzed. Hearing her, the dog dropped the chalk and ran to her, its tail wagging and held high, and jumped on her skirt. Aunt Matilde's laughter subsided, but Uncle Armando, vexed, left the room to avoid witnessing this collapse of order through the intrusion of the absurd. Uncle Gustavo and my father kept on playing billiards; now more than ever it was essential not to see, not to see anything, not to make remarks, not even to allude to the episode, and perhaps in this way to keep something from moving forward.

I did not find Aunt Matilde's guffaws amusing. It was only too clear that something dark had happened. The dog lay still on her lap. The crack of the billiard balls as they collided, precise and discrete, seemed to lead Aunt Matilde's hand first from its place on the sofa to her skirt, and then to the back of the sleeping dog. Seeing that expressionless hand resting there, I also observed that the tension I had never before recognized on my aunt's face—I never suspected it was anything other than dignity—had dissolved, and a great peace was softening her features. I could not resist what I did. Obeying something stronger than my own will, I slid closer to her on the sofa. I waited for her to beckon to me with a look or include me with a smile, but she didn't, because their new relationship was too exclusive; there was no place for me. There were only those two united beings. I didn't like it, but I was left out. And the men remained isolated, because they had not paid attention to the dangerous invitation to which Aunt Matilde had dared to listen.

5

Coming home from school in the afternoon, I would go straight downstairs and, mounting my new bicycle, would circle round and round in the narrow garden behind the house, around the elm tree and the pair of iron benches. On the other side of the wall, the neighbors' walnut trees were beginning to show signs of spring, but I didn't keep track of the seasons and their gifts because I had more serious things to think about. And as I knew nobody came down to the garden until the suffocations of midsummer made it essential, it was the best place to think about what was happening in our house.

Superficially it might be said nothing was happening. But how could one remain calm in the face of the curious relationship that had arisen between my aunt and the white dog? It was as if Aunt Matilde, after punctiliously serving and conforming to her unequal life, had at last found her equal, someone who spoke her innermost language, and as among women, they carried on an intimacy full of pleasantries and agreeable refinements. They ate bonbons that came in boxes tied with frivolous bows. My aunt arranged oranges, pineapples, grapes on the tall fruit stands, and the dog watched as if to criticize her taste or deliver an opinion. She seemed to have discovered a more benign region of life in this sharing of pleasantries, so much so that now everything had lost its importance in the shadow of this new world of affection.

Frequently, when passing her bedroom door, I would hear a guffaw like the one that had dashed the old order of her life to the ground that night, or I would hear her conversing—not soliloquizing as when talking to me—with someone whose voice I could not hear. It was the new life. The culprit, the dog, slept in her room in a basket—elegant, feminine, and absurd to my way of thinking—and followed her everywhere, except into the dining room. It was forbidden to go in there, but waited for its friend to emerge, followed her to the library or the billiard room, wherever we were going, and sat beside her or on her lap, and from time to time, sly looks of understanding would pass between them.

How was this possible? I asked myself. Why had she waited until now to overflow and begin a dialogue for the first time in her life? At times she seemed insecure about the dog, as if afraid the day might come when it would go away, leaving her alone with all this new abundance on her hands. Or was she still concerned about the dog's health? It was too strange. These ideas floated like blurs in my imagination while I listened to the gravel crunching under the wheels of my bicycle. What was not blurry, on the other hand, was my vehement desire to fall seriously ill, to see if that way I too could gain a similar relationship. The dog's illness had been the cause of it all. Without that, my aunt would never have become linked to it. But I had an iron constitution, and furthermore it was clear that inside Aunt Matilde's heart there was room for only one love at a time, especially if it were so intense.

My father and uncles didn't seem to notice any change at all. The dog was quiet, and abandoning its street manners it seemed to acquire Aunt Matilde's somewhat dignified mien; but it preserved all the impudence of a female whom the vicissitudes of life have not been able to shock, as well as its good temper and its liking for adventure. It was easier for the men to accept than reject it since the latter would at least have meant speaking, and perhaps even an uncomfortable revision of their standards of security.

One night, when the pitcher of lemonade had already made its appearance on the library credenza, cooling that corner of the shadows, and the windows had been opened to the air, my father stopped abruptly at the entrance to the billiard room.

'What is this?' he exclaimed, pointing at the floor.

The three men gathered in consternation to look at a tiny round puddle on the waxed floor.

'Matilde!' Uncle Gustavo cried.

She came over to look and blushed with shame. The dog had taken refuge under the billiard table in the next room. Turning toward the table, my father saw it there, and suddenly changing course he left the room, followed by his brothers, heading toward the bedrooms, where each of them locked himself in, silent and alone.

Aunt Matilde said nothing. She went up to her room followed by the dog. I stayed in the library with a glass of lemonade in my hand, looking out at the summer sky and listening, anxiously listening to distant foghorns and the noise of the unknown city, terrible and at the same time desirable, stretched out under the stars.

Then I heard Aunt Matilde descend. She appeared with her hat on and her keys jingling in her hand.

'Go to bed,' she said. 'I'm taking her for a walk on the street so she can take care of her business there.'

Then she added something that made me nervous: 'The night's so pretty . . .

And she went out.

From that night on, instead of going upstairs after dinner to turn down her brothers' beds, she went to her room, put on her hat, and came down again, her keys jingling. She went out with the dog, not saying a word to anybody. My uncles and my father and I stayed in the billiard room, or, as the season wore on, sat on the benches in the garden, with the rustling elm and the clear sky pressing down on us. These nightly walks of Aunt Matilde's were never mentioned, there was never any indication that anybody knew anything important had changed in the house; but an element had been introduced there that contradicted all order.

At first Aunt Matilde would stay out at most fifteen or twenty minutes, returning promptly to take coffee with us and exchange a few commonplaces. Later, her outings inexplicably took more time. She was no longer a woman who walked her dog for reasons of hygiene; out there in the streets, in the city, there was something powerful attracting her. Waiting for her, my father glanced furtively at his pocket watch, and if she was very late, Uncle Gustavo went up to the second floor, as if he had forgotten something there, to watch from the balcony. But they never said anything. Once when Aunt Matilde's walk had taken too long, my father paced back and forth along the path between the hydrangeas, their flowers like blue eyes watching the night. Uncle Gustavo threw away a cigar he couldn't light satisfactorily, and then another, stamping it out under his heel. Uncle Armando overturned a cup of coffee. I watched, waiting for an eventual explosion, for them to say something, for them to express their anxiety and fill those endless minutes stretching on and on without the presence of Aunt Matilde. It was half past twelve when she came home.

'Why did you wait up for me?' she said smiling.

She carried her hat in her hand and her hair, ordinarily so neat, was disheveled. I noted that daubs of mud stained her perfect shoes.

'What happened to you?'

'Nothing,' was her answer, and with that she closed forever any possible right her brothers might have had to interfere with those unknown hours, happy or tragic or insignificant, which were now her life.

I say they were her life, because in those instants she remained with us before going to her room, with the dog, muddy too, next to her, I perceived an animation in her eyes, a cheerful restlessness like the animal's, as if her eyes had recently bathed in scenes never before witnessed, to which we had no access. These two were companions. The night protected them. They belonged to the noises, to the foghorns that wafted over docks, dark or lamplit streets, houses, factories, and parks, finally reaching my ears.

Her walks with the dog continued. Now she said good night to us right after dinner, and all of us went to our rooms, my father, Uncle Gustavo, Uncle Armando, and myself. But none of us fell asleep until we heard her come in, late, sometimes very late, when the light of dawn already brightened the top of our elm tree. Only after she was heard closing her bedroom door would the paces by which my father measured his room stop, and a window be closed by one of her brothers to shut out the night, which had ceased being dangerous for the time being.

Once after she had come in very late, I thought I heard her singing very softly and sweetly, so I cracked open my door and looked out. She passed in front of my door, the white dog cuddled in her arms. Her face looked surprisingly young and perfect, although it was a little dirty, and I saw there was a tear in her skirt. This woman was capable of anything; she had her whole life before her. I went to bed terrified that this would be the end.

And I wasn't wrong. Because one night shortly afterwards, Aunt Matilde went out for a walk with the dog and never came back.

We waited up all night long, each one of us in his room, and she didn't come home. The next day nobody said anything. But the silent waiting went on, and we all hovered silently, without seeming to, around the windows of the house, watching for her. From that first day fear made the harmonious dignity of the three brothers' faces collapse, and they aged rapidly in a very short time.

'Your aunt went on a trip,' the cook told me once, when I finally dared to ask. But I knew it wasn't true.

Life went on in our house as if Aunt Matilde were still living with us. It's true they had a habit of gathering in the library, and perhaps locked in there they talked, managing to overcome the wall of fear that isolated them, giving free rein to their fears and doubts. But I'm not sure. Several times a visitor came who didn't belong to our world, and they would lock themselves in with him. But I don't believe he had brought them news of a possible investigation; perhaps he was nothing more than the boss of a longshoremen's union who was coming to claim damages for some accident. The door of the library was too thick, too heavy, and I never knew if Aunt Matilde, dragged along by the white dog, had got lost in the city, or in death, or in a region more mysterious than either.

GUSTAVE FLAUBERT

(1821–1880)

GUSTAVE FLAUBERT was born in Rouen, France; his father was a prominent surgeon. Acceding to his father's wishes, Flaubert studied law in Paris from 1841 until 1843; in that period he suffered a nervous breakdown. He gave up the study of law to pursue literature, spending most of his life in Croisset, near Rouen, where he lived with his mother and sister. His classic *Madame Bovary,* which portrays the adulterous love and suicide of a young wife, appeared in 1856. Notwithstanding the novel's exemplary control of technique and language, its author faced prosecution, ultimately unsuccessful, on moral grounds. *Salammbô,* a novel of ancient Carthage, was published in 1863, followed by *L'éducation sentimentale* in 1870, *The Temptation of St. Anthony* in 1874, and in 1877, *Three Tales,* one of which is his masterly story "A Simple Heart." An unfinished satire, *Bouvard and Pécuchet,* was published posthumously in 1881. Nine volumes of his letters appeared between 1926 and 1933. In his later years, Flaubert achieved considerable literary fame. Henry James, Ivan Turgenev, and Guy de Maupassant were among those who gathered on Sunday afternoons at his Paris home.

The "simple heart" of Flaubert's story belongs to Félicité, who after her parents' death grows up without encountering love of any kind. She finds it for herself over and over again, only to lose it each time. That she loves despite repeated sorrows and disappointments is a given of her nature; it is tied, Flaubert suggests, precisely to her unworldliness. After her young girl's romanticism has been both stirred and betrayed in a first, furtive affair, she lives out her life on the strength of her ability to recognize love in its various forms: romantic, maternal, between friends, filial, of creatures, religious. The story of Félicité's simple heart becomes a story of love's all-encompassing strength.

A *Simple Heart*

I

Madame Aubain's servant Félicité was the envy of the ladies of Pont-l'Évêque for half a century.

She received four pounds a year. For that she was cook and general servant, and did the sewing, washing, and ironing; she could bridle a horse, fatten poultry, and churn butter—and she remained faithful to her mistress, unamiable as the latter was.

Mme Aubain had married a gay bachelor without money who died at the beginning of 1809, leaving her with two small children and a quantity of debts. She then sold all her property except the farms of Toucques and Geffosses, which brought in two hundred pounds a year at most, and left her house in Saint-Melaine for a less expensive one that had belonged to her family and was situated behind the market.

This house had a slate roof and stood between an alley and a lane that went down to the river. There was an unevenness in the levels of the rooms which made you stumble. A narrow hall divided the kitchen from the "parlor" where Mme Aubain spent her day, sitting in a wicker easy chair by the window. Against the panels, which were painted white, was a row of eight mahogany chairs. On an old piano under the barometer a heap of wooden and cardboard boxes rose like a pyramid. A stuffed armchair stood on either side of the Louis Quinze chimney piece, which was in yellow marble with a clock in the middle of it modeled like a temple of Vesta. The whole room was a little musty, as the floor was lower than the garden.

The first floor began with "Madame's" room: very large, with a pale-flowered wallpaper and a portrait of "Monsieur" as a dandy of the period. It led to a smaller room, where there were two children's cots without mattresses. Next came the drawing room, which was always shut up and full of furniture covered with sheets. Then there was a corridor leading to a study. The shelves of a large bookcase were respectably lined with books and papers, and its three wings surrounded a broad writing table in dark wood. The two panels at the end of the room were covered with pen drawings, water-color landscapes, and engravings by Audran, all relics of better days and vanished splendor. Félicité's room on the top floor got its light from a dormer window, which looked over the meadows.

She rose at daybreak to be in time for Mass, and worked till evening without stopping. Then, when dinner was over, the plates and dishes in order, and the door shut fast, she thrust the log under the ashes and went to sleep in front of the hearth with her rosary in her hand. Félicité was the stubbornest of all bargainers; and as for cleanness, the polish on her saucepans was the despair of other servants. Thrifty in all things, she ate slowly, gathering off the table in her fingers the crumbs of her loaf—a twelve-pound loaf expressly baked for her, which lasted for three weeks.

At all times of year she wore a print handkerchief fastened with a pin behind, a bonnet that covered her hair, gray stockings, a red skirt, and a bibbed apron—such as hospital nurses wear—over her jacket.

Her face was thin and her voice sharp. At twenty-five she looked like forty. From fifty onwards she seemed of no particular age; and with her silence, straight figure, and precise movements she was like a woman made of wood, and going by clockwork.

II

She had had her love story like another.

Her father, a mason, had been killed by falling off some scaffolding. Then her mother died, her sisters scattered, and a farmer took her in and employed her, while she was still quite little, to herd the cows at pasture. She shivered in rags and would lie flat on the ground to drink water from the ponds; she was beaten for nothing, and finally turned out for the theft of a shilling which she did not steal. She went to another farm, where she became dairymaid; and as she was liked by her employers her companions were jealous of her.

One evening in August (she was then eighteen) they took her to the assembly at Colleville. She was dazed and stupefied in an instant by the noise of the fiddlers, the lights in the trees, the gay medley of dresses, the lace, the gold crosses, and the throng of people jigging all together. While she kept shyly apart a young man with a well-to-do air, who was leaning on the shaft of a cart and smoking his pipe, came up to ask her to dance. He treated her to cider, coffee, and cake, and bought her a silk handkerchief; and then, imagining she had guessed his meaning, offered to see her home. At the edge of a field of oats he pushed her roughly down. She was frightened and began to cry out; and he went off.

One evening later she was on the Beaumont road. A big hay wagon was moving slowly along; she wanted to get in front of it, and as she brushed past the wheels she recognized Theodore. He greeted her quite calmly, saying she must excuse it all because it was "the fault of the drink." She could not think of any answer and wanted to run away.

He began at once to talk about the harvest and the worthies of the commune, for his father had left Colleville for the farm at Les Écots, so that now he and she were neighbors. "Ah!" she said. He added that they thought of settling him in life. Well, he was in no hurry; he was waiting for a wife to his fancy. She dropped her head; and then he asked her if she thought of marrying. She answered with a smile that it was meant to make fun of her.

"But I am not, I swear!"—and he passed his left hand round her waist. She walked in the support of his embrace; their steps grew slower. The wind was soft, the stars glittered, the huge wagonload of hay swayed in front of them, and dust rose from the dragging steps of the four horses. Then, without a word of command, they turned to the right. He clasped her once more in his arms, and she disappeared into the shadow.

The week after Theodore secured some assignations with her.

They met at the end of farmyards, behind a wall, or under a solitary tree. She was not innocent as young ladies are—she had learned knowledge from the animals—but her reason and the instinct of her honor would not let her fall. Her resistance exasperated Theodore's passion; so much so that to satisfy it—or perhaps quite artlessly—he made her an offer of marriage. She was in doubt whether to trust him, but he swore great oaths of fidelity.

Soon he confessed to something troublesome; the year before his parents had bought him a substitute for the army, but any day he might be taken again, and the idea of serving was a terror to him. Félicité took this cowardice of his as a sign of affection, and it redoubled hers. She stole away at night to see him, and when she reached their meeting place Theodore racked her with his anxieties and urgings.

At last he declared that he would go himself to the prefecture for information, and would tell her the result on the following Sunday, between eleven and midnight.

When the moment came she sped toward her lover. Instead of him she found one of his friends.

He told her that she would not see Theodore any more. To ensure himself against conscription he had married an old woman, Madame Lehoussais, of Toucques, who was very rich.

There was an uncontrollable burst of grief. She threw herself on the ground, screamed, called to the God of mercy, and moaned by herself in the fields till daylight came. Then she came back to the farm and announced that she was going to leave; and at the end of the month she received her wages, tied all her small belongings with a handkerchief, and went to Pont-l-Évêque.

In front of the inn there she made inquiries of a woman in a widow's cap, who, as it happened, was just looking for a cook. The girl did not know much, but her willingness seemed so great and her demands so small that Mme Aubain ended by saying:

"Very well, then, I will take you."

A quarter of an hour afterwards Félicité was installed in her house.

She lived there at first in a tremble, as it were, at "the style of the house" and the memory of "Monsieur" floating over it all. Paul and Virginie, the first aged seven and the other hardly four, seemed to her beings of a precious substance; she carried them on her back like a horse; it was a sorrow to her that Mme Aubain would not let her kiss them every minute. And yet she was happy there. Her grief had melted in the pleasantness of things all round.

Every Thursday regular visitors came in for a game of boston, and Félicité got the cards and foot-warmers ready beforehand. They arrived punctually at eight and left before the stroke of eleven.

On Monday mornings the dealer who lodged in the covered passage spread out all his old iron on the ground. Then a hum of voices began to fill the town, mingled with the neighing of horses, bleating of lambs, grunting of pigs, and the sharp rattle of carts along the street. About noon, when the market was at its height, you might see a tall, hook-nosed old countryman with his cap pushed back making his appearance at the door. It was Robelin, the farmer of Geffosses. A little later came Liébard, the farmer from Toucques—short, red, and corpulent—in a gray jacket and gaiters shod with spurs.

Both had poultry or cheese to offer their landlord. Félicité was invariably a match for their cunning and they went away filled with respect for her.

At vague intervals Mme Aubain had a visit from the Marquis de Gremanville, one of her uncles, who had ruined himself by debauchery and now lived at Falaise on his last remaining morsel of land. He invariably came at the luncheon hour, with a dreadful poodle whose paws left all the furniture in a mess. In spite of efforts to show his breeding, which he carried to the point of raising his hat every time he mentioned "my late father," habit was too strong for him; he poured himself out glass after glass and fired off improper remarks. Félicité edged him politely out of the house—"You have had enough, Monsieur de Gremanville! Another time!"—and she shut the door on him.

She opened it with pleasure to M. Bourais, who had been a lawyer. His boldness, his white stock, frilled shirt, and roomy brown coat, his way of rounding the arm as he took snuff—his whole person, in fact, created that disturbance of mind which overtakes us at the sight of extraordinary men.

As he looked after the property of "Madame" he remained shut up with her for hours in "Monsieur's" study, though all the time he was afraid of compromising himself. He respected the magistracy immensely, and had some pretensions to Latin.

To combine instruction and amusement he gave the children a geography book made up of a series of prints. They represented scenes in different parts of the world: cannibals with feathers on their heads, a monkey carrying off a young lady, Bedouins in the desert, the harpooning of a whale, and so on. Paul explained these engravings to Félicité; and that, in fact, was the whole of her literary education. The children's education was undertaken by Guyot, a poor creature employed at the town hall, who was famous for his beautiful hand and sharpened his penknife on his boots.

When the weather was bright the household set off early for a day at Geffosses Farm.

Its courtyard is on a slope, with the farmhouse in the middle, and the sea looks like a gray streak in the distance.

Félicité brought slices of cold meat out of her basket, and they breakfasted in a room adjoining the dairy. It was the only surviving fragment of a country house which was now no more. The wallpaper hung in tatters, and quivered in the drafts. Mme Aubain sat with bowed head, overcome by her memories; the children became afraid to speak. "Why don't you play, then?" she would say, and off they went.

Paul climbed into the barn, caught birds, played at ducks and drakes over the pond, or hammered with his stick on the big casks which boomed like drums. Virginie fed the rabbits or dashed off to pick cornflowers, her quick legs showing their embroidered little drawers.

One autumn evening they went home by the fields. The moon was in its first quarter, lighting part of the sky; and mist floated like a scarf over the windings of the Toucques. Cattle, lying out in the middle of the grass, looked quietly at the four people as they passed. In the third meadow some of them got up and made a half circle in front of the walkers. "There's nothing to be afraid of," said Félicité, as she stroked the nearest on the back with a kind of crooning song; he wheeled round and others did the same. But when they crossed the next pasture there was a formidable bellow. It was a bull, hidden by the mist. Mme Aubain was about to run. "No! no! don't go so fast!" They mended their pace, however, and heard a loud breathing behind them which came nearer. His hoofs thudded on the meadow grass like hammers; why, he was galloping now! Félicité turned round, and tore up clods of earth with both hands and threw them in his eyes. He lowered his muzzle, waved his horns, and quivered with fury, bellowing terribly. Mme Aubain, now at the end of the pasture with her two little ones, was looking wildly for a place to get over the high bank. Félicité was retreating, still with her face to the bull, keeping up a shower of clods which blinded him, and crying all the time, "Be quick! be quick!"

Mme Aubain went down into the ditch, pushed Virginie first and then Paul, fell several times as she tried to climb the bank, and managed it at last by dint of courage.

The bull had driven Félicité to bay against a rail fence; his slaver was streaming into her face; another second, and he would have gored her. She had just time to slip between two of the rails and the big animal stopped short in amazement.

This adventure was talked of at Pont-l'Évêque for many a year. Félicité did not pride herself on it in the least, not having the barest suspicion that she had done anything heroic.

Virginie was the sole object of her thoughts, for the child developed a nervous complaint as a result of her fright, and M. Poupart, the doctor, advised seabathing at Trouville. It was not a frequented place then. Mme Aubain collected information, consulted Bourais, and made preparations as though for a long journey.

Her luggage started a day in advance, in Liébard's cart. The next day he brought round two horses, one of which had a lady's saddle with a velvet back to it, while a cloak was rolled up to make a kind of seat on the crupper of the other. Mme Aubain rode on that, behind the farmer. Félicité took charge of Virginie, and Paul mounted M. Lechaptois' donkey, lent on condition that great care was taken of it.

The road was so bad that its five miles took two hours. The horses sank in the mud up to their pasterns, and their haunches jerked abruptly in the effort to get out; or else they stumbled in the ruts, and at other moments had to jump. In some places Liébard's mare came suddenly to a halt. He waited patiently until she went on again, talking about the people who had properties along the road, and adding moral reflections to their history. So it was that as they were in the middle of Toucques, and passed under some windows bowered with nasturtiums, he shrugged his shoulders and said: "There's a Mme Lehoussais lives there; instead of taking a young man she . . ." Félicité did not hear the rest; the horses were trotting and the donkey galloping. They all turned down a bypath; a gate swung open and two boys appeared; and the party dismounted in front of a manure heap at the very threshold of the farmhouse door.

When Mme Liébard saw her mistress she gave lavish signs of joy. She served her a luncheon with a sirloin of beef, tripe, black pudding, a fricassee of chicken, sparkling cider, a fruit tart, and brandied plums; seasoning it all with compliments to Madame, who seemed in better health; Mademoiselle, who was "splendid" now; and Monsieur Paul, who had "filled out" wonderfully. Nor did she forget their deceased grandparents, whom the Liébards had known, as they had been in the service of the family for several generations. The farm, like them, had the stamp of antiquity. The beams on the ceiling were worm-eaten, the walls blackened with smoke, and the windowpanes gray with dust. There was an oak dresser laden with every sort of useful article—jugs, plates, pewter bowls, wolftraps, and sheep shears; and a huge syringe made the children laugh. There was not a tree in the three courtyards without mushrooms growing at the bottom of it or a tuft of mistletoe on its boughs. Several of them had been thrown down by the wind. They had taken root again at the middle; and all were bending under their wealth of apples. The thatched roofs, like brown velvet and of varying thickness, withstood the heaviest squalls. The cart shed, however, was falling into ruin. Mme Aubain said she would see about it, and ordered the animals to be saddled again.

It was another half-hour before they reached Trouville. The little caravan dismounted to pass Écores—it was an overhanging cliff with boats below it—and three minutes later they were at the end of the quay and entered the courtyard of the Golden Lamb, kept by good Mme David.

From the first days of their stay Virginie began to feel less weak, thanks to the change of air and the effect of the sea baths. These, for want of a bathing dress, she took in her chemise; and her nurse dressed her afterwards in a coastguard's cabin which was used by the bathers.

In the afternoons they took the donkey and went off beyond the Black Rocks, in the direction of Hennequeville. The path climbed at first through ground with dells in it like the green sward of a park, and then reached a plateau where grass fields and arable lay side by side. Hollies rose stiffly out of the briary tangle at the edge of the road; and here and there a great withered tree made zigzags in the blue air with its branches.

They nearly always rested in a meadow, with Deauville on their left, Havre on their right, and the open sea in front. It glittered in the sunshine, smooth as a mirror and so quiet that its murmur was scarcely to be heard; sparrows chirped in hiding and the immense sky arched over it all. Mme Aubain sat doing her needlework; Virginie plaited rushes by her side; Félicité pulled up lavender, and Paul was bored and anxious to start home.

Other days they crossed the Toucques in a boat and looked for shells. When the tide went out sea urchins, starfish, and jellyfish were left exposed; and the children ran in pursuit of the foam flakes which scudded in the wind. The sleepy waves broke on the sand and unrolled all along the beach; it stretched away out of sight, bounded on the land side by the dunes which parted it from the Marsh, a wide meadow shaped like an arena. As they came home that way, Trouville, on the hill slope in the background, grew bigger at every step, and its miscellaneous throng of houses seemed to break into a gay disorder.

On days when it was too hot they did not leave their room. From the dazzling brilliance outside light fell in streaks between the laths of the blinds. There were no sounds in the village; and on the pavement below not a soul. This silence round them deepened the quietness of things. In the distance, where men were calking, there was a tap of hammers as they plugged the hulls, and a sluggish breeze wafted up the smell of tar.

The chief amusement was the return of the fishing boats. They began to tack as soon as they had passed the buoys. The sails came down on two of the three masts; and they drew on with the foresail swelling like a balloon, glided through the splash of the waves, and when they had reached the middle of the harbor suddenly dropped anchor. Then the boats drew up against the quay. The sailors threw quivering fish over the side; a row of carts was waiting, and women in cotton bonnets darted out to take the baskets and give their men a kiss.

One of them came up to Félicité one day, and she entered the lodgings a little later in a state of delight. She had found a sister again—and then Nastasie Barette, "wife of Leroux," appeared, holding an infant at her breast and another child with her right hand, while on her left was a little cabin boy with his hands on his hips and a cap over his ear.

After a quarter of an hour Mme Aubain sent them off; but they were always to be found hanging about the kitchen, or encountered in the course of a walk. The husband never appeared.

Félicité was seized with affection for them. She bought them a blanket, some shirts, and a stove; it was clear that they were making a good thing out of her. Mme Aubain was annoyed by this weakness of hers, and she did not like the liberties taken by the nephew, who said "thee" and "thou" to Paul. So as Virginie was coughing and the fine weather gone, she returned to Pont-l'Évêque.

There M. Bourais enlightened her on the choice of a boys' school. The one at Caen was reputed to be the best, and Paul was sent to it. He said his good-bys bravely, content enough at going to live in a house where he would have companions.

Mme Aubain resigned herself to her son's absence as a thing that had to be. Virginie thought about it less and less. Félicité missed the noise he made. But she found an occupation to distract her; from Christmas onward she took the little girl to catechism every day.

III

After making a genuflexion at the door she walked up between the double row of chairs under the lofty nave, opened Mme Aubain's pew, sat down, and began to look about her. The choir stalls were filled with the boys on the right and the girls on the left, and the curé stood by the lectern. On a painted window in the apse the Holy Ghost looked down upon the Virgin. Another window showed her on her knees before the child Jesus, and a group carved in wood behind the altar shrine represented St. Michael overthrowing the dragon.

The priest began with a sketch of sacred history. The Garden, the Flood, the Tower of Babel, cities in flames, dying nations, and overturned idols passed like a dream before her eyes; and the dizzying vision left her with reverence for the Most High and fear of His wrath. Then she wept at the story of the Passion. Why had they crucified Him, when He loved the children, fed the multitudes, healed the blind, and had willed, in His meekness, to be born among the poor, on the dung heap of a stable? The sowings, harvests, wine presses, all the familiar things the Gospel speaks of, were a part of her life. They had been made holy by God's passing; and she loved the lambs more tenderly for her love of the Lamb, and the doves because of the Holy Ghost.

She found it hard to imagine Him in person, for He was not merely a bird, but a flame as well, and a breath at other times. It may be His light, she thought, which flits at night about the edge of the marshes, His breathing which drives on the clouds, His voice which gives harmony to the bells; and she would sit rapt in adoration, enjoying the cool walls and the quiet of the church.

Of doctrines she understood nothing—did not even try to understand. The curé discoursed, the children repeated their lesson, and finally she went to sleep, waking up with a start when their wooden shoes clattered on the flagstones as they went away.

It was thus that Félicité, whose religious education had been neglected in her youth, learned the catechism by dint of hearing it; and from that time she copied all Virginie's observances, fasting as she did and confessing with her. On Corpus Christi Day they made a festal altar together.

The first communion loomed distractingly ahead. She fussed over the shoes, the rosary, the book and gloves; and how she trembled as she helped Virginie's mother to dress her!

All through the Mass she was racked with anxiety. She could not see one side of the choir because of M. Bourais; but straight in front of her was the flock of maidens, with white crowns above their hanging veils, making the impression of a field of snow; and she knew her dear child at a distance by her dainty neck and thoughtful air. The bell tinkled. The heads bowed, and there was silence. As the organ pealed, singers and congregation took up the *Agnus Dei*; then the procession of the boys began, and after them the girls rose. Step by step, with their hands joined in prayer, they went toward the lighted altar, knelt on the first step, received the sacrament in turn, and came back in the same order to their places. When Virginie's turn came Félicité leaned forward to see her; and with the imaginativeness of deep and tender feeling it seemed to her that she actually was the child; Virginie's face became hers, she was dressed in her clothes, it was her heart beating in her breast. As the moment came to open her mouth she closed her eyes and nearly fainted.

She appeared early in the sacristy next morning for monsieur the curé to give her the communion. She took it with devotion, but it did not give her the same exquisite delight.

Mme Aubain wanted to make her daughter into an accomplished person; and as Guyot could not teach her music or English she decided to place her in the Ursuline Convent at Honfleur as a boarder. The child made no objection. Félicité sighed and thought that Madame lacked feeling. Then she reflected that her mistress might be right; matters of this kind were beyond her.

So one day an old spring van drew up at the door, and out of it stepped a nun to fetch the young lady. Félicité hoisted the luggage on to the top, admonished the driver, and put six pots of preserves, a dozen pears, and a bunch of violets under the seat.

At the last moment Virginie broke into a fit of sobbing; she threw her arms round her mother, who kissed her on the forehead, saying over and over, "Come, be brave! be brave!" The step was raised, and the carriage drove off.

Then Mme Aubain's strength gave way; and in the evening all her friends—the Lormeau family, Mme Lechaptois, the Rochefeuille ladies, M. de Houppeville, and Bourais—came in to console her.

To be without her daughter was very painful for her at first. But she heard from Virginie three times a week, wrote to her on the other days, walked in the garden, and so filled up the empty hours.

From sheer habit Félicité went into Virginie's room in the mornings and gazed at the walls. It was boredom to her not to have to comb the child's hair now, lace up her boots, tuck her into bed—and not to see her charming face perpetually and hold her hand when they went out together. In this idle condition she tried making lace. But her fingers were too heavy and broke the threads; she could not attend to anything, she had lost her sleep, and was, in her own words, "destroyed."

To "divert herself" she asked leave to have visits from her nephew Victor.

He arrived on Sundays after Mass, rosy-cheeked, bare-chested, with the scent of the country he had walked through still about him. She laid her table promptly and they had lunch, sitting opposite each other. She ate as little as possible herself to save expense, but stuffed him with food so generously that at last he went to sleep. At the first stroke of vespers she woke him up, brushed his trousers, fastened his tie, and went to church, leaning on his arm with maternal pride.

Victor was always instructed by his parents to get something out of her—a packet of moist sugar, it might be, a cake of soap, spirits, or even money at times.

He brought his things for her to mend and she took over the task, only too glad to have a reason for making him come back.

In August his father took him off on a coasting voyage. It was holiday time, and she was consoled by the arrival of the children. Paul, however, was getting selfish, and Virginie was too old to be called "thou" any longer; this put a constraint and barrier between them.

Victor went to Morlaix, Dunkirk, and Brighton in succession and made Félicité a present on his return from each voyage. It was a box made of shells the first time, a coffee cup the next, and on the third occasion a large gingerbread man. Victor was growing handsome. He was well made, had a hint of a mustache, good honest eyes, and a small leather hat pushed backwards like a pilot's. He entertained her by telling stories embroidered with nautical terms.

On a Monday, July 14, 1819 (she never forgot the date), he told her that he had signed on for the big voyage and next night but one he would take the Honfleur boat and join his schooner, which was to weigh anchor from Havre before long. Perhaps he would be gone two years.

The prospect of this long absence threw Félicité into deep distress; one more good-by she must have, and on the Wednesday evening, when Madame's dinner was finished, she put on her clogs and made short work of the twelve miles between Pont-l'Évêque and Honfleur.

When she arrived in front of the Calvary she took the turn to the right instead of the left, got lost in the timber yards, and retraced her steps; some people to whom she spoke advised her to be quick. She went all round the harbor basin, full of ships, and knocked against hawsers; then the ground fell away, lights flashed across each other, and she thought her wits had left her, for she saw horses up in the sky.

Others were neighing by the quayside, frightened at the sea. They were lifted by a tackle and deposited in a boat, where passengers jostled each other among cider casks, cheese baskets, and sacks of grain; fowls could be heard clucking, the captain swore; and a cabin boy stood leaning over the bows, indifferent to it all. Félicité, who had not recognized him, called "Victor!" and he raised his head; all at once, as she was darting forwards, the gangway was drawn back.

The Honfleur packet, women singing, as they hauled it, passed out of harbor. Its framework creaked and the heavy waves whipped its bows. The canvas had swung round, no one could be seen on board now; and on the moon-silvered sea the boat made a black speck which paled gradually, dipped, and vanished.

As Félicité passed by the Calvary she had a wish to commend to God what she cherished most, and she stood there praying a long time with her face bathed in tears and her eyes toward the clouds. The town was asleep, coast guards were walking to and fro; and water poured without cessation through the hole in the sluice, with the noise of a torrent. The clocks struck two.

The convent parlor would not be open before day. If Félicité were late Madame would most certainly be annoyed; and in spite of her desire to kiss the other child she turned home. The maids at the inn were waking up as she came in to Pont-l'Évêque.

So the poor slip of a boy was going to toss for months and months at sea! She had not been frightened by his previous voyages. From England or Brittany you came back safe enough; but America, the colonies, the islands—these were lost in a dim region at the other end of the world.

Félicité's thoughts from that moment ran entirely on her nephew. On sunny days she was harassed by the idea of thirst; when there was a storm she was afraid of the lightning on his account. As she listened to the wind growling in the chimney or carrying off the slates she pictured him lashed by that same tempest, at the top of a shattered mast, with his body thrown backwards under a sheet of foam; or else (with a reminiscence of the illustrated geography) he was being eaten by savages, captured in a wood by monkeys, or dying on a desert shore. And never did she mention her anxieties.

Mme Aubain had anxieties of her own, about her daughter. The good sisters found her an affectionate but delicate child. The slightest emotion unnerved her. She had to give up the piano.

Her mother stipulated for regular letters from the convent. She lost patience one morning when the postman did not come, and walked to and fro in the parlor from her armchair to the window. It was really amazing; not a word for four days!

To console Mme Aubain by her own example Félicité remarked:

"As for me, Madame, it's six months since I heard . . ."

"From whom, pray?"

"Why . . . from my nephew," the servant answered gently.

"Oh! your nephew!" And Mme Aubain resumed her walk with a shrug of the shoulders, as much as to say: "I was not thinking of him! And what is more, it's absurd! A scamp of a cabin boy—what does he matter? . . . whereas my daughter . . . why, just think!"

Félicité, though she had been brought up on harshness, felt indignant with Madame—and then forgot. It seemed the simplest thing in the world to her to lose one's head over the little girl. For her the two children were equally important; a bond in her heart made them one, and their destinies must be the same.

She heard from the chemist that Victor's ship had arrived at Havana. He had read this piece of news in a gazette.

Cigars—they made her imagine Havana as a place where no one does anything but smoke, and there was Victor moving among the Negroes in a cloud of tobacco. Could you, she wondered, "in case you needed," return by land? What was the distance from Pont-l'Évêque? She questioned M. Bourais to find out.

He reached for his atlas and began explaining the longitudes; Félicité's consternation provoked a fine pedantic smile. Finally he marked with his pencil a black, imperceptible point in the indentations of an oval spot, and said as he did so, "Here it is." She went over the map; the maze of colored lines wearied her eyes without conveying anything; and on an invitation from Bourais to tell him her difficulty she begged him to show her the house where Victor was living. Bourais threw up his arms, sneezed, and laughed immensely: a simplicity like hers was a positive joy. And Félicité did not understand the reason; how could she when she expected, very likely, to see the actual image of her nephew—so stunted was her mind!

A fortnight afterwards Liébard came into the kitchen at market time as usual and handed her a letter from her brother-in-law. As neither of them could read she took it to her mistress.

Mme Aubain, who was counting the stitches in her knitting, put the work down by her side, broke the seal of the letter, started, and said in a low voice, with a look of meaning:

"It is bad news . . . that they have to tell you. Your nephew . . ."

He was dead. The letter said no more.

Félicité fell onto a chair, leaning her head against the wainscot; and she closed her eyelids, which suddenly flushed pink. Then with bent forehead, hands hanging, and fixed eyes, she said at intervals:

"Poor little lad! poor little lad!"

Liébard watched her and heaved sighs. Mme Aubain trembled a little.

She suggested that Félicité should go to see her sister at Trouville. Félicité answered by a gesture that she had no need.

There was a silence. The worthy Liébard thought it was time for them to withdraw.

Then Félicité said:

"They don't care, not they!"

Her head dropped again; and she took up mechanically, from time to time, the long needles on her worktable.

Women passed in the yard with a barrow of dripping linen.

As she saw them through the windowpanes she remembered her washing; she had put it to soak the day before, today she must wring it out; and she left the room.

Her plank and tub were at the edge of the Toucques. She threw a pile of linen on the bank, rolled up her sleeves, and taking her wooden beater dealt lusty blows whose sound carried to the neighboring gardens. The meadows were empty, the river stirred in the wind; and down below long grasses wavered, like the hair of corpses floating in the water. She kept her grief down and was very brave until the evening; but once in her room she surrendered to it utterly, lying stretched on the mattress with her face in the pillow and her hands clenched against her temples.

Much later she heard, from the captain himself, the circumstances of Victor's end. They had bled him too much at the hospital for yellow fever. Four doctors held him at once. He had died instantly, and the chief had said:

"Bah! there goes another!"

His parents had always been brutal to him. She preferred not to see them again; and they made no advances, either because they forgot her or from the callousness of the wretchedly poor.

Virginie began to grow weaker.

Tightness in her chest, coughing, continual fever, and veinings on her cheek-bones betrayed some deep-seated complaint. M. Poupart had advised a stay in Provence. Mme Aubain determined on it, and would have brought her daughter home at once but for the climate of Pont-l'Évêque.

She made an arrangement with a jobmaster, and he drove her to the convent every Tuesday. There is a terrace in the garden, with a view over the Seine. Virginie took walks there over the fallen vine leaves, on her mother's arm. A shaft of sunlight through the clouds made her blink sometimes, as she gazed at the sails in the distance and the whole horizon from the castle of Tancarville to the light-houses at Havre. Afterwards they rested in the arbor. Her mother had secured a little cask of excellent Malaga; and Virginie, laughing at the idea of getting tipsy, drank a thimbleful of it, no more.

Her strength came back visibly. The autumn glided gently away. Félicité reassured Mme Aubain. But one evening, when she had been out on a commission in the neighborhood, she found M. Poupart's gig at the door. He was in the hall, and Mme Aubain was tying her bonnet.

"Give me my foot warmer, purse, gloves! Quicker, come!"

Virginie had inflammation of the lungs; perhaps it was hopeless.

"Not yet!" said the doctor, and they both got into the carriage under whirling flakes of snow. Night was coming on and it was very cold.

Félicité rushed into the church to light a taper. Then she ran after the gig, came up with it in an hour, and jumped lightly in behind. As she hung on by the fringes a thought came into her mind: "The courtyard has not been shut up; supposing burglars got in!" And she jumped down.

At dawn next day she presented herself at the doctor's. He had come in and started for the country again. Then she waited in the inn, thinking that a letter would come by some hand or other. Finally, when it was twilight, she took the Lisieux coach.

The convent was at the end of a steep lane. When she was about halfway up it she heard strange sounds—a death bell tolling. "It is for someone else," thought Félicité, and she pulled the knocker violently.

After some minutes there was a sound of trailing slippers, the door opened ajar, and a nun appeared.

The good sister, with an air of compunction, said that "she had just passed away." On the instant the bell of St. Leonard's tolled twice as fast.

Félicité went up to the second floor.

From the doorway she saw Virginie stretched on her back, with her hands joined, her mouth open, and head thrown back under a black crucifix that leaned toward her, between curtains that hung stiffly, less pale than was her face. Mme Aubain, at the foot of the bed which she clasped with her arms, was choking with sobs of agony. The mother superior stood on the right. Three candlesticks on the chest of drawers made spots of red, and the mist came whitely through the windows. Nuns came and took Mme Aubain away.

For two nights Félicité never left the dead child. She repeated the same prayers, sprinkled holy water over the sheets, came and sat down again, and watched her. At the end of the first vigil she noticed that the face had grown yellow, the lips turned blue, the nose was sharper, and the eyes sunk in. She kissed them several times, and would not have been immensely surprised if Virginie had opened them again; to minds like hers the supernatural is quite simple. She made the girl's toilette, wrapped her in her shroud, lifted her down into her bier, put a garland on her head, and spread out her hair. It was fair, and extraordinarily long for her age. Félicité cut off a big lock and slipped half of it into her bosom, determined that she should never part with it.

The body was brought back to Pont-l'Évêque, as Mme Aubain intended; she followed the hearse in a closed carriage.

It took another three quarters of an hour after the Mass to reach the cemetery. Paul walked in front, sobbing. M. Bourais was behind, and then came the chief residents, the women shrouded in black mantles, and Félicité. She thought of her nephew; and because she had not been able to pay these honors to him her grief was doubled, as though the one were being buried with the other.

Mme Aubain's despair was boundless. It was against God that she first rebelled, thinking it unjust of Him to have taken her daughter from her—she had never done evil and her conscience was so clear! Ah, no!—she ought to have taken Virginie off to the south. Other doctors would have saved her. She accused herself now, wanted to join her child, and broke into cries of distress in the middle of her dreams. One dream haunted her above all. Her husband, dressed as a sailor, was returning from a long voyage, and shedding tears he told her that he had been ordered to take Virginie away. Then they consulted how to hide her somewhere.

She came in once from the garden quite upset. A moment ago—and she pointed out the place—the father and daughter had appeared to her, standing side by side, and they did nothing, but they looked at her.

For several months after this she stayed inertly in her room. Félicité lectured her gently; she must live for her son's sake, and for the other, in remembrance of "her."

"Her," answered Mme Aubain, as though she were just waking up. "Ah, yes! . . . yes! . . . You do not forget her!" This was an allusion to the cemetery, where she was strictly forbidden to go.

Félicité went there every day.

Precisely at four she skirted the houses, climbed the hill, opened the gate, and came to Virginie's grave. It was a little column of pink marble with a stone underneath and a garden plot enclosed by chains. The beds were hidden under a coverlet of flowers. She watered their leaves, freshened the gravel, and knelt down to break up the earth better. When Mme Aubain was able to come there she felt a relief and a sort of consolation.

Then years slipped away, one like another, and their only episodes were the great festivals as they recurred—Easter, the Assumption, All Saints' Day. Household occurrences marked dates that were referred to afterwards. In 1825, for instance, two glaziers whitewashed the hall; in 1827 a piece of the roof fell into the courtyard and nearly killed a man. In the summer of 1828 it was Madame's turn to offer the consecrated bread; Bourais, about this time, mysteriously absented himself; and one by one the old acquaintances passed away: Guyot, Liébard, Mme Lechaptois, Robelin, and Uncle Gremanville, who had been paralyzed for a long time.

One night the driver of the mail coach announced the Revolution of July in Pont-l'Évêque. A new subprefect was appointed a few days later—Baron de Larsonnière, who had been consul in America, and brought with him, besides his wife, a sister-in-law and three young ladies, already growing up. They were to be seen about on their lawn, in loose blouses, and they had a Negro and a parrot. They paid a call on Mme Aubain which she did not fail to return. The moment they were seen in the distance Félicité ran to let her mistress know. But only one thing could really move her feelings—the letters from her son.

He was swallowed up in a tavern life and could follow no career. She paid his debts, he made new ones; and the sighs that Mme Aubain uttered as she sat knitting by the window reached Félicité at her spinning wheel in the kitchen.

They took walks together along the espaliered wall, always talking of Virginie and wondering if such and such a thing would have pleased her and what, on some occasion, she would have been likely to say.

All her small belongings filled a cupboard in the two-bedded room. Mme Aubain inspected them as seldom as she could. One summer day she made up her mind to it—and some moths flew out of the wardrobe.

Virginie's dresses were in a row underneath a shelf, on which there were three dolls, some hoops, a set of toy pots and pans, and the basin that she used. They took out her petticoats as well, and the stockings and handkerchiefs, and laid them out on the two beds before folding them up again. The sunshine lit up these poor things, bringing out their stains and the creases made by the body's movements. The air was warm and blue, a blackbird warbled, life seemed bathed in a deep sweetness. They found a little plush hat with thick, chestnut-colored pile; but it was eaten all over by moths. Félicité begged it for her own. Their eyes met fixedly and filled with tears; at last the mistress opened her arms, the servant threw herself into them, and they embraced each other, satisfying their grief in a kiss that made them equal.

It was the first time in their lives, Mme Aubain's nature not being expansive. Félicité was as grateful as though she had received a favor, and cherished her mistress from that moment with the devotion of an animal and a religious worship.

The kindness of her heart unfolded.

When she heard the drums of a marching regiment in the street she posted herself at the door with a pitcher of cider and asked the soldiers to drink. She nursed cholera patients and protected the Polish refugees; one of these even declared that he wished to marry her. They quarreled, however; for when she came back from the Angelus one morning she found that he had got into her kitchen and made himself a vinegar salad which he was quietly eating.

After the Poles came Father Colmiche, an old man who was supposed to have committed atrocities in '93. He lived by the side of the river in the ruins of a pigsty. The little boys watched him through the cracks in the wall, and threw pebbles at him which fell on the pallet where he lay constantly shaken by a catarrh; his hair was very long, his eyes inflamed, and there was a tumor on his arm bigger than his head. She got him some linen and tried to clean up his miserable hole; her dream was to establish him in the bakehouse, without letting him annoy Madame. When the tumor burst she dressed it every day; sometimes she brought him cake, and would put him in the sunshine on a truss of straw. The poor old man, slobbering and trembling, thanked her in his worn-out voice, was terrified that he might lose her, and stretched out his hands when he saw her go away. He died; and she had a Mass said for the repose of his soul.

That very day a great happiness befell her; just at dinnertime appeared Mme de Larsonnière's Negro, carrying the parrot in its cage, with perch, chain, and padlock. A note from the baroness informed Mme Aubain that her husband had been raised to a prefecture and they were starting that evening; she begged her to accept the bird as a memento and mark of her regard.

For a long time he had absorbed Félicité's imagination, because he came from America; and that name reminded her of Victor, so much so that she made inquiries of the Negro. She had once gone so far as to say "How Madame would enjoy having him!"

The Negro repeated the remark to his mistress; and as she could not take the bird away with her she chose this way of getting rid of him.

IV

His name was Loulou. His body was green and the tips of his wings rose-pink; his forehead was blue and his throat golden.

But he had the tiresome habits of biting his perch, tearing out his feathers, sprinkling his dirt about, and spattering the water of his tub. He annoyed Mme Aubain, and she gave him to Félicité for good.

She endeavored to train him; soon he could repeat, "Nice boy! Your servant, sir! Good morning, Marie!" He was placed by the side of the door, and astonished several people by not answering to the name Jacquot, for all parrots are called Jacquot. People compared him to a turkey and a log of wood, and stabbed Félicité to the heart each time. Strange obstinacy on Loulou's part!—directly you looked at him he refused to speak.

None the less he was eager for society; for on Sundays, while the Rochefeuille ladies, M. de Houppeville, and new familiars—Onfroy the apothecary, Monsieur Varin, and Captain Mathieu—were playing their game of cards, he beat the windows with his wings and threw himself about so frantically that they could not hear each other speak.

Bourais' face, undoubtedly, struck him as extremely droll. Directly he saw it he began to laugh—and laugh with all his might. His peals rang through the courtyard and were repeated by the echo; the neighbors came to their windows and laughed too; while M. Bourais, gliding along under the wall to escape the parrot's eye, and hiding his profile with his hat, got to the river and then entered by the garden gate. There was a lack of tenderness in the looks which he darted at the bird.

Loulou had been slapped by the butcher boy for making so free as to plunge his head into his basket; and since then he was always trying to nip him through his shirt. Fabu threatened to wring his neck, although he was not cruel, for all his tattooed arms and large whiskers. Far from it; he really rather liked the parrot, and in a jovial humor even wanted to teach him to swear. Félicité, who was alarmed by such proceedings, put the bird in the kitchen. His little chain was taken off and he roamed about the house.

His way of going downstairs was to lean on each step with the curve of his beak, raise the right foot, and then the left; and Félicité was afraid that these gymnastics brought on fits of giddiness. He fell ill and could not talk or eat any longer. There was a growth under his tongue, such as fowls have sometimes. She cured him by tearing the pellicle off with her fingernails. M. Paul was thoughtless enough one day to blow some cigar smoke into his nostrils, and another time when Mme Lormeau was teasing him with the end of her umbrella he snapped at the ferrule. Finally he got lost.

Félicité had put him on the grass to refresh him, and gone away for a minute, and when she came back—no sign of the parrot! She began by looking for him in the shrubs, by the waterside, and over the roofs, without listening to her mistress's cries of "Take care, do! You are out of your wits!" Then she investigated all the gardens in Pont-l'Évêque, and stopped the passers-by. "You don't ever happen to have seen my parrot, by any chance, do you?" And she gave a description of the parrot to those who did not know him. Suddenly, behind the mills at the foot of the hill she thought she could make out something green that fluttered. But on the top of the hill there was nothing. A hawker assured her that he had come across the parrot just before, at Saint-Melaine, in Mère Simon's shop. She rushed there; they had no idea of what she meant. At last she came home exhausted, with her slippers in shreds and despair in her soul; and as she was sitting in the middle of the garden seat at Madame's side, telling the whole story of her efforts, a light weight dropped on to her shoulder—it was Loulou! What on earth had he been doing? Taking a walk in the neighborhood, perhaps!

She had some trouble in recovering from this, or rather never did recover. As the result of a chill she had an attack of quinsy, and soon afterwards an earache. Three years later she was deaf; and she spoke very loud, even in church. Though Félicité's sins might have been published in every corner of the diocese without dishonor to her or scandal to anybody, his reverence the priest thought it right now to hear her confession in the sacristy only.

Imaginary noises in the head completed her upset. Her mistress often said to her, "Heavens! how stupid you are!" "Yes, Madame," she replied, and looked about for something.

Her little circle of ideas grew still narrower; the peal of church bells and the lowing of cattle ceased to exist for her. All living beings moved as silently as ghosts. One sound only reached her ears now—the parrot's voice.

Loulou, as though to amuse her, reproduced the click-clack of the turnspit, the shrill call of a man selling fish, and the noise of the saw in the joiner's house opposite; when the bell rang he imitated Mme Aubain's "Félicité! the door! the door!"

They carried on conversations, he endlessly reciting the three phrases in his repertory, to which she replied with words that were just as disconnected but uttered what was in her heart. Loulou was almost a son and a lover to her in her isolated state. He climbed up her fingers, nibbled at her lips, and clung to her kerchief; and when she bent her forehead and shook her head gently to and fro, as nurses do, the great wings of her bonnet and the bird's wings quivered together.

When the clouds massed and the thunder rumbled Loulou broke into cries, perhaps remembering the downpour in his native forests. The streaming rain made him absolutely mad; he fluttered wildly about, dashed up to the ceiling, upset everything, and went out through the window to dabble in the garden; but he was back quickly to perch on one of the firedogs and hopped about to dry himself, exhibiting his tail and his beak in turn.

One morning in the terrible winter of 1837 she had put him in front of the fireplace because of the cold. She found him dead, in the middle of his cage: head downwards, with his claws in the wires. He had died from congestion, no doubt. But Félicité thought he had been poisoned with parsley, and though there was no proof of any kind her suspicions inclined to Fabu.

She wept so piteously that her mistress said to her, "Well, then, have him stuffed!"

She asked advice from the chemist, who had always been kind to the parrot. He wrote to Havre, and a person called Fallacher undertook the business. But as parcels sometimes got lost in the coach she decided to take the parrot as far as Honfleur herself.

Along the sides of the road were leafless apple trees, one after the other. Ice covered the ditches. Dogs barked about the farms; and Félicité, with her hands under her cloak, her little black sabots and her basket, walked briskly in the middle of the road.

She crossed the forest, passed High Oak, and reached St. Gatien.

A cloud of dust rose behind her, and in it a mail coach, carried away by the steep hill, rushed down at full gallop like a hurricane. Seeing this woman who would not get out of the way, the driver stood up in front and the postilion shouted too. He could not hold in his four horses, which increased their pace, and the two leaders were grazing her when he threw them to one side with a jerk of the reins. But he was wild with rage, and lifting his arm as he passed at full speed, gave her such a lash from waist to neck with his big whip that she fell on her back.

Her first act, when she recovered consciousness, was to open her basket. Loulou was happily none the worse. She felt a burn in her right cheek, and when she put her hands against it they were red; the blood was flowing.

She sat down on a heap of stones and bound up her face with her handkerchief. Then she ate a crust of bread which she had put in the basket as a precaution, and found a consolation for her wound in gazing at the bird.

When she reached the crest of Ecquemauville she saw the Honfleur lights sparkling in the night sky like a company of stars; beyond, the sea stretched dimly. Then a faintness overtook her and she stopped; her wretched childhood, the disillusion of her first love, her nephew's going away, and Virginie's death all came back to her at once like the waves of an oncoming tide, rose to her throat, and choked her.

Afterwards, at the boat, she made a point of speaking to the captain, begging him to take care of the parcel, though she did not tell him what was in it.

Fellacher kept the parrot a long time. He was always promising it for the following week. After six months he announced that a packing case had started, and then nothing more was heard of it. It really seemed as though Loulou was never coming back. "Ah, they have stolen him!" she thought.

He arrived at last, and looked superb. There he was, erect upon a branch which screwed into a mahogany socket, with a foot in the air and his head on one side, biting a nut which the bird stuffer—with a taste for impressiveness—had gilded.

Félicité shut him up in her room. It was a place to which few people were admitted, and held so many religious objects and miscellaneous things that it looked like a chapel and bazaar in one.

A big cupboard impeded you as you opened the door. Opposite the window commanding the garden a little round one looked into the court; there was a table by the folding bed with a water jug, two combs, and a cube of blue soap in a chipped plate. On the walls hung rosaries, medals, several benign Virgins, and a holy-water vessel made out of coconut; on the chest of drawers, which was covered with a cloth like an altar, was the shell box that Victor had given her, and after that a watering can, a toy balloon, exercise books, the illustrated geography, and a pair of young lady's boots; and, fastened by its ribbons to the nail of the looking glass, hung the little plush hat! Félicité carried observances of this kind so far as to keep one of Monsieur's frock coats. All the old rubbish which Mme Aubain did not want any longer she laid hands on for her room. That was why there were artificial flowers along the edge of the chest of drawers and a portrait of the Comte d'Artois in the little window recess.

With the aid of a bracket Loulou was established over the chimney, which jutted into the room. Every morning when she woke up she saw him there in the dawning light, and recalled old days and the smallest details of insignificant acts in a deep quietness which knew no pain.

Holding, as she did, no communication with anyone, Félicité lived as insensibly as if she were walking in her sleep. The Corpus Christi processions roused her to life again. Then she went round begging mats and candlesticks from the neighbors to decorate the altar they put up in the street.

In church she was always gazing at the Holy Ghost in the window, and observed that there was something of the parrot in him. The likeness was still clearer, she thought, on a crude color print representing the baptism of Our Lord. With his purple wings and emerald body he was the very image of Loulou.

She bought him, and hung him up instead of the Comte d'Artois, so that she could see them both together in one glance. They were linked in her thoughts; and the parrot was consecrated by his association with the Holy Ghost, which became more vivid to her eye and more intelligible. The Father could not have chosen to express Himself through a dove, for such creatures cannot speak; it must have been one of Loulou's ancestors, surely. And though Félicité looked at the picture while she said her prayers she swerved a little from time to time toward the parrot.

She wanted to join the Ladies of the Virgin, but Mme Aubain dissuaded her.

And then a great event loomed up before them—Paul's marriage.

He had been a solicitor's clerk to begin with, and then tried business, the Customs, the Inland Revenue, and made efforts, even, to get into the Rivers and Forests. By an inspiration from heaven he had suddenly, at thirty-six, discovered his real line—the Registrar's Office. And there he showed such marked capacity that an inspector had offered him his daughter's hand and promised him his influence.

So Paul, grown serious, brought the lady to see his mother.

She sniffed at the ways of Pont-l'Évêque, gave herself great airs, and wounded Félicité's feelings. Mme Aubain was relieved at her departure.

The week after came news of M. Bourais' death in an inn in Lower Brittany. The rumor of suicide was confirmed, and doubts arose as to his honesty. Mme Aubain studied his accounts, and soon found out the whole tale of his misdoings—embezzled arrears, secret sales of wood, forged receipts, etc. Besides that he had an illegitimate child, and "relations with a person at Dozulé."

These shameful facts distressed her greatly. In March, 1853, she was seized with a pain in the chest; her tongue seemed to be covered with film, and leeches did not ease the difficult breathing. On the ninth evening of her illness she died, just at seventy-two.

She passed as being younger, owing to the bands of brown hair which framed her pale, pockmarked face. There were few friends to regret her, for she had a stiffness of manner which kept people at a distance.

But Félicité mourned for her as one seldom mourns for a master. It upset her ideas and seemed contrary to the order of things, impossible and monstrous, that Madame should die before her.

Ten days afterwards, which was the time it took to hurry there from Besançon, the heirs arrived. The daughter-in-law ransacked the drawers, chose some furniture, and sold the rest; and then they went back to their registering.

Madame's armchair, her small round table, her foot warmer, and the eight chairs were gone! Yellow patches in the middle of the panels showed where the engravings had hung. They had carried off the two little beds and the mattresses, and all Virginie's belongings had disappeared from the cupboard. Félicité went from floor to floor dazed with sorrow.

The next day there was a notice on the door, and the apothecary shouted in her ear that the house was for sale.

She tottered, and was obliged to sit down. What distressed her most of all was to give up her room, so suitable as it was for poor Loulou. She enveloped him with a look of anguish when she was imploring the Holy Ghost, and formed the idolatrous habit of kneeling in front of the parrot to say her prayers. Sometimes the sun shone in at the attic window and caught his glass eye, and a great luminous ray shot out of it and put her in an ecstasy.

She had a pension of fifteen pounds a year which her mistress had left her. The garden gave her a supply of vegetables. As for clothes, she had enough to last her to the end of her days, and she economized in candles by going to bed at dusk.

She hardly ever went out, as she did not like passing the dealer's shop, where some of the old furniture was exposed for sale. Since her fit of giddiness she dragged one leg; and as her strength was failing Mère Simon, whose grocery business had collapsed, came every morning to split the wood and pump water for her.

Her eyes grew feeble. The shutters ceased to be thrown open. Years and years passed, and the house was neither let nor sold.

Félicité never asked for repairs because she was afraid of being sent away. The boards on the roof rotted; her bolster was wet for a whole winter. After Easter she spat blood.

Then Mère Simon called in a doctor. Félicité wanted to know what was the matter with her. But she was too deaf to hear, and the only word which reached her was "pneumonia." It was a word she knew, and she answered softly, "Ah! like Madame," thinking it natural that she should follow her mistress.

The time for the festal shrines was coming near. The first one was always at the bottom of the hill, the second in front of the post office, and the third toward the middle of the street. There was some rivalry in the matter of this one, and the women of the parish ended by choosing Mme Aubain's courtyard.

The hard breathing and fever increased. Félicité was vexed at doing nothing for the altar. If only she could at least have put something there! Then she thought of the parrot. The neighbors objected that it would not be decent. But the priest gave her permission, which so intensely delighted her that she begged him to accept Loulou, her sole possession, when she died.

From Tuesday to Saturday, the eve of the festival, she coughed more often. By the evening her face had shriveled, her lips stuck to her gums, and she had vomitings; and at twilight next morning, feeling herself very low, she sent for a priest.

Three kindly women were round her during the extreme unction. Then she announced that she must speak to Fabu. He arrived in his Sunday clothes, by no means at his ease in the funeral atmosphere.

"Forgive me," she said, with an effort to stretch out her arm: "I thought it was you who had killed him."

What did she mean by such stories? She suspected him of murder—a man like him! He waxed indignant, and was on the point of making a row.

"There," said the woman, "she is no longer in her senses, you can see it well enough!"

Félicité spoke to shadows of her own from time to time. The women went away, and Mère Simon had breakfast. A little later she took Loulou and brought him close to Félicité with the words:

"Come, now, say good-by to him!"

Loulou was not a corpse, but the worms devoured him; one of his wings was broken, and the tow was coming out of his stomach. But she was blind now; she kissed him on the forehead and kept him close against her cheek. Mère Simon took him back from her to put him on the altar.

V

Summer scents came up from the meadows; flies buzzed; the sun made the river glitter and heated the slates. Mère Simon came back into the room and fell softly asleep.

She woke at the noise of bells; the people were coming out from vespers. Félicité's delirium subsided. She thought of the procession and saw it as if she had been there.

All the school children, the church singers, and the firemen walked on the pavement, while in the middle of the road the verger armed with his halleberd and the beadle with a large cross advanced in front. Then came the schoolmaster, with an eye on the boys, and the sister, anxious about her little girls; three of the daintiest, with angelic curls, scattered rose petals in the air; the deacon controlled the band with outstretched arms; and two censer bearers turned back at every step toward the Holy Sacrament, which was borne by monsieur the curé, wearing his beautiful chasuble, under a canopy of dark-red velvet held up by four churchwardens. A crowd of people pressed behind, between the white cloths covering the house walls, and they reached the bottom of the hill.

A cold sweat moistened Félicité's temples. Mère Simon sponged her with a piece of linen, saying to herself that one day she would have to go that way.

The hum of the crowd increased, was very loud for an instant, and then went further away.

A fusillade shook the windowpanes. It was the postilions saluting the monstrance. Félicité rolled her eyes and said as audibly as she could: "Does he look well?" The parrot was weighing on her mind.

Her agony began. A death rattle that grew more and more convulsed made her sides heave. Bubbles of froth came at the corners of her mouth and her whole body trembled.

Soon the booming of the ophicleides, the high voices of the children, and the deep voices of the men were distinguishable. At intervals all was silent, and the tread of feet, deadened by the flowers they walked on, sounded like a flock pattering on grass.

The clergy appeared in the courtyard. Mère Simon clambered on to a chair to reach the attic window, and so looked down straight upon the shrine. Green garlands hung over the altar, which was decked with a flounce of English lace. In the middle was a small frame with relics in it; there were two orange trees at the corners, and all along stood silver candlesticks and china vases, with sunflowers, lilies, peonies, foxgloves, and tufts of hortensia. This heap of blazing color slanted from the level of the altar to the carpet which went on over the pavement; and some rare objects caught the eye. There was a silver-gilt sugar basin with a crown of violets; pendants of Alençon stone glittered on the moss, and two Chinese screens displayed their landscapes. Loulou was hidden under roses, and showed nothing but his blue forehead, like a plaque of lapis lazuli.

The churchwardens, singers, and children took their places round the three sides of the court. The priest went slowly up the steps, and placed his great, radiant golden sun upon the lace. Everyone knelt down. There was a deep silence; and the censers glided to and fro on the full swing of their chains.

An azure vapor rose up into Félicité's room. Her nostrils met it; she inhaled it sensuously, mystically; and then closed her eyes. Her lips smiled. The beats of her heart lessened one by one, vaguer each time and softer, as a fountain sinks, an echo disappears; and when she sighed her last breath she thought she saw an opening in the heavens, and a gigantic parrot hovering above her head.

GAIL GODWIN

(1937–)

GAIL GODWIN was born in Birmingham, Alabama. She received a B.A. in journalism from the University of North Carolina in 1959, and an M.A. (1968) and Ph.D. (1971) in English from the University of Iowa. From 1959 to 1960 she worked as a reporter on the *Miami Herald*, from 1961 to 1965 as a consultant in London to the United States Travel Service, and in 1966 as an editorial assistant at the *Saturday Evening Post*. She has taught at the University of Iowa Writers' Workshop, at Vassar College, and in Columbia University's Writing Program. In addition to numerous stories, her publications include reviews and essays, as well as two short story collections. She is also the author of several novels, including *The Odd Woman* (1974), *A Mother and Two Daughters* (1982), *Father Melancholy's Daughter* (1991), and *The Good Husband* (1994). She was the librettist for several operas by the composer Robert Starer. Among her many awards are a literature award from the American Academy and Institute of Arts and Letters (1981), a Guggenheim Fellowship (1975–76), and a National Endowment for the Arts Fellowship (1974–75). Godwin lives in Woodstock, New York.

Godwin's work—her early work particularly—explores the sensibilities of women, odd in different ways, usually driven by talent or ambition. These women seek to fulfill a desire or realize a gift and must confront the past while negotiating the present's pitfalls and challenges. The utter accuracy of Godwin's eye and ear give her stories singular life. For her protagonists, the aesthetic is also a consistent touchstone. A woman, writing of her lover's summer vacation, addresses a letter to Charlotte Brontë in a sudden self-possessed moment.

"My Lover, His Summer Vacation" is from Godwin's collection, *Dream Children* (1976). A motif of these wholly original, deftly spun stories has people *imagining* other people's lives as a way of living their own. Here, the protagonist refers to herself as "his mistress," while she gives an account, with time pinpointed, of her lover's vacation with his wife. Despite its self-effacement, the voice is knowing, with a rueful understanding threaded through the yearning. Godwin confers on her heroine an intelligent, ironic sensibility that observes even as it suffers. The story moves seamlessly between the concrete particulars of her plight and the generic issues it raises. His mistress may be shortchanged, but her unique powers of imagination, including her ability to place herself in the lineage of Brontë's *Jane Eyre*, suggest that her life may be less diminished than his.

My Lover, His Summer Vacation

First Day

7:15 A.M. He leaves town. He packed the car last evening before going to see his mistress. The luggage is neatly strapped down, beneath a canvas, on the new carrier rack. The ends were too long so he sawed them off himself. He is proud of the job. His son, thirteen, sits on the other bucket seat, blank and noncommunicative, picking at a hangnail. Between them, on the carpeted hump, is an AAA Trip-Tik. (Prepared Expressly for You, M——— L———. Have a Safe Trip! Jim.) Jim is a nice fellow, so agreeable. His competent blue marker leads this man and his boy out of their city and shows them exactly where to get on Interstate 74 going east. Jim might have ordered the weather as well. Clean blue skies, a few harmless clouds. He is tense as he enters his body and his son's into the right lane of the highway. So many cars, going so fast. As always, he wonders if he can ever accelerate enough to match their speeds. Fifty, fifty-five, sixty, seventy. Yes, he is one of them. He sits back a little. His face relaxes. He says to his son, "We couldn't have asked for a better day." His son grunts. He is dying to turn on the radio and his fingers twitch a couple of times, getting up nerve to flutter toward the dial, but no. His father never plays the radio while driving. His mother does. She says music insulates her, keeps her from being scared stiff of all those fools on the road, including herself. She has gone on ahead, to visit her mother.

The man thinks of last night. He took his mistress a present. ("Here is a little going-away gift.") He stayed till half past three, two hours longer than usual. She said, "I am going to miss you more than you will miss me. You won't keep saying to yourself, 'I wonder what she is doing right this minute.'" He said, "It's true I don't have obsessive thoughts about people. I really don't think about people a lot, except when they are in trouble." He added, "I do the best I can."

They could have left at 7:00 a.m., but his son wanted to finish watching a cartoon. Did other people's sons watch as much TV as his did? When he was that age . . . what was he doing at that age? He remembers so little. His mistress is always asking him little things about his childhood. "Why do we want to drag up all that mess?" he says. Then later he had remembered that when he was nine he had flown. His mistress was delighted. Kept pressing for details. "Well, it's not too clear. It only happened once. I just lifted up my arms and jumped, and I flew for a minute. Then I wondered whether such things were possible and I hit the ground with a thud." "Ah, you shouldn't have thought," she said.

He passes a truck. Easily. Using his signal lights both times. The truck driver flashes his headlights "Thank you." Now they have achieved a steady seventy-five. He feels good.

10:03 A.M. His mistress's confidante comes by. Pilar. She is from Buenos Aires. Pili for short. She just walks in the screen door, calls out, "Anybody here?" His mistress comes out of the bathroom where she has been doing various things to her hair and face. The women embrace, Pili naturally, it is the custom of her country, the other woman shrinking slightly, because she would not want anyone to mistake her for a lesbian. "I'm glad to see you," says his mistress; "you have saved me from my mirror." The two women laugh. His mistress makes tea. They sit facing each other on the sofa, legs tucked under, and talk about men, men and women. "Do you think men are basically more remote than women?" his mistress asks. "Yes," says Pili, "they are, but it's not a physiologically caused thing; it's because they've been protected, they've been excused from all the efforts we make because we make them for them." Her voice trips piquantly over "physiologically," making the word lyrical and delicate and foreign, like Pili herself. "Do you think it might be a sign that the marriage is breaking up when the wife leaves ten days early to go and see her mother?" his mistress asks. "No, that is bourgeois to think like that," Pili says. "It simply means that they have lived together so long that each can go off and do what he likes. It is no small thing to have someone who lets you go when you please. The reason I stay with Ricardo is because he has learned not to bother me." "I'm so depressed," says his mistress. "That is because you are stuck midway in the water," says Pili solemnly. "You want to surface but cannot. Perhaps you should touch bottom and then start up. Go against your own tides. Make it difficult for him sometimes. You are an attractive woman. You are attractive even to me. I think it is important for a woman to be attractive to other women. I think you will find a man of your own. I like the way you move, the way you walk, the way you get excited about things. There is something sweet about you. I have often thought . . . well . . . that he is not enough for you. Whenever I see him at parties, there is like a glass tube around him. He looks interested in what you are saying but he is not really listening. Now have I hurt your feelings?" "No," says the other, "you have made me more cheerful." They laugh. Pili tells more anecdotes about the year, before her marriage to Ricardo, when she worked as a model at Elizabeth Arden's. "I would put on anything and walk around and all the fat ladies on their massage tables would want what I had on. They would look at me—I was exquisite in those days—and buy whatever I was wearing right off my back. Lace negligées, bathing suits, little-nothing bed jackets. They thought they could buy the way I looked by buying the garment. One day I sold two hundred dollars' worth of colored wooden beads. The manager said, 'Pili, we have got to get rid of these awful beads,' so I flung a few strands around myself and walked by this lady and she looked at me hard and said, 'How much are those beads?' I told her we had a whole tableful, but she said, 'No, I want those, the ones you have around your neck.' So I took them off and sold them to her and she put them around her neck where they didn't do a thing. By the end of the day, I had sold all of my beads."

He does not know his mistress has a confidante. It would annoy him intensely, after he recovered from the fright. She was so loyal at first, handling their secret like a blessed icon. Then one night he didn't call and Pili was there and . . . She has moments of terror and regret. She shouldn't have told. What if he finds out? ("I am disappointed in you. I thought you understood that I value my privacy more than anything.") Would he leave her? Then at other times, when she gets in a rage, she is glad Pili knows, she is glad she has sent her own secret spy into his precious privacy like a worm into his garden. She counts her betrayal of him as an evening of the score.

10:45 A.M.　He takes the exit marked "GAS FOOD LODGING," drives round to the side of the Shell station, parks in front of the rest rooms. Unbuckles his seat belt and looks at his son. "I don't need to," says the son. The father frowns. "You'd better anyway. I don't want to stop again. We're having lunch at that place in Kentucky the man at the AAA recommended and we won't get there till after one." "I couldn't go if I tried," protests the son. The father sighs, uplifts his palms in that familiar gesture of resignation, and leaves the car. As soon as he disappears into the MEN'S, the son grabs for the radio dial. Wonderful noise blares through the car: static, music, a confusion of excited voices. He finds a good song. His face goes beatific and slack as he loses himself in the song, its last bar synchronizing with his father's reappearance. Quickly, furtively, he snaps off the radio as his father reenters the air-conditioned silence. "Sure you won't change your mind?" says the father.

1:09 P.M.　He takes the Berea exit off I-75 and drives through a shady college town. All the young people on the street look cheerful. That is because they are working their way through college, he thinks. He will have to send his own son; otherwise he might refuse to go. They find a parking place right in front of the Boone Tavern Hotel, lock up the car. He puts a dime in the meter. The dining room is pleasantly uncrowded. "If we'd come at noon, no telling how long we'd have had to wait," he tells his son, pleased with their good timing. Several people look up as they are shown to their table: a tall, shy-looking man in his forties and a tall, rosy-faced son who walks just like the father. They have a fine meal with many courses, breads, choice of desserts. Cooked by the students, served by the students, even the chairs they are sitting on have been made by students. Different students come by, offering and describing various breads and cakes they have made. There is one young man, rather pale and plump, peddling a spoon bread. He speaks with a very precise diction, moving his soft, pale hands as he describes this bread. "Yes, we'll try it, thank you," says the father, annoyed because his son is giggling behind his hand. The plump young man looks hurt, serves the two of them quickly and leaves. "What was that all about?" he asks his son. "He's a fem," says the boy. "Well, this bread is certainly very tasty," says the father. "There's this guy in our class who's a fem," the son continues, animated for the first time during the trip. "What has he done to earn your endearing label?" "Oh, it's not just me, all the guys call him fem." The son stuffs spoon bread into his mouth. The father waits. "He has this funny way of talking, see, he uses this huge vocabulary nobody can understand, and he hates sports; he would rather talk to girls, or the teacher. We had this creative-writing project; everybody had to make a box, decorate this shoebox and put things in it that would represent this imaginary person, this imaginary person whose box it was supposed to be. He covered his box with flowered paper! His imaginary person was a girl! He was the only person in the whole class that did a girl. Even the girls chose men. He had feathers in the box and an old valentine with lace and all sorts of stupid things." "Who was your imaginary person?" asks the father, glancing covertly at his watch; he does not want to get a ticket. "It was a sports hero. A football hero. Only he dies tragically, you see, he has a heart attack, right on the field after he makes this touchdown that wins the game." The father calls for their check.

3:45 P.M.   His mistress shops. She buys a week's worth of porterhouse steaks, a large carton of nonfat cottage cheese, assorted fresh vegetables, a dozen grapefruits. She has decided to lose ten pounds during the two weeks. Where is she going to find them to lose? Nevertheless, going on a diet is bound to change something. She needs the discipline. She wants to be changed. She wants him to come back and say, "You look different." She buys *Jane Eyre*, a book she has always loved, and drives her dusty car home, feeling hopeful about these purchases. This is the first day of her vacation as well.

8:10 P.M.   The man and the boy are in bed watching TV. They are staying at the Holiday Inn—Central. There are three Holiday Inns in Knoxville. Jim at the AAA called ahead and made reservations for one double room tonight, and a double and a single tomorrow night. This room is enormous. It is decorated in a Spanish style: heavy furniture of dark pine, bedspreads in dark gold and black and turquoise, a sort of Moorish design. There is one lamp on (the son wanted them to turn all the lamps off, but the father explained it was bad for the eyes), and the room is full of distances and shadows. They had steaks for supper and baked potatoes with sour cream, butter, and little bits of chives and bacon. Each has a king-sized bed to himself. During a commercial, the son says, "You know why you always win everything? It's because you won't get involved." "Did your mother say that?" he asks. "No," says the boy, "I figured it out myself."

Second Day

8:45 A.M.   Humid. It wasn't supposed to get humid in the mountains. There is an implacable white film over the entire sky, edging down into I-40. They will miss all the views Jim marked for them to see between Knoxville and Asheville.

199

His mistress wanted to know everywhere he was going so she could follow along in her imagination. "To tell the truth, I'm kind of dreading it," he said. "It's so laced through with duty." Then he had added prudently, " I'm not complaining, since I chose it, but I'm saying it's less than ideal." His wife will be on the early-afternoon plane from New York, where she has been visiting her mother. He and Carl will pick her up at the Raleigh-Durham Airport, they will spend the night at the Holiday Inn in Goldsboro and drive to Ocracoke the next day. The trip is expertly planned by Jim.

10:30 A.M. His mistress and her confidante go swimming at the YMCA's new health club. Women can swim from 9:30 till 11:30, but must be cleared out by noon. The two women use Ricardo's locker, since women are not allowed to rent lockers. Pili tells her friend that she really ought to wear a cap in that chlorine, and put protein conditioner on her split ends before she puts on the cap. But his mistress cannot wear a cap, because even while she is swimming laps, she imagines that he is watching her. Pili has a specific number of laps to exercise different sections of her petite, trim figure. So many for crawl, so many for breaststroke, so many for the kickboard. She wears a pink cap with a pointed tip that makes her look like an imp. Her face bobs up and down in the water, serious with Exercise. Afterward, in the shower, she smacks and slaps herself to encourage circulation and break down fatty tissue, Muzak leaks out of the walls, surrounding them with platitudes of melody. "Really," says Pili, rubbing cream into her elbows and kneecaps, "when we get to my house, we are going to sit down and each write a postcard protesting that music. It won't take two minutes. I keep a stack of stamped postcards for just such occasions." "Oh, they would never turn it off for just the two of us," says the other. "Two is also a group," says Pili.

2:22 P.M. Raleigh-Durham Airport. They had cheeseburgers, French fries, and a waxy apple pie for dessert. He sits at the table by the window, watching planes taxi in and out, land, take off. He wishes for a 747, but his wish is not granted. His son is slouched over the magazine rack, reading a comic book, his face devoid of any intellectual struggle. Do other people's sons read comic books all the time? A dark speck materializes upon the whitish surface of sky. At 2:30 precisely, his wife's plane, an ordinary DC-4, touches the runway. He has already paid the check. He parts Carl reluctantly from his comic. They go through the terminal, which is being enlarged, he leading a polite trail between soldiers and families with too much luggage or too many children to handle both successfully. A power saw grates against his eardrum. In the waiting room for Gate 4, they can look through the window and watch the passengers disembark. Where is his wife? Once she missed a plane. What if she missed it today? They would have to wait here for hours, maybe even spend the night in Raleigh, where they don't have reservations. Jim's schedule ruined. He feels annoyance, then hears his son say, "There's

Mom." She looks apprehensive descending the metal steps, her eyes cast down as though she is terrified she might fall down and make a fool of herself. She smiles too gratefully at the airline official who stands at the bottom of the steps handing people down. It's his job, after all.

8:17 P.M.   Blue dusk fills the town he has abandoned. It gets darker earlier every evening now. His mistress drives by his house, a routine she has often indulged in. But tonight she cruises slowly, blatantly by. Even if she did have a blowout right in front of his house, no curtains would part, no startled face peer out, recognizing the guilty Mustang. The house is dark, a mere silhouette, a mere sketch of a house. No life there tonight. No having to guess who is in what room, doing what. No one weeps, cooks, watches TV, increases the ties that bind in that house tonight. Good. Apples are falling off the tree, rotting in his yard by the dozens. Good. Pili went to a party in his house last spring. She made frequent trips to the bathroom in order to investigate the upstairs for her friend. "What I want to know is, how many bedrooms," said his mistress when Pili came by afterward to report. "Well," replied the secret agent, "one has football players pasted all over the walls. I do not think that room is his. Then the other—I am sorry, my dear, but I could only find two—has a double bed in it. It is a very low bed, with a madras spread. It is practically on the floor. I don't know how people can sleep in those low beds." "How long was it? You know he is very tall," persisted his mistress. "Well," said Pili, reconsidering, "now I think of it, it was a very *short* double bed . . ." "I knew it," said the mistress. "You know, he told me he has a darkroom in the attic. . . ." "Ha!" cried Pili. "Our mystery is solved. He has a bed in his darkroom. Even Ricardo has a daybed in his study for when we have fights."

9:15 P.M.   Holiday Inn, Goldsboro. Carl has a room all to himself. He is in bed watching TV. The room is in total blackness except for the TV screen. There is a great show on. It is a weekly show about a doctor and all the different cases this doctor has. Tonight it is about this basketball player who has to have this dangerous operation on his knee, which may mean that he cannot go on to be a star. The first time Carl saw this particular show he could hardly watch it he was so nervous. Would the operation succeed or fail? This time he can really enjoy the show, because he knows what is coming next. Now it is that scene where the doctor is explaining to the boy that he will be able to lead a perfectly normal life, etc., etc., even if he can't fulfill his dream of being a great basketball star. He wishes he could get this boy on the TV to himself after the doctor leaves the room and say, "Don't worry! I know how it is going to end. You are still going to win that game and get the championship for your team!" The light from the TV screen dances upon his face. His eyes narrow, his lips grow slack, revealing healthy young teeth. At this moment, his face is an exact youthful replica of his father's at the moment of orgasm.

Third Day

9:30 A.M.   A whole hour behind Jim's schedule. She was in the bathroom for thirty-five minutes. Now she is in the bucket seat, wearing both kinds of safety belts, and Carl is in the back, looking out the window at nothing. They will reach Cape Lookout by early afternoon if they don't dawdle over lunch. They are renting a beach house with Bob and Mildred Taylor. Bob, a linguist, has written many articles on the Hatteras dialect. Mildred weaves rugs of gorgeous design and sells them for hundreds of dollars.

11:43 A.M.   His mistress sketches Pili's garden with felt-tip drawing pens. It is a late-summer garden whose colors are bright and sharp. She uses carmine, magenta, burnt orange, clear yellow. Pili has told her the names of the flowers, but she keeps forgetting. She has not sketched in years. The pens, bought this morning, are a joy. They move easily and make the garden look brighter than it is already. Pili is snipping dill weed from her herb garden. "You could still go to Mexico for your vacation," she scolds from beneath her garden hat. "Tomorrow afternoon you could be strutting up and down the beach in your bikini, attracting men like flies." "It's better I stay here," says his mistress. "I owe hundreds on my charge accounts." "Oh, yes, I know. You have bought too many clothes. You are so far gone that you would curl up and die for him under a palm tree instead of enjoying yourself," says Pili. "I was like that with Alistair." "Who was Alistair?" "Oh, some ridiculous creature I suffered over before I met Ricardo."

3:10 P.M.   "I got the carrier rack home from Sears," he is saying as they wait in their car for the ferry to Ocracoke, "and the ends were too long for the car. I borrowed a metal saw from Jack Atkinson and trimmed them down to fit."

"That's wonderful," she says.

10:00 P.M.   His mistress opens *Jane Eyre*. The beginning seems to have changed. Didn't the story open in an orphanage? Or was that the movie? Did she read this book before, or did she only imagine she had? Oh, well, it is going to be a wonderful book, she knows. But she can't concentrate. Her eyelids have sandbags attached and she keeps replaying dialogues from two nights ago in this bed.

Fourth Day

8:00 P.M.   Too much sun. His face is hot. Mildred's good supper. Oyster stew and what was the extra green in the salad, sort of bitter? He praised it, so his wife will find out and put it in their salads. She and Mildred in the kitchen. He just heard his wife say, ". . . I wish I had some talent, something of my own. . . ." Bob has lit his pipe. "I am going to the Hebrides this fall," he says. "I got that grant." "Mmm," replies his friend appreciatively, "good." Bob says, "Would you like to go over to this tiny island with me tomorrow? It's marvelously peaceful.

Just gulls and egrets and wild birds." "That sounds fine," says the other. Carl is happy, too. He sits by himself on the dark screened-in porch, impervious to the sound of the sea, watching his regular programs on TV.

8:00 P.M. Dinner at Pili and Ricardo's. Pili has the knack of making the simplest fare elegant. They are having a spicy hamburger casserole baked inside pastry, marinated cucumbers with the dill she snipped yesterday, carrots cooked with baby onions, fresh pineapple flavored with Benedictine, and plenty of decanted Valpolicella. The table is set with one of her great-grandmother's hand-embroidered tablecloths, and each piece of cutlery (sent from Tiffany's to Buenos Aires in the nineteenth century) has a wild animal carved on it. His mistress's knife has a rabbit peeping out from behind some graceful leaves. Ricardo is courteous but distant. He has a way of treating each woman. He teases Pili a little, compliments her, makes demands. With their guest he is more gentle, but more impersonal. He is an architect, a small man who looks larger. He has a mustache like Marlon Brando's in *Viva Zapata!* and wears smoked, gold-rimmed glasses and impeccable white cotton shirts with tucks in them. During the pineapple, the phone rings. It is one of Ricardo's clients. "Americans eat so early and expect everyone else to do likewise," he says, going out of the room. He calls back to Pili for her to hang up when he takes it in his study and to please bring him coffee.

The women clear the dishes. The guest loiters in a corner of the pretty kitchen while Pili whisks about, an efficient sprite. How she yearns for an order comparable to Pili's life: spices on their little spinning racks, homegrown herbs in their airproof glass jars. . . . Ricardo's voice drones above, explaining building specifications. Safe in his own house, planning the houses of others. "Let's take our coffee to my study," says Pili. "I want you to read what I have done on the new chapter." Pili is writing a book about the beauty secrets of her family: her great-aunt Isabel, who is now ninety and has the skin of a young girl, her mother's facial that any woman can make from the ingredients in her own kitchen. . . . "When I finish the book, Ricardo's secretary will type it on the Selectric. Then I shall get out my good clothes and go to New York and visit the publishers." "You will be a walking advertisement for your book," says her friend, thinking: *Ah, married, passion over with (except for the* 'cariñitos'), *able to devote your days to snipping dill in your garden, dispatching angry postcards to encroachers on your freedom, writing a leisurely, humorous book about women putting mayonnaise and vinegar on their faces to make themselves irresistible to men.* . . .

Fifth Day

11:00 A.M. The two men row out to Bob's island, which turns out to be less than one hundred yards long. They tie their boat to a tree and tramp around, serious as scouts. Wild cries of birds. No human sounds other than their own feet in the grassy sand. Suddenly Bob breaks the beautiful peace. "I might as well tell you. Mildred and I are splitting at the end of this summer." His friend does not answer. "I'm going to the Hebrides alone. No, that's not true. Someone is going with me. We're terribly in love. She's so young, I could almost be her father. But it's not like *that*, she's no little empty-head, Susan isn't. Do you know, she has made a movie? A feature-length film! Shot the thing herself with a sixteen-milli-meter. Why, she's not even beautiful." He shakes his head, dazed by his luck. Then, embarrassed by his friend's silence, he fills his pipe and puffs it vigorously. The other man watches an egret tuck his ungainly feet under him and float hero-ically up the warm sky. Finally he says, "There will probably be lots of material for a filmmaker in a place like the Hebrides." Bob explodes with laughter. "Oh, Matthew, you'll never change!" Bob has grown a droopy mustache this past year, and when he laughs he resembles a sad old walrus trying to be young and gay.

Sixth Day

ANYTIME.

> Lands of the Outer Banks are constantly undergoing changes caused by wind and wave action. Some believe the landmass is moving a minute distance toward the mainland each year and will continue to do so as long as the ocean remains at its present level or until the mainland is reached. Inlets connecting the ocean and sounds sometimes have had a lifetime of less than 100 years. They appear or disap-pear as the result of storms. . . .   —AAA Tour Book, Southeastern Region.

She paid $26 to join, just so she could get the maps and books to follow him.

11:30 P.M.   Jane Eyre locked in the red room without a candle because she stood up for her rights.

Seventh Day

In one week he comes home.

What are *cariñitos?* They are what has replaced passion in the twelve-year-old marriage of Pili and Ricardo. *Cariño* means affection, kindness. When Pili, or sometimes it is Ricardo, has had a horrible day, she, or sometimes it is he, falls face down on the bed and implores the other: "*Cariñitos, por favor.*" Then the stronger of the two at that moment (i.e., the one implored) gives the other a back rub.

Eighth Day

SOMETIME.   The four adults have dragged Carl to Kill Devil Hill. It is so histori-cal. In the year——, Wilbur and Orville Wright flew the first airplane, blah, blah, blah. Mr. Taylor: "Oh, you don't know how it killed me to see that bridge go up, that pure Elizabethan dialect gone forever. . . ." Carl's mother in her shy, uncertain voice: "Sometimes I think progress is awful." If progress is awful, why have they dragged him all the way up here to see this useless monument?

Ninth Day

In five days he comes home.

She will have to make herself small again, move over and share this city with him. He won't have missed her. He'll smile and say, "Gee, I'm glad to see you. Let's go to bed." Perhaps she should buy an animal of some kind.

Tenth Day

AROUND NOON

His Wife: How are my shoulders?

Mildred: They're O.K. You were careful the first week. I'm not really too depressed about it. After all, the girls are grown, there will be enough money because this Susan's father is in sausages or something, and I have my rugs and can go back to being a vegetarian. Bob told Matthew, you know.

His Wife: No, I didn't. What did Matthew say?

Mildred: He said there would be lots of things to film in the Hebrides.

His Wife (laughing): Poor Matthew!

11:59

Dear Charlotte Brontë:

I am writing to you from the late-twentieth century. I just this minute finished your novel and felt like chatting. The novel has done extraordinarily well since your early death in 1855. You were taking a risk. Even today when we can do heart transplants and good-looking young poets no longer die from TB, it is incautious to have a first baby at 39. I am 32 myself next birthday, and for two years have been doing something Jane refused to do. Yes, I am mistress to the man I love. His wife is still living, and, unfortunately, not confined to the attic. I don't think he is capable of loving me as much as Mr. Rochester loves Jane, for, you see, he has never known solitude. If you were writing your novel today, you could have saved yourself the trouble of that last 132 pages in the Signet paperback* edition.

*A paperback is a book printed on cheap paper with an illustrated cardboard cover that usually misrepresents the story.

You could have saved yourself that whole episode with that prick** St. John,

**Prick (noun) is a modern pejorative term usually applied to a selfish man, a sexually inconsiderate man, or a man one happens to be furious with.

marking time till Rochester's wife could burn up. Today it is accepted that sometimes even nice girls sleep with (when they can) men they are unable to marry.

A MISTRESS
(circa 1970)

P.S. It must be gratifying to know that one's art product will live longer than some landmasses.

Eleventh Day

Tomorrow he starts home.

Swimming and lunch with Pili. In the afternoon paper, his mistress sees an ad for six-week-old seal-point Siamese kittens, already litter-trained. Calls the woman. "They really are darling, we have only two left. A little boy and a little girl. They really are inseparable. I'd probably sell them both for the price of one just so they could stay together." She has plenty of room, a fenced-in back yard, a perfect place for the litter bin. Winter nights with a fire in the fireplace, two elegant, independent creatures leaping and cuffing each other on her green-and-turquoise Danish rug. But what if he is allergic to cats?

In the evening she goes to see *Blow-Up* again with Pili and Ricardo. Afterward they have a terrible fight in the parking lot. He says the movie was meaningless, it had no value system. "Oh, your values! Your systems!" screams Pili. It gets so bad they have to switch to Spanish. She stands a discreet distance away, burrowing the toes of her sandals in the gravel. She thinks how she will offer him this scene as a humorous anecdote.

Twelfth Day

Jim gets them almost clear across North Carolina via 70 and 85, then it's into Winston-Salem on 40, overnight at the Blue Bird Motel. (Rating, Good, but giving them a head start on 52 next morning.) The good thing about Jim is that he's dependable but keeps the journey from becoming monotonous.

Thirteenth Day

MORNING.   She gets up, dresses in anything. So much to get done! Forces self to make coffee so won't faint downtown. Paces while it perks, checking herself nervously in mirrors. Dirty hair! Legs and underarms unshaved for fourteen days! Gulps coffee, backs down driveway, drives halfway to town before releasing hand brake. First stop: Bronson's Department Store. Can't wait for elevator. Escalator to fourth, Household Goods. August White Sale. She needs towels, thick towels. He told her once he could not stand drying on a thin towel. How thick does a towel have to be for him to consider it thick? She imagines miraculous towels in his own bathroom, weighing five or six pounds, discovered by his wife at some incredible bargain in some store she would be denied admission to. Goes around feeling the edges of towels. Finds some. They are not on sale. She buys four, sucking in her breath and strolling about nonchalantly while the saleslady calls up to Credit to check her charge card. The thing is, she has already gone over her $300 limit with that green crêpe dress she bought for the night before he left. She gets away with it. Bronson's probably wants her to, probably flourishes on fools like her. Passing through Shoes, she sees these sandals, dark blue with red stitching, an arrogant little heel. The summer's almost over. She needs boots, not sandals. Once he said, "You have such nice, slim feet." Charges the sandals, feeling positively hubristic. Bronson's wouldn't dare stop her now. Bronson's doesn't. Liquor store. He likes good Scotch, sometimes imported beer, depending on his mood and where he's supposed to have been. She buys a fifth of Johnnie Walker Black Label and a six-pack of Tuborg dark, sucking in her breath as she writes the check. Now she has $9.17 left in her account. To supermarket. More cottage cheese, more grapefruit, more milk. Must make it till next payday without meat. Driving home, decides to have her car washed. Free if she buys gas. But her tank is full; she has gone nowhere in two weeks. Charges the car wash on credit card. As she drives the left front tire onto the rack, she sees a sign advertising hot or cold wax. "What is the difference between hot and cold wax?" she asks the black man who is pushing down her aerial. "Hot is fifty cents more." "I'll have the hot," she says. Goes into a little waiting alley where she can watch her car being cleaned for his homecoming. An enormous green sponge, cut in strips, undulates across the hood like a fat hula dancer. When time comes for the wax, red and yellow lights flash, bells ring, and a sign saying "YOUR CAR IS NOW GETTING HOT WAX" flicks on and off, on and off. She drives home sparkling, euphoric, to clean her house.

EVENING. Columbus, Ohio. Jim really understands the rhythm of a vacation. He understands that, going away, one wants to spread out, wants more luxury, more views. Coming home, it doesn't matter so much; one's thoughts return to the convenient, the economical. Only the average-sized double bed in this room. His wife goes first in the bathroom, because she knows he takes his bath in the evening. She splashes water quickly on her face; he will not know the difference. Actually she is too tired, but this is one of those Institutional Times. Thanksgiving, Christmas, Anniversaries, Last Night of Vacation. A sort of test. She slips her gown over her head. It smells of suntan oil. She runs a brush through her hair.

He is sitting in his undershirt and shorts on the side of their bed, his reading glasses on, studying the map. She puts her hand on his neck, leans her hip against the side of his head, and looks down with him at all those confusing, possible routes. She says, "Poor Mildred and Bob." "Yes, it's complicated," he says.

She savors her solitude in bed. Cool sheets. Hears him splashing in the bathroom, but she is already at home, back in her house, going from room to room checking the damage. What lights did they leave on? Did they remember to empty the garbage? What will be rotted in the refrigerator? She cruises the aisles of the A & P, filling her basket with the staples they have forgotten to replace. The apple tree. All those apples will be ripe, rotting. Baked apples, apple pies, apple turnovers, apple chutney . . .

He comes out, releasing a gust of steamy air into the dark room. She has switched off the lamp and he feels his way cautiously till his eyes adjust, till he can make out her hair like dark feathers on the pillow. "Boy, am I beat," he says, getting in on his side. "Yes, I know you are," she says. They lie in the dark, not touching. He puts his hand on her arm. "How are you?" "I'm fine, Matthew, I'm always fine." "Yes, I know," he says. He raises up on his elbow, looks for her mouth, then bends to kiss her, his lips puckering like a child. She wraps her arms about him. She really is tired, but he's aroused and it seems a sort of tribute to her, when he has been driving since morning. Would she be happier if she could weave rugs or make speeches on the floor of the Senate? How many times over the years she has cried herself dry. But now she no longer expects miracles, even wants them. How unsettling a miracle would be.

After he is asleep, she lies there planning meals for the rest of their week.

Fourteenth Day

9:10 A.M. "Do you want me to trim it, or what?"

"Yes, please. No, don't. Wait, could you just snip off these dead ends?"

Under the dryer, she opens the map and traces her finger along 70, just this side of Dayton.

AFTERNOON. Waiting. Mirror. Lie down on bed. No, ruin hair. This beautiful sunshine. Her last day of vacation. Should call up Pili and go for a stimulating walk. Back to mirror. *What is that?*

Regards with fatalistic horror the Thing growing on her left jaw. Oh, no, oh, damn!

Backs down driveway, forgets hand brake all the way to town. Parks outside Bronson's. Rushes in. Cosmetics. Where, what? Scans the cases: Ultimate, Intimate . . . Urgent!

"May I help you, honey?"

"Oh, yes, I don't know. . . . Listen, do you see this thing on my face, this bump? Well, I've got to get rid of it before tonight. Tonight is the most important night of my life. It's my—it's my wedding rehearsal. Tomorrow is my wedding!"

"Donna, will you come over here a minute? This young lady's wedding day is tomorrow. What do you think?" The two women scrutinize the spoiler on their customer's face.

"Disaster Cream," prescribes Donna.

That much money for this little tube? Charge it. Sucks in breath and strolls nonchalantly. Gets away with it again. Perhaps Bronson's is seeing how far a fool will go before clapping her into jail. Perhaps they are televising her with secret cameras, using her as an example.

There is a yellow ticket on her windshield. She gets in the car, rips open the slim cardboard box, unswivels the tube, applies the white, gritty potion.

EVENING

7:30 P.M.—Bathes, shaves legs and underarms, applies skin lotion liberally to entire body. Disaster spot under control and camouflage.

8:00 P.M.—Sits on sofa, fully dressed, wearing new sandals.

8:30 P.M.—Calls a number. "You park free while banking in First National, your full-service bank. Time: 8:28."

9:00 P.M.—Opens the Johnnie Walker.

9:30 P.M.—This is degrading.

9:40 P.M.—An accident. State Highway Police picking through debris. What and whose debris? All three? Mother and son? Father and husband? How much damage? Seriously? Critically? Abrasions and contusions, released from————Hospital? DOA? The two women meet in the waiting room. In the mortuary. "I've decided to keep the coffin closed." "You can't do that to me! I loved him, too!"

9:50 P.M.—Jane was right to leave Thornfield till she could have all or nothing.

10:10 P.M.—Prick.

10:17 P.M.—Drives furtively by his house, her Mustang absolutely exploding in his face with shining HOT WAX! All their lights are on.

10:33 P.M.—Calls up Pili. "Did I wake you? Did I disturb the two of you?" (Murderously.) "Oh, no, we were just watching an old Greta Garbo movie," says Pili. "Well, I just wanted to tell you it's all over. I've given him up. I wanted you to be the first to know." "Sweetie! How marvelous!" cries Pili. "Let's go swimming at ten and have a long lunch, okay? You can tell me all about it." "I can't. I have to go back to work tomorrow." "Oh, *pobrecita*, I forgot. I know! Come for dinner Tuesday night. That is Ricardo's squash night. We can have a good long chat." "Okay. Fine. I'd love to, Pili. See you Tuesday." Goes to bathroom, scrubs face till bump shines, combs hair flat for bed, kicks sandals behind toilet. Uses one of the Sacred Towels. More Johnnie Walker. So long, Prick.

11:15 P.M.—Phone rings. Awakens her out of dream in which the wife is saying, "Yes, I know it's hard, but do you know, he really loves you. What he loves most, he told me, was the way you appreciate our house. He is always begging me to ask you over."

"This is Matthew. I'm down at the office. I thought I'd give you a call. Were you asleep?"

"No. Yes. I don't know."

She hears him laugh softly. His voice sounds younger than she remembered it.

"How are you?" he says, going slowly, risking nothing.

"I'm great. How was your vacation?"

"Oh, you know how vacations go. It rained quite a bit. Carl got a pretty bad bee sting. Now I come back and see these piles of letters waiting for me. I was hoping we could see each other perhaps tomorrow evening—"

"Well, we could!"

"But I hadn't bargained on these dozens and dozens of letters. I was thinking maybe Tuesday evening, but even that's not certain. We could make tentative plans, unless you already have something. . . ."

Rain! Bee stings! Will she ever be able to know everything about him? There is always one more fact she hadn't counted on. And dozens and dozens of letters! She will be kept busy from now until Tuesday trying to imagine the contents of those letters. And how he will answer them. And what he will be doing in between. And what if he can't make it Tuesday? And how is she going to get through now until Tuesday?

"I'll save Tuesday," she hears herself say.

"And now tell me," he says (she can see him smiling attentively in his dark office as he speaks softly into the receiver), "what have you been up to these past two weeks?"

MYRA GOLDBERG

(1943–   )

MYRA GOLDBERG was born in New York City and graduated from the University of California at Berkeley in 1964. In 1977 she received an M.A. degree from the City University of New York, where she studied with Donald Barthelme. Her short stories have appeared in such magazines as the *New England Review, Tikkun, Kenyon Review, Ploughshares, Massachusetts Review, Feminist Quarterly,* and the *Transatlantic Review;* her nonfiction has appeared in, among other publications, the *Village Voice, Cross Currents,* and *American Book Review.* Goldberg's awards include the W. H. Hudson Fellowship, two Goodman Memorial Awards for short fiction, and a Lebensberger Foundation grant. Her collection, *Whistling and Other Stories* (1993), received wide critical acclaim, and was cited by the *New York Times Book Review* as one of the notable books of the year. She is a member of the fiction writing faculty of Sarah Lawrence College.

Goldberg's voice has been likened to Grace Paley's. Her style is fresh, intimately conversational, deceptively matter-of-fact. Characters' voices overlap, building symphonically, their music being a kind of pure speech, rendered with startling accuracy. While the idiom is contemporary American, the sensibility informing the stories is European-Jewish and literary. The stories have impressive technical sophistication; one of the things Goldberg typically does is tell two stories at once, with the "real" story intertwining with or overlapping another. It is a technique that seems to reflect the stories' overall theme of human connectedness—our disparate lives run on intersecting or collision courses (the latter, often inadvertent). And we connect as we always have, in love as in other essential matters, through storytelling itself.

In "Whistling," the title story of Goldberg's collection, a man and a woman at once tell and enact a roundabout story of love. The protagonists, Laura and Louie, are deep in courtship's ritual throes. When, for example, she balks at spending the night with him because the presence of his young son makes her uncomfortable, Louie blurts out by way of reassurance that the child is used to all the women his father entertains. Perhaps to insulate their mutually jangled nerves, perhaps as a delaying action for their own story, Laura begins to tell Louie a story of a friend's peripatetic love. Louie, seduced and seducing, is along with us instructed by the story and the woman.

Whistling

Louie and Laura were on their way to Brooklyn when Laura said: Stop the car. Louie couldn't stop the car, he said. There were too many cars behind them. Besides, why should he stop the car?

Because they hadn't agreed on a restaurant yet and driving without a destination would get them nowhere, said Laura. Nope, said Louie. Driving without a destination would get them to Brooklyn, to that restaurant he'd mentioned, near his wife Iz's apartment, where his son Josh was waiting to be picked up after supper and taken to Louie's house for the weekend.

How long, asked Laura, to this place, to this restaurant?

Oh about ten minutes, not counting traffic, Louie said. Laura could tell him a story to pass the time. He liked her stories. He thought she liked telling them to him.

No.

Okay. See if I care. Louie began whistling. Stopped whistling and explained professorially that he had just whistled the first verse of an eleven minute song in Yiddish that his mother sang to him. It was a song about love, happy and unhappy. He'd forgotten the words, but maybe Laura could remember them.

Laura had never heard the song. But she could make something up, she told him. In English, of course, and about her friend Pru, who was on her mind these days. Only it wouldn't be a song, but a story. Now let's see:

This story takes place in the Catskills. Near Sparta, near where I spent my summers as a child. It was beautiful there. It's still beautiful there, but when I was a child . . .

—Laura, said Louie. I thought you were telling me a love story.

—Right, said Laura. This is a story about Pru and John. And what I meant to say was that Pru met John in the Catskills. And where I wanted to begin was with Pru and me renting a house near Sparta because I'd remembered the place from my childhood—pine trees and berry-picking expeditions and whole days spent rocking in the hammock reading and a million cousins to play with. I thought a summer like that might be good for Pru, who'd been miserable all spring, pale and quiet and hardly eating anything unless I dragged her to a restaurant.

But that's another story. About David, the anthropologist Pru had been living with. He made her get an abortion because he didn't want kids. Then he went back to his wife and had one. A kid, I mean. It was awful.

Louie agreed it was awful.

Our first few weeks in Sparta were awful too. All my relatives were gone, which at first I thought was a blessing, but the town had been turned into a ski resort and we were the only summer people for miles around. All that was left were the pine trees and the berry bushes, so I put up a hammock and Pru went berry picking. Then at night, I read "Uncle Vanya" out loud in the kitchen, while Pru made preserves and we waited for something to happen, anything.

—I spent years like that, said Louie. Waiting.

—One day, said Laura, the hottest day of the summer, a motorcycle drove into the yard and a man in a crash helmet and leather chaps and big stomper boots got off.

—And raped you.

—God no, Louie. He waved at Pru who said she'd met him near the berry patch. She thought he'd moved in next door, but wasn't sure, because she hadn't listened very carefully. He sounded stupid, she added.

I looked over at the man again. He was sitting on the ground, polishing his bike, replacing parts. Periodically, he would start the motor up and Pru would wince and pick a berry from her basket and reject it for spots or mold or missing seeds. Then the man would kill the motor and look over at us and shrug.

Finally we went in to make supper. I set the table, while Pru stared out the window. The man was gone, she said. So was the motorcycle. Maybe we would have some peace and quiet again. I ate supper. Pru picked at a salad. I suggested she bake a pie afterwards and took up "Uncle Vanya" again.

Act one. The doctor enters. He begins to speak about a patient of his who died at Lent. He is conscience stricken. 'I sat down, closed my eyes—just like this—and I started to think. I wondered whether the people who come after us in a hundred years' time, the people for whom we are now blazing a trail—would they remember us and think kindly of us?'

"I've had enough of that play," said Pru. "And enough of this." She gestured towards the pie, "I feel ridiculous. I can't even remember why we came here. I should go back to the city and figure out what I want to do with myself. Go into therapy maybe."

Then she sat down, perfectly still, still pale in spite of the sun over the berry bushes and stared at the star she'd pricked into the pie with a toothpick.

It was a star of David. The black juice oozed out at the points. I had failed. I hadn't done a thing for Pru. And just then—Thank God—there was a knock on the door. I went to open it.

A tall man stood on the porch with the moonlight shining around him. "We're neighbors," he said. "I thought you might like some of this."

He lifted up a bottle of white wine. It was all he could find in town, he said, pointing to the motorcycle underneath the pine trees.

I took another look at him. He was slight, with a blonde silky beard and wire rimmed glasses and soft faded blue jeans.

"So you're the guy next door," I said, surprised enough to lead him back into the kitchen where Pru was sitting.

"Oh, it's you," said Pru.

—I knew it, said Louie. I knew that motorcycle man had to be John, at last.

I ran for the corkscrew. John opened the bottle and poured the wine into paper cups. Pru sat motionless, her blonde braid crowning her head, her bright blue bathrobe wrapped around her. Then she picked up a knife and cut the pie into pieces. Silence fell. Quite suddenly.

"Why don't you read us some more? Laura was reading," Pru told John, who smiled encouragingly at me.

I read: 'Do stay, I beg you. You must admit you have absolutely nothing whatsoever to do, you have no object in life, nothing to occupy your mind with, so sooner or later, you'll be bound to give way to your feelings—it's inevitable. And it will be better if it happens not in Harkov or somewhere in Kursk, but down here, in the lap of nature. At least it's poetical here . . .'

I looked up. Pru was frowning at me. "I'm a doctor," said John. "I don't get time to do much reading."

—What kind of doctor is he? asked Louie.

—A psychiatrist. Community Mental Health. John goes out visiting people in their homes in Bedford Stuyvesant.

—They let him in? said Louie.

—That's what Pru wanted to know. Poor people had pride, she said. What made John so sure they wanted him on their doorsteps.

John traced a circle on the oilcloth with his fingers. Then another. "They need all the help they can get," he said. "We all do."

"Have another piece of pie," I said.

"I'd love one," he said. "I really appreciate this."

He acted appreciative too—seriously considering each mouthful, telling Pru between mouthfuls about his mother, who burned the vegetables and made meatloaf with oatmeal in it and not enough salt.

"I was always hungry," he said. "Except at my grandmother's farm in the summertime."

Pru leaned forward. "In my family, they counted the stringbeans so we'd all get the same amount."

They both laughed. I was horrified.

John began telling a story about his grandmother's farm.

I excused myself and started up the stairs to bed. The murmurings continued in the kitchen. I lay in bed listening. John's voice was low and careful. Pru broke in periodically. Then they got quiet. Footsteps started for the door. The screendoor slammed. "Shhh," said Pru. "We'll wake up Laura."

The next morning a record was playing when I came downstairs. A fire had been lit in the fireplace. Pru was in the kitchen cooking bacon and eggs. John was gone. He's shy, actually, when you get to know him and Pru was embarrassed because they'd stayed up all night.

—Fucking, said Louie.

—Something like that, said Laura.

—Go on, said Louie. What's the matter?

—Where do you want me to go? That's it, isn't it? He rescued her. She didn't have to go into therapy.

—I'm surprised at you, said Louie. Obviously she rescued him. The poor guy. Polishing his bike. Visiting the poor in Brooklyn. Community Mental Health.

—It's next May, said Laura. Memorial Day weekend. Breakfast time. Pru is out buying groceries. John is in her kitchen ripping up the linoleum. He's reaching the floorboards. Wide. 18th century. The phone rings. John picks it up. Pru walks in with the groceries.

"It's your father," John writes on a notepad. "He wants to know if you'll be down for the weekend. Do you want to speak to him?"

"God no," says Pru. "Tell him I'm not here right now. Tell him I'll take the Metroliner."

"She'll take the Metroliner, sir," says John into the phone. "And she's not here right now."

—Where did you get that dialogue? asked Louie. It's peculiar. What's wrong with them?

—Pru's father is a judge, said Laura. Pru is terrified of him. John is a well brought up person. They talk like that.

—You're making it up, said Louie. The father. The judge.

—I am not. Pru told me. Also, she told John that he couldn't stay at her house anymore. The phone might ring at any moment and . . .

—That's enough detail, said Louie. We're almost there. Tell me what happened.

—What happened was that Pru went home to Philadelphia for the weekend and John went uptown to his place and a few weeks later, I found a note under my door:

Join us for a wedding picnic on the lawn of
the Madison Thorndike Memorial Estate
in Ossining. Saturday, June 30th. 5 p.m.
                    Pru and John

—It's a research center, said Laura. There was a map on the other side.

—We're here, said Louie. This is the restaurant.

—Two for a booth? asked the manager when they got inside.

Louie passed the breadbasket, but Laura refused it. She wanted to talk about the weekend. She loved staying over at Louie's place, she said, but not with Josh around. Josh got upset. Laura got upset, said Louie. Why make an issue out of everything?

Laura? said Louie, after awhile.

What do you want, Louie.

I want to know if your friend Pru finally got married.

Who? Pru? Are you kidding?

I'm perfectly serious, said Louie.

Laura laughed. Where was I?

You were sulking, said Louie. And in the story, you had just gotten the message.

Oh yes. The message. I got the message and went over to Pru's house to congratulate her. A guy I'd never seen before opened the door. He was short and stocky with his sleeves rolled up and the button over here—on the chest—undone. He kissed me. "Pru," he shouted. "It's that friend of yours."

—You married him, said Louie.

—He's already married. He's a family therapist, an old friend of John's. His name is Michael. He was just feeling expansive that day.

—He's always feeling expansive, said Louie. Besides, he knew you. You're a soft touch.

—He knew all of us, said Laura. That's his profession. He sat in the kitchen puffing on a pipe while Pru and John went back and forth about who should marry them—a minister, a judge, a justice of the peace—all out of the question. Then he tapped his pipe against the ashtray. Everyone looked up at him. "How about writing your own ceremony?" he said. "You can get a friend to marry you and go to City Hall afterwards for the legalities."

—This time you objected, said Louie.

—Only to the ceremony, said Laura.

—You didn't like the words they used.

—John wanted to begin with: 'In an effort to secure our mutual growth and satisfaction.' I said it was awful. Pru agreed. John went to sit with Michael. Two hours later, we had a page and a half written out and Clara, from across the hall, promising to play the flute in the background.

—Pru and John asked Michael to deliver the ceremony, said Louie. You felt hurt.

—How did you know?

—That reminds me of Morrison, said Louie. He's chairman of the department. I practically wrote his last article for him. Now he's stuck me with a second section of Contemporary American Problems to teach this summer.

—That's nice, said Laura. We can go to the Catskills when you're finished. You'll have some money.

Louie fingered the oil and vinegar bottles.

—You're giving the money to Iz, said Laura. You've decided to go back to her. Josh needs you.

—Stop jumping to conclusions, said Louie. We were talking about the wedding. We'll talk about this afterwards.

—The wedding, said Laura, was set for a Saturday. On Wednesday, Pru called me. Something had happened. John had decided that he couldn't go to City Hall. Not after the last marriage. Did I say he was married before?

Well, he was. Just after he got out of the Peace Corps. It was all nonsense, he said, that marriage, but he couldn't make those promises again and take the chance of another divorce.

"What should I do?" asked Pru.

"Gee, that's too bad, Pru," I said.

"But what do you think, Laura?"

"I don't know, Pru. I can see why he's nervous."

—What kind of crap is that? shouted Louie. You knew perfectly well what you thought. You always do. Pru is your friend. You should have told her.

—What could I say? 'Don't marry a man who doesn't want to marry you.' Or, 'Don't marry a man who wants to marry you, but not legally.' How did I know what she should do? Anyway, I was probably right to keep quiet because Pru was deciding to go through with it—the picnic part. "Call, if there's anything you need help with," I said. "Thanks," said Pru. "But I've already made the Greek salad." Then the minute she'd hung up, I called my father.

—Aha, said Louie. Your father enters the scene.

—Don't be silly. He was horrified. He started telling me a long story about some peddler in his village in Poland. Six children from five different women. Phoney ceremonies. Rabbis nobody had ever laid eyes on before. "Is she crazy?" he said. "A psychiatrist and a flute player? She agreed to that?"

"This is America, Dad," I said. "It's different here. John was in the Peace Corps. Pru taught kindergarten. They're very ethical people. John's just nervous."

"Who isn't?" asked my father. "The man's no fool. He knows it's not binding. Call her back. Talk to her. Tell her to talk to a lawyer if she won't listen to anybody else."

"I'll tell her," I said. "When she calls back."

Pru never called back. I bought a dress. I got a ride up to Ossining with Michael who assured me there would be appetizers first, so it didn't matter if we were a little late. There were no appetizers. Pru's face was as white as her dress. "Five o'clock," she said, "means five o'clock." Michael rushed to the bottom of the lawn where the young people sat crosslegged in a circle. A flute was play- ing. The Water Music. Michael composed himself. His Indian shirt floated in the breeze. "We are gathered together," he began, "to celebrate a joyous oc- casion."

I breathed deeply and sat down on a bridge chair with the relatives.

When the ceremony was over, we all signed a petition that Pru brought around saying we were a community of witnesses to the event. "That's not a bad idea," said my father, when I told him. "Maybe the girl's got a head on her shoulders, after all."

—I like the way your father changes his mind, said Louie. He's a good man.

—He likes you too, said Laura. He thinks the world of you, Louie.

Louie beamed. Laura looked across the table. A shining face beneath a high balding forehead looked back at her. A fringe of soft black hair blew in strands around his head as the electric fan behind him whirled and whirled.

—Louie, said Laura. I think I'll stay over with you and Josh tonight.

Louie was very sorry on the phone afterwards, but Laura didn't see what he had to be sorry for. So she'd taken the F train home. She liked the F train, liked watching it emerge from the tunnel, a mighty F blazoned across its forehead in red.

That's enough, Laura, said Louie. You said that you'd stay with me. Then ten minutes later, you were shouting "Stop the Car" and running away to the subway.

You left out the part in the car where you reassured me, Louie. Where you said: Josh is used to it. There are women in and out of there all the time.

Did I say that?

Laura looked over at the postcard on the bulletin board.

Join us. It's beautiful here. Can you
and Louie make it up for a weekend?
　　　Pru and John

Let me come over and comfort you, said Louie.

Comfort me?

I could whistle. You could finish telling me that story. We could make love. Okay.

Laura? Can I call you back? Josh is about to wake up. I have to take him to the bathroom.

Laura pressed her finger against the black plastic button and laid the phone back into its cradle.

For Christ's sake. You've done it again, Josh. You were supposed to wake up, said Louie.

You were supposed to wake me, Daddy. Josh began to cry. Louie sat down on the hideabed beside him. Let me tell you a story, he said.

I'm coming, said Laura on the phone the next morning. I'm coming to the Catskills, Pru, to see you and John again.

"Do you remember David?" asked Pru. She was chewing on a pine needle, watching John who was perched in the rafters of the summer cottage they'd just bought, hammering. "Well, all the time we were living together, his wife kept calling. About the bills and the washing machine. I thought she was crazy, Laura. I pitied her. David had been gone for a year and a half."

"Louie's wife doesn't call," said Laura. "Except about Josh. To make arrangements."

"Lunchtime," called John from the house.

"Okay, John. In a minute. Look, Laura, John says I was just an episode in David's marriage, a digression. It happens a lot, he says. To his patients." Pru stood up.

"I'm not hungry," said Laura, walking over to the log where her book sat, the paper still marking her place inside, the pen between the pages. She took the paper out.

Dear Louie,
I never got to finish telling you that story.

Laura looked up from her letter. Pru was walking towards the house. John was climbing down from the rafters.

When we last met, Pru and John had just gotten back from their honeymoon. Pru called me. The honeymoon was fine, she said. Backpacking was fine. Then one day, on the top of Mt. Marcy, John asked her to marry him. Legally, this time. At City Hall. At first, she said yes.

Then she started to think about it, all the way down the mountain, in the car going home, with the radio playing and not a word from John between Scroon Lake and Schenectady and the more she thought about it, the less she liked the idea.

John was right in the first place, she saw, passing Ossining and the wedding grove. It was absurd to rush into things before you knew what you were talking about.

"What are you talking about?" I asked her.

"The marriage laws," said Pru. "I want to know what I'm agreeing to. I've decided to talk to a lawyer. That makes sense, doesn't it?"

"Let me call you back," I said, because just then, there was a whistle underneath my window. It was you, Louie. We were going to see your mother in Brooklyn that night. I was nervous. You had a wife, a child. What would your mother think of me? 'She'll like you, take my word for it,' you said. You were right. Your mother liked me. 'You're a nice girl,' she said. 'They're all nice girls, Louie's friends.'

Laura looked up at the house. Pru and John had disappeared. It was hard to go on with her letter. She folded the paper, slipped it into an envelope, addressed it:

Louie Lichtman
c/o Dept. of History
Brooklyn College
Brooklyn, New York

'The point,' wrote Louie, on the term paper in front of him, 'is not that the Wobblies were stupid or old fashioned. They just didn't see what you see, because they were inside the struggle, instead of writing papers about it. Besides, transitional periods are difficult for everyone.

B+'

But all periods are transitional periods, remembered Louie, reconsidering the grade, as the phone rang. No he was not Professor Morrison, Louie told the caller. Professor Morrison was down the hall with the medievalists and what the fuck was wrong with Laura, he thought, hanging up, not a word from her for weeks. For a week, anyway. He dialed her number. Still no answer. Thank God. She might assume something. He picked up the next term paper to grade.

"There's a letter for you," said Professor Morrison, sticking his head in the doorway. "They put it in my box. Somebody doesn't know how to read."

Louie opened up the envelope and read: 'Dear Louie, I never got to finish telling you that story.' 'Good girl' he wrote in the margin. Then he read on. Down the mountain, past Scroon Lake and Schenectady, to Ossining and the wedding grove and Pru telephoning Laura and Laura hanging up the phone. 'It was you, Louie. We were going to see your mother in Brooklyn that night.' Louie sucked his pencil, went back to the beginning. Wrote: 'So Pru wouldn't marry John after all' to the left of the wedding grove. Wrote: 'That makes sense, considering what he'd done to her' next to Pru's decision to consult a lawyer. Then he stopped. There was a blank on the bottom of the page.

'Good work' wrote Louie. 'As I said in the margins, everything she did made perfect sense, considering. But was she serious? Is this a joke? The point is,' he scrawled, triumphant, vigorous, 'is this the end?'

No Louie, began the postcard, because when I called Pru back the next day, she was already out of town looking for land in the Catskills with John. As for the wedding, they got married sometime between the decision to buy land and the closing of the title or the deed, whatever you call it. They are both scrupulous people and they didn't want to lie on a legal document. Then Pru called one night to find out what procedures you could follow to keep your maiden name intact so I congratulated her and she said, 'oh well, it seems simpler this way' and besides, they are going to have a baby.

Louie stared at the postcard. 'The hills around Carthage' said the printed explanation of the view. 'Laura, in care of Pru and John' had been written underneath. Not an inch of space for a comment had been left. Louie would have to write a letter, but what would he say in it? He rummaged in the desk drawer for a postcard. A Raphael Madonna smiled up at him. Mondrian's view of Broadway lay behind. Then a map of New York State, by Esso. Louie closed the drawer and picked the telephone up.

There was no number, said the operator, in the Carthage, New York directory for a Doctor and Mrs. John Summerfield or a Ms. Prudence Merryweather or a Pru and John Summerfield-Merryweather.

Check the listings for the next town, said Louie.

Which town do you want? asked the operator. Sparta? Victory Falls?

Forget it. Louie put the telephone down and picked the map out of the drawer.

Several hours later, in Carthage, a real estate salesman directed Louie to the last summer cottage on the road up the mountain. A motorcycle was parked in the front yard. A hammock was swinging from between two ancient pine trees. Louie got out of the car. Anybody home? he called. Nobody answered. Louie walked over to the hammock. There was Laura, asleep, a book open on her stomach, the spine rising and falling as she breathed. Louie leaned over. Laura, he said. Laura stirred. Laura, it's me, he said. Laura rubbed her eyes. Louie picked the book off her stomach and closed it. Laura opened her eyes and smiled. It's about time, she said.

Goodbye, said Pru. Goodbye, said John.

Goodbye, said Louie and Laura from the car.

A few yards down the road, Louie and Laura heard shouts from behind them. Louie stopped the car. Pru ran up with a quart of blackberries and some advice: The Red Herring on Route Nine was a great place to stop if they were looking for a restaurant on their way home.

Laura took the berries through the open window.

Louie started the car again. John told me to take the thruway, he said. What's with Pru?

She's giving us the benefit of her experience, said Laura.

Louie laughed. Then he began whistling. Stopped whistling at the entrance to the thruway to say that Pru and John had inspired him. The words to the eleven minute love song in Yiddish were coming back.

Sing a minute's worth, said Laura.

Louie shook his head. There's some background material you need to know first, he said. It's a prerequisite to the song.

In English, please, said Laura.

A brilliant young Talmudic scholar and his girlfriend, a beautiful maidele, are parted by circumstances, said Louie.

—What are the circumstances? asked Laura.

—They have a fight. The maidele disappears. The scholar is distraught. Cryptic messages begin arriving at the Yeshiva for him. The messages, deciphered, reveal the whereabouts of the maidele. The scholar rushes to the mountaintop where he finds the maidele in a deep sleep and carries her home via the thruway.

—What's the Yiddish for thruway? asked Laura.

—It loses in translation, said Louie. Anyway, there's a test coming up for the scholar and the maidele, so you'll have to be quiet. He pointed to the sign ahead of them: REST STOP EXIT 10 FOOD GAS COMFORT. The scholar is thirsty, said Louie. Before him lies a long journey. Beside him there's an inn. Between the inn and the scholar sits the maidele.

—Can't they find someplace more exciting to stop than a Hot Shoppe? asked Laura.

—Not on the thruway, said Louie. But how will the scholar convince the maidele that he's right before the exit has passed? She doesn't trust him. She doesn't know how much he cares for her.

—How much does he care for her? asked Laura.

—Enough to rush to the mountaintop and back, said Louie.

Laura looked out of the window. We're about to miss the exit, she said. Click click click went the directional signals as Louie changed lanes. The scholar and the maidele had passed the test, announced Louie in the Hot Shoppe parking lot. The background material had been covered.

What happened to the song? asked Laura.

Louie unsnapped his seat belt and rubbed the place beneath where the metal had pressed. Then he looked over at Laura. She was sticking hairpins into the mass of curls on top of her head.

I like your hair down better, said Louie.

Laura let her hair down.

A shower of hairpins hit the dashboard.

Louie leaned over and touched her forehead with his lips.

The beginning, he said.

JEWELLE L. GOMEZ
(1948–)

JEWELLE L. GOMEZ has lived in Boston, Brooklyn, and San Francisco. She received a B.A. from Northeastern University in 1971, and in 1973, an M.S. from the Columbia School of Journalism. She has worked in a variety of positions, as a writer, a script editor, and as a television production assistant for several networks. She has also served as Director of the Literature Program of the New York State Council on the Arts; on the executive board of PEN American Center; the board of directors of the Open Meadows Foundation; the board of advisors in the Women's Studies Department at Hunter College, where she taught as well; and the board of advisors of the Human Sexuality Archives at Cornell University. She has acted as consulting editor of *Belles Lettres* and *Multi-Cultural Review*. Her publications include two books of poetry, *The Lipstick Papers* (1980) and *Flamingoes and Bears* (1987); *The Gilda Stories* (1991) featuring a benevolent black lesbian vampire as protagonist; and a collection of essays, *Forty-Three Septembers* (1993). She has contributed reviews to such publications as the *New York Times*, the *Village Voice*, *Ms. Magazine*, *Kenyon Review*, *Outlook*, and the *Nation*. Her awards include a National Negro Service Tuition Award (1968–71), a Ford Foundation Fellowship (1972), Barbara Deming/Money for Women Award (1988), and the Lambda Literary Award for fiction and science fiction (1991).

In a *Village Voice* interview (June 28, 1988) conducted by Lisa Kennedy, Gomez says her job, as a writer who is also a lesbian and a black, is "to keep confronting people and making them accountable."

"Don't Explain" (1987) takes place two weeks after the death of Billie Holiday. The protagonist, Letty, a lesbian, waits tables at the 411 Lounge in Boston, where she has lived since leaving Virginia some years back. She serves meals to the men who frequent the place, nimbly handling their mechanical small talk and passes. She is mourning the end of an affair and is weary with secrets kept, with desires banked. And she's stopped playing Billie Holiday on the 411 jukebox. A young coworker befriends her and invites her home for an evening with a group of women; they are sociable, close. A Billie Holiday tune plays. Letty observes, "The song sounded different here, among these women." The story sounds a note of permission, given by the women and the song, to love whom you choose.

Don't Explain

Boston 1959

Letty deposited the hot platters on the table, effortlessly. She slid one deep-fried chicken, a club-steak with boiled potatoes and a fried porgie platter down her thick arm as if removing beaded bracelets. Each plate landed with a solid clink on the shiny Formica, in its appropriate place. The last barely settled before Letty turned back to the kitchen to get Bo John his lemonade and extra biscuits and then to put her feet up. Out of the corner of her eye she saw Tip come in the lounge. His huge shoulders, draped in sharkskin, barely cleared the narrow door frame.

"Damn! He's early tonight!" she thought but kept going. Tip was known for his generosity, that's how he'd gotten his nickname. He always sat at Letty's station because they were both from Virginia, although neither had been back in years. Letty had come up to Boston in 1946 and been waiting tables in the 411 Lounge since '52. She liked the people: the pimps were limited but flashy; the musicians who hung around were unpredictable in their pursuit of a good time and the "business" girls were generous and always willing to embroider a wild story. After Letty's mother died there'd been no reason to go back to Burkeville.

Letty took her newspaper from the locker behind the kitchen and filled a large glass with the tart grape juice punch for which the cook, Mabel, was famous.

"I'm going on break, Mabel. Delia's takin' my station."

She sat in the back booth nearest the kitchen beneath the large blackboard which displayed the menu. When Delia came out of the bathroom Letty hissed to get her attention. The reddish-brown skin of Delia's face was shiny with a country freshness that always made Letty feel a little warm.

"What's up, Miss Letty?" Her voice was soft and saucy.

"Take my tables for twenty minutes. Tip just came in."

The girl's already bright smile widened, as she started to thank Letty.

"Go 'head, go 'head. He don't like to wait. You can thank me if he don't run you back and forth fifty times."

Delia hurried away as Letty sank into the coolness of the overstuffed booth and removed her shoes. After a few sips of her punch she rested her head on the back of the seat with her eyes closed. The sounds around her were as familiar as her own breathing: squeaking Red Cross shoes as Delia and Vinnie passed, the click of high heels around the bar, the clatter of dishes in the kitchen and ice clinking in glasses. The din of conversation rose, levelled and rose again over the juke box. Letty had not played her record in days but the words spun around in her head as if they were on the turntable:

> ". . . right or wrong don't matter
> when you're with me sweet

224

Don't Explain

Hush now, don't explain
You're my joy and pain."

Letty sipped her cool drink; sweat ran down her spine soaking into the nylon uniform. July weather promised to give no breaks and the fans were working overtime like everybody else.

She saw Delia cross to Tip's table again. In spite of the dyed red hair, no matter how you looked at her, Delia was still a country girl: long and self-conscious, shy and bold because she didn't know any better. She'd moved up from Anniston with her cousin a year before and landed the job at the 411 immediately. She worked hard and sometimes Letty and she shared a cab going uptown after work, when Delia's cousin didn't pick them up in her green Pontiac.

Letty caught Tip eyeing Delia as she strode on long, tight-muscled legs back to the kitchen. "That lounge lizard!" Letty thought to herself. Letty had trained Delia: how to balance plates, how to make tips and how to keep the customer's hands on the table. She was certain Delia would have no problem putting Tip in his place. In the year she'd been working Delia hadn't gone out with any of the bar flies, though plenty had asked. Letty figured that Delia and her cousin must run with a different crowd. They talked to each other sporadically in the kitchen or during their break but Letty never felt that wire across her chest like Delia was going to ask her something she couldn't answer.

She closed her eyes again for the few remaining minutes. The song was back in her head and Letty had to squeeze her lips together to keep from humming aloud. She pushed her thoughts onto something else. But when she did she always stumbled upon Maxine. Letty opened her eyes. When she'd quit working at Salmagundi's and come to the 411 she'd promised herself never to think about any woman like that again. She didn't know why missing Billie so much brought it all back to her. She'd not thought of that time or those feelings for a while.

She heard Abe shout a greeting at Duke behind the bar as he surveyed his domain. That was Letty's signal. No matter whether it was her break or not she knew white people didn't like to see their employees sitting down, especially with their shoes off. By the time Abe was settled on his stool near the door, Letty was up, her glass in hand and on her way through the kitchen's squeaky swinging door.

"You finished your break already?" Delia asked.

"Abe just come in."

"Uh oh, let me git this steak out there to that man. Boy he sure is nosey!"

"Who, Tip?"

"Yeah, he ask me where I live, who I live with, where I come from like he supposed to know me!"

"Well just don't take nothing he say to heart and you'll be fine. And don't take no rides from him!"

"Yeah, he asked if he could take me home after I get off. I told him me and you had something to do."

Letty was silent as she sliced the fresh bread and stacked it on plates for the next orders.

"My cousin's coming by, so it ain't a lie, really. She can ride us."

"Yeah," Letty said as Delia giggled and turned away with her platter.

Vinnie burst through the door like she always did, looking breathless and bossy. "Abe up there, girl! You better get back on station. You got a customer."

Letty drained her glass with deliberation, wiped her hands on her thickly starched white apron and walked casually past Vinnie as if she'd never spoken. She heard Mabel's soft chuckle float behind her. She went over to Tip who was digging into the steak like his life depended on devouring it before the plate got dirty.

"Everything alright tonight?" Letty asked, her ample brown body towering over the table.

"Yeah, baby, everything alright. You ain't workin' this side no more?"

"I was on break. My feet can't wait for your stomach, you know."

Tip laughed. "Break! What you need a break for, big and healthy as you is!"

"We all gets old, Tip. But the feet get old first, let me tell you that!"

"Not in my business, baby. Why you don't come on and work for me and you ain't got to worry 'bout your feet."

Letty sucked her teeth loudly, the exaggeration a part of the game they played over the years. "Man, I'm too old for that mess!"

"You ain't too old for me."

"Ain't nobody too old for you! Or too young neither, looks like."

"Where you and that gal goin' tonight?"

"To a funeral," Letty responded dryly.

"Aw woman get on away from my food!" The gold cap on his front tooth gleamed from behind his greasy lips when he laughed. Letty was pleased. Besides giving away money Tip liked to hurt people. It was better when he laughed.

The kitchen closed at 11:00 p.m. Delia and Letty slipped out of their uniforms in the tiny bathroom and were on their way out the door by 11:15. Delia looked even younger in her knife-pleated skirt and white cotton blouse. Letty did feel old tonight in her slacks and long-sleeved shirt. The movement of car headlights played across her face, which was set in exhaustion. The dark green car pulled up and they slipped in quietly, both anticipating tomorrow, Sunday, the last night of their work week.

Delia's cousin was a stocky woman who looked forty, Letty's age. She never spoke much. Not that she wasn't friendly. She always greeted Letty with a smile and laughed at Delia's stories about the customers. "Just close to the chest like me, that's all," Letty often thought. As they pulled up to the corner of Columbus Avenue and Cunard Street, Letty opened the rear door. Delia turned to her and said, "I'm sorry you don't play your record on your break no more, Miss Letty. I know you don't want to, but I'm sorry just the same."

Delia's cousin looked back at them with a puzzled expression but said nothing. Letty slammed the car door shut and turned to climb the short flight of stairs to her apartment. Cunard Street was quiet outside her window and the guy upstairs wasn't blasting his record player for once. Still, Letty lay awake and restless in her single bed. The fan was pointed at the ceiling, bouncing warm air over her, rustling her sheer nightgown.

Inevitably the strains of Billie Holiday's songs brushed against her, much like the breeze that fanned around her. She felt silly when she thought about it, but the melodies gripped her like a solid presence. It was more than the music. Billie had been her hero. Letty saw Billie as big, like herself, with big hungers, and some secret that she couldn't tell anyone. Two weeks ago, when Letty heard that the Lady had died, sorrow enveloped her. A refuge had been closed that she could not consciously identify to herself or to anyone. It embarrassed her to think about. Like it did when she remembered Maxine.

When Letty first started working at the 411 she met Billie when she'd come into the club with several musicians on her way back from the Jazz Festival. There the audience, curious to see what a real, live junkie looked like, had sat back waiting for Billie to fall on her face. Instead she'd killed them dead with her liquid voice and rough urgency. Still, the young, thin horn player kept having to reassure her: "Billie you were the show, the whole show!"

Once convinced, Billie became the show again, loud and commanding. She demanded her food be served at the bar and sent Mabel, who insisted on waiting on her personally, back to the kitchen fifteen times. Billie laughed at jokes that Letty could barely hear as she bustled back and forth between the abandoned kitchen and her own tables. The sound of that laugh from the bar penetrated her bones. She'd watched and listened, certain she saw something no one else did. When Billie had finished eating and gathered her entourage to get back on the road she left a tip, not just for Mabel but for each of the waitresses and the bartender. "Generous just like the 'business' girls," Letty was happy to note. She still had the two one dollar bills in an envelope at the back of her lingerie drawer.

After that, Letty felt even closer to Billie. She played one of the few Lady Day records on the juke box every night during her break. Everyone at the 411 had learned not to bother her when her song came on. Letty realized, as she lay waiting for sleep, that she'd always felt that if she had been able to say or do something that night to make friends with Billie, it might all have been different. In half sleep the faces of Billie, Maxine and Delia blended in her mind. Letty slid her hand along the soft nylon of her gown to rest it between her full thighs. She pressed firmly, as if holding desire inside herself. Letty could have loved her enough to make it better. That was Letty's final thought as she dropped off to sleep.

Sunday nights at the 411 were generally mellow. Even the pimps and prostitutes used it as a day of rest. Letty came in early and had a drink at the bar and talked with the bartender before going to the back to change into her uniform. She saw Delia through the window as she stepped out of the green Pontiac, looking as if she'd just come from Concord Baptist Church. "Satin Doll" was on the juke box, wrapping the bar in cool nostalgia.

Abe let Mabel close the kitchen early on Sunday and Letty looked forward to getting done by 10:00 or 10:30, and maybe enjoying some of the evening. When her break time came Letty started for the juke box automatically. She hadn't played anything by Billie in two weeks; now, looking down at the inviting glare, she knew she still couldn't do it. She punched the buttons that would bring up Jackie Wilson's "Lonely Teardrops" and went to the back booth.

She'd almost dropped off to sleep when she heard Delia whisper her name. She opened her eyes and looked up into the girl's smiling face. Her head was haloed in tight, shiny curls.

"Miss Letty, won't you come home with me tonight?"

"What?"

"I'm sorry to bother you, but your break time almost up. I wanted to ask if you'd come over to the house tonight . . . after work. My cousin'll bring you back home after."

Letty didn't speak. Her puzzled look prompted Delia to start again.

"Sometime on Sunday my cousin's friends from work come over to play cards, listen to music, you know. Nothin' special, just some of the girls from the office building down on Winter Street where she work, cleaning. She, I mean we, thought you might want to come over tonight. Have a drink, play some cards . . ."

"I don't play cards much."

"Well not everybody play cards . . . just talk . . . sitting around talking. My cousin said you might like to for a change."

Letty wasn't sure she liked the last part: "for a change," as if they had to entertain an old aunt.

"I really want you to come, Letty. They always her friends but none of them is my own friends. They alright, I don't mean nothin' against them, but it would be fun to have my own personal friend there, you know?"

Delia was a good girl. Those were the perfect words to describe her, Letty thought smiling. "Sure honey, I'd just as soon spend my time with you as lose my money with some fools."

They got off at 10:15 and Delia apologized that they had to take a cab uptown. Her cousin and her friends didn't work on Sunday so they were already at home. Afraid that the snag would give Letty an opportunity to back out Delia hadn't mentioned it until they were out of their uniforms and on the sidewalk. Letty almost declined, tempted to go home to the safe silence of her room. But she didn't. She stepped into the street and waved down a Red and White cab. All the way uptown Delia apologized that the evening wasn't a big deal and cautioned Letty not to expect much. "Just a few friends, hanging around, drinking and talking." She was jumpy and Letty tried to put her at ease. She had not expected her first visit would make Delia so anxious.

The apartment was located halfway up Blue Hill Avenue in an area where a few blacks had recently been permitted to rent. They entered a long, carpeted hallway and heard the sounds of laughter and music ringing from the rooms at the far end.

Once inside, with the door closed, Delia's personality took on another dimension. This was clearly her home and Letty could not believe she ever really needed an ally to back her up. Delia stepped out of her shoes at the door and walked to the back with her same, long-legged gait. They passed a closed door, which Letty assumed to be one of the bedrooms, then came to a kitchen ablaze with light. Food and bottles were strewn across the pink and gray Formica-top table. A counter opened from the kitchen into the dining room, which was the center of activity. Around a large mahogany table sat five women in smoke-filled concentration, playing poker.

Delia's cousin looked up from her cards with the same slight smile as usual. Here it seemed welcoming, not guarded as it did in those brief moments in her car. She wore brown slacks and a matching sweater. The pink, starched points of her shirt collar peeked out at the neck.

Delia crossed to her and kissed her cheek lightly. Letty looked around the table to see if she recognized anyone. The women all seemed familiar in the way that city neighbors can, but Letty was sure she hadn't met any of them before. Delia introduced her to each one: Karen, a short, round woman with West Indian bangles up to her pudgy elbow; Betty, who stared intently at her cards through thick eyeglasses encased in blue cat-eye frames; Irene, a big, dark woman with long black hair and a gold tooth in front. Beside her sat Myrtle who was wearing army fatigues and a gold Masonic ring on her pinky finger. She said hello in the softest voice Letty had ever heard. Hovering over her was Clara, a large red woman whose hair was bound tightly in a bun at the nape of her neck. She spoke with a delectable southern accent that drawled her "How're you doin' " into a full paragraph that was draped around an inquisitive smile.

Delia became ill-at-ease again as she pulled Letty by the arm toward the French doors behind the players. There was a small den with a desk, some books and a television set. Through the next set of glass doors was a livingroom. At the record player was an extremely tall, brown-skinned woman. She bent over the wooden cabinet searching for the next selection, oblivious to the rest of the gathering. Two women sat on the divan in deep conversation, which they punctuated with constrained giggles.

"Maryalice, Sheila, Dolores . . . this is Letty."

They looked up at her quickly, smiled, then went back to their preoccupations: two to their gossip, the other returning to the record collection. Delia directed Letty back toward the foyer and the kitchen.

"Come on, let me get you a drink. You know, I don't even know what you drink!"

"Delia?" Her cousin's voice reached them over the counter, just as they stepped into the kitchen. "Bring a couple of beers back when you come, OK?"

"Sure, babe," Delia went to the refrigerator and pulled out two bottles. "Let me just take these in. I'll be right back."

"Go 'head, I can take care of myself in this department, girl." Letty surveyed the array of bottles on the table. Delia went to the dining room and Letty mixed a Scotch and soda. She poured slowly as the reality settled on her. These women were friends, perhaps lovers, like she and Maxine had been. The name she'd heard for women like these burst inside her head: bulldagger. Letty flinched, angry she had let it in, angry that it frightened her. "Ptuh!" Letty blew air through her teeth as if spitting the word back at the air.

She did know these women, Letty thought, as she stood at the counter smiling out at the poker game. They were oblivious to her, except for Terry. Letty remembered that was Delia's cousin's name. As Letty took her first sip, Terry called over to her. "We gonna be finished with this game in a minute Letty, then we can talk."

"Take your time," Letty said, then went out through the foyer door and around to the livingroom. She walked slowly on the carpet and adjusted her eyes to the light, which was a bit softer. The tall woman, Maryalice, had just put a record on the turntable and sat down on a love seat across from the other two women. Letty stood in the doorway a moment before the tune began:

"Hush now, don't explain
Just say you'll remain
I'm glad you're back
Don't explain . . ."

Letty was stunned, but the song sounded different here, among these women. Billie sang just to them, here. The isolation and sadness seemed less inevitable with these women listening. Letty watched Maryalice sitting with her long legs stretched out tensely in front of her. She was wrapped in her own thoughts, her eyes closed. She appeared curiously disconnected, after what had clearly been a long search for this record. Letty watched her face as she swallowed several times. Then Letty moved to sit on the seat beside her. They listened to the music while the other two women spoke in low voices.

When the song was over Maryalice didn't move. Letty rose from the sofa and went to the record player. Delia stood tentatively in the doorway of the livingroom. Letty picked up the arm of the phonograph and replaced it at the beginning of the record. When she sat again beside Maryalice she noticed the drops of moisture on the other woman's lashes. Maryalice relaxed as Letty settled onto the seat beside her. They both listened to Billie together, for the first time.

NADINE GORDIMER

(1923–)

NADINE GORDIMER was born in Springs, a small South African town near Johannes-
burg, and educated at the University of Witwatersrand. A brief first marriage ended in
divorce, and she remarried in 1954. Her first short story was published when she was
fifteen; her first collection, *Face to Face,* was published in 1949. She is the author of
numerous collections of short stories and novels. Her work is permeated by her passionately held antiapartheid convictions. Two of her novels were banned by the South
African government, in 1958, *A World of Strangers,* and in 1979, *Burger's Daughter.*
Gordimer is not, she contends, a political writer; in fact, she takes issue with such
characterizations. Apartheid, which was as pervasive as the air South Africa's people
breathed, functions as an all-encompassing fact of the world Gordimer's fiction depicts; in it, the usual classifications, like "political," don't apply. She is a writer of
extraordinary intelligence and humanity, with a profound understanding of the how
and why of human behavior; her rigorous ethical vision is grounded in that understanding. Her language is both a poet's and a thinker's. Her voices are various, often
juxtaposed; she can render in one breath the murmurs of an uneasy schoolgirl, in the
next, the shallow rhetoric of the well-meaning ideologue. Among her novels are *The
Laughing Days* (1953), *A World of Strangers* (1958), *The Conservationist* (joint winner
in 1974 of the Booker Prize), *July's People* (1981), and *My Son's Story* (1990). Her
short story collections include *Livingston's Companions* (1971), *A Soldier's Embrace*
(1980), and *Jump and Other Stories* (1991). Her many awards include honorary degrees from Harvard, Yale, and the New School for Social Research, and honorary
membership in the American Academy of Arts and Sciences and the American Academy of Literature and Art. She is a member of International PEN, the Congress of South
African Writers, and the Royal Society of Literature. In 1991 she won the Nobel Prize
for literature, its first woman recipient in twenty-six years.

"A Find" (1991) gives a cool, knowing account of an unnamed man, down on his
luck with women, who tells himself he wants to do without them. Accordingly, he
takes a solo vacation in a beach resort, where there is little to gaze upon but women.
When the women leave the stony beach and he is left to contemplate only the stones
themselves, he unexpectedly turns up a jewel. One find leads to another, in this wise,
ironic tale of games played and replayed between the sexes. It is a story told with
wonderful adroitness and economy.

A *Find*

To hell with them.

A man who had bad luck with women decided to live alone for a while. He was twice married for love. He cleared the house of whatever his devoted second wife had somehow missed out when she left with the favourite possessions they had collected together—paintings, rare glass, even the best wines lifted from the cellar. He threw away books on whose flyleaf the first wife had lovingly written her new name as a bride. Then he went on holiday without taking some woman along. For the first time he could remember; but those tarts and tramps with whom he had believed himself to be in love had turned out unfaithful as the honest wives who had vowed to cherish him forever.

He went alone to a resort where the rocks flung up the sea in ragged fans, the tide sizzled and sucked in the pools. There was no sand. On stones like boiled sweets, striped and flecked and veined, people—women—lay on salt-faded mattresses and caressed themselves with scented oils. Their hair was piled up and caught in elastic garlands of artificial flowers, that year, or dripped—as they came out of the water with crystal beads studding glossy limbs—from gilt clasps that flashed back and forth to the hoops looped in their ears. Their breasts were bared. They wore inverted triangles of luminescent cloth over the pubis, secured by a string that went up through the divide of the buttocks to meet two strings coming round from over the belly and hip-bones. In his line of vision, as they walked away down to the sea they appeared totally naked; when they came up out of the sea, gasping with pleasure, coming towards his line of vision, their breasts danced, drooped as the women bent, laughing, for towels and combs and the anointing oil. The bodies of some were patterned like tie-dyed fabric: strips and patches white or red where garments had covered bits of them from the fiery immersion of sun. The nipples of others were raw as strawberries, it could be observed that they could scarcely bear to touch them with balm. There were men, but he didn't see men. When he closed his eyes and listened to the sea he could smell the women—the oil.

He swam a great deal. Far out in the calm bay between wind-surfers crucified against their gaudy sails, closer in shore where the surf trampled his head under hordes of white waters. A shoal of young mothers carried their infants about in the shallows. Denting its softness, naked against their mothers' flesh the children clung, so lately separated from it that they still seemed part of those female bodies in which they had been planted by males like himself. He lay on the stones to dry. He liked the hard nudging of the stones, fidgeting till he adjusted his bones to them, wriggling them into depressions until his contours were contained rather than resisted. He slept. He woke to see their shaven legs passing his head—women. Drops shaken from their wet hair fell on his warm shoulders. Sometimes he found himself swimming underwater beneath them, his tough-skinned body grazing past like a shark.

As men do at the shore when they are alone, he flung stones at the sea, remembering—regaining—the art of making them skim and skip across the water. Lying face-down out of reach of the last rills, he sifted handfuls of sea-polished stones and, close up, began to see them as adults cease to see: the way a child will look and look at a flower, a leaf—a stone, following its alluvial stripes, its fragments of mysterious colour, its buried sprinklings of mica, feeling (he did) its egg- or lozenge-shape smoothed by the sea's oiled caressing hand.

Not all the stones were really stones. There were flattish amber ovals the gem-cutter ocean had buffed out of broken beer bottles. There were cabochons of blue and green glass (some other drowned bottle) that could have passed for aquamarines and emeralds. Children collected them in hats or buckets. And one afternoon among these treasures mixed with bits of Styrofoam discarded from cargo ships and other plastic jetsam that is cast, refloated and cast again, on shores all round the world, he found in the stones with which he was occupying his hand like a monk telling his beads, a real treasure. Among the pebbles of coloured glass was a diamond and sapphire ring. It was not on the surface of the stony beach, so evidently had not been dropped there that day by one of the women. Some darling, some rich man's treasure (or ensconced wife), diving off a yacht, out there, wearing her jewels while she fashionably jettisoned other coverings, must have felt one of the rings slipped from her finger by the water. Or didn't feel it, noticed the loss only when back on deck, rushed to find the insurance policy, while the sea drew the ring deeper and deeper down; and then, tiring of it over days, years, slowly pushed and washed it up to dump on land. It was a beautiful ring. The sapphire a large oblong surrounded by round diamonds with a baguette-cut diamond, set horizontally on either side of this brilliant mound, bridging it to an engraved circle.

Although it had been dug up from a good six inches down by his random fingering, he looked around as if the owner were sure to be standing over him.

But they were oiling themselves, they were towelling their infants, they were plucking their eyebrows in the reflection of tiny mirrors, they were sitting cross-legged with their breasts lolling above the squat tables where the waiter from the restaurant had placed their salads and bottles of white wine. He took the ring up to the restaurant; perhaps someone had reported a loss. The patronne drew back. She might have been being offered stolen goods by a fence. It's valuable. Take it to the police.

Suspicion arouses alertness; perhaps, in this foreign place, there was some cause to be suspicious. Even of the police. If no one claimed the ring, some local would pocket it. So what was the difference—he put it into his own pocket, or rather into the shoulder-bag that held his money, his credit cards, his car keys and sunglasses. And he went back to the beach and lay down again, on the stones, among the women. To think.

He put an advertisement in the local paper. *Ring found on Blue Horizon Beach, Tuesday 1st,* and the telephone and room number at his hotel. The patronne was right; there were many calls. A few from men, claiming their wives, mothers, girl-friends had, indeed, lost a ring on that beach. When he asked them to describe the ring, they took a chance: a diamond ring. But they could only prevaricate when pressed for more details. If a woman's voice was the wheedling, ingratiating one (even weepy, some of them) recognizable as that of some middle-aged con-woman, he cut off the call the moment she tried to describe her lost ring. But if the voice was attractive and sometimes clearly young, soft, even hesitant in its lying boldness, he asked the owner to come to his hotel to identify the ring.

Describe it.

He seated them comfortably before his open balcony with the light from the sea interrogating their faces. Only one convinced him she really had lost a ring; she described it in detail and went away, sorry to have troubled him. Others— some quite charming or even extremely pretty, dressed to seduce—would have settled for something else come of the visit, if they could not get away with their invented descriptions of a ring. They seemed to calculate that a ring is a ring; if it's valuable, it must have diamonds, and one or two were ingenious enough to say, yes, there were other precious stones with it, but it was an heirloom (grand-mother, aunt) and they didn't really know the names of the stones.

But the colour? The shape?

They left as if affronted; or they giggled guiltily, they'd come just for a dare, a bit of fun. And they were quite difficult to get rid of politely.

Then there was one with a voice unlike that of any of the other callers, the controlled voice of a singer or an actress, maybe, expressing diffidence. I have given up hope. Of finding it . . . my ring. She had seen the advertisement and thought, no, no, it's no use. But if there were a million-to-one chance . . . He asked her to come to the hotel.

She was certainly forty, a born beauty with great, still, grey-green eyes and no help needed except to keep her hair peacock-black. It grew from a peak like a beak high on her round forehead and was drawn up to a coil on her crown, glossy as smoothed feathers. There was no sign of a fold where her breasts met, firmly spaced in the neck of a dress black as her hair. Her hands were made for rings; she spread long thumbs and fingers, turned palms out: And then it was gone, I saw a gleam a moment in the water—

Describe it.

She gazed straight at him, turned her head to direct those eyes away, and began to speak. Very elaborate, she said, platinum and gold . . . you know, it's difficult to be precise about an object you've worn so long you don't notice it any more. A large diamond . . . several. And emeralds, and red stones . . . rubies, but I think they had fallen out before . . .

He went to the drawer in the hotel desk-cum-dressing-table and from under folders describing restaurants, cable TV programmes and room service available, he took an envelope. Here's your ring, he said.

Her eyes did not change. He held it out to her.

Her hand wafted slowly towards him as if under water. She took the ring from him and began to put it on the middle finger of her right hand. It would not fit but she corrected the movement with swift conjuring and it slid home over the third finger.

He took her out to dinner and the subject was not referred to. Ever again. She became his third wife. They live together with no more unsaid, between them, than any other couple.

NATHANIEL HAWTHORNE

(1804–1864)

NATHANIEL HAWTHORNE, novelist and short-story writer, is one of the great writers of American fiction. He was born in Salem, Massachusetts, to a prominent New England family whose Puritan roots traced back to the early seventeenth century. At Bowdoin College in Maine, Hawthorne met Henry Wadsworth Longfellow and Franklin Pierce, the future president, for whom Hawthorne later wrote a campaign biography. (During his presidency, Pierce appointed Hawthorne as U.S. consul in Liverpool and Manchester, England.) Hawthorne graduated from Bowdoin in 1825 and for the next dozen years lived reclusively in Salem with his sisters and his widowed mother, writing stories and sketches for newspapers. Solitariness, in fact, was a mark both of his temperament and situation; it was considerably alleviated by his marriage to Sophie Peabody (the sister of Elizabeth Peabody, the educator and social reformer) in 1842. In 1828 he published a novel, *Fanshawe*, anonymously; as a matter of literary judgment, he recalled most of the copies after publication and burned them. *Twice-Told Tales*, a volume of stories appearing in 1837, was his next published work. In 1839, he took a job as a surveyor in the Boston Customs House. In that period, he reestablished his contacts with Longfellow and others in the New England literary community. He spent a brief, unsatisfying time at Bronson Alcott's Brook Farm (*The Blithedale Romance* [1852] is loosely based on his stay in this utopian community); its visionary idealism went against his conservative grain. After their marriage, he and Sophia Peabody settled in Concord, Massachusetts, where he wrote the stories collected in *Mosses from an Old Manse*. Herman Melville, a neighbor, was among the first to praise his genius. From mid-century on, Hawthorne produced his best-known works, including *The Scarlet Letter* (1850), *The House of the Seven Gables* (1851), *The Blithedale Romance*, and *The Marble Faun* (1860). The latter was completed during Hawthorne's travels in Europe. He died while on a trip to the White Mountains with Franklin Pierce.

Hawthorne's fiction reflects his preoccupation with America's Puritan past. His stories are allegorical cautionary tales. In "The Birthmark" (1846), the theme of love intersects with an essential fatalism about the human condition. Hawthorne sees lovers as driven by the overpowering desire to control love. Aylmer, a man of science, becomes obsessed with the single flaw in the appearance of his lovely wife Georgiana—an imprint, like the hand of a tiny cherub, on her face. Aylmer believes that science can remove this single impediment to his wife's perfection; for him, the birthmark has come to mirror Georgiana herself. The story has to do with what happens to the couple's lives when Aylmer's science is applied to love.

The Birthmark

In the latter part of the last century there lived a man of science, an eminent proficient in every branch of natural philosophy, who not long before our story opens had made experience of a spiritual affinity more attractive than any chemical one. He had left his laboratory to the care of an assistant, cleared his fine countenance from the furnace smoke, washed the stain of acids from his fingers, and persuaded a beautiful woman to become his wife. In those days when the comparatively recent discovery of electricity and other kindred mysteries of Nature seemed to open paths into the region of miracle, it was not unusual for the love of science to rival the love of woman in its depth and absorbing energy. The higher intellect, the imagination, the spirit, and even the heart might all find their congenial aliment in pursuits which, as some of their ardent votaries believed, would ascend from one step of powerful intelligence to another, until the philosopher should lay his hand on the secret of creative force and perhaps make new worlds for himself. We know not whether Aylmer possessed this degree of faith in man's ultimate control over Nature. He had devoted himself, however, too unreservedly to scientific studies ever to be weaned from them by any second passion. His love for his young wife might prove the stronger of the two; but it could only be by intertwining itself with his love of science, and uniting the strength of the latter to his own.

Such a union accordingly took place, and was attended with truly remarkable consequences and a deeply impressive moral. One day, very soon after their marriage, Aylmer sat gazing at his wife with a trouble in his countenance that grew stronger until he spoke.

"Georgiana," said he, "has it never occurred to you that the mark upon your cheek might be removed?"

"No, indeed," said she, smiling; but perceiving the seriousness of his manner, she blushed deeply. "To tell you the truth it has been so often called a charm that I was simple enough to imagine it might be so."

"Ah, upon another face perhaps it might," replied her husband; "but never on yours. No, dearest Georgiana, you came so nearly perfect from the hand of Nature that this slightest possible defect, which we hesitate whether to term a defect or a beauty, shocks me, as being the visible mark of earthly imperfection."

"Shocks you, my husband!" cried Georgiana, deeply hurt; at first reddening with momentary anger, but then bursting into tears. "Then why did you take me from my mother's side? You cannot love what shocks you!"

To explain this conversation it must be mentioned that in the centre of Georgiana's left cheek there was a singular mark, deeply interwoven, as it were, with the texture and substance of her face. In the usual state of her complexion—a healthy though delicate bloom—the mark wore a tint of deeper crimson, which imperfectly defined its shape amid the surrounding rosiness. When she blushed it gradually became more indistinct, and finally vanished amid the triumphant rush of blood that bathed the whole cheek with its brilliant glow. But if any shifting motion caused her to turn pale there was the mark again, a crimson stain upon the snow, in what Aylmer sometimes deemed an almost fearful distinctness. Its shape bore not a little similarity to the human hand, though of the smallest pygmy size. Georgiana's lovers were wont to say that some fairy at her birth hour had laid her tiny hand upon the infant's cheek, and left this impress there in token of the magic endowments that were to give her such sway over all hearts. Many a desperate swain would have risked life for the privilege of pressing his lips to the mysterious hand. It must not be concealed, however, that the impression wrought by this fairy sign manual varied exceedingly, according to the difference of temperament in the beholders. Some fastidious persons—but they were exclusively of her own sex—affirmed that the bloody hand, as they chose to call it, quite destroyed the effect of Georgiana's beauty, and rendered her countenance even hideous. But it would be as reasonable to say that one of those small blue stains which sometimes occur in the purest statuary marble would convert the Eve of Powers to a monster. Masculine observers, if the birthmark did not heighten their admiration, contented themselves with wishing it away, that the world might possess one living specimen of ideal loveliness without the semblance of a flaw. After his marriage,—for he thought little or nothing of the matter before,—Aylmer discovered that this was the case with himself.

Had she been less beautiful,—if Envy's self could have found aught else to sneer at,—he might have felt his affection heightened by the prettiness of this mimic hand, now vaguely portrayed, now lost, now stealing forth again and glimmering to and fro with every pulse of emotion that throbbed within her heart; but seeing her otherwise so perfect, he found this one defect grow more and more intolerable with every moment of their united lives. It was the fatal flaw of humanity which Nature, in one shape or another, stamps ineffaceably on all her productions, either to imply that they are temporary and finite, or that their perfection must be wrought by toil and pain. The crimson hand expressed the ineludible gripe in which mortality clutches the highest and purest of earthly mould, degrading them into kindred with the lowest, and even with the very brutes, like whom their visible frames return to dust. In this manner, selecting it as the symbol of his wife's liability to sin, sorrow, decay, and death, Aylmer's sombre imagination was not long in rendering the birthmark a frightful object, causing him more trouble and horror than ever Georgiana's beauty, whether of soul or sense, had given him delight.

At all the seasons which should have been their happiest, he invariably and without intending it, nay, in spite of a purpose to the contrary, reverted to this one disastrous topic. Trifling as it at first appeared, it so connected itself with innumerable trains of thought and modes of feeling that it became the central point of all. With the morning twilight Aylmer opened his eyes upon his wife's face and recognized the symbol of imperfection; and when they sat together at the evening hearth his eyes wandered stealthily to her cheek, and beheld, flickering with the blaze of the wood fire, the spectral hand that wrote mortality where he would fain have worshipped. Georgiana soon learned to shudder at his gaze. It needed but a glance with the peculiar expression that his face often wore to change the roses of her cheek into a deathlike paleness, amid which the crimson hand was brought strongly out, like a bass-relief of ruby on the whitest marble.

Late one night when the lights were growing dim, so as hardly to betray the stain on the poor wife's cheek, she herself, for the first time, voluntarily took up the subject.

"Do you remember, my dear Aylmer," said she, with a feeble attempt at a smile, "have you any recollection of a dream last night about this odious hand?"

"None! none whatever!" replied Aylmer, starting; but then he added, in a dry, cold tone, affected for the sake of concealing the real depth of his emotion, "I might well dream of it; for before I fell asleep it had taken a pretty firm hold of my fancy."

"And you did dream of it?" continued Georgiana, hastily; for she dreaded lest a gush of tears should interrupt what she had to say. "A terrible dream! I wonder that you can forget it. Is it possible to forget this one expression?—'It is in her heart now; we must have it out!' Reflect, my husband; for by all means I would have you recall that dream."

The mind is in a sad state when Sleep, the all-involving, cannot confine her spectres within the dim region of her sway, but suffers them to break forth, affrighting this actual life with secrets that perchance belong to a deeper one. Aylmer now remembered his dream. He had fancied himself with his servant Aminadab, attempting an operation for the removal of the birthmark; but the deeper went the knife, the deeper sank the hand, until at length its tiny grasp appeared to have caught hold of Georgiana's heart; whence, however, her husband was inexorably resolved to cut or wrench it away.

When the dream had shaped itself perfectly in his memory, Aylmer sat in his wife's presence with a guilty feeling. Truth often finds its way to the mind close muffled in robes of sleep, and then speaks with uncompromising directness of matters in regard to which we practise an unconscious self-deception during our waking moments. Until now he had not been aware of the tyrannizing influence acquired by one idea over his mind, and of the lengths which he might find in his heart to go for the sake of giving himself peace.

"Aylmer," resumed Georgiana, solemnly, "I know not what may be the cost to both of us to rid me of this fatal birthmark. Perhaps its removal may cause cureless deformity; or it may be the stain goes as deep as life itself. Again: do we know that there is a possibility, on any terms, of unclasping the firm gripe of this little hand which was laid upon me before I came into the world?"

"Dearest Georgiana, I have spent much thought upon the subject," hastily interrupted Aylmer. "I am convinced of the perfect practicability of its removal."

"If there be the remotest possibility of it," continued Georgiana, "let the attempt be made at whatever risk. Danger is nothing to me; for life, while this hateful mark makes me the object of your horror and disgust,—life is a burden which I would fling down with joy. Either remove this dreadful hand, or take my wretched life! You have deep science. All the world bears witness of it. You have achieved great wonders. Cannot you remove this little, little mark, which I cover with the tips of two small fingers? Is this beyond your power, for the sake of your own peace, and to save your poor wife from madness?"

"Noblest, dearest, tenderest wife," cried Aylmer, rapturously, "doubt not my power. I have already given this matter the deepest thought—thought which might almost have enlightened me to create a being less perfect than yourself. Georgiana, you have led deeper than ever into the heart of science. I feel myself fully competent to render this dear cheek as faultless as its fellow; and then, most beloved, what will be my triumph when I shall have corrected what Nature left imperfect in her fairest work! Even Pygmalion, when his sculptured woman assumed life, felt not greater ecstasy than mine will be."

"It is resolved, then," said Georgiana, faintly smiling. "And, Aylmer, spare me not, though you should find the birthmark take refuge in my heart at last."

Her husband tenderly kissed her cheek—her right cheek—not that which bore the impress of the crimson hand.

The next day Aylmer apprised his wife of a plan that he had formed whereby he might have opportunity for the intense thought and constant watchfulness which the proposed operation would require; while Georgiana, likewise, would enjoy the perfect repose essential to its success. They were to seclude themselves in the extensive apartments occupied by Aylmer as a laboratory, and where, during his toilsome youth, he had made discoveries in the elemental powers of Nature that had roused the admiration of all the learned societies in Europe. Seated calmly in this laboratory, the pale philosopher had investigated the secrets of the highest cloud region and of the profoundest mines; he had satisfied himself of the causes that kindled and kept alive the fires of the volcano; and had explained the mystery of the fountains, and how it is that they gush forth, some so bright and pure, and others with such rich medicinal virtues, from the dark bosom of the earth. Here, too, at an earlier period, he had studied the wonders of the human frame, and attempted to fathom the very process by which Nature assimilates all her precious influences from earth and air, and from the spiritual world, to create and foster man, her masterpiece. The latter pursuit, however, Aylmer had long laid aside in unwilling recognition of the truth—against which all seekers sooner or later stumble—that our great creative Mother, while she amuses us with apparently working in the broadest sunshine, is yet severely careful to keep her own secrets, and, in spite of her pretended openness, shows us nothing but results. She permits us, indeed, to mar, but seldom to mend, and, like a jealous patentee, on no account to make. Now, however, Aylmer resumed these half-forgotten investigations; not, of course, with such hopes or wishes as first suggested them; but because they involved much physiological truth and lay in the path of his proposed scheme for the treatment of Georgiana.

As he led her over the threshold of the laboratory, Georgiana was cold and tremulous. Aylmer looked cheerfully into her face, with intent to reassure her, but was so startled with the intense glow of the birthmark upon the whiteness of her cheek that he could not restrain a strong convulsive shudder. His wife fainted.

"Aminadab! Aminadab!" shouted Aylmer, stamping violently on the floor.

Forthwith there issued from an inner apartment a man of low stature, but bulky frame, with shaggy hair hanging about his visage, which was grimed with the vapors of the furnace. This personage had been Aylmer's underworker during his whole scientific career, and was admirably fitted for that office by his great mechanical readiness, and the skill with which, while incapable of comprehending a single principle, he executed all the details of his master's experiments. With his vast strength, his shaggy hair, his smoky aspect, and the indescribable earthiness that incrusted him, he seemed to represent man's physical nature; while Aylmer's slender figure, and pale, intellectual face, were no less apt a type of the spiritual element.

"Throw open the door of the boudoir, Aminadab," said Aylmer, "and burn a pastil."

"Yes, master," answered Aminadab, looking intently at the lifeless form of Georgiana; and then he muttered to himself, "If she were my wife, I'd never part with that birthmark."

When Georgiana recovered consciousness she found herself breathing an atmosphere of penetrating fragrance, the gentle potency of which had recalled her from her deathlike faintness. The scene around her looked like enchantment. Aylmer had converted those smoky, dingy, sombre rooms, where he had spent his brightest years in recondite pursuits, into a series of beautiful apartments not unfit to be the secluded abode of a lovely woman. The walls were hung with gorgeous curtains, which imparted the combination of grandeur and grace that no other species of adornment can achieve; and as they fell from the ceiling to the floor, their rich and ponderous folds, concealing all angles and straight lines, appeared to shut in the scene from infinite space. For aught Georgiana knew, it might be a pavilion among the clouds. And Aylmer, excluding the sunshine, which would have interfered with his chemical processes, had supplied its place with perfumed lamps, emitting flames of various hue, but all uniting in a soft, impurpled radiance. He now knelt by his wife's side, watching her earnestly, but without alarm; for he was confident in his science, and felt that he could draw a magic circle round her within which no evil might intrude.

"Where am I? Ah, I remember," said Georgiana, faintly; and she placed her hand over her cheek to hide the terrible mark from her husband's eyes.

"Fear not, dearest!" exclaimed he. "Do not shrink from me! Believe me, Georgiana, I even rejoice in this single imperfection, since it will be such a rapture to remove it."

"Oh, spare me!" sadly replied his wife. "Pray do not look at it again. I never can forget that convulsive shudder."

In order to soothe Georgiana, and, as it were, to release her mind from the burden of actual things, Aylmer now put in practice some of the light and playful secrets which science had taught him among its profounder lore. Airy figures, absolutely bodiless ideas, and forms of unsubstantial beauty came and danced before her, imprinting their momentary footsteps on beams of light. Though she had some indistinct idea of the method of these optical phenomena, still the illusion was almost perfect enough to warrant the belief that her husband possessed sway over the spiritual world. Then again, when she felt a wish to look forth from her seclusion, immediately, as if her thoughts were answered, the procession of external existence flitted across a screen. The scenery and the figures of actual life were perfectly represented, but with that bewitching, yet indescribable difference which always makes a picture, an image, or a shadow so much more attractive than the original. When wearied of this Aylmer bade her cast her eyes upon a vessel containing a quantity of earth. She did so, with little interest at first; but was soon startled to perceive the germ of a plant shooting upward from the soil. Then came the slender stalk; the leaves gradually unfolded themselves; and amid them was a perfect and lovely flower.

"It is magical!" cried Georgiana. "I dare not touch it."

"Nay, pluck it," answered Aylmer,—"pluck it, and inhale its brief perfume while you may. The flower will wither in a few moments and leave nothing save its brown seed vessels; but thence may be perpetuated a race as ephemeral as itself."

But Georgiana had no sooner touched the flower than the whole plant suffered a blight, its leaves turning coal-black as if by the agency of fire.

"There was too powerful a stimulus," said Aylmer, thoughtfully.

To make up for this abortive experiment, he proposed to take her portrait by a scientific process of his own invention. It was to be effected by rays of light striking upon a polished plate of metal. Georgiana assented; but, on looking at the result, was affrighted to find the features of the portrait blurred and indefinable; while the minute figure of a hand appeared where the cheek should have been. Aylmer snatched the metallic plate and threw it into a jar of corrosive acid.

Soon, however, he forgot these mortifying failures. In the intervals of study and chemical experiment he came to her flushed and exhausted, but seemed invigorated by her presence, and spoke in glowing language of the resources of his art. He gave a history of the long dynasty of the alchemists, who spent so many ages in quest of the universal solvent by which the golden principle might be elicited from all things vile and base. Aylmer appeared to believe that, by the plainest scientific logic, it was altogether within the limits of possibility to discover this long-sought medium; "but," he added, "a philosopher who should go deep enough to acquire the power would attain too lofty a wisdom to stoop to the exercise of it." Not less singular were his opinions in regard to the elixir vitæ. He more than intimated that it was at his option to concoct a liquid that should prolong life for years, perhaps interminably; but that it would produce a discord in Nature which all the world, and chiefly the quaffer of the immortal nostrum, would find cause to curse.

"Aylmer, are you in earnest?" asked Georgiana, looking at him with amazement and fear. "It is terrible to possess such power, or even to dream of possessing it."

"Oh, do not tremble, my love," said her husband. "I would not wrong either you or myself by working such inharmonious effects upon our lives; but I would have you consider how trifling, in comparison, is the skill requisite to remove this little hand."

At the mention of the birthmark, Georgiana, as usual, shrank as if a redhot iron had touched her cheek.

Again Aylmer applied himself to his labors. She could hear his voice in the distant furnace room giving directions to Aminadab, whose harsh, uncouth, misshapen tones were audible in response, more like the grunt or growl of a brute than human speech. After hours of absence, Aylmer reappeared and proposed that she should now examine his cabinet of chemical products and natural treasures of the earth. Among the former he showed her a small vial, in which, he remarked, was contained a gentle yet most powerful fragrance, capable of impregnating all the breezes that blow across a kingdom. They were of inestimable value, the contents of that little vial; and, as he said so, he threw some of the perfume into the air and filled the room with piercing and invigorating delight.

"And what is this?" asked Georgiana, pointing to a small crystal globe containing a gold-colored liquid. "It is so beautiful to the eye that I could imagine it the elixir of life."

"In one sense it is," replied Aylmer; "or, rather, the elixir of immortality. It is the most precious poison that ever was concocted in this world. By its aid I could apportion the lifetime of any mortal at whom you might point your finger. The strength of the dose would determine whether he were to linger out years, or drop dead in the midst of a breath. No king on his guarded throne could keep his life if I, in my private station, should deem that the welfare of millions justified me in depriving him of it."

"Why do you keep such a terrific drug?" inquired Georgiana in horror.

"Do not mistrust me, dearest," said her husband, smiling; "its virtuous potency is yet greater than its harmful one. But see! here is a powerful cosmetic. With a few drops of this in a vase of water, freckles may be washed away as easily as the hands are cleansed. A stronger infusion would take the blood out of the cheek, and leave the rosiest beauty a pale ghost."

"Is it with this lotion that you intend to bathe my cheek?" asked Georgiana, anxiously.

"Oh, no," hastily replied her husband; "this is merely superficial. Your case demands a remedy that shall go deeper."

In his interviews with Georgiana, Aylmer generally made minute inquiries as to her sensations and whether the confinement of the rooms and the temperature of the atmosphere agreed with her. These questions had such a particular drift that Georgiana began to conjecture that she was already subjected to certain physical influences, either breathed in with the fragrant air or taken with her food. She fancied likewise, but it might be altogether fancy, that there was a stirring up of her system—a strange, indefinite sensation creeping through her veins, and tingling, half painfully, half pleasurably, at her heart. Still, whenever she dared to look into the mirror, there she beheld herself pale as a white rose and with the crimson birthmark stamped upon her cheek. Not even Aylmer now hated it so much as she.

To dispel the tedium of the hours which her husband found it necessary to devote to the processes of combination and analysis, Georgiana turned over the volumes of his scientific library. In many dark old tomes she met with chapters full of romance and poetry. They were the works of philosophers of the middle ages, such as Albertus Magnus, Cornelius Agrippa, Paracelsus, and the famous friar who created the prophetic Brazen Head. All these antique naturalists stood in advance of their centuries, yet were imbued with some of their credulity, and therefore were believed, and perhaps imagined themselves to have acquired from the investigation of Nature a power above Nature, and from physics a sway over the spiritual world. Hardly less curious and imaginative were the early volumes of the Transactions of the Royal Society, in which the members, knowing little of the limits of natural possibility, were continually recording wonders or proposing methods whereby wonders might be wrought.

But to Georgiana the most engrossing volume was a large folio from her husband's own hand, in which he had recorded every experiment of his scientific career, its original aim, the methods adopted for its development, and its final success or failure, with the circumstances to which either event was attributable. The book, in truth, was both the history and emblem of his ardent, ambitious, imaginative, yet practical and laborious life. He handled physical details as if there were nothing beyond them; yet spiritualized them all, and redeemed himself from materialism by his strong and eager aspiration towards the infinite. In his grasp the veriest clod of earth assumed a soul. Georgiana, as she read, reverenced Aylmer and loved him more profoundly than ever, but with a less entire dependence on his judgment than heretofore. Much as he had accomplished, she could not but observe that his most splendid successes were almost invariably failures, if compared with the ideal at which he aimed. His brightest diamonds were the merest pebbles, and felt to be so by himself, in comparison with the inestimable gems which lay hidden beyond his reach. The volume, rich with achievements that had won renown for its author, was yet as melancholy a record as ever mortal hand had penned. It was the sad confession and continual exemplification of the shortcomings of the composite man, the spirit burdened with clay and working in matter, and of the despair that assails the higher nature at finding itself so miserably thwarted by the earthly part. Perhaps every man of genius in whatever sphere might recognize the image of his own experience in Aylmer's journal.

So deeply did these reflections affect Georgiana that she laid her face upon the open volume and burst into tears. In this situation she was found by her husband.

"It is dangerous to read in a sorcerer's books," said he with a smile, though his countenance was uneasy and displeased. "Georgiana, there are pages in that volume which I can scarcely glance over and keep my senses. Take heed lest it prove as detrimental to you."

"It has made me worship you more than ever," said she.

"Ah, wait for this one success," rejoined he, "then worship me if you will. I shall deem myself hardly unworthy of it. But come, I have sought you for the luxury of your voice. Sing to me, dearest."

So she poured out the liquid music of her voice to quench the thirst of his spirit. He then took his leave with a boyish exuberance of gayety, assuring her that her seclusion would endure but a little longer, and that the result was already certain. Scarcely had he departed when Georgiana felt irresistibly impelled to follow him. She had forgotten to inform Aylmer of a symptom which for two or three hours past had begun to excite her attention. It was a sensation in the fatal birthmark, not painful, but which induced a restlessness throughout her system. Hastening after her husband, she intruded for the first time into the laboratory.

The first thing that struck her eye was the furnace, that hot and feverish worker, with the intense glow of its fire, which by the quantities of soot clustered above it seemed to have been burning for ages. There was a distilling apparatus in full operation. Around the room were retorts, tubes, cylinders, crucibles, and other apparatus of chemical research. An electrical machine stood ready for immediate use. The atmosphere felt oppressively close, and was tainted with gaseous odors which had been tormented forth by the processes of science. The severe and homely simplicity of the apartment, with its naked walls and brick pavement, looked strange, accustomed as Georgiana had become to the fantastic elegance of her boudoir. But what chiefly, indeed almost solely, drew her attention, was the aspect of Aylmer himself.

He was pale as death, anxious and absorbed, and hung over the furnace as if it depended upon his utmost watchfulness whether the liquid which it was distilling should be the draught of immortal happiness or misery. How different from the sanguine and joyous mien that he had assumed for Georgiana's encouragement!

"Carefully now, Aminadab; carefully, thou human machine; carefully, thou man of clay!" muttered Aylmer, more to himself than his assistant. "Now if there be a thought too much or too little, it is all over."

"Ho! ho!" mumbled Aminadab. "Look, master! look!"

Aylmer raised his eyes hastily, and at first reddened, then grew paler than ever, on beholding Georgiana. He rushed towards her and seized her arm with a gripe that left the print of his fingers upon it.

"Why do you come hither? Have you no trust in your husband?" cried he, impetuously. "Would you throw the blight of that fatal birthmark over my labors? It is not well done. Go, prying woman, go!"

"Nay, Aylmer," said Georgiana with the firmness of which she possessed no stinted endowment, "it is not you that have a right to complain. You mistrust your wife; you have concealed the anxiety with which you watch the development of this experiment. Think not so unworthily of me, my husband. Tell me all the risk we run, and fear not that I shall shrink; for my share in it is far less than your own."

"No, no, Georgiana!" said Aylmer, impatiently; "it must not be."

"I submit," replied she calmly. "And, Aylmer, I shall quaff whatever draught you bring me; but it will be on the same principle that would induce me to take a dose of poison if offered by your hand."

"My noble wife," said Aylmer, deeply moved, "I knew not the height and depth of your nature until now. Nothing shall be concealed. Know, then, that this crimson hand, superficial as it seems, has clutched its grasp into your being with a strength of which I had no previous conception. I have already administered agents powerful enough to do aught except to change your entire physical system. Only one thing remains to be tried. If that fail us we are ruined."

"Why did you hesitate to tell me this?" asked she.

"Because, Georgiana," said Aylmer, in a low voice, "there is danger."

"Danger? There is but one danger—that this horrible stigma shall be left upon my cheek!" cried Georgiana. "Remove it, remove it, whatever be the cost, or we shall both go mad!"

"Heaven knows your words are too true," said Aylmer, sadly. "And now, dearest, return to your boudoir. In a little while all will be tested."

He conducted her back and took leave of her with a solemn tenderness which spoke far more than his words how much was now at stake. After his departure, Georgiana became rapt in musings. She considered the character of Aylmer, and did it completer justice than at any previous moment. Her heart exulted, while it trembled, at his honorable love—so pure and lofty that it would accept nothing less than perfection nor miserably make itself contented with an earthlier nature than he had dreamed of. She felt how much more precious was such a sentiment than that meaner kind which would have borne with the imperfection for her sake, and have been guilty of treason to holy love by degrading its perfect idea to the level of the actual; and with her whole spirit she prayed that, for a single moment, she might satisfy his highest and deepest conception. Longer than one moment she well knew it could not be; for his spirit was ever on the march, ever ascending, and each instant required something that was beyond the scope of the instant before.

The sound of her husband's footsteps aroused her. He bore a crystal goblet containing a liquor colorless as water, but bright enough to be the draught of immortality. Aylmer was pale; but it seemed rather the consequence of a highly-wrought state of mind and tension of spirit than of fear or doubt.

"The concoction of the draught has been perfect," said he, in answer to Georgiana's look. "Unless all my science have deceived me, it cannot fail."

"Save on your account, my dearest Aylmer," observed his wife, "I might wish to put off this birthmark of mortality by relinquishing mortality itself in preference to any other mode. Life is but a sad possession to those who have attained precisely the degree of moral advancement at which I stand. Were I weaker and blinder it might be happiness. Were I stronger, it might be endured hopefully. But being what I find myself, methinks I am of all mortals the most fit to die."

"You are fit for heaven without tasting death!" replied her husband. "But why do we speak of dying? The draught cannot fail. Behold its effect upon this plant."

On the window seat there stood a geranium diseased with yellow blotches, which had overspread all its leaves. Aylmer poured a small quantity of the liquid upon the soil in which it grew. In a little time, when the roots of the plant had taken up the moisture, the unsightly blotches began to be extinguished in a living verdure.

"There needed no proof," said Georgiana, quietly. "Give me the goblet. I joyfully stake all upon your word."

"Drink, then, thou lofty creature!" exclaimed Aylmer, with fervid admiration. "There is no taint of imperfection on thy spirit. Thy sensible frame, too, shall soon be all perfect."

She quaffed the liquid and returned the goblet to his hand.

"It is grateful," said she with a placid smile. "Methinks it is like water from a heavenly fountain; for it contains I know not what of unobtrusive fragrance and deliciousness. It allays a feverish thirst that had parched me for many days. Now, dearest, let me sleep. My earthly senses are closing over my spirit like the leaves around the heart of a rose at sunset."

She spoke the last words with a gentle reluctance, as if it required almost more energy than she could command to pronounce the faint and lingering syllables. Scarcely had they loitered through her lips ere she was lost in slumber. Aylmer sat by her side, watching her aspect with the emotions proper to a man the whole value of whose existence was involved in the process now to be tested. Mingled with this mood, however, was the philosophic investigation characteristic of the man of science. Not the minutest symptom escaped him. A heightened flush of the cheek, a slight irregularity of breath, a quiver of the eyelid, a hardly perceptible tremor through the frame,—such were the details which, as the moments passed, he wrote down in his folio volume. Intense thought had set its stamp upon every previous page of that volume, but the thoughts of years were all concentrated upon the last.

While thus employed, he failed not to gaze often at the fatal hand, and not without a shudder. Yet once, by a strange and unaccountable impulse, he pressed it with his lips. His spirit recoiled, however, in the very act; and Georgiana, out of the midst of her deep sleep, moved uneasily and murmured as if in remonstrance. Again Aylmer resumed his watch. Nor was it without avail. The crimson hand, which at first had been strongly visible upon the marble paleness of Georgiana's cheek, now grew more faintly outlined. She remained not less pale than ever; but the birthmark, with every breath that came and went, lost somewhat of its former distinctness. Its presence had been awful; its departure was more awful still. Watch the stain of the rainbow fading out the sky, and you will know how that mysterious symbol passed away.

"By Heaven! it is well-nigh gone!" said Aylmer to himself, in almost irrepressible ecstasy. "I can scarcely trace it now. Success! success! And now it is like the faintest rose color. The lightest flush of blood across her cheek would overcome it. But she is so pale!"

He drew aside the window curtain and suffered the light of natural day to fall into the room and rest upon her cheek. At the same time he heard a gross, hoarse chuckle, which he had long known as his servant Aminadab's expression of delight.

"Ah, clod! ah, earthly mass!" cried Aylmer, laughing in a sort of frenzy, "you have served me well! Matter and spirit—earth and heaven—have both done their part in this! Laugh, thing of the senses! You have earned the right to laugh."

These exclamations broke Georgiana's sleep. She slowly unclosed her eyes and gazed into the mirror which her husband had arranged for that purpose. A faint smile flitted over her lips when she recognized how barely perceptible was now that crimson hand which had once blazed forth with such disastrous brilliancy as to scare away all their happiness. But then her eyes sought Aylmer's face with a trouble and anxiety that he could by no means account for.

"My poor Aylmer!" murmured she.

"Poor? Nay, richest, happiest, most favored!" exclaimed he. "My peerless bride, it is successful! You are perfect!"

"My poor Aylmer," she repeated, with a more than human tenderness, "you have aimed loftily; you have done nobly. Do not repent that with so high and pure a feeling, you have rejected the best the earth could offer. Aylmer, dearest Aylmer, I am dying!"

Alas! it was too true! the fatal hand had grappled with the mystery of life, and was the bond by which an angelic spirit kept itself in union with a mortal frame. As the last crimson tint of the birthmark—that sole token of human imperfection—faded from her cheek, the parting breath of the now perfect woman passed into the atmosphere, and her soul, lingering a moment near her husband, took its heavenward flight. Then a hoarse, chuckling laugh was heard again! Thus ever does the gross fatality of earth exult in its invariable triumph over the immortal essence which, in this dim sphere of half development, demands the completeness of a higher state. Yet, had Aylmer reached a profounder wisdom, he need not thus have flung away the happiness which would have woven his mortal life of the selfsame texture with the celestial. The momentary circumstance was too strong for him; he failed to look beyond the shadowy scope of time, and, living once for all in eternity, to find the perfect future in the present.

HENRY JAMES
(1843–1916)

HENRY JAMES was born in New York City, to a gifted family. His father, Henry James, Sr., was a philosopher and theologian. His brother was William James, the philosopher and psychologist. Educated privately by tutors in the United States and Europe, he entered Harvard Law School in 1862 and withdrew a year later. In Cambridge, he met William Dean Howells, who became a key source of encouragement and a lifelong friend. With the support of Howells and others in the Cambridge literary circle, James began publishing critical essays in the *Atlantic Monthly*. His first story, "A Tragedy of Error," appeared in the *North American Review* in 1864. He made frequent trips to Europe, and in 1876 he settled there permanently, living first in Paris, then London; he became a British subject in 1915. Literature and travel were his essential activities. In his long and productive life, he wrote one-hundred-twelve stories and twenty novels. His works include *Daisy Miller* (1879), *Portrait of a Lady* (1881), *The Bostonians* (1886), *The Turn of the Screw* (1898), *The Wings of the Dove* (1902), *The Ambassadors* (1903), and *The Golden Bowl* (1904). In 1976, sixty years after his death, James was named to Westminster Abbey's Poets' Corner.

James's contribution to literature is his mastery of psychological realism—his sense of relationships, including those of lovers, as revealing essential truths of character and culture. The intricacies of relationships and states of being, as revealed especially in his late writings, are reflected in a highly nuanced prose style.

One of his principal concerns was the influence of Europeans on Americans. "Adina" (1874) represents a relatively early illustration of James's international theme, in which the values and cultures of France and Italy are associated with a moral sense more mysterious, less cut-and-dried than ours, as well as with a greater capacity for enjoying life's pleasures.

In "Adina," two young men, Sam Scrope and the narrator, are on holiday in Rome. The narrator reports: "It was [Scrope's] fancy to pretend that he enjoyed nothing." Scrope's facade, if it is one, drops utterly when the pair encounters a "picturesque" Italian, who holds in his palm a possibly precious and ancient gem. Scrope, who at long last has found something to enjoy, covets the gem. As love arrives in the person of Adina, the gem becomes a catalyst for romance as well as the moral center of the story.

Adina

I

We had been talking of Sam Scrope round the fire—mindful, such of us, of the rule *de mortuis*. Our host, however, had said nothing; rather to my surprise, as I knew he had been particularly intimate with our friend. But when our group had dispersed, and I remained alone with him, he brightened the fire, offered me another cigar, puffed his own awhile with a retrospective air, and told me the following tale:

Eighteen years ago Scrope and I were together in Rome. It was the beginning of my acquaintance with him, and I had grown fond of him, as a mild, meditative youth often does of an active, irreverent, caustic one. He had in those days the germs of the eccentricities,—not to call them by a hard name,—which made him afterwards the most intolerable of the friends we did not absolutely break with; he was already, as they say, a crooked stick. He was cynical, perverse, conceited, obstinate, brilliantly clever. But he was young, and youth, happily, makes many of our vices innocent. Scrope had his merits, or our friendship would not have ripened. He was not an amiable man, but he was an honest one—in spite of the odd caprice I have to relate; and half my kindness for him was based in a feeling that at bottom, in spite of his vanity, he enjoyed his own irritability as little as other people. It was his fancy to pretend that he enjoyed nothing, and that what sentimental travelers call picturesqueness was a weariness to his spirit; but the world was new to him and the charm of fine things often took him by surprise and stole a march on his premature cynicism. He was an observer in spite of himself, and in his happy moods, thanks to his capital memory and ample information, an excellent critic and most profitable companion. He was a punctilious classical scholar. My boyish journal, kept in those days, is stuffed with learned allusions; they are all Scrope's. I brought to the service of my Roman experience much more loose sentiment than rigid science. It was indeed a jocular bargain between us that in our wanderings, picturesque and archaeological, I should undertake the sentimental business—the raptures, the reflections, the sketching, the quoting from Byron. He considered me absurdly Byronic, and when, in the manner of tourists at that period, I breathed poetic sighs over the subjection of Italy to the foreign foe, he used to swear that Italy had got no more than she deserved, that she was a land of vagabonds and declaimers, and that he had yet to see an Italian whom he would call a man. I quoted to him from Alfieri that the "human plant" grew stronger in Italy than anywhere else, and he retorted, that nothing grew strong there but lying and cheating, laziness, beggary and vermin. Of course we each said more than we believed. If we met a shepherd on the Campagna, leaning on his crook and gazing at us darkly from under the shadow of his matted

251

locks, I would proclaim that he was the handsomest fellow in the world, and demand of Scrope to stop and let me sketch him. Scrope would confound him for a filthy scarecrow and me for a drivelling album-poet. When I stopped in the street to stare up at some mouldering *palazzo* with a patched petticoat hanging to dry from the drawing-room window, and assured him that its haunted disrepair was dearer to my soul than the neat barred front of my Aunt Esther's model mansion in Mount Vernon street, he would seize me by the arm and march me off, pinching me till I shook myself free, and whelming me, my soul and my *palazzo* in a ludicrous torrent of abuse. The truth was that the picturesque of Italy, both in man and in nature, fretted him, depressed him strangely. He was consciously a harsh note in the midst of so many mellow harmonies; every thing seemed to say to him—"Don't you wish you were as easy, as lovable, as carelessly beautiful as we?" In the bottom of his heart he did wish it. To appreciate the bitterness of this dumb disrelish of the Italian atmosphere, you must remember how very ugly the poor fellow was. He was uglier at twenty than at forty, for as he grew older it became the fashion to say that his crooked features were "distinguished." But twenty years ago, in the infancy of modern aesthetics, he could not have passed for even a bizarre form of ornament. In a single word, poor Scrope looked *common:* that was where the shoe pinched. Now you know that in Italy almost everything has, to the outer sense, what artists call style.

In spite of our clashing theories, our friendship *did* ripen, and we spent together many hours, deeply seasoned with the sense of youth and freedom. The best of these, perhaps, were those we passed on horseback, on the Campagna; you remember such hours; you remember those days of early winter, when the sun is as strong as that of a New England June, and the bare, purple-drawn slopes and hollows lie bathed in the yellow light of Italy. On such a day, Scrope and I mounted our horses in the grassy terrace before St John Lateran, and rode away across the broad meadows over which the Claudian Aqueduct drags its slow length—stumbling and lapsing here and there, as it goes, beneath the burden of the centuries. We rode a long distance—well towards Albano, and at last stopped near a low fragment of ruin, which seemed to be all that was left of an ancient tower. Was it indeed ancient, or was it a relic of one of the numerous mediæval fortresses, with which the grassy desert of the Campagna is studded? This was one of the questions which Scrope, as a competent classicist, liked to ponder; though when I called his attention to the picturesque effect of the fringe of wild plants which crowned the ruin, and detached their clear filaments in the deep blue air, he shrugged his shoulders, and said they only helped the brickwork to crumble. We tethered our horses to a wild fig tree hard by, and strolled around the tower. Suddenly, on the sunny side of it, we came upon a figure asleep on the grass. A young man lay there, all unconscious, with his head upon a pile of weed-smothered stones. A rusty gun was on the ground beside him, and an empty game-bag, lying near it, told of his being an unlucky sportsman. His heavy sleep seemed to point to a long morning's fruitless tramp. And yet he must have been either very unskilled, or very little in earnest, for the Campagna is alive with small game, every month in the year—or was, at least, twenty years ago. It was no more than I owed to my reputation for Byronism, to discover a careless, youthful grace in the young fellow's attitude. One of his legs was flung over the other; one of his arms was thrust back under his head, and the other resting loosely on the grass; his head drooped backward, and exposed a strong, young throat; his hat was pulled over his eyes, so that we could see nothing but his mouth and chin. "An American rustic asleep is an ugly fellow," said I; "but this young Roman clodhopper, as he lies snoring there, is really statuesque;" "clodhopper," was for argument, for our rustic Endymion, judging by his garments, was something better than a mere peasant. He turned uneasily, as we stood above him, and muttered something. "It's not fair to wake him," I said, and passed my arm into Scrope's, to lead him away; but he resisted, and I saw that something had struck him.

In his change of position, our picturesque friend had opened the hand which was resting on the grass. The palm, turned upward, contained a dull-colored oval object, of the size of a small snuff-box. "What has he got there?" I said to Scrope; but Scrope only answered by bending over and looking at it. "Really, we are taking great liberties with the poor fellow," I said. "Let him finish his nap in peace." And I was on the point of walking away. But my voice had aroused him; he lifted his hand, and, with the movement, the object I have compared to a snuff-box caught the light, and emitted a dull flash.

"It's a gem," said Scrope, "recently disinterred and encrusted with dirt."

The young man awoke in earnest, pushed back his hat, stared at us, and slowly sat up. He rubbed his eyes, to see if he were not still dreaming, then glanced at the gem, if gem it was, thrust his hand mechanically into his pocket, and gave us a broad smile. "Gentle, serene Italian nature!" I exclaimed. "A young New England farmer, whom we should have disturbed in this fashion, would wake up with an oath and a kick."

"I mean to test his gentleness," said Scrope. "I'm determined to see what he has got there." Scrope was very fond of small *bric-a-brac*, and had ransacked every curiosity shop in Rome. It was an oddity among his many oddities, but it agreed well enough with the rest of them. What he looked for and relished in old prints and old china was not, generally, beauty of form nor romantic association; it was elaborate and patient workmanship, fine engraving, skillful method.

"Good day," I said to our young man; "we didn't mean to interrupt you."

He shook himself, got up, and stood before us, looking out from under his thick curls, and still frankly smiling. There was something very simple,—a trifle silly,—in his smile, and I wondered whether he was not under-witted. He was young, but he was not a mere lad. His eyes were dark and heavy, but they gleamed with a friendly light, and his parted lips showed the glitter of his strong, white teeth. His complexion was of a fine, deep brown, just removed from coarseness by that vague suffused pallor common among Italians. He had the frame of a young Hercules; he was altogether as handsome a vagabond as you could wish for the foreground of a pastoral landscape.

"You've not earned your rest," said Scrope, pointing to his empty game-bag; "you've got no birds."

He looked at the bag and at Scrope, and then scratched his head and laughed. "I don't want to kill them," he said. "I bring out my gun because it's stupid to walk about pulling a straw! And then my uncle is always grumbling at me for not doing something. When he sees me leave the house with my gun, he thinks I may, at least, get my dinner. He didn't know the lock's broke; even if I had powder and shot, the old blunderbuss wouldn't go off. When I'm hungry I go to sleep." And he glanced, with his handsome grin, at his recent couch. "The birds might come and perch on my nose, and not wake me up. My uncle never thinks of asking me what I have brought home for supper. He is a holy man, and lives on black bread and beans."

"Who is your uncle?" I inquired.

"The Padre Girolamo at Lariccia."

He looked at our hats and whips, asked us a dozen questions about our ride, our horses, and what we paid for them, our nationality, and our way of life in Rome, and at last walked away to caress our browsing animals and scratch their noses. "He has got something precious there," Scrope said, as we strolled after him. "He has evidently found it in the ground. The Campagna is full of treasures yet." As we overtook our new acquaintance he thrust his indistinguishable prize behind him, and gave a foolish laugh, which tried my companion's patience. "The fellow's an idiot!" he cried. "Does he think I want to snatch the thing?"

"What is it you've got there?" I asked kindly.

"Which hand will you have?" he said, still laughing.

"The right."

"The left," said Scrope, as he hesitated.

He fumbled behind him a moment more, and then produced his treasure with a flourish. Scrope took it, wiped it off carefully with his handkerchief, and bent his near-sighted eyes over it. I left him to examine it. I was more interested in watching the Padre Girolamo's nephew. The latter stood looking at my friend gravely, while Scrope rubbed and scratched the little black stone, breathed upon it and held it up to the light. He frowned and scratched his head; he was evidently trying to concentrate his wits on the fine account he expected Scrope to give of it. When I glanced towards Scrope, I found he had flushed excitedly, and I immediately bent my nose over it too. It was of about the size of a small hen's-egg, of a dull brown color, stained and encrusted by long burial, and deeply corrugated on one surface. Scrope paid no heed to my questions, but continued to scrape and polish. At last—"How did you come by this thing?" he asked dryly.

"I found it in the earth, a couple of miles from here, this morning." And the young fellow put out his hand nervously, to take it back. Scrope resisted a moment, but thought better, and surrendered it. As an old mouser, he began instinctively to play at indifference. Our companion looked hard at the little stone, turned it over and over, then thrust it behind him again, with his simple-souled laugh.

"Here's a precious chance," murmured Scrope.

"But in Heaven's name, what is it," I demanded, impatiently.

"Don't ask me. I don't care to phrase the conjecture audibly—it's immense—if it's what I think it is; and here stands this giggling lout with a prior claim to it. What shall I do with him? I should like to knock him in the head with the butt end of his blunderbuss."

"I suppose he'll sell you the thing, if you offer him enough."

"Enough? What does he know about enough? He don't know a topaz from a turnip."

"Is it a topaz, then?"

"Hold your tongue, and don't mention names. He must sell it as a turnip. Make him tell you just where he found it."

He told us very frankly, still smiling from ear to ear. He had observed in a solitary ilex-tree, of great age, the traces of a recent lightning-stroke. (A week of unseasonably sultry weather had, in fact some days before, culminated in a terrific thunder-storm.) The tree had been shivered and killed, and the earth turned up at its foot. The bolt, burying itself, had dug a deep, straight hole, in which one might have planted a stake. "I don't know why," said our friend, "but as I stood looking at it, I thrust the muzzle of my old gun into the aperture. It descended for some distance and stopped with a strange noise, as if it were striking a metallic surface. I rammed it up and down, and heard the same noise. Then I said to myself—'Something is hidden there—*quattrini*, perhaps; let us see.' I made a spade of one of the shivered ilex-boughs, dug, and scraped and scratched; and, in twenty minutes, fished up a little, rotten, iron box. It was so rotten that the lid and sides were as thin as letter-paper. When I gave them a knock, they crumbled. It was filled with other bits of iron of the same sort, which seemed to have formed the compartments of a case; and with the damp earth, which had oozed in through the holes and crevices. In the middle lay this stone, embedded in earth and mold. There was nothing else. I broke the box to pieces and kept the stone. *Ecco!*"

Scrope, with a shrug, repossessed himself of the moldy treasure, and our friend, as he gave it up, declared it was a thousand years old. Julius Caesar had worn it in his crown!

"Julius Caesar wore no crown, my dear friend," said Scrope urbanely. "It may be a thousand years old, and it may be ten. It may be an—agate, and it may be a flint! I don't know. But if you will sell it on the chance?——" And he tossed it three times high into the air, and caught it as it fell.

"I have my idea it's precious," said the young man. "Precious things are found here very day—why shouldn't I stumble on something as well as another? Why should the lightning strike just that spot, and no other? It was sent there by my patron, the blessed Saint Angelo!"

He was not such a simpleton, after all; or rather he was a puzzling mixture of simplicity and sense. "If you really want the thing," I said to Scrope, "make him an offer, and have done with it."

" 'Have done with it,' is easily said. How little do you suppose he will take?"

"I haven't the smallest idea of its value."

"It's value has nothing to do with the matter. Estimate it at its value and we may as well put it back into its hole—of its probable value, he knows nothing; he need never know," and Scrope, musing an instant, counted, and flung them down on the grass, ten silver *scudi*—the same number of dollars. Angelo,—he virtually told us his name,—watched them fall, one by one, but made no movement to pick them up. But his eyes brightened; his simplicity and his shrewdness were debating the question. The little heap of silver was most agreeable; to make a poor bargain, on the other hand, was not. He looked at Scrope with a dumb appeal to his fairness which quite touched me. It touched Scrope, too, a trifle; for, after a moment's hesitation, he flung down another *scudi*. Angelo gave a puzzled sigh, and Scrope turned short about and began to mount. In another moment we were both in the saddle. Angelo stood looking at his money. "Are you satisfied?" said my companion, curtly.

The young fellow gave a strange smile. "Have *you* a good conscience?" he demanded.

"Hang your impudence!" cried Scrope, very red. "What's my conscience to you?" And he thrust in his spurs and galloped away. I waved my hand to our friend and followed more slowly. Before long I turned in the saddle and looked back. Angelo was standing as we had left him, staring after us, with his money evidently yet untouched. But, of course, he would pick it up!

I rode along with my friend in silence; I was wondering over his off-hand justice. I was youthful enough to shrink from being thought a Puritan or a casuist, but it seemed to me that I scented sophistry in Scrope's double valuation of Angelo's treasure. If it was a prize for him, it was a prize for Angelo, and ten *scudi*,— and one over,—was meager payment for a prize. It cost me some discomfort to find rigid Sam Scrope, of all men, capable of a piece of bargaining which needed to be ingeniously explained. Such as it was, he offered his explanation at last— half angrily, as if he knew his logic was rather grotesque. "Say it out; say it, for Heaven's sake!" he cried. "I know what you're thinking—I've played that pretty-faced simpleton a trick, eh?—and I'm no better than a swindler, evidently! Let me tell you, once for all, that I'm not ashamed of having got my prize cheap. It was ten *scudi* or nothing! If I had offered a farthing more I should have opened those sleepy eyes of his. It was a case to pocket one's scruples and *act*. That silly boy was not to be trusted with the keeping of such a prize for another half hour; the deuce knows what might have become of it. I rescued it in the interest of art, of science, of taste. The proper price of the thing I couldn't have dreamed of offering; where was I to raise ten thousand dollars to buy a bauble? Say I had offered a hundred—forthwith our picturesque friend, thick-witted though he is, would have pricked up his ears and held fast! He would have asked time to reflect and take advice, and he would have hurried back to his village and to his uncle, the shrewd old priest, Padre Girolamo. The wise-heads of the place would have held a conclave, and decided—I don't know what; that they must go up to Rome and see Signor Castillani, or the director of the Papal excavations. Some knowing person would have got wind of the affair, and whispered to the Padre Girolamo that his handsome nephew had been guided by a miracle to a fortune, and might marry a *contessina*. And when all was done, where should I be for my pains? As it is, I discriminate; I look at the matter all round, and I decide. I get my prize; the ingenious Angelo gets a month's carouse,—he'll enjoy it,—and goes to sleep again. Pleasant dreams to him! What does he want of money? Money would have corrupted him! I've saved the *contessina*, too; I'm sure he would have beaten her. So, if we're all satisfied, is it for you to look black? My mind's at ease; I'm neither richer nor poorer. I'm not poorer, because against my eleven *scudi* may stand the sense of having given a harmless treat to an innocent lad; I'm not richer, because,—I hope you understand,—I mean never to turn my stone into money. There it is that delicacy comes in. It's a stone and nothing more; and all the income I shall derive from it will be enjoying the way people open their eyes and hold their breath when I make it sparkle under the lamp, and tell them just what stone it is."

"What stone is it, then, in the name of all that's demoralizing?" I asked, with ardor.

Scrope broke into a gleeful chuckle, and patted me on the arm. "*Pazienza!* Wait till we get under the lamp, some evening, and then I'll make it sparkle and tell you. I must be sure first," he added, with sudden gravity.

But it was the feverish elation of his tone, and not its gravity, that struck me. I began to hate the stone; it seemed to have corrupted him. His ingenious account of his motives left something vaguely unexplained—almost inexplicable. There are dusky corners in the simplest natures; strange, moral involutions in the healthiest. Scrope was not simple, and, in virtue of his defiant self-consciousness, he might have been called morbid; so that I came to consider his injustice in this particular case as the fruit of a vicious seed which I find it hard to name. Everything in Italy seemed mutely to reproach him with his meager faculty of pleasing; the indefinable gracefulness of nature and man murmured forever in his ears that he was an angular cynic. This was the real motive of his intolerance of my sympathetic rhapsodies, and it prompted him now to regale himself, once for all, with the sense of an advantage wrested, if not by fair means, then by foul, from some sentient form of irritating Italian felicity. This is a rather metaphysical account of the matter; at the time I guessed the secret, without phrasing it.

Scrope carried his stone to no appraiser, and asked no archæological advice about it. He quietly informed himself, as if from general curiosity, as to the best methods of cleansing, polishing, and restoring antique gems, laid in a provision of delicate tools and acids, turned the key in his door, and took the measure of his prize. I asked him no questions, but I saw that he was intensely preoccupied, and was becoming daily better convinced that it was a rare one. He went about whistling and humming odd scraps of song, like a lover freshly accepted. Whenever I heard him I had a sudden vision of our friend Angelo staring blankly after us, as we rode away like a pair of ravishers in a German ballad. Scrope and I lodged in the same house, and one evening, at the end of a week, after I had gone to bed, he made his way into my room, and shook me out of my slumbers as if the house were on fire. I guessed his errand before he had told it, shuffled on my dressing-gown, and hurried to his own apartment. "I couldn't wait till morning," he said, "I've just given it the last touch; there it lies in its imperial beauty!"

There it lay, indeed, under the lamp, flashing back the light from its glowing heart—a splendid golden topaz on a cushion of white velvet. He thrust a magnifying glass into my hand, and pushed me into a chair by the table. I saw the surface of the stone was worked in elaborate intaglio, but I was not prepared for the portentous character of image and legend. In the center was a full-length naked figure, which I supposed at first to be a pagan deity. Then I saw the orb of sovereignty in one outstretched hand, the chiseled imperial scepter in the other, and the laurel-crown on the low-browed head. All round the face of the stone, near the edges, ran a chain of carven figures—warriors, and horses, and chariots, and young men and women interlaced in elaborate confusion. Over the head of the image, within this concave frieze, stood the inscription:

DIVUS TIBERIUS CÆSAR TOTIUS ORBIS IMPERATOR

The workmanship was extraordinarily delicate; beneath the powerful glass I held in my hand, the figures revealed the perfection and finish of the most renowned of antique marbles. The color of the stone was superb, and, now that its purity had been restored, its size seemed prodigious. It was in every way a gem among gems, a priceless treasure.

"Don't you think it was worth while getting up to shake hands with the Emperor Tiberius?" cried Scrope, after observing my surprise. "Shabby Nineteenth Century Yankees, as we are, we are having our audience. Down on your knees, barbarian, we're in a tremendous presence! Haven't I worked all these days and nights, with my little rags and files, to some purpose? I've annulled the centuries—I've resuscitated a *totius orbis imperator*. Do you conceive, do you apprehend, does your heart thump against your ribs? Not as it should, evidently. This is where Cæsar wore it, dull modern—here, on his breast, near the shoulder, framed in chiselled gold, circled about with pearls as big as plums, clasping together the two sides of his gold-stiffened mantle. It was the agraffe of the imperial purple. Tremble, sir!" and he took up the splendid jewel, and held it against my breast. "No doubts—no objections—no reflections—or we're mortal enemies. How do I know it—where's my warrant? It simply must be! It's too precious to have been anything else. It's the finest intaglio in the world. It has told me its secret; it has lain whispering classic Latin to me by the hour all this week past."

"And has it told you how it came to be buried in its iron box?"

"It has told me everything—more than I can tell you now. Content yourself for the present with admiring it."

Admire it I did for a long time. Certainly, if Scrope's hypothesis was not sound, it ought to have been, and if the Emperor Tiberius had never worn the topaz in his mantle, he was by so much the less imperial. But the design, the legend, the shape of the stone, were all very cogent evidence that the gem had played a great part. "Yes, surely," I said, "it's the finest of known intaglios."

Scrope was silent a while. "Say of unknown," he answered at last. "No one shall ever know it. You I hereby hold pledged to secresy. I shall show it to no one else—except to my mistress, if I ever have one. I paid for the chance of its turning out something great. I couldn't pay for the renown of possessing it. That only a princely fortune could have purchased. To be known as the owner of the finest intaglio in the world would make a great man of me, and that would hardly be fair to our friend Angelo. I shall sink the glory, and cherish my treasure for its simple artistic worth."

"And how would you express that simple artistic worth in Roman *scudi*?"

"It's impossible. Fix upon any sum you please."

I looked again at the golden topaz, gleaming in its velvet nest; and I felt that there could be no successful effort to conceal such a magnificent negation of obscurity. "I recommend you," I said at last, "to think twice before showing it to your mistress."

I had no idea, when I spoke, that my words were timely; for I had vaguely taken for granted that my friend was foredoomed to dispense with this graceful appendage, very much as Peter Schlemihl, in the tale, was condemned to have no shadow. Nevertheless, before a month had passed, he was in a fair way to become engaged to a charming girl. "Juxtaposition is much," says Clough; especially juxtaposition, he implies, in foreign countries; and in Scrope's case it had been particularly close. His cousin, Mrs Waddington, arrived in Rome, and with her a young girl who, though really no relative, offered him all the opportunities of cousinship, added to the remoter charm of a young lady to whom he had to be introduced. Adina Waddington was her companion's stepdaughter, the elder lady having, some eight years before, married a widower with a little girl. Mr Waddington had recently died, and the two ladies were just emerging from their deep mourning. These dusky emblems of a common grief helped them to seem united, as indeed they really were, although Mrs Waddington was but ten years older than her stepdaughter. She was an excellent woman, without a fault that I know of, but that of thinking all the world as good as herself and keeping dinner waiting sometimes while she sketched the sunset. She was stout and fresh-colored, she laughed and talked rather loud, and generally, in galleries and temples, caused a good many stiff British necks to turn round.

She had a mania for excursions, and at Frascati and Tivoli she inflicted her good-humored ponderosity on diminutive donkeys with a relish which seemed to prove that a passion for scenery, like all our passions, is capable of making the best of us pitiless. I had often heard Scrope say that he detested boisterous women, but he forgave his cousin her fine spirits, and stepped into his place as her natural escort and adviser. In the vulgar sense he was not selfish; he had a very definite theory as to the sacrifices a gentleman should make to formal courtesy; but I was nevertheless surprised at the easy terms on which the two ladies secured his services. The key to the mystery was the one which fits so many locks; he was in love with Miss Waddington. There was a sweet stillness about her which balanced the widow's exuberance. Her pretty name of Adina seemed to me to have somehow a mystic fitness to her personality. She was short and slight and blonde, and her black dress gave a sort of infantine bloom to her fairness. She wore her auburn hair twisted into a thousand fantastic braids, like a coiffure in a Renaissance drawing, and she looked out at you from grave blue eyes, in which, behind a cold shyness, there seemed to lurk a tremulous promise to be franker when she knew you better. She never consented to know me well enough to be very frank; she talked very little, and we hardly exchanged a dozen words a day; but I confess that I found a perturbing charm in those eyes. As it was all in silence, though, there was no harm.

Scrope, however, ventured to tell his love—or, at least, to hint at it eloquently enough. I was not so deeply smitten as to be jealous, and I drew a breath of relief when I guessed his secret. It made me think better of him again. The stand he had taken about poor Angelo's gem, in spite of my efforts to account for it philosophically, had given an uncomfortable twist to our friendship. I asked myself if he really had no heart; I even wondered whether there was not a screw loose in his intellect. But here was a hearty, healthy, natural passion, such as only an honest man could feel—such as no man could feel without being the better for it. I began to hope that the sunshine of his fine sentiment would melt away his aversion to giving Angelo his dues. He was charmed, soul and sense, and for a couple of months he really forgot himself, and ceased to send forth his unsweetened wit to do battle for his ugly face. His happiness rarely made him "gush," as they say; but I could see that he was vastly contented with his prospects. More than once, when we were together, he broke into a kind of nervous, fantastic laugh, over his own thoughts; and on his refusal to part with them for the penny which one offers under those circumstances, I said to myself, that this was humorous surprise at his good luck. How had *he* come to please that exquisite creature? Of course, I learned even less from the young girl about her own view of the case; but Mrs Waddington and I, not being in love with each other, had nothing to do but to gossip about our companions whenever (which was very often) they consigned us to a *tête-à-tête*.

"She tells me nothing," the good-humored widow said; "and if I'm to know the answer to a riddle, I must have it in black and white. My cousin is not what is called 'attractive,' but I think Adina, nevertheless, is interested in him. How do you and I know how passion may transfigure and exalt him? And who shall say beforehand what a fanciful young girl shall do with that terrible little piece of machinery she calls her heart? Adina is a strange child; she is fanciful without being capricious. For all I know, she may admire my cousin for his very ugliness and queerness. She has decided, very likely, that she wants an 'intellectual' husband, and if Mr Scrope is not handsome, nor frivolous, nor over-polite, there's a greater chance of his being wise." Why Adina should have listened to my friend, however, was her own business. Listen to him she did, and with a sweet attentiveness which may well have flattered and charmed him.

We rarely spoke of the imperial topaz; it seemed not a subject for light allusions. It might properly make a man feel solemn to possess it; the mere memory of its luster lay like a weight on my own conscience. I had felt, as we lost sight of our friend Angelo that, in one way or another, we should hear of him again; but the weeks passed by without his re-appearing, and my conjectures as to the sequel, on his side, of his remarkable bargain remained quite unanswered. Christmas arrived, and with it the usual ceremonies. Scrope and I took the requisite vigorous measures,—it was a matter, you know, of fists and elbows and knees,—and obtained places for the two ladies at the Midnight Mass at the Sistine Chapel. Mrs Waddington was my especial charge, and on coming out we found we had lost sight of our companions in the crowd. We waited awhile in the Colonnade, but they were not among the passers, and we supposed that they had gone home independently, and expected us to do likewise. But on reaching Mrs Waddington's lodging we found they had not come in. As their prolonged absence demanded an explanation, it occurred to me that they had wandered into Saint Peter's, with many others of the attendants at the Mass, and were watching the tapers twinkle in its dusky immensity. It was not perfectly regular that a young lady should be wandering about at three o'clock in the morning with a very "unattractive" young man; but "after all," said Mrs Waddington, "she's almost his cousin." By the time they returned she was much more. I went home, went to bed, and slept as late as the Christmas bells would allow me. On rising, I knocked at Scrope's door to wish him the compliments of the season, but on his coming to open it for me, perceived that such common-place greetings were quite below the mark. He was but half undressed, and had flung himself, on his return, on the outside of his bed. He had gone with Adina, as I supposed, into Saint Peter's, and they had found the twinkling tapers as picturesque as need be. He walked about the room for some time restlessly, and I saw that he had something to say. At last he brought it out. "I say, I'm accepted. I'm engaged. I'm what's called a happy man."

Of course I wished him joy on the news; and could assure him, with ardent conviction, that he had chosen well. Miss Waddington was the loveliest, the purest, the most interesting of young girls. I could see that he was grateful for my sympathy, but he disliked "expansion," and he contented himself, as he shook hands with me, with simply saying—"Oh yes; she's the right thing." He took two or three more turns about the room, and then suddenly stopped before his toilet-table, and pulled out a tray in his dressing-case. There lay the great intaglio; larger even than I should have dared to boast. "That would be a pretty thing to offer one's *fiancée*," he said, after gazing at it for some time. "How could she wear it—how could one have it set?"

"There could be but one way," I said; "as a massive medallion, depending from a necklace. It certainly would light up the world more, on the bosom of a beautiful woman, than thrust away here, among your brushes and razors. But, to my sense, only a beauty of a certain type could properly wear it—a splendid, dusky beauty, with the brow of a Roman Empress, and the shoulders of an antique statue. A fair, slender girl, with blue eyes, and sweet smile, would seem, somehow, to be overweighted by it, and if I were to see it hung, for instance, round Miss Waddington's white neck, I should feel as if it were pulling her down to the ground, and giving her a mysterious pain."

He was a trifle annoyed, I think, by this rather fine-spun objection; but he smiled as he closed the tray. "Adina may not have the shoulders of the Venus of Milo," he said, "but I hope it will take more than a bauble like this to make her stoop."

I don't always go to church on Christmas Day; but I have a life-long habit of taking a solitary walk, in all weathers, and harboring Christian thoughts if they come. This was a Southern Christmas, without snow on the ground, or sleighbells in the air, or the smoke of crowded firesides rising into a cold, blue sky. The day was mild, and almost warm, the sky gray and sunless. If I was disposed toward Christmas thoughts, I confess, I sought them among Pagan memories. I strolled about the forums, and then walked along to the Coliseum. It was empty, save for a single figure, sitting on the steps at the foot of the cross in the center—a young man, apparently, leaning forward, motionless, with his elbows on his knees, and his head buried in his hands. As he neither stirred nor observed me when I passed near him, I said to myself that, brooding there so intensely in the shadow of the sign of redemption, he might pass for an image of youthful remorse. Then, as he never moved, I wondered whether it was not a deeper passion even than repentance. Suddenly he looked up, and I recognized our friend Angelo—not immediately, but in response to a gradual movement of recognition in his own face. But seven weeks had passed since our meeting, and yet he looked three years older. It seemed to me that he had lost flesh, and gained expression. His simple-souled smile was gone; there was no trace of it in the shy mistrust of his greeting. He looked graver, manlier, and very much less rustic. He was equipped in new garments of a pretentious pattern, though they were carelessly worn, and bespattered with mud. I remember he had a flaming orange necktie, which harmonized admirably with his picturesque coloring. Evidently he was greatly altered; as much altered as if he had made a voyage round the world. I offered him my hand, and asked if he remembered me.

"*Per Dio!*" he cried. "With good reason." Even his voice seemed changed; it was fuller and harsher. He bore us a grudge. I wondered how his eyes had been opened. He fixed them on me with a dumb reproachfulness, which was half appealing and half ominous. He had been brooding and brooding on his meager bargain till the sense of wrong had become a kind of smothered fear. I observed all this with poignant compassion, for it seemed to me that he had parted with something more precious even than his imperial intaglio. He had lost his boyish ignorance—that pastoral piece of mind which had suffered him to doze there so gracefully with his head among the flowers. But even in his resentment he was simple still. "Where is the other one—your friend?" he asked.

"He's at home—he's still in Rome."

"And the stone—what has he done with it?"

"Nothing. He has it still."

He shook his head dolefully. "Will he give it back to me for twenty-five *scudi?*"

"I'm afraid not. He values it."

"I believe so. Will he let me see it?"

"That you must ask him. He shows it to no one."

"He's afraid of being robbed, eh? That proves its value! He hasn't shown it to a jeweler—to a, what do they call them?—a lapidary?"

"To no one. You must believe me."

"But he has cleaned it, and polished it, and discovered what it is?"

"It's very old. It's hard to say."

"Very old! Of course it's old. There are more years in it than it brought me *scudi*. What does it look like? Is it red, blue, green, yellow?"

"Well, my friend," I said, after a moment's hesitation, "it's yellow."

He gave me a searching stare; then quickly—"It's what's called a topaz," he cried.

"Yes, it's what's called a topaz."

"And it's sculptured—that I could see! It's an intaglio. Oh, I know the names, and I've paid enough for my learning. What's the figure? A king's head—or a Pope's, perhaps, eh? Or the portrait of some beautiful woman that you read about?"

"It is the figure of an Emperor."

"What is his name?"

"Tiberius."

"*Corpo di Cristo!*" his face flushed, and his eyes filled with angry tears.

"Come," I said, "I see you're sorry to have parted with the stone. Some one has been talking to you, and making you discontented."

"Every one, *per Dio!* Like the finished fool I was, I couldn't keep my folly to myself. I went home with my eleven *scudi*, thinking I should never see the end of them. The first thing I did was to buy a gilt hair-pin from a peddler, and give it to the Ninetta—a young girl of my village, with whom I had a friendship. She stuck it into her braids, and looked at herself in the glass, and then asked how I had suddenly got so rich! 'Oh, I'm richer than you suppose,' said I, and showed her my money, and told her the story of the stone. She is a very clever girl, and it would take a knowing fellow to have the last word with her. She laughed in my face, and told me I was an idiot, that the stone was surely worth five hundred *scudi*; that my *forestiere* was a pitiless rascal; that I ought to have brought it away, and shown it to my elders and betters; in fine, that I might take her word for it, I had held a fortune in my hand, and thrown it to the dogs. And, to wind up this sweet speech, she took out her hairpin, and tossed it into my face. She never wished to see me again; she had as lief marry a blind beggar at a cross-road. What was I to say? She had a sister who was waiting-maid to a fine lady in Rome,—a *marchesa*,—who had a priceless necklace made of fine old stones picked up on the Campagna. I went away hanging my head, and cursing my folly: I flung my money down in the dirt, and spat upon it! At last, to ease my spirit, I went to drink a *foglietta* at the wine-shop. There I found three or four young fellows I knew; I treated them all round; I hated my money, and wanted to get rid of it. Of course they too wanted to know how I came by my full pockets. I told them the truth. I hoped they would give me a better account of things than that vixen of a Ninetta. But they knocked their glasses on the table, and jeered at me in chorus. Any donkey, out a-grazing, if he had turned up such a treasure with his nose, would have taken it in his teeth and brought it home to his master. This was cold comfort; I drowned my rage in wine. I emptied one flask after another; for the first time in my life I got drunk. But I can't speak of that night! The next day I took what was left of my money to my uncle, and told him to give it to the poor, to buy new candlesticks for his church, or to say masses for the redemption of my blaspheming soul. He looked at it very hard, and hoped I had come by it honestly. I was in for it; I told *him* too! He listened to me in silence, looking at me over his spectacles. When I had done, he turned over the money in his hands, and then sat for three minutes with his eyes closed. Suddenly he thrust it back into my own hands. 'Keep it—keep it, my son,' he said, 'your wits will never help you to a supper, make the most of what you've got!' Since then, do you see, I've been in a fever. I can think of nothing else but the fortune I've lost."

"Oh, a fortune!" I said, deprecatingly. "You exaggerate."

"It would have been a fortune to me. A voice keeps ringing in my ear night and day, and telling me I could have got a thousand *scudi* for it."

I'm afraid I blushed; I turned away a moment; when I looked at the young man again, his face had kindled. "Tiberius eh? A Roman emperor sculptured on a big topaz—that's fortune enough for me! Your friend's a rascal—do you know that? I don't say it for you; I like your face, and I believe that, if you can, you'll help me. But your friend is an ugly little monster. I don't know why the devil I trusted him; I saw he wished me no good. Yet, if ever there was a harmless fellow, I was. *Ecco!* it's my fate. That's very well to say; I say it and say it, but it helps me no more than an empty glass helps your thirst. I'm not harmless now. If I meet your friend, and he refuses me justice, I won't answer for these two hands. You see—they're strong; I could easily strangle him! Oh, at first, I shall speak him fair, but if he turns me off, and answers me with English oaths, I shall think only of my *revenge!*" And with a passionate gesture he pulled off his hat, and flung it on the ground, and stood wiping the perspiration from his forehead.

I answered him briefly but kindly enough. I told him to leave his case in my hands, go back to Lariccia and try and find some occupation which would divert him from his grievance. I confess that even as I gave this respectable advice, I but half believed in it. It was none of poor Angelo's mission to arrive at virtue through tribulation. His indolent nature, active only in immediate feeling, would have found my prescription of wholesome labor more intolerable even than his wrong. He stared gloomily and made no answer, but he saw that I had his interests at heart, and he promised me, at least, to leave Rome, and believe that I would fairly plead his cause. If I had good news for him I was to address him at Lariccia. It was thus I learned his full name,—a name, certainly, that ought to have been to its wearer a sort of talisman against trouble,—Angelo Beati.

II

Sam Scrope looked extremely annoyed when I began to tell him of my encounter with our friend, and I saw there was still a cantankerous something in the depths of his heart intensely hostile to fairness. It was characteristic of his peculiar temper that his happiness, as an accepted lover, had not disposed him to graceful concessions. He treated his bliss as his own private property, and was as little in the humor to diffuse its influence as he would have been to send out in charity a choice dish from an unfinished dinner. Nevertheless, I think he might have stiffly admitted that there was a grain of reason in Angelo's claim, if I had not been too indiscreetly accurate in my report of our interview. I had been impressed, indeed, with something picturesquely tragic in the poor boy's condition, and, to do perfect justice to the picture, I told him he had flung down his hat on the earth as a gauntlet of defiance and talked about his *revenge*. Scrope hereupon looked fiercely disgusted and pronounced him a theatrical jackanapes; but he authorized me to drop him a line saying that he would speak with him a couple of days later. I was surprised at Scrope's consenting to see him, but I perceived that he was making a conscientious effort to shirk none of the disagreeables of the matter. "I won't have him stamping and shouting in the house here," he said. "I'll also meet him at the Coliseum." He named his hour and I despatched to Lariccia three lines of incorrect but courteous Italian.

It was better,—far better,—that they should not have met. What passed between them Scrope requested me on his return to excuse him from repeating; suffice it that Angelo was an impudent puppy, and that he hoped never to hear of him again. Had Angelo, at last, I asked, received any compensation? "Not a farthing!" cried Scrope, and walked out of the room. Evidently the two young men had been a source of immitigable offense to each other. Angelo had promised to speak to him fair, and I inclined to believe had done so; but the very change in his appearance, by seeming to challenge my companion's sympathy in too peremptory a fashion, had had the irritating effect of a menace. Scrope had been contemptuous, and his awkward, ungracious Italian had doubtless made him seem more so. One can't handle Italians with contempt; those who know them have learned what may be done with a moderate amount of superficial concession. Angelo had replied in wrath, and, as I afterwards learned, had demanded, as a right, the restitution of the topaz in exchange for the sum received for it. Scrope had rejoined that if he took that tone he should get nothing at all, and the injured youth had retorted with reckless and insulting threats. What had prevented them from coming to blows, I know not, no sign of flinching, certainly, on my companion's part. Face to face, he had not seemed to Angelo so easy to strangle, and that saving grain of discretion which mingles with all Italian passion had whispered to the young man to postpone his revenge. Without taking a melodramatic view of things, it seemed to me that Scrope had an evil chance in waiting for him. I had, perhaps, no definite vision of a cloaked assassin lurking under a dark archway, but I thought it perfectly possible that Angelo might make himself intolerably disagreeable. His simply telling his story up and down Rome to whomsoever would listen to him, might be a grave annoyance; though indeed Scrope had the advantage that most people might refuse to believe in the existence of a gem of which its owner was so little inclined to boast. The whole situation, at all events, made me extremely nervous. I cursed my companion one day for a hungrier Jew than Shylock, and pitied him the next as the victim of a moral hallucination. If we gave him time, he *would* come to his senses; he would repay poor Angelo with interest. Meanwhile, however, I could do nothing, for I felt that it was worse than useless to suggest to Scrope that he was in danger. He would have scorned the idea of a ranting Italian making him swerve an inch from his chosen path.

I am unable to say whether Angelo's "imprudence" had seemed to relieve him, generally, from his vow to conceal the intaglio; a few words, at all events, from Miss Waddington, a couple of evenings later, reminded me of the original reservation he had made to the vow. Mrs Waddington was at the piano, deciphering a new piece of music, and Scrope, who was fond of a puzzle, as a puzzle, was pretending, half jocosely, to superintend and correct her. "I've seen it," Adina said to me, with grave, expanded eyes; "I've seen the wonderful topaz. He says you are in the secret. He won't tell me how he came by it. Honestly, I hope."

I tried to laugh. "You mustn't investigate too closely the honesty of hunters for antiquities. It's hardly dishonest in their code to treat loose cameos and snuff-boxes as pickpockets treat purses."

She looked at me in shy surprise, as if I had made a really cruel joke. "He says that I must wear it one of these days as a medallion." she went on. "But I shall not. The stone is beautiful, but I should feel most uncomfortable in carrying the Emperor Tiberius so near my heart. Wasn't he one of the bad Emperors—one of the worst? It is almost a pollution to have a thing that *he* had looked at and touched coming to one in such direct descent. His image almost spoils for me the beauty of the stone and I'm very glad Mr Scrope keeps it out of sight." This seemed a very becoming state of mind in a blonde angel of New England origin.

The days passed by and Angelo's "revenge" still hung fire. Scrope never met his fate at a short turning of one of the dusky Roman streets; he came in punctually every evening at eleven o'clock. I wondered whether our brooding friend had already spent the sinister force of a nature formed to be lazily contented. I hoped so, but I was wrong. We had gone to walk one afternoon,—the ladies, Scrope and I,—in the charming Villa Borghese, and, to escape from the rattle of the fashionable world and its distraction, we had wandered away to an unfrequented corner where the old moldering wall and the slim black cypresses and the untrodden grass made, beneath the splendid Roman sky, the most harmonious of pictures. Of course there was a mossy stone hemicycle not far off, and cracked benches with griffins' feet, where one might sit and gossip and watch the lizards scamper in the sun. We had done so for some half an hour when Adina espied the first violet of the year glimmering at the root of a cypress. She made haste to rise and gather it, and then wandered further, in the hope of giving it a few companions. Scrope sat and watched her as she moved slowly away, trailing her long shadow on the grass and drooping her head from side to side in her charming quest. It was not, I know, that he felt no impulse to join her; but that he was in love, for the moment, with looking at her from where he sat. Her search carried her some distance and at last she passed out of sight behind a bend in the villa wall. Mrs Waddington proposed in a few moments that we should overtake her, and we moved forward. We had not advanced many paces before she re-appeared, glancing over her shoulder as she came towards us with an air of suppressed perturbation. In an instant I saw she was being followed; a man was close behind her—a man in whom my second glance recognized Angelo Beati. Adina was pale; something had evidently passed between them. By the time she had met us, we were also face to face with Angelo. He was pale, as well, and, between these two pallors, Scrope had flushed crimson. I was afraid of an explosion and stepped toward Angelo to avert it. But to my surprise, he was evidently following another line. He turned the cloudy brightness of his eyes upon each of us and poised his hand in the air as if to say, in answer to my unspoken charge—"Leave me alone, I know what I am about." I exchanged a glance with Scrope, urging him to pass on with the ladies and let me deal with the intruder. Miss Waddington stopped; she was gazing at Angelo with soft intentness. Her lover, to lead her away, grasped her arm almost rudely, and as she went with him I saw her faintly flushing. Mrs Waddington, unsuspicious of evil, saw nothing but a very handsome young man.

"What a beautiful creature for a sketch!" I heard her exclaim, as she followed her step-daughter.

"I'm not going to make a noise," said Angelo, with a somber smile; "don't be frightened! I know what good manners are. These three weeks now that I've been hanging about Rome, I've learned to play the gentleman. Who is that young lady?"

"My dear young man, it's none of your business. I hope you had not the hardihood to speak to her."

He was silent a moment, looking after her as she retreated on her companion's arm. "Yes, I spoke to her—and she understood me. Keep quiet; I said nothing she mightn't hear. But such as it was, she understood it. She's your friend's *amica*; I know that. I've been watching you for half an hour from behind those trees. She is wonderfully beautiful. Farewell; I wish you no harm, but tell your friend I've not forgotten *him*. I'm only awaiting my chance; I think it will come. I don't want to kill him; I want to give him some hurt that he'll survive and *feel*—forever!" He was turning away, but he paused and watched my companions till they disappeared. At last—"He has more than his share of good luck," he said, with a sort of forced coldness. "A topaz—and a pearl! both at once! Eh, farewell!" And he walked rapidly away, waving his hand. I let him go. I was unsatisfied, but his unexpected sobriety left me nothing to say.

When a startling event comes to pass, we are apt to waste a good deal of time in trying to recollect the correct signs and portents which preceded it, and when they seem fewer than they should be, we don't scruple to imagine them—we invent them after the fact. Therefore it is that I don't pretend to be sure that I was particularly struck, from this time forward, with something strange in our quiet Adina. She had always seemed to me vaguely, innocently strange; it was part of her charm that in the daily noiseless movement of her life a mystic undertone seemed to murmur—"You don't half know me!" Perhaps we three prosaic mortals were not quite worthy to know her: yet I believe that if a practised man of the world had whispered to me, one day, over his wine, after Miss Waddington had rustled away from the table, that *there* was a young lady who, sooner or later, would treat her friends to a first class surprise, I should have laid my finger on his sleeve and told him with a smile that he phrased my own thought. Was she more silent than usual, was she preoccupied, was she melancholy, was she restless? Picturesquely, she ought to have been all these things; but in fact, she was still to the unillumined eye simply a very pretty blonde maiden, who smiled more than she spoke, and accepted her lover's devotion with a charming demureness which savored much more of humility than of condescension. It seemed to me useless to repeat to Scrope the young Italian's declaration that he had spoken to her, and poor Sam never intimated to me either that he had questioned her in suspicion of the fact, or that she had offered him any account of it. I was sure, however, that something must have passed between the young girl and her lover in the way of question and answer, and I privately wondered what the deuce Angelo had meant by saying she had understood him. What had she understood? Surely not the story of Scrope's acquisition of the gem; for granting—what was unlikely—that Angelo had had time to impart it, it was unnatural that Adina should not have frankly demanded an explanation. At last I broke the ice and asked Scrope if he supposed Miss Waddington had reason to connect the great intaglio with the picturesque young man she had met in the Villa Borghese.

My question caused him visible discomfort. "Picturesque?" he growled. "Did she tell you she thought him picturesque?"

"By no means. But he is! You must at least allow him that."

"He hadn't brushed his hair for a week—if that's what you mean. But it's a charm which I doubt that Adina appreciates. But she has certainly taken," he added in a moment, "an unaccountable dislike to the topaz. She says the Emperor Tiberius spoils it for her. It's carrying historical antipathies rather far: I supposed nothing could spoil a fine gem for a pretty woman. It appears," he finally said, "that that rascal spoke to her."

"What did he say?"

"He asked her if she was engaged to me."

"And what did she answer?"

"Nothing."

"I suppose she was frightened."

"She might have been; but she says she was not. He begged her not to be; he told her he was a poor harmless fellow looking for justice. She left him, without speaking. I told her he was crazy—it's not a lie."

"Possibly!" I rejoined. Then, as a last attempt—"You know it wouldn't be quite a lie," I added, "to say that *you* are not absolutely sane. You're very erratic, about the topaz; obstinacy, pushed under certain circumstances beyond a certain point, bears a dangerous likeness to craziness."

I suppose that if one could reason with a mule it would make him rather more mulish to know one called him stubborn. Scrope gave me a chilling grin. "I deny your circumstances. If I'm mad, I claim the madman's privilege of believing myself peculiarly sane. If you wish to preach to me, you must catch me in a lucid interval."

The breath of early spring in Rome, though magical, as you know, in its visible influence on the dark old city, is often rather trying to the foreign constitution. After a fortnight of uninterrupted sirocco, Mrs Waddington's fine spirits confessed to depression. She was afraid, of course, that she was going to have "the fever," and made haste to consult a physician. He reassured her, told her she simply needed change of air, and recommended a month at Albano. To Albano, accordingly, the two ladies repaired, under Scrope's escort. Mrs Waddington kindly urged my going with them; but I was detained in Rome by the arrival of some relations of my own, for whom I was obliged to play *cicerone*. I could only promise to make an occasional visit to Albano. My uncle and his three daughters were magnificent sight-seers, and gave me plenty to do; nevertheless, at the end of a week I was able to redeem my promise. I found my friends lodging at the inn, and the two ladies doing their best to merge the sense of dirty stone floors and crumpled yellow table-cloth in ecstatic contemplation, from their windows, of the great misty sea-like level of the Campagna. The view apart, they were passing delightful days. You remember the loveliness of the place and its pictur-esque neighborhood of strange old mountain towns. The country was blooming with early flowers and foliage, and my friends lived in the open air. Mrs Wad-dington sketched in water colors. Adina gathered wild nosegays, and Scrope hov-ered contentedly between them—not without an occasional frank stricture on the elder lady's use of her pigments and Adina's combinations of narcissus and cycla-men. All seemed to me very happy and, without ill-nature, I felt almost tempted to wonder whether the most desirable gift of the gods is not a thick-and-thin conviction of one's own impeccability. Yet even a lover with a bad conscience might be cheated into a disbelief in retribution by the unbargained sweetness of such a presence in his life as Adina Waddington's.

I spent the night at Albano, but as I had pledged myself to go the next morn-ing to a funzione with my fair cousins in Rome,—"fair" is for rhetoric; but they were excellent girls:—I was obliged to rise and start at dawn. Scrope had offered to go with me part of the way, and walk back to the inn before breakfast; but I declined to accept so onerous a favor, and departed alone, in the early twilight. A rickety diligence made the transit across the Campagna, and I had a five minutes' walk to the post-office, while it stood waiting for its freight. I made my way through the little garden of the inn, as this saved me some steps. At the sound of my tread on the gravel, a figure rose slowly from a bench at the foot of a crippled grim statue, and I found myself staring at Angelo Beati. I greeted him with an exclamation, which was virtually a challenge of his right to be there. He stood and looked at me fixedly, with a strangely defiant, unembarrassed smile, and at last, in answer to my repeated inquiry as to what the deuce he was about, he said he supposed he had a right to take stroll in a neighbor's garden.

"A neighbor?" said I. "How——?"

"Eh, *per Dio!* don't I live at Lariccia?" And he laughed in almost as simple a fashion as when we had awaked him from his dreamless sleep in the meadows.

I had had so many other demands on my attention during my friend's absence that it never occurred to me that Scrope had lodged himself in the very jaws of the enemy. But I began to believe that, after all, the enemy was very harmless. If Angelo confined his machinations to sitting about in damp gardens at malarial hours, Scrope would not be the first to suffer. I had fancied at first that his sense of injury had made a man of him; but there seemed still to hang about him a sort of a romantic ineffectiveness. His painful impulsion toward maturity had lasted but a day and he had become again an irresponsible lounger in Arcady. But he must have had an Arcadian constitution to brave the Roman dews at that rate. "And you came here for a purpose," I said. "It ought to be a very good one to warrant your spending your nights out of doors in this silly fashion. If you are not careful you'll get the fever and die, and that will be the end of everything."

He seemed grateful for my interest in his health. "No, no, *Signorino mio*, I'll not get the fever. I've a fever here"—and he struck a blow on his breast—"that's a safeguard against the other. I've had a purpose in coming here, but you'll never guess it. Leave me alone; I shan't harm you! But now, that day is beginning, I must go; I must not be seen."

I grasped him by the arm, looked at him hard and tried to penetrate his meaning. He met my eyes frankly and gave a little contented laugh. Whatever his secret was, he was not ashamed of it; I saw with some satisfaction that it was teaching him patience. Something in his face, in the impression it gave me of his nature, reassured me, at the same time, that it contradicted my hypothesis of a moment before. There was no evil in it and no malignity, but a deep, insistent, natural desire which seemed to be slumbering for the time in a mysterious prevision of success. He thought, apparently, that his face was telling too much. He gave another little laugh, and began to whistle softly. "You are meant for something better," I said, "than to skulk about here like a burglar. How would you like to go to America and do some honest work?" I had an absurd momentary vision of helping him on his way, and giving him a letter of introduction to my brother-in-law, who was in the hardware business.

He took off his hat and passed his hand through his hair. "You think, then, I am meant for something good?"

"If you will! If you'll give up your idle idea of 'revenge' and trust to time to right your wrong."

"Give it up?—Impossible!" he said, grimly. "Ask me rather to chop off my arm. This is the same thing. It's part of my life. I *have* trusted to time—I've waited four long months, and yet here I stand as poor and helpless as at the beginning. No, no, I'm not to be treated like a dog. If he had been just, I would have done anything for him. I'm not a bad fellow; I never had an unkind thought. Very likely I was too simple, too stupid, too contented with being poor and shabby. The Lord does with us as he pleases; he thought I needed a little shaking up. I've got it, surely! But did your friend take counsel of the Lord? No, no! He took counsel of his own selfishness, and he thought himself clever enough to steal the sweet and never taste the bitter. But the bitter will come; and it will be my sweet."

"That's fine talk! Tell me in three words what it means."

"*Aspetti!*—If you are going to Rome by the coach, as I suppose, you should be moving. You may lose your place. I have an idea we shall meet again." He walked away, and in a moment I heard the great iron gate of the garden creaking on its iron hinges.

I was puzzled, and for a moment, I had a dozen minds to stop over with my friends. But on the one hand, I saw no definite way in which I could preserve them from annoyance; and on the other, I was confidently expected in Rome. Besides, might not the dusky cloud be the sooner dissipated by letting Angelo's project,—substance or shadow, whatever it was,—play itself out? To Rome accordingly I returned; but for several days I was haunted with a suspicion that something ugly, something sad, something strange, at any rate, was taking place at Albano. At last it became so oppressive that I hired a light carriage and drove back again. I reached the inn toward the close of the afternoon, and but half expected to find my friends at home. They had in fact gone out to walk, and the landlord had not noticed in what direction. I had nothing to do but to stroll about the dirty little town till their return. Do you remember the Capuchin convent at the edge of the Alban lake? I walked up to it and, seeing the door of the church still open, made my way in. The dusk had gathered in the corners, but the altar, for some pious reason, was glowing with an unusual number of candles. They twinkled picturesquely in the gloom; here and there a kneeling figure defined itself vaguely; it was a pretty piece of chiaroscuro, and I sat down to enjoy it. Presently I noticed the look of intense devotion of a young woman sitting near me. Her hands were clasped on her knees, her head thrown back and her eyes fixed in strange expansion on the shining altar. We make out pictures, you know, in the glow of the hearth at home; this young girl seemed to be reading an ecstatic vision in the light of the tapers. Her expression was so peculiar that for some moments it disguised her face and left me to perceive with a sudden shock that I was watching Adina Waddington. I looked round for her companions, but she was evidently alone. It seemed to me then that I had no right to watch her covertly, and yet I was indisposed either to disturb her or to retire and leave her. The evening was approaching; how came it that she was unaccompanied? I concluded that she was waiting for the others; Scrope, perhaps, had gone in to see the sunset from the terrace of the convent garden—a privilege denied to ladies; and Mrs Waddington was lingering outside the church to take memoranda for a sketch. I turned away, walked round the church and approached the young girl on the other side. This time my nearness aroused her. She removed her eyes from the altar, looked at me, let them rest on my face, and yet gave no sign of recognition. But at last she slowly rose and I saw that she knew me. Was she turning Catholic and preparing to give up her heretical friends? I greeted her, but she continued to look at me with intense gravity, as if her thoughts were urging her beyond frivolous civilities. She seemed not in the least flurried—as I had feared she would be—at having been observed; she was preoccupied, excited, in a deeper fashion. In suspecting that something strange was happening at Albano, apparently I was not far wrong— "What are you doing, my dear young lady," I asked brusquely, "in this lonely church?"

"I'm asking for light," she said.

"I hope you've found it!" I answered smiling.

"I think so!" and she moved toward the door. "I'm alone," she added, "will you take me home?" She accepted my arm and we passed out; but in front of the church she paused. "Tell me," she said suddenly, "are you a very intimate friend of Mr Scrope's?"

"You must ask him," I answered, "if he considers me so. I at least aspire to the honor." The intensity of her manner embarrassed me, and I tried to take refuge in jocosity.

"Tell me then this: will he bear a disappointment—a keen disappointment?"

She seemed to appeal to me to say yes! But I felt that she had a project in hand, and I had no warrant to give her a license. I looked at her a moment; her solemn eyes seemed to grow and grow till they made her whole face a mute entreaty.

"No," I said resolutely, "decidedly not!"

She gave a heavy sigh and we walked on. She seemed buried in her thoughts; she gave no heed to my attempts at conversation, and I had to wait till we reached the inn for an explanation of her solitary visit to Capuccini. Her companions had come in, and from them, after their welcome, I learned that the three had gone out together, but that Adina had presently complained of fatigue, and obtained leave to go home. "If I break down on the way," she had said, "I will go into a church to rest." They had been surprised at not finding her at the inn, and were grateful for my having met her. Evidently, they, too, had discovered that the young girl was in a singular mood. Mrs Waddington had a forced smile, and Scrope had no smile at all. Adina quietly sat down to her needlework, and we confessed, even tacitly, to no suspicion of her being "nervous." Common nervousness it certainly was not; she bent her head calmly over her embroidery, and drew her stitches with a hand innocent of the slightest tremor. At last we had dinner; it passed somewhat oppressively, and I was thankful for Scrope's proposal, afterwards, to go and smoke a cigar in the garden. Poor Scrope was unhappy; I could see that, but I hardly ventured to hope that he would tell me off-hand what was the matter with Adina. It naturally occurred to me that she had shown a disposition to retract her engagement. I gave him a dozen chances to say so, but he evidently could not trust himself to utter his fears. To give an impetus to our conversation, I reminded him of his nearness to Lariccia, and asked whether he had had a glimpse of Angelo Beati.

"Several," he said. "He has passed me in the village, or on the roads, some half a dozen times. He gives me an impudent stare and goes his way. He takes it out in looking daggers from his dark eyes; you see how much there is to be feared from him!"

"He doesn't quite take it out," I presently said, "in looking daggers. He hangs about the inn at night; he roams about the garden while you're in bed, as if he thought that he might give you bad dreams by staring at your windows." And I described our recent interview at dawn.

Scrope stared in great surprise, then slowly flushed in rising anger. "Curse the meddling idiot!" he cried. "If he doesn't know where to stop, I'll show him."

"Buy him off!" I said sturdily.

"I'll buy him a horsewhip and give it to him over his broad back!"

I put my hands in my pockets, I believe, and strolled away, whistling. Come what might, I washed my hands of mediation! But it was not irritation, for I felt a strange, half-reasoned increase of pity for my friend's want of pliancy. He stood puffing his cigar gloomily, and by way of showing him that I didn't altogether give up, I asked him at last whether it had yet been settled when he should marry. He had told me shortly before that this was still an open question, and that Miss Waddington preferred to leave it so.

He made no immediate answer, but looked at me hard, "Why do you ask—just now?"

"Why, my dear fellow, friendly curiosity—" I began.

He tossed the end of his cigar nervously upon the ground. "No, no; it's not friendly curiosity!" he cried. "You've noticed something—you suspect something!"

Since he insisted, I confessed that I did. "That beautiful girl," I said, "seems to me agitated and preoccupied; I wondered whether you had been having a quarrel."

He seemed relieved at being pressed to speak.

"That beautiful girl is a puzzle. I don't know what's the matter with her; it's all very painful; she's a very strange creature. I never dreamed there was an obstacle to our happiness—to our union. She has never protested and promised; it's not her way, nor her nature; she is always humble, passive, gentle; but always extremely grateful for every sign of tenderness. Till within three or four days ago, she seemed to me more so than ever; her habitual gentleness took the form of a sort of shrinking, almost suffering, deprecation of my attentions, my *petits soins*, my lover's nonsense. It was as if they oppressed and mortified her—and she would have liked me to bear more lightly. I did not see directly that it was not the excess of my devotion, but my devotion itself—the very fact of my love and her engagement that pained her. When I did it was a blow in the face. I don't know what under heaven I've done! Women are fathomless creatures. And yet Adina is not capricious, in the common sense. Mrs Waddington told me that it was a 'girl's mood,' that we must not seem to heed it,—it would pass over. I've been waiting, but the situation don't mend; you've guessed at trouble without a hint. So these are *peines d'amour?*" he went on, after brooding a moment. "I didn't know how fiercely I was in love!"

I don't remember with what well-meaning foolishness I was going to attempt to console him; Mrs Waddington suddenly appeared and drew him aside. After a moment's murmured talk with her, he went rapidly into the house. She remained with me and, as she seemed greatly perplexed, and we had, moreover, often discussed our companion's situation and prospects, I immediately told her that Scrope had just been relating his present troubles. "They are very unexpected," she cried. "It's thunder in a clear sky. Just now Adina laid down her work and told me solemnly that she would like to see Mr Scrope alone; would I kindly call him? Would she kindly tell me, I inquired, what in common sense was the matter with her, and what she proposed to say to him." She looked at me a moment as if I were a child of five years old interrupting family prayers; then came up gently and kissed me, and said I would know everything in good time. Does she mean to stand there in that same ghostly fashion and tell him that, on the whole, she has decided not to marry him? What has the poor man done?"

"She has ceased to love him," I suggested.

"Why ceased, all of a sudden?"

"Perhaps it's not so sudden as you suppose. Such things have happened, in young women's hearts, as a gradual revision of a first impression."

"Yes, but not without a particular motive—another fancy. Adina is fanciful, that I know; with all respect be it said, it was fanciful to accept poor Sam to begin with. But her choice deliberately made, what has put her out of humor with it?—in a word the only possible explanation would be that our young lady has transferred her affections. But it's impossible!"

"Absolutely so?" I asked.

"Absolutely. Judge for yourself. To whom, pray? She hasn't seen another man in a month. Who could have so mysteriously charmed her? The little hunchback who brings us mandarin oranges every morning? Perhaps she has lost her heart to Prince Doria! I believe he has been staying at his villa yonder."

I found no smile for this mild sarcasm. I was wondering—wondering. "Has she literally seen no one else?" I asked when my wonderings left me breath.

"I can't answer for whom she may have *seen*; she's not blind. But she has spoken to no one else, nor been spoken to; that's very certain. Love at sight—at sight only—used to be common in the novels I devoured when I was fifteen; but I doubt whether it exists anywhere else."

I had a question on my tongue's end, but I hesitated some time to risk it. I debated some time in silence and at last I uttered it, with a prefatory apology. "On which side of the house is Adina's room?"

"Pray, what are you coming to?" said my companion. "On this side."

"It looks into the garden?"

"There it is in the second story."

"Be so good——which one?"

"The third window—the one with the shutters tied back with a handkerchief."

The shutters and the handkerchief suddenly acquired a mysterious fascination for me. I looked at them for some time, and when I glanced back at my companion our eyes met. I don't know what she thought—what she thought I thought. I thought it *might* be out of a novel—such a thing as love at sight; such a thing as an unspoken dialogue, between a handsome young Italian with a "wrong," in a starlit garden, and a fanciful western maid at a window. From her own sudden impression Mrs Waddington seemed slowly to recoil. She gathered her shawl about her, shivered, and turned towards the house. "The thing to do," I said, offering her my arm, "is to leave Albano to-morrow."

On the inner staircase we paused; Mrs Waddington was loth to interrupt Adina's interview with Scrope. While she was hesitating whither to turn, the door of her sitting-room opened, and the young girl passed out. Scrope stood behind her, very pale, his face distorted with an emotion he was determined to repress. She herself was pale, but her eyes were lighted up like two wind-blown torches. Meeting the elder lady, she stopped, stood for a moment, looking down and hesitating, and then took Mrs Waddington's two hands and silently kissed her. She turned to me, put out her hand, and said "Good night!" I shook it, I imagine, with sensible ardor, for somehow, I was deeply impressed. There was a nameless force in the girl, before which one had to stand back. She lingered but an instant and rapidly disappeared towards her room, in the dusky corridor. Mrs Waddington laid her hand kindly upon Scrope's arm and led him back into the parlor. He evidently was not going to be plaintive; his pride was rankling and burning, and it seasoned his self-control.

"Our engagement is at an end," he simply said.

Mrs Waddington folded her hands. "And for what reason?"

"None."

It was cruel, certainly; but what could we say? Mrs Waddington sank upon the sofa and gazed at the poor fellow in mute, motherly compassion. Her large, caressing pity irritated him; he took up a book and sat down with his back to her. I took up another, but I couldn't read; I sat noticing that he never turned his own page. Mrs Waddington at last transferred her gaze uneasily, appealingly, to me; she moved about restlessly in her place; she was trying to shape my vague intimations in the garden into something palpable to common credulity. I could give her now no explanation that would not have been a gratuitous offense to Scrope. But I felt more and more nervous; my own vague previsions oppressed me. I flung down my book at last, and left the room. In the corridor Mrs Waddington overtook me, and requested me to tell her what I meant by my extraordinary allusions to—"in plain English," she said, "to an intrigue."

"It would be needless, and it would be painful," I answered, "to tell you now and here. But promise me to return to Rome to-morrow. There we can take breath and talk."

"Oh, we shall bundle off, I promise!" she cried. And we separated. I mounted the stairs to go to my room; as I did so I heard her dress rustling in the corridor, undecidedly. Then came the sound of a knock; she had stopped at Adina's door. Involuntarily I paused and listened. There was a silence, and then another knock; another silence and a third knock; after this, despairing, apparently, of obtaining admission, she moved away, and I went to my room. It was useless going to bed; I knew I should not sleep. I stood a long time at my open window, wondering whether I had anything to say to Scrope. At the end of half an hour I wandered down into the garden again, and strolled through all the alleys. They were empty, and there was a light in Adina's window. No; it seemed to me that there was nothing I could bring myself to say to Scrope, but that he should leave Albano the next day, and Rome and Italy as soon after as possible, wait a year, and then try his fortune with Miss Waddington again. Towards morning I *did* sleep.

Breakfast was served in Mrs Waddington's parlor, and Scrope appeared punctually, as neatly shaved and brushed as if he were still under tribute to a pair of blue eyes. He really, of course, felt less serene than he looked. It can never be comfortable to meet at breakfast the young lady who has rejected you over night. Mrs Waddington kept us waiting some time, but at last she entered with surprising energy. Her comely face was flushed from brow to chin, and in her hand she clasped a crumpled note. She flung herself upon the sofa and burst into tears; I had only time to turn the grinning *cameriera* out of the room. "She's gone, gone, gone!" she cried, among her sobs. "Oh the crazy, wicked, ungrateful girl!"

Scrope, of course, knew no more than a tea-pot what she meant; but I understood her more promptly—and yet I believe I gave a long whistle. Scrope stood staring at her as she thrust out the crumpled note: that she meant that Adina— that Adina had left us in the night—was too large a horror for his unprepared sense. His dumb amazement was an almost touching sign of the absence of a thought which could have injured the girl. He saw by my face that I knew something, and he let me draw the note from Mrs Waddington's hand and read it aloud:

> "Good-bye to everything! Think me crazy if you will. I could never explain. Only forget me and believe that I am happy, happy, happy!
> Adina Beati."

I laid my hand on his shoulder; even yet he seemed powerless to apprehend. "Angelo Beati," I said gravely, "has at last taken his revenge!"

"Angelo Beati!" he cried. "An Italian beggar! It's a lie!"

I shook my head and patted his shoulder. "He has insisted on payment. He's a clever fellow!"

He saw that I knew, and slowly, distractedly he answered with a burning blush!

It was a most extraordinary occurrence; we had ample time to say so, and to say so again, and yet never really to understand it. Neither of my companions ever saw the young girl again; Scrope never mentioned her but once. He went about for a week in absolute silence; when at last he spoke I saw that the fold was taken, that he was going to be a professional cynic for the rest of his days. Mrs Waddington was a good-natured woman, as I have said, and, better still, she was a just woman. But I assure you, she never forgave her step-daughter. In after years, as I grew older, I took an increasing satisfaction in having assisted, as they say, at this episode. As mere *action*, it seemed to me really superb, and in judging of human nature I often weighed it mentally against the perpetual spectacle of strong impulses frittered in weakness and perverted by prudence. There has been no prudence here, certainly, but there has been ardent, full-blown, positive passion. We see the one every day, the other once in five years. More than once I ventured to ventilate this heresy before the kindly widow, but she always stopped me short. "The thing was odious," she said; "I thank heaven the girl's father did not live to see it."

We didn't finish that dismal day at Albano, but returned in the evening to Rome. Before our departure I had an interview with the Padre Girolamo of Laric-cia, who failed to strike me as the holy man whom his nephew had described. He was a swarthy, snuffy little old priest, with a dishonest eye—quite capable, I believed, of teaching his handsome nephew to play his cards. But I had no reproaches to waste upon him; I simply wished to know whither Angelo had taken the young girl. I obtained the information with difficulty and only after a solemn promise that if Adina should reiterate, *vivâ voce*, to a person delegated by her friends, the statement that she was happy, they would take no steps to recover possession of her. She was in Rome, and in that holy city they should leave her. "Remember," said the Padre, very softly, "that she is of age, and her own mistress, and can do what she likes with her money;—she has a good deal of it, eh?" She had less than he thought, but evidently the Padre knew his ground. It was he, he admitted, who had united the young couple in marriage, the day before; the ceremony had taken place in the little old circular church on the hill, at Albano, at five o'clock in the morning. "You see, Signor," he said, slowly rubbing his yellow hands, "she had taken a great fancy!" I gave him no chance, by any remark of my own, to remind me that Angelo had a grudge to satisfy, but he professed the assurance that his nephew was the sweetest fellow in the world. I heard and departed in silence; my curiosity, at least, had not yet done with Angelo.

Mrs Waddington, also, had more of this sentiment than she confessed to; her kindness wondered, under protest of her indignation, how on earth the young girl was living, and whether the smells on her staircase were very bad indeed. It was, therefore, at her tacit request that I repaired to the lodging of the young pair, in the neighborhood of the Piazza Barberini. The quarters were modest, but they looked into the quaint old gardens of the Capuchin Friars; and in the way of smells, I observed nothing worse than the heavy breath of a great bunch of pinks in a green jug on the window sill. Angelo stood there, pulling one of the pinks to pieces, and looking quite the proper hero of his romance. He eyed me shyly and a trifle coldly at first, as if he were prepared to stand firm against a possible blowing up; but when he saw that I chose to make no allusions whatever to the past, he suffered his dark brow to betray his serene contentment. I was no more disposed than I had been a week before, to call him a bad fellow; but he was a mystery,—his character was as great an enigma as the method of his courtship. That he was in love I don't pretend to say; but I think he had already forgotten how his happiness had come to him, and that he was basking in a sort of primitive natural, sensuous delight in being adored. It was like the warm sunshine, or like plenty of good wine. I don't believe his fortune in the least surprised him; at the bottom of every genuine Roman heart,—even if it beats beneath a beggar's rags,—

you'll find an ineradicable belief that we are all barbarians, and made to pay them tribute. He was welcome to all his grotesque superstitions, but what sort of a future did they promise for Adina? I asked leave to speak with her; he shrugged his shoulders, said she was free to choose, and went into an adjoining room with my proposal. Her choice apparently was difficult; I waited some time, wondering how she would look on the other side of the ugly chasm she had so audaciously leaped. She came in at last, and I immediately saw that she was vexed by my visit. She wished to utterly forget her past. She was pale and very grave; she seemed to wear a frigid mask of reserve. If she had seemed to me a singular creature before, it didn't help me to understand her to see her there, beside her extraordinary husband. My eyes went from one to the other and, I suppose, betrayed my reflections; she suddenly begged me to inform her of my errand.

"I have been asked," I said, "to enquire whether you are contented. Mrs Waddington is unwilling to leave Rome while there is a chance of your——" I hesitated for a word, and she interrupted me.

"Of my repentance, is what you mean to say?" She fixed her eyes on the ground for a moment, then suddenly raised them. "Mrs Waddington may leave Rome," she said softly. I turned in silence, but waited a moment for some slight message of farewell. "I only ask to be forgotten!" she added, seeing me stand.

Love is said to be *par excellence* the egotistical passion; if so Adina was far gone. "I can't promise to forget you," I said; "you and my friend here deserve to be remembered!"

She turned away; Angelo seemed relieved at the cessation of our English. He opened the door for me, and stood for a moment with a significant, conscious smile.

"She's happy, eh?" he asked.

"So she says!"

He laid his hand on my arm, "So am I!—She's better than the topaz!"

"You're a queer fellow!" I cried; and, pushing past him, I hurried away.

Mrs Waddington gave her step-daughter another chance to repent, for she lingered in Rome a fortnight more. She was disappointed at my being able to bring her no information as to how Adina had eluded observation—how she had played her game and kept her secret. My own belief was that there had been a very small amount of courtship, and that until she stole out of the house the morning before her flight, to meet the Padre Girolamo and his nephew at the church, she had barely heard the sound of her lover's voice. There had been signs, and glances, and other unspoken vows, two or three notes, perhaps. Exactly who Angelo was, and what had originally secured for us the honor of his attentions, Mrs Waddington never learned; it was enough for her that he was a friendless, picturesque Italian. Where everything was a painful puzzle, a shade or two, more or less, of obscurity hardly mattered. Scrope, of course, never attempted to account for his own blindness, though to his silent thoughts it must have seemed bitterly strange. He spoke of Adina, as I said, but once.

He knew by instinct, by divination,—for I had not told him,—that I had been to see her, and late on the evening following my visit, he proposed to me to take a stroll through the streets. It was a soft, damp night, with vague, scattered cloud masses through which the moon was slowly drifting. A warm south wind had found its way into the dusky heart of the city. "Let us go to St Peter's," he said, "and see the fountains play in the fitful moonshine." When we reached the bridge of St Angelo, he paused and leaned some time on the parapet, looking over into the Tiber. At last, suddenly raising himself—"You've seen her?" he asked.

"Yes."

"What did she say?"

"She said she was happy."

He was silent, and we walked on. Half-way over the bridge he stopped again and gazed at the river. Then he drew a small velvet case from his pocket, opened it, and let something shine in the moonlight. It was the beautiful, the imperial, the baleful topaz. He looked at me and I knew what his look meant. It made my heart beat, but I did not say—no! It had been a curse, the golden gem, with its cruel emblems; let it return to the moldering underworld of the Roman past! I shook his hand firmly, he stretched out the other and, with a great flourish, tossed the glittering jewel into the dusky river. There it lies! Some day, I suppose, they will dredge the Tiber for treasures, and, possible, disinter our topaz, and recognize it. But who will guess at this passionate human interlude to its burial of centuries?

YASUNARI KAWABATA

(1899–1972)

YASUNARI KAWABATA was born in Osaka, Japan. By the time he was three, he was orphaned. In 1920 he entered Tokyo Imperial University, and he received a degree in Japanese literature in 1924. He was the recipient of every major Japanese literary award; of Germany's Goethe Medal (1959); and of several French awards, including the Ordre des Arts et Lettres (1960). He became the president of Japan's PEN Club in 1948. In 1968 he became the first Japanese writer to receive the Nobel Prize in literature. In the course of his career he was responsible for the discovery of a number of younger Japanese writers, including Yukio Mishima. He was a leading figure of the neoperceptionist school of Japanese writing, marked by lyricism and image, that followed the naturalism of the twenties. Among Kawabata's best-known works are *Snow Country*, which he worked on for thirteen years before completing it in 1948 (tr. 1956); *Thousand Cranes* (tr. 1959); *The Sound of the Mountain* (tr. 1970); *The Lake* (tr. 1974); and *The House of the Sleeping Beauties and Other Stories* (tr. 1969). In 1972, four years after receiving the Nobel Prize, Kawabata committed suicide.

"The Moon on the Water," (tr. 1962), as the title suggests, subtly traces variations on the theme of reflection. Kyoko's first marriage was to a man who shortly becomes an invalid and then remains bedridden until he dies. She brings the world to him through a mirror, and the world in the mirror, being one they can share, increasingly becomes her world as well. When Kyoko enters into a second marriage with a man she loves, the mirror becomes a metaphor for the reflection, in her present life, of the earlier love. The story renders her attempt to reconcile the two loves with a piercing simplicity.

The Moon on the Water

It occurred to Kyoko one day to let her husband, in bed upstairs, see her vegetable garden by reflecting it in her hand mirror. To one who had been so long confined, this opened a new life. The hand mirror was part of a set in Kyoko's trousseau. The mirror stand was not very big. It was made of mulberry wood, as was the frame of the mirror itself. It was the hand mirror that still reminded her of the bashfulness of her early married years when, as she was looking into it at the reflection of her back hair in the stand mirror, her sleeve would slip and expose her elbow.

When she came from the bath, her husband seemed to enjoy reflecting the nape of her neck from all angles in the hand mirror. Taking the mirror from her, he would say: "How clumsy you are! Here, let me hold it." Maybe he found something new in the mirror. It was not that Kyoko was clumsy, but that she became nervous at being looked at from behind.

Not enough time had passed for the color of the mulberry-wood frame to change. It lay in a drawer. War came, followed by flight from the city and her husband's becoming seriously ill; by the time it first occurred to Kyoko to have her husband see the garden through the mirror, its surface had become cloudy and the rim had been smeared with face powder and dirt. Since it still reflected well enough, Kyoko did not worry about this cloudiness—indeed she scarcely noticed it. Her husband, however, would not let the mirror go from his bedside and polished it and its frame in his idleness with the peculiar nervousness of an invalid. Kyoko sometimes imagined that tuberculosis germs had found their way into the imperceptible cracks in the frame. After she had combed her husband's hair with a little camellia oil, he sometimes ran the palm of his hand through his hair and then rubbed the mirror. The wood of the mirror stand remained dull, but that of the mirror grew lustrous.

When Kyoko married again, she took the same mirror stand with her. The hand mirror, however, had been burned in the coffin of her dead husband. A hand mirror with a carved design had now taken its place. She never told her second husband about this.

According to custom, the hands of her dead husband had been clasped and his fingers crossed, so that it was impossible to make them hold the hand mirror after he had been put into the coffin. She laid the mirror on his chest.

"Your chest hurt you so. Even this must be heavy."

Kyoko moved the mirror down to his stomach. Because she thought of the important role that the mirror had played in their marital life, Kyoko had first laid it on his chest. She wanted to keep this little act as much as possible from the eyes even of her husband's family. She had piled white chrysanthemums on the mirror. No one had noticed it. When the ashes were being gathered after the cremation, people noticed the glass which had been melted into a shapeless mass, partly sooty and partly yellowish. Someone said: "It's glass. What is it, I wonder?" She had in fact placed a still smaller mirror on the hand mirror. It was the sort of mirror usually carried in a toilet case, a long, narrow, double-faced mirror. Kyoko had dreamed of using it on her honeymoon trip. The war had made it impossible for them to go on a honeymoon. During her husband's lifetime she never was able to use it on a trip.

With her second husband, however, she went on a honeymoon. Since her leather toilet case was now very musty, she bought a new one—with a mirror in it too.

On the very first day of their trip, her husband touched Kyoko and said: "You are like a little girl. Poor thing!" His tone was not in the least sarcastic. Rather it suggested unexpected joy. Possibly it was good for him that Kyoko was like a little girl. At this remark, Kyoko was assailed by an intense sorrow. Her eyes filled with tears and she shrank away. He might have taken that to be girlish too.

Kyoko did not know whether she had wept for her own sake or for the sake of her dead husband. Nor was it possible to know. The moment this idea came to her, she felt very sorry for her second husband and thought she had to be co-quettish.

"Am I so different?" No sooner had she spoken than she felt very awkward, and shyness came over her.

He looked satisfied and said: "You never had a child . . ."

His remark pierced her heart. Before a male force other than her former husband Kyoko felt humiliated. She was being made sport of.

"But it was like looking after a child all the time."

This was all she said by way of protest. It was as if her first husband, who had died after a long illness, had been a child inside her. But if he was to die in any case, what good had her continence done?

"I've only seen Mori from the train window." Her second husband drew her to him as he mentioned the name of her hometown. "From its name it sounds like a pretty town in the woods. How long did you live there?"

"Until I graduated from high school. Then I was drafted to work in a munitions factory in Sanjo."

"Is Sanjo near, then? I've heard a great deal about Sanjo beauties. I see why you're so beautiful."

"No, I'm not." Kyoko brought her hand to her throat.

"Your hands are beautiful, and I thought your body should be beautiful too."

"Oh no."

Finding her hands in the way, Kyoko quietly drew them back.

"I'm sure I'd have married you even if you had had a child. I could have adopted the child and looked after it. A girl would have been better," he whispered in Kyoko's ear. Maybe it was because he had a boy, but his remark seemed odd even as an expression of love. Possibly he had planned the long, ten-day honeymoon so that she would not have to face the stepson quite so soon.

Her husband had a toilet case for traveling, made of what seemed to be good leather. Kyoko's did not compare with it. His was large and strong, but it was not new. Maybe because he often traveled or because he took good care of it, the case had a mellow luster. Kyoko thought of the old case, never used, which she had left to mildew. Only its small mirror had been used by her first husband, and she had sent it with him in death.

The small glass had melted into the hand mirror, so that no one except Kyoko could tell that they had been separate before. Since Kyoko had not said that the curious mass had been mirrors, her relatives had no way of knowing.

283

Kyoko felt as if the numerous worlds reflected in the two mirrors had vanished in the fire. She felt the same kind of loss when her husband's body was reduced to ashes. It had been with the hand mirror that came with the mirror stand that Kyoko first reflected the vegetable garden. Her husband always kept that mirror beside his pillow. Even the hand mirror seemed to be too heavy for the invalid, and Kyoko, worried about his arms and shoulders, gave him a lighter and smaller one.

It was not only Kyoko's vegetable garden that her husband had observed through the two mirrors. He had seen the sky, clouds, snow, distant mountains, and nearby woods. He had seen the moon. He had seen wild flowers, and birds of passage had made their way through the mirror. Men walked down the road in the mirror and children played in the garden.

Kyoko was amazed at the richness of the world in the mirror. A mirror which had until then been regarded only as a toilet article, a hand mirror which had served only to show the back of one's neck, had created for the invalid a new life. Kyoko used to sit beside his bed and talk about the world in the mirror. They looked into it together. In the course of time it became impossible for Kyoko to distinguish between the world that she saw directly and the world in the mirror. Two separate worlds came to exist. A new world was created in the mirror and it came to seem like the real world.

"The sky shines silver in the mirror," Kyoko said. Looking up through the window, she added: "When the sky itself is grayish." The sky in the mirror lacked the leaden and heavy quality of the actual sky. It was shining.

"Is it because you are always polishing the mirror?"

Though he was lying down, her husband could see the sky by turning his head.

"Yes, it's a dull gray. But the color of the sky is not necessarily the same to dogs' eyes and sparrows' eyes as it is to human eyes. You can't tell which eyes see the real color."

"What we see in the mirror—is that what the mirror eye sees?"

Kyoko wanted to call it the eye of their love. The trees in the mirror were a fresher green than real trees, and the lilies a purer white.

"This is the print of your thumb, Kyoko. Your right thumb."

He pointed to the edge of the mirror. Kyoko was somehow startled. She breathed on the mirror and erased the fingerprint.

"That's all right, Kyoko. Your fingerprint stayed on the mirror when you first showed me the vegetable garden."

"I didn't notice it."

"You may not have noticed it. Thanks to this mirror, I've memorized the prints of your thumbs and index fingers. Only an invalid could memorize his wife's fingerprints."

Her husband had done almost nothing but lie in bed since their marriage. He had not gone to war. Toward the end of the war he had been drafted, but he fell

284

ill after several days of labor at an airfield and came home at the end of the war. Since he was unable to walk, Kyoko went with his elder brother to meet him. After her husband had been drafted, she stayed with her parents. They had left the city to avoid the bombings. Their household goods had long since been sent away. As the house where their married life began had been burned down, they had rented a room in the home of a friend of Kyoko's. From there her husband commuted to his office. A month in their honeymoon house and two months at the house of a friend—that was all the time Kyoko spent with her husband before he fell ill.

It was then decided that her husband should rent a small house in the mountains and convalesce there. Other families had been in the house, also fugitives from the city, but they had gone back to Tokyo after the war ended. Kyoko took over their vegetable garden. It was only some six yards square, a clearing in the weeds. They could easily have bought vegetables, but Kyoko worked in the garden. She became interested in vegetables grown by her own hand. It was not that she wanted to stay away from her sick husband, but such things as sewing and knitting made her gloomy. Even though she thought of him always, she had brighter hopes when she was out in the garden. There she could indulge her love for her husband. As for reading, it was all she could do to read aloud at his bedside. Then Kyoko thought that by working in the garden she might regain that part of herself which it seemed she was losing in the fatigue of the long nursing.

It was in the middle of September that they moved to the mountains. The summer visitors had almost all gone and a long spell of early autumn rains came, chilly and damp.

One afternoon the sun came out to the clear song of a bird. When she went into the garden, she found the green vegetables shining. She was enraptured by the rosy clouds on the mountaintops. Startled by her husband's voice calling her, she hurried upstairs, her hands covered with mud, and found him breathing painfully.

"I called and called. Couldn't you hear me?"

"I'm sorry. I couldn't."

"Stop working in the garden. I'd be dead in no time if I had to keep calling you like that. In the first place, I can't see where you are and what you're doing."

"I was in the garden. But I'll stop."

He was calmer.

"Did you hear the lark?"

That was all he had wanted to tell her. The lark sang in the nearby woods again. The woods were clear against the evening glow. Thus Kyoko learned to know the song of the lark.

"A bell will help you, won't it? How about having something you can throw until I get a bell for you?"

"Shall I throw a cup from here? That would be fun."

It was settled that Kyoko might continue her gardening; but it was after spring had come to end the long, harsh mountain winter that Kyoko thought of showing him the garden in the mirror.

The single mirror gave him inexhaustible joy, as if a lost world of fresh green had come back. It was impossible for him to see the worms she picked from the vegetables. She had to come upstairs to show him. "I can see the earthworms from here, though," he used to say as he watched her digging in the earth.

When the sun was shining into the house, Kyoko sometimes noticed a light and, looking up, discovered that her husband was reflecting the sun in the mirror. He insisted that Kyoko remake the dark-blue kimono he had used during his student days into pantaloons for herself. He seemed to enjoy the sight of Kyoko in the mirror as she worked in the garden, wearing the dark blue with its white splashes.

Kyoko worked in the garden half-conscious and half-unconscious of the fact that she was being seen. Her heart warmed to see how different her feelings were now from the very early days of her marriage. Then she had blushed even at showing her elbow when she held the smaller glass behind her head. It was, however, only when she remarried that she started making up as she pleased, released from the long years of nursing and the mourning that had followed. She saw that she was becoming remarkably beautiful. It now seemed that her husband had really meant it when he said that her body was beautiful.

Kyoko was no longer ashamed of her reflection in the mirror—after she had had a bath, for instance. She had discovered her own beauty. But she had not lost that unique feeling that her former husband had planted in her toward the beauty in the mirror. She did not doubt the beauty she saw in the mirror. Quite the reverse: she could not doubt the reality of that other world. But between her skin as she saw it and her skin as reflected in the mirror she could not find the difference that she had found between that leaden sky and the silver sky in the mirror. It may not have been only the difference in distance. Maybe the longing of her first husband confined to his bed had acted upon her. But then, there was now no way of knowing how beautiful she had looked to him in the mirror as she worked in the garden. Even before his death, Kyoko herself had not been able to tell.

Kyoko thought of, indeed longed for, the image of herself working in the garden, seen through the mirror in her husband's hand, and for the white of the lilies, the crowd of village children playing in the field, and the morning sun rising above the far-off snowy mountains—for that separate world she had shared with him. For the sake of her present husband, Kyoko suppressed this feeling, which seemed about to become an almost physical yearning, and tried to take it for something like a distant view of the celestial world.

One morning in May, Kyoko heard the singing of wild birds over the radio. It was a broadcast from a mountain near the heights where she had stayed with her first husband until his death. As had become her custom, after seeing her present husband off to work, Kyoko took the hand mirror from the drawer of the stand and reflected the clear sky. Then she gazed at her face in the mirror. She was astonished by a new discovery. She could not see her own face unless she reflected it in the mirror. One could not see one's own face. One felt one's own face, wondering if the face in the mirror was one's actual face. Kyoko was lost in thought for some time. Why had God created man's face so that he might not see it himself?

"Suppose you could see your own face, would you lose your mind? Would you become incapable of acting?"

Most probably man had evolved in such a way that he could not see his own face. Maybe dragonflies and praying mantises could see their own faces.

But then perhaps one's own face was for others to see. Did it not resemble love? As she was putting the hand mirror back in the drawer, Kyoko could not even now help noticing the odd combination of carved design and mulberry. Since the former mirror had burned with her first husband, the mirror stand might well be compared to a widow. But the hand mirror had had its advantages and disadvantages. Her husband was constantly seeing his face in it. Perhaps it was more like seeing death itself. If his death was a psychological suicide by means of a mirror, then Kyoko was the psychological murderer. Kyoko had once thought of the disadvantages of the mirror, and tried to take it from him. But he would not let her.

"Do you intend to have me see nothing? As long as I live, I want to keep loving something I can see," her husband said. He would have sacrificed his life to keep the world in the mirror. After heavy rains they would gaze at the moon through the mirror, the reflection of the moon from the pool in the garden. A moon which could hardly be called even the reflection of a reflection still lingered in Kyoko's heart.

"A sound love dwells only in a sound person." When her second husband said this, Kyoko nodded shyly, but she could not entirely agree with him. When her first husband died, Kyoko wondered what good her continence had done; but soon the continence became a poignant memory of love, a memory of days brimming with love, and her regrets quite disappeared. Probably her second husband regarded woman's love too lightly. "Why did you leave your wife, when you are such a tenderhearted man?" Kyoko would ask him. He never answered. Kyoko had married him because the elder brother of her dead husband had insisted. After four months as friends they were married. He was fifteen years older.

When she became pregnant, Kyoko was so terrified that her very face changed.

"I'm afraid. I'm afraid." She clung to her husband. She suffered intensely from morning sickness and she even became deranged. She crawled into the garden barefooted and gathered pine needles. She had her stepson carry two lunch boxes to school, both boxes filled with rice. She sat staring blankly into the mirror, thinking that she saw straight through it. She rose in the middle of night, sat on the bed, and looked into her husband's sleeping face. Assailed by terror at the knowledge that man's life is a trifle, she found herself loosening the sash of her night robe. She made as if to strangle him. The next moment she was sobbing hysterically. Her husband awoke and retied her sash gently. She shivered in the summer night.

"Trust the child in you, Kyoko." Her husband rocked her in his arms.

The doctor suggested that she be hospitalized. Kyoko resisted, but was finally persuaded.

"I will go to the hospital. Please let me go first to visit my family for a few days."

Some time later her husband took her to her parents' home. The next day Kyoko slipped out of the house and went to the heights where she had lived with her first husband. It was early in September, ten days earlier than when she had moved there with him. Kyoko felt like vomiting. She was dizzy in the train and obsessed by an impulse to jump off. As the train passed the station on the heights, the crisp air brought her relief. She regained control of herself, as if the devil possessing her had gone. She stopped, bewildered, and looked at the mountains surrounding the high plateau. The outline of the blue mountains where the color was now growing darker was vivid against the sky, and she felt in them a living world. Wiping her eyes, moist with warm tears, she walked toward the house where he and she had lived. From the woods which had loomed against the rosy evening glow that day there came again the song of a lark. Someone was living in the house and a white lace curtain hung at the window upstairs. Not going too near, she gazed at the house.

"What if the child should look like you?" Startled at her own words, she turned back, warm and at peace.

HEINRICH VON KLEIST
(1777–1811)

HEINRICH VON KLEIST was born in Frankfurt on the Oder, Germany, the son of a retired army major. At the age of fifteen he entered the Prussian army, where he served unhappily for seven years. In 1799 he resigned his commission and enrolled at the university at Frankfurt, where he studied mathematics and philosophy. He began writing in 1801, and in 1803 completed one of his best-known plays, *The Broken Jug* (tr. 1964), followed by an adaptation of Molière's *Amphitryon* (1807). His tragedies include *Penthesilea* (1808), a chivalric drama, *Käthchen von Heilbronn* (1810), and *The Prince of Homburg* (1821), a historical, nationalistic play. His novellas include *Michael Kohlhaas* (1810–11, tr. 1967, published in *Phöbus,* a magazine he founded in Dresden, with his friend Adam Müller), and *The Marquise of O——* (1810–11, tr. 1960). In 1810, von Kleist and Müller began a joint editorship of *Berliner Abendblätter* (Berlin Evening News), for which von Kleist wrote patriotic, anti-Napoleon editorials. The government shut down the newspaper in 1811. Von Kleist, who seemingly never recovered from the melancholy that commenced during his early military service, committed suicide at the age of thirty-four.

The Marquise of O—— is adroitly plotted and passionately told. Its headlong pace and hairpin turns make it read like an adventure tale whose ingredients include near-rape, the dangers of war, heroic rescue, operatically unfolding family rifts, and a twisty denouement. The telling may be old-fashioned, but the tale, in its quite modern and psychologically accurate rendering of a tangle of affections, has unusual prescience.

The Marquise of O——

In M——, a large town in northern Italy, the widowed Marquise of O——, a lady of unblemished reputation and the mother of several well-bred children, published the following notice in the newspapers: that, without her knowing how, she was in the family way; that she would like the father of the child she was going to bear to report himself; and that her mind was made up, out of consideration for her people, to marry him. The lady whom unalterable circumstances forced to take this unusual step, which she did so bravely in the face of the derision it was bound to excite in the world, was the daughter of Colonel G——, Commandant of the citadel of M——. Three years or so previously, her husband, the Marquis of O——, to whom she had been devoted heart and soul, had died during a trip to Paris on family business. After his death, yielding to the wishes of Madam G——, her worthy mother, she left the estate near V—— where she had lived until then and returned to the Commandant's house with her two children. There she spent the following years in strict seclusion, occupying her time with painting, reading, educating her children, and caring for her parents: until the —— War suddenly filled the neighborhood with troops of nearly all the powers, including those of Russia. Colonel G——, who was under orders to defend the fortress, urged his wife and daughter to retire to the latter's estate near V—— or to his son's place. But before the ladies could make up their minds as between the hardships of a siege or the horrors they might be exposed to in the open country, the citadel was invested by Russian troops and commanded to surrender. Announcing to his family that he would carry on as if they were not there, the Colonel retorted with shot and shell. The enemy in turn bombarded the fortress. He set the magazines ablaze, captured an outworks, and, when the Colonel delayed to answer a second summons to surrender, ordered a night assault and carried the fort by storm.

Just as the Russian troops, supported by a violent cannonade, were breaking into the citadel, the left wing of the Commandant's residence caught fire and the women were forced to flee. The Colonel's wife panted after her daughter, who was flying down the stairs with her children, and shouted for them all to keep together and take refuge in the cellars; but a shell exploding in the house at that very moment made the confusion there complete. The Marquise, flinging open a door, found herself in the citadel square, where the flashing of the cannon in violent action lit up the night and drove her, helpless to know where she should turn, back inside the burning building. Here, unluckily, just as she was about to escape by the back door, she ran into a troop of enemy sharpshooters who fell silent the instant they laid eyes on her, slung their muskets, and, gesturing obscenely, marched her off with them. In vain the Marquise screamed for help to her terror-stricken women fleeing through the back gate as she was flung back and forth among the horrible gang of quarreling soldiers. They dragged her to the rear castle yard, where she was on the point of collapsing to the ground under the filthy abuse inflicted on her when a Russian officer, hearing her screams, came running up and began to lay about him with furious strokes, scattering the dogs panting after their prey. To the Marquise he seemed a very angel from heaven. He smashed the last of the murderous brutes, whose arms were wound about her slender figure, in the face with the hilt of his sword and made him reel back with the blood gushing from his mouth; then, saluting her courteously in French, he offered her his arm and led her, speechless from all she had gone through, to the other wing of the residence, which had not caught fire yet, where she fainted dead away. A little while after, when her terrified women appeared, he told them to call a doctor; promised them, as he put his hat on, that she would soon recover; and returned to the fray.

In a short time the square was entirely in the hands of the Russians, and the Commandant, who kept up a resistance only because no quarter was offered him, was just falling back with his dwindling force on the entrance door to the residence when the Russian officer, with a heated face, came out of that very door and called on him to surrender. The Commandant answered that that was just what he had been waiting for, handed him his sword, and asked permission to go into the castle and look for his family. The Russian officer who, judging by his actions, was one of the leaders of the assault, granted his request on condition that he was accompanied by a guard; he placed himself hurriedly at the head of a detachment, threw his force into the fighting wherever it was still in doubt, and posted men as fast as possible at all the strong points of the fort. No sooner was this done than he ran back to the drill square and ordered his men to battle the roaring flames which were threatening to spread in every direction, himself performing prodigies of exertion when his orders were not carried out with the necessary zeal. One minute he was scrambling among the burning gables, hose in hand, aiming the stream of water at the flames, the next minute he had darted into the magazines and, striking terror to the souls of his fellow Asiatics, was rolling out powder kegs and live grenades. Meanwhile the Commandant had passed inside the house and was horrified to learn about the misfortune that had befallen his daughter. The Marquise, however, who had entirely recovered without the help of any doctor, just as the Russian officer said she would, and who was overjoyed to find all her people safe and sound and stayed in bed only to allay their extreme anxiety about her, assured him that her one wish was to get up and tell her rescuer how grateful she was to him. She already knew that he was Count F——, Lieutenant-Colonel of the T——th Rifle Corps and Knight of the Order of Merit and of several others. She asked her father to beg him not to leave the citadel before he had made an appearance, if only for a minute or so, at the residence. The Commandant, who respected his daughter's feeling, returned without delay to the fort, where he found the Count on the ramparts, going up and down among his battered troops and issuing an uninterrupted stream of orders; and, no better opportunity offering, he then and there conveyed his grateful daughter's wish to him. The Count promised him that he was only waiting to snatch a moment from his duties to pay her his respects. He had been anxious all along to hear how the Marquise was, but the reports of some of his officers had drawn him back into the thick of the fighting.

At daybreak the Commanding General of the Russian forces arrived to inspect the fort. He paid his respects to the Commandant, regretted that his bravery had not been helped by better luck, and gave him leave to go wherever he liked on his parole. The Commandant thanked him earnestly and said how much this day had put him in debt to the Russians in general and to the young Count F——, Lieutenant-Colonel of the T——th Rifle Corps, in particular. The General asked what had happened; when he was told the story of the criminal attack on the Commandant's daughter, he became furious. Calling the Count forward by name, he praised his noble-spirited conduct in a short speech, which caused the officer to blush furiously, and ended his words by ordering the villains who had dishonored the Czar's name to be shot; would he tell him who they were? Count F—— gave a confused reply, in which he said that he could not give the General their names because it had been impossible to recognize their faces by the feeble glimmer of the castle-yard lamps. The General, who had heard that the castle was already in flames at the time of the episode, looked surprised; it was possible, he remarked, to recognize people one knew well by their voices in the dark; and ordered him, when the Count shrugged his shoulders with an embarrassed air, to investigate the matter at once. But just then somebody pressed forward from the back of the circle and reported that one of the villains whom the Count had wounded had fallen in the corridor and that the Commandant's people had lugged him into a closet where he still was. The General sent a guard to fetch the man; questioned him briefly; and, when he had revealed the names of the others, had the whole crew, five all told, shot. When this was done, the General posted a small garrison in the fort and issued marching orders to the rest of his troops; the officers scattered on the double to their different corps; the Count made his way through the crowd of hurrying soldiers to the Commandant and said how very sorry he was, but under the circumstances he could only send his warmest regards to the Marquise; and in less than an hour the entire fort was clear of Russians again.

The family now began to think how they might find some occasion in the future to tell the Count how grateful they felt toward him; imagine their horror, then, when they learned that he had been killed in a skirmish on the very same day that he had marched away from the fort. The messenger who brought this news to M—— had with his own eyes seen him carried off, mortally wounded in the chest, toward P——, where he had died, according to a reliable report, at the very moment when the bearers were lifting him from their shoulders. The Commandant went in person to the post-house to see if he could learn anything more about the Russian's death. He discovered that when the Count was hit on the battlefield he had cried out, "Julietta, with this shot you are avenged!" and after that had never opened his lips again. The Marquise was inconsolable for having let the chance slip to throw herself at his feet. She made the most violent accusations against herself for not having gone to him in the fort when he declined (probably, as she thought, from modesty) to come to her in the castle; pitied the unfortunate lady, with the same name as her own, whom he had been thinking about even as he was dying; tried in vain to learn her whereabouts so as to tell her the unhappy news; and could not get the thought of him out of her own mind until several months had passed.

At this time the family were obliged to move out of the Commandant's residence to make room for the Russian commander. At first they thought of going to Colonel G——'s estate, which was very much the Marquise's inclination; but as the Colonel had no liking for country life, they ended by taking a house in town and fixing it up to live there permanently. Their life now flowed back into its accustomed channels. The Marquise had resumed the long-interrupted education of her children, and in her leisure hours turned to her easel and her books, when, quite unaccountably for someone who had always been a paragon of good health, she found herself troubled by a persistent indisposition that made it impossible for her to see anyone for weeks on end. She suffered from nausea, dizziness, and fainting spells, and was at a loss to explain her strange condition. One morning, as the family sat at tea and her father had gone out of the room for a moment, the Marquise, rousing herself from a lengthy fit of abstraction, said to her mother, "If a woman were to tell me that she felt the way I did just now when I picked up the cup, I should certainly think to myself that she was pregnant." Madam G—— said she didn't know what her daughter meant. The Marquise explained that she had just felt the same sort of twinge she had had when she was carrying her second child. Madam G—— said it was perhaps the spirit of fantasy that her daughter was going to be delivered of, and laughed. Yes, the Marquise replied in the same humorous spirit, and Morpheus was the father or one of his attendant dreams. But then the Colonel came back, the conversation was interrupted, and when the Marquise recovered a few days later the whole thing was forgotten.

Not long after this, just when the Commandant's son, who was Forest Warden, happened to be at home, the family were frightened out of their wits to hear a servant enter the room and announce that Count F—— was there. "Count F——!" gasped father and daughter together, and they all fell speechless. The servant swore that his eyes and ears had not deceived him and that the visitor was already waiting in the anteroom. The Commandant immediately jumped up to open the door himself, and the Count entered, handsome as a young god, even if his face was rather pale. After they had gotten over their surprise and the Count had assured the parents—who said no, it couldn't be, he must be dead—that he was very much alive, he turned, with an expression of great tenderness on his face, to the daughter; and the very first thing he asked her was, how did she feel? Very well, the Marquise said, she only wanted to know how he had come back from the dead. But he would not let his question drop and said she was not telling him the truth; her face showed signs of unusual fatigue; unless he was much mistaken, she was feeling ill. The Marquise, softened by the warmth with which he spoke, replied: very well, her fatigue, since he would have it so, was perhaps the last trace of an indisposition that had troubled her several weeks ago; she did not think that anything more would come of it. To which he replied, with an outburst of delight: nor did he!—and he asked her if she would marry him. The Marquise did not know what to make of such behavior. Blushing deeply, she looked at her mother who, in turn, was staring in embarrassment at her husband and son; whereupon the Count went up to the Marquise and, taking her hand as if to kiss it, asked her if she had understood him. The Commandant inquired if he would not like to sit down; and with elaborate courtesy, touched nevertheless with some solemnity, he drew a chair up for the Count.

"Indeed," said the Colonel's wife, "we shall go on thinking you are a ghost until you've told us how you rose up out of the grave in which they buried you at P——." Letting go the lady's hand, the Count sat down and said that he was forced to be very brief: he had been wounded mortally in the breast and carried to P——; for months there he had despaired of his life; during this time his only thoughts had been for the Marquise; he could not describe the pleasure and the pain that coupled together in his image of her; after his recovery, he had returned to the army, where he had felt a terrible restlessness; more than once he had reached for a pen to pour his heart out to the Colonel and the Marquise; but unexpectedly he was sent to Naples with dispatches; he could not be sure that he wouldn't be sent from there to Constantinople—he might even have to go to St. Petersburg; meanwhile it was impossible for him to go on living any longer without a clear understanding about something that was absolutely necessary for his soul's peace; he had not been able to resist taking a few steps in that direction while passing through M——; in short, he cherished the hope of obtaining the Marquise's hand, and he implored them as earnestly as he knew how to give his suit an immediate answer.

After a long pause, the Commandant replied that the offer, if seriously intended, as he did not doubt it was, was a very flattering one. But his daughter had made up her mind, after the death of her husband, the Marquis of O——, never to marry again. However, as the Count had recently laid so great an obligation on her, it was not impossible that this should sway her from her resolution; he asked him to allow her a little time to think the matter over quietly. The Count assured him that his friendly answer was a great encouragement to his hopes; that in other circumstances it would have made him perfectly content; that he appreciated fully how boorish it seemed for him to ask for more; but that compelling reasons, into which it was impossible for him to go, made a definite answer extremely desirable; that the horses which were to take him to Naples were already hitched to his carriage; and that he implored them with all his heart and soul, if there was anybody in that house to take his part—here he shot a look at the Marquise—not to let him ride away without a more favorable reply. The Colonel, rather taken aback by such insistence, said that although the gratitude his daughter felt for him justified his assuming a great deal, it did not justify his assuming so much; she could not take a step on which the happiness of her life depended without giving it prudent consideration beforehand. It was absolutely necessary for his daughter to enjoy the pleasure of his closer acquaintance before declaring herself. He invited him to return to M—— after his trip was done and be their guest for a while. If after that—but not before—the Marquise thought that she could find her happiness with him, he would be only too happy to hear that she had given him the answer he wanted. The Count blushed and said that during the whole trip he had foreseen that his impatient desires would meet with this fate; that he looked forward to being utterly miserable during the interim period; that although he could hardly like the unhappy part he was now compelled to play, he would not deny that a closer acquaintance was all to the good; that he believed he could answer for his reputation, although it was a question whether any consideration should be given to that most deceptive of all things; that the only dishonorable act he had ever committed was a secret from the world and he was already on the way to making it good—in short, that he was an honorable man, and he begged the Commandant to accept his assurance of the truthfulness of all he said. The Commandant smiled faintly, though without a trace of irony, and said that he quite agreed with everything the Count had said. He had never come across a young man who in so short a time had revealed so many superior traits of character. He was pretty well convinced that a brief period of reflection would overcome all present hesitation; but before he talked things over with his own family as well as with the Count's, no other course was possible. At this, the Count announced that his parents were dead and he was his own master. His uncle was General K——, on whose assent to the marriage he could rely. He added that he possessed considerable means and would be able to make Italy his home.

The Commandant bowed politely, explained his wishes once again, and requested him not to press his suit any further until he returned from his trip. The Count, after a short pause in which he showed every sign of extreme uneasiness, turned to the Marquise's mother and said that he had done everything possible to get out of having to make the trip; that he had gone as far as he dared in importuning the Commanding General and General K——, his uncle, to be relieved of the mission, but that they hoped that the journey would rouse him out of the melancholy still weighing on him from his illness; and that, for this reason, he was now completely miserable.

The family did not know what to say to this. The Count rubbed his forehead and went on, saying that if there were any hope of his coming nearer the goal he sought, he would put off his departure for a day or even more. And he looked in turn at the Commandant, the Marquise, and her mother. The Commandant stared at the floor with an expression of displeasure and did not speak. His wife said, "Go along, why don't you, and make your trip to Naples; then come back to M—— and give us the pleasure of your company for a while; we'll see about everything else after that."

The Count sat where he was for a minute and seemed to be trying to decide what he should do. Then, getting up and putting his chair aside, he said that since he was forced to recognize that the hopes with which he had entered their house were premature, and since the family insisted on a closer acquaintance, which he was far from blaming them for, he would send his dispatches back to the headquarters at Z——, for them to be forwarded by some other means, and accept their kind invitation to be a guest in their house for a few weeks. Then he paused for a moment, standing by the wall with his hand on the chair, and gazed at the Commandant. The latter replied that he would feel extremely sorry if the passion that the Count seemed to cherish for his daughter should get him into serious trouble; right now the Count must know what he absolutely had to do and what he didn't, and whether he could send the dispatches back and occupy the room they had for him. At these words they saw the Count change color; he kissed Madam G——'s hand, bowed to the others, and withdrew.

The family did not know what to make of such behavior. The mother said that surely it was not possible that he should think of sending the dispatches he was carrying to Naples back to Z—— simply because he had not been able, on his way through M——, during a five minutes' conversation, to persuade a lady whom he did not know at all to consent to his proposal of marriage. The Forest Warden exclaimed that such reckless behavior would certainly be punished by nothing less than imprisonment in a fortress! And such a man would be dismissed into the bargain, added the Commandant. However, the latter continued, there was no danger of that. The Count had only been talking wildly; he would think twice before returning the dispatches. But the mother, when she learned about this danger, was extremely apprehensive that he would send them back. His head-strong, single-minded nature, she thought, was capable of just such a deed. She begged her son to run after him and dissuade him from a step that promised nothing but disaster. The Forest Warden replied that his interfering in that way would have the opposite effect and only encourage the Count to hope that he could gain his purpose by this stratagem. The Marquise thought the same thing, although she was convinced that, unless her brother did something, the Count would certainly send the dispatches back; he would rather bring disaster on himself than show himself up for an empty talker. All were agreed that his behavior was extraordinary and that he seemed accustomed to capturing ladies' hearts, like fortresses, by storm.

At this moment the Commandant noticed that the Count's coach was standing ready before the door. He called his family to the window and asked a servant, who came into the room just then, whether the Count was still in the house. The servant said that he was below in the servants' hall, in the company of an adjutant, writing letters and sealing packets. The Commandant, repressing his dismay, hurried downstairs with his son and asked the Count, whom he found conducting his business at a most unsuitable table, if he didn't care to step into his own room, and if there was not anything else he might do for him. The Count's pen continued to dash across the paper as he said no, thank you, his business was already done; he asked the Commandant what the time was as he sealed the letter, and, after giving the adjutant the whole portfolio, wished the latter a pleasant journey. The Commandant, who could not believe his eyes, said to the Count, as the adjutant left the house, "Sir, unless you have very weighty reasons——"

"The most compelling reasons," the Count interrupted, and walked with the adjutant to the carriage and opened the door for him.

"In that case," the Commandant continued, "I would at least send along the dispatches——"

"Impossible," the Count retorted as he helped the adjutant to his seat. "The dispatches wouldn't do any good in Naples without me. I thought of that too. Drive on!"

"And your uncle's letters?" called the adjutant, leaning out of the coach door.

"They can reach me," replied the Count, "at M——."

"Drive on!" the adjutant called, and away went the carriage.

Count F—— now turned to the Commandant and asked him if he would be good enough to have somebody show him to his room. He would have the honor of doing that himself, the disconcerted Colonel replied; he called to the Count's servants and his own to look after the luggage, and conducted him to the guest room; after which he stiffly said good day. The Count dressed; left the house to report to the military governor of the place; and for the rest of the day was nowhere to be seen, only returning to the house just before dinner.

Meanwhile the family were feeling extremely upset. The Forest Warden described how peremptorily the Count had answered the Commandant's questions; said his returning the dispatches looked to him quite deliberately done; and asked what on earth could be the reason for wooing at a post-horse gallop. The Commandant said that he could not make head or tail of the business and ordered his family not to mention it again in his presence. The mother kept peering out of the window from one minute to the next to see if the Count had not come back regretting his hasty decision and wanting to undo it. Finally when it got dark she sat down next to the Marquise, who was working busily at a table and seemed to shun conversation, and asked her in an undertone, while the father was pacing up and down the room, what she made of the whole thing. Looking hesitantly toward the Commandant, the Marquise said that if her father had prevailed on him to go to Naples, everything would have been all right. "To Naples!" exclaimed the Commandant, who had overheard what she said. "Should I have had the priest sent for? Or should I have had him locked up and sent to Naples under guard?"

"No, no," the Marquise said. "But a real effort to remonstrate with him would have had an effect." And she bent down, a trifle unwillingly, over her work again.

At last, toward evening, the Count appeared. They were only waiting for the matter to come up again, after the first greetings were over, so as to attack him with their combined force and get him to retrieve what he had done, if that was still possible. But they waited in vain. During the entire dinner he carefully skirted everything that might have touched on the subject and talked instead to the Commandant about the war and to the Forest Warden about hunting. When he happened to mention the skirmish at P—— in which he had been wounded, the mother drew him into an account of his illness, asking him how it had been in the little town and if he had had everything he needed there. In the course of this conversation he told them a number of things that were interesting for what they revealed about his passion for the Marquise: how she had seemed always to be at his bedside during his illness; how in his feverish delirium he kept confusing her image with that of a swan that he had seen as a boy on his uncle's estate; how he was especially moved by the recollection of a time when he had spattered the swan with mud and it had dived silently under the water to rise up pure and shining again; how the Marquise, in the shape of the swan, was always swimming about on a flaming flood and he had called out Thinka, which was the name of the swan from his boyhood, but had not been able to make her come to him, for all her pleasure lay in gliding up and down and haughtily puffing out her breast—suddenly he said, with a deep blush, that he was terribly in love with her; looked down at his plate again, and was silent. At last it was time to get up from the table; the Count, after a few words with the mother, bowed to the company and retired to his room, leaving them standing there in complete perplexity again. The Commandant thought that they should let matters take their course. In doing what he did, the Count was probably counting on the influence of his relatives, for otherwise he would be ignominiously dismissed. Madam G—— asked her daughter what she thought of him after all this, and whether she could find it in her to say something to him that would avert a catastrophe. "Mother dear," replied the Marquise, "I am afraid I can't. I am sorry that my gratitude should be put to such a hard test. But I had made up my mind not to remarry; I really shouldn't want to put my happiness at stake a second time, and certainly not without giving the whole matter a lot of thought." The Forest Warden said that if that was her firm resolve, it would be a help to the Count, even so, to know it; it seemed evident to him that he needed to be given some sort of definite answer. The Colonel's wife replied that since this young man, who was the possessor of so many unusual qualities, had said that he was willing to live in Italy, she thought it was only fair to give his offer some consideration and to test the Marquise's determination not to remarry. The Forest Warden dropped into a chair next to his sister and asked her if she liked the way the Count looked. The Marquise answered with some embarrassment, "I like him and I don't like him," and appealed to the way the others felt.

"Supposing," said Madam G——, "that nothing that we are able to learn about him while he is away in Naples contradicts the general impression you have of him now, and supposing he renews his offer on his return, what answer would you give him then?"

"In that case," replied the Marquise, "since in fact his desire to marry me seems so strong—" she hesitated at this point and her eyes glistened—"in that case I would be ready to satisfy it for the sake of what I owe him."

Her mother, who had always wished her daughter to remarry, was hard put to it to conceal the joy this declaration gave her, and wondered what it would lead to. The Forest Warden got up restlessly from his chair and said that if the Marquise thought there was any possibility of her favoring the Count with her hand, then something ought to be said to him right away which would make it possible to avert the consequences of the crazy thing he had done. His mother thought so too. After all, she said, with a man like that there was no great risk, since one need hardly fear that the rest of his life would not be in keeping with all those superior qualities he had demonstrated on the night the Russians stormed the fortress. The Marquise looked down at the ground with a tense and nervous expression. "Perhaps he might be told," her mother went on, as she took her hand, "something to the effect that until he returns from Naples, you won't enter into any other engagement."

"I can promise him that," the Marquise said. "Only I am afraid that it won't be enough for him and will get us all embroiled."

"Let me worry about that!" her mother said with elation, and turned her head to look for the Commandant. "Lorenzo," she asked, "what do you think?" and she began to rise from her chair. The Commandant, who had heard everything, continued standing at the window and looking out into the street without saying anything. The Forest Warden promised them that with this harmless assurance he would guarantee to get the Count out of the house.

"Well, go ahead and do it! Do it right now!" his father exclaimed, turning away from the window. "Here I am, surrendering to this Russian a second time!"

His wife jumped up at these words, kissed him and her daughter, and, while her husband smiled at her bustling energy, wanted to know how they could tell the Count about it right away. It was decided, at the Forest Warden's suggestion, to ask him if he would not care to join the family for a moment if he were still dressed. The Count sent back the answer that he would be honored to join them at once, and hardly had the valet returned with this message than he himself burst into the room, with great strides of joy, and threw himself down at the Marquise's feet in a state of intense emotion. The Commandant was about to speak when the Count, springing to his feet, said that he knew everything that he needed to know, kissed his hand and that of his wife, hugged the Marquise's brother, and asked them if they would do him the favor of helping him to find a traveling coach. The Marquise, though her feelings had been stirred by this scene, said, "I really am afraid, Count F——, lest your impetuous hopes——"

"Not at all! Not at all!" replied the Count. "You've agreed to nothing, if the reports you get about me should clash with the feeling that moved you to call me back into this room." On hearing this, the Commandant gave him a hearty hug, the Forest Warden offered him his own carriage on the spot, a soldier was sent running to the posthouse to hire horses, and, all in all, his leaving occasioned more rejoicing than ever they had known at anybody's coming. He hoped, said the Count, to overtake the adjutant with the dispatches at B——, from where he would go on to Naples by a shorter way than through M——; in Naples he would do everything possible to get out of having to make the trip to Constantinople; and since his mind was made up, if the worst came to worst, to sham illness, he promised them that, unless he ran into unavoidable delays, he would be back in M—— without fail in about four to six weeks. Just then his orderly reported that the horses were harnessed and everything was ready for his departure. The Count picked up his hat, went up to the Marquise, and took her hand. "Well, Julietta," he said, "I feel a great deal easier now,"—and he put his hand in hers—"although it was my dearest wish to marry you before I left."

"Marry her!" they all exclaimed.

"Marry her," the Count reiterated, kissed the Marquise's hand, and assured her, when she asked him if he had taken leave of his senses, that a day would come when she would understand his meaning. The family were ready to get angry; but he immediately bade goodbye to them all very warmly, begged them not to bother their heads about what he had just said, and took his departure.

Several weeks passed, during which the family anxiously awaited, with very different feelings, the outcome of this strange affair. The Commandant received a polite letter from General K——, the Count's uncle; the Count himself wrote from Naples; the answers the family received to their inquiries spoke quite well of him; in short, the engagement seemed as good as concluded when the Marquise's indisposition came back again stronger than ever. And for the first time she noticed an inexplicable change in her figure. She spoke frankly to her mother about her condition and said she did not know what to make of it. Her mother, who felt very anxious about her daughter's health because of these strange attacks, wanted her to call a doctor in for consultation. But the Marquise was against the idea and hoped that her natural vigor would prevail; she suffered the sharpest pains for several days without following her mother's advice, until recurrent sensations of so unusual a kind filled her with such alarm that she had the doctor called; he was a man who enjoyed her father's fullest confidence. Inviting him to sit down on the divan—her mother was away just then—after a brief introduction she told him jokingly what her condition looked like to her. The doctor gave her a searching look; deliberated a while after he had finished his careful examination; and then said, with an expression of great earnestness, that the Marquise's diagnosis was perfectly correct. When she asked him what he meant and he had explained himself quite clearly, observing with a smile he was unable to repress that she was in perfect health and needed no physician, the Marquise tugged the bell cord while she looked at him very hard from the side, and asked him to leave. Speaking under her breath as if he were not worth bothering about, she muttered that it was no pleasure for her to joke with him about such things. The doctor testily replied that he wished she had always been as little inclined to joking as she was now, took his hat and stick, and got up to go. The Marquise promised him that she would report his insults to her father. The physician retorted that he would swear to his opinion in a court of law, opened the door, bowed, and began to leave the room. As he stooped to pick up a glove that he had dropped, the Marquise asked, "But how is it possible, Doctor?" The doctor said he didn't really see any need for him to tell her about the ultimate causes of things, bowed once more, and left.

The Marquise stood there as if thunderstruck. Then she pulled herself together and was about to run to her father when she recalled the intensely serious manner of the man who she thought had insulted her, and her limbs were paralyzed. She threw herself down on the couch in a state of violent agitation. Mistrusting herself, she reviewed every minute of the past year, and decided she had gone mad when she thought about what had just happened. At last her mother came in; when she asked her in alarm why she was so upset, her daughter told her what the physician had said. Madam G—— unhesitatingly called him a shameless, frivolous quack and encouraged her daughter in her determination to tell her father how the doctor had insulted her. The Marquise assured her that the doctor had spoken in deadly earnest and that he seemed perfectly prepared to repeat his mad opinion to her father's face. Madam G——, now more than a little frightened, wanted to know if she thought there was any possibility of her being in such a condition.

"Graves would start to teem first," the Marquise said, "and the womb of a corpse give birth!"

"You are a strange child," her mother said, giving her a tight hug. "Why are you so upset then? If you *know* that it isn't so, why should a doctor's opinion, even the opinion of a whole panel of doctors, bother you? He either made a mistake or he was being malicious, but what difference does it make to you? I think, however, that the right thing for us to do is to tell your father."

"Oh my God!" exclaimed the Marquise, with a convulsive start. "How can I feel calm about it? Don't my own internal sensations, which I am only too familiar with, argue against me? If I knew that somebody else had these symptoms, wouldn't I myself think that she was pregnant?"

"Oh, how awful!" the Colonel's wife replied.

"Malice or mistake!" the Marquise continued. "Why should a man who seemed to deserve our respect until today try to hurt me in such a mean and wanton way? Me, who never once offended him? Who received him with absolute confidence, anticipating in advance the gratitude I would feel toward him? And whose own wish, as his first words showed, seemed an honest and straightforward one to help, not to cause me greater pain than I have ever felt before? But if, since a choice has to be made," she went on, while her mother steadily regarded her, "I conclude that he made a mistake, how is it possible for me to believe that a physician, even a mediocre one, could err in such a matter?"

Her mother said, with a touch of sharpness, "And yet it has to be one or the other."

"Yes indeed, Mother dear," the Marquise replied, her face reddening with an expression of injured innocence as she kissed her hand, "so it does. Although my condition is such an enigma that you must allow me to have my doubts. I swear, for such an assurance is needed, that I am as innocent as my own children; your own conscience cannot be clearer, more honorable. Nevertheless, I must ask you to send for a midwife; I need to convince myself about the way things really are with me and, whatever the result, find some peace of mind."

"A midwife!" Madam G—— cried in a shocked voice. "A clear conscience and a midwife!" And she was unable to speak.

"A midwife, Mother dear," the Marquise repeated, falling on her knees before her, "and this very instant, or I'll go mad."

"Very well," the Colonel's wife replied. "But please make sure you don't have the confinement under my roof." And she got up to leave the room. The Marquise, following her with outstretched arms, prostrated herself on the ground and embraced her knees. "If a life against which it was impossible to level one reproach," she cried with the eloquence of grief, "a life that followed your example, gives me a right to your respect, if any maternal feeling still pleads for me in your heart as long as my guilt is still not absolutely clear, please don't forsake me at this terrible time!"

"Please tell me why you are so upset," her mother said. "Is it just because of what the doctor said? Just because of those internal sensations you have?"

"Yes, Mother," the Marquise said, with her hand on her heart. "There is no other reason."

"No other, Julietta?" her mother asked. "Think a moment. A misstep, as unspeakably painful as it would be to me, does, well, sometimes happen, and in the end I should have to forgive you; but if you went and invented some fairy tale about a revolution in nature in order to escape your mother's censure, and piled one blasphemous oath on another so as to impose on a heart that is only too ready to believe everything you say, that would be more shameful than I know how to say; I could never love you again."

"May the kingdom of heaven lie as open to me some day as my heart is open to you now," cried the Marquise. "I have concealed nothing from you, Mother."

This exclamation, which was uttered with so much pathos, shook her mother deeply. "Oh heavens!" she cried. "My darling child, how sorry I am for you!" And she raised her daughter up, kissed her, and held her in her arms. "What in the world are you afraid of, then? Come, you look quite ill to me." And she wanted to take her to her bed. But the Marquise, whose tears were flowing copious and fast, protested that she was very well and that there was nothing wrong with her except for that strange and inexplicable condition.

"Condition!" her mother burst out again. "What condition? If you are so sure about your memory, isn't it madness to be so terribly afraid? Can't these vague internal sensations of yours have deceived you?"

"No, no!" the Marquise said. "I haven't deceived myself! If you'll just call the midwife in, you will see that this dreadful thing which is destroying me is true."

"Come, my darling," said Madam G——, who was beginning to fear for her reason. "Come along with me and lie down. Whatever was it that you think the doctor told you? How flushed your face is! All your limbs are trembling! What could the doctor have told you?"—and now completely skeptical of what the Marquise said had passed between her and the doctor, she drew her daughter away with her.

"Dear, best Mother!" the Marquise said, smiling through her tears. "I've not gone out of my mind. The doctor told me that I was pregnant. Send for the midwife and, the instant she says it isn't so, I'll feel easy again."

"Good, fine," the Colonel's wife said, stifling her fear. "She'll come right away; since you are absolutely set on having her laugh in your face, I'll get her in right away so she can tell you what a dreamer you are, and not quite right in the head." And she pulled the bell cord and immediately sent one of her people to fetch the midwife.

The Marquise was still lying in her mother's arms, her breast heaving apprehensively, when the woman appeared and heard Madam G——'s explanation of the strange idea that was making her daughter ill: the Marquise swore that her behavior had always been virtuous and yet, deluded by some kind of mysterious sensations, she insisted on being examined by an experienced woman. The midwife, as she probed the Marquise, gabbled about young blood and the cunning of the world; when she finished, she said she had had to do with similar cases in the past; all the young widows who found themselves in her predicament would absolutely have it that they had been living on a desert island; at the same time she spoke soothingly to the Marquise and promised her that the lighthearted buccaneer who had landed in the night would soon come back to her. When the Marquise heard this, she fainted dead away. The Colonel's wife could not subdue her motherly feelings and, with the help of the midwife, labored to revive her; but her anger got the better of her when her daughter came to. "Julietta!" she cried, in accents of intense suffering, "Won't you please, please tell me the truth and say who the father is?" She still seemed ready to forgive her. But when the Marquise said she would lose her mind, her mother got up from the couch and shouted, "Go on, then! You are a contemptible creature! I curse the hour I bore you!" and she ran out of the room.

The Marquise, who was about to swoon again, drew the midwife down to her and laid her violently trembling head on her breast. In a faltering voice she asked her how inflexible the laws of nature were: was it possible to conceive without one's knowing it? The midwife smiled, undid the Marquise's dress, and said that that was not the present case. No, no, of course not, the Marquise hastened to say, she had known when she conceived, she only wanted to know in general whether such an occurrence was possible in nature. The midwife answered that, with the exception of the Holy Virgin, no such thing had ever happened to any woman on this earth. The Marquise trembled more and more violently. Fearing that she was going to give birth any minute, she clutched the midwife in terror and begged her not to leave her. The woman tried to reassure her, telling her that her confinement was still a long way off, advising her how in such cases one could escape the cackling of the world, and promising her that everything would turn out all right. But as these words, which were meant to comfort her, only pierced her bosom like so many knife thrusts, the Marquise managed to get a grip on herself, announced that she was feeling better, and asked her companion to leave.

Hardly was the midwife out of the room when the Marquise received a note from her mother that read as follows: "It is Colonel G——'s wish that in view of the existing circumstances the Marquise should leave his house. He sends her herewith all the papers concerning her property, and trusts that God will spare him the misery of ever seeing her again."

The letter, however, was wet with tears and in one corner a word—"dictated"—had been erased. The Marquise burst into tears. Weeping over her parents' mistake and the injustice into which these good people were led, she stumbled to her mother's apartment. Madam G—— was with her father, she was told; she tottered to her father's apartment. When she found the door shut against her, she sank to the ground in front of it and in a pitiable voice called all the saints to witness that she was innocent. She must have been there for several minutes or so before the Forest Warden came out and, with an inflamed face, said that the Commandant refused to see her. The Marquise, sobbing brokenly, exclaimed, "Dear brother!" pushed against him into the room, cried, "My beloved father!" and stretched her arms out to the Commandant. He turned his back on her and hurried into his bedroom. When she followed him there he shouted, "Go away!" and tried to slam the door; but she wailed and pleaded and would not let him do it, until he suddenly gave up and retreated, pursued by the Marquise, to the far wall of the room, where he stood with his back to her. Just as she threw herself at his feet and hugged his knees in her trembling arms, a pistol that he had snatched from the wall went off and the shot crashed into the ceiling.

"Dear God!" cried the Marquise, got up from her knees as white as a corpse, and ran from her father's apartment. "Order the carriage for me," she shouted as she came into her apartment; dropped into a chair deathly tired; dressed her children as fast as possible; and had her things packed. Just as she was holding her younger child between her knees and wrapping a last shawl around him before getting into the coach, the Forest Warden entered and said that her father had ordered her to leave the children behind in his care.

"My children!" she exclaimed, and stood up. "Go and tell that unnatural father of yours that he can come and put a pistol bullet through me, but that he won't take my children away from me!" And with all the pride of innocence she picked her two children up in her arms, carried them into the coach without her brother's daring to stop her, and drove away.

Having learned how strong she was through this courageous effort, she was suddenly able to raise herself, as if by her own bootstraps, out of the depths into which fate had cast her. The turmoil in her breast quieted as soon as she was on the open road, she kissed her children, the precious spoils of her struggle, over and over again, and felt quite pleased with herself when she thought about the victory she had won over her brother, thanks to the strength of her unspotted conscience. Her reason, which had been strong enough not to crack under the strain of her uncanny situation, now bowed before the great, holy and inscrutable scheme of things. She saw the impossibility of persuading her family of her innocence, understood that she must accept that fact if she did not want to be destroyed, and in a matter of days after her arrival at V—— her grief had given way to a heroic resolution to arm herself with pride against the onslaughts of the world. She decided to withdraw into herself entirely, to concentrate all her energies on the education of the two children she already possessed, and to lavish all her mother love on the third that God had made her a gift of. She made plans for restoring her beautiful estate, which, owing to her long absence, had fallen a little into disrepair, once she was over her confinement; sat in the summerhouse and knitted little caps and stockings for little limbs, while she thought about a comfortable arrangement of the rooms; and also which one she would fill with books and which would be best to put her easel in. And so, before the date of Count F——'s return from Naples arrived, she had become quite reconciled to living a life of ever greater seclusion. The porter was given orders to let nobody into the house. One thought only she could not endure, that the young being whom she had conceived in the purest innocence and whose origin seemed more divine to her than other people's just because it was more mysterious, should bear a stigma in society. An unusual means to discover its father occurred to her, a means that, when she first thought of it, made her start in pure terror and drop her knitting. Tossing restlessly through long sleepless nights, she kept turning the idea, which wounded her in her most sensitive feelings, over in her mind so as to accustom herself to it. Meanwhile she tried repeatedly to get in touch with the man who had deceived her so, even though she had made up her mind that he must belong beyond all redemption to the scum of his sex, and could only have sprung from the blackest and filthiest mire, whatever one might think of the place he now occupied in the world. But as her own feelings of independence grew stronger and stronger, and as she reflected that a gem keeps its value regardless of how it is mounted, she plucked up her courage, one morning when the new life stirred inside her, and had inserted in the newspapers of M—— that extraordinary appeal of which the reader was apprised at the beginning of this story.

Count F——, whom unavoidable business detained in Naples, had meanwhile written to the Marquise a second time to say that other circumstances might arise which would make it desirable for her to keep the tacit promise she had given him. As soon as he could get excused from making the trip to Constantinople, and his other obligations permitted, he left Naples and came right to M——, arriving only a few days after the time he had said he would. The Commandant received him with an embarrassed expression, said that urgent business called him away from the house, and asked the Forest Warden to entertain the guest in the meantime. The Forest Warden led him to his room and, after a brief exchange of greetings, inquired if he knew anything about what had occurred in the Commandant's house during his absence. The Count paled and answered, "No." Whereupon the Forest Warden told him about the shame that the Marquise had brought upon the family, recounting the whole story that our readers have just heard. The Count struck his forehead. "Why were so many obstacles put in my way!" he cried, forgetting himself. "If the marriage had taken place, we should have been spared all this shame and suffering!" The Forest Warden gaped at him and asked whether he was crazy enough to want to marry someone so contemptible. The Count retorted that she was worth more than the whole world that contemned her; that he had absolute confidence in her innocence, and that he would go to V—— today and renew his marriage proposal. At once he picked up his hat, said goodbye to the Forest Warden, who thought he had taken leave of his senses, and left.

Jumping on a horse, he galloped off to V——. When he dismounted at the gate and tried to enter the hall, the porter told him that the Marquise would not see anyone. The Count asked him whether this ban applied to a friend of the house as well as to strangers, to which the porter replied that there were no exceptions he knew of, and right after inquired with a doubtful air if he were not Count F——. "No," replied the Count, after looking at him sharply, and, turning to his servant and speaking loud enough for the porter to hear, he said that in that case they would stop at an inn and he would announce himself to the Marquise in writing. As soon as he was out of the porter's sight, he turned a corner and slipped along the wall of a great garden that stretched behind the house. Entering the garden through an open gate that he discovered, he walked up a path and was just about to climb the slope at the rear of the house when he caught sight, in a summerhouse off to one side, of the charming and mysterious figure of the Marquise, who was busily working at a small table. He walked silently toward her and stood in the entrance to the summerhouse before she noticed him, three short steps away from her.

"Count F——!" exclaimed the Marquise, looking up in surprise and blushing. The Count smiled, stood for a moment in the entrance without moving, then sat down next to her with such modest importunity that it was impossible for her to take alarm, and slipped his arm around her waist before she could think what to do. "Where did you come from, Count, how is it possible——?" the Marquise asked, and looked shyly at the ground.

"From M——," the Count replied, pressing her gently to him, "through a back gate that I found standing open. I was sure you would forgive me if I came in."

"Didn't they say anything to you in M—— about ——?" she said, without moving in his arms, and stopped.

"They told me everything, dear Lady," replied the Count. "But as I am absolutely convinced of your innocence——"

"What!" exclaimed the Marquise, standing up and trying to free herself from his embrace. "In spite of that you are willing to come here——!"

"In spite of the world," he said, holding her fast, "in spite of your family, even in spite of your own lovely self," and he kissed her fervently on the breast.

"Please go away!" the Marquise cried.

"As convinced," he said, "my darling Julietta, as if I were omniscient, as if my own soul lived in your bosom."

"Let me go!" she cried.

"I've come here," he said—and he would not let her go—"to repeat my proposal and to receive my happiness from your hand if you will hear my suit."

"Let me go this instant! I order you to!" And she wrenched herself from his arms and started from the summerhouse.

"Darling! Paragon!" he whispered, getting up and reaching out to hold her.

"Did you hear me!" the Marquise panted, turning and eluding his grasp.

"Only let me whisper one secret to you!" begged the Count as he grabbed clumsily at the smooth arm slipping through his hands.

"I won't hear a word," the Marquise retorted, gave him a push against his chest, fled up the slope, and disappeared.

He was halfway up the slope in pursuit, determined to make her listen to him at whatever cost, when the door banged shut in front of him and he heard the bolt shoot home in rattling haste. He stopped short, not knowing what to do and wondering if he should climb through an open window at the side of the house and keep on until he reached his goal; but as hard as it was for him in every way to give up, he saw no help for it now. Angry with himself for letting her get away from him, he stole down the slope and left the garden to look for his horses. He felt that his attempt to explain himself to her directly had irretrievably failed, and, going at a slow walk back toward M——, he revolved in his mind the letter he now saw himself condemned to write. But in the evening, when he was in the blackest mood possible, whom should he run into at the common table of an inn but the Forest Warden, who immediately wanted to know if his suit had succeeded at V——. The Count answered with a short "No" and was tempted to say something nasty and snubbing; but for the sake of courtesy, he added after a while that he had decided to write to her and would shortly have the whole thing cleared up. The Forest Warden said that he was sorry that the Count's passion for the Marquise had robbed him of his senses. He had to tell him, however, that she was already getting ready to make another choice; he rang for the latest papers and handed the Count the sheet that contained her appeal to the father of her child. The blood rushed to his face as the Count read it through. His mood changed abruptly. The Forest Warden asked him whether he thought the man the Marquise was looking for would appear? "Without a doubt!" the Count retorted as he bent over the paper and greedily devoured what it said. Then, after going to the window for a moment while folding up the paper, he said, "Now everything is all right! Now I know what I have to do!" He turned around and courteously asked the Forest Warden if he would see him again soon; said goodbye, and went away fully reconciled to his fate.

Meanwhile some lively scenes had taken place at the Commandant's house. The Colonel's wife was very angry at her husband's violent rage and at her own weakness in tamely submitting to the tyrannical expulsion of her daughter from her home. When the shot had sounded in the Commandant's bedroom and her daughter had come rushing out, she had fainted away; true, she had recovered at once, but all the Commandant had said when she awoke was that he was sorry she had been frightened for nothing, and he had tossed the discharged pistol on a table. Later, when they were talking about demanding the children from the Marquise, she had timidly remarked that they had no right to take such a step; she pleaded, in a voice still weak and pathetic from the fainting fit, that there should be no more violent scenes in the house; but the Commandant had only turned to the Forest Warden and, livid with rage, had said, "Go and bring them here!" When Count F——'s second letter arrived, the Commandant ordered it sent to the Marquise at V——; she, as they learned later from the messenger, merely laid it aside and said thank you. The Colonel's wife, who was in the dark about so many things in the whole affair, and especially about her daughter's intention to enter into a new marriage for which she had not the slightest desire, vainly tried to bring the subject of the Count's proposal up again. But the Colonel always asked her, in a way that resembled an order more than a request, not to speak to him about it; on one such occasion, when he happened to be taking down a portrait of his daughter that still hung on the wall, he told his wife that he wanted to wipe the Marquise out of his memory completely, and that he no longer had a daughter. It was at this point that the Marquise's extraordinary appeal appeared in the newspapers. Madam G——, absolutely dazed by it, went holding the newspaper, which her husband had given her, into his room, where she found him working at a table, and asked him what in the world he thought about it all? The Commandant, without looking up from his writing, said, "Oh, of course, she's innocent."

"What!" Madam G—— burst out in complete astonishment; "Innocent?"

"She did it in her sleep," the Commandant said, without looking up.

"In her sleep!" Madam G—— replied; "Such a terrible thing could ——?"

"Idiot!" shouted the Commandant, pushed his papers into a heap, and left the room.

The next time the newspapers appeared, the Colonel's wife read the following reply, the ink of which was still wet, in one of them, as she and her husband were sitting at breakfast: "If the Marquise of O—— will come to the house of her father, Colonel G——, at eleven o'clock in the morning on the 3rd of——, the person whom she is looking for will appear there to throw himself at her feet."

Before she had read halfway through the announcement, the Colonel's wife was struck speechless; hastily glancing at the end, she handed the paper to the Commandant. The Colonel read it through three times, as if he could not believe his eyes. "Now for heaven's sake, Lorenzo," exclaimed his wife, "tell me what you think about it!"

"The vile creature!" replied the Commandant and stood up. "The cunning impostor! Ten times the shamelessness of a bitch joined to ten times the slyness of a fox would not equal hers! What a face! Did you ever see two such eyes? A cherub's look is no truer!" And he went on in this vein and could not calm himself.

"But if it is a trick," his wife asked, "what in the world can she hope to gain by it?"

"What does she hope to gain by it? She wants to carry her contemptible pretense to the bitter end," the Colonel replied. "She has already learned by heart the story that the two of them, he and she, intend to tell us here at eleven o'clock in the morning of the third. 'My dear little daughter,' I am supposed to say, 'I didn't realize that, who could have believed it, I beg your pardon, receive my blessing, all is forgiven.' But there is a bullet here for the man who crosses my threshold on the morning of the third! I think, therefore, that it would be better to have the servants put him out of the house."

After reading the newspaper notice over again, Madam G—— said that, if it were a choice between two incredibilities, she would rather believe in some mysterious action of fate than in the infamy of a daughter otherwise so excellent. But before she had a chance to finish what she was saying, the Commandant shouted, "Do me the favor of keeping still! I can't stand hearing one more word about it!" and he left the room.

A few days later the Commandant received a letter from the Marquise in which she asked him, with the most touching respect, to have the goodness to send on to her at V——, since she was denied the favor of being allowed to enter her father's house, the man who would appear on the morning of the third. The Colonel's wife happened to be there when he received the letter; and, noticing the confusion of feelings plainly reflected in his face—for if the whole thing were a deception, what motive could he impute to his daughter now that she did not seem to be asking for his forgiveness—she was emboldened to propose a plan to him that she had been nursing for some time in her troubled breast. While the Colonel continued to stare vacuously at the newspaper, she said that a notion had occurred to her: would he allow her to visit V—— for a day or so? If the Marquise really knew the man who had published the reply to her appeal and he was only pretending to be a stranger to her, she knew how to put her in a position where she would have to betray herself even though she were the most cunning dissembler in the world. The Commandant answered her by tearing the letter to bits with sudden violence: she knew very well that he wanted to have nothing to do with the Marquise, and he forbade her to communicate with her in any way. He sealed the torn pieces in an envelope, addressed it to the Marquise, and gave it back to the messenger; that was his answer. Hiding the exasperation she felt at his crazy obstinacy, which destroyed any possibility of getting to the bottom of the business, his wife decided to carry out her plan in spite of him. The following morning, taking one of the Commandant's soldiers with her, she rode over to V—— while her husband was still in bed. When her carriage drew up before the gates of the estate, the porter told her that nobody was allowed to see the Marquise. Madam G—— said that she had been told that that was so, but asked him nevertheless to go in and announce that Madam G—— was there. He said it would not do any good, since there was not a person in the world that the Marquise would speak to. Madam G—— replied that the Marquise must certainly have mentioned her, as she was her mother, and that he was not to dawdle any longer but to do his duty. It was hardly a moment between the porter's going into the house on what he considered to be a useless errand and the Marquise's bursting out of the door, running toward the gate, and falling on her knees before the coach. Madam G—— got out of the carriage with the help of the soldier and, more than a little moved, lifted her daughter from the ground. Overcome with emotion, the Marquise bent over her mother's hand and, while the tears streamed down her face, she led her, with great deference, into the house.

"Dear, dear Mother," she said, after showing her to the couch but remaining standing herself and drying her eyes, "what happy chance must I thank for your coming to visit me?" Madam G—— gave her daughter an affectionate hug and said she simply had to come to see her to beg her pardon for the brutal way in which she had been turned out of her father's house.

"Pardon!" the Marquise broke in, and wanted to kiss her hands. But her mother would not let her and went on, "Not only did the answer that just appeared in the newspapers to your advertisement convince me as well as your father that you are innocent; I also have to tell you that the man himself appeared in person at the house, to our great and pleasant surprise."

"Who appeared——?" the Marquise exclaimed, sitting down beside her mother; "which man appeared in person?"—and her face was tense with expectation.

"The one who wrote that answer," Madam G—— replied, "the very man you addressed your appeal to, he himself in person."

"Then for goodness' sake," the Marquise said, her breast heaving violently, "who is he?" And again, "Who is he?"

"That," Madam G—— replied, "I would rather let you guess. Just imagine it—yesterday when we were having tea, right in the middle of our reading the answer in the newspaper, a man whom all of us know very well rushed into the room in wild despair and fell at your father's feet and, a moment after, at mine. We didn't know what to make of it all and asked him to explain himself. His conscience, he said, left him no peace, he was the scoundrel who had deceived the Marquise; he must know how his crime was judged and, if vengeance on him was demanded, he came himself to satisfy that demand."

"But who is he? Who? Who?" the Marquise cried.

"As I have said," continued Madam G——, "a young and otherwise well-bred man whom we should never have thought capable of such a despicable act. But I hope, my daughter, that you won't be horrified to learn that he is of humble station and lacks all those qualities which we should otherwise require of a husband for you."

"Just the same, Mother dear," the Marquise said, "he can't be entirely unworthy, since he threw himself at your feet before mine. But who is he, won't you please tell me who he is?"

"Well," her mother replied, "he is Leopardo, the chasseur, whom your father had come from the Tyrol not long ago and whom I have brought along with me, as you may have noticed, to introduce to you as your bridegroom."

"Leopardo, the chasseur!" cried the Marquise, clapping her hand to her forehead in despair.

"What are you afraid of?" the Colonel's wife asked. "Have you any reason to doubt he is the one?"

"How? Where? When?" the Marquise asked in bewilderment.

"He will only tell you that," she said. "Shame and love, he says, make it impossible for him to talk to anyone else but you. But, if you like, we can open the door to the anteroom where he is waiting with a beating heart, and while I go off somewhere you can see if you can get him to tell his secret."

"Oh, my God!" the Marquise exclaimed. "I once dozed off on the couch in the midday heat and when I woke up I saw him slinking away!" And she hid her shame-reddened face in her small hands.

Her mother dropped on her knees in front of her. "Oh my daughter!" she cried. "Oh my wonderful daughter!" and she threw her arms around her. "And oh your contemptible mother!" she said, burying her face in her daughter's lap.

"What's the matter, Mother?" the Marquise asked in dismay.

"I want you to know," her mother continued, "you who are purer than the angels, that there is not a word of truth in anything I said; that my soul is so corrupt that I could not believe in such radiant innocence as yours; and that I needed to play this shameful trick in order to convince myself."

"My darling mother," said the Marquise, and full of joy she bent down to lift her up.

"No," she said, "I won't budge from here, you marvelous, saintly girl, until you say you can forgive my vicious behavior."

"I forgive you, Mother, oh I do! Stand up," cried the Marquise. "Oh please do!"

"First tell me," said Madam G——, "if you can ever love and respect me as you used to."

"My adored mother!" the Marquise said, and also went down on her knees. "I never lost the reverence and love I feel for you. How could anybody have believed me when the circumstances were so queer? I am so happy that you don't blame me."

"From now on," Madam G—— said, getting to her feet with the help of her daughter, "I will wait upon you hand and foot, my darling child. You shall have your confinement in my house; if the circumstances were different and I were expecting you to present me with a young prince, I shouldn't take care of you with greater tenderness and consideration. I'll not budge from your side again the

311

rest of my days. I defy the whole world; from now on your shame is the only glory I wish, if only you will think well of me again and forget the cruel way in which I repudiated you." The Marquise tried to comfort her with endless caresses and reassurances, but the evening came, and then midnight, before she succeeded. The following day, when the old lady's excitement, which gave her a fever during the night, had somewhat abated, mother, daughter, and grandchildren drove back to M——. The journey was like a triumph. They were as jolly as they could be and joked about Leopardo, the chasseur, who was sitting up front in the coachman's box; her mother said to the Marquise that she saw her blush every time she looked at his broad back. The Marquise responded to this with something between a sigh and a smile. "Who knows," she said, "who will finally show up at eleven o'clock on the morning of the third!"

Thereafter, the closer they drew to M——, the more serious they became, in anticipation of the fateful scene that was about to take place. When they alighted in front of the house, Madam G——, saying not a word about her plans, took her daughter to her old rooms, told her to make herself at home, and, declaring that she would be back shortly, slipped away. An hour later she returned, her face quite flushed. "Did you ever see such a fellow?" she said, secretly pleased nevertheless. "Such a doubting Thomas! It took me a whole hour to convince him, and now of course he is sitting there and crying!"

"Who?" the Marquise asked.

"Who else but the one who has the most reason to cry."

"You don't mean Father?" the Marquise said.

"Like a baby!" her mother said. "If I hadn't had to wipe the tears out of my own eyes, I would have burst out laughing as soon as I was out of the room."

"And all because of me?" the Marquise asked, getting up. "And I sit here——?"

"Don't you budge!" Madam G—— exclaimed. "Why did he dictate that letter to me? Let him come looking for you here if he ever wants to see me again."

"Mother dear!" begged the Marquise.

"I won't relent!" her mother interrupted. "Why did he reach for that pistol!"

"I implore you!"

"No, you won't," Madam G—— replied, pushing her daughter back into her chair. "And if he doesn't come here by this evening, you and I will go away tomorrow." The Marquise said it would be cruel and unjust to do that. But her mother said: "Be quiet"—for just then she heard a sound of sobbing drawing near; "Here he is now!"

"Where?" the Marquise asked, and listened. "Can that be someone at the door, that terrible——?"

"Of course," Madam G—— replied. "He wants us to let him in."

"Let me go!" cried the Marquise and jumped out of her chair.

"If you love me, Julietta," replied the Colonel's wife, "then stay where you are." And at that very instant the Commandant entered, holding his handkerchief to his eyes. Madam G—— took up a position in front of her daughter, as if to protect her, and turned her back to the Colonel.

"Dear, dear Father," cried the Marquise and stretched her arms out to him.

"Don't you budge!" commanded her mother. "Do you hear?" The Commandant stood in the middle of the room and wept. "Let him apologize to you," continued Madam G——. "Why must he be so violent! And why must he be so obstinate! I love him, but I love you too; I honor him, but you too. And if I must make a choice, then I'll stay with you because you are the better one." The Commandant bent down until he was almost doubled over and roared so loudly that the walls rang.

"Oh my God!" exclaimed the Marquise, gave in to her mother all at once, reached for her handkerchief, and let her own tears flow.

Madam G—— said, "He can't even speak," and moved a little to one side. At which her daughter got up, put her arms around the Commandant, and begged him to calm himself. She herself was weeping furiously. She asked him if he would not sit down; she tried to persuade him to sit down; she pushed a chair toward him for him to sit on; but he would not say one word; there was no budging him from where he was, and yet he would not take a seat, just stood there in the center of the room, his head bowed to the ground, and cried. The Marquise turned halfway toward her mother as she held him up and said that he would get ill; even her mother seemed to waver in her firmness when she saw how convulsed he was. But when the Commandant yielded to the incessant pleadings of his daughter and finally sat down, and she crouched at his feet and caressed and comforted him incessantly, the mother started talking again, said that it served him right and that perhaps he would now come back to his senses, walked out of the room and left them alone.

Once outside, she wiped her own tears away, and wondered if the violent agitation of feeling to which she had exposed him might not be a danger to his health and if it were perhaps advisable to send for a doctor. For the evening meal, she prepared everything that she could think of that had a fortifying and soothing effect, turned back the coverlets of his bed and warmed the sheets so that she could tuck him in as soon as he appeared on his daughter's arm, and, when he still did not come and the table was already laid, tip-toed to the Marquise's room to hear what was going on. As she listened with her ear against the door, she heard a soft whisper that subsided into silence at that very moment; it seemed to have come from the Marquise; and as she was able to see through the keyhole, her daughter was sitting on the Commandant's lap, something he never in his life had allowed her to do. Finally she opened the door and peered in—and her heart leaped for joy: her daughter lay motionless in her father's arms, her head thrown back and her eyes closed, while he sat in the armchair, with tear-choked, glistening eyes, and pressed long, warm and avid kisses on her mouth: just as if he were her lover! Her daughter did not speak, her husband did not speak; he hung over her as if she were his first love and held her mouth and kissed it. The mother's delight was indescribable; standing unobserved behind the chair, she hesitated to disturb the joy of reconciliation that had come to her home. At last she moved nearer and, peering around one side of the chair, she saw her husband again take his daughter's face between his hands and with unspeakable delight bend down and press his lips against her mouth. On catching sight of her, the Commandant looked away with a frown and was about to say something; but calling out, "Oh, what a face!" she kissed him in her turn so that his frown went away, and with a joke dispelled the intense emotion filling the hushed room. She invited them both to supper, and they followed her to the table like a pair of newlyweds; the Commandant, to be sure, seemed quite cheerful during the meal, but he ate and spoke little, from time to time a sob escaped him, and he stared down at his plate and played with his daughter's hand.

Next day the great question was, who would appear at eleven o'clock of the following morning, for it was now the eve of the dreaded third. Father and mother, and the brother as well—for he too had made it up with his sister—were all agreed that, if the man were at all passable, the Marquise should marry him; everything that could possibly make the Marquise's position a happy one should be done. But if his circumstances were such that even with their help a marked discrepancy would still exist between his position and the Marquise's, then her parents were against the marriage; the Marquise could stay with them as before and they would adopt the child. She, however, seemed inclined to stick to her promise, providing the man was not an out-and-out scoundrel, and to give her child a father at whatever cost to herself. In the evening the mother asked how they should receive the visitor. The Commandant thought the best thing would be to leave the Marquise alone around eleven o'clock. But the Marquise insisted that she wanted her two parents present, and her brother too, since she had no wish to share any kind of secrets with the person. Also she thought that their visitor's answer to her advertisement, in which he proposed the Commandant's house as the meeting place, suggested that he too wished to have her family present—a fact about the reply, she had to confess, that had won her good opinion. Madam G—— pointed out that her father and her brother would have very awkward parts indeed to play in the proceeding, and asked her daughter to excuse the men; but she was perfectly agreeable to being present herself. After a moment's reflection her daughter accepted this suggestion.

And finally, after a night of the most anxious suspense, the morning of the dreaded third arrived. As the clock struck eleven, the two women were sitting in the reception room, dressed as if for a betrothal; you could have heard the pounding of their hearts if the clatter of the morning had been hushed. The eleventh stroke was still shivering in the air when the door opened to admit Leopardo, the chasseur, whom their father had sent to the Tyrol for. The women paled when they saw him. "Count F——'s carriage," he announced, "is at the door and he begs to be received."

"Count F——!" the two exclaimed together, in utter consternation. The Marquise shouted, "Bolt the door! We are not at home to him," jumped up and was about to push the chasseur, who was standing in her way, out of the room and bar the door herself when the Count entered, wearing the same uniform, plus his decorations and sword, that he had worn during the capture of the fortress. The Marquise felt like sinking into the ground with confusion; she snatched up a handkerchief she had left on the chair and meant to fly into a neighboring room; but Madam G—— caught hold of her hand, cried, "Julietta!"—and as if choking on her own thoughts, her voice failed her. Riveting her eyes on the Count, Madam G—— repeated, "Julietta, please!" and tried to pull her daughter back. "After all, whom were we waiting for——?"

"Oh no, surely not for him!" she cried, suddenly turning around and shooting the Count a look that crackled like lightning while a deathlike pallor spread across her face. The Count went down on one knee to her; his right hand was pressed against his heart, his head hung down on his breast, and he stared with burning intensity in front of him, saying nothing.

"Whom else!" gasped the Colonel's wife. "We are such idiots—whom else but him——?"

The Marquise stood stiffly erect over him and said, "I am going out of my mind, Mother."

"You goose!" her mother retorted, pulled her to her and whispered something in her ear. The Marquise turned away and, hiding her face in her hands, went and fell on the sofa. "What's the matter with you!" her mother cried. "What has happened that you weren't expecting?" The Count did not move from the mother's side; still kneeling, he caught up the hem of her dress and kissed it. "Dear, kind, gracious lady!" he whispered and a tear rolled down his cheek.

"Get up, Count, please get up!" the Colonel's wife said. "Go over there and make her feel better; that way we shall all be reconciled and everything will be forgiven and forgotten." The Count stood up, crying. Getting down again before the Marquise, he took her hand as delicately as if it were made of gold that his slightest touch would tarnish. But she stood erect, crying, "Go away! Go away! Go away! I was ready for some villain of a fellow, but not—not—not the devil!" and, walking around him as if he had the plague, she opened the door and said, "Call the Colonel!"

"Julietta!" her mother panted. The Marquise looked with murderous fierceness first at the Count and then at her mother; her breast heaved, her eyes blazed; one of the Furies could not have looked more terrible. The Colonel and the Forest Warden entered. "Father," she called out before he had even come through the doorway, "I can't marry this man!" thrust her hand into a vessel of holy water fastened behind the door, with a sweep of her arm sprinkled her father, mother and brother with the water, and disappeared.

The Commandant looked surprised and asked what had happened; his face went white when he saw Count F—— in the room. The mother took the Count's hand and said, "Don't ask any questions. This young man is sincerely sorry for what he has done; give him your blessing, come, give it to him, and all will end well." The Count looked completely crushed. The Commandant laid his hand on him; his eyelids twitched, his lips were as white as chalk. "May God's curse avoid this head!" he cried. "When do you mean to get married?"

"Tomorrow," the mother answered for him, for he was absolutely speechless. "Tomorrow or today. Whatever you wish; the Count, who has shown such praiseworthy eagerness to redeem his offense, will certainly prefer the earliest possible date."

"Then I shall have the pleasure of meeting you tomorrow morning at eleven at St. Augustine's Church," the Commandant said, bowed to him, asked his wife and son to accompany him to the Marquise's room, and left the Count standing there.

They tried in vain to get the Marquise to explain her strange behavior; she was in a violent fever, would not hear of the marriage, and begged them to leave her alone. When they asked her why she had suddenly changed her mind and what made the Count more obnoxious to her than somebody else, she stared blankly at her father and did not answer. Madam G—— asked her if she had forgotten that she was going to be a mother; she said that in this case she had to think of herself more than of her child and, calling on all the angels and saints as witnesses, she swore again that she would never marry. Her father, seeing that she was extremely overwrought, said that she must keep her word, left the room, and, after duly exchanging notes with the Count, gave all the necessary orders for the wedding. He also submitted a marriage contract to the Count in which the latter renounced all his rights as a husband, at the same time that he agreed to do anything and everything that might be required of him. The Count signed the paper and sent it back moistened with his tears. The next morning, when the Commandant brought the contract to the Marquise, he found her somewhat more composed. Sitting up in bed, she read it over several times, folded it up reflectively, unfolded it, and read it over again; and then announced that she would be at St. Augustine's Church at eleven o'clock.

She got up, dressed herself without a word, got into the coach with all her family when the hour sounded, and drove to the church.

The Count was not allowed to join them until they were at the church door. During the entire ceremony the Marquise stared straight ahead at the altar painting; she did not even vouchsafe the man with whom she exchanged rings a passing glance. After the service the Count gave her his arm; but as soon as they were out of the church the Countess bowed to him; the Commandant asked him if he might have the honor of seeing him occasionally in his daughter's apartment, to which the Count stammered something in reply that nobody could understand, pulled his hat off to the company, and went away. He took a place in M—— and several months went by without his so much as setting foot in the Commandant's house, where the Countess continued to stay.

Thanks only to the delicate, honorable, and exemplary way he behaved whenever he encountered the family, he was invited, after the Countess was duly delivered of a son, to the latter's baptism. The Countess, sitting up in bed with rugs around her shoulders, saw him only for a moment as he stood in the doorway and bowed respectfully to her from the distance. Into the cradle among the gifts with which the guests welcomed the newborn child he tossed two papers, one of which, as it turned out when he departed, was a gift of 20,000 rubles to the boy, the other a will making the mother, in case he died, the heiress of everything he owned. From that day on, thanks to Madam G——'s management, he was invited to the house more often; he was free to come and go, and soon no evening passed in which he did not appear there. When his feelings told him that everybody, seeing what an imperfect place the world in general was, had pardoned him, he began to court his wife the Countess anew. After a year she consented for the second time, and a second marriage was celebrated, happier than the first, after which the whole family moved to V——. A whole line of young Russians now followed the first; and when the Count once asked his wife, in a happy moment, why on that terrible third of the month, when she seemed ready to accept any villain of a fellow that came along, she had fled from him as if from the Devil, she threw her arms around his neck and said: he wouldn't have looked like a devil to her then if he had not seemed like an angel to her at his first appearance.

MILAN KUNDERA

(1929–)

MILAN KUNDERA, a novelist, essayist, poet, playwright, and short-story writer, was born in Brno, Czechoslovakia. He was educated in Prague, at Charles University and at the Academy of Music and Dramatic Arts. Later he taught in Prague, at the Institute for Advanced Cinematographic Studies, a post he lost after the 1968 Soviet invasion of Czechoslovakia. The Czech Communist regime imposed literary and travel bans on Kundera, and ultimately revoked his citizenship. He and his wife, Vera Hrabankova, whom he married in 1967, then settled in France. His novels include *The Joke* (tr. 1969), *Life is Elsewhere* (tr. 1974), *The Book of Laughter and Forgetting* (tr. 1980), *The Unbearable Lightness of Being* (1984), and *Immortality* (1991). His work has been translated into fifteen languages. His honors and awards include the Czechoslovak Writers Union Prize for *The Joke;* France's Prix Médicis for *Life is Elsewhere;* and the Jerusalem Prize for Literature.

"The Hitchhiking Game" (from *Laughable Loves,* tr. 1974) is a characteristic work in that the lovers' story is played out against the implied backdrop of the totalitarian state's constraints. The young man and young woman, on vacation together, fall into a game she initiates: she pretends not to be the sensitive, shy young girl who has always compelled his tenderness, but a hitchhiking stranger, boldly thumbing a ride. How close these originally innocent erotic games come to imprisoning the players suggests, on the one hand, that they may be fated to internalize the state's restrictions on spontaneous human activity such as love. On the other hand, the story may indicate that love has the power to outwit and outdistance repressive forces, having, after all, a long history of narrow escapes.

The Hitchhiking Game

1

The needle on the gas gauge suddenly dipped toward empty and the young driver of the sports car declared that it was maddening how much gas the car ate up. "See that we don't run out of gas again," protested the girl (about twenty-two), and reminded the driver of several places where this had already happened to them. The young man replied that he wasn't worried, because whatever he went through with her had the charm of adventure for him. The girl objected; when-ever they had run out of gas on the highway it had, she said, always been an adventure only for her. The young man had hidden and she had had to make ill use of her charms by thumbing a ride and letting herself be driven to the nearest gas station, then thumbing a ride back with a can of gas. The young man asked the girl whether the drivers who had given her a ride had been unpleasant, since she spoke as if her task had been a hardship. She replied (with awkward flirta-tiousness) that sometimes they had been *very* pleasant but that it hadn't done her any good as she had been burdened with the can and had had to leave them before she could get anything going. "Pig," said the young man. The girl protested that she wasn't a pig, but that he really was. God knows how many girls stopped him on the highway, when he was driving the car alone! Still driving, the young man put his arm around the girl's shoulders and kissed her gently on the forehead. He knew that she loved him and that she was jealous. Jealousy isn't a pleasant quality, but if it isn't overdone (and if it's combined with modesty), apart from its inconvenience there's even something touching about it. At least that's what the young man thought. Because he was only twenty-eight, it seemed to him that he was old and knew everything that a man could know about women. In the girl sitting beside him he valued precisely what, until now, he had met with least in women: purity.

The needle was already on empty, when to the right the young man caught sight of a sign, announcing that the station was a quarter of a mile ahead. The girl hardly had time to say how relieved she was before the young man was signal-ing left and driving into a space in front of the pumps. However, he had to stop a little way off, because beside the pumps was a huge gasoline truck with a large metal tank and a bulky hose, which was refilling the pumps. "We'll have to wait," said the young man to the girl and got out of the car. "How long will it take?" he shouted to the man in overalls. "Only a moment," replied the attendant, and the young man said: "I've heard that one before." He wanted to go back and sit in the car, but he saw that the girl had gotten out the other side. "I'll take a little walk in the meantime," she said. "Where to?" the young man asked on purpose, want-ing to see the girl's embarrassment. He had known her for a year now but she would still get shy in front of him. He enjoyed her moments of shyness, partly because they distinguished her from the women he'd met before, partly because he was aware of the law of universal transience, which made even his girl's shy-ness a precious thing to him.

2

The girl really didn't like it when during the trip (the young man would drive for several hours without stopping) she had to ask him to stop for a moment some-where near a clump of trees. She always got angry when, with feigned surprise, he asked her why he should stop. She knew that her shyness was ridiculous and old-fashioned. Many times at work she had noticed that they laughed at her on account of it and deliberately provoked her. She always got shy in advance at the thought of how she was going to get shy. She often longed to feel free and easy about her body, the way most of the women around her did. She had even invented a special course in self-persuasion: she would repeat to herself that at birth every human being received one out of the millions of available bodies, as one would receive an allotted room out of the millions of rooms in an enormous hotel. Consequently, the body was fortuitous and impersonal, it was only a ready-made, borrowed thing. She would repeat this to herself in different ways, but she could never manage to feel it. This mind-body dualism was alien to her. She was too much one with her body; that is why she always felt such anxiety about it.

She experienced this same anxiety even in her relations with the young man, whom she had known for a year and with whom she was happy, perhaps because he never separated her body from her soul and she could live with him *wholly*. In this unity there was happiness, but right behind the happiness lurked suspicion, and the girl was full of that. For instance, it often occurred to her that the other women (those who weren't anxious) were more attractive and more seductive and that the young man, who did not conceal the fact that he knew this kind of woman well, would someday leave her for a woman like that. (True, the young man declared that he'd had enough of them to last his whole life, but she knew that he was still much younger than he thought.) She wanted him to be completely hers and she to be completely his, but it often seemed to her that the more she tried to give him everything, the more she denied him something: the very thing that a light and superficial love or a flirtation gives to a person. It worried her that she was not able to combine seriousness with lightheartedness.

But now she wasn't worrying and any such thoughts were far from her mind. She felt good. It was the first day of their vacation (of their two-week vacation, about which she had been dreaming for a whole year), the sky was blue (the whole year she had been worrying about whether the sky would really be blue), and he was beside her. At his, "Where to?" she blushed, and left the car without a word. She walked around the gas station, which was situated beside the highway in total isolation, surrounded by fields. About a hundred yards away (in the direction in which they were traveling), a wood began. She set off for it, vanished behind a little bush, and gave herself up to her good mood. (In solitude it was possible for her to get the greatest enjoyment from the presence of the man she loved. If his presence had been continuous, it would have kept on disappearing. Only when alone was she able to *hold on* to it.)

When she came out of the wood onto the highway, the gas station was visible. The large gasoline truck was already pulling out and the sports car moved forward toward the red turret of the pump. The girl walked on along the highway and only at times looked back to see if the sports car was coming. At last she caught sight of it. She stopped and began to wave at it like a hitchhiker waving at a stranger's car. The sports car slowed down and stopped close to the girl. The young man leaned toward the window, rolled it down, smiled, and asked, "Where are you headed, miss?" "Are you going to Bystritsa?" asked the girl, smiling flirtatiously at him. "Yes, please get in," said the young man, opening the door. The girl got in and the car took off.

3

The young man was always glad when his girl friend was gay. This didn't happen too often; she had a quite tiresome job in an unpleasant environment, many hours of overtime without compensatory leisure and, at home, a sick mother. So she often felt tired. She didn't have either particularly good nerves or self-confidence and easily fell into a state of anxiety and fear. For this reason he welcomed every manifestation of her gaiety with the tender solicitude of a foster parent. He smiled at her and said: "I'm lucky today. I've been driving for five years, but I've never given a ride to such a pretty hitchhiker."

The girl was grateful to the young man for every bit of flattery; she wanted to linger for a moment in its warmth and so she said, "You're very good at lying."

"Do I look like a liar?"

"You look like you enjoy lying to women," said the girl, and into her words there crept unawares a touch of the old anxiety, because she really did believe that her young man enjoyed lying to women.

The girl's jealousy often irritated the young man, but this time he could easily overlook it for, after all, her words didn't apply to him but to the unknown driver. And so he just casually inquired, "Does it bother you?"

"If I were going with you, then it would bother me," said the girl and her words contained a subtle, instructive message for the young man; but the end of her sentence applied only to the unknown driver, "but I don't know you, so it doesn't bother me."

"Things about her own man always bother a woman more than things about a stranger" (this was now the young man's subtle, instructive message to the girl), "so seeing that we are strangers, we could get on well together."

The girl purposely didn't want to understand the implied meaning of his message, and so she now addressed the unknown driver exclusively:

"What does it matter, since we'll part company in a little while?"

"Why?" asked the young man.

"Well, I'm getting out at Bystritsa."

"And what if I get out with you?"

At these words the girl looked up at him and found that he looked exactly as she imagined him in her most agonizing hours of jealousy. She was alarmed at how he was flattering her and flirting with her (an unknown hitchhiker), and *how becoming it was to him*. Therefore she responded with defiant provocativeness, "What would *you* do with me, I wonder?"

"I wouldn't have to think too hard about what to do with such a beautiful woman," said the young man gallantly and at this moment he was once again speaking far more to his own girl than to the figure of the hitchhiker.

But this flattering sentence made the girl feel as if she had caught him at something, as if she had wheedled a confession out of him with a fraudulent trick. She felt toward him a brief flash of intense hatred and said, "Aren't you rather too sure of yourself?"

The young man looked at the girl. Her defiant face appeared to him to be completely convulsed. He felt sorry for her and longed for her usual, familiar expression (which he used to call childish and simple). He leaned toward her, put his arm around her shoulders, and softly spoke the name with which he usually addressed her and with which he now wanted to stop the game.

But the girl released herself and said: "You're going a bit too fast!"

At this rebuff the young man said: "Excuse me, miss," and looked silently in front of him at the highway.

4

The girl's pitiful jealousy, however, left her as quickly as it had come over her. After all, she was sensible and knew perfectly well that all this was merely a game. Now it even struck her as a little ridiculous that she had repulsed her man out of jealous rage. It wouldn't be pleasant for her if he found out why she had done it. Fortunately women have the miraculous ability to change the meaning of their actions after the event. Using this ability, she decided that she had repulsed him not out of anger but so that she could go on with the game, which, with its whimsicality, so well suited the first day of their vacation.

So again she was the hitchhiker, who had just repulsed the overenterprising driver, but only so as to slow down his conquest and make it more exciting. She half turned toward the young man and said caressingly:

"I didn't mean to offend you, mister!"

"Excuse me, I won't touch you again," said the young man.

He was furious with the girl for not listening to him and refusing to be herself when that was what he wanted. And since the girl insisted on continuing in her role, he transferred his anger to the unknown hitchhiker whom she was portraying. And all at once he discovered the character of his own part: he stopped making the gallant remarks with which he had wanted to flatter his girl in a roundabout way, and began to play the tough guy who treats women to the coarser aspects of his masculinity: willfulness, sarcasm, self-assurance.

This role was a complete contradiction of the young man's habitually solicitous approach to the girl. True, before he had met her, he had in fact behaved roughly rather than gently toward women. But he had never resembled a heartless tough guy, because he had never demonstrated either a particularly strong will or ruthlessness. However, if he did not resemble such a man, nonetheless he had *longed* to at one time. Of course it was a quite naive desire, but there it was. Childish desires withstand all the snares of the adult mind and often survive into ripe old age. And this childish desire quickly took advantage of the opportunity to embody itself in the proffered role.

The young man's sarcastic reserve suited the girl very well—it freed her from herself. For she herself was, above all, the epitome of jealousy. The moment she stopped seeing the gallantly seductive young man beside her and saw only his inaccessible face, her jealousy subsided. The girl could forget herself and give herself up to her role.

Her role? What was her role? It was a role out of trashy literature. The hitchhiker stopped the car not to get a ride, but to seduce the man who was driving the car. She was an artful seductress, cleverly knowing how to use her charms. The girl slipped into this silly, romantic part with an ease that astonished her and held her spellbound.

5

There was nothing the young man missed in his life more than lightheartedness. The main road of his life was drawn with implacable precision. His job didn't use up merely eight hours a day, it also infiltrated the remaining time with the compulsory boredom of meetings and home study, and, by means of the attentiveness of his countless male and female colleagues, it infiltrated the wretchedly little time he had left for his private life as well. This private life never remained secret and sometimes even became the subject of gossip and public discussion. Even two weeks' vacation didn't give him a feeling of liberation and adventure; the gray shadow of precise planning lay even here. The scarcity of summer accommodations in our country compelled him to book a room in the Tatras six months in advance, and since for that he needed a recommendation from his office, its omnipresent brain thus did not cease knowing about him even for an instant.

He had become reconciled to all this, yet all the same from time to time the terrible thought of the straight road would overcome him—a road along which he was being pursued, where he was visible to everyone, and from which he could not turn aside. At this moment that thought returned to him. Through an odd and brief conjunction of ideas the figurative road became identified with the real highway along which he was driving—and this led him suddenly to do a crazy thing.

"Where did you say you wanted to go?" he asked the girl.

"To Banska Bystritsa," she replied.

"And what are you going to do there?"

"I have a date there."

"Who with?"

"With a certain gentleman."

The car was just coming to a large crossroads. The driver slowed down so he could read the road signs, then turned off to the right.

"What will happen if you don't arrive for that date?"

"It would be your fault and you would have to take care of me."

"You obviously didn't notice that I turned off in the direction of Nove Zamky."

"Is that true? You've gone crazy!"

"Don't be afraid, I'll take care of you," said the young man.

So they drove and chatted thus—the driver and the hitchhiker who did not know each other.

The game all at once went into a higher gear. The sports car was moving away not only from the imaginary goal of Banska Bystritsa, but also from the real goal, toward which it had been heading in the morning: the Tatras and the room that had been booked. Fiction was suddenly making an assault upon real life. The young man was moving away from himself and from the implacable straight road, from which he had never strayed until now.

"But you said you were going to the Low Tatras!" The girl was surprised.

"I am going, miss, wherever I feel like going. I'm a free man and I do what I want and what it pleases me to do."

6

When they drove into Nove Zamky it was already getting dark.

The young man had never been here before and it took him a while to orient himself. Several times he stopped the car and asked the passersby directions to the hotel. Several streets had been dug up, so that the drive to the hotel, even though it was quite close by (as all those who had been asked asserted), necessitated so many detours and roundabout routes that it was almost a quarter of an hour before they finally stopped in front of it. The hotel looked unprepossessing, but it was the only one in town and the young man didn't feel like driving on. So he said to the girl, "Wait here," and got out of the car.

Out of the car he was, of course, himself again. And it was upsetting for him to find himself in the evening somewhere completely different from his intended destination—the more so because no one had forced him to do it and as a matter of fact he hadn't even really wanted to. He blamed himself for this piece of folly, but then became reconciled to it. The room in the Tatras could wait until tomorrow and it wouldn't do any harm if they celebrated the first day of their vacation with something unexpected.

He walked through the restaurant—smoky, noisy, and crowded—and asked for the reception desk. They sent him to the back of the lobby near the staircase, where behind a glass panel a superannuated blonde was sitting beneath a board full of keys. With difficulty, he obtained the key to the only room left.

The girl, when she found herself alone, also threw off her role. She didn't feel ill-humored, though, at finding herself in an unexpected town. She was so devoted to the young man that she never had doubts about anything he did, and confidently entrusted every moment of her life to him. On the other hand the idea once again popped into her mind that perhaps—just as she was now doing—other women had waited for her man in his car, those women whom he met on business trips. But surprisingly enough this idea didn't upset her at all now. In fact, she smiled at the thought of how nice it was that today she was this other woman, this irresponsible, indecent other woman, one of those women of whom she was so jealous. It seemed to her that she was cutting them all out, that she had learned how to use their weapons; how to give the young man what until now she had not known how to give him: lightheartedness, shamelessness, and dissoluteness. A curious feeling of satisfaction filled her, because she alone had the ability to be all women and in this way (she alone) could completely captivate her lover and hold his interest.

The young man opened the car door and led the girl into the restaurant. Amid the din, the dirt, and the smoke he found a single, unoccupied table in a corner.

7

"So how are you going to take care of me now?" asked the girl provocatively.

"What would you like for an aperitif?"

The girl wasn't too fond of alcohol, still she drank a little wine and liked vermouth fairly well. Now, however, she purposely said: "Vodka."

"Fine," said the young man. "I hope you won't get drunk on me."

"And if I do?" said the girl.

The young man did not reply but called over a waiter and ordered two vodkas and two steak dinners. In a moment the waiter brought a tray with two small glasses and placed it in front of them.

The man raised his glass, "To you!"

"Can't you think of a wittier toast?"

Something was beginning to irritate him about the girl's game. Now sitting face to face with her, he realized that it wasn't just the *words* which were turning her into a stranger, but that her *whole persona* had changed, the movements of her body and her facial expression, and that she unpalatably and faithfully resembled that type of woman whom he knew so well and for whom he felt some aversion.

And so (holding his glass in his raised hand), he corrected his toast: "O.K., then I won't drink to you, but to your kind, in which are combined so successfully the better qualities of the animal and the worse aspects of the human being."

"By 'kind' do you mean all women?" asked the girl.

"No, I mean only those who are like you."

"Anyway it doesn't seem very witty to me to compare a woman with an animal."

"O.K.," the young man was still holding his glass aloft, "then I won't drink to your kind, but to your soul. Agreed? To your soul, which lights up when it descends from your head into your belly, and which goes out when it rises back up to your head."

The girl raised her glass. "O.K., to my soul, which descends into my belly."

"I'll correct myself once more," said the young man. "To your belly, into which your soul descends."

"To my belly," said the girl, and her belly (now that they had named it specifically), as it were, responded to the call; she felt every inch of it.

Then the waiter brought their steaks and the young man ordered them another vodka and some soda water (this time they drank to the girl's breasts), and the conversation continued in this peculiar, frivolous tone. It irritated the young man more and more how *well able* the girl was to become the lascivious miss. If she was able to do it so well, he thought, it meant that she really *was* like that. After all, no alien soul had entered into her from somewhere in space. What she was acting now was she herself; perhaps it was that part of her being which had formerly been locked up and which the pretext of the game had let out of its cage. Perhaps the girl supposed that by means of the game she was *disowning* herself, but wasn't it the other way around? Wasn't she becoming herself only through the game? Wasn't she freeing herself through the game? No, opposite him was not sitting a strange woman in his girl's body; it was his girl, herself, no one else. He looked at her and felt growing aversion toward her.

However, it was not only aversion. The more the girl withdrew from him *psychically*, the more he longed for her *physically*. The alien quality of her soul drew attention to her body, yes, as a matter of fact it turned her body into a body for *him* as if until now it had existed for the young man hidden within clouds of compassion, tenderness, concern, love, and emotion, as if it had been lost in these clouds (yes, as if this body had been lost!). It seemed to the young man that today he was seeing his girl's body for the first time.

After her third vodka and soda the girl got up and said flirtatiously, "Excuse me."

The young man said, "May I ask you where you are going, miss?"

"To piss, if you'll permit me," said the girl and walked off between the tables back toward the plush screen.

8

She was pleased with the way she had astounded the young man with this word, which—in spite of all its innocence—he had never heard from her. Nothing seemed to her truer to the character of the woman she was playing than this flirtatious emphasis placed on the word in question. Yes, she was pleased, she was in the best of moods. The game captivated her. It allowed her to feel what she had not felt till now: a *feeling of happy-go-lucky irresponsibility*.

She, who was always uneasy in advance about her every next step, suddenly felt completely relaxed. The alien life in which she had become involved was a life without shame, without biographical specifications, without past or future, without obligations. It was a life that was extraordinarily free. The girl, as a hitchhiker, could do anything, *everything was permitted her*. She could say, do, and feel whatever she liked.

She walked through the room and was aware that people were watching her from all the tables. It was a new sensation, one she didn't recognize: *indecent joy caused by her body*. Until now she had never been able to get rid of the fourteen-year-old girl within herself who was ashamed of her breasts and had the disagreeable feeling that she was indecent, because they stuck out from her body and were visible. Even though she was proud of being pretty and having a good figure, this feeling of pride was always immediately curtailed by shame. She rightly suspected that feminine beauty functioned above all as sexual provocation and she found this distasteful. She longed for her body to relate only to the man she loved. When men stared at her breasts in the street it seemed to her that they were invading a piece of her most secret privacy which should belong only to herself and her lover. But now she was the hitchhiker, the woman without a destiny. In this role she was relieved of the tender bonds of her love and began to be intensely aware of her body. And her body became more aroused the more alien the eyes watching it.

She was walking past the last table when an intoxicated man, wanting to show off his worldliness, addressed her in French: "*Combien, mademoiselle?*"

The girl understood. She thrust out her breasts and fully experienced every movement of her hips, then disappeared behind the screen.

9

It was a curious game. This curiousness was evidenced, for example, in the fact that the young man, even though he himself was playing the unknown driver remarkably well, did not for a moment stop seeing his girl in the hitchhiker. And it was precisely this that was tormenting. He saw his girl seducing a strange man, and had the bitter privilege of being present, of seeing at close quarters how she looked and of hearing what she said when she was cheating on him (when she had cheated on him, when she would cheat on him). He had the paradoxical honor of being himself the pretext for her unfaithfulness.

This was all the worse because he worshipped rather than loved her. It had always seemed to him that her inward nature was *real* only within the bounds of fidelity and purity, and that beyond these bounds it simply didn't exist. Beyond these bounds she would cease to be herself, as water ceases to be water beyond the boiling point. When he now saw her crossing this horrifying boundary with nonchalant elegance, he was filled with anger.

The girl came back from the rest room and complained: "A guy over there asked me: *Combien, mademoiselle?*"

"You shouldn't be surprised," said the young man, "after all, you look like a whore."

"Do you know that it doesn't bother me in the least?"

"Then you should go with the gentleman!"

"But I have you."

"You can go with him after me. Go and work out something with him."

"I don't find him attractive."

"But in principle you have nothing against it, having several men in one night."

"Why not, if they're good-looking."

"Do you prefer them one after the other or at the same time?"

"Either way," said the girl.

The conversation was proceeding to still greater extremes of rudeness; it shocked the girl slightly but she couldn't protest. Even in a game there lurks a lack of freedom; even a game is a trap for the players. If this had not been a game and they had really been two strangers, the hitchhiker could long ago have taken offense and left. But there's no escape from a game. A team cannot flee from the playing field before the end of the match, chess pieces cannot desert the chessboard: the boundaries of the playing field are fixed. The girl knew that she had to accept whatever form the game might take, just because it was a game. She knew that the more extreme the game became, the more it would be a game and the more obediently she would have to play it. And it was futile to evoke good sense and warn her dazed soul that she must keep her distance from the game and not take it seriously. Just because it was only a game her soul was not afraid, did not oppose the game, and narcotically sank deeper into it.

The young man called the waiter and paid. Then he got up and said to the girl, "We're going."

"Where to?" The girl feigned surprise.

"Don't ask, just come on," said the young man.

"What sort of way is that to talk to me?"

"The way I talk to whores," said the young man.

10

They went up the badly lit staircase. On the landing below the second floor a group of intoxicated men was standing near the rest room. The young man caught hold of the girl from behind so that he was holding her breast with his hand. The men by the rest room saw this and began to call out. The girl wanted to break away, but the young man yelled at her: "Keep still!" The men greeted this with general ribaldry and addressed several dirty remarks to the girl. The young man and the girl reached the second floor. He opened the door of their room and switched on the light.

It was a narrow room with two beds, a small table, a chair, and a washbasin. The young man locked the door and turned to the girl. She was standing facing him in a defiant pose with insolent sensuality in her eyes. He looked at her and tried to discover behind her lascivious expression the familiar features which he loved tenderly. It was as if he were looking at two images through the same lens, at two images superimposed one upon the other with the one showing through the other. These two images showing through each other were telling him that *everything* was in the girl, that her soul was terrifyingly amorphous, that it held faithfulness and unfaithfulness, treachery and innocence, flirtatiousness and chastity. This disorderly jumble seemed disgusting to him, like the variety to be found in a pile of garbage. Both images continued to show through each other and the young man understood that the girl differed only on the surface from other women, but deep down was the same as they: full of all possible thoughts, feelings, and vices, which justified all his secret misgivings and fits of jealousy. The impression that certain outlines delineated her as an individual was only a delusion to which the other person, the one who was looking, was subject—namely himself. It seemed to him that the girl he loved was a creation of his desire, his thoughts, and his faith and that the *real* girl now standing in front of him was hopelessly alien, hopelessly *ambiguous*. He hated her.

"What are you waiting for? Strip," he said.

The girl flirtatiously bent her head and said, "Is it necessary?"

The tone in which she said this seemed to him very familiar; it seemed to him that once long ago some other woman had said this to him, only he no longer knew which one. He longed to humiliate her. Not the hitchhiker, but his own girl. The game merged with life: The game of humiliating the hitchhiker became only a pretext for humiliating his girl. The young man had forgotten that he was playing a game. He simply hated the woman standing in front of him. He stared at her and took a fifty-crown bill from his wallet. He offered it to the girl. "Is that enough?"

The girl took the fifty crowns and said: "You don't think I'm worth much."

The young man said: "You aren't worth more."

The girl nestled up against the young man. "You can't get around me like that! You must try a different approach, you must work a little!"

She put her arms around him and moved her mouth toward his. He put his fingers on her mouth and gently pushed her away. He said: "I only kiss women I love."

"And you don't love me?"

"No."

"Whom do you love?"

"What's that got to do with you? Strip!"

11

She had never undressed like this before. The shyness, the feeling of inner panic, the dizziness, all that she had always felt when undressing in front of the young man (and she couldn't hide in the darkness), all this was gone. She was standing in front of him self-confident, insolent, bathed in light, and astonished at where she had all of a sudden discovered the gestures, heretofore unknown to her, of a slow, provocative striptease. She took in his glances, slipping off each piece of clothing with a caressing movement and enjoying each individual stage of this exposure.

But then suddenly she was standing in front of him completely naked and at this moment it flashed through her head that now the whole game would end, that, since she had stripped off her clothes, she had also stripped away her dissimulation, and that being naked meant that she was now herself and the young man ought to come up to her now and make a gesture with which he would wipe out everything and after which would follow only their most intimate lovemaking. So she stood naked in front of the young man and at this moment stopped playing the game. She felt embarrassed and on her face appeared the smile, which really belonged to her—a shy and confused smile.

But the young man didn't come to her and didn't end the game. He didn't notice the familiar smile. He saw before him only the beautiful, alien body of his own girl, whom he hated. Hatred cleansed his sensuality of any sentimental coating. She wanted to come to him, but he said: "Stay where you are, I want to have a good look at you." Now he longed only to treat her as a whore. But the young man had never had a whore and the ideas he had about them came from literature and hearsay. So he turned to these ideas and the first thing he recalled was the image of a woman in black underwear (and black stockings) dancing on the shiny top of a piano. In the little hotel room there was no piano, there was only a small table covered with a linen cloth leaning against the wall. He ordered the girl to climb up on it. The girl made a pleading gesture, but the young man said, "You've been paid."

When she saw the look of unshakable obsession in the young man's eyes, she tried to go on with the game, even though she no longer could and no longer knew how. With tears in her eyes she climbed onto the table. The top was scarcely three feet square and one leg was a little bit shorter than the others so that standing on it the girl felt unsteady.

But the young man was pleased with the naked figure, now towering above him, and the girl's shy insecurity merely inflamed his imperiousness. He wanted to see her body in all positions and from all sides, as he imagined other men had seen it and would see it. He was vulgar and lascivious. He used words that she had never heard from him in her life. She wanted to refuse, she wanted to be released from the game. She called him by his first name, but he immediately yelled at her that she had no right to address him so intimately. And so eventually in confusion and on the verge of tears, she obeyed, she bent forward and squatted according to the young man's wishes, saluted, and then wiggled her hips as she did the Twist for him. During a slightly more violent movement, when the cloth slipped beneath her feet and she nearly fell, the young man caught her and dragged her to the bed.

He had intercourse with her. She was glad that at least now finally the unfortunate game would end and they would again be the two people they had been before and would love each other. She wanted to press her mouth against his. But the young man pushed her head away and repeated that he only kissed women he loved. She burst into loud sobs. But she wasn't even allowed to cry, because the young man's furious passion gradually won over her body, which then silenced the complaint of her soul. On the bed there were soon two bodies in perfect harmony, two sensual bodies, alien to each other. This was exactly what the girl had most dreaded all her life and had scrupulously avoided till now: love-making without emotion or love. She knew that she had crossed the forbidden boundary, but she proceeded across it without objections and as a full participant—only somewhere, far off in a corner of her consciousness, did she feel horror at the thought that she had never known such pleasure, never so much pleasure as at this moment—beyond that boundary.

12

Then it was all over. The young man got up off the girl and, reaching out for the long cord hanging over the bed, switched off the light. He didn't want to see the girl's face. He knew that the game was over, but didn't feel like returning to their customary relationship. He feared this return. He lay beside the girl in the dark in such a way that their bodies would not touch.

After a moment he heard her sobbing quietly. The girl's hand diffidently, childishly touched his. It touched, withdrew, then touched again, and then a pleading, sobbing voice broke the silence, calling him by his name and saying, "I am me, I am me . . ."

The young man was silent, he didn't move, and he was aware of the sad emptiness of the girl's assertion, in which the unknown was defined in terms of the same unknown quantity.

And the girl soon passed from sobbing to loud crying and went on endlessly repeating this pitiful tautology: "I am me, I am me, I am me . . ."

The young man began to call compassion to his aid (he had to call it from afar, because it was nowhere near at hand), so as to be able to calm the girl. There were still thirteen days' vacation before them.

D. H. LAWRENCE

(1885–1930)

DAVID HERBERT LAWRENCE was born in Nottinghamshire, England. His father was a coal miner; his mother had been a teacher and she hoped that a good education for her gifted, often sickly son would help him rise above the poverty and deprivation of a miner's life. In 1905 he graduated from a two-year teacher-training course at University College, Nottingham, and took a job outside London as a schoolmaster. In 1909 the *English Review,* edited by Ford Madox Ford, published a few of Lawrence's poems; Ford also helped secure the publication in 1911 of Lawrence's first novel, *The White Peacock. Sons and Lovers* appeared in 1913. In 1914, after her divorce, Lawrence married Frieda von Richthofen, a native of Germany. During World War I the couple lived in England, where Lawrence's well-known opposition to the war, coupled with his wife's German ancestry, made them targets of harrassment. The situation was compounded when the British police declared *The Rainbow* (1915) obscene. For the balance of their lives together, Lawrence and Frieda lived nomadically, traveling to the Continent, Ceylon, Australia, and eventually to the United States and Mexico. Lawrence's other novels include *Women in Love* (1920), *Aaron's Rod* (1922), *Kangaroo* (1923), *The Plumed Serpent* (1926), and *Lady Chatterly's Lover,* which appeared in an expurgated edition in 1928; publication of the unexpurgated version in England and the United States was deferred for more than thirty years. In addition to the novels and poems, Lawrence was the author of numerous volumes of short stories, as well as several works of nonfiction.

The importance of sexuality and its connection to nature—to the elemental—is among Lawrence's key preoccupations. The cadences of his prose seem tidal; the language has a kind of scriptural authority at the same time that it reflects immersion in sensory experience.

In "The Horse Dealer's Daughter" (1922) the characters respond to forces larger than themselves—the pull of earth and air and water. Mabel, the horse dealer's daughter, and her three brothers are facing poverty. Their parents are gone, the horses are gone, the "morning's post had given the final tap to the family fortunes, and all was over." Mabel steals out to tend her mother's grave; though her mother died years ago, Mabel's love for her remains unextinguished. The question the story addresses is whether intimacy has the power to frustrate grief and despair.

The Horse Dealer's Daughter

"Well, Mabel, and what are you going to do with yourself?" asked Joe, with foolish flippancy. He felt quite safe himself. Without listening for an answer, he turned aside, worked a grain of tobacco to the tip of his tongue, and spat it out. He did not care about anything, since he felt safe himself.

The three brothers and the sister sat round the desolate breakfast-table, attempting some sort of desultory consultation. The morning's post had given the final tap to the family fortunes, and all was over. The dreary dining-room itself, with its heavy mahogany furniture, looked as if it were waiting to be done away with.

But the consultation amounted to nothing. There was a strange air of ineffectuality about the three men, as they sprawled at table, smoking and reflecting vaguely on their own condition. The girl was alone, a rather short, sullen-looking young woman of twenty-seven. She did not share the same life as her brothers. She would have been good-looking, save for the impressive fixity of her face, 'bull-dog,' as her brothers called it.

There was a confused tramping of horses' feet outside. The three men all sprawled round in their chairs to watch. Beyond the dark holly bushes that separated the strip of lawn from the high-road, they could see a cavalcade of shire horses swinging out of their own yard, being taken for exercise. This was the last time. These were the last horses that would go through their hands. The young men watched with critical, callous look. They were all frightened at the collapse of their lives, and the sense of disaster in which they were involved left them no inner freedom.

Yet they were three fine, well-set fellows enough. Joe, the eldest, was a man of thirty-three, broad and handsome in a hot, flushed way. His face was red, he twisted his black moustache over a thick finger, his eyes were shallow and restless. He had a sensual way of uncovering his teeth when he laughed, and his bearing was stupid. Now he watched the horses with a glazed look of helplessness in his eyes, a certain stupor of downfall.

The great draught-horses swung past. They were tied head to tail, four of them, and they heaved along to where a lane branched off from the high-road, planting their great hoofs floutingly in the fine black mud, swinging their great rounded haunches sumptuously, and trotting a few sudden steps as they were led into the lane, round the corner. Every movement showed a massive, slumbrous strength, and a stupidity which held them in subjection. The groom at the head looked back, jerking the leading rope. And the cavalcade moved out of sight up the lane, the tail of the last horse, bobbed up tight and stiff, held out taut from the swinging great haunches as they rocked behind the hedges in a motion-like sleep.

Joe watched with glazed hopeless eyes. The horses were almost like his own body to him. He felt he was done for now. Luckily he was engaged to a woman as old as himself, and therefore her father, who was steward of a neighbouring estate, would provide him with a job. He would marry and go into harness. His life was over, he would be a subject animal now.

He turned uneasily aside, the retreating steps of the horses echoing in his ears. Then, with foolish restlessness, he reached for the scraps of bacon-rind from the plates, and making a faint whistling sound, flung them to the terrier that lay against the fender. He watched the dog swallow them, and waited till the creature looked into his eyes. Then a faint grin came on his face, and in a high, foolish voice he said:

"You won't get much more bacon, shall you, you little b——?"

The dog faintly and dismally wagged its tail, then lowered its haunches, circled round, and lay down again.

There was another helpless silence at the table. Joe sprawled uneasily in his seat, not willing to go till the family conclave was dissolved. Fred Henry, the second brother, was erect, clean-limbed, alert. He had watched the passing of the horses with more *sang-froid*. If he was an animal, like Joe, he was an animal which controls, not one which is controlled. He was master of any horse, and he carried himself with a well-tempered air of mastery. But he was not master of the situations of life. He pushed his coarse brown moustache upwards, off his lip, and glanced irritably at his sister, who sat impassive and inscrutable.

"You'll go and stop with Lucy for a bit, shan't you?" he asked. The girl did not answer.

"I don't see what else you can do," persisted Fred Henry.

"Go as a skivvy," Joe interpolated laconically.

The girl did not move a muscle.

"If I was her, I should go in for training for a nurse," said Malcolm, the youngest of them all. He was the baby of the family, a young man of twenty-two, with a fresh, jaunty *museau*.

But Mabel did not take any notice of him. They had talked at her and round her for so many years, that she hardly heard them at all.

The marble clock on the mantelpiece softly chimed the half-hour, the dog rose uneasily from the hearth-rug and looked at the party at the breakfast-table. But still they sat on in ineffectual conclave.

"Oh, all right," said Joe suddenly, apropos of nothing. "I'll get a move on."

He pushed back his chair, straddled his knees with a downward jerk, to get them free, in horsey fashion, and went to the fire. Still he did not go out of the room; he was curious to know what the others would do or say. He began to charge his pipe, looking down at the dog and saying in a high, affected voice:

"Going wi' me? Going wi' me are ter? Tha'rt goin' further than tha counts on just now, dost hear?"

The dog faintly wagged its tail, the man stuck out his jaw and covered his pipe with his hands, and puffed intently, losing himself in the tobacco, looking down all the while at the dog with an absent brown eye. The dog looked up at him in mournful distrust. Joe stood with his knees stuck out, in real horsey fashion.

"Have you had a letter from Lucy?" Fred Henry asked of his sister.

"Last week," came the neutral reply.

"And what does she say?"

There was no answer.

"Does she *ask* you to go and stop there?" persisted Fred Henry.

"She says I can if I like."

"Well, then, you'd better. Tell her you'll come on Monday."

This was received in silence.

"That's what you'll do then, is it?" said Fred Henry, in some exasperation.

But she made no answer. There was a silence of futility and irritation in the room. Malcolm grinned fatuously.

"You'll have to make up your mind between now and next Wednesday," said Joe loudly, "or else find yourself lodgings on the kerbstone."

The face of the young woman darkened, but she sat on immutable.

"Here's Jack Fergusson!" exclaimed Malcolm, who was looking aimlessly out of the window.

"Where?" exclaimed Joe loudly.

"Just gone past."

"Coming in?"

Malcolm craned his neck to see the gate.

"Yes," he said.

There was a silence. Mabel sat on like one condemned, at the head of the table. Then a whistle was heard from the kitchen. The dog got up and barked sharply. Joe opened the door and shouted:

"Come on."

After a moment a young man entered. He was muffled up in overcoat and a purple woollen scarf, and his tweed cap, which he did not remove, was pulled down on his head. He was of medium height, his face was rather long and pale, his eyes looked tired.

"Hello, Jack! Well, Jack!" exclaimed Malcolm and Joe. Fred Henry merely said: "Jack."

"What's doing?" asked the newcomer, evidently addressing Fred Henry.

"Same. We've got to be out by Wednesday. Got a cold?"

"I have—got it bad, too."

"Why don't you stop in?"

"*Me* stop in? When I can't stand on my legs, perhaps I shall have a chance." The young man spoke huskily. He had a slight Scotch accent.

"It's a knock-out, isn't it," said Joe, boisterously, "if a doctor goes round croaking with a cold. Looks bad for the patients, doesn't it?"

The young doctor looked at him slowly.

"Anything the matter with *you*, then?" he asked sarcastically.

"Not as I know of. Damn your eyes, I hope not. Why?"

"I thought you were very concerned about the patients, wondered if you might be one yourself."

"Damn it, no, I've never been patient to no flaming doctor, and hope I never shall be," returned Joe.

At this point Mabel rose from the table, and they all seemed to become aware of her existence. She began putting the dishes together. The young doctor looked at her, but did not address her. He had not greeted her. She went out of the room with the tray, her face impassive and unchanged.

"When are you off then, all of you?" asked the doctor.

"I'm catching the eleven-forty," replied Malcolm. "Are you goin' down wi' th' trap, Joe?"

"Yes, I've told you I'm going down wi' th' trap, haven't I?"

"We'd better be getting her in then. So long, Jack, if I don't see you before I go," said Malcolm, shaking hands.

He went out, followed by Joe, who seemed to have his tail between his legs.

"Well, this is the devil's own," exclaimed the doctor, when he was left alone with Fred Henry. "Going before Wednesday, are you?"

"That's the orders," replied the other.

"Where, to Northampton?"

"That's it."

"The devil!" exclaimed Fergusson, with quiet chagrin.

And there was silence between the two.

"All settled up, are you?" asked Fergusson.

"About."

There was another pause.

"Well, I shall miss yer, Freddy, boy," said the young doctor.

"And I shall miss thee, Jack," returned the other.

"Miss you like hell," mused the doctor.

Fred Henry turned aside. There was nothing to say. Mabel came in again, to finish clearing the table.

"What are *you* going to do, then, Miss Pervin?" asked Fergusson. "Going to your sister's, are you?"

Mabel looked at him with her steady, dangerous eyes, that always made him uncomfortable, unsettling his superficial ease.

"No," she said.

"Well, what in the name of fortune *are* you going to do? Say what you mean to do," cried Fred Henry, with futile intensity.

But she only averted her head, and continued her work. She folded the white table-cloth, and put on the chenille cloth.

"The sulkiest bitch that ever trod!" muttered her brother.

But she finished her task with perfectly impassive face, the young doctor watching her interestedly all the while. Then she went out.

Fred Henry stared after her, clenching his lips, his blue eyes fixing in sharp antagonism, as he made a grimace of sour exasperation.

"You could bray her into bits, and that's all you'd get out of her," he said, in a small, narrowed tone.

The doctor smiled faintly.

"What's she *going* to do, then?" he asked.

"Strike me if *I* know!" returned the other.

There was a pause. Then the doctor stirred.

"I'll be seeing you to-night, shall I?" he said to his friend.

"Ay—where's it to be? Are we going over to Jessdale?"

"I don't know. I've got such a cold on me. I'll come round to the 'Moon and Stars', anyway."

"Let Lizzie and May miss their night for once, eh?"

"That's it—if I feel as I do now."

"All's one——"

The two young men went through the passage and down to the back door together. The house was large, but it was servantless now, and desolate. At the back was a small bricked house-yard and beyond that a big square, gravelled fine and red, and having stables on two sides. Sloping, dank, winter-dark fields stretched away on the open sides.

But the stables were empty. Joseph Pervin, the father of the family, had been a man of no education, who had become a fairly large horse dealer. The stables had been full of horses, there was a great turmoil and come-and-go of horses and of dealers and grooms. Then the kitchen was full of servants. But of late things had declined. The old man had married a second time, to retrieve his fortunes. Now he was dead and everything was gone to the dogs, there was nothing but debt and threatening.

For months, Mabel had been servantless in the big house, keeping the home together in penury for her ineffectual brothers. She had kept house for ten years. But previously it was with unstinted means. Then, however brutal and coarse everything was, the sense of money had kept her proud, confident. The men might be foul-mouthed, the women in the kitchen might have bad reputations, her brothers might have illegitimate children. But so long as there was money, the girl felt herself established, and brutally proud, reserved.

No company came to the house, save dealers and coarse men. Mabel had no associates of her own sex, after her sister went away. But she did not mind. She went regularly to church, she attended to her father. And she lived in the memory of her mother, who had died when she was fourteen, and whom she had loved. She had loved her father, too, in a different way, depending upon him, and feeling secure in him, until at the age of fifty-four he married again. And then she had set hard against him. Now he had died and left them all hopelessly in debt.

She had suffered badly during the period of poverty. Nothing, however, could shake the curious, sullen, animal pride that dominated each member of the family. Now, for Mabel, the end had come. Still she would not cast about her. She would follow her own way just the same. She would always hold the keys of her own situation. Mindless and persistent, she endured from day to day. Why should she think? Why should she answer anybody? It was enough that this was the end, and there was no way out. She need not pass any more darkly along the main street of the small town, avoiding every eye. She need not demean herself any more, going into the shops and buying the cheapest food. This was at an end. She thought of nobody, not even of herself. Mindless and persistent, she seemed in a sort of ecstasy to be coming nearer to her fulfillment, her own glorification, approaching her dead mother, who was glorified.

In the afternoon she took a little bag, with shears and sponge and a small scrubbing-brush, and went out. It was a grey, wintry day, with saddened, dark green fields and an atmosphere blackened by the smoke of foundries not far off. She went quickly, darkly along the causeway, heeding nobody, through the town to the churchyard.

There she always felt secure, as if no one could see her, although as a matter of fact she was exposed to the stare of everyone who passed along under the churchyard wall. Nevertheless, once under the shadow of the great looming church, among the graves, she felt immune from the world, reserved within the thick churchyard wall as in another country.

Carefully she clipped the grass from the grave, and arranged the pinky white, small chrysanthemums in the tin cross. When this was done, she took an empty jar from a neighbouring grave, brought water, and carefully, most scrupulously sponged the marble headstone and the coping-stone.

It gave her sincere satisfaction to do this. She felt in immediate contact with the world of her mother. She took minute pains, went through the park in a state bordering on pure happiness, as if in performing this task she came into a subtle, intimate connection with her mother. For the life she followed here in the world was far less real than the world of death she inherited from her mother.

The doctor's house was just by the church. Fergusson, being a mere hired assistant, was slave to the country-side. As he hurried now to attend to the out-patients in the surgery, glancing across the graveyard with his quick eye, he saw the girl at her task at the grave. She seemed so intent and remote, it was like looking into another world. Some mystical element was touched in him. He slowed down as he walked, watching her as if spellbound.

She lifted her eyes, feeling him looking. Their eyes met. And each looked again at once, each feeling, in some way, found out by the other. He lifted his cap and passed on down the road. There remained distinct in his consciousness, like a vision, the memory of her face, lifted from the tombstone in the church-yard, and looking at him with slow, large, portentous eyes. It *was* portentous, her face. It seemed to mesmerise him. There was a heavy power in her eyes which laid hold of his whole being, as if he had drunk some powerful drug. He had been feeling weak and done before. Now the life came back into him, he felt delivered from his own fretted, daily self.

He finished his duties at the surgery as quickly as might be, hastily filling up the bottles of the waiting people with cheap drugs. Then, in perpetual haste, he set off again to visit several cases in another part of his round, before tea-time. At all times he preferred to walk if he could, but particularly when he was not well. He fancied the motion restored him.

The afternoon was falling. It was grey, deadened, and wintry, with a slow, moist, heavy coldness sinking in and deadening all the faculties. But why should he think or notice? He hastily climbed the hill and turned across the dark green fields, following the black cinder-track. In the distance, across a shallow dip in the country, the small town was clustered like smouldering ash, a tower, a spire, a heap of low, raw, extinct houses. And on the nearest fringe of the town, sloping into the dip, was Oldmeadow, the Pervins' house. He could see the stables and the outbuildings distinctly, as they lay towards him on the slope. Well, he would not go there many more times! Another resource would be lost to him, another place gone: the only company he cared for in the alien, ugly little town he was losing. Nothing but work, drudgery, constant hastening from dwelling to dwelling among the colliers and the iron-workers. It wore him out, but at the same time he had a craving for it. It was a stimulant to him to be in the homes of the working people, moving, as it were, through the innermost body of their life. His nerves were excited and gratified. He could come so near, into the very lives of the rough, inarticulate, powerfully emotional men and women. He grumbled, he said he hated the hellish hole. But as a matter of fact it excited him, the contact with the rough, strongly-feeling people was a stimulant applied direct to his nerves.

Below Oldmeadow, in the green, shallow, soddened hollow of fields, lay a square, deep pond. Roving across the landscape, the doctor's quick eye detected a figure in black passing through the gate of the field, down towards the pond. He looked again. It would be Mabel Pervin. His mind suddenly became alive and attentive.

Why was she going down there? He pulled up on the path on the slope above, and stood staring. He could just make sure of the small black figure moving in the hollow of the failing day. He seemed to see her in the midst of such obscurity, that he was like a clairvoyant, seeing rather with the mind's eye than with ordinary sight. Yet he could see her positively enough, whilst he kept his eye attentive. He felt, if he looked away from her, in the thick, ugly falling dusk, he would lose her altogether.

He followed her minutely as she moved, direct and intent, like something transmitted rather than stirring in voluntary activity, straight down the field towards the pond. There she stood on the bank for a moment. She never raised her head. Then she waded slowly into the water.

He stood motionless as the small black figure walked slowly and deliberately towards the centre of the pond, very slowly, gradually moving deeper into the motionless water, and still moving forward as the water got up to her breast. Then he could see her no more in the dusk of the dead afternoon.

"There!" he exclaimed. "Would you believe it?"

And he hastened straight down, running over the wet, soddened fields, pushing through the hedges, down into the depression of callous wintry obscurity. It took him several minutes to come to the pond. He stood on the bank, breathing heavily. He could see nothing. His eyes seemed to penetrate the dead water. Yes, perhaps that was the dark shadow of her black clothing beneath the surface of the water.

He slowly ventured into the pond. The bottom was deep, soft clay, he sank in, and the water clasped dead cold round his legs. As he stirred he could smell the cold, rotten clay that fouled up into the water. It was objectionable in his lungs. Still, repelled and yet not heeding, he moved deeper into the pond. The cold water rose over his thighs, over his loins, upon his abdomen. The lower part of his body was all sunk in the hideous cold element. And the bottom was so deeply soft and uncertain, he was afraid of pitching with his mouth underneath. He could not swim, and was afraid.

He crouched a little, spreading his hands under the water and moving them round, trying to feel for her. The dead cold pond swayed upon his chest. He moved again, a little deeper, and again, with his hands underneath, he felt all around under the water. And he touched her clothing. But it evaded his fingers. He made a desperate effort to grasp it.

And so doing he lost his balance and went under, horribly, suffocating in the foul earthy water, struggling madly for a few moments. At last, after what seemed an eternity, he got his footing, rose again into the air and looked around. He gasped, and knew he was in the world. Then he looked at the water. She had risen near him. He grasped her clothing, and drawing her nearer, turned to take his way to land again.

He went very slowly, carefully, absorbed in the slow progress. He rose higher, climbing out of the pond. The water was now only about his legs; he was thankful, full of relief to be out of the clutches of the pond. He lifted her and staggered on to the bank, out of the horror of wet, grey clay.

He laid her down on the bank. She was quite unconscious and running with water. He made the water come from her mouth, he worked to restore her. He did not have to work very long before he could feel the breathing begin again in her; she was breathing naturally. He worked a little longer. He could feel her live beneath his hands; she was coming back. He wiped her face, wrapped her in his overcoat, looked round into the dim, dark grey world, then lifted her and staggered down the bank and across the fields.

It seemed an unthinkably long way, and his burden so heavy he felt he would never get to the house. But at last he was in the stable-yard, and then in the house-yard. He opened the door and went into the house. In the kitchen he laid her down on the hearth-rug and called. The house was empty. But the fire was burning in the grate.

Then again he kneeled to attend to her. She was breathing regularly, her eyes were wide open and as if conscious, but there seemed something missing in her look. She was conscious in herself, but unconscious of her surroundings.

He ran upstairs, took blankets from a bed, and put them before the fire to warm. Then he removed her saturated, earthy-smelling clothing, rubbed her dry with a towel, and wrapped her naked in the blankets. Then he went into the dining-room, to look for spirits. There was a little whisky. He drank a gulp himself, and put some into her mouth.

The effect was instantaneous. She looked full into his face, as if she had been seeing him for some time, and yet had only just become conscious of him.

"Dr. Fergusson?" she said.

"What?" he answered.

He was divesting himself of his coat, intending to find some dry clothing upstairs. He could not bear the smell of the dead, clayey water, and he was mortally afraid for his own health.

"What did I do?" she asked.

"Walked into the pond," he replied. He had begun to shudder like one sick, and could hardly attend to her. Her eyes remained full on him, he seemed to be going dark in his mind, looking back at her helplessly. The shuddering became quieter in him, his life came back to him, dark and unknowing, but strong again.

"Was I out of my mind?" she asked, while her eyes were fixed on him all the time.

"Maybe, for the moment," he replied. He felt quiet, because his strength had come back. The strange fretful strain had left him.

"Am I out of my mind now?" she asked.

"Are you?" he reflected a moment. "No," he answered truthfully. "I don't see that you are." He turned his face aside. He was afraid now, because he felt dazed, and felt dimly that her power was stronger than his, in this issue. And she continued to look at him fixedly all the time. "Can you tell me where I shall find some dry things to put on?" he asked.

"Did you dive into the pond for me?" she asked.

"No," he answered. "I walked in. But I went in overhead as well."

There was silence for a moment. He hesitated. He very much wanted to go upstairs to get into dry clothing. But there was another desire in him. And she seemed to hold him. His will seemed to have gone to sleep, and left him, standing there slack before her. But he felt warm inside himself. He did not shudder at all, though his clothes were sodden on him.

"Why did you?" she asked.

"Because I didn't want you to do such a foolish thing," he said.

"It wasn't foolish," she said, still gazing at him as she lay on the floor, with a sofa cushion under her head. "It was the right thing to do. *I* knew best, then."

"I'll go and shift these wet things," he said. But still he had not the power to move out of her presence, until she sent him. It was as if she had the life of his body in her hands, and he could not extricate himself. Or perhaps he did not want to.

Suddenly she sat up. Then she became aware of her own immediate condition. She felt the blankets about her, she knew her own limbs. For a moment it seemed as if her reason were going. She looked round, with wild eye, as if seeking something. He stood still with fear. She saw her clothing lying scattered.

"Who undressed me?" she asked, her eyes resting full and inevitable on his face.

"I did," he replied, "to bring you round."

For some moments she sat and gazed at him awfully, her lips parted.

"Do you love me, then?" she asked.

He only stood and stared at her, fascinated. His soul seemed to melt.

She shuffled forward on her knees, and put her arms round him, round his legs, as he stood there, pressing her breasts against his knees and thighs, clutching him with strange, convulsive certainty, pressing his thighs against her, drawing him to her face, her throat, as she looked up at him with flaring, humble eyes of transfiguration, triumphant in first possession.

"You love me," she murmured, in strange transport, yearning and triumphant and confident. "You love me. I know you love me, I know."

And she was passionately kissing his knees, through the wet clothing, passionately and indiscriminately kissing his knees, his legs, as if unaware of everything.

He looked down at the tangled wet hair, the wild, bare, animal shoulders. He was amazed, bewildered, and afraid. He had never thought of loving her. He had never wanted to love her. When he rescued her and restored her, he was a doctor, and she was a patient. He had had no single personal thought of her. Nay, this introduction of the personal element was very distasteful to him, a violation of his professional honour. It was horrible to have her there embracing his knees. It was horrible. He revolted from it, violently. And yet—and yet—he had not the power to break away.

She looked at him again, with the same supplication of powerful love, and that same transcendent, frightening light of triumph. In view of the delicate flame which seemed to come from her face like a light, he was powerless. And yet he had never intended to love her. He had never intended. And something stubborn in him could not give way.

"You love me," she repeated, in a murmur of deep, rhapsodic assurance. "You love me."

Her hands were drawing him, drawing him down to her. He was afraid, even a little horrified. For he had, really, no intention of loving her. Yet her hands were drawing him towards her. He put out his hand quickly to steady himself, and grasped her bare shoulder. A flame seemed to burn the hand that grasped her soft shoulder. He had no intention of loving her: his whole will was against his yielding. It was horrible. And yet wonderful was the touch of her shoulders, beautiful the shining of her face. Was she perhaps mad? He had a horror of yielding to her. Yet something in him ached also.

He had been staring away at the door, away from her. But his hand remained on her shoulder. She had gone suddenly very still. He looked down at her. Her eyes were now wide with fear, with doubt, the light was dying from her face, a shadow of terrible greyness was returning. He could not bear the touch of her eyes' question upon him, and the look of death behind the question.

With an inward groan he gave way, and let his heart yield towards her. A sudden gentle smile came on his face. And her eyes, which never left his face, slowly, slowly filled with tears. He watched the strange water rise in her eyes, like some slow fountain coming up. And his heart seemed to burn and melt away in his breast.

He could not bear to look at her any more. He dropped on his knees and caught her head with his arms and pressed her face against his throat. She was very still. His heart, which seemed to have broken, was burning with a kind of agony in his breast. And he felt her slow, hot tears wetting his throat. But he could not move.

He felt the hot tears wet his neck and the hollows of his neck, and he remained motionless, suspended through one of man's eternities. Only now it had become indispensable to him to have her face pressed close to him; he could never let her go again. He could never let her head go away from the close clutch of his arm. He wanted to remain like that for ever, with his heart hurting him in a pain that was also life to him. Without knowing, he was looking down on her damp, soft brown hair.

Then, as it were suddenly, he smelt the horrid stagnant smell of that water. And at the same moment she drew away from him and looked at him. Her eyes were wistful and unfathomable. He was afraid of them, and he fell to kissing her, not knowing what he was doing. He wanted her eyes not to have that terrible, wistful, unfathomable look.

When she turned her face to him again, a faint delicate flush was glowing, and there was again dawning that terrible shining of joy in her eyes, which really terrified him, and yet which he now wanted to see, because he feared the look of doubt still more.

"You love me?" she said, rather faltering.

"Yes." The word cost him a painful effort. Not because it wasn't true. But because it was too newly true, the *saying* seemed to tear open again his newly-torn heart. And he hardly wanted it to be true, even now.

She lifted her face to him, and he bent forward and kissed her on the mouth, gently, with the one kiss that is an eternal pledge. And as he kissed her his heart strained again in his breast. He never intended to love her. But now it was over. He had crossed over the gulf to her, and all that he had left behind had shrivelled and become void.

After the kiss, her eyes again slowly filled with tears. She sat still, away from him, with her face drooped aside, and her hands folded in her lap. The tears fell very slowly. There was complete silence. He too sat there motionless and silent on the hearth-rug. The strange pain of his heart that was broken seemed to consume him. That he should love her? That this was love! That he should be ripped open in this way! Him, a doctor! How they would all jeer if they knew! It was agony to him to think they might know.

In the curious naked pain of the thought he looked again to her. She was sitting there drooped into a muse. He saw a tear fall, and his heart flared hot. He saw for the first time that one of her shoulders was quite uncovered, one arm bare, he could see one of her small breasts; dimly, because it had become almost dark in the room.

"Why are you crying?" he asked, in an altered voice.

She looked up at him, and behind her tears the consciousness of her situation for the first time brought a dark look of shame to her eyes.

"I'm not crying, really," she said, watching him, half frightened.

He reached his hand, and softly closed it on her bare arm.

"I love you! I love you!" he said in a soft, low vibrating voice, unlike himself.

She shrank, and dropped her head. The soft, penetrating grip of his hand on her arm distressed her. She looked up at him.

"I want to go," she said. "I want to go and get you some dry things."

"Why?" he said. "I'm all right."

"But I want to go," she said. "And I want you to change your things."

He released her arm, and she wrapped herself in the blanket, looking at him rather frightened. And still she did not rise.

"Kiss me," she said wistfully.

He kissed her, but briefly, half in anger.

Then, after a second, she rose nervously, all mixed up in the blanket. He watched her in her confusion as she tried to extricate herself and wrap herself up so that she could walk. He watched her relentlessly, as she knew. And as she went, the blanket trailing, and as he saw a glimpse of her feet and her white leg, he tried to remember her as she was when he had wrapped her in the blanket. But then he didn't want to remember, because she had been nothing to him then, and his nature revolted from remembering her as she was when she was nothing to him.

A tumbling, muffled noise from within the dark house startled him. Then he heard her voice: "There are clothes." He rose and went to the foot of the stairs, and gathered up the garments she had thrown down. Then he came back to the fire, to rub himself down and dress. He grinned at his own appearance when he had finished.

The fire was sinking, so he put on coal. The house was now quite dark, save for the light of a street-lamp that shone in faintly from beyond the holly trees. He lit the gas with matches he found on the mantelpiece. Then he emptied the pockets of his own clothes, and threw all his wet things in a heap into the scullery. After which he gathered up her sodden clothes, gently, and put them in a separate heap on the copper-top in the scullery.

It was six o'clock on the clock. His own watch had stopped. He ought to go back to the surgery. He waited, and still she did not come down. So he went to the foot of the stairs and called:

"I shall have to go."

Almost immediately he heard her coming down. She had on her best dress of black voile, and her hair was tidy, but still damp. She looked at him—and in spite of herself, smiled.

"I don't like you in those clothes," she said.

"Do I look a sight?" he answered.

They were shy of one another.

"I'll make you some tea," she said.

"No, I must go."

"Must you?" And she looked at him again with the wide, strained, doubtful eyes. And again, from the pain of his breast, he knew how he loved her. He went and bent to kiss her, gently, passionately, with his heart's painful kiss.

"And my hair smells so horrible," she murmured in distraction. "And I'm so awful, I'm so awful! Oh no, I'm too awful." And she broke into bitter, heart-broken sobbing. "You can't want to love me, I'm horrible."

"Don't be silly, don't be silly," he said, trying to comfort her, kissing her, holding her in his arms. "I want you, I want to marry you, we're going to be married, quickly, quickly—to-morrow if I can."

But she only sobbed terribly, and cried:

"I feel awful. I feel awful. I feel I'm horrible to you."

"No, I want you, I want you," was all he answered, blindly, with that terrible intonation which frightened her almost more than her horror lest he should *not* want her.

DAVID LEAVITT
(1961–   )

DAVID LEAVITT was born in Pittsburgh and grew up in Palo Alto, California. He graduated from Yale University in 1983, with a B.A. in English, awarded summa cum laude. His books include *Family Dancing,* his first collection of stories, published in 1984 when he was twenty-three years old; a novel, *The Lost Language of Cranes,* (1986) subsequently adapted for television; *A Place I've Never Been,* a second story collection (1990); and the novel *Equal Affections* (1988). He is coeditor with Mark Mitchell of the *Penguin Book of Gay Stories,* an anthology (1994). His awards include an O. Henry Prize for the story "Counting Mouths"; *Family Dancing* won him nominations for the Pen/Faulkner Prize and the National Book Critics Circle Award. He is the recipient of a National Endowment for the Arts grant (1985) and a Guggenheim Fellowship (1990). His books have also been widely translated.

"Territory" is from *Family Dancing*. In a clear, plain voice marked by distribution of sympathy among his characters, Leavitt maps in this story the warring territories of love, past and present. Neil Campbell brings his lover, Wayne, home to California to meet his mother. She is enlightened; she has marched in gay pride parades and for other causes as well. One sees, however, in Neil's sensitively wrought uneasiness with his mother, and in her eagerness to please, how brittle the ground between them is. Here, the new territory of love is not carved out of the old. In the end the lovers, on a flight home, are airborne. So love, defying even the elements, establishes itself as a ground lovers stand on wherever they are.

Territory

Neil's mother, Mrs. Campbell, sits on her lawn chair behind a card table outside the food co-op. Every few minutes, as the sun shifts, she moves the chair and table several inches back so as to remain in the shade. It is a hundred degrees outside, and bright white. Each time someone goes in or out of the co-op a gust of air-conditioning flies out of the automatic doors, raising dust from the cement.

Neil stands just inside, poised over a water fountain, and watches her. She has on a sun hat, and a sweatshirt over her tennis dress; her legs are bare, and shiny with coca butter. In front of her, propped against the table, a sign proclaims:

MOTHERS, FIGHT FOR YOUR CHILDREN'S RIGHTS—SUPPORT A NON-NUCLEAR FUTURE. Women dressed exactly like her pass by, notice the sign, listen to her brief spiel, finger pamphlets, sign petitions or don't sign petitions, never give money. Her weary eyes are masked by dark glasses. In the age of Reagan, she has declared, keeping up the causes of peace and justice is a futile, tiresome, and unrewarding effort; it is therefore an effort fit only for mothers to keep up. The sun bounces off the window glass through which Neil watches her. His own reflection lines up with her profile.

Later that afternoon, Neil spreads himself out alongside the pool and imagines he is being watched by the shirtless Chicano gardener. But the gardener, concentrating on his pruning, is neither seductive nor seducible. On the lawn, his mother's large Airedales—Abigail, Lucille, Fern—amble, sniff, urinate. Occasionally, they accost the gardener, who yells at them in Spanish.

After two years' absence, Neil reasons, he should feel nostalgia, regret, gladness upon returning home. He closes his eyes and tries to muster the proper background music for the cinematic scene of return. His rhapsody, however, is interrupted by the noises of his mother's trio—the scratchy cello, whining violin, stumbling piano—as she and Lillian Havalard and Charlotte Feder plunge through Mozart. The tune is cheery, in a Germanic sort of way, and utterly inappropriate to what Neil is trying to feel. Yet it *is* the music of his adolescence; they have played it for years, bent over the notes, their heads bobbing in silent time to the metronome.

It is getting darker. Every few minutes, he must move his towel so as to remain within the narrowing patch of sunlight. In four hours, Wayne, his lover of ten months and the only person he has ever imagined he could spend his life with, will be in this house, where no lover of his has ever set foot. The thought fills him with a sense of grand terror and curiosity. He stretches, tries to feel seductive, desirable. The gardener's shears whack at the ferns; the music above him rushes to a loud, premature conclusion. The women laugh and applaud themselves as they give up for the day. He hears Charlotte Feder's full nasal twang, the voice of a fat woman in a pink pants suit—odd, since she is a scrawny, arthritic old bird, rarely clad in anything other than tennis shorts and a blouse. Lillian is the fat woman in the pink pants suit; her voice is thin and warped by too much crying. Drink in hand, she calls out from the porch, "Hot enough!" and waves. He lifts himself up and nods to her.

The women sit on the porch and chatter; their voices blend with the clink of ice in glasses. They belong to a small circle of ladies all of whom, with the exception of Neil's mother, are widows and divorcées. Lillian's husband left her twenty-two years ago, and sends her a check every month to live on; Charlotte has been divorced twice as long as she was married, and has a daughter serving a long sentence for terrorist acts committed when she was nineteen. Only Neil's mother has a husband, a distant sort of husband, away often on business. He is away on business now. All of them feel betrayed—by husbands, by children, by history.

Neil closes his eyes, tries to hear the words only as sounds. Soon, a new noise accosts him: his mother arguing with the gardener in Spanish. He leans on his elbows and watches them; the syllables are loud, heated, and compressed, and seem on the verge of explosion. But the argument ends happily; they shake hands. The gardener collects his check and walks out the gate without so much as looking at Neil.

He does not know the gardener's name; as his mother has reminded him, he does not know most of what has gone on since he moved away. Her life has gone on, unaffected by his absence. He flinches at his own egoism, the egoism of sons.

"Neil! Did you call the airport to make sure the plane's coming in on time?"

"Yes," he shouts to her. "It is."

"Good. Well, I'll have dinner ready when you get back."

"Mom—"

"What?" The word comes out in a weary wail that is more of an answer than a question.

"What's wrong?" he says, forgetting his original question.

"Nothing's wrong," she declares in a tone that indicates that everything is wrong. "The dogs have to be fed, dinner has to be made, and I've got people here. Nothing's wrong."

"I hope things will be as comfortable as possible when Wayne gets here."

"Is that a request or a threat?"

"Mom—"

Behind her sunglasses, her eyes are inscrutable. "I'm tired," she says. "It's been a long day. I . . . I'm anxious to meet Wayne. I'm sure he'll be wonderful, and we'll all have a wonderful, wonderful time. I'm sorry. I'm just tired."

She heads up the stairs. He suddenly feels an urge to cover himself; his body embarrasses him, as it has in her presence since the day she saw him shirtless and said with delight, "Neil! You're growing hair under your arms!"

Before he can get up, the dogs gather round him and begin to sniff and lick at him. He wriggles to get away from them, but Abigail, the largest and stupidest, straddles his stomach and nuzzles his mouth. He sputters and, laughing, throws her off. "Get away from me, you goddamn dogs," he shouts, and swats at them. They are new dogs, not the dog of his childhood, not dogs he trusts.

He stands, and the dogs circle him, looking up at his face expectantly. He feels renewed terror at the thought that Wayne will be here so soon: Will they sleep in the same room? Will they make love? He has never had sex in his parents' house. How can he be expected to be a lover here, in this place of his childhood, of his earliest shame, in this household of mothers and dogs?

"Dinnertime! Abbylucyferny, Abbylucyferny, dinnertime!" His mother's litany disperses the dogs, and they run for the door.

"Do you realize," he shouts to her, "that no matter how much those dogs love you they'd probably kill you for the leg of lamb in the freezer?"

Neil was twelve the first time he recognized in himself something like sexuality. He was lying outside, on the grass, when Rasputin—the dog, long dead, of his childhood—began licking his face. He felt a tingle he did not recognize, pulled off his shirt to give the dog access to more of him. Rasputin's tongue tickled coolly. A wet nose started to sniff down his body, toward his bathing suit. What he felt frightened him, but he couldn't bring himself to push the dog away. Then his mother called out, "Dinner," and Rasputin was gone, more interested in food than in him.

It was the day after Rasputin was put to sleep, years later, that Neil finally stood in the kitchen, his back turned to his parents, and said, with unexpected ease, "I'm a homosexual." The words seemed insufficient, reductive. For years, he had believed his sexuality to be detachable from the essential him, but now he realized that it was part of him. He had the sudden, despairing sensation that though the words had been easy to say, the fact of their having been aired was incurably damning. Only then, for the first time, did he admit that they were true, and he shook and wept in regret for what he would not be for his mother, for having failed her. His father hung back, silent; he was absent for that moment as he was mostly absent—a strong absence. Neil always thought of him sitting on the edge of the bed in his underwear, captivated by something on television. He said, "It's O.K., Neil." But his mother was resolute; her lower lip didn't quaver. She had enormous reserves of strength to which she only gained access at moments like this one. She hugged him from behind, wrapped him in the childhood smells of perfume and brownies, and whispered, "It's O.K., honey." For once, her words seemed as inadequate as his. Neil felt himself shrunk to an embarrassed adolescent, hating her sympathy, not wanting her to touch him. It was the way he would feel from then on whenever he was in her presence—even now, at twenty-three, bringing home his lover to meet her.

All through his childhood, she had packed only the most nutritious lunches, had served on the PTA, had volunteered at the children's library and at his school, had organized a successful campaign to ban a racist history textbook. The day after he told her, she located and got in touch with an organization called the Coalition of Parents of Lesbians and Gays. Within a year, she was president of it. On weekends, she and the other mothers drove their station wagons to San Francisco, set up their card tables in front of the Bulldog Baths, the Liberty Baths, passed out literature to men in leather and denim who were loath to admit they even had mothers. These men, who would habitually do violence to each other, were strangely cowed by the suburban ladies with their informational booklets, and bent their heads. Neil was a sophomore in college then, and lived in San Francisco. She brought him pamphlets detailing the dangers of bath-houses and back rooms, enemas and poppers, wordless sex in alleyways. His excursion into that world had been brief and lamentable, and was over. He winced at the thought that she knew all his sexual secrets, and vowed to move to the East Coast to escape her. It was not very different from the days when she had campaigned for a better playground, or tutored the Hispanic children in the audiovisual room. Those days, as well, he had run away from her concern. Even today, perched in front of the co-op, collecting signatures for nuclear disarmament, she was quintessentially a mother. And if the lot of mothers was to expect nothing in return, was the lot of sons to return nothing?

Driving across the Dumbarton Bridge on his way to the airport, Neil thinks, I have returned nothing; I have simply returned. He wonders if she would have given birth to him had she known what he would grow up to be.

Then he berates himself: Why should he assume himself to be the cause of her sorrow? She has told him that her life is full of secrets. She has changed since he left home—grown thinner, more rigid, harder to hug. She has given up baking, taken up tennis; her skin has browned and tightened. She is no longer the woman who hugged him and kissed him, who said, "As long as you're happy, that's all that's important to us."

The flats spread out around him; the bridge floats on purple and green silt, and spongy bay fill, not water at all. Only ten miles north, a whole city has been built on gunk dredged up from the bay.

He arrives at the airport ten minutes early, to discover that the plane has landed twenty minutes early. His first view of Wayne is from behind, by the baggage belt. Wayne looks as he always looks—slightly windblown—and is wearing the ratty leather jacket he was wearing the night they met. Neil sneaks up on him and puts his hands on his shoulders; when Wayne turns around, he looks relieved to see him.

They hug like brothers; only in the safety of Neil's mother's car do they dare to kiss. They recognize each other's smells, and grow comfortable again. "I never imagined I'd actually see you out here," Neil says, "but you're exactly the same here as there."

"It's only been a week."

They kiss again. Neil wants to go to a motel, but Wayne insists on being pragmatic. "We'll be there soon. Don't worry."

"We could go to one of the bathhouses in the city and take a room for a couple of aeons," Neil says. "Christ, I'm hard up. I don't even know if we're going to be in the same bedroom."

"Well, if we're not," Wayne says, "we'll sneak around. It'll be romantic."

They cling to each other for a few more minutes, until they realize that people are looking in the car window. Reluctantly, they pull apart. Neil reminds himself that he loves this man, that there is a reason for him to bring this man home.

He takes the scenic route on the way back. The car careers over foothills, through forests, along white four-lane highways high in the mountains. Wayne tells Neil that he sat next to a woman on the plane who was once Marilyn Monroe's psychiatrist's nurse. He slips his foot out of his shoe and nudges Neil's ankle, pulling Neil's sock down with his toe.

"I have to drive," Neil says. "I'm very glad you're here."

There is a comfort in the privacy of the car. They have a common fear of walking hand in hand, of publicly showing physical affection, even in the permissive West Seventies of New York—a fear that they have admitted only to one another. They slip through a pass between two hills, and are suddenly in residential Northern California, the land of expensive ranch-style houses.

As they pull into Neil's mother's driveway, the dogs run barking toward the car. When Wayne opens the door, they jump and lap at him, and he tries to close it again. "Don't worry. Abbylucyferny! Get in the house, damn it!"

His mother descends from the porch. She has changed into a blue flower-print dress, which Neil doesn't recognize. He gets out of the car and halfheartedly chastises the dogs. Crickets chirp in the trees. His mother looks radiant, even beautiful, illuminated by the headlights, surrounded by the now quiet dogs, like a Circe with her slaves. When she walks over to Wayne, offering her hand, and says, "Wayne, I'm Barbara," Neil forgets that she is his mother.

"Good to meet you, Barbara," Wayne says, and reaches out his hand. Craftier than she, he whirls her around to kiss her cheek.

Barbara! He is calling his mother Barbara! Then he remembers that Wayne is five years older than he is. They chat by the open car door, and Neil shrinks back—the embarrassed adolescent, uncomfortable, unwanted.

So the dreaded moment passes and he might as well not have been there. At dinner, Wayne keeps the conversation smooth, like a captivated courtier seeking Neil's mother's hand. A faggot son's sodomist—such words spit into Neil's head. She has prepared tiny meatballs with fresh coriander, fettucine with pesto. Wayne talks about the street people in New York; El Salvador is a tragedy; if only Sadat had lived; Phyllis Schlafly—what can you do?

"It's a losing battle," she tells him. "Every day I'm out there with my card table, me and the other mothers, but I tell you, Wayne, it's a losing battle. Sometimes I think us old ladies are the only ones with enough patience to fight."

Occasionally, Neil says something, but his comments seem stupid and clumsy. Wayne continues to call her Barbara. No one under forty has ever called her Barbara as long as Neil can remember. They drink wine; he does not.

Now is the time for drastic action. He contemplates taking Wayne's hand, then checks himself. He has never done anything in her presence to indicate that the sexuality he confessed to five years ago was a reality and not an invention. Even now, he and Wayne might as well be friends, college roommates. Then Wayne, his savior, with a single, sweeping gesture, reaches for his hand, and clasps it, in the midst of a joke he is telling about Saudi Arabians. By the time he is laughing, their hands are joined. Neil's throat contracts; his heart begins to beat violently. He notices his mother's eyes flicker, glance downward; she never breaks the stride of her sentence. The dinner goes on, and every taboo nurtured since childhood falls quietly away.

She removes the dishes. Their hands grow sticky; he cannot tell which fingers are his and which Wayne's. She clears the rest of the table and rounds up the dogs.

"Well, boys, I'm very tired, and I've got a long day ahead of me tomorrow, so I think I'll hit the sack. There are extra towels for you in Neil's bathroom, Wayne. Sleep well."

"Good night, Barbara," Wayne calls out. "It's been wonderful meeting you."

They are alone. Now they can disentangle their hands.

"No problem about where we sleep, is there?"

"No," Neil says. "I just can't imagine sleeping with someone in this house."

His leg shakes violently. Wayne takes Neil's hand in a firm grasp and hauls him up.

Later that night, they lie outside, under redwood trees, listening to the hysteria of the crickets, the hum of the pool cleaning itself. Redwood leaves prick their skin. They fell in love in bars and apartments, and this is the first time that they have made love outdoors. Neil is not sure he has enjoyed the experience. He kept sensing eyes, imagined that the neighborhood cats were staring at them from behind a fence of brambles. He remembers he once hid in this spot when he and some of the children from the neighborhood were playing sardines, remembers the intoxication of small bodies packed together, the warm breath of suppressed laughter on his neck. "The loser had to go through the spanking machine," he tells Wayne.

"Did you lose often?"

"Most of the time. The spanking machine never really hurt—just a whirl of hands. If you moved fast enough, no one could actually get you. Sometimes, though, late in the afternoon, we'd get naughty. We'd chase each other and pull each other's pants down. That was all. Boys and girls together!"

"Listen to the insects," Wayne says, and closes his eyes.

Neil turns to examine Wayne's face, notices a single, small pimple. Their lovemaking usually begins in a wrestle, a struggle for dominance, and ends with a somewhat confusing loss of identity—as now, when Neil sees a foot on the grass, resting against his leg, and tries to determine if it is his own or Wayne's.

From inside the house, the dogs begin to bark. Their yelps grow into alarmed falsettos. Neil lifts himself up. "I wonder if they smell something," he says.

"Probably just us," says Wayne.

"My mother will wake up. She hates getting waked up."

Lights go on in the house; the door to the porch opens.

"What's wrong, Abby? What's wrong?" his mother's voice calls softly.

Wayne clamps his hand over Neil's mouth. "Don't say anything," he whispers.

"I can't just—" Neil begins to say, but Wayne's hand closes over his mouth again. He bites it, and Wayne starts laughing.

"What was that?" Her voice projects into the garden. "Hello?" she says.

The dogs yelp louder. "Abbylucyferny, it's O.K., it's O.K." Her voice is soft and panicked. "Is anyone there?" she asks loudly.

The brambles shake. She takes a flashlight, shines it around the garden. Wayne and Neil duck down; the light lands on them and hovers for a few seconds. Then it clicks off and they are in the dark—a new dark, a darker dark, which their eyes must readjust to.

"Let's go to bed, Abbylucyferny," she says gently. Neil and Wayne hear her pad into the house. The dogs whimper as they follow her, and the lights go off.

Once before, Neil and his mother had stared at each other in the glare of bright lights. Four years ago, they stood in the arena created by the headlights of her car, waiting for the train. He was on his way back to San Francisco, where he was marching in a Gay Pride Parade the next day. The train station was next door to the food co-op and shared its parking lot. The co-op, familiar and boring by day, took on a certain mystery in the night. Neil recognized the spot where he had skidded on his bicycle and broken his leg. Through the glass doors, the brightly lit interior of the store glowed, its rows and rows of cans and boxes forming their own horizon, each can illuminated so that even from outside Neil could read the labels. All that was missing was the ladies in tennis dresses and sweatshirts, pushing their carts past bins of nuts and dried fruits.

"Your train is late," his mother said. Her hair fell loosely on her shoulders, and her legs were tanned. Neil looked at her and tried to imagine her in labor with him—bucking and struggling with his birth. He felt then the strange, sexless love for women which through his whole adolescence he had mistaken for heterosexual desire.

A single bright light approached them; it preceded the low, haunting sound of the whistle. Neil kissed his mother, and waved goodbye as he ran to meet the train. It was an old train, with windows tinted a sort of horrible lemon-lime. It stopped only long enough for him to hoist himself on board, and then it was moving again. He hurried to a window, hoping to see her drive off, but the tint of the window made it possible for him to make out only vague patches of light—street lamps, cars, the co-op.

He sank into the hard, green seat. The train was almost entirely empty; the only other passenger was a dark-skinned man wearing bluejeans and a leather jacket. He sat directly across the aisle from Neil, next to the window. He had rough skin and a thick mustache. Neil discovered that by pretending to look out the window he could study the man's reflection in the lemon-lime glass. It was only slightly hazy—the quality of a bad photograph. Neil felt his mouth open, felt sleep closing in on him. Hazy red and gold flashes through the glass pulsed in the face of the man in the window, giving the curious impression of muscle spasms. It took Neil a few minutes to realize that the man was staring at him, or, rather, staring at the back of his head—staring at his staring. The man smiled as though to say, I know exactly what you're staring at, and Neil felt the sickening sensation of desire rise in his throat.

Right before they reached the city, the man stood up and sat down in the seat next to Neil's. The man's thigh brushed deliberately against his own. Neil's eyes were watering; he felt sick to his stomach. Taking Neil's hand, the man said, "Why so nervous, honey? Relax."

Neil woke up the next morning with the taste of ashes in his mouth. He was lying on the floor, without blankets or sheets or pillows. Instinctively, he reached for his pants, and as he pulled them on came face to face with the man from the train. His name was Luis; he turned out to be a dog groomer. His apartment smelled of dog.

"Why such a hurry?" Luis said.

"The parade. The Gay Pride Parade. I'm meeting some friends to march."

"I'll come with you," Luis said. "I think I'm too old for these things, but why not?"

Neil did not want Luis to come with him, but he found it impossible to say so. Luis looked older by day, more likely to carry diseases. He dressed again in a torn T-shirt, leather jacket, bluejeans. "It's my everyday apparel," he said, and laughed. Neil buttoned his pants, aware that they had been washed by his mother the day before. Luis possessed the peculiar combination of hypermasculinity and effeminacy which exemplifies faggotry. Neil wanted to be rid of him, but Luis's mark was on him, he could see that much. They would become lovers whether Neil liked it or not.

They joined the parade midway. Neil hoped he wouldn't meet anyone he knew; he did not want to have to explain Luis, who clung to him. The parade was full of shirtless men with oiled, muscular shoulders. Neil's back ached. There were floats carrying garishly dressed prom queens and cheerleaders, some with beards, some actually looking like women. Luis said, "It makes me proud, makes me glad to be what I am." Neil supposed that by darting into the crowd ahead of him he might be able to lose Luis forever, but he found it difficult to let him go; the prospect of being alone seemed unbearable.

Neil was startled to see his mother watching the parade, holding up a sign. She was with the Coalition of Parents of Lesbians and Gays; they had posted a huge banner on the wall behind them proclaiming: OUR SONS AND DAUGHTERS, WE ARE PROUD OF YOU. She spotted him; she waved, and jumped up and down.

"Who's that woman?" Luis asked.

"My mother. I should go say hello to her."

"O.K.," Luis said. He followed Neil to the side of the parade. Neil kissed his mother. Luis took off his shirt, wiped his face with it, smiled.

"I'm glad you came," Neil said.

"I wouldn't have missed it, Neil. I wanted to show you I cared."

He smiled, and kissed her again. He showed no intention of introducing Luis, so Luis introduced himself.

"Hello, Luis," Mrs. Campbell said. Neil looked away. Luis shook her hand, and Neil wanted to warn his mother to wash it, warned himself to check with a V.D. clinic first thing Monday.

"Neil, this is Carmen Bologna, another one of the mothers," Mrs. Campbell said. She introduced him to a fat Italian woman with flushed cheeks, and hair arranged in the shape of a clamshell.

"Good to meet you, Neil, good to meet you," said Carmen Bologna. "You know my son, Michael? I'm so proud of Michael! He's doing so well now. I'm proud of him, proud to be his mother I am, and your mother's proud, too!"

The woman smiled at him, and Neil could think of nothing to say but "Thank you." He looked uncomfortably toward his mother, who stood listening to Luis. It occurred to him that the worst period of his life was probably about to begin and he had no way to stop it.

A group of drag queens ambled over to where the mothers were standing. "Michael! Michael!" shouted Carmen Bologna, and embraced a sticklike man wrapped in green satin. Michael's eyes were heavily dosed with green eyeshadow, and his lips were painted pink.

Neil turned and saw his mother staring, her mouth open. He marched over to where Luis was standing, and they moved back into the parade. He turned and waved to her. She waved back; he saw pain in her face, and then, briefly, regret. That day, he felt she would have traded him for any other son. Later, she said to him, "Carmen Bologna really was proud, and, speaking as a mother, let me tell you, you have to be brave to feel such pride."

Neil was never proud. It took him a year to dump Luis, another year to leave California. The sick taste of ashes was still in his mouth. On the plane, he envisioned his mother sitting alone in the dark, smoking. She did not leave his mind until he was circling New York, staring down at the dawn rising over Queens. The song playing in his earphones would remain hovering on the edges of his memory, always associated with her absence. After collecting his baggage, he took a bus into the city. Boys were selling newspapers in the middle of highways, through the windows of stopped cars. It was seven in the morning when he reached Manhattan. He stood for ten minutes on East Thirty-fourth Street, breathed the cold air, and felt bubbles rising in his blood.

Neil got a job as a paralegal—a temporary job, he told himself. When he met Wayne a year later, the sensations of that first morning returned to him. They'd been up all night, and at six they walked across the park to Wayne's apartment with the nervous, deliberate gait of people aching to make love for the first time. Joggers ran by with their dogs. None of them knew what Wayne and he were about to do, and the secrecy excited him. His mother came to mind, and the song, and the whirling vision of Queens coming alive below him. His breath solidified into clouds, and he felt happier than he had ever felt before in his life.

The second day of Wayne's visit, he and Neil go with Mrs. Campbell to pick up the dogs at the dog parlor. The grooming establishment is decorated with pink ribbons and photographs of the owner's champion pit bulls. A fat, middle-aged woman appears from the back, leading the newly trimmed and fluffed Abigail, Lucille, and Fern by three leashes. The dogs struggle frantically when they see Neil's mother, tangling the woman up in their leashes. "Ladies, behave!" Mrs. Campbell commands, and collects the dogs. She gives Fern to Neil and Abigail to Wayne. In the car on the way back, Abigail begins pawing to get on Wayne's lap.

"Just push her off," Mrs. Campbell says. "She knows she's not supposed to do that."

"You never groomed Rasputin," Neil complains.

"Rasputin was a mutt."

"Rasputin was a beautiful dog, even if he did smell."

"Do you remember when you were a little kid, Neil, you used to make Rasputin dance with you? Once you tried to dress him up in one of my blouses."

"I don't remember that," Neil says.

"Yes. I remember," says Mrs. Campbell. "Then you tried to organize a dog beauty contest in the neighborhood. You wanted to have runners-up—everything."

"A dog beauty contest?" Wayne says.

"Mother, do we have to—"

"I think it's a mother's privilege to embarrass her son," Mrs. Campbell says, and smiles.

When they are about to pull into the driveway, Wayne starts screaming, and pushes Abigail off his lap. "Oh, my God!" he says. "The dog just pissed all over me."

Neil turns around and sees a puddle seeping into Wayne's slacks. He suppresses his laughter, and Mrs. Campbell hands him a rag.

"I'm sorry, Wayne," she says. "It goes with the territory."

"This is really disgusting," Wayne says, swatting at himself with the rag.

Neil keeps his eyes on his own reflection in the rearview mirror and smiles.

At home, while Wayne cleans himself in the bathroom, Neil watches his mother cook lunch—Japanese noodles in soup. "When you went off to college," she says, "I went to the grocery store. I was going to buy you ramen noodles, and I suddenly realized you weren't going to be around to eat them. I started crying right then, blubbering like an idiot."

Neil clenches his fists inside his pockets. She has a way of telling him little sad stories when he doesn't want to hear them—stories of dolls broken by her brothers, lunches stolen by neighborhood boys on the way to school. Now he has joined the ranks of male children who have made her cry.

"Mama, I'm sorry," he says.

She is bent over the noodles, which steam in her face. "I didn't want to say anything in front of Wayne, but I wish you had answered me last night. I was very frightened—and worried."

"I'm sorry," he says, but it's not convincing. His fingers prickle. He senses a great sorrow about to be born.

"I lead a quiet life," she says. "I don't want to be a disciplinarian. I just don't have the energy for these—shenanigans. Please don't frighten me that way again."

"If you were so upset, why didn't you say something?"

"I'd rather not discuss it. I lead a quiet life. I'm not used to getting woken up late at night. I'm not used—"

"To my having a lover?"

"No, I'm not used to having other people around, that's all. Wayne is charming. A wonderful young man."

"He likes you, too."

"I'm sure we'll get along fine."

She scoops the steaming noodles into ceramic bowls. Wayne returns, wearing shorts. His white, hairy legs are a shocking contrast to hers, which are brown and sleek.

"I'll wash those pants, Wayne," Mrs. Campbell says. "I have a special detergent that'll take out the stain."

She gives Neil a look to indicate that the subject should be dropped. He looks at Wayne, looks at his mother; his initial embarrassment gives way to a fierce pride—the arrogance of mastery. He is glad his mother knows that he is desired, glad it makes her flinch.

Later, he steps into the back yard; the gardener is back, whacking at the bushes with his shears. Neil walks by him in his bathing suit, imagining he is on parade.

That afternoon, he finds his mother's daily list on the kitchen table:

TUESDAY
7:00—breakfast
Take dogs to groomer
Groceries(?)

Campaign against Draft—4–7

Buy underwear
Trios—2:00
Spaghetti
Fruit
Asparagus if sale
Peanuts
Milk

Doctor's Appointment (make)
Write Cranston/Hayakawa
re disarmament

Handi-Wipes
Mozart
Abigail
Top Ramen
Pedro

Her desk and trash can are full of such lists; he remembers them from the earliest days of his childhood. He had learned to read from them. In his own life, too, there have been endless lists—covered with check marks and arrows, at least one item always spilling over onto the next day's agenda. From September to November, "Buy plane ticket for Christmas" floated from list to list to list.

The last item puzzles him: Pedro. Pedro must be the gardener. He observes the accretion of names, the arbitrary specifics that give a sense of his mother's life. He could make a list of his own selves: the child, the adolescent, the promiscuous faggot son, and finally the good son, settled, relatively successful. But the divisions wouldn't work; he is today and will always be the child being licked by the dog, the boy on the floor with Luis; he will still be everything he is ashamed of. The other lists—the lists of things done and undone—tell their own truth: that his life is measured more properly in objects than in stages. He knows himself as "jump rope," "book," "sunglasses," "underwear."

"Tell me about your family, Wayne," Mrs. Campbell says that night, as they drive toward town. They are going to see an Esther Williams movie at the local revival house: an underwater musical, populated by mermaids, underwater Rockettes.

"My father was a lawyer," Wayne says. "He had an office in Queens, with a neon sign. I think he's probably the only lawyer in the world who had a neon sign. Anyway, he died when I was ten. My mother never remarried. She lives in Queens. Her great claim to fame is that when she was twenty-two she went on 'The $64,000 Question.' Her category was mystery novels. She made it to sixteen thousand before she got tripped up."

"When I was about ten, I wanted you to go on 'Jeopardy,' " Neil says to his mother. "You really should have, you know. You would have won."

"You certainly loved 'Jeopardy,' " Mrs. Campbell says. "You used to watch it during dinner. Wayne, does your mother work?"

"No," he says. "She lives off investments."

"You're both only children," Mrs. Campbell says. Neil wonders if she is ruminating on the possible connection between that coincidence and their "alternative life style."

The movie theater is nearly empty. Neil sits between Wayne and his mother. There are pillows on the floor at the front of the theater, and a cat is prowling over them. It casts a monstrous shadow every now and then on the screen, disturbing the sedative effect of water ballet. Like a teen-ager, Neil cautiously reaches his arm around Wayne's shoulder. Wayne takes his hand immediately. Next to them, Neil's mother breathes in, out, in, out. Neil timorously moves his other arm and lifts it behind his mother's neck. He does not look at her, but he can tell from her breathing that she senses what he is doing. Slowly, carefully, he lets his hand drop on her shoulder; it twitches spasmodically, and he jumps, as if he had received an electric shock. His mother's quiet breathing is broken by a gasp; even Wayne notices. A sudden brightness on the screen illuminates the panic in her eyes, Neil's arm frozen above her, about to fall again. Slowly, he lowers his arm until his fingertips touch her skin, the fabric of her dress. He has gone too far to go back now; they are all too far.

Wayne and Mrs. Campbell sink into their seats, but Neil remains stiff, holding up his arms, which rest on nothing. The movie ends, and they go on sitting just like that.

"I'm old," Mrs. Campbell says later, as they drive back home. "I remember when those films were new. Your father and I went to one on our first date. I loved them, because I could pretend that those women underwater were flying—they were so graceful. They really took advantage of Technicolor in those days. Color was something to appreciate. You can't know what it was like to see a color movie for the first time, after years of black-and-white. It's like trying to explain the surprise of snow to an East Coaster. Very little is new anymore, I fear."

Neil would like to tell her about his own nostalgia, but how can he explain that all of it revolves around her? The idea of her life before he was born pleases him. "Tell Wayne how you used to look like Esther Williams," he asks her.

She blushes. "I was told I looked like Esther Williams, but really more like Gene Tierney," she says. "Not beautiful, but interesting. I like to think I had a certain magnetism."

"You still do," Wayne says, and instantly recognizes the wrongness of his comment. Silence and a nervous laugh indicate that he has not yet mastered the family vocabulary.

When they get home, the night is once again full of the sound of crickets. Mrs. Campbell picks up a flashlight and calls the dogs. "Abbylucyferny, Abbylucyferny," she shouts, and the dogs amble from their various corners. She pushes them out the door to the back yard and follows them. Neil follows her. Wayne follows Neil, but hovers on the porch. Neil walks behind her as she tramps through the garden. She holds out her flashlight, and snails slide from behind bushes, from under rocks, to where she stands. When the snails become visible, she crushes them underfoot. They make a wet, cracking noise, like eggs being broken.

"Nights like this," she says, "I think of children without pants on, in hot South American countries. I have nightmares about tanks rolling down our street."

"The weather's never like this in New York," Neil says. "When it's hot, it's humid and sticky. You don't want to go outdoors."

"I could never live anywhere else but here. I think I'd die. I'm too used to the climate."

"Don't be silly."

"No, I mean it," she says. "I have adjusted too well to the weather."

The dogs bark and howl by the fence. "A cat, I suspect," she says. She aims her flashlight at a rock, and more snails emerge—uncountable numbers, too stupid to have learned not to trust light.

"I know what you were doing at the movie," she says.

"What?"

"I know what you were doing."

"What? I put my arm around you."

"I'm sorry, Neil," she says. "I can only take so much. Just so much."

"What do you mean?" he says. "I was only trying to show affection."

"Oh, affection—I know about affection."

He looks up at the porch, sees Wayne moving toward the door, trying not to listen.

"What do you mean?" Neil says to her.

She puts down the flashlight and wraps her arms around herself. "I remember when you were a little boy," she says. "I remember, and I have to stop remembering. I wanted you to grow up happy. And I'm very tolerant, very understanding. But I can only take so much."

His heart seems to have risen into his throat. "Mother," he says, "I think you know my life isn't your fault. But for God's sake, don't say that your life is my fault."

"It's not a question of fault," she says. She extracts a Kleenex from her pocket and blows her nose. "I'm sorry, Neil. I guess I'm just an old woman with too much on her mind and not enough to do." She laughs halfheartedly. "Don't worry. Don't say anything," she says. "Abbylucyferny, Abbylucyferny, time for bed!"

He watches her as she walks toward the porch, silent and regal. There is the pad of feet, the clinking of dog tags as the dogs run for the house.

He was twelve the first time she saw him march in a parade. He played the tuba, and as his elementary-school band lumbered down the streets of their then small town she stood on the sidelines and waved. Afterward, she had taken him out for ice cream. He spilled some on his red uniform, and she swiped at it with a napkin. She had been there for him that day, as well as years later, at that more memorable parade; she had been there for him every day.

Somewhere over Iowa, a week later, Neil remembers this scene, remembers other days, when he would find her sitting in the dark, crying. She had to take time out of her own private sorrow to appease his anxiety. "It was part of it," she told him later. "Part of being a mother."

"The scariest thing in the world is the thought that you could unknowingly ruin someone's life," Neil tells Wayne. "Or even change someone's life. I hate the thought of having such control. I'd make a rotten mother."

"You're crazy," Wayne says. "You have this great mother, and all you do is complain. I know people whose mothers have disowned them."

"Guilt goes with the territory," Neil says.

"Why?" Wayne asks, perfectly seriously.

Neil doesn't answer. He lies back in his seat, closes his eyes, imagines he grew up in a house in the mountains of Colorado, surrounded by snow—endless white snow on hills. No flat places, and no trees; just white hills. Every time he has flown away, she has come into his mind, usually sitting alone in the dark, smoking. Today she is outside at dusk, skimming leaves from the pool.

"I want to get a dog," Neil says.

Wayne laughs. "In the city? It'd suffocate."

The hum of the airplane is druglike, dazing. "I want to stay with you a long time," Neil says.

"I know." Imperceptibly, Wayne takes his hand.

"It's very hot there in the summer, too. You know, I'm not thinking about my mother now."

"It's O.K."

For a moment, Neil wonders what the stewardess or the old woman on the way to the bathroom will think, but then he laughs and relaxes.

Later, the plane makes a slow circle over New York City, and on it two men hold hands, eyes closed, and breathe in unison.

DORIS LESSING

(1919–)

DORIS LESSING was born in Persia to English parents. When she was five Lessing's family moved to a farm in Southern Rhodesia, where she grew up. In 1949, having written her first novel, *The Grass Is Singing* (1950), she moved to London, where she still lives. Her second work, whose overall title is *The Children of Violence*, consists of five volumes, including *Martha Quest* (1952), the name of the series' autobiographical protagonist and *The Four-Gated City* (1969). Other important novels include *The Golden Notebook* (1962), *Briefing for a Descent into Hell* (1971), and *The Good Terrorist* (1985). She is also the author of a series of five science-fiction novels, collectively titled *Canopus in Argos: Archives.* Her volumes of short fiction include *The Habit of Loving* (1957), *A Man and Two Women* (which includes "One off the Short List"; 1963), and *The Sun Between Their Feet* (1973). Lessing has also written several plays. Among her prizes and honors are the 1976 Prix Médicis Award for work translated into French, awarded to *The Golden Notebook;* the nomination of *The Sirian Experiments* (1981) for the Booker McConnell Prize; and in 1986–87, the W. H. Smith Literary Award, the Palermo Prize, and the Premio Internazionale Mondello, all for *The Good Terrorist.* Among her themes are the political Left and the situation of women. Lessing puts an unusual spin on the latter in "One off the Short List."

The narrative has Graham Spence, the protagonist as heel, put forward an inadvertently self-exposing account of a campaign to conquer a woman. What Lessing has him reveal takes the form of perverse premeditation and savage helplessness brilliantly mixed. The story is a stunning orchestration of points of view, effected via the projections of Graham Spence's shabby psyche onto Barbara Coles, the talented, attractive woman he is hell-bent to seduce. Love of self, with its concomitants of self-pity and self-hatred, is what Lessing portrays here through the character of Graham Spence. In Barbara's emerald-green eyes, though he doesn't know it, Graham sees his own envy. At the same time, he is blind to her secret weapon of self-respect.

One off the Short List

When he had first seen Barbara Coles, some years before, he only noticed her because someone said: "That's Johnson's new girl." He certainly had not used of her the private erotic formula: *Yes, that one.* He even wondered what Johnson

saw in her. "She won't last long," he remembered thinking, as he watched Johnson, a handsome man, but rather flushed with drink, flirting with some unknown
girl while Barbara stood by a wall looking on. He thought she had a sullen expression.

She was a pale girl, not slim, for her frame was generous, but her figure could
pass as good. Her straight yellow hair was parted on one side in a way that struck
him as gauche. He did not notice what she wore. But her eyes were all right, he
remembered: large, and solidly green, square-looking because of some trick of the
flesh at their corners. Emeraldlike eyes in the face of a school-girl, or young
schoolmistress who was watching her lover flirt and would later sulk about it.

Her name sometimes cropped up in the papers. She was a stage decorator, a
designer, something on those lines.

Then a Sunday newspaper had a competition for stage design and she won it.
Barbara Coles was one of the "names" in the theatre, and her photograph was
seen about. It was always serious. He remembered having thought her sullen.

One night he saw her across the room at a party. She was talking with a
well-known actor. Her yellow hair was still done on one side, but now it looked
sophisticated. She wore an emerald ring on her right hand that seemed deliberately to invite comparison with her eyes. He walked over and said: "We have met
before, Graham Spence." He noted, with discomfort, that he sounded abrupt.
"I'm sorry, I don't remember, but how do you do?" she said, smiling. And continued her conversation.

He hung around a bit, but soon she went off with a group of people she was
inviting to her home for a drink. She did not invite Graham. There was about
her an assurance, a carelessness, that he recognised as the signature of success. It
was then, watching her laugh as she went off with her friends, that he used the
formula: "Yes, *that one*." And he went home to his wife with enjoyable expectation, as if his date with Barbara Coles were already arranged.

His marriage was twenty years old. At first it had been stormy, painful,
tragic—full of partings, betrayals and sweet reconciliations. It had taken him at
least a decade to realise that there was nothing remarkable about this marriage
that he had lived through with such surprise of the mind and the senses. On the
contrary, the marriages of most of the people he knew, whether they were first,
second or third attempts, were just the same. His had run true to form even to
the serious love affair with the young girl for whose sake he had *almost* divorced
his wife—yet at the last moment had changed his mind, letting the girl down so
that he must have her for always (not unpleasurably) on his conscience. It was
with humiliation that he had understood that this drama was not at all the unique
thing he had imagined. It was nothing more than the experience of everyone in
his circle. And presumably in everybody else's circle too?

Anyway, round about the tenth year of his marriage he had seen a good many
things clearly, a certain kind of emotional adventure went from his life, and the
marriage itself changed.

His wife had married a poor youth with a great future as a writer. Sacrifices had been made, chiefly by her, for that future. He was neither unaware of them, nor ungrateful; in fact he felt permanently guilty about it. He at last published a decently successful book, then a second which now, thank God, no one remembered. He had drifted into radio, television, book reviewing.

He understood he was not going to make it; that he had become—not a hack, no one could call him that—but a member of that army of people who live by their wits on the fringes of the arts. The moment of realisation was when he was in a pub one lunchtime near the B.B.C. where he often dropped in to meet others like himself: he understood that was why he went there—they *were* like him. Just as that melodramatic marriage had turned out to be like everyone else's—except that it had been shared with one woman instead of with two or three—so it had turned out that his unique talent, his struggles as a writer had led him here, to this pub and the half dozen pubs like it, where all the men in sight had the same history. They all had their novel, their play, their book of poems, a moment of fame, to their credit. Yet here they were, running television programmes about which they were cynical (to each other or to their wives) or writing reviews about other people's books. Yes, that's what he had become, an impresario of other people's talent. These two moments of clarity, about his marriage and about his talent, had roughly coincided; and (perhaps not by chance) had coincided with his wife's decision to leave him for a man younger than himself who had a future, she said, as a playwright. Well, he had talked her out of it. For her part she had to understand he was not going to be the T. S. Eliot or Graham Greene of our time—but after all, how many were? She must finally understand this, for he could no longer bear her awful bitterness. For his part he must stop coming home drunk at five in the morning, and starting a new romantic affair every six months which he took so seriously that he made her miserable because of her implied deficiencies. In short he was to be a good husband. (He had always been a dutiful father.) And she a good wife. And so it was: the marriage became stable, as they say.

The formula: *Yes, that one* no longer implied a necessarily sexual relationship. In its more mature form, it was far from being something he was ashamed of. On the contrary, it expressed a humorous respect for what he was, for his real talents and flair, which had turned out to be not artistic after all, but to do with emotional life, hard-earned experience. It expressed an ironical dignity, a proving to himself not only: I can be honest about myself, but also: I have earned the best in *that* field whenever I want it.

He watched the field for the women who were well known in the arts, or in politics; looked out for photographs, listened for bits of gossip. He made a point of going to see them act, or dance, or orate. He built up a not unshrewd picture of them. He would either quietly pull strings to meet her or—more often, for there was a gambler's pleasure in waiting—bide his time until he met her in the natural course of events, which was bound to happen sooner or later. He would be seen out with her a few times in public, which was in order, since his work meant he had to entertain well-known people, male and female. His wife always knew, he told her. He might have a brief affair with this woman, but more often than not it was the appearance of an affair. Not that he didn't get pleasure from other people envying him—he would make a point, for instance, of taking this woman into the pubs where his male colleagues went. It was that his real pleasure came when he saw her surprise at how well she was understood by him. He enjoyed the atmosphere he was able to set up between an intelligent woman and himself: a humorous complicity which had in it much that was unspoken, and which almost made sex irrelevant.

Onto the list of women with whom he planned to have this relationship went Barbara Coles. There was no hurry. Next week, next month, next year, they would meet at a party. The world of well-known people in London is a small one. Big and little fishes, they drift around, nose each other, flirt their fins, wriggle off again. When he bumped into Barbara Coles, it would be time to decide whether or not to sleep with her.

Meanwhile he listened. But he didn't discover much. She had a husband and children, but the husband seemed to be in the background. The children were charming and well brought up, like everyone else's children. She had affairs, they said; but while several men he met sounded familiar with her, it was hard to determine whether they had slept with her, because none directly boasted of her. She was spoken of in terms of her friends, her work, her house, a party she had given, a job she had found someone. She was liked, she was respected, and Graham Spence's self-esteem was flattered because he had chosen her. He looked forward to saying in just the same tone: "Barbara Coles asked me what I thought about the set and I told her quite frankly. . . ."

Then by chance he met a young man who did boast about Barbara Coles; he claimed to have had the great love affair with her, and recently at that; and he spoke of it as something generally known. Graham realised how much he had already become involved with her in his imagination because of how perturbed he was now, on account of the character of this youth, Jack Kennaway. He had recently become successful as a magazine editor—one of those young men who, not as rare as one might suppose in the big cities, are successful from sheer impertinence, effrontery. Without much talent or taste, yet he had the charm of his effrontery. "Yes, I'm going to succeed, because I've decided to; yes, I may be stupid, but not so stupid that I don't know my deficiencies. Yes, I'm going to be successful because you people with integrity, etc., etc., simply don't believe in the possibility of people like me. You are too cowardly to stop me. Yes, I've taken your measure and I'm going to succeed because I've got the courage, not only to be unscrupulous, but to be quite frank about it. And besides, you admire me, you must, or otherwise you'd stop me. . . ." Well, that was young Jack Kennaway, and he shocked Graham. He was a tall, languishing young man, handsome in a dark melting way, and, it was quite clear, he was either asexual or homosexual.

And this youth boasted of the favours of Barbara Coles; boasted, indeed, of her love. Either she was a raving neurotic with a taste for neurotics; or Jack Kennaway was a most accomplished liar; or she slept with anyone. Graham was intrigued. He took Jack Kennaway out to dinner in order to hear him talk about Barbara Coles. There was no doubt the two were pretty close—all those dinners, theatres, weekends in the country—Graham Spence felt he had put his finger on the secret pulse of Barbara Coles; and it was intolerable that he must wait to meet her; he decided to arrange it.

It became unnecessary. She was in the news again, with a run of luck. She had done a successful historical play, and immediately afterwards a modern play, and then a hit musical. In all three, the sets were remarked on. Graham saw some interviews in newspapers and on television. These all centered around the theme of her being able to deal easily with so many different styles of theatre; but the real point was, of course, that she was a woman, which naturally added piquancy to the thing. And now Graham Spence was asked to do a half-hour radio interview with her. He planned the questions he would ask her with care, drawing on what people had said of her, but above all on his instinct and experience with women. The interview was to be at nine-thirty at night; he was to pick her up at six from the theatre where she was currently at work, so that there would be time, as the letter from the B.B.C. had put it, "for you and Miss Coles to get to know each other."

At six he was at the stage door, but a message from Miss Coles said she was not quite ready, could he wait a little. He hung about, then went to the pub opposite for a quick one, but still no Miss Coles. So he made his way backstage, directed by voices, hammering, laughter. It was badly lit, and the group of people at work did not see him. The director, James Poynter, had his arm around Barbara's shoulders. He was newly well-known, a carelessly good-looking young man reputed to be intelligent. Barbara Coles wore a dark blue overall, and her flat hair fell over her face so that she kept pushing it back with the hand that had the emerald on it. These two stood close, side by side. Three young men, stagehands, were on the other side of a trestle which had sketches and drawings on it. They were studying some sketches. Barbara said, in a voice warm with energy: "Well, so I thought if we did *this*—do you see, James? What do you think, Steven?" "Well, love," said the young man she called Steven, "I see your idea, but I wonder if . . ." "I think you're right, Babs," said the director. "Look," said Barbara, holding one of the sketches towards Steven, "look, let me show you." They all leaned forward, the five of them, absorbed in the business.

Suddenly Graham couldn't stand it. He understood he was shaken to his depths. He went off stage, and stood with his back against a wall in the dingy passage that led to the dressing rooms. His eyes were filled with tears. He was seeing what a long way he had come from the crude, uncompromising, admirable young egomaniac he had been when he was twenty. That group of people there—working, joking, arguing, yes, that's what he hadn't known for years. What bound them was the democracy of respect for each other's work, a confidence in themselves and in each other. They looked like people banded together against a world which they—no, not despised, but which they measured, understood, would fight to the death, out of respect for what *they* stood for, for what *it* stood for. It was a long time since he felt part of that balance. And he understood that he had seen Barbara Coles when she was most herself, at ease with a group of people she worked with. It was then, with the tears drying on his eyelids, which felt old and ironic, that he decided he would sleep with Barbara Coles. It was a necessity for him. He went back through the door onto the stage, burning with this single determination.

The five were still together. Barbara had a length of blue gleaming stuff which she was draping over the shoulder of Steven, the stagehand. He was showing it off, and the others watched. "What do you think, James?" she asked the director. "We've got that sort of dirty green, and I thought . . ." "Well," said James, not sure at all, "well, Babs, well . . ."

Now Graham went forward so that he stood beside Barbara, and said: "I'm Graham Spence, we've met before." For the second time she smiled socially and said: "Oh I'm sorry, I don't remember." Graham nodded at James, whom he had known, or at least had met off and on, for years. But it was obvious James didn't remember him either.

"From the B.B.C.," said Graham to Barbara, again sounding abrupt, against his will. "Oh I'm sorry, I'm so sorry, I forgot all about it. I've got to be interviewed," she said to the group. "Mr. Spence is a journalist." Graham allowed himself a small smile ironical of the word journalist, but she was not looking at him. She was going on with her work. "We should decide tonight," she said. "Steven's right." "Yes, I am right," said the stagehand. "She's right, James, we need that blue with that sludge-green everywhere." "James," said Barbara, "James, what's wrong with it? You haven't said." She moved forward to James, passing Graham. Remembering him again, she became contrite. "I'm sorry," she said, "we can none of us agree. Well, look"—she turned to Graham—"you advise us, we've got so involved with it that . . ." At which James laughed, and so did the stagehands. "No, Babs," said James, "of course Mr. Spence can't advise. He's just this moment come in. We've got to decide. Well I'll give you till tomorrow morning. Time to go home, it must be six by now."

"It's nearly seven," said Graham, taking command.

"It isn't!" said Barbara, dramatic. "My God, how terrible, how appalling, how could I have done such a thing. . . ." She was laughing at herself. "Well, you'll have to forgive me, Mr. Spence, because you haven't got any alternative."

They began laughing again: this was clearly a group joke. And now Graham took his chance. He said firmly, as if he were her director, in fact copying James Poynter's manner with her: "No, Miss Coles, I won't forgive you, I've been kicking my heels for nearly an hour." She grimaced, then laughed and accepted it. James said: "There, Babs, that's how you ought to be treated. We spoil you." He

367

kissed her on the cheek, she kissed him on both his, the stagehands moved off. "Have a good evening, Babs," said James, going, and nodding to Graham. Who stood concealing his pleasure with difficulty. He knew, because he had had the courage to be firm, indeed, peremptory, with Barbara, that he had saved himself hours of maneuvering. Several drinks, a dinner—perhaps two or three evenings of drinks and dinners—had been saved because he was now on this footing with Barbara Coles, a man who could say: "No, I won't forgive you, you've kept me waiting."

She said: "I've just got to . . ." and went ahead of him. In the passage she hung her overall on a peg. She was thinking, it seemed, of something else, but seeing him watching her, she smiled at him, companionably: he realised with triumph it was the sort of smile she would offer one of the stagehands, or even James. She said again: "Just one second . . ." and went to the stage-door office. She and the stage doorman conferred. There was some problem. Graham said, taking another chance: "What's the trouble, can I help?"—as if he could help, as if he expected to be able to. "Well . . ." she said, frowning. Then, to the man: "No, it'll be all right. Good night." She came to Graham. "We've got ourselves into a bit of a fuss because half the set's in Liverpool and half's here and—but it will sort itself out." She stood, at ease, chatting to him, one colleague to another. All this was admirable, he felt; but there would be a bad moment when they emerged from the special atmosphere of the theatre into the street. He took another decision, grasped her arm firmly, and said: "We're going to have a drink before we do anything at all, it's a terrible evening out." Her arm felt resistant, but remained within his. It was raining outside, luckily. He directed her, authoritative: "No, not that pub, there's a nicer one around the corner." "Oh, but I like this pub," said Barbara, "we always use it."

"Of course you do," he said to himself. But in that pub there would be the stagehands, and probably James, and he'd lose contact with her. He'd become a *journalist* again. He took her firmly out of danger around two corners, into a pub he picked at random. A quick look around—no, they weren't there. At least, if there were people from the theatre, she showed no sign. She asked for a beer. He ordered her a double Scotch, which she accepted. Then, having won a dozen preliminary rounds already, he took time to think. Something was bothering him—what? Yes, it was what he had observed backstage, Barbara and James Poynter. Was she having an affair with him? Because if so, it would all be much more difficult. He made himself see the two of them together, and thought with a jealousy surprisingly strong: *Yes, that's it.* Meantime he sat looking at her, seeing himself look at her, *a man gazing in calm appreciation at a woman*: waiting for her to feel it and respond. She was examining the pub. Her white woollen suit was belted, and had a not unprovocative suggestion of being a uniform. Her flat yellow hair, hastily pushed back after work, was untidy. Her clear white skin, without any colour, made her look tired. Not very exciting, at the moment, thought Graham, but maintaining his appreciative pose for when she would turn and see it. He knew what she would see: he was relying not only on the "warm kindly" beam of his gaze, for this was merely a reinforcement of the impression he knew he made. He had black hair, a little greyed. His clothes were loose and bulky—masculine. His eyes were humorous and appreciative. He was not, never had been, concerned to lessen the impression of being settled, dependable: the husband and father. On the contrary, he knew women found it reassuring.

When she at last turned she said, almost apologetic: "Would you mind if we sat down? I've been lugging great things around all day." She had spotted two empty chairs in a corner. So had he, but rejected them, because there were other people at the table. "But my dear, of course!" They took the chairs, and then Barbara said: "If you'll excuse me a moment." She had remembered she needed makeup. He watched her go off, annoyed with himself. She was tired; and he could have understood, protected, sheltered. He realised that in the other pub, with the people she had worked with all day, she would not have thought: "I must make myself up, I must be on show." That was for outsiders. She had not, until now, considered Graham an outsider, because of his taking his chance to seem one of the working group in the theatre; but now he had thrown this opportunity away. She returned armoured. Her hair was sleek, no longer defenceless. And she had made up her eyes. Her eyebrows were untouched, pale gold streaks above the brilliant green eyes whose lashes were blackened. Rather good, he thought, the contrast. Yes, but the moment had gone when he could say: Did you know you had a smudge on your cheek? Or—my dear girl!—pushing her hair back with the edge of a brotherly hand. In fact, unless he was careful, he'd be back at starting point.

He remarked: "That emerald is very cunning"—smiling into her eyes.

She smiled politely, and said: "It's not cunning, it's an accident, it was my grandmother's." She flirted her hand lightly by her face, though, smiling. But that was something she had done before, to a compliment she had had before, and often. It was all social, she had become social entirely. She remarked: "Didn't you say it was half past nine we had to record?"

"My dear Barbara, we've got two hours. We'll have another drink or two, then I'll ask you a couple of questions, then we'll drop down to the studio and get it over, and then we'll have a comfortable supper."

"I'd rather eat now, if you don't mind. I had no lunch, and I'm really hungry."

"But my dear, of course." He was angry. Just as he had been surprised by his real jealousy over James, so now he was thrown off balance by his anger: he had been counting on the long quiet dinner afterwards to establish intimacy. "Finish your drink and I'll take you to Nott's." Nott's was expensive. He glanced at her assessingly as he mentioned it. She said: "I wonder if you know Butler's? It's good and it's rather close." Butler's was good, and it was cheap, and he gave her a good mark for liking it. But Nott's it was going to be. "My dear, we'll get into a taxi and be at Nott's in a moment, don't worry."

She obediently got to her feet: the way she did it made him understand how badly he had slipped. She was saying to herself: Very well, he's like that, then all right, I'll do what he wants and get it over with. . . .

Swallowing his own drink he followed her, and took her arm in the pub doorway. It was polite within his. Outside it drizzled. No taxi. He was having bad luck now. They walked in silence to the end of the street. There Barbara glanced into a side street where a sign said: BUTLER'S. Not to remind him of it, on the contrary, she concealed the glance. And here she was, entirely at his disposal, they might never have shared the comradely moment in the theatre.

They walked half a mile to Nott's. No taxis. She made conversation: this was, he saw, to cover any embarrassment he might feel because of a half-mile walk through rain when she was tired. She was talking about some theory to do with the theatre, with designs for theatre building. He heard himself saying, and repeatedly: Yes, yes, yes. He thought about Nott's, how to get things right when they reached Nott's. There he took the headwaiter aside, gave him a pound, and instructions. They were put in a corner. Large Scotches appeared. The menus were spread. "And now, my dear," he said, "I apologise for dragging you here, but I hope you'll think it's worth it."

"Oh, it's charming, I've always liked it. It's just that . . ." She stopped herself saying: it's such a long way. She smiled at him, raising her glass, and said: "It's one of my very favourite places, and I'm glad you dragged me here." Her voice was flat with tiredness. All this was appalling; he knew it; and he sat thinking how to retrieve his position. Meanwhile she fingered the menu. The headwaiter took the order, but Graham made a gesture which said: Wait a moment. He wanted the Scotch to take effect before she ate. But she saw his silent order; and, without annoyance or reproach, leaned forward to say, sounding patient: "Graham, please, I've got to eat, you don't want me drunk when you interview me, do you?"

"They are bringing it as fast as they can," he said, making it sound as if she were greedy. He looked neither at the headwaiter nor at Barbara. He noted in himself, as he slipped further and further away from contact with her, a cold determination growing in him; one apart from, apparently, any conscious act of will, that come what may, if it took all night, he'd be in her bed before morning. And now, seeing the small pale face, with the enormous green eyes, it was for the first time that he imagined her in his arms. Although he had said: Yes, *that one*, weeks ago, it was only now that he imagined her as a sensual experience. Now he did, so strongly that he could only glance at her, and then away towards the waiters who were bringing food.

"Thank the Lord," said Barbara, and all at once her voice was gay and intimate. "Thank heavens. Thank every power that is. . . ." She was making fun of her own exaggeration; and, as he saw, because she wanted to put him at his ease after his boorishness over delaying the food. (She hadn't been taken in, he saw, humiliated, disliking her.) "Thank all the gods of Nott's," she went on, "because if I hadn't eaten inside five minutes I'd have died, I tell you." With which she picked up her knife and fork and began on her steak. He poured wine, smiling with her, thinking that *this* moment of closeness he would not throw away. He watched her frank hunger as she ate, and thought: Sensual—it's strange I hadn't wondered whether she would be or not.

"Now," she said, sitting back, having taken the edge off her hunger: "Let's get to work."

He said: "I've thought it over very carefully—how to present you. The first thing seems to me, we must get away from that old chestnut: Miss Coles, how extraordinary for a woman to be so versatile in her work . . . I hope you agree?" This was his trump card. He had noted, when he had seen her on television, her polite smile when this note was struck. (The smile he had seen so often tonight.) This smile said: All right, if you *have* to be stupid, what can I do?

Now she laughed and said: "What a relief. I was afraid you were going to do the same thing."

"Good, now you eat and I'll talk."

In his carefully prepared monologue he spoke of the different styles of theatre she had shown herself mistress of, but not directly: he was flattering her on the breadth of her experience; the complexity of her character, as shown in her work. She ate, steadily, her face showing nothing. At last she asked: "and how did you plan to introduce this?"

He had meant to spring that on her as a surprise, something like: Miss Coles, a surprisingly young woman for what she has accomplished (she was thirty? thirty-two?) and a very attractive one. . . . "Perhaps I can give you an idea of what she's like if I say she could be taken for the film star Marie Carletta. . . ." The Carletta was a strong earthy blonde, known to be intellectual. He now saw he could not possibly say this: he could imagine her cool look if he did. She said: "Do you mind if we get away from all that—my manifold talents, et cetera. . . ." He felt himself stiffen with annoyance; particularly because this was not an accusation, he saw she did not think him worth one. She had assessed him: This is the kind of man who uses this kind of flattery and therefore. . . . It made him angrier that she did not even trouble to say: Why did you do exactly what you promised you wouldn't? She was being invincibly polite, trying to conceal her patience with his stupidity.

"After all," she was saying, "It is a stage designer's job to design what comes up. Would anyone take, let's say Johnnie Cranmore" (another stage designer) "onto the air or television and say: How very versatile you are because you did that musical about Java last month and a modern play about Irish labourers this?"

He battened down his anger. "My dear Barbara, I'm sorry. I didn't realise that what I said would sound just like the mixture as before. So what shall we talk about?"

"What I was saying as we walked to the restaurant: can we get away from the personal stuff?"

371

Now he almost panicked. Then, thank God, he laughed from nervousness, for she laughed and said: "You didn't hear one word I said."

"No, I didn't. I was frightened you were going to be furious because I made you walk so far when you were tired."

They laughed together, back to where they had been in the theatre. He leaned over, took her hand, kissed it. He said: "Tell me again." He thought: Damn, now she's going to be earnest and intellectual.

But he understood he had been stupid. He had forgotten himself at twenty— or, for that matter, at thirty; forgotten one could live inside an idea, a set of ideas, with enthusiasm. For in talking about her ideas (also the ideas of the people she worked with) for a new theatre, a new style of theatre, she was as she had been with her colleagues over the sketches or the blue material. She was easy, informal, almost chattering. This was how, he remembered, one talked about ideas that were a breath of life. The ideas, he thought, were intelligent enough; and he would agree with them, with her, if he believed it mattered a damn one way or another, if any of these enthusiasms mattered a damn. But at least he now had the key, he knew what to do. At the end of not more than half an hour, they were again two professionals, talking about ideas they shared, for he remembered caring about all this himself once. *When? How many years ago was it that he had been able to care?*

At last he said: "My dear Barbara, do you realise the impossible position you're putting me in? Margaret Ruyen who runs this programme is determined to do you personally, the poor woman hasn't got a serious thought in her head."

Barbara frowned. He put his hand on hers, teasing her for the frown: "No, wait, trust me, we'll circumvent her." She smiled. In fact Margaret Ruyen had left it all to him, had said nothing about Miss Coles.

"They aren't very bright—the brass," he said. "Well, never mind: we'll work out what we want, do it, and it'll be a *fait accompli*."

"Thank you, what a relief. How lucky I was to be given you to interview me." She was relaxed now, because of the whisky, the food, the wine, above all because of this new complicity against Margaret Ruyen. It would all be easy. They worked out five or six questions, over coffee, and took a taxi through rain to the studios. He noted that the cold necessity to have her, to make her, to beat her down, had left him. He was even seeing himself, as the evening ended, kissing her on the cheek and going home to his wife. This comradeship was extraordinarily pleasant. It was balm to the wound he had not known he carried until that evening, when he had had to accept the justice of the word *journalist*. He felt he could talk forever about the state of the theatre, its finances, the stupidity of the government, the philistinism of . . .

At the studios he was careful to make a joke so that they walked in on the laugh. He was careful that the interview began at once, without conversation with Margaret Ruyen; and that from the moment the green light went on, his voice lost its easy familiarity. He made sure that not one personal note was struck during the interview. Afterwards, Margaret Ruyen, who was pleased, came forward to say so; but he took her aside to say that Miss Coles was tired and needed to be taken home at once: for he knew this must look to Barbara as if he were squaring a producer who had been expecting a different interview. He led Barbara off, her hand held tight in his against his side. "Well," he said, "we've done it, and I don't think she knows what hit her."

"Thank you," she said, "it really was pleasant to talk about something sensible for once."

He kissed her lightly on the mouth. She returned it, smiling. By now he felt sure that the mood need not slip again, he could hold it.

"There are two things we can do," he said. "You can come to my club and have a drink. Or I can drive you home and you can give me a drink. I have to go past you."

"Where do you live?"

"Wimbledon." He lived, in fact, at Highgate; but she lived in Fulham. He was taking another chance, but by the time she found out, they would be in a position to laugh over his ruse.

"Good," she said. "You can drop me home then. I have to get up early." He made no comment. In the taxi he took her hand; it was heavy in his, and he asked: "Does James slave-drive you?"

"I didn't realize you knew him—no, he doesn't."

"Well, I don't know him intimately. What's he like to work with?"

"Wonderful," she said at once. "There's no one I enjoy working with more."

Jealousy spurted in him. He could not help himself: "Are you having an affair with him?"

She looked: what's it to do with you? but said: "No, I'm not."

"He's very attractive," he said, with a chuckle of worldly complicity. She said nothing, and he insisted: "If I were a woman I'd have an affair with James."

It seemed she might very well say nothing. But she remarked: "He's married."

His spirits rose in a swoop. It was the first stupid remark she had made. It was a remark of such staggering stupidity that . . . he let out a humoring snort of laughter, put his arm around her, kissed her, said: "My dear little Babs."

She said: "Why Babs?"

"Is that the prerogative of James. And of the stagehands?" he could not prevent himself adding.

"I'm only called that at work." She was stiff inside his arm.

"My dear Barbara, then . . ." He waited for her to enlighten and explain, but she said nothing. Soon she moved out of his arm, on the pretext of lighting a cigarette. He lit it for her. He noted that his determination to lay her, and at all costs, had come back. They were outside her house. He said quickly: "And now, Barbara, you can make me a cup of coffee and give me a brandy." She hesitated; but he was out of the taxi, paying, opening the door for her. The house had no lights on, he noted. He said: "We'll be very quiet so as not to wake the children."

She turned her head slowly to look at him. She said, flat, replying to his real question: "My husband is away. As for the children, they are visiting friends tonight." She now went ahead of him to the door of the house. It was a small house, in a terrace of small and not very pretty houses. Inside a little, bright, intimate hall, she said: "I'll go and make some coffee. Then, my friend, you must go home because I'm very tired."

The *my friend* struck him deep, because he had become vulnerable during their comradeship. He said, gabbling: "You're annoyed with me—oh, please don't, I'm sorry."

She smiled, from a cool distance. He saw, in the small light from the ceiling, her extraordinary eyes. "Green" eyes are hazel, are brown with green flecks, are even blue. Eyes are chequered, flawed, changing. Hers were solid green, but really, he had never seen anything like them before. They were like very deep water. They were like—well, emeralds; or the absolute clarity of green in the depths of a tree in summer. And now, as she smiled almost perpendicularly up at him, he saw a darkness come over them. Darkness swallowed the clear green. She said: "I'm not in the least annoyed." It was as if she had yawned with boredom. "And now I'll get the things . . . in there." She nodded at a white door and left him. He went into a long, very tidy white room, that had a narrow bed in one corner, a table covered with drawings, sketches, pencils. Tacked to the walls with drawing pins were swatches of coloured stuffs. Two small chairs stood near a low round table: an area of comfort in the working room. He was thinking: I wouldn't like it if my wife had a room like this. I wonder what Barbara's husband . . . ? He had not thought of her till now in relation to her husband, or to her children. Hard to imagine her with a frying pan in her hand, or for that matter, cosy in the double bed.

A noise outside: he hastily arranged himself, leaning with one arm on the mantelpiece. She came in with a small tray that had cups, glasses, brandy, coffeepot. She looked abstracted. Graham was on the whole flattered by this: it probably meant she was at ease in his presence. He realised he was a little tight and rather tired. Of course, she was tired too, that was why she was vague. He remembered that earlier that evening he had lost a chance by not using her tiredness. Well now, if he were intelligent . . . She was about to pour coffee. He firmly took the coffeepot out of her hand, and nodded at a chair. Smiling, she obeyed him. "That's better," he said. He poured coffee, poured brandy, and pulled the table towards her. She watched him. Then he took her hand, kissed it, patted it, laid it down gently. Yes, he thought, I did that well.

Now, a problem. He wanted to be closer to her, but she was fitted into a damned silly little chair that had arms. If he were to sit by her on the floor . . . ? But no, for him, the big bulky reassuring man, there could be no casual gestures, no informal postures. Suppose I scoop her out of the chair onto the bed? He drank his coffee as he plotted. Yes, he'd carry her to the bed, but not yet.

"Graham," she said, setting down her cup. She was, he saw with annoyance, looking tolerant. "Graham, in about half an hour I want to be in bed and asleep."

As she said this, she offered him a smile of amusement at this situation—man and woman maneuvering, the great comic situation. And with part of himself he could have shared it. Almost, he smiled with her, laughed. (Not till days later he exclaimed to himself: Lord what a mistake I made, not to share the joke with her then: that was where I went seriously wrong.) But he could not smile. His face was frozen, with a stiff pride. Not because she had been watching him plot; the amusement she now offered him took the sting out of that; but because of his revived determination that he was going to have his own way, he was going to have her. He was not going home. But he felt that he held a bunch of keys, and did not know which one to choose.

He lifted the second small chair opposite to Barbara, moving aside the coffee table for this purpose. He sat in this chair, leaned forward, took her two hands, and said: "My dear, don't make me go home yet, don't, I beg you." The trouble was, nothing had happened all evening that could be felt to lead up to these words and his tone—simple, dignified, human being pleading with human being for surcease. He saw himself leaning forward, his big hands swallowing her small ones; he saw his face, warm with the appeal. And he realised he had meant the words he used. They were nothing more than what he felt. He wanted to stay with her because she wanted him to, because he was her colleague, a fellow worker in the arts. He needed this desperately. But she was examining him, curious rather than surprised, and from a critical distance. He heard himself saying: "If James were here, I wonder what you'd do?" His voice was aggrieved; he saw the sudden dark descend over her eyes, and she said: "Graham, would you like some more coffee before you go?"

He said: "I've been wanting to meet you for years. I know a good many people who know you."

She leaned forward, poured herself a little more brandy, sat back, holding the glass between her two palms on her chest. An odd gesture: Graham felt that this vessel she was cherishing between her hands was herself. A patient, long-suffering gesture. He thought of various men who had mentioned her. He thought of Jack Kennaway, wavered, panicked, said: "For instance, Jack Kennaway."

And now, at the name, an emotion lit her eyes—what was it? He went on, deliberately testing this emotion, adding to it: "I had dinner with him last week—oh, quite by chance!—and he was talking about you."

"Was he?"

He remembered he had thought her sullen, all those years ago. Now she seemed defensive, and she frowned. He said: "In fact he spent most of the evening talking about you."

She said in short, breathless sentences, which he realised were due to anger:

"I can very well imagine what he says. But surely you can't think I enjoy being reminded that . . ." She broke off, resenting him, he saw, because he forced her down onto a level she despised. But it was not his level either: it was all her fault, all hers! He couldn't remember not being in control of a situation with a woman for years. Again he felt like a man teetering on a tightrope. He said, trying to make good use of Jack Kennaway, even at this late hour: "Of course, he's a charming boy, but not a man at all."

She looked at him, silent, guarding her brandy glass against her breasts.

"Unless appearances are totally deceptive, of course." He could not resist probing, even though he knew it was fatal.

She said nothing.

"Do you know you are supposed to have had the great affair with Jack Kennaway?" he exclaimed, making this an amused expostulation against the fools who could believe it.

"So I am told." She set down her glass. "And now," she said, standing up, dismissing him. He lost his head, took a step forward, grabbed her in his arms, and groaned: "Barbara!"

She turned her face this way and that under his kisses. He snatched a diagnostic look at her expression—it was still patient. He placed his lips against her neck, groaned "Barbara" again, and waited. She would have to do something. Fight free, respond, something. She did nothing at all. At last she said: "For the Lord's sake, Graham!" She sounded amused: he was again being offered amusement. But if he shared it with her, it would be the end of this chance to have her. He clamped his mouth over hers, silencing her. She did not fight him off so much as blow him off. Her mouth treated his attacking mouth as a woman blows and laughs in water, puffing off waves or spray with a laugh, turning aside her head. It was a gesture half annoyance, half humour. He continued to kiss her while she moved her head and face about under the kisses as if they were small attacking waves.

And so began what, when he looked back on it afterwards, was the most embarrassing experience of his life. Even at the time he hated her for his ineptitude. For he held her there for what must have been nearly half an hour. She was much shorter than he, he had to bend, and his neck ached. He held her rigid, his thighs on either side of hers, her arms clamped to her side in a bear's hug. She was unable to move, except for her head. When his mouth ground hers open and his tongue moved and writhed inside it, she still remained passive. And he could not stop himself. While with his intelligence he watched this ridiculous scene, he was determined to go on, because sooner or later her body must soften in wanting his. And he could not stop because he could not face the horror of the moment when he set her free and she looked at him. And he hated her more, every moment. Catching glimpses of her great green eyes, open and dismal beneath his, he knew he had never disliked anything more than those "jewelled" eyes. They were repulsive to him. It occurred to him at last that even if by now she wanted him, he wouldn't know it, because she was not able to move at all. He cautiously loosened his hold so that she had an inch or so leeway. She remained quite passive. As if, he thought derisively, she had read or been told that the way to incite men maddened by lust was to fight them. He found he was thinking: Stupid cow, so you imagine I find you attractive, do you? You've got the conceit to think that!

The sheer, raving insanity of this thought hit him, opened his arms, his thighs, and lifted his tongue out of her mouth. She stepped back, wiping her mouth with the back of her hand, and stood dazed with incredulity. The embarrassment that lay in wait for him nearly engulfed him, but he let anger postpone it. She said positively apologetic, even, at this moment, humorous: "You're crazy, Graham. What's the matter, are you drunk? You don't seem drunk. You don't even find me attractive."

The blood of hatred went to his head and he gripped her again. Now she had got her face firmly twisted away so that he could not reach her mouth, and she repeated steadily as he kissed the parts of her cheeks and neck that were available to him: "Graham, let me go, do let me go, Graham." She went on saying this; he went on squeezing, grinding, kissing and licking. It might go on all night: it was a sheer contest of wills, nothing else. He thought: It's only a really masculine woman who wouldn't have given in by now out of sheer decency of the flesh! One thing he knew, however: that she would be in that bed, in his arms, and very soon. He let her go, but said: "I'm going to sleep with you tonight, you know that, don't you?"

She leaned with hand on the mantlepiece to steady herself. Her face was colourless, since he had licked all the makeup off. She seemed quite different: small and defenceless with her large mouth pale now, her smudged green eyes fringed with gold. And now, for the first time, he felt what it might have been supposed (certainly by her) he felt hours ago. Seeing the small damp flesh of her face, he felt kinship, intimacy with her, he felt intimacy of the flesh, the affection and good humour of sensuality. He felt she was flesh of his flesh, his sister in the flesh. He felt desire for her, instead of the will to have her; and because of this, was ashamed of the farce he had been playing. Now he desired simply to take her into bed in the affection of his senses.

She said: "What on earth am I supposed to do? Telephone for the police, or what?" He was hurt that she still addressed the man who had ground her into sulky apathy; she was not addressing *him* at all.

She said: "Or scream for the neighbours, is that what you want?"

The gold-fringed eyes were almost black, because of the depth of the shadow of boredom over them. She was bored and weary to the point of falling to the floor, he could see that.

He said. "I'm going to sleep with you."

"But how can you possibly want to?"—a reasonable, a civilised demand addressed to a man who (he could see) she believed would respond to it. She said:

"You know I don't want to, and I know you don't really give a damn one way or the other."

He was stung back into being the boor because she had not the intelligence to see that the boor no longer existed; because she could not see that this was a man who wanted her in a way which she must respond to.

There she stood, supporting herself with one hand, looking small and white and exhausted, and utterly incredulous. She was going to turn and walk off out of simple incredulity, he could see that. "Do you think I don't mean it?" he demanded, grinding this out between his teeth. She made a movement—she was on the point of going away. His hand shot out on its own volition and grasped her wrist. She frowned. His other hand grasped her other wrist. His body hove up against hers to start the pressure of a new embrace. Before it could, she said: "Oh Lord, no, I'm not going through all that again. Right, then."

"What do you mean—right, then?" he demanded.

She said: "You're going to sleep with me. O.K. Anything rather than go through that again. Shall we get it over with?"

He grinned, saying in silence: "No darling, oh no you don't, I don't care what words you use, I'm going to have you now and that's all there is to it."

She shrugged. The contempt, the weariness of it, had no effect on him, because he was now again hating her so much that wanting her was like needing to kill something or someone.

She took her clothes off, as if she were going to bed by herself: her jacket, skirt, petticoat. She stood in white bra and panties, a rather solid girl, brown-skinned still from the summer. He felt a flash of affection for the brown girl with her loose yellow hair as she stood naked. She got into bed and lay there, while the green eyes looked at him in civilised appeal: Are you really going through with this? Do you have to? Yes, his eyes said back: I do have to. She shifted her gaze aside, to the wall, saying silently: Well, if you want to take me without any desire at all on my part, then go ahead, if you're not ashamed. He was not ashamed, because he was maintaining the flame of hate for her which he knew quite well was all that stood between him and shame. He took off his clothes, and got into bed beside her. As he did so, knowing he was putting himself in the position of raping a woman who was making it elaborately clear he bored her, his flesh subsided completely, sad, and full of reproach because a few moments ago it was reaching out for his sister whom he could have made happy. He lay on his side by her, secretly at work on himself, while he supported himself across her body on his elbow, using the free hand to manipulate her breasts. He saw that she gritted her teeth against his touch. At least she could not know that after all this fuss he was not potent.

In order to incite himself, he clasped her again. She felt his smallness, writhed free of him, sat up and said: "Lie down."

While she had been lying there, she had been thinking: The only way to get this over with is to make him big again, otherwise I've got to put up with him all night. His hatred of her was giving him a clairvoyance: he knew very well what went on through her mind. She had switched on, with the determination to *get it all over with*, a sensual good humour, a patience. He lay down. She squatted beside him, the light from the ceiling blooming on her brown shoulders, her flat fair hair falling over her face. But she would not look at his face. Like a bored, skilled wife, she was; or like a prostitute. She administered to him, she was setting herself to please him. Yes, he thought, she's sensual, or she could be. Meanwhile she was succeeding in defeating the reluctance of his flesh, which was the tender token of a possible desire for her, by using a cold skill that was the result of her contempt for him. Just as he decided: Right, it's enough, now I shall have her properly, she made him come. It was not a trick, to hurry or cheat him, what defeated him was her transparent thought: Yes, that's what he's worth.

Then, having succeeded, and waited for a moment or two, she stood up, naked, the fringes of gold at her loins and in her armpits speaking to him a language quite different from that of her green, bored eyes. She looked at him and thought, showing it plainly: What sort of man is it who . . .? He watched the slight movement of her shoulders: a just-checked shrug. She went out of the room: then the sound of running water. Soon she came back in a white dressing gown, carrying a yellow towel. She handed him the towel, looking away in politeness as he used it. "Are you going home now?" she enquired hopefully, at this point.

"No, I'm not." He believed that now he would have to start fighting her again, but she lay down beside him, not touching him (he could feel the distaste of her flesh for his) and he thought: Very well, my dear, but there's a lot of the night left yet. He said aloud: "I'm going to have you properly tonight." She said nothing, lay silent, yawned. Then she remarked consolingly, and he could have laughed outright from sheer surprise: "Those were hardly conducive circumstances for making love." She was *consoling* him. He hated her for it. A proper little slut: I force her into bed, she doesn't want me, but she still has to make me feel good, like a prostitute. But even while he hated her he responded in kind, from the habit of sexual generosity. "It's because of my admiration for you, because . . . after all, I was holding in my arms one of the thousand women."

A pause. "The thousand?" she enquired, carefully.

"The thousand especial women."

"In Britain or in the world? You choose them for their brains, their beauty—what?"

"Whatever it is that makes them outstanding," he said, offering her a compliment.

"Well," she remarked at last, inciting him to be amused again: "I hope that at least there's a short list you can say I am on, for politeness' sake."

He did not reply for he understood he was sleepy. He was still telling himself that he must stay awake when he was slowly waking and it was morning. It was about eight. Barbara was not there. He thought: My God! What on earth shall I tell my wife? Where was Barbara? He remembered the ridiculous scenes of last night and nearly succumbed to shame. Then he thought, reviving anger: If she didn't sleep beside me here I'll never forgive her. . . . He sat up, quietly, determined to go through the house until he found her and, having found her, to possess her, when the door opened and she came in. She was fully dressed in a green suit, her hair done, her eyes made up. She carried a tray of coffee, which she set down beside the bed. He was conscious of his big loose hairy body, half uncovered. He said to himself that he was not going to lie in bed, naked, while she was dressed. He said: "Have you got a gown of some kind?" She handed him, without speaking, a towel, and said: "The bathroom's second on the left." She went out. He followed, the towel around him. Everything in this house was gay, intimate—not at all like her efficient working room. He wanted to find out where she had slept, and opened the first door. It was the kitchen, and she was in it, putting a brown earthenware dish into the oven. "The next door," said Barbara. He went hastily past the second door, and opened (he hoped quietly) the third. It was a cupboard full of linen. "This door," said Barbara, behind him.

"So all right then, where did you sleep?"

"What's it to do with you? Upstairs, in my own bed. Now, if you have everything, I'll say goodbye, I want to get to the theatre."

"I'll take you," he said at once.

He saw again the movement of her eyes, the dark swallowing the light in deadly boredom. "I'll take you," he insisted.

"I'd prefer to go by myself," she remarked. Then she smiled: "However, you'll take me. Then you'll make a point of coming right in, so that James and everyone can see—that's what you want to take me for, isn't it?"

He hated her, finally, and quite simply, for her intelligence; that not once had he got away with anything, that she had been watching, since they had met yesterday, every movement of his campaign for her. However, some fate or inner urge over which he had no control made him say sentimentally: "My dear, you must see that I'd like at least to take you to your work."

"Not at all, have it on me," she said, giving him the lie direct. She went past him to the room he had slept in. "I shall be leaving in ten minutes," she said.

He took a shower, fast. When he returned, the workroom was already tidied, the bed made, all signs of the night gone. Also, there were no signs of the coffee she had brought in for him. He did not like to ask for it, for fear of an outright refusal. Besides, she was ready, her coat on, her handbag under her arm. He went, without a word, to the front door, and she came after him, silent.

He could see that every fibre of her body signalled a simple message: Oh God, for the moment when I can be rid of this boor! She was nothing but a slut, he thought.

A taxi came. In it she sat as far away from him as she could. He thought of what he should say to his wife.

Outside the theatre she remarked: "You could drop me here, if you liked." It was not a plea, she was too proud for that. "I'll take you in," he said, and saw her thinking: Very well, I'll go through with it to shame him. He was determined to take her in and hand her over to her colleagues, he was afraid she would give him the slip. But far from playing it down, she seemed determined to play it his way. At the stage door, she said to the doorman: "This is Mr. Spence, Tom—do you remember, Mr. Spence from last night?" "Good morning, Babs," said the man, examining Graham, politely, as he had been ordered to do.

Barbara went to the door to the stage, opened it, held it open for him. He went in first, then held it open for her. Together they walked into the cavernous, littered, badly lit place and she called out: "James, James!" A man's voice called out from the front of the house: "Here, Babs, why are you so late?"

The auditorium opened before them, darkish, silent, save for an early-morning busyness of charwomen. A vacuum cleaner roared, smally, somewhere close. A couple of stagehands stood looking up at a drop which had a design of blue and green spirals. James stood with his back to the auditorium, smoking. "You're late, Babs," he said again. He saw Graham behind her, and nodded. Barbara and James kissed. Barbara said, giving allowance to every syllable: "You remember Mr. Spence from last night?" James nodded: How do you do? Barbara stood beside him, and they looked together up at the blue-and-green backdrop. Then Barbara looked again at Graham, asking silently: All right now, isn't that enough? He could see her eyes, sullen with boredom.

He said: "Bye, Babs. Bye, James. I'll ring you, Babs." No response, she ignored him. He walked off slowly, listening for what might be said. For instance: "Babs, for God's sake, what are you doing with him?" Or she might say: "Are you wondering about Graham Spence? Let me explain."

Graham passed the stagehands who, he could have sworn, didn't recognise him. Then at last he heard James's voice to Barbara: "It's no good, Babs, I know you're enamoured of that particular shade of blue, but do have another look at it, there's a good girl. . . ." Graham left the stage, went past the office where the stage doorman sat reading a newspaper. He looked up, nodded, went back to his paper. Graham went to find a taxi, thinking: I'd better think up something convincing, then I'll telephone my wife.

Luckily he had an excuse not to be at home that day, for this evening he had to interview a young man (for television) about his new novel.

YUKIO MISHIMA
(1925–1970)

YUKIO MISHIMA (the pseudonym of Kimitake Hiraoka) was born in Tokyo, the son of an important government official. In 1947 he graduated from the Tokyo University Law School, having compiled a distinguished record, and went to work in the Finance Ministry. Shortly thereafter he resigned in order to devote himself to writing. But Mishima's early work even predates that decision. "The Grove in Bloom," written when he was sixteen, appeared three years later as the title story in a short-story collection. His literary reputation had already been achieved by 1946, when *Tobacco* was published with the endorsement of Yasunari Kawabata. *Confessions of a Mask* in 1949 (tr. 1958) secured and enhanced for Mishima the reputation of being among the most conspicuously gifted of postwar Japanese writers. His other titles include *The Thirst for Love* (tr. 1969), *Forbidden Colors* (tr. 1968), *After the Banquet* (tr. 1963), *The Sailor Who Fell from Grace with the Sea* (tr. 1965), and a tetralogy, *The Sea of Fertility,* containing *Spring Snow* (tr. 1972), *Galloping Horses* (tr. 1973), *The Temple of the Dawn* (tr. 1973), and *The Divinity's Five Omens* (1971). He is, in addition, the author of numerous books of essays, short stories, poems, and plays.

Mishima was also deeply preoccupied with the past glory of Imperial Japan, and with the samurai code of honor. In the sixties he established a private army of some one hundred men to revive the samurai tradition. Ultimately, discouraged by his inability to affect a larger society, he committed suicide by the ritual *seppuku.*

In "Patriotism" (tr. 1966), the lieutenant, Shinji, age thirty-one, explains to his new wife Reiko, age twenty-three, that as the wife of a soldier, she must accept the possibility that her husband's death could occur at any time. Wordlessly, she places a dagger her mother has given her ("the most prized of her new possessions") on the mat alongside her husband's sword. These images, integral to Mishima's sensibility, shadow the account that follows of the couple's first half-year, their tender domestic intimacy, their passionate and joyous sex.

Patriotism

1

On the twenty-eighth of February, 1936 (on the third day, that is, of the February 26 Incident), Lieutenant Shinji Takeyama of the Konoe Transport Battalion— profoundly disturbed by the knowledge that his closest colleagues had been with the mutineers from the beginning, and indignant at the imminent prospect of Imperial troops attacking Imperial troops—took his officer's sword and ceremonially disemboweled himself in the eight-mat room of his private residence in the sixth block of Aoba-chō, in Yotsuya Ward. His wife, Reiko, followed him, stabbing herself to death. The lieutenant's farewell note consisted of one sentence: "Long live the Imperial Forces." His wife's, after apologies for her unfilial conduct in thus preceding her parents to the grave, concluded: "The day which, for a soldier's wife, had to come, has come. . . ." The last moments of this heroic and dedicated couple were such as to make the gods themselves weep. The lieutenant's age, it should be noted, was thirty-one, his wife's twenty-three; and it was not half a year since the celebration of their marriage.

2

Those who saw the bride and bridegroom in the commemorative photograph— perhaps no less than those actually present at the lieutenant's wedding—had exclaimed in wonder at the bearing of this handsome couple. The lieutenant, majestic in military uniform, stood protectively beside his bride, his right hand resting upon his sword, his officer's cap held at his left side. His expression was severe, and his dark brows and wide-gazing eyes well conveyed the clear integrity of youth. For the beauty of the bride in her white over-robe no comparisons were adequate. In the eyes, round beneath soft brows, in the slender, finely shaped nose, and in the full lips, there was both sensuousness and refinement. One hand, emerging shyly from a sleeve of the over-robe, held a fan, and the tips of the fingers, clustering delicately, were like the bud of a moon-flower.

After the suicide, people would take out this photograph and examine it, and sadly reflect that too often there was a curse on these seemingly flawless unions. Perhaps it was no more than imagination, but looking at the picture after the tragedy it almost seemed as if the two young people before the gold-lacquered screen were gazing, each with equal clarity, at the deaths which lay before them.

Thanks to the good offices of their go-between, Lieutenant General Ozeki, they had been able to set themselves up in a new home at Aoba-chō in Yotsuya. "New home" is perhaps misleading. It was an old three-room rented house backing onto a small garden. As neither the six- nor the four-and-a-half-mat room downstairs was favored by the sun, they used the upstairs eight-mat room as both bedroom and guest room. There was no maid, so Reiko was left alone to guard the house in her husband's absence.

The honeymoon trip was dispensed with on the grounds that these were times of national emergency. The two of them had spent the first night of their marriage at this house. Before going to bed, Shinji, sitting erect on the floor with his sword laid before him, had bestowed upon his wife a soldierly lecture. A woman who had become the wife of a soldier should know and resolutely accept that her husband's death might come at any moment. It could be tomorrow. It could be the day after. But, no matter when it came—he asked—was she steadfast in her resolve to accept it? Reiko rose to her feet, pulled open a drawer of the cabinet, and took out what was the most prized of her new possessions, the dagger her mother had given her. Returning to her place, she laid the dagger without a word on the mat before her, just as her husband had laid his sword. A silent understanding was achieved at once, and the lieutenant never again sought to test his wife's resolve.

In the first few months of her marriage Reiko's beauty grew daily more radiant, shining serene like the moon after rain.

As both were possessed of young, vigorous bodies, their relationship was passionate. Nor was this merely a matter of the night. On more than one occasion, returning home straight from maneuvers, and begrudging even the time it took to remove his mud-splashed uniform, the lieutenant had pushed his wife to the floor almost as soon as he had entered the house. Reiko was equally ardent in her response. For a little more or a little less than a month, from the first night of their marriage Reiko knew happiness, and the lieutenant, seeing this, was happy too.

Reiko's body was white and pure, and her swelling breasts conveyed a firm and chaste refusal; but, upon consent, those breasts were lavish with their intimate, welcoming warmth. Even in bed these two were frighteningly and awesomely serious. In the very midst of wild, intoxicating passions, their hearts were sober and serious.

By day the lieutenant would think of his wife in the brief rest periods between training; and all day long, at home, Reiko would recall the image of her husband. Even when apart, however, they had only to look at the wedding photograph for their happiness to be once more confirmed. Reiko felt not the slightest surprise that a man who had been a complete stranger until a few months ago should now have become the sun about which her whole world revolved.

All these things had a moral basis, and were in accordance with the Education Rescript's injunction that "husband and wife should be harmonious." Not once did Reiko contradict her husband, nor did the lieutenant ever find reason to scold his wife. On the god shelf below the stairway, alongside the tablet from the Great Ise Shrine, were set photographs of their Imperial Majesties, and regularly every morning, before leaving for duty, the lieutenant would stand with his wife at this hallowed place and together they would bow their heads low. The offering water was renewed each morning, and the sacred sprig of *sasaki* was always green and fresh. Their lives were lived beneath the solemn protection of the gods and were filled with an intense happiness which set every fiber in their bodies trembling.

3

Although Lord Privy Seal Saitō's house was in their neighborhood, neither of them heard any noise of gunfire on the morning of February 26. It was a bugle, sounding muster in the dim, snowy dawn, when the ten-minute tragedy had already ended, which first disrupted the lieutenant's slumbers. Leaping at once from his bed, and without speaking a word, the lieutenant donned his uniform, buckled on the sword held ready for him by his wife, and hurried swiftly out into the snow-covered streets of the still darkened morning. He did not return until the evening of the twenty-eighth.

Later, from the radio news, Reiko learned the full extent of this sudden eruption of violence. Her life throughout the subsequent two days was lived alone, in complete tranquility, and behind locked doors.

In the lieutenant's face, as he hurried silently out into the snowy morning, Reiko had read the determination to die. If her husband did not return, her own decision was made: she too would die. Quietly she attended to the disposition of her personal possessions. She chose her sets of visiting kimonos as keepsakes for friends of her schooldays, and she wrote a name and address on the stiff paper wrapping in which each was folded. Constantly admonished by her husband never to think of the morrow, Reiko had not even kept a diary and was now denied the pleasure of assiduously rereading her record of the happiness of the past few months and consigning each page to the fire as she did so. Ranged across the top of the radio were a small china dog, a rabbit, a squirrel, a bear, and a fox. There were also a small vase and a water pitcher. These comprised Reiko's one and only collection. But it would hardly do, she imagined, to give such things as keepsakes. Nor again would it be quite proper to ask specifically for them to be included in the coffin. It seemed to Reiko, as these thoughts passed through her mind, that the expressions on the small animals' faces grew even more lost and forlorn.

Reiko took the squirrel in her hand and looked at it. And then, her thoughts turning to a realm far beyond these childlike affections, she gazed up into the distance at the great sunlike principle which her husband embodied. She was ready, and happy, to be hurtled along to her destruction in that gleaming sun chariot—but now, for these few moments of solitude, she allowed herself to luxuriate in this innocent attachment to trifles. The time when she had genuinely loved these things, however, was long past. Now she merely loved the memory of having once loved them, and their place in her heart had been filled by more intense passions, by a more frenzied happiness. . . . For Reiko had never, even to herself, thought of those soaring joys of the flesh as a mere pleasure. The February cold, and the icy touch of the china squirrel, had numbed Reiko's slender fingers; yet, even so, in her lower limbs, beneath the ordered repetition of the pattern which crossed the skirt of her trim *meisen* kimono, she could feel now, as she thought of the lieutenant's powerful arms reaching out toward her, a hot moistness of the flesh which defied the snows.

She was not in the least afraid of the death hovering in her mind. Waiting alone at home, Reiko firmly believed that everything her husband was feeling or thinking now, his anguish and distress, was leading her—just as surely as the power in his flesh—to a welcome death. She felt as if her body could melt away with ease and be transformed to the merest fraction of her husband's thought.

Listening to the frequent announcements on the radio, she heard the names of several of her husband's colleagues mentioned among those of the insurgents. This was news of death. She followed the developments closely, wondering anxiously, as the situation became daily more irrevocable, why no Imperial ordinance was sent down, and watching what had at first been taken as a movement to restore the nation's honor come gradually to be branded with the infamous name of mutiny. There was no communication from the regiment. At any moment, it seemed, fighting might commence in the city streets, where the remains of the snow still lay.

Toward sundown on the twenty-eighth Reiko was startled by a furious pounding on the front door. She hurried downstairs. As she pulled with fumbling fingers at the bolt, the shape dimly outlined beyond the frosted-glass panel made no sound, but she knew it was her husband. Reiko had never known the bolt on the sliding door to be so stiff. Still it resisted. The door just would not open.

In a moment, almost before she knew she had succeeded, the lieutenant was standing before her on the cement floor inside the porch, muffled in a khaki greatcoat, his top boots heavy with slush from the street. Closing the door behind him, he returned the bolt once more to its socket. With what significance, Reiko did not understand.

"Welcome home."

Reiko bowed deeply, but her husband made no response. As he had already unfastened his sword and was about to remove his greatcoat, Reiko moved around behind to assist. The coat, which was cold and damp and had lost the odor of horse dung it normally exuded when exposed to the sun, weighed heavily upon her arm. Draping it across a hanger, and cradling the sword and leather belt in her sleeves, she waited while her husband removed his top boots and then followed behind him into the "living room." This was the six-mat room downstairs.

Seen in the clear light from the lamp, her husband's face, covered with a heavy growth of bristle, was almost unrecognizably wasted and thin. The cheeks were hollow, their luster and resilience gone. In his normal good spirits he would have changed into old clothes as soon as he was home and have pressed her to get supper at once, but now he sat before the table still in his uniform, his head drooping dejectedly. Reiko refrained from asking whether she should prepare the supper.

After an interval the lieutenant spoke.

"I knew nothing. They hadn't asked me to join. Perhaps out of consideration, because I was newly married. Kanō, and Homma too, and Yamaguchi."

Reiko recalled momentarily the faces of high-spirited young officers, friends of her husband, who had come to the house occasionally as guests.

"There may be an Imperial ordinance sent down tomorrow. They'll be posted as rebels, I imagine. I shall be in command of a unit with orders to attack them. . . . I can't do it. It's impossible to do a thing like that."

He spoke again.

"They've taken me off guard duty, and I have permission to return home for one night. Tomorrow morning, without question, I must leave to join the attack. I can't do it, Reiko."

Reiko sat erect with lowered eyes. She understood clearly that her husband had spoken of his death. The lieutenant was resolved. Each word, being rooted in death, emerged sharply and with powerful significance against this dark, unmovable background. Although the lieutenant was speaking of his dilemma, already there was no room in his mind for vacillation.

However, there was a clarity, like the clarity of a stream fed from melting snows, in the silence which rested between them. Sitting in his own home after the long two-day ordeal, and looking across at the face of his beautiful wife, the lieutenant was for the first time experiencing true peace of mind. For he had at once known, though she said nothing, that his wife divined the resolve which lay beneath his words.

"Well, then . . ." The lieutenant's eyes opened wide. Despite his exhaustion they were strong and clear, and now for the first time they looked straight into the eyes of his wife. "Tonight I shall cut my stomach."

Reiko did not flinch.

Her round eyes showed tension, as taut as the clang of a bell.

"I am ready," she said. "I ask permission to accompany you."

The lieutenant felt almost mesmerized by the strength in those eyes. His words flowed swiftly and easily, like the utterances of a man in delirium, and it was beyond his understanding how permission in a matter of such weight could be expressed so casually.

"Good. We'll go together. But I want you as a witness, first, for my own suicide. Agreed?"

When this was said a sudden release of abundant happiness welled up in both their hearts. Reiko was deeply affected by the greatness of her husband's trust in her. It was vital for the lieutenant, whatever else might happen, that there should be no irregularity in his death. For that reason there had to be a witness. The fact that he had chosen his wife for this was the first mark of his trust. The second, and even greater, mark was that though he had pledged that they should die together he did not intend to kill his wife first—he had deferred her death to a time when he would no longer be there to verify it. If the lieutenant had been a suspicious husband, he would doubtless, as in the usual suicide pact, have chosen to kill his wife first.

When Reiko said, "I ask permission to accompany you," the lieutenant felt these words to be the final fruit of the education which he had himself given his wife, starting on the first night of their marriage, and which had schooled her, when the moment came, to say what had to be said without a shadow of hesitation. This flattered the lieutenant's opinion of himself as a self-reliant man. He was not so romantic or conceited as to imagine that the words were spoken spontaneously, out of love for her husband.

With happiness welling almost too abundantly in their hearts, they could not help smiling at each other. Reiko felt as if she had returned to her wedding night.

Before her eyes was neither pain nor death. She seemed to see only a free and limitless expanse opening out into vast distances.

"The water is hot. Will you take your bath now?"

"Ah yes, of course."

"And supper . . . ?"

The words were delivered in such level, domestic tones that the lieutenant came near to thinking, for the fraction of a second, that everything had been a hallucination.

"I don't think we'll need supper. But perhaps you could warm some sake?"

"As you wish."

As Reiko rose and took a *tanzen* gown from the cabinet for after the bath, she purposely directed her husband's attention to the opened drawer. The lieutenant rose, crossed to the cabinet, and looked inside. From the ordered array of paper wrappings he read, one by one, the addresses of the keepsakes. There was no grief in the lieutenant's response to this demonstration of heroic resolve. His heart was filled with tenderness. Like a husband who is proudly shown the childish purchases of a young wife, the lieutenant, overwhelmed by affection, lovingly embraced his wife from behind and implanted a kiss upon her neck.

Reiko felt the roughness of the lieutenant's unshaven skin against her neck. This sensation, more than being just a thing of this world, was for Reiko almost the world itself, but now—with the feeling that it was soon to be lost forever—it had freshness beyond all her experience. Each moment had its own vital strength, and the senses in every corner of her body were reawakened. Accepting her husband's caresses from behind, Reiko raised herself on the tips of her toes, letting the vitality seep through her entire body.

"First the bath, and then, after some sake . . . lay out the bedding upstairs, will you?"

The lieutenant whispered the words into his wife's ear. Reiko silently nodded.

Flinging off his uniform, the lieutenant went to the bath. To faint background noises of slopping water Reiko tended the charcoal brazier in the living room and began the preparations for warming the sake.

Taking the *tanzen*, a sash, and some underclothes, she went to the bathroom to ask how the water was. In the midst of a coiling cloud of steam the lieutenant was sitting cross-legged on the floor, shaving, and she could dimly discern the rippling movements of the muscles on his damp, powerful back as they responded to the movement of his arms.

There was nothing to suggest a time of any special significance. Reiko, going busily about her tasks, was preparing side dishes from odds and ends in stock. Her hands did not tremble. If anything, she managed even more efficiently and smoothly than usual. From time to time, it is true, there was a strange throbbing deep within her breast. Like distant lightning, it had a moment of sharp intensity and then vanished without trace. Apart from that, nothing was in any way out of the ordinary.

The lieutenant, shaving in the bathroom, felt his warmed body miraculously healed at last of the desperate tiredness of the days of indecision and filled—in spite of the death which lay ahead—with pleasurable anticipation. The sound of his wife going about her work came to him faintly. A healthy physical craving, submerged for two days, reasserted itself.

The lieutenant was confident there had been no impurity in that joy they had experienced when resolving upon death. They had both sensed at that moment—though not, of course, in any clear and conscious way—that those permissible pleasures which they shared in private were once more beneath the protection of Righteousness and Divine Power, and of a complete and unassailable morality. On looking into each other's eyes and discovering there an honorable death, they had felt themselves safe once more behind steel walls which none could destroy, encased in an impenetrable armor of Beauty and Truth. Thus, so far from seeing any inconsistency or conflict between the urges of his flesh and the sincerity of his patriotism, the lieutenant was even able to regard the two as parts of the same thing.

Thrusting his face close to the dark, cracked, misted wall mirror, the lieutenant shaved himself with great care. This would be his death face. There must be no unsightly blemishes. The clean-shaven face gleamed once more with a youthful luster, seeming to brighten the darkness of the mirror. There was a certain elegance, he even felt, in the association of death with this radiantly healthy face.

Just as it looked now, this would become his death face! Already, in fact, it had half departed from the lieutenant's personal possession and had become the bust above a dead soldier's memorial. As an experiment he closed his eyes tight. Everything was wrapped in blackness, and he was no longer a living, seeing creature.

Returning from the bath, the traces of the shave glowing faintly blue beneath his smooth cheeks, he seated himself beside the now well-kindled charcoal brazier. Busy though Reiko was, he noticed, she had found time lightly to touch up her face. Her cheeks were gay and her lips moist. There was no shadow of sadness to be seen. Truly, the lieutenant felt, as he saw this mark of his young wife's passionate nature, he had chosen the wife he ought to have chosen.

As soon as the lieutenant had drained his sake cup he offered it to Reiko. Reiko had never before tasted sake, but she accepted without hesitation and sipped timidly.

"Come here," the lieutenant said.

Reiko moved to her husband's side and was embraced as she leaned backward across his lap. Her breast was in violent commotion, as if sadness, joy, and the potent sake were mingling and reacting within her. The lieutenant looked down into his wife's face. It was the last face he would see in this world, the last face he would see of his wife. The lieutenant scrutinized the face minutely, with the eyes of a traveler bidding farewell to splendid vistas which he will never revisit. It was a face he could not tire of looking at—the features regular yet not cold, the lips lightly closed with a soft strength. The lieutenant kissed those lips, unthinkingly. And suddenly, though there was not the slightest distortion of the face into the unsightliness of sobbing, he noticed that tears were welling slowly from beneath the long lashes of the closed eyes and brimming over into a glistening stream.

When, a little later, the lieutenant urged that they should move to the upstairs bedroom, his wife replied that she would follow after taking a bath. Climbing the stairs alone to the bedroom, where the air was already warmed by the gas heater, the lieutenant lay down on the bedding with arms outstretched and legs apart. Even the time at which he lay waiting for his wife to join him was no later and no earlier than usual.

He folded his hands beneath his head and gazed at the dark boards of the ceiling in the dimness beyond the range of the standard lamp. Was it death he was now waiting for? Or a wild ecstasy of the senses? The two seemed to overlap, almost as if the object of this bodily desire was death itself. But, however that might be, it was certain that never before had the lieutenant tasted such total freedom.

There was the sound of a car outside the window. He could hear the screech of its tires skidding in the snow piled at the side of the street. The sound of its horn re-echoed from near-by walls. . . . Listening to these noises he had the feeling that this house rose like a solitary island in the ocean of a society going as restlessly about its business as ever. All around, vastly and untidily, stretched the country for which he grieved. He was to give his life for it. But would that great country, with which he was prepared to remonstrate to the extent of destroying himself, take the slightest heed of his death? He did not know; and it did not matter. His was a battlefield without glory, a battlefield where none could display deeds of valor: it was the front line of the spirit.

Reiko's footsteps sounded on the stairway. The steep stairs in this old house creaked badly. There were fond memories in that creaking, and many a time, while waiting in bed, the lieutenant had listened to its welcome sound. At the thought that he would hear it no more he listened with intense concentration, striving for every corner of every moment of this precious time to be filled with the sound of those soft footfalls on the creaking stairway. The moments seemed transformed to jewels, sparkling with inner light.

Reiko wore a Nagoya sash about the waist of her *yukata*, but as the lieutenant reached toward it, its redness sobered by the dimness of the light, Reiko's hand moved to his assistance and the sash fell away, slithering swiftly to the floor. As she stood before him, still in her *yukata*, the lieutenant inserted his hands through the side slits beneath each sleeve, intending to embrace her as she was; but at the touch of his finger tips upon the warm naked flesh, and as the armpits closed gently about his hands, his whole body was suddenly aflame.

In a few moments the two lay naked before the glowing gas heater.

Neither spoke the thought, but their hearts, their bodies, and their pounding breasts blazed with the knowledge that this was the very last time. It was as if the words "The Last Time" were spelled out, in invisible brushstrokes, across every inch of their bodies.

The lieutenant drew his wife close and kissed her vehemently. As their tongues explored each other's mouths, reaching out into the smooth, moist interior, they felt as if the still-unknown agonies of death had tempered their senses to the keenness of red-hot steel. The agonies they could not yet feel, the distant pains of death, had refined their awareness of pleasure.

"This is the last time I shall see your body," said the lieutenant. "Let me look at it closely." And, tilting the shade on the lampstand to one side, he directed the rays along the full length of Reiko's outstretched form.

Reiko lay still with her eyes closed. The light from the low lamp clearly revealed the majestic sweep of her white flesh. The lieutenant, not without a touch of egocentricity, rejoiced that he would never see this beauty crumble in death.

At his leisure, the lieutenant allowed the unforgettable spectacle to engrave itself upon his mind. With one hand he fondled the hair, with the other he softly stroked the magnificent face, implanting kisses here and there where his eyes lingered. The quiet coldness of the high, tapering forehead, the closed eyes with their long lashes beneath faintly etched brows, the set of the finely shaped nose, the gleam of teeth glimpsed between full, regular lips, the soft cheeks and the small, wise chin . . . these things conjured up in the lieutenant's mind the vision of a truly radiant death face, and again and again he pressed his lips tight against the white throat—where Reiko's own hand was soon to strike—and the throat reddened faintly beneath his kisses. Returning to the mouth he laid his lips against it with the gentlest of pressures, and moved them rhythmically over Reiko's with the light rolling motion of a small boat. If he closed his eyes, the world became a rocking cradle.

Wherever the lieutenant's eyes moved his lips faithfully followed. The high, swelling breasts, surmounted by nipples like the buds of a wild cherry, hardened as the lieutenant's lips closed about them. The arms flowed smoothly downward from each side of the breast, tapering toward the wrists, yet losing nothing of their roundness or symmetry, and at their tips were those delicate fingers which had held the fan at the wedding ceremony. One by one, as the lieutenant kissed them, the fingers withdrew behind their neighbor as if in shame. . . . The natural hollow curving between the bosom and the stomach carried in its lines a suggestion not only of softness but of resilient strength, and while it gave forewarning of the rich curves spreading outward from here to the hips it had, in itself, an appearance only of restraint and proper discipline. The whiteness and richness of the stomach and hips was like milk brimming in a great bowl, and the sharply shadowed dip of the navel could have been the fresh impress of a raindrop, fallen there that very moment. Where the shadows gathered more thickly, hair clustered, gentle and sensitive, and as the agitation mounted in the now no longer passive body there hung over this region a scent like the smoldering of fragrant blossoms, growing steadily more pervasive.

At length, in a tremulous voice, Reiko spoke.

"Show me. . . . Let me look too, for the last time."

Never before had he heard from his wife's lips so strong and unequivocal a request. It was as if something which her modesty had wished to keep hidden to the end had suddenly burst its bonds of constraint. The lieutenant obediently lay back and surrendered himself to his wife. Lithely she raised her white, trembling body, and—burning with an innocent desire to return to her husband what he had done for her—placed two white fingers on the lieutenant's eyes, which gazed fixedly up at her, and gently stroked them shut.

Suddenly overwhelmed by tenderness, her cheeks flushed by a dizzying uprush of emotion, Reiko threw her arms about the lieutenant's close-cropped head. The bristly hairs rubbed painfully against her breast, the prominent nose was cold as it dug into her flesh, and his breath was hot. Relaxing her embrace, she gazed down at her husband's masculine face. The severe brows, the closed eyes, the splendid bridge of the nose, the shapely lips drawn firmly together . . . the blue, clean-shaven cheeks reflecting the light and gleaming smoothly. Reiko kissed each of these. She kissed the broad nape of the neck, the strong, erect shoulders, the powerful chest with its twin circles like shields and its russet nipples. In the armpits, deeply shadowed by the ample flesh of the shoulders and chest, a sweet and melancholy odor emanated from the growth of hair, and in the sweetness of this odor was contained, somehow, the essence of young death. The lieutenant's naked skin glowed like a field of barley, and everywhere the muscles showed in sharp relief, converging on the lower abdomen about the small, unassuming navel. Gazing at the youthful, firm stomach, modestly covered by a vigorous growth of hair, Reiko thought of it as it was soon to be, cruelly cut by the sword, and she laid her head upon it, sobbing in pity, and bathed it with kisses.

At the touch of his wife's tears upon his stomach the lieutenant felt ready to endure with courage the cruelest agonies of his suicide.

What ecstasies they experienced after these tender exchanges may well be imagined. The lieutenant raised himself and enfolded his wife in a powerful embrace, her body now limp with exhaustion after her grief and tears. Passionately they held their faces close, rubbing cheek against cheek. Reiko's body was trembling. Their breasts, moist with sweat, were tightly joined, and every inch of the young and beautiful bodies had become so much one with the other that it seemed impossible there should ever again be a separation. Reiko cried out. From the heights they plunged into the abyss, and from the abyss they took wing and soared once more to dizzying heights. The lieutenant panted like the regimental standard-bearer on a route march. . . . As one cycle ended, almost immediately a new wave of passion would be generated, and together—with no trace of fatigue—they would climb again in a single breathless movement to the very summit.

4

When the lieutenant at last turned away, it was not from weariness. For one thing, he was anxious not to undermine the considerable strength he would need in carrying out his suicide. For another, he would have been sorry to mar the sweetness of these last memories by overindulgence.

Since the lieutenant had clearly desisted, Reiko too, with her usual compliance, followed his example. The two lay naked on their backs, with fingers interlaced, staring fixedly at the dark ceiling. The room was warm from the heater, and even when the sweat had ceased to pour from their bodies they felt no cold. Outside, in the hushed night, the sounds of passing traffic had ceased. Even the noises of the trains and streetcars around Yotsuya station did not penetrate this far. After echoing through the region bounded by the moat, they were lost in the heavily wooded park fronting the broad driveway before Akasaka Palace. It was hard to believe in the tension gripping this whole quarter, where the two factions of the bitterly divided Imperial Army now confronted each other, poised for battle.

Savoring the warmth glowing within themselves, they lay still and recalled the ecstasies they had just known. Each moment of the experience was relived. They remembered the taste of kisses which had never wearied, the touch of naked flesh, episode after episode of dizzying bliss. But already, from the dark boards of the ceiling, the face of death was peering down. These joys had been final, and their bodies would never know them again. Not that joy of this intensity—and the same thought had occurred to them both—was ever likely to be reexperienced, even if they should live on to old age.

The feel of their fingers intertwined—this too would soon be lost. Even the wood-grain patterns they now gazed at on the dark ceiling boards would be taken from them. They could feel death edging in, nearer and nearer. There could be no hesitation now. They must have the courage to reach out to death themselves, and to seize it.

"Well, let's make our preparations," said the lieutenant. The note of determination in the words was unmistakable, but at the same time Reiko had never heard her husband's voice so warm and tender.

After they had risen, a variety of tasks awaited them.

The lieutenant, who had never once before helped with the bedding, now cheerfully slid back the door of the closet, lifted the mattress across the room by himself, and stowed it away inside.

Reiko turned off the gas heater and put away the lamp standard. During the lieutenant's absence she had arranged this room carefully, sweeping and dusting it to a fresh cleanness, and now—if one overlooked the rosewood table drawn into one corner—the eight-mat room gave all the appearance of a reception room ready to welcome an important guest.

"We've seen some drinking here, haven't we? With Kanō and Homma and Noguchi . . ."

"Yes, they were great drinkers, all of them."

"We'll be meeting them before long, in the other world. They'll tease us, I imagine, when they find I've brought you with me."

Descending the stairs, the lieutenant turned to look back into this calm, clean room, now brightly illuminated by the ceiling lamp. There floated across his mind the faces of the young officers who had drunk there, and laughed, and innocently bragged. He had never dreamed then that he would one day cut open his stomach in this room.

In the two rooms downstairs husband and wife busied themselves smoothly and serenely with their respective preparations. The lieutenant went to the toilet, and then to the bathroom to wash. Meanwhile Reiko folded away her husband's padded robe, placed his uniform tunic, his trousers, and a newly cut bleached loincloth in the bathroom, and set out sheets of paper on the living room table for the farewell notes. Then she removed the lid from the writing box and began rubbing ink from the ink tablet. She had already decided upon the wording of her own note.

Reiko's fingers pressed hard upon the cold gilt letters of the ink tablet, and the water in the shallow well at once darkened, as if a black cloud had spread across it. She stopped thinking that this repeated action, this pressure from her fingers, this rise and fall of faint sound, was all and solely for death. It was a routine domestic task, a simple paring away of time until death should finally stand before her. But somehow, in the increasingly smooth motion of the tablet rubbing on the stone, and in the scent from the thickening ink, there was unspeakable darkness.

Neat in his uniform, which he now wore next to his skin, the lieutenant emerged from the bathroom. Without a word he seated himself at the table, bolt upright, took a brush in his hand, and stared undecidedly at the paper before him.

Reiko took a white silk kimono with her and entered the bathroom. When she reappeared in the living room, clad in the white kimono and with her face lightly made up, the farewell note lay completed on the table beneath the lamp. The thick black brushstrokes said simply:

"Long Live the Imperial Forces—Army Lieutenant Takeyama Shinji."

While Reiko sat opposite him writing her own note, the lieutenant gazed in silence, intensely serious, at the controlled movement of his wife's pale fingers as they manipulated the brush.

With their respective notes in their hands—the lieutenant's sword strapped to his side, Reiko's small dagger thrust into the sash of her white kimono—the two of them stood before the god shelf and silently prayed. Then they put out all the downstairs lights. As he mounted the stairs the lieutenant turned his head and gazed back at the striking, white-clad figure of his wife, climbing behind him, with lowered eyes, from the darkness beneath.

The farewell notes were laid side by side in the alcove of the upstairs room.

They wondered whether they ought not to remove the hanging scroll, but since it had been written by their go-between, Lieutenant General Ozeki, and consisted, moreover, of two Chinese characters signifying "Sincerity," they left it where it was. Even if it were to become stained with splashes of blood, they felt that the lieutenant general would understand.

The lieutenant, sitting erect with his back to the alcove, laid his sword on the floor before him.

Reiko sat facing him, a mat's width away. With the rest of her so severely white the touch of rouge on her lips seemed remarkably seductive.

Across the dividing mat they gazed intently into each other's eyes. The lieutenant's sword lay before his knees. Seeing it, Reiko recalled their first night and was overwhelmed with sadness. The lieutenant spoke, in a hoarse voice:

"As I have no second to help me I shall cut deep. It may look unpleasant, but please do not panic. Death of any sort is a fearful thing to watch. You must not be discouraged by what you see. Is that all right?"

"Yes."

Reiko nodded deeply.

Looking at the slender white figure of his wife the lieutenant experienced a bizarre excitement. What he was about to perform was an act in his public capacity as a soldier, something he had never previously shown his wife. It called for a resolution equal to the courage to enter battle; it was a death of no less degree and quality than death in the front line. It was his conduct on the battlefield that he was now to display.

Momentarily the thought led the lieutenant to a strange fantasy. A lonely death on the battlefield, a death beneath the eyes of his beautiful wife . . . in the sensation that he was now to die in these two dimensions, realizing an impossible union of them both, there was sweetness beyond words. This must be the very pinnacle of good fortune, he thought. To have every moment of his death observed by those beautiful eyes—it was like being borne to death on a gentle, fragrant breeze. There was some special favor here. He did not understand precisely what it was, but it was a domain unknown to others; a dispensation granted to no one else had been permitted to himself. In the radiant, bridelike figure of his white-robed wife the lieutenant seemed to see a vision of all those things he had loved and for which he was to lay down his life—the Imperial Household, the Nation, the Army Flag. All these, no less than the wife who sat before him, were presences observing him closely with clear and never-faltering eyes.

Reiko too was gazing intently at her husband, so soon to die, and she thought that never in this world had she seen anything so beautiful. The lieutenant always looked well in uniform, but now, as he contemplated death with severe brows and firmly closed lips, he revealed what was perhaps masculine beauty at its most superb.

"It's time to go," the lieutenant said at last.

Reiko bent her body low to the mat in a deep bow. She could not raise her face. She did not wish to spoil her make-up with tears, but the tears could not be held back.

When at length she looked up she saw hazily through the tears that her husband had wound a white bandage around the blade of his now unsheathed sword, leaving five or six inches of naked steel showing at the point.

Resting the sword in its cloth wrapping on the mat before him, the lieutenant rose from his knees, resettled himself cross-legged, and unfastened the hooks of his uniform collar. His eyes no longer saw his wife. Slowly, one by one, he undid the flat brass buttons. The dusky brown chest was revealed, and then the stomach. He unclasped his belt and undid the buttons of his trousers. The pure whiteness of the thickly coiled loincloth showed itself. The lieutenant pushed the cloth down with both hands, further to ease his stomach, and then reached for the white-bandaged blade of his sword. With his left hand he massaged his abdomen, glancing downward as he did so.

To reassure himself on the sharpness of his sword's cutting edge the lieutenant folded back the left trouser flap, exposing a little of his thigh, and lightly drew the blade across the skin. Blood welled up in the wound at once, and several streaks of red trickled downward, glistening in the strong light.

It was the first time Reiko had ever seen her husband's blood, and she felt a violent throbbing in her chest. She looked at her husband's face. The lieutenant was looking at the blood with calm appraisal. For a moment—though thinking at the same time that it was hollow comfort—Reiko experienced a sense of relief.

The lieutenant's eyes fixed his wife with an intense, hawk-like stare. Moving the sword around to his front, he raised himself slightly on his hips and let the upper half of his body lean over the sword point. That he was mustering his whole strength was apparent from the angry tension of the uniform at his shoulders. The lieutenant aimed to strike deep into the left of his stomach. His sharp cry pierced the silence of the room.

Despite the effort he had himself put into the blow, the lieutenant had the impression that someone else had struck the side of his stomach agonizingly with a thick rod of iron. For a second or so his head reeled and he had no idea what had happened. The five or six inches of naked point had vanished completely into his flesh, and the white bandage, gripped in his clenched fist, pressed directly against his stomach.

He returned to consciousness. The blade had certainly pierced the wall of the stomach, he thought. His breathing was difficult, his chest thumped violently, and in some far deep region, which he could hardly believe was a part of himself, a fearful and excruciating pain came welling up as if the ground had split open to disgorge a boiling stream of molten rock. The pain came suddenly nearer, with terrifying speed. The lieutenant bit his lower lip and stifled an instinctive moan.

Was this *seppuku*?—he was thinking. It was a sensation of utter chaos, as if the sky had fallen on his head and the world was reeling drunkenly. His will power and courage, which had seemed so robust before he made the incision, had now dwindled to something like a single hairlike thread of steel, and he was assailed by the uneasy feeling that he must advance along this thread, clinging to it with desperation. His clenched fist had grown moist. Looking down, he saw that both his hand and the cloth about the blade were drenched in blood. His loincloth too was dyed a deep red. It struck him as incredible that, amidst this terrible agony, things which could be seen could still be seen, and existing things existed still.

The moment the lieutenant thrust the sword into his left side and she saw the deathly pallor fall across his face, like an abruptly lowered curtain, Reiko had to struggle to prevent herself from rushing to his side. Whatever happened, she must watch. She must be a witness. That was the duty her husband had laid upon her. Opposite her, a mat's space away, she could clearly see her husband biting his lip to stifle the pain. The pain was there, with absolute certainty, before her eyes. And Reiko had no means of rescuing him from it.

The sweat glistened on her husband's forehead. The lieutenant closed his eyes, and then opened them again, as if experimenting. The eyes had lost their luster, and seemed innocent and empty like the eyes of a small animal.

The agony before Reiko's eyes burned as strong as the summer sun, utterly remote from the grief which seemed to be tearing herself apart within. The pain resolved into pain, a prisoner in a cage of pain where no hand could reach out to him. But Reiko felt no pain at all. Her grief was not pain. As she thought about this, Reiko began to feel as if someone had raised a cruel wall of glass high between herself and her husband.

Ever since her marriage her husband's existence had been her own existence, and every breath of his had been a breath drawn by herself. But now, while her husband's existence in pain was a vivid reality, Reiko could find in this grief of hers no certain proof at all of her own existence.

With only his right hand on the sword the lieutenant began to cut sideways across his stomach. But as the blade became entangled with the entrails it was pushed constantly outward by their soft resilience; and the lieutenant realized that it would be necessary, as he cut, to use both hands to keep the point pressed deep into his stomach. He pulled the blade across. It did not cut as easily as he had expected. He directed the strength of his whole body into his right hand and pulled again. There was a cut of three or four inches.

The pain spread slowly outward from the inner depths until the whole stomach reverberated. It was like the wild clanging of a bell. Or like a thousand bells which jangled simultaneously at every breath he breathed and every throb of his pulse, rocking his whole being. The lieutenant could no longer stop himself from moaning. But by now the blade had cut its way through to below the navel, and when he noticed this he felt a sense of satisfaction, and a renewal of courage.

The volume of blood had steadily increased, and now it spurted from the wound as if propelled by the beat of the pulse. The mat before the lieutenant was drenched red with splattered blood, and more blood overflowed onto it from pools which gathered in the folds of the lieutenant's khaki trousers. A spot, like a bird, came flying across to Reiko and settled on the lap of her white silk kimono.

By the time the lieutenant had at last drawn the sword across to the right side of his stomach, the blade was already cutting shallow and had revealed its naked tip, slippery with blood and grease. But, suddenly stricken by a fit of vomiting, the lieutenant cried out hoarsely. The vomiting made the fierce pain fiercer still, and the stomach, which had thus far remained firm and compact, now abruptly heaved, opening wide its wound, and the entrails burst through, as if the wound too were vomiting. Seemingly ignorant of their master's suffering, the entrails gave an impression of robust health and almost disagreeable vitality as they slipped smoothly out and spilled over into the crotch. The lieutenant's head drooped, his shoulders heaved, his eyes opened to narrow slits, and a thin trickle of saliva dribbled from his mouth. The gold markings on his epaulettes caught the light and glinted.

Blood was scattered everywhere. The lieutenant was soaked in it to his knees, and he sat now in a crumpled and listless posture, one hand on the floor. A raw smell filled the room. The lieutenant, his head drooping, retched repeatedly, and the movement showed vividly in his shoulders. The blade of the sword, now pushed back by the entrails and exposed to its tip, was still in the lieutenant's right hand.

It would be difficult to imagine a more heroic sight than that of the lieutenant at this moment, as he mustered his strength and flung back his head. The move-ment was performed with sudden violence, and the back of his head struck with a sharp crack against the alcove pillar. Reiko had been sitting until now with her face lowered, gazing in fascination at the tide of blood advancing toward her knees, but the sound took her by surprise and she looked up.

The lieutenant's face was not the face of a living man. The eyes were hollow, the skin parched, the once so lustrous cheeks and lips the color of dried mud. The right hand alone was moving. Laboriously gripping the sword, it hovered shakily in the air like the hand of a marionette and strove to direct the point at the base of the lieutenant's throat. Reiko watched her husband make this last, most heart-rending, futile exertion. Glistening with blood and grease, the point was thrust at the throat again and again. And each time it missed its aim. The strength to guide it was no longer there. The straying point struck the collar and the collar badges. Although its hooks had been unfastened, the stiff military collar had closed together again and was protecting the throat.

Reiko could bear the sight no longer. She tried to go to her husband's help, but she could not stand. She moved through the blood on her knees, and her white skirts grew deep red. Moving to the rear of her husband, she helped no more than by loosening the collar. The quivering blade at last contacted the naked flesh of the throat. At that moment Reiko's impression was that she herself had propelled her husband forward; but that was not the case. It was a movement planned by the lieutenant himself, his last exertion of strength. Abruptly he threw his body at the blade, and the blade pierced his neck, emerging at the nape. There was a tremendous spurt of blood and the lieutenant lay still, cold blue-tinged steel protruding from his neck at the back.

5

Slowly, her socks slippery with blood, Reiko descended the stairway. The upstairs room was now completely still.

Switching on the ground-floor lights, she checked the gas jet and the main gas plug and poured water over the smoldering, half-buried charcoal in the brazier. She stood before the upright mirror in the four-and-a-half-mat room and held up her skirts. The bloodstains made it seem as if a bold, vivid pattern was printed across the lower half of her white kimono. When she sat down before the mirror, she was conscious of the dampness and coldness of her husband's blood in the region of her thighs, and she shivered. Then, for a long while, she lingered over her toilet preparations. She applied the rouge generously to her cheeks, and her lips too she painted heavily. This was no longer make-up to please her husband. It was make-up for the world which she would leave behind, and there was a touch of the magnificent and the spectacular in her brushwork. When she rose, the mat before the mirror was wet with blood. Reiko was not concerned about this.

Returning from the toilet, Reiko stood finally on the cement floor of the porchway. When her husband had bolted the door here last night it had been in preparation for death. For a while she stood immersed in the consideration of a simple problem. Should she now leave the bolt drawn? If she were to lock the door, it could be that the neighbors might not notice their suicide for several days. Reiko did not relish the thought of their two corpses putrifying before discovery. After all, it seemed, it would be best to leave it open. . . . She released the bolt, and also drew open the frosted-glass door a fraction. . . . At once a chill wind blew in. There was no sign of anyone in the midnight streets, and stars glittered ice-cold through the trees in the large house opposite.

Leaving the door as it was, Reiko mounted the stairs. She had walked here and there for some time and her socks were no longer slippery. About halfway up, her nostrils were already assailed by a peculiar smell.

The lieutenant was lying on his face in a sea of blood. The point protruding from his neck seemed to have grown even more prominent than before. Reiko walked heedlessly across the blood. Sitting beside the lieutenant's corpse, she stared intently at the face, which lay on one cheek on the mat. The eyes were opened wide, as if the lieutenant's attention had been attracted by something. She raised the head, folding it in her sleeve, wiped the blood from the lips, and bestowed a last kiss.

Then she rose and took from the closet a new white blanket and a waist cord. To prevent any derangement of her skirts, she wrapped the blanket about her waist and bound it there firmly with the cord.

399

Reiko sat herself on a spot about one foot distant from the lieutenant's body. Drawing the dagger from her sash, she examined its dully gleaming blade intently, and held it to her tongue. The taste of the polished steel was slightly sweet.

Reiko did not linger. When she thought how the pain which had previously opened such a gulf between herself and her dying husband was now to become a part of her own experience, she saw before her only the joy of herself entering a realm her husband had already made his own. In her husband's agonized face there had been something inexplicable which she was seeing for the first time. Now she would solve that riddle. Reiko sensed that at last she too would be able to taste the true bitterness and sweetness of that great moral principle in which her husband believed. What had until now been tasted only faintly through her husband's example she was about to savor directly with her own tongue.

Reiko rested the point of the blade against the base of her throat. She thrust hard. The wound was only shallow. Her head blazed, and her hands shook uncontrollably. She gave the blade a strong pull sideways. A warm substance flooded into her mouth, and everything before her eyes reddened, in a vision of spouting blood. She gathered her strength and plunged the point of the blade deep into her throat.

VLADIMIR NABOKOV

(1899–1977)

VLADIMIR NABOKOV was born in St. Petersburg to a Russian aristocratic family. After the Russian Revolution the family emigrated to Germany, while Nabokov went on to England to study. He had by this time already published a small book of poems. He graduated from Trinity College, Cambridge, in 1922. Returning to Berlin in 1923, he began writing, in Russian, under the pen name V. Sirin. In 1937 Nabokov left Berlin for Paris, and in 1940 he emigrated to the United States where, from 1948 to 1959, he was a professor of Russian literature at Cornell University. In 1959 he and his wife moved to Montreux, Switzerland, where he remained until his death.

His work is notable for its intricacy and intensity of focus; its opulent language, dense with allusion and word play; the breadth of his intellectual and philosophic concerns, including the preoccupation with time and memory. *Lolita* (1958), his best-known novel (which contributed the word *nymphet* to the language), follows a European intellectual's obsessive pursuit from motel to motel of a seductive twelve-year-old American girl; at the time of its publication, it was viewed as scandalous. Nabokov's other titles include *The Real Life of Sebastian Knight* (1938), his first book in English; *Ada or Ardor: A Family Chronicle* (1969); *Bend Sinister* (1947); and *Pnin* (1957). He was also the author of short stories, poetry, critical works, and memoir, of which perhaps the best known is *Speak, Memory* (1966). Nabokov received numerous literary awards, including two Guggenheim fellowships. He was also an internationally known lepidopterist; butterflies and moths are netted as well in his narratives.

"First Love" (1958) is told through the prism of memory. The narrator is ten years old when he falls in love with the "little French girl, Colette." Their meeting on the beach in Biarritz is preceded by an indelibly rendered account of a train ride, which has the limitlessly refracted, curving character of life itself.

First Love

1

In the early years of this century, a travel agency on Nevski Avenue displayed a three-foot-long model of an oak-brown international sleeping car. In delicate verisimilitude it completely outranked the painted tin of my clockwork trains. Unfortunately it was not for sale. One could make out the blue upholstery inside, the embossed leather lining of the compartment walls, their polished panels, inset mirrors, tulip-shaped reading lamps, and other maddening details. Spacious windows alternated with narrower ones, single or geminate, and some of these were of frosted glass. In a few of the compartments, the beds had been made.

The then great and glamorous Nord Express (it was never the same after World War One when its elegant brown became a nouveau-riche blue), consisting solely of such international cars and running but twice a week, connected St. Petersburg with Paris. I would have said: directly with Paris, had passengers not been obliged to change from one train to a superficially similar one at the Russo-German frontier (Verzhbolovo-Eydtkuhnen), where the ample and lazy Russian sixty-and-a-half-inch gauge was replaced by the fifty-six-and-a-half-inch standard of Europe and coal succeeded birch logs.

In the far end of my mind I can unravel, I think, at least five such journeys to Paris, with the Riviera or Biarritz as their ultimate destination. In 1909, the year I now single out, our party consisted of eleven people and one dachshund. Wearing gloves and a traveling cap, my father sat reading a book in the compartment he shared with our tutor. My brother and I were separated from them by a washroom. My mother and her maid, Natasha, occupied a compartment adjacent to ours. Next came my two small sisters, their English governess, Miss Lavington, and a Russian nurse. The odd one of our party, my father's valet, Osip (whom, a decade later, the pedantic Bolsheviks were to shoot, because he appropriated our bicycles instead of turning them over to the nation), had a stranger for a companion.

Historically and artistically, the year had started with a political cartoon in *Punch:* goddess England bending over goddess Italy, on whose head one of Messina's bricks has landed—probably, the worst picture *any* earthquake has ever inspired. In April of that year, Peary had reached the North Pole. In May, Shalyapin had sung in Paris. In June, bothered by rumors of new and better Zeppelins, the United States War Department had told reporters of plans for an aerial Navy. In July, Blériot had flown from Calais to Dover (with a little additional loop when he lost his bearings). It was late August now. The firs and marshes of Northwestern Russia sped by, and on the following day gave way to German pine-woods and heather.

At a collapsible table, my mother and I played a card game called *durachki.* Although it was still broad daylight, our cards, a glass, and on a different plane the locks of a suitcase were reflected in the window. Through forest and field, and in sudden ravines, and among scuttling cottages, those discarnate gamblers kept steadily playing on for steadily sparkling stakes. It was a long, very long game: on this gray winter morning, in the looking glass of my bright hotel room, I see shining the same, the very same, locks of that now seventy-year-old valise, a highish, heavish *nécessaire de voyage* of pigskin, with "H.N." elaborately interwoven in thick silver under a similar coronet, which had been bought in 1897 for my mother's wedding trip to Florence. In 1917 it transported from St. Petersburg to the Crimea and then to London a handful of jewels. Around 1930, it lost to a pawnbroker its expensive receptacles of crystal and silver leaving empty the cunningly contrived leather holders on the inside of the lid. But that loss has been amply recouped during the thirty years it then traveled with me—from Prague to Paris, from St. Nazaire to New York and through the mirrors of more than two hundred motel rooms and rented houses, in forty-six states. The fact that of our Russian heritage the hardiest survivor proved to be a traveling bag is both logical and emblematic.

"*Ne budet-li, tï ved' ustal* [Haven't you had enough, aren't you tired]?" my mother would ask, and then would be lost in thought as she slowly shuffled the cards. The door of the compartment was open and I could see the corridor window, where the wires—six thin black wires—were doing their best to slant up, to ascend skywards, despite the lightning blows dealt them by one telegraph pole after another; but just as all six, in a triumphant swoop of pathetic elation, were about to reach the top of the window, a particularly vicious blow would bring them down, as low as they had ever been, and they would have to start all over again.

When, on such journeys as these, the train changed its pace to a dignified amble and all but grazed housefronts and shop signs, as we passed through some big German town, I used to feel a twofold excitement, which terminal stations could not provide. I saw a city, with its toylike trams, linden trees, and brick walls enter the compartment, hobnob with the mirrors, and fill to the brim the windows on the corridor side. This informal contact between train and city was one part of the thrill. The other was putting myself in the place of some passerby who, I imagined, was moved as I would be moved myself to see the long, romantic, auburn cars, with their intervestibular connecting curtains as black as bat wings and their metal lettering copper-bright in the low sun, unhurriedly negotiate an iron bridge across an everyday thoroughfare and then turn, with all windows suddenly ablaze, around a last block of houses.

There were drawbacks to those optical amalgamations. The wide-windowed dining car, a vista of chaste bottles of mineral water, miter-folded napkins, and dummy chocolate bars (whose wrappers—Cailler, Kohler, and so forth—enclosed nothing but wood), would be perceived at first as a cool haven beyond a consecution of reeling blue corridors; but as the meal progressed toward its fatal last course, and more and more dreadfully one equilibrist with a full tray would back against our table to let another equilibrist pass with another full tray, I would keep catching the car in the act of being recklessly sheathed, lurching waiters and all, in the landscape, while the landscape itself went through a complex system of motion, the day-time moon stubbornly keeping abreast of one's plate, the distant meadows opening fanwise, the near trees sweeping up on invisible swings toward the track, a parallel rail line all at once committing suicide by anastomosis, a bank of nictitating grass rising, rising, rising, until the little witness of mixed velocities was made to disgorge his portion of *omelette aux confitures de fraises*.

It was at night, however, that the *Compagnie Internationale des Wagons-Lits et des Grands Express Européens* lived up to the magic of its name. From my bed under my brother's bunk (Was he asleep? Was he there at all?), in the semidarkness of our compartment, I watched things, and parts of things, and shadows, and sections of shadows cautiously moving about and getting nowhere. The woodwork gently creaked and crackled. Near the door that led to the toilet, a dim garment on a peg and, higher up, the tassel of the blue, bivalved night light swung rhythmically. It was hard to correlate those halting approaches, that hooded stealth, with the headlong rush of the outside night, which I knew *was* rushing by, spark-streaked, illegible.

I would put myself to sleep by the simple act of identifying myself with the engine driver. A sense of drowsy well-being invaded my veins as soon as I had everything nicely arranged—the carefree passengers in their rooms enjoying the ride I was giving them, smoking, exchanging knowing smiles, nodding, dozing; the waiters and cooks and train guards (whom I had to place somewhere) carousing in the diner; and myself, goggled and begrimed, peering out of the engine cab at the tapering track, at the ruby or emerald point in the black distance. And then, in my sleep, I would see something totally different—a glass marble rolling under a grand piano or a toy engine lying on its side with its wheels still working gamely.

A change in the speed of the train sometimes interrupted the current of my sleep. Slow lights were stalking by; each, in passing, investigated the same chink, and then a luminous compass measured the shadows. Presently, the train stopped with a long-drawn Westinghousian sigh. Something (my brother's spectacles, as it proved next day) fell from above. It was marvelously exciting to move to the foot of one's bed, with part of the bedclothes following, in order to undo cautiously the catch of the window shade, which could be made to slide only halfway up, impeded as it was by the edge of the upper berth.

Like moons around Jupiter, pale moths revolved about a lone lamp. A dismembered newspaper stirred on a bench. Somewhere on the train one could hear muffled voices, somebody's comfortable cough. There was nothing particularly interesting in the portion of station platform before me, and still I could not tear myself away from it until it departed of its own accord.

Next morning, wet fields with misshapen willows along the radius of a ditch or a row of poplars afar, traversed by a horizontal band of milky-white mist, told one·that the train was spinning through Belgium. It reached Paris at 4 P.M., and even if the stay was only an overnight one, I had always time to purchase something—say, a little brass *Tour Eiffel*, rather roughly coated with silver paint—before we boarded, at noon on the following day, the Sud-Express, which, on its way to Madrid, dropped us around 10 P.M. at the La Négresse station of Biarritz, a few miles from the Spanish frontier.

2

Biarritz still retained its quiddity in those days. Dusty blackberry bushes and weedy *terrains à vendre* bordered the road that led to our villa. The Carlton was still being built. Some thirty-six years had to elapse before Brigadier General Samuel McCroskey would occupy the royal suite of the Hôtel du Palais, which stands on the site of a former palace, where, in the sixties, that incredibly agile medium, Daniel Home, is said to have been caught stroking with his bare foot (in imitation of a ghost hand) the kind, trustful face of Empress Eugénie. On the promenade near the Casino, an elderly flower girl, with carbon eyebrows and a painted smile, nimbly slipped the plump torus of a carnation into the buttonhole of an intercepted stroller whose left jowl accentuated its royal fold as he glanced down sideways at the coy insertion of the flower.

The rich-hued Oak Eggars questing amid the brush were quite unlike ours (which did not breed on oak, anyway), and here the Speckled Woods haunted not woods, but hedges and had tawny, not pale-yellowish, spots. Cleopatra, a tropical-looking, lemon-and-orange Brimstone, languorously flopping about in gardens, had been a sensation in 1907 and was still a pleasure to net.

Along the back line of the *plage*, various seaside chairs and stools supported the parents of straw-hatted children who were playing in front on the sand. I could be seen on my knees trying to set a found comb aflame by means of a magnifying glass. Men sported white trousers that to the eye of today would look as if they had comically shrunk in the washing; ladies wore, that particular season, light coats with silk-faced lapels, hats with big crowns and wide brims, dense embroidered white veils, frill-fronted blouses, frills at their wrists, frills on their parasols. The breeze salted one's lips. At a tremendous pace a stray Clouded Yellow came dashing across the palpitating *plage*.

Additional movement and sound were provided by venders hawking *cacahuètes*, sugared violets, pistachio ice cream of a heavenly green, cachou pellets, and huge convex pieces of dry, gritty, waferlike stuff that came from a red barrel. With a distinctness that no later superpositions have dimmed, I see that waffleman stomp along through deep mealy sand, with the heavy cask on his bent back. When called, he would sling it off his shoulder by a twist of its strap, bang it down on the sand in a Tower of Pisa position, wipe his face with his sleeve, and proceed to manipulate a kind of arrow-and-dial arrangement with numbers on the lid of the cask. The arrow rasped and whirred around. Luck was supposed to fix the size of a sou's worth of wafer. The bigger the piece, the more I was sorry for him.

The process of bathing took place on another part of the beach. Professional bathers, burly Basques in black bathing suits, were there to help ladies and children enjoy the terrors of the surf. Such a *baigneur* would place the *client* with his back to the incoming wave and hold him by the hand as the rising, rotating mass of foamy, green water violently descended from behind, knocking one off one's feet with one mighty wallop. After a dozen of these tumbles, the *baigneur*, glistening like a seal, would lead his panting, shivering, moistly snuffling charge landward, to the flat foreshore, where an unforgettable old woman with gray hairs on her chin promptly chose a bathing robe from several hanging on a clothesline. In the security of a little cabin, one would be helped by yet another attendant to peel off one's soggy, sand-heavy bathing suit. It would plop onto the boards, and, still shivering, one would step out of it and trample on its bluish, diffuse stripes. The cabin smelled of pine. The attendant, a hunchback with beaming wrinkles, brought a basin of steaming-hot water, in which one immersed one's feet. From him I learned, and have preserved ever since in a glass cell of my memory, that "butterfly" in the Basque language is *misericoletea*—or at least it sounded so (among the seven words I have found in dictionaries the closest approach is *micheletea*).

3

On the browner and wetter part of the *plage*, that part which at low tide yielded the best mud for castles, I found myself digging, one day, side by side with a little French girl called Colette.

She would be ten in November, I had been ten in April. Attention was drawn to a jagged bit of violet mussel shell upon which she had stepped with the bare sole of her narrow long-toed foot. No, I was not English. Her greenish eyes seemed flecked with the overflow of the freckles that covered her sharp-featured face. She wore what might now be termed a playsuit, consisting of a blue jersey with rolled-up sleeves and blue knitted shorts. I had taken her at first for a boy and then had been puzzled by the bracelet on her thin wrist and the cork-screw brown curls dangling from under her sailor cap.

She spoke in birdlike bursts of rapid twitter, mixing governess English and Parisian French. Two years before, on the same *plage*, I had been much attached to Zina, the lovely, sun-tanned, bad-tempered little daughter of a Serbian naturopath—she had, I remember (absurdly, for she and I were only eight at the time), a *grain de beauté* on her apricot skin just below the heart, and there was a horrible collection of chamber pots, full and half-full, and one with surface bubbles, on the floor of the hall in her family's boardinghouse lodgings which I visited early one morning to be given by her, as she was being dressed, a dead hummingbird moth found by the cat. But when I met Colette, I knew at once that this was the real thing. Colette seemed to me so much stranger than all my other chance playmates at Biarritz! I somehow acquired the feeling that she was less happy than I, less loved. A bruise on her delicate, downy forearm gave rise to awful conjectures. "He pinches as bad as my mummy," she said, speaking of a crab. I evolved various schemes to save her from her parents, who were *"des bourgeois de Paris"* as I heard somebody tell my mother with a slight shrug. I interpreted the disdain in my own fashion, as I knew that those people had come all the way from Paris in their blue-and-yellow limousine (a fashionable adventure in those days) but had drably sent Colette with her dog and governess by an ordinary coach-train. The dog was a female fox terrier with bells on her collar and a most waggly behind. From sheer exuberance, she would lap up salt water out of Colette's toy pail. I remembered the sail, the sunset, and the lighthouse pictured on that pail, but I cannot recall the dog's name, and this bothers me.

During the two months of our stay at Biarritz, my passion for Colette all but surpassed my passion for Cleopatra. Since my parents were not keen to meet hers, I saw her only on the beach; but I thought of her constantly. If I noticed she had been crying, I felt a surge of helpless anguish that brought tears to my own eyes. I could not destroy the mosquitoes that had left their bites on her frail neck, but I could, and did, have a successful fistfight with a red-haired boy who had been rude to her. She used to give me warm handfuls of hard candy. One day, as we were bending together over a starfish, and Colette's ringlets were tickling my ear, she suddenly turned toward me and kissed me on the cheek. So great was my emotion that all I could think of saying was, "You little monkey."

I had a gold coin that I assumed would pay for our elopement. Where did I want to take her? Spain? America? The mountains above Pau? "*Là-bas, là-bas, dans la montagne*," as I had heard Carmen sing at the opera. One strange night, I lay awake, listening to the recurrent thud of the ocean and planning our flight. The ocean seemed to rise and grope in the darkness and then heavily fall on its face.

Of our actual getaway, I have little to report. My memory retains a glimpse of her obediently putting on rope-soled canvas shoes, on the lee side of a flapping tent, while I stuffed a folding butterfly net into a brown-paper bag. The next glimpse is of our evading pursuit by entering a pitch-dark *cinéma* near the Casino (which, of course, was absolutely out of bounds). There we sat, holding hands across the dog, which now and then gently jingled in Colette's lap, and were shown a jerky, drizzly, but highly exciting bullfight at St. Sebástian. My final glimpse is of myself being led along the promenade by Linderovski. His long legs move with a kind of ominous briskness and I can see the muscles of his grimly set jaw working under the tight skin. My bespectacled brother, aged nine, whom he happens to hold with his other hand, keeps trotting out forward to peer at me with awed curiosity, like a little owl.

Among the trivial souvenirs acquired at Biarritz before leaving, my favorite was not the small bull of black stone and not the sonorous sea shell but something which now seems almost symbolic—a meerschaum penholder with a tiny peephole of crystal in its ornamental part. One held it quite close to one's eye, screwing up the other, and when one had got rid of the shimmer of one's own lashes, a miraculous photographic view of the bay and of the line of cliffs ending in a lighthouse could be seen inside.

And now a delightful thing happens. The process of recreating that penholder and the microcosm in its eyelet stimulates my memory to a last effort. I try again to recall the name of Colette's dog—and, triumphantly, along those remote beaches, over the glassy evening sands of the past, where each footprint slowly fills up with sunset water, here it comes, here it comes, echoing and vibrating: Floss, Floss, Floss!

Colette was back in Paris by the time we stopped there for a day before continuing our homeward journey; and there, in a fawn park under a cold blue sky, I saw her (by arrangement between our mentors, I believe) for the last time. She carried a hoop and a short stick to drive it with, and everything about her was extremely proper and stylish in an autumnal, Parisian, *tenue-de-ville-pour-fillettes* way. She took from her governess and slipped into my brother's hand a farewell present, a box of sugar-coated almonds, meant, I knew, solely for me; and instantly she was off, tap-tapping her glinting hoop through light and shade, around and around a fountain choked with dead leaves, near which I stood. The leaves mingle in my memory with the leather of her shoes and gloves, and there was, I remember, some detail in her attire (perhaps a ribbon on her Scottish cap, or the pattern of her stockings) that reminded me then of the rainbow spiral in a glass marble. I still seem to be holding that wisp of iridescence, not knowing exactly where to fit it, while she runs with her hoop ever faster around me and finally dissolves among the slender shadows cast on the graveled path by the interlaced arches of its low looped fence.

JOHN O'HARA
(1905–1970)

JOHN O'HARA, a physician's son, was born in Pottsville, Pennsylvania, the model for the town O'Hara called Gibbsville, where many of his novels and stories are set—among them, the novella *Imagine Kissing Pete.* His literary output, spanning 1934–1974, includes seventeen novels, among them, *A Rage to Live* 1949; *Ten North Frederick,* 1955; *From the Terrace,* 1958; the book for the 1941 Broadway musical comedy *Pal Joey;* some screenplays, as well as several hundred stories, many of them crafted with stunning skill. O'Hara's writing is situated in the mainstream of American realism. It is marked by a meticulous delineation of social aspiration, pretension, and ambition—what these days might be called upward mobility; a cross section of characters in diverse social and economic strata; a climate of compassion without sentiment; and an ear for dialogue, uncanny and unerring, in which O'Hara took altogether justified pride.

After appearing first in the *New Yorker, Imagine Kissing Pete* was published in Thanksgiving of 1960 as one in a boxed set of three novellas with the overall title *Sermons and Soda-Water.* (The other two were *The Girl on the Baggage Truck* and *We're Friends Again.*) As a love story, *Imagine Kissing Pete* is as unlikely as it is convincing. It is fashioned as ingeniously as a detective story, with the masterly denouement running through the story and along its numerous detours as a kind of secret thread. "Imagine *kissing* Pete, let alone any of the rest of it," comments one of the characters at the outset, to narrator Jim Malloy. The occasion is the engagement of Gibbsville's Bobbie Hammersmith and Pete McCrea, whose "spite marriage" follows.

Exhibited in the story is O'Hara's penchant for linked and overlapping characters; Malloy is a frequent O'Hara narrator, appearing in the two companion novellas as well as in other Gibbsville stories and the novel *Butterfield Eight* (1935). The fate of Julian English, protagonist of *Appointment in Samarra* (1934), O'Hara's first novel, is briefly recounted in *Imagine Kissing Pete* as well. And the dialogue has O'Hara's typical pinpoint accuracy and wit. A drunken party of Gibbsville couples, linked by long acquaintance, are forced in the midst of their sloppy revels to abandon a car in the snow. A state highway patrolman hails them: " 'What happened to you fellows?' he said. 'You have a wreck?' " Comes the pithy reply: " 'I married one,' said Joe." It is characteristic of O'Hara that a minor character can articulate, in an almost throwaway line, a major theme.

Imagine Kissing Pete

To those who knew the bride and groom, the marriage of Bobbie Hammersmith and Pete McCrea was the surprise of the year. As late as April of '29 Bobbie was still engaged to a fellow who lived in Greenwich, Connecticut, and she had told friends that the wedding would take place in September. But the engagement was broken and in a matter of weeks the invitations went out for her June wedding to Pete. One of the most frequently uttered comments was that Bobbie was not giving herself much opportunity to change her mind again. The comment was doubly cruel, since it carried the implication that if she gave herself time to think, Pete McCrea would not be her ideal choice. It was not only that she was marrying Pete on the rebound; she seemed to be going out of her way to find someone who was so unlike her other beaus that the contrast was unavoidable. And it was.

I was working in New York and Pete wrote to ask me to be an usher. Pete and I had grown up together, played together as children, and gone to dancing school and to the same parties. But we had never been close friends and when Pete and I went away to our separate prep schools and, later, Pete to Princeton and I to work, we drifted into that relationship of young men who had known each other all their lives without creating anything that was enduring or warm. As a matter of fact, I had never in my life received a written communication from Pete McCrea, and his handwriting on the envelope was new to me, as mine in my reply was to him. He mentioned who the best man and the other ushers would be—all Gibbsville boys—and this somewhat pathetic commentary on his four years in prep school and four years in college made an appeal to home town and boyhood loyalty that I could not reject. I had some extra days coming to me at the office, and so I told Pete I would be honored to be one of his ushers. My next step was to talk to a Gibbsville girl who lived in New York, a friend of Bobbie Hammersmith's. I took her to dinner at an Italian speakeasy where my credit was good, and she gave me what information she had. She was to be a bridesmaid.

"Bobbie isn't saying a word," said Kitty Clark. "That is, nothing about the inner turmoil. Nothing *intime*. Whatever happened happened the last time she was in New York, four or five weeks ago. All she'd tell me was that Johnny White was impossible. Impossible. Well, he'd been very possible all last summer and fall."

"What kind of a guy was he?" I asked.

"Oh—*attractive*," she said. "Sort of wild, I guess, but not a roué. Maybe he is a roué, but I'd say more just wild. I honestly don't know a thing about it, but it wouldn't surprise me if Bobbie was ready to settle down, and he wasn't. She was probably more in love with him than he was with her."

"I doubt that. She wouldn't turn around and marry Pete if she were still in love with this White guy."

"Oh, *wouldn't* she? Oh, are you ever wrong there. If she wanted to thumb her nose at Johnny, I can't think of a better way. Poor Pete. You know *Pete.* Ichabod McCrea. Remember when Mrs. McCrea made us stop calling him Ichabod? Lord and Taylor! She went to see my mother and I guess all the other mothers and said it just had to stop. Bad enough calling her little Angus by such a common nickname as Pete. But calling a boy Ichabod. I don't suppose Pete ever knew his mother went around like that."

"Yes he did. It embarrassed him. It always embarrassed him when Mrs. McCrea did those things."

"Yes, she was uncanny. I can remember when I was going to have a party, practically before I'd made out the list Mrs. McCrea would call Mother to be sure Pete wasn't left out. Not that I ever would have left him out. We all always had the same kids to our parties. But Mrs. McCrea wasn't leaving anything to chance. I'm dying to hear what she has to say about this marriage. I'll bet she doesn't like it, but I'll bet she's in fear and trembling in case Bobbie changes her mind again. Ichabod McCrea and Bobbie Hammersmith. Beauty and the beast. And actually he's not even a beast. It would be better if he were. She's the third of our old bunch to get married, but much as I hate to say it, I'll bet she'll be the first to get a divorce. Imagine *kissing* Pete, let alone any of the rest of it."

The wedding was on a Saturday afternoon; four o'clock in Trinity Church, and the reception at the country club. It had been two years since I last saw Bobbie Hammersmith and she was now twenty-two, but she could have passed for much more than that. She was the only girl in her crowd who had not bobbed her hair, which was jet-black and which she always wore with plaited buns over the ears. Except in the summer her skin was like Chinese white and it was always easy to pick her out first in group photographs; her eyes large dark dots, quite far apart, and her lips small but prominent in the whiteness of her face beneath the two small dots of her nose. In summer, with a tan, she reminded many non-operagoers of Carmen. She was a striking beauty, although it took two years' absence from her for me to realize it. In the theatre they have an expression, "walked through the part," which means that an actress played a role without giving it much of herself. Bobbie walked through the part of bride-to-be. A great deal of social activity was concentrated in the three days—Thursday, Friday, and Saturday—up to and including the wedding reception; but Bobbie walked through the part. Today, thirty years later, it would be assumed that she had been taking tranquilizers, but this was 1929.

Barbara Hammersmith had never been anything but a pretty child; if she had ever been homely it must have been when she was a small baby, when I was not bothering to look at her. We—Pete McCrea and the other boys—were two, three, four years older than Bobbie, but when she was fifteen or sixteen she began to pass among us, from boy to boy, trying one and then another, causing several fist fights, and half promising but never delivering anything more than the "soul kisses" that were all we really expected. By the time she was eighteen she had been in and out of love with all of us with the solitary exception of Pete McCrea. When she broke off with a boy, she would also make up with the girl he had temporarily deserted for Bobbie, and all the girls came to understand that every boy in the crowd had to go through a love affair with her. Consequently Bobbie was popular; the boys remembered her kisses, the girls forgave her because the boys had been returned virtually intact. We used the word hectic a lot in those days; Kitty Clark explained the short duration of Bobbie's love affairs by observing that being in love with Bobbie was too hectic for most boys. It was also true that it was not hectic enough. The boys agreed that Bobbie was a hot little number, but none of us could claim that she was not a virgin. At eighteen Bobbie entered a personal middle age, and for the big social occasions her beaus came from out-of-town. She was also busy at the college proms and football games, as far west as Ann Arbor, as far north as Brunswick, Maine. I was working on the Gibbsville paper during some of those years, the only boy in our crowd who was not away at college, and I remember Ann Arbor because Bobbie went there wearing a Delta Tau Delta pin and came back wearing the somewhat larger Psi U. "Now don't you say anything in front of Mother," she said. "She thinks they're both the same."

We played auction bridge, the social occupation in towns like ours, and Bobbie and I were assimilated into an older crowd: the younger married set and the youngest of the couples who were in their thirties. We played for prizes—flasks, cigarette lighters, vanity cases, cartons of cigarettes—and there was a party at someone's house every week. The hostess of the evening usually asked me to stop for Bobbie, and I saw her often. Her father and mother would be reading the evening paper and sewing when I arrived to pick up Bobbie. Philip Hammersmith was not a native of Gibbsville, but he had lived there long enough to have gone to the Mexican Border in 1916 with the Gibbsville company of mounted engineers, and he had gone to France with them, returning as a first lieutenant and with the Croix de Guerre with palm. He was one of the best golfers in the club, and everyone said he was making money hand-over-fist as an independent coal operator. He wore steel-rim glasses and he had almost completely gray hair, cut short. He inspired trust and confidence. He was slow-moving, taller than six feet, and always thought before speaking. His wife, a Gibbsville girl, was related, as she said, to half the town; a lively little woman who took her husband's arm even if they were walking only two doors away. I always used to feel that whatever he may have wanted out of life, yet unattained or unattainable, she had just what she wanted: a good husband, a nice home, and a pretty daughter who would not long remain unmarried. At home in the evening, and whenever I saw him on the street, Mr. Hammersmith was wearing a dark-gray worsted suit, cut loose and with a soft roll to the lapel; black knit four-in-hand necktie; white shirt; heavy gray woolen socks, and thick-soled brogues. This costume, completely unadorned—he wore a wrist watch—was what he always wore except for formal occasions, and the year-to-year sameness of his attire constituted his only known eccentricity. He was on the board of the second most conservative bank, the trustees of Gibbsville

Hospital, the armory board, the Y.M.C.A., and the Gibbsville and Lantenengo country clubs. Nevertheless I sensed that that was not all there was to Philip Hammersmith, that the care he put into the creation of the general picture of himself—hard work, quiet clothes, thoughtful manner, conventional associations—was done with a purpose that was not necessarily sinister but was extraordinarily private. It delighted me to discover, one night while waiting for Bobbie, that he knew more about what was going on than most of us suspected he would know. "Jimmy, you know Ed Charney, of course," he said.

I knew Ed Charney, the principal bootlegger in the area. "Yes, I know him pretty well," I said.

"Then do you happen to know if there's any truth to what I heard? I heard that his wife is threatening to divorce him."

"I doubt it. They're Catholics."

"Do you know her?"

"Yes. I went to Sisters' school with her."

"Oh, then maybe you can tell me something else. I've heard that she's the real brains of those two."

"She quit school after eighth grade, so I don't know about that. I don't remember her being particularly bright. She's about my age but she was two grades behind me."

"I see. And you think their religion will keep them from getting a divorce?"

"Yes, I do. I don't often see Ed at Mass, but I know he carries rosary beads. And she's at the eleven o'clock Mass every Sunday, all dolled up."

This conversation was explained when Repeal came and with it public knowledge that Ed Charney had been quietly buying bank stock, one of several moves he had made in the direction of respectability. But the chief interest to me at the time Mr. Hammersmith and I talked was in the fact that he knew anything at all about the Charneys. It was so unlike him even to mention Ed Charney's name.

To get back to the weekend of Bobbie Hammersmith's wedding: it was throughout that weekend that I first saw Bobbie have what we called that faraway look, that another generation called Cloud 90. If you happened to catch her at the right moment, you would see her smiling up at Pete in a way that must have been reassuring to Mrs. McCrea and to Mrs. Hammersmith, but I also caught her at several wrong moments and I saw something I had never seen before: a resemblance to her father that was a subtler thing than the mere duplication of such features as mouth, nose, and set of the eyes. It was almost the same thing I have mentioned in describing Philip Hammersmith; the wish yet unattained or unattainable. However, the pre-nuptial parties and the wedding and reception went off without a hitch, or so I believed until the day after the wedding.

Kitty Clark and I were on the same train going back to New York and I made some comment about the exceptional sobriety of the ushers and how everything had gone according to plan. "Amazing, considering," said Kitty.

"Considering what?"

"That there was almost no wedding at all," she said. "You must promise word of honor, Jimmy, or I won't tell you."

"I promise. Word of honor."

"Well, after Mrs. McCrea's very-dull-I-must-say luncheon, when we all left to go to Bobbie's? A little after two o'clock?"

"Yes."

"Bobbie asked me if I'd go across the street to our house and put in a long distance call to Johnny White. I said I couldn't do that, and what on earth was she thinking of. And Bobbie said, 'You're my oldest and best friend. The least you can do is make this one last effort, to keep me from ruining my life.' So I gave in and I dashed over to our house and called Johnny. He was out and they didn't know where he could be reached or what time he was coming home. So I left my name. *My* name, not Bobbie's. Six o'clock, at the reception, I was dancing with—I was dancing with *you*."

"When the waiter said you were wanted on the phone."

"It was Johnny. He'd been sailing and just got in. I made up some story about why I'd called him, but he didn't swallow it. '*You* didn't call me,' he said. '*Bobbie* did.' Well of course I wouldn't admit that. By that time she was married, and if her life was already ruined it would be a darned sight more ruined if I let him talk to her. Which he wanted to do. Then he tried to pump me. Where were they going on their wedding trip? I said nobody knew, which was a barefaced lie. I knew they were going to Bermuda. Known it since Thursday. But I wouldn't tell Johnny . . . I don't like him a bit after yesterday. I'd thought he was attractive, and he *is*, but he's got a mean streak that I never knew before. Feature this, if you will. When he realized I wasn't going to get Bobbie to come to the phone, or give him any information, he said, 'Well, no use wasting a long-distance call. What are you doing next weekend? How about coming out here?' 'I'm not that hard up,' I said, and banged down the receiver. I hope I shattered his eardrum."

I saw Pete and Bobbie McCrea when I went home the following Christmas. They were living in a small house on Twin Oaks Road, a recent real-estate development that had been instantly successful with the sons and daughters of the big two- and three-servant mansions. They were not going to any of the holiday dances; Bobbie was expecting a baby in April or early May.

"You're not losing any time," I said.

"I don't want to lose any time," said Bobbie. "I want to have a lot of children. Pete's an only child and so am I, and we don't think it's fair, if you can afford to have more."

"If we can afford it. The way that stock market is going, we'll be lucky to pay for this one," said Pete.

"Oh, don't start on that, Pete. That's all Father talks about," said Bobbie. "My father *was* hit pretty hard, but I wish he didn't have to keep talking about it all the time. Everybody's in the same boat."

"No, they're not. *We're* on a *raft*."

"I asked you, please, Pete. Jimmy didn't come here to listen to our financial woes. Do you see much of Kitty? I've owed her a letter for ages."

"No, I haven't seen her since last summer, we went out a few times," I said.

"Kitty went to New York to try to rope in a millionaire. She isn't going to waste her time on Jim."

"That's not what she went to New York for at all. And as far as wasting her time on Jim, Jim may not want to waste his time on her." She smiled. "Have you got a girl, Jim?"

"Not really."

"Wise. Very wise," said Pete McCrea.

"I don't know how wise. It's just that I have a hell of a hard time supporting myself, without trying to support a wife, too," I said.

"Why I understood you were selling articles to magazines, and going around with all the big shots."

"I've had four jobs in two years, and the jobs didn't last very long. If things get any tougher I may have to come back here. At least I'll have a place to sleep and something to eat."

"But I see your name in magazines," said Pete. "I don't always read your articles, but they must pay you well."

"They don't. At least I can't live on the magazine pieces without a steady job. Excuse me, Bobbie. Now you're getting *my* financial woes."

"She'll listen to yours. It's mine she doesn't want to hear about."

"That's because I know about ours. I'm never allowed to forget them," said Bobbie. "Are you going to all the parties?"

"Yes, stag. I have to bum rides. I haven't got a car."

"We resigned from the club," said Pete.

"Well we didn't *have* to do that," said Bobbie. "Father was going to give it to us for a Christmas present. And you have your job."

"We'll see how much longer I have it. Is that the last of the gin?"

"Yes."

Pete rose. "I'll be back."

"Don't buy any more for me," I said.

"You flatter yourself," he said. "I wasn't only getting it for you." He put on his hat and coat. "No funny business while I'm gone. I remember you two."

He kept a silly grin on his face while saying the ugly things, but the grin was not genuine and the ugly things were.

"I don't know what's the matter with him," said Bobbie. "Oh, I do, but why talk about it?"

"He's only kidding."

"You know better than that. He says worse things, much worse, and I'm only hoping they don't get back to Father. Father has enough on his mind. I thought if I had this baby right away it would—you know—give Pete confidence. But it's had just the opposite effect. He says it isn't his child. *Isn't his child!* Oh, I married him out of spite. I'm sure Kitty must have told you that. But it *is* his child, I swear it, Jim. It couldn't be anybody else's."

"I guess it's the old inferiority complex," I said.

"The first month we were married—Pete was a virgin—and I admit it, I wasn't. I stayed with two boys before I was married. But I was certainly not pregnant when I married Pete, and the first few weeks he was loving and sweet, and grateful. But then something happened to him, and he made a pass at I-won't-say-who. It was more than a pass. It was quite a serious thing. I might as well tell you. It was Phyllis. We were all at a picnic at the Dam and several people got pretty tight, Pete among them. And there's no other word for it, he tried to rape Phyllis. Tore her bathing suit and slapped her and did other things. She got away from him and ran back to the cottage without anyone seeing her. Luckily Joe didn't see her or I'm sure he'd have killed Pete. You know, Joe's strong as an ox and terribly jealous. I found out about it from Phyllis herself. She came here the next day and told me. She said she wasn't going to say anything to Joe, but that we mustn't invite her to our house and she wasn't going to invite us to hers."

"I'm certainly glad Joe didn't hear about it. He would do something drastic," I said. "But didn't he notice that you two weren't going to his house, and they to yours? It's a pretty small group."

She looked at me steadily. "We haven't been going anywhere. My excuse is that I'm pregnant, but the truth is, we're not being asked. It didn't end with Phyllis, Jim. One night at a dinner party Mary Lander just slapped his face, in front of everybody. Everybody laughed and thought Pete must have said something, but it wasn't something he'd said. He'd taken her hand and put it—you know. This is *Pete! Ichabod!* Did you ever know any of this about him?"

"You mean have I heard any of this? No."

"No, I didn't mean that. I meant, did he go around making passes and I never happened to hear about it?"

"No. When we'd talk dirty he'd say, 'Why don't you fellows get your minds above your belts?' "

"I wish your father were still alive. I'd go see him and try to get some advice. I wouldn't think of going to Dr. English."

"Well, you're not the one that needs a doctor. Could you get Pete to go to one? He's a patient of Dr. English's, isn't he?"

"Yes, but so is Mrs. McCrea, and Pete would never confide in Dr. English."

"Or anyone else at this stage, I guess," I said. "I'm not much help, am I?"

"Oh, I didn't expect you to have a solution. You know, Jim, I wish you would come back to Gibbsville. Other girls in our crowd have often said it was nice to have you to talk to. Of course you were a very bad boy, too, but a lot of us miss you."

"That's nice to hear, Bobbie. Thank you. I may be back, if I don't soon make a go of it in New York. I won't have any choice."

During that Christmas visit I heard other stories about Pete McCrea. In general they were told as plain gossip, but two or three times there was a hint of a lack of sympathy for Bobbie. "She knew what she was doing . . . she made her bed . . ." And while there was no lack of righteous indignation over Pete's behavior, he had changed in six months from a semi-comic figure to an unpleasant man, but a man nevertheless. In half a year he had lost most of his old friends; they all said, "You've never seen such a change come over anybody in all your life," but when they remembered to call him Ichabod it was only to emphasize the change.

Bobbie's baby was born in April, but lived only a few weeks. "She was determined to have that baby," Kitty Clark told me. "She had to prove to Pete that it was anyway *conceived* after she married him. But it must have taken all her strength to hold on to it that long. All her strength *and* the baby's. Now would be a good time for her to divorce him. She can't go on like that."

But there was no divorce, and Bobbie was pregnant again when I saw her at Christmas, 1930. They no longer lived in the Twin Oaks Road house, and her father and mother had given up their house on Lantenengo Street. The Hammersmiths were living in an apartment on Market Street, and Bobbie and Pete were living with Mrs. McCrea. "Temporarily, till Pete decides whether to take this job in Tulsa, Oklahoma," said Bobbie.

"Who do you think you're kidding?" said Pete. "It isn't a question of me deciding. It's a cousin of mine deciding if he'll take me on. And why the hell should he?"

"Well, you've had several years' banking experience," she said.

"Yes. And if I was so good, why did the bank let me go? Jim knows all this. What else have you heard about us, Jim? Did you hear Bobbie was divorcing me?"

"It doesn't look that way from here," I said.

"You mean because she's pregnant? That's elementary biology, and God knows you're acquainted with the facts of life. But if you want to be polite, all right. Pretend you didn't hear she was getting a divorce. You might as well pretend Mr. and Mrs. Hammersmith are still living on Lantenengo Street. If they were, Bobbie'd have got her divorce."

"Everybody tells me what I *was* going to do or *am* going to do," said Bobbie. "Nobody ever consults me."

"I suppose that's a crack at my mother."

"Oh, for Christ's sake, Pete, lay off, at least while I'm here," I said.

"Why? You like to think of yourself as an old friend of the family, so you might as well get a true picture. When you get married, if you ever do, I'll come and see you, and maybe your wife will cry on my shoulder." He got up and left the house.

"Well, it's just like a year ago," said Bobbie. "When you came to call on us last Christmas?"

"Where will he go now?"

"Oh, there are several places where he can charge drinks. They all think Mrs. McCrea has plenty of money, but they're due for a rude awakening. She's living on capital, but she's not going to sell any bonds to pay his liquor bills."

"Then maybe *he's* due for a rude awakening."

"Any awakening would be better than the last three months, since the bank fired him. He sits here all day long, then after Mrs. McCrea goes to bed he goes to one of his speakeasies." She sat up straighter. "He has a lady friend. Or have you heard?"

"No."

"Yes. He graduated from making passes at all my friends. He had to. We were never invited anywhere. Yes, he has a girl friend. Do you remember Muriel Nierhaus?"

"The chiropractor's wife. Sure. Big fat Muriel Minzer till she married Nierhaus, then we used to say he gave her some adjustments. Where is Nierhaus?"

"Oh, he's opened several offices. Very prosperous. He divorced her but she gets alimony. She's Pete's girl friend. Muriel Minzer is *Angus McCrea's* girl friend."

"You don't seem too displeased," I said.

"Would you be, if you were in my position?"

"I guess I know what you mean. But—well, nothing."

"But why don't I get a divorce?" She shook her head. "A spite marriage is a terrible thing to do to anybody. If I hadn't deliberately selected Pete out of all the boys I knew, he'd have gone on till Mrs. McCrea picked out somebody for him, and it would almost have had to be the female counterpart of Pete. A girl like— oh—Florence. Florence Temple."

"Florence Temple, with her cello. Exactly right."

"But I did that awful thing to Pete, and the first few weeks of marriage were just too much for him. He went haywire. I'd slept with two boys before I was married, so it wasn't as much of a shock to me. But Pete almost wore me out. And such adoration, I can't tell you. Then when we came back from Bermuda he began to see all the other girls he'd known all his life, and he'd ask me about them. It was as though he'd never seen them before, in a way. In other ways, it was as though he'd just been waiting all his life to start ripping their clothes off. He was dangerous, Jim. He really was. I could almost tell who would be next by the questions he'd ask. Before we'd go to a party, he'd say 'Who's going to be there tonight?' And I'd say I thought the usual crowd. Then he'd rattle off the list of names of our friends, and leave out one name. That was supposed to fool me, but it didn't for long. The name he left out, that girl was almost sure to be in for a bad time."

"And now it's all concentrated on Muriel Minzer?"

"As far as I know."

"Well, that's a break for you, *and* the other girls. Did you ever talk to him about the passes he made at the others?"

"Oh, how could we avoid it? Whoever it was, she was always 'that little whore.' "

"Did he ever get anywhere with any of them?"

She nodded. "One, but I won't tell you who. There was one girl that didn't stop him, and when that happened he wanted me to sleep with her husband."

"Swap, eh?"

"Yes. But I said I wasn't interested. Pete wanted to know why not? Why wouldn't I? And I almost told him. The boy was one of the two boys I'd stayed with before I was married—oh, when I was seventeen. And he never told anybody and neither have I, or ever will."

"You mean one of our old crowd actually did get somewhere with you, Bobbie?"

"One did. But don't try to guess. It won't do you any good to guess, because I'd never, never tell."

"Well, whichever one it was, he's the best liar I ever knew. And I guess the nicest guy in our whole crowd. You know, Bobbie, the whole damn bunch are going to get credit now for being as honorable as one guy."

"You were all nice, even if you all did talk too much. If it had been you, you would have lied, too."

"No, I don't think I would have."

"You lied about Kitty. Ha ha ha. You didn't know I knew about you and Kitty. I knew it the next day. The very next day. If you don't believe me, I'll tell you where it happened and how it happened, and all about it. That was the great bond we had in common. You and Kitty, and I and this other boy."

"Then Kitty's a gentleman, because she never told me a word about you."

"I kissed every boy in our crowd except Pete, and I necked, heavy-necked two, as you well know, and stayed with one."

"The question is, did you stay with the other one that you heavy-necked with?"

"You'll never know, Jim, and please don't try to find out."

"I won't, but I won't be able to stop theorizing," I said.

We knew everything, everything there was to know. We were so far removed from the technical innocence of eighteen, sixteen, nineteen. I was a man of the world, and Bobbie was indeed a woman, who had borne a child and lived with a husband who had come the most recently to the knowledge we had acquired, but was already the most intricately involved in the complications of sex. We—Bobbie and I—could discuss him and still remain outside the problems of Pete McCrea. We could almost remain outside our own problems. We knew so much, and since what we knew seemed to be all there was to know, we were shockproof. We had come to our maturity and our knowledgeability during the long decade of cynicism that was usually dismissed as "a cynical disregard of the law of the land," but that was something else, something deeper. The law had been passed with a

419

"noble" but nevertheless cynical disregard of men's right to drink. It was a law that had been imposed on some who took pleasure in drinking by some who did not. And when the law was an instant failure, it was not admitted to be a failure by those who had imposed it. They fought to retain the law in spite of its immediate failure and its proliferating corruption, and they fought as hard as they would have for a law that had been an immediate success. They gained no recruits to their own way; they had only deserters, who were not brave deserters but furtive ones; there was no honest mutiny but only grumbling and small disobediences. And we grew up listening to the grumbling, watching the small disobediences; laughing along when the grumbling was intentionally funny, imitating the small disobediences in other ways besides the customs of drinking. It was not only a cynical disregard for a law of the land; the law was eventually changed. Prohibition, the zealots' attempt to force total abstinence on a temperate nation, made liars of a hundred million men and cheats of their children; the West Point cadets who cheated in examinations, the basketball players who connived with gamblers, the thousands of uncaught cheats in the high schools and colleges. We had grown up and away from our earlier esteem of God and country and valor, and had matured at a moment when riches were vanishing for reasons that we could not understand. We were the losing, not the lost, generation. We could not blame Pete McCrea's troubles—and Bobbie's—on the Southern Baptists and the Northern Methodists. Since we knew everything, we knew that Pete's sudden release from twenty years of frustrations had turned him loose in a world filled with women. But Bobbie and I sat there in her mother-in-law's house, breaking several laws of possession, purchase, transportation and consumption of liquor, and with great calmness discussing the destruction of two lives—one of them hers—and the loss of her father's fortune, the depletion of her mother-in-law's, the allure of a chiropractor's divorcée, and our own promiscuity. We knew everything, but we were incapable of recognizing the meaning of our complacency.

I was wearing my dinner jacket, and someone was going to pick me up and take me to a dinner dance at the club. "Who's stopping for you?" said Bobbie.

"It depends. Either Joe or Frank. Depends on whether they go in Joe's car or in Frank's. I'm to be ready when they blow their horn."

"Do me a favor, Jim. Make them come in. Pretend you don't hear the horn."

"If it's Joe, he's liable to drive off without me. You know Joe if he's had a few too many."

In a few minutes there was a blast of a two-tone horn, repeated. "That's Joe's car," said Bobbie. "You'd better go." She went to the hall with me and I kissed her cheek. The front door swung open and it was Joe Whipple.

"Hello, Bobbie," he said.

"Hello, Joe. Won't you all come in? Haven't you got time for one drink?" She was trying not to sound suppliant, but Joe was not deceived.

"Just you and Jim here?" he said.

"Yes. Pete went out a little while ago."

420

"I'll see what the others say," said Joe. He left to speak to the three in the sedan, and obviously he was not immediately persuasive, but they came in with him. They would not let Bobbie take their coats, but they were nice to her and with the first sips of our drinks we were all six almost back in the days when Bobbie Hammersmith's house was where so many of our parties started from. Then we heard the front door thumping shut and Pete McCrea looked in.

There were sounds of hello, but he stared at us over his horn-rims and said to Bobbie: "You didn't have to invite me, but you could have told me." He turned and again the front door thumped.

"Get dressed and come with us," said Joe Whipple.

"I can't do that," said Bobbie.

"She can't, Joe," said Phyllis Whipple. "That would only make more trouble."

"What trouble? She's going to have to sit here alone till he comes home. She might as well be with us," said Joe.

"Anyway, I haven't got a dress that fits," said Bobbie. "But thanks for asking me."

"I won't have you sitting here—"

"Now don't make matters worse, Joe, for heaven's sake," said his wife.

"I could lend you a dress, Bobbie, but I think Phyllis is right," said Mary Lander. "Whatever *you* want to do."

"*Want* to do! That's not the question," said Bobbie. "Go on before I change my mind. Thanks, everybody. Frank, you haven't said a word."

"Nothing much for me to say," said Frank Lander. But as far as I was concerned he, and Bobbie herself, had said more than anyone else. I caught her looking at me quickly.

"Well, all right, then," said Joe. "I'm outnumbered. Or outpersuaded or something."

I was the last to say goodbye, and I whispered to Bobbie: "Frank, eh?"

"You're only guessing," she said. "Goodnight, Jim." Whatever they would be after we left, her eyes were brighter than they had been in years. She had very nearly gone to a party, and for a minute or two she had been part of it.

I sat in the back seat with Phyllis Whipple and Frank Lander. "If you'd had any sense you'd know there'd be a letdown," said Phyllis.

"Oh, drop it," said Joe.

"It might have been worth it, though, Phyllis," said Mary Lander. "How long is it since she's seen anybody but that old battle-ax, Mrs. McCrea? God, I hate to think what it must be like, living in that house with Mrs. McCrea."

"I'm sure it would have been a *lot* easier if Bobbie'd come with us," said Phyllis. "That would have fixed things just right with Mrs. McCrea. She's just the type that wants Bobbie to go out and have a good time. Especially without Pete. You forget how the old lady used to call up all the mothers as soon as she heard there was a party planned. What Joe did was cruel because it was so downright stupid. Thoughtless. Like getting her all excited and then leaving her hung up."

"You've had too much to drink," said Joe.

"I have?"

"Yes, you don't say things like that in front of a bachelor," said Joe.

"Who's—oh, Jim? It is to laugh. Did I shock you, Jim?"

"Not a bit. I didn't know what you meant. Did you say something risqué?"

"My husband thinks I did."

"Went right over my head," I said. "I'm innocent about such things."

"So's your old man," said Joe.

"Do you think she should have come with us, Frank?" I said.

"Why ask me? No. I'm with Phyllis. What's the percentage for Bobbie? You saw that son of a bitch in the doorway, and you know damn well when he gets home from Muriel Nierhaus's, he's going to raise hell with Bobbie."

"Then Bobbie had nothing to lose," said Joe. "If Pete's going to raise hell with her, anyway, she might as well have come with us."

"How does he raise hell with her?" I said.

No one said anything.

"Do you know, Phyllis?" I said.

"What?" said Phyllis.

"Oh, come on. You heard me," I said. "Mary?"

"I'm sure I don't know."

"Oh, nuts," I said.

"Go ahead, tell him," said Frank Lander.

"Nobody ever knew for sure," said Phyllis, quietly.

"That's not true. Caroline English, for one. She knew for sure."

Phyllis spoke: "A few weeks before Bobbie had her baby she rang Caroline's doorbell in the middle of the night and asked Caroline if she could stay there. Naturally Caroline said yes, and she saw that Bobbie had nothing but a coat over her nightgown and had bruises all over her arms and shoulders. Julian was away, a lucky break because he'd have gone over and had a fight with Pete. As it was, Caroline made Bobbie have Dr. English come out and have a look at her, and nothing more was said. I mean, it was kept secret from everybody, especially Mr. Hammersmith. But the story got out somehow. Not widespread, but we all heard about it."

"We don't want it to get back to Mr. Hammersmith," said Mary Lander.

"He knows," said Frank Lander.

"You keep saying that, but I don't believe he does," said Mary.

"I don't either," said Joe Whipple. "Pete wouldn't be alive today if Phil Hammersmith knew."

"That's where I think you're wrong," said Phyllis. "Mr. Hammersmith might want to kill Pete, but killing him is another matter. And what earthly good would it do? The Hammersmiths have lost every penny, so I'm told, and at least with Pete still alive, Mrs. McCrea supports Bobbie. Barely. But they have food and a roof over their heads."

"Phil Hammersmith knows the whole damn story, you can bet anything on that. And it's why he's an old man all of a sudden. Have you seen him this trip, Jim?" said Frank Lander.

"I haven't seen him since the wedding."

"Oh, well—" said Mary.

"You won't—" said Joe.

"You won't recognize him," said Frank Lander. "He's bent over—"

"They say he's had a stroke," said Phyllis Whipple.

"And on top of everything else he got a lot of people sore at him by selling his bank stock to Ed Charney," said Joe. "Well, not a lot of people, but some that could have helped him. My old man, to name one. And I don't think that was so hot. Phil Hammersmith was a carpetbagger himself, and damn lucky to be in the bank. Then to sell his stock to a lousy stinking bootlegger . . . You should hear Harry Reilly on the subject."

"I don't want to hear Harry Reilly on any subject," said Frank Lander. "Cheap Irish Mick."

"I don't like him any better than you do, Frank, but call him something else," I said.

"I'm sorry, Jim. I didn't mean that," said Frank Lander.

"No. It just slipped out," I said.

"I apologize," said Frank Lander.

"Oh, all right."

"Don't be sensitive, Jim," said Mary.

"Stay out of it, Mary," said Frank Lander.

"*Everybody* calm down," said Joe. "Everybody knows that Harry Reilly is a cheap Irish Mick, and nobody knows it better than Jim, an Irish Mick but not a cheap one. So shut the hell up, everybody."

"Another country heard from," said Phyllis.

"Now *you*, for Christ's sake," said Joe. "Who has the quart?"

"I have my quart," said Frank Lander.

"I have mine," I said.

"I asked who has mine. Phyllis?"

"When we get to the club, time enough," said Phyllis.

"Hand it over," said Joe.

"Three quarts of whiskey between five people. I'd like to know how we're going to get home tonight," said Mary Lander.

"Drunk as a monkey, if you really want to know," said Joe. "Tight as a nun's."

"Well, at least we're off the subject of Bobbie and Pete," said Phyllis.

"I'm not. I was coming back to it. Phyllis. The quart," said Joe.

"No," said Phyllis.

"Here," I said. "And remember where it came from." I handed him my bottle. Joe took a swig in the corner of his mouth, swerving the car only slightly.

"Thanks," he said, and returned the bottle. "Now, Mary, if you'll light me a cigarette like a dear little second cousin."

"Once removed," said Mary Lander.

"Once removed, and therefore related to Bobbie through her mother."

"No, *you* are but I'm not," said Mary Lander.

"Well, you're in it some way, through me. Now for the benefit of those who are not related to Bobbie or Mrs. Hammersmith, or Mary or me. Permit me to give you a little family history that will enlighten you on several points."

"Is this going to be about Mr. Hammersmith?" said Phyllis. "I don't think you'd better tell that."

"You're related only by marriage, so kindly keep your trap shut. If I want to tell it, I can."

"Everybody remember that I asked him not to," said Phyllis.

"Don't tell it, Joe, whatever it is," said Mary Lander.

"Yeah, what's the percentage?" said Frank Lander. "They have enough trouble without digging up past history."

"Oh, you're so noble, Lander," said Joe. "You fool nobody."

"If you're going to tell the story, go ahead, but stop insulting Frank," said Mary Lander.

"We'll be at the club before he gets started," said Phyllis.

"Then we'll sit there till I finish. Anyway, it doesn't take that long. So, to begin at the beginning. Phil Hammersmith. Phil Hammersmith came here before the war, just out of Lehigh."

"You're not even telling it right," said Phyllis.

"Phyllis is right. I'm screwing up my own story. Well, I'll begin again. Phil Hammersmith graduated from Lehigh, then a few years *later* he came to Gibbsville."

"That's better," said Phyllis.

"The local Lehigh contingent all knew him. He'd played lacrosse and he was a Sigma Nu around the time Mr. Chew was there. So he already had friends in Gibbsville."

"Now you're on the right track," said Phyllis.

"Thank you, love," said Joe.

"Where was he from originally?" I asked.

"Don't ask questions, Jim. It only throws me. He was from some place in New Jersey. So anyway he arrived in Gibbsville and got a job with the Coal & Iron Company. He was a civil engineer, and he had the job when he arrived. That is, he didn't come here looking for a job. He was hired before he got here."

"You've made that plain," said Phyllis.

"Well, it's important," said Joe.

"Yes, but you don't have to say the same thing over and over again," said Phyllis.

"Yes I do. Anyway, apparently the Coal & Iron people hired him on the strength of his record at Lehigh, plus asking a few questions of the local Lehigh contingent, that knew him, *plus* a very good recommendation he'd had from some firm in Bethlehem. Where he'd worked after getting out of college. But after he'd been here a while, and was getting along all right at the Coal & Iron, one day a construction engineer from New York arrived to talk business at the C. & I. Building. They took him down-cellar to the drafting-room and who should he see but Phil Hammersmith. But apparently Phil didn't see him. Well, the New York guy was a real wet smack, because he tattled on Phil.

"Old Mr. Duncan was general superintendent then and he sent for Phil. Was it true that Phil had once worked in South America, and if so, why hadn't he mentioned it when he applied for a job? Phil gave him the obvious answer. 'Because if I had, you wouldn't have hired me.' 'Not necessarily,' said Mr. Duncan. 'We might have accepted your explanation.' 'You say that now, but I tried telling the truth and I couldn't get a job.' 'Well, tell me the truth now,' said Mr. Duncan. 'All right,' said Phil. So he told Mr. Duncan what had happened.

"He was working in South America. Peru, I think. Or maybe Bolivia. In the jungle. And the one thing they didn't want the natives, the Indians, to get hold of was firearms. But one night he caught a native carrying an armful of rifles from the shanty, and when Phil yelled at him, the native ran, and Phil shot him. Killed him. The next day one of the other engineers was found with his throat cut. And the day after that the native chief came and called on the head man of the construction outfit. Either the Indians thought they'd killed the man that had killed their boy, or they didn't much care. But the chief told the white boss that the next time an Indian was killed, two white men would be killed. And not just killed. Tortured. Well, there were four or maybe five engineers, including Phil and the boss. The only white men in an area as big as Pennsylvania, and I guess they weighed their chances and being mathematicians, the odds didn't look so hot. So they quit. No hero stuff. They just quit. Except Phil. He was fired. The boss blamed Phil for everything and in his report to the New York office he put in a lot of stuff that just about fixed Phil for good. The boss, of course, was the same man that spotted Phil at the C. & I. drafting-room."

"You told it very well," said Phyllis.

"So any time you think of Phil Hammersmith killing Pete McCrea, it wouldn't be the first time," said Joe.

"And the war," I said. "He probably killed a few Germans."

"On the other hand, he never got over blaming himself for the other engineer's getting his throat cut," said Joe. "This is all the straight dope. Mr. Duncan to my old man."

We were used to engineers, their travels and adventures in far-off places, but engineers came and went and only a few became fixtures in our life. Phil Hammersmith's story was all new to Mary and Frank and me, and in the cold moonlight, as we sat in a heated automobile in a snow-covered parking area of a Pennsylvania country club, Joe Whipple had taken us to a dark South American jungle, given us a touch of fear, and in a few minutes covered Phil Hammersmith in mystery and then removed the mystery.

"Tell us more about Mr. Hammersmith," said Mary Lander.

Mary Lander. I had not had time to realize the inference that must accompany my guess that Frank Lander was the one boy in our crowd who had stayed with Bobbie. Mary Lander was the only girl who had not fought off Pete McCrea. She was the last girl I would have suspected of staying with Pete, and yet the one that surprised me the least. She had always been the girl our mothers like us to take out, a kind of mothers' ideal for their sons, and possibly even for themselves. Mary Morgan Lander was the third generation of a family that had always been in the grocery business, the only store in the county that sold caviar and English biscuits and Sportsmen's Bracer chocolate, as well as the most expensive domestic items of fruit, vegetables, and tinned goods. Her brother Llewellyn Morgan still scooped out dried prunes and operated the rotary ham slicer, but no one seriously believed that all the Morgan money came from the store. Lew Morgan taught Sunday School in the Methodist Episcopal Church and played basketball at the Y.M.C.A., but he had been to Blair Academy and Princeton, and his father had owned one of the first Pierce-Arrows in Gibbsville. Mary had been unfairly judged a teaser, in previous years. She was not a teaser, but a girl who would kiss a boy and allow him to wander all over her body so long as he did not touch bare skin. Nothing surprised me about Mary. It was in character for her to have slapped Pete McCrea at a dinner party, and then to have let him stay with her and to have discussed with him a swap of husbands and wives. No casual dirty remark ever passed unnoticed by Mary; when someone made a slip we would all turn to see how Mary was taking it, and without fail she had heard it, understood it, and taken a pious attitude. But in our crowd she was the one person most conscious of sex and scatology. She was the only one of whom I would say she had a dirty mind, but I kept that observation to myself along with my theory that she hated Frank Lander. My theory, based on no information whatever, was that marriage and Frank Lander had not been enough for her and that Pete McCrea had become attractive to her because he was so awful.

"There's no more to tell," said Joe Whipple. We got out of the car and Mary took Joe's arm, and her evening was predictable: fathers and uncles and older brothers would cut in on her, and older women would comment as they always did that Mary Lander was *such* a sensible girl, *so* considerate of her elders, a *wonderful* wife to Frank. And we of her own age would dance with her because under cover of the dancing crowd Mary would wrap both legs around our right legs with a promise that had fooled us for years. Quiet little Mary Lander, climbing up a boy's leg but never forgetting to smile her Dr. Lyons smile at old Mrs. Ginyan and old Mr. Heff. And yet through some mental process that I did not take time to scrutinize, I was less annoyed with Mary than I had been since we were children. I was determined not to dance with her, and I did not, but my special knowledge about her and Pete McCrea reduced her power to allure. Bobbie had married Pete McCrea and she was still attractive in spite of it; but Mary's seductiveness vanished with the revelation that she had picked Pete as her lover, if only for once, twice, or how many times. I had never laughed at Mary before, but now she was the fool, not we, not I.

I got quite plastered at the dance, and so did a lot of other people. On the way home we sang a little—"Body and Soul" was the song, but Phyllis was the only one who could sing the middle part truly—and Frank Lander tried to tell about an incident in the smoking-room, where Julian English apparently had thrown a drink in Harry Reilly's face. It did not seem worth making a fuss about, and Frank never finished his story. Mary Lander attacked me: "You never danced with me, not once," she said.

"I didn't?"

"No, you didn't, and you know you didn't," she said. "And you always do."

"Well, this time I guess I didn't."

"Well, *why* didn't you?"

"Because he didn't want to," said Frank Lander. "You're making a fool of yourself. I should think you'd have more pride."

"Yeah, why don't you have more pride, Mary?" said Joe Whipple. "You'd think it was an honor to dance with this Malloy guy."

"It is," I said.

"That's it. You're getting so conceited," said Mary. "Well, I'm sure I didn't have to sit any out."

"Then why all the fuss?" said Frank Lander.

"Such popularity must be deserved," I said, quoting an advertising slogan.

"Whose? Mary's or yours?" said Phyllis.

"Well, I was thinking of Mary's, but now that you mention it . . ." I said.

"How many times did he dance with *you*, Phyllis?" said Joe.

"Three or four," said Phyllis.

"In that case, Frank, Jim has insulted your wife. I don't see any other way out of it. You have to at least slap his face. Shall I stop the car?"

"My little trouble-maker," said Phyllis.

"Come on, let's have a fight," said Joe. "Go ahead, Frank. Give him a punch in the nose."

"Yeah, like you did at the Dam, Frank," I said.

"Oh, God. I remember that awful night," said Phyllis. "What did you fight over?"

"Bobbie," I said.

"Bobbie was the cause of *more* fights," said Mary Lander.

"Well, we don't need her to fight over now. We have you," said Joe. "Your honor's been attacked and your husband wants to defend it. The same as I would if Malloy hadn't danced with *my* wife. It's a good thing you danced with Phyllis, Malloy, or you and I'd get out of this car and start slugging."

"Why did you fight over Bobbie? I don't remember that," said Mary.

"Because she came to the picnic with Jim and then went off necking with Frank," said Phyllis. "I remember the whole thing."

"Stop *talking* about fighting and let's *fight*," said Joe.

"All right, stop the car," I said.

"Now you're talking," said Joe.

"Don't be ridiculous," said Phyllis.

"Oh, shut up," said Joe. He pulled up on the side of the road. "I'll referee." He got out of the car, and so did Frank and I and Phyllis. "All right, put up your dukes." We did so, moved around a bit in the snow and slush. "Go on, mix it," said Joe, whereupon Frank rushed me and hit me on the left cheek. All blows were directed at the head, since all three of us were armored in coonskin coats. "That was a good one, Frank. Now go get him, Jim." I swung my right hand and caught Frank's left eye, and at that moment we were all splashed by slush, taken completely by surprise as Phyllis, whom we had forgotten, drove the car away.

"That bitch!" said Joe. He ran to the car and got hold of a door handle but she increased her speed and he fell in the snow. "God damn that bitch, I should have known she was up to something. Now what? Let's try to bum a ride." The fight, such as it was, was over, and we tried to flag down cars on their way home from the dance. We recognized many of them, but not one would stop.

"Well, thanks to you, we've got a nice three-mile walk to Swedish Haven," said Frank Lander.

"Oh, she'll be back," said Joe.

"I'll bet you five bucks she's not," I said.

"Well, I won't bet, but I'll be damned if I'm going to walk three miles. I'm just going to wait till we can bum a ride."

"If you don't keep moving you'll freeze," said Frank.

"We're nearer the club than we are Swedish Haven. Let's go back there," I said.

"And have my old man see me?" said Joe.

"Your old man went home hours ago," I said.

"Well, somebody'll see me," said Joe.

"Listen, half the club's seen you already, and they wouldn't even stop," I said.

"Who has a cigarette?" said Joe.

"Don't give him one," said Frank.

"I have no intention of giving him one," I said. "Let's go back to the club. My feet are soaking wet."

"So are mine," said Frank. We were wearing pumps, and our feet had been wet since we got out of the car.

"That damn Phyllis, she knows I just got over a cold," said Joe.

"Maybe that's why she did it," I said. "It'd serve you right if you got pneumonia."

We began to walk in the middle of the road, in the direction of the clubhouse, which we could see, warm and comfortable on top of a distant plateau. "That old place never looked so good," said Joe. "Let's spend the night there."

"The rooms are all taken. The orchestra's staying there," I said.

We walked about a mile, our feet getting sorer at every step, and the combination of exhaustion and the amount we had had to drink made even grumbling an effort. Then a Dodge touring car, becurtained, stopped about fifty yards from us and a spotlight was turned on each of our faces. A man in a short overcoat and fur-lined cap came toward us. He was a State Highway patrolman. "What happened to you fellows?" he said. "You have a wreck?"

"I married one," said Joe.

"Oh, a weisscrackah," said the patrolman, a Pennsylvania Dutchman. "Where's your car?"

"We got out to take a leak and my wife drove off with it," said Joe.

"You from the dance at the gulf club?"

"Yes," said Joe. "How about giving us a lift?"

"Let me see you' driwah's license," said the cop.

Joe took out his billfold and handed over the license. "So? From Lantenengo street yet? All right, get in. Whereabouts you want to go to?"

"The country club," said Joe.

"The hell with that," said Frank. "Let's go on to Gibbsville."

"This aint no taxi service," said the cop. "And I aint taking you to no Gippsfille. I'm on my way to my substation. Swedish Haven. You can phone there for a taxi. Privileged characters, you think you are. A bunch of drunks, you ask me."

I had to go back to New York on the morning train and the events of the next few days, so far as they concerned Joe and Phyllis Whipple and Frank and Mary Lander, were obscured by the suicide, a day or two later, of Julian English, the man who had thrown a drink at Harry Reilly. The domestic crisis of the Whipples and the Landers and even the McCreas seemed very unimportant. And yet when I heard about English, who had not been getting along with his wife, I wondered about my own friends, people my own age but not so very much younger than Julian and Caroline English. English had danced with Phyllis and Mary that night, and now he was dead. I knew very little about the causes of the difficulties between him and Caroline, but they could have been no worse than the problems that existed in Bobbie's marriage and that threatened the marriage of Frank and Mary Lander. I was shocked and saddened by the English suicide; he was an attractive man whose shortcomings seemed out of proportion to the magnitude of killing himself. He had not been a friend of mine, only an acquaintance with whom I had had many drinks and played some golf; but friends of mine, my closest friends in the world, boys-now-men like myself, were at the beginning of the same kind of life and doing the same kind of thing that for Julian English ended in a sealed-up garage with a motor running. I hated what I thought those next few days and weeks. There is nothing young about killing oneself, no matter when it happens, and I hated this being deprived of the sweetness of youth. And that was what it was, that was what was happening to us. I, and I think the others, had looked upon our squabbles as unpleasant incidents but belonging to our youth. Now they were plainly recognizable as symptoms of life without youth, without youth's excuses or youth's recoverability. I wanted to love someone, and during the next year or two I confused the desperate need for love with love itself. I had put a hopeless love out of my life; but that is not part of this story, except to state it and thus to show that I knew what I was looking for.

2

When you have grown up with someone it is much easier to fill in gaps of five years, ten years, in which you do not see him, than to supply those early years in the life of a friend you meet in maturity. I do not know why this is so, unless it is a mere matter of insufficient time. With the friends of later life you may exchange boyhood stories that seem worth telling, but boyhood is not all stories. It is mostly not stories, but day-to-day, unepisodic living. And most of us are too polite to burden our later-life friends with unexciting anecdotes about people they will never meet. (Likewise we hope they will not burden us.) But it is easy to bring old friends up to date in your mental dossiers by the addition of a few vital facts. Have they stayed married? Have they had many more children? Have they made money or lost it? Usually the basic facts will do, and then you tell yourself that Joe Whipple is still Joe Whipple, plus two sons, a new house, a hundred thousand dollars, forty pounds, bifocals, fat in the neck, and a new concern for the state of the nation.

Such additions I made to my friends' dossiers as I heard about them from time to time; by letters from them, conversations with my mother, an occasional newspaper clipping. I received these facts with joy for the happy news, sorrow for the sad, and immediately went about my business, which was far removed from any business of theirs. I seldom went back to Gibbsville during the Thirties—mine and the century's—and when I did I stayed only long enough to stand at a grave, to toast a bride, to spend a few minutes beside a sickbed. In my brief encounters with my old friends I got no information about Bobbie and Pete McCrea, and only after I had returned to New York or California would I remember that I had intended to inquire about them.

There is, of course, some significance in the fact that no one volunteered information about Bobbie and Pete. It was that they had disappeared. They continued to live in Gibbsville, but in parts of the town that were out of the way for their old friends. There is no town so small that that cannot happen, and Gibbsville, a third-class city, was large enough to have all the grades of poverty and wealth and the many half grades in between, in which $10 a month in the husband's income could make a difference in the kind and location of the house in which he lived. No one had volunteered any information about Bobbie and

Pete, and I had not remembered to inquire. In five years I had had no new facts about them, none whatever, and their disappearance from my ken might have continued but for a broken shoelace.

I was in Gibbsville for a funeral, and the year was 1938. I had broken a shoelace, it was evening and the stores were closed, and I was about to drive back to New York. The only place open that might have shoelaces was a poolroom that in my youth had had a two-chair bootblack stand. The poolroom was in a shabby section near the railroad stations and a couple of cheap hotels, four or five saloons, an automobile tire agency, a barber shop, and a quick-lunch counter. I opened the poolroom door, saw that the bootblack's chairs were still there, and said to the man behind the cigar counter: "Have you got any shoelaces?"

"Sorry I can't help you, Jim," said the man. He was wearing an eyeshade, but as soon as he spoke I recognized Pete McCrea.

"Pete, for God's sake," I said. We shook hands.

"I thought you might be in town for the funeral," he said. "I should have gone, too, I guess, but I decided I wouldn't. It was nice of you to make the trip."

"Well, you know. He was a friend of my father's. Do you own this place?"

"I run it. I have a silent partner, Bill Charney. You remember Ed Charney? His younger brother. I don't know where to send you to get a shoelace."

"The hell with the shoelace. How's Bobbie?"

"Oh, Bobbie's fine. *You* know. A lot of changes, but this is better than nothing. Why don't you call her up? She'd love to hear from you. We're living out on Mill Street, but we have a phone. Call her up and say hello. The number is 3385-J. If you have time maybe you could go see her. I have to stay here till I close up at one o'clock, but she's home."

"What number on Mill Street? You call her up and tell her I'm coming? Is that all right?"

"Hell, yes."

Someone thumped the butt of a cue on the floor and called out: "Rack 'em up, Pete?"

"I have to be here. You go on out and I'll call her up," he said. "Keep your shirt on," he said to the pool player, then, to me: "It's 402 Mill Street, across from the open hearth, second house from the corner. I guess I won't see you again, but I'm glad we had a minute. You're looking very well." I could not force a comment on his appearance. His nose was red and larger, his eyes watery, the dewlaps sagging, and he was wearing a blue denim work shirt with a dirty leather bow tie.

"Think I could get in the Ivy Club if I went back to Princeton?" he said. "I didn't make it the first time around, but now I'm a big shot. So long, Jim. Nice to've seen you."

The open hearth had long since gone the way of all the mill equipment, the mill itself had been inactive for years, and as a residential area the mill section was only about a grade and a half above the poorest Negro slums. But in front of most of the houses in the McCreas' row there were cared-for plots; there always had been, even when the mill was running and the air was full of smoke and acid. It was an Irish and Polish neighborhood, but knowledge of that fact did not keep me from locking all the doors of my car. The residents of the neighborhood would not have touched my father's car, but this was not his car and I was not he.

The door of Number 402 opened as soon as I closed my car door. Bobbie waited for me to lock up and when I got to the porch, she said: "Jim. Jim, Jim, Jim. How nice. I'm so glad to see you." She quickly closed the door behind me and then kissed me. "Give me a real kiss and a real hug. I didn't dare while the door was open." I kissed her and held her for a moment and then she said: "Hey, I guess we'd better cut this out."

"Yes," I said. "It's nice, though."

"Haven't done that since we were—God!" She stood away and looked at me. "You could lose some weight, but you're not so bad. How about a bottle of beer? Or would you rather have some cheap whiskey?"

"What are you drinking?"

"Cheap whiskey, but I'm used to it," she said.

"Let's both have some cheap whiskey," I said.

"Straight? With water? Or how?"

"Oh, a small slug of whiskey and a large slug of water in it. I'm driving back to New York tonight."

She went to the kitchen and prepared the drinks. I recognized some of the furniture from the Hammersmith and McCrea houses. "Brought together by a shoestring," she said. "Here's to it. How do I look?"

"If you want my frank and candid opinion, good enough to go right upstairs and make up for the time we lost. Pete won't be home till one o'clock."

"If then," she said. "Don't think I wouldn't, but it's too soon after my baby. Didn't Pete tell you I finally produced a healthy son?"

"No."

"You'll hear him in a little while. We have a daughter, two years old, and now a son. Angus McCrea, Junior. Seven pounds two ounces at birth."

"Good for you," I said.

"Not so damn good for me, but it's over, and he's healthy."

"And what about your mother and father?" I said.

"Oh, poor Jim. You didn't know? Obviously you didn't, and you're going to be so sorry you asked. Daddy committed suicide two years ago. He shot himself. And Mother's in Swedish Haven." Swedish Haven was local lore for the insane asylum. "I'm sorry I had to tell you."

"God, why won't they lay off you?" I said.

"Who is they? Oh, you mean just—life?"

"Yes."

"I don't know, Jim," she said. "I've had about as much as I can stand, or so I keep telling myself. But I must be awfully tough, because there's always something else, and I go right on. Will you let me complain for just a minute, and then I'll stop? The only one of the old crowd I ever see is Phyllis. She comes out and never forgets to bring a bottle, so we get tight together. But some things we don't discuss, Phyllis and I. Pete is a closed subject."

"What's he up to?"

"Oh, he has his women. I don't even know who they are any more, and couldn't care less. Just as long as he doesn't catch a disease. I told him that, so he's been careful about it." She sat up straight. "I haven't been the soul of purity, either, but it's Pete's son. Both children are Pete's. But I haven't been withering on the vine."

"Why should you?"

"That's what *I* said. Why should I have nothing? Nothing? The children are mine, and I love them, but I need more than that, Jim. Children don't love you back. All they do is depend on you to feed them and wash them and all the rest of it. But after they're in bed for the night—I never know whether Pete will be home at two o'clock or not at all. So I've had two tawdry romances, I guess you'd call them. Not you, but Mrs. McCrea would."

"Where is dear Mrs. McCrea?"

"She's living in Jenkintown, with an old maid sister. Thank heaven they can't afford carfare, so I'm spared that."

"Who are your gentlemen friends?"

"Well, the first was when we were living on the East Side. A gentleman by the name of Bill Charney. Yes, Ed's brother and Pete's partner. I was crazy about him. Not for one single minute in love with him, but I never even thought about love with him. He wanted to marry me, too, but I was a nasty little snob. I *couldn't* marry Bill Charney, Jim. I just couldn't. So he married a nice little Irish girl and they're living on Lantenengo Street in the house that used to belong to old Mr. Duncan. And I'm holding court on Mill Street, thirty dollars a month rent."

"Do you want some money?"

"Will you give me two hundred dollars?"

"More than that, if you want it."

"No, I'd just like to have two hundred dollars to hide, to keep in case of emergency."

"In case of emergency, you can always send me a telegram in care of my publisher." I gave her $200.

"Thank you. Now I have some money. For the last five or six years I haven't had any money of my own. You don't care how I spend this, do you?"

"As long as you spend it on yourself."

"I've gotten so stingy I probably won't spend any of it. But this is wonderful. Now I can read the ads and say to myself I could have some expensive lingerie. I think I will get a permanent, next month."

"Is that when you'll be back in circulation again?"

"Good guess. Yes, about a month," she said. "But not the same man. I didn't tell you about the second one. You don't know him. He came here after you left Gibbsville. His name is McCormick and he went to Princeton with Pete. They sat next to each other in a lot of classes, McC, McC, and he was sent here to do some kind of an advertising survey and ran into Pete. They'd never been exactly what you'd call pals, but they *knew* each other and Mac took one look and sized up the situation and—well, I thought, why not? He wasn't as exciting as Mr. Charney, but at one time I would have married him. *If* he'd asked me. He doesn't live here any more."

"But you've got the next one picked out?"

"No, but I know there will be a next one. Why lie to myself? And why lie to you? I don't think I ever have."

"Do you ever see Frank?"

"Frank? Frank Lander? What made you think of him?"

"Bobbie," I said.

"Oh, of course. That was a guess of yours, a long time ago," she said. "No, I never see Frank." She was smoking a cigarette, and sitting erect with her elbow on the arm of her chair, holding the cigarette high and with style. If her next words had been "Jeeves, have the black Rolls brought round at four o'clock" she would not have been more naturally grand. But her next words were: "I haven't even thought about Frank. There was another boy, Johnny White, the one I was engaged to. *Engaged to.* That close to spending the rest of my life with him—or at least part of it. But because he wanted me to go away with him before we were married, I broke the engagement and married Pete."

"Is that all it was? That he wanted you to go away with him?"

"That's really all it was. I got huffy and said he couldn't really love me if he wanted to take that risk. Not that we hadn't been taking risks, but a pre-marital trip, that was something else again. My five men, Jim. Frank. Johnny. Bill and Mac. And Pete."

"Why didn't you and Frank ever get engaged?"

"I wonder. I *have* thought about *that*, so I was wrong when I said I never think of Frank. But Frank in the old days, not Frank now. What may have happened was that Frank was the only boy I'd gone all the way with, and then I got scared because I didn't want to give up the fun, popularity, good times. Jim, I have a confession to make. About you."

"Oh?"

"I told Frank I'd stayed with you. He wouldn't believe he was my first and he kept harping on it, so I really got rid of Frank by telling him you were the first."

"Why me?"

"Because the first time I ever stayed with Frank, or anybody, it was at a picnic at the Dam, and I'd gone to the picnic with you. So you were the logical one."

"Did you tell him that night?"

434

"No. Later. Days later. But you had a fight with him that night, and the fight made it all the more convincing."

"Well, thanks, little pal," I said.

"Oh, you don't care, do you?"

"No, not really."

"You had Kitty, after all," she said. "Do you ever see Kitty?"

"No. Kitty lives in Cedarhurst and they keep to themselves, Cedarhurst people."

"What was your wife like?"

"She was nice. Pretty. Wanted to be an actress. I still see her once in a while. I like her, and always will, but if ever there were two people that shouldn't have got married . . ."

"I can name two others," said Bobbie.

"You and Pete. But you've stuck to him."

"Don't be polite. I'm stuck with him. Can you imagine what Pete would be like if I left him?"

"Well, to be brutally frank, what's he like anyway? You don't have to go on paying for a dirty trick the rest of your life."

"It wasn't just a dirty trick. It would have been a dirty trick if I'd walked out on him the day we were getting married. But I went through with it, and that made it more than a dirty trick. I *should have* walked out on him, the day we got married. I even tried. And he'd have recovered—then. Don't forget, Pete McCrea was used to dirty tricks being played on him, and he might have got over it if I'd left him at the church. But once I'd married him, he became a different person, took himself much more seriously, and so did everyone else. They began to dislike him, but that was better than being laughed at." She sipped her drink.

"Well, who did it? I did. Your little pal," she said. "How about some more cheap whiskey?"

"No thanks, but you go ahead," I said.

"The first time I ever knew there *was* a Mill Street was the day we rented this house," she said, as she poured herself a drink. "I'd never been out this way before."

"You couldn't have lived here when the mill was operating. The noise and the smoke."

"I can live anywhere," she said. "So can anyone else. And don't be too surprised if you find us back on Lantenengo. Do you know the big thing nowadays? Slot machines and the numbers racket. Pete wants to get into The Numbers, but he hasn't decided how to go about it. Bill Charney is the kingpin in the county, although not the real head. It's run by a syndicate in Jersey City."

"Don't let him do it, Bobbie," I said. "Really don't."

"Why not? He's practically in it already. He has slot machines in the poolroom, and that's where people call up to find out what number won today. He might as well be in it."

"No."

"It's the only way Pete will ever have any money, and if he ever gets his hands on some money, maybe he'll divorce me. Then I could take the children and go away somewhere. California."

"That's a different story. If you're planning it that way. But stay out of The Numbers if you ever have any idea of remaining respectable. You can't just go in for a few years and then quit."

"Respectable? Do you think my son's going to be able to get into Princeton? His father is the proprietor of a poolroom, and they're going to know that when Angus gets older. Pete will never be anything else. He's found his niche. But if I took the children to California they might have a chance. And *I* might have a chance, before it's too late. It's our only hope, Jim. Phyllis agrees with me."

I realized that I would be arguing against a hope and a dream, and if she had that much left, and only that much, I had no right to argue. She very nearly followed my thinking. "It's what I live on, Jim," she said. "That—and this." She held up her glass. "And a little admiration. A little—admiration. Phyllis wants to give me a trip to New York. Would you take us to '21' and those places?"

"Sure."

"Could you get someone for Phyllis?"

"I think so. Sure. Joe wouldn't go on this trip?"

"And give up a chance to be with Mary Lander?"

"So now it's Joe and Mary?"

"Oh, that's old hat in Gibbsville. They don't even pretend otherwise."

"And Frank? What about him?"

"Frank is the forgotten man. If there were any justice he ought to pair off with Phyllis, but they don't like each other. Phyllis calls Frank a wishy-washy namby-pamby, and Frank calls Phyllis a drunken trouble-maker. We've all grown up, Jim. Oh, haven't we just? Joe doesn't like Phyllis to visit me because Mary says all we do is gossip. Although how she'd know *what* we do . . ."

"They were all at the funeral, and I thought what a dull, stuffy little group they've become," I said.

"But that's what they are," said Bobbie. "Very stuffy and very dull. What else is there for them to do? If I were still back there with them I'd be just as bad. Maybe worse. In a way, you know, Pete McCrea has turned out to be the most interesting man in our crowd, present company excepted. Joe was a very handsome young man and so was Frank, and their families had lots of money and all the rest of it. But you saw Joe and Frank today. I haven't seen them lately, but Joe looks like a professional wrestler and I remember how hairy he was, all over his chest and back and his arms and legs. And Frank just the opposite, skin like a girl's and slender, but now we could almost call *him* Ichabod. He looks like a cranky schoolteacher, and his glasses make him look like an owl. Mary, of course, beautifully dressed I'm sure, and not looking a day older."

"Several days older, but damn good-looking," I said.

A baby cried and Bobbie made no move. "That's my daughter. Teething. Now she'll wake up my son and you're in for a lot of howling." The son began to cry, and Bobbie excused herself. She came back in a few minutes with the infant in her arms. "It's against my rules to pick them up, but I wanted to show him to you. Isn't he an ugly little creature? The answer is yes." She took him away and returned with the daughter. "She's begun to have a face."

"Yes, I can see that. Your face, for which she can be thankful."

"Yes, I wouldn't want a girl to look like Pete. It doesn't matter so much with a boy." She took the girl away and when she rejoined me she refilled her glass.

"Are you sorry you didn't have children?" she said.

"Not the way it turned out, I'm not," I said.

"These two haven't had much of a start in life, the poor little things. They haven't even been christened. Do you know why? There was nobody we could ask to be their godfathers." Her eyes filled with tears. "That was when I really saw what we'd come to."

"Bobbie, I've got a four-hour drive ahead of me, so I think I'd better get started."

"Four hours to New York? In that car?"

"I'm going to stop and have a sandwich halfway."

"I could give you a sandwich and make some coffee."

"I don't want it now, thanks."

We looked at each other. "I'd like to show how much I appreciate your coming out to see me," she said. "But it's probably just as well I can't. But I'll be all right in New York, Jim. That is, if I ever get there. I won't believe that, either, till I'm on the train."

If she came to New York I did not know about it, and during the war years Bobbie and her problems receded from my interest. I heard that Pete was working in a defense plant, from which I inferred that he had not made the grade in the numbers racket. Frank Lander was in the Navy, Joe Whipple in the War Production Board, and by the time the war was over I discovered that so many other people and things had taken the place of Gibbsville in my thoughts that I had almost no active curiosity about the friends of my youth. I had even had a turn-over in my New York friendships. I had married again, I was working hard, and most of my social life originated with my wife's friends. I was making, for me, quite a lot of money, and I was a middle-aged man whose physician had made some honest, unequivocal remarks about my life expectancy. It took a little time and one illness to make me realize that if I wanted to see my child grow to maturity, I had to retire from night life. It was not nearly so difficult as I had always anticipated it would be.

After I became reconciled to middle age and the quieter life I made another discovery: that the sweetness of my early youth was a persistent and enduring thing, so long as I kept it at the distance of years. Moments would come back to me, of love and excitement and music and laughter that filled my breast as they had thirty years earlier. It was not nostalgia, which only means homesickness, nor was it a wish to be living that excitement again. It was a splendid contentment with the knowledge that once I had felt those things so deeply and well that the throbbing urging of George Gershwin's "Do It Again" could evoke the original sensation and the pictures that went with it: a tea dance at the club and a girl in a long black satin dress and my furious jealousy of a fellow who wore a yellow foulard tie. I wanted none of it ever again, but all I had I wanted to keep. I could remember precisely the tone in which her brother had said to her: "Are you coming or aren't you?" and the sounds of his galoshes after she said: "I'm going home with Mr. Malloy." They were the things I knew before we knew everything, and, I suppose, before we began to learn. There was always a girl, and nearly always there was music; if the Gershwin tune belonged to that girl, a Romberg tune belonged to another and "When Hearts Are Young" became a personal anthem, enduringly sweet and safe from all harm, among the protected memories. In middle age I was proud to have lived according to my emotions at the right time, and content to live that way vicariously and at a distance. I had missed almost nothing, escaped very little, and at fifty I had begun to devote my energy and time to the last, simple but big task of putting it all down as well as I knew how.

In the midst of putting it all down, as novels and short stories and plays, I would sometimes think of Bobbie McCrea and the dinginess of her history. But as the reader will presently learn, the "they"—life—that had once made me cry out in anger, were not through with her yet. (Of course "they" are never through with anyone while he still lives, and we are not concerned here with the laws of compensation that seem to test us, giving us just enough strength to carry us in another trial.) I like to think that Bobbie got enough pleasure out of a pair of nylons, a permanent wave, a bottle of Phyllis Whipple's whiskey, to recharge the brightness in her. As we again take up her story I promise the reader a happy ending, if only because I want it that way. It happens also to be the true ending. . . .

Pete McCrea did not lose his job at the end of the war. His Princeton degree helped there. He had gone into the plant, which specialized in aluminum extrusion, as a manual laborer, but his IBM card revealed that he had taken psychology courses in college, and he was transferred to Personnel. It seemed an odd choice, but it is not hard to imagine that Pete was better fitted by his experience as a poolroom proprietor than as a two-year student of psychology. At least he spoke both languages, he liked the work, and in 1945 he was not bumped by a returning veteran.

Fair Grounds, the town in which the plant was situated, was only three miles from Gibbsville. For nearly a hundred years it had been the trading center for the Pennsylvania Dutch farmers in the area, and its attractions had been Becker's general store, the Fair Grounds Bank, the freight office of the Reading Railway, the Fair Grounds Hotel, and five Protestant churches. Clerks at Becker's and at the bank and the Reading, and bartenders at the hotel and the pastors of the churches, all had to speak Pennsylvania Dutch. English was desirable but not a requirement. The town was kept scrubbed, dusted and painted, and until the erection of the aluminum plant, jobs and trades were kept in the same families. An engineman's son worked as waterboy until he was old enough to take the examinations for brakeman; a master mechanic would give his boy calipers for Christmas. There were men and women in Fair Grounds who visited Gibbsville only to serve on juries or to undergo surgery at the Gibbsville Hospital. There were some men and women who had never been to Gibbsville at all and regarded Gibbsville as some Gibbsville citizens regarded Paris, France. That was the pre-aluminum Fair Grounds.

To this town in 1941 went Pete and Bobbie McCrea. They rented a house no larger than the house on Mill Street but cleaner and in better repair. Their land-lord and his wife went to live with his mother-in-law, and collected the $50 legally frozen monthly rent and $50 side payment for the use of the radio and the gas stove. But in spite of under-the-table and black-market prices Peter and Bobbie McCrea were financially better off then they had been since their marriage, and nylons at black-market prices were preferable to the no nylons she had on Mill Street. The job, and the fact that he continued to hold it, restored some respect-ability to Pete, and they discussed rejoining the club. "Don't try it, I warn you," said Phyllis Whipple. "The club isn't run by your friends any more. Now it's been taken over by people that couldn't have got in ten years ago."

"Well, we'd have needed all our old friends to go to bat for us, and I guess some would think twice about it," said Pete. "So we'll do our drinking at the Tavern."

The Dan Patch Tavern, which was a new name for the renovated Fair Grounds Hotel bar, was busy all day and all night, and it was one of the places where Pete could take pleasure in his revived respectability. It was also one of the places where Bobbie could count on getting that little admiration that she needed to live on. On the day of Pearl Harbor she was only thirty-four years old and at the time of the Japanese surrender she was only thirty-eight. She was accorded admiration in abundance. Some afternoons just before the shift changed she would walk the three blocks to the Tavern and wait for Pete. The bartender on duty would say "Hi, Bobbie," and bring her currently favorite drink to her booth. Sometimes there would be four men sitting with her when Pete arrived from the plant; she was never alone for long. If one man tried to persuade her to leave, and became annoyingly insistent, the bartenders came to her rescue. The bartend-ers and the proprietor knew that in her way Bobbie was as profitable as the juke box. She was an attraction. She was a good-looking broad who was not a whore or a falling-down lush, and all her drinks were paid for. She was the Tavern's favorite customer, male or female, and if she had given the matter any thought she could have been declared in. All she wanted in return was a steady supply of Camels and protection from being mauled. The owner of the Tavern, Rudy Schau, was the only one who was aware that Bobbie and Pete had once lived on

Lantenengo Street in Gibbsville, but far from being impressed by their background, he had a German opinion of aristocrats who had lost standing. He was actively suspicious of Bobbie in the beginning, but in time he came to accept her as a wife whose independence he could not condone and a good-looking woman whose morals he had not been able to condemn. And she was good for business. Beer business was good, but at Bobbie's table nobody drank beer, and the real profit was in the hard stuff.

In the Fair Grounds of the pre-aluminum days Bobbie would have had few women friends. No decent woman would have gone to a saloon every day—or any day. She most likely would have received warnings from the Ku Klux Klan, which was concerned with personal conduct in a town that had only a dozen Catholic families, no Negroes and no Jews. But when the aluminum plant (which was called simply The Aluminum or The Loomy) went into war production the population of Fair Grounds immediately doubled and the solid Protestant character of the town was changed in a month. Eight hundred new people came to town and they lived in apartments in a town where there were no apartments: in rooms in private houses, in garages and old stables, in rented rooms and haylofts out in the farming area. The newcomers wasted no time with complaints of double-rent, inadequate heating, holes in the roof, insufficient sanitation. The town was no longer scrubbed, dusted or painted, and thousands of man-hours were lost while a new shift waited for the old to vacate parking space in the streets of the town. Bobbie and Pete were among the lucky early ones: they had a house. That fact of itself gave Bobbie some distinction. The house had two rooms and kitchen on the first floor, three rooms and bath on the second, and it had a cellar and an attic. In the identical houses on both sides there were a total of four families and six roomers. As a member of Personnel it was one of Pete's duties to find housing for workers, but Bobbie would have no roomers. "The money wouldn't do us much good, so let's live like human beings," she said.

"You mean there's nothing to buy with the money," said Pete. "But we could save it."

"If we had it, we'd spend it. You've never saved a cent in your life and neither have I. If you're thinking of the children's education, buy some more war bonds and have it taken out of your pay. But I'm not going to share my bathroom with a lot of dirty men. I'd have to do all the extra work, not you."

"You could make a lot of money doing their laundry. Fifty cents a shirt."

"Are you serious?"

"No."

"It's a good thing you're not, because I could tell you how else I could make a lot more money."

"Yes, a lot more," said Pete.

"Well, then, keep your ideas to yourself. I won't have boarders and I won't do laundry for fifty cents a shirt. That's final."

And so Bobbie had her house, she got the admiration she needed, and she achieved a moderate popularity among the women of her neighborhood by little friendly acts that came spontaneously out of her friendly nature. There was a dinginess to the new phase: the house was not much, the men who admired her and the women who welcomed her help were the ill-advantaged, the cheap, the vulgar, and sometimes the evil. But the next step down from Mill Street would have been hopeless degradation, and the next step up, Fair Grounds, was at least up. She was envied for her dingy house, and when Pete called her the Queen of the Klondike she was not altogether displeased. There was envy in the epithet, and in the envy was the first sign of respect he had shown her in ten years. He had never suspected her of an affair with Mac McCormick, and if he had suspected her during her infatuation with Bill Charney he had been afraid to make an accusation; afraid to anticipate his own feelings in the event that Charney would give him a job in The Numbers. When Charney brought in a Pole from Detroit for the job Pete had wanted, Pete accepted $1,000 for his share of the poolroom and felt only grateful relief. Charney did not always buy out his partners, and Pete refused to wonder if the money and the easy dissolution of the partnership had been paid for by Bobbie. It was not a question he wanted to raise, and when the war in Europe created jobs at Fair Grounds he believed that his luck had begun to change.

Whatever the state of Pete's luck, the pace of his marriage had begun to change. The pace of his marriage—and not his alone—was set by the time he spent at home and what he did during that time. For ten years he had spent little more time at home than was necessary for sleeping and eating. He could not sit still in the same room with Bobbie, and even after the children were born he did not like to have her present during the times he would play with them. He would arrive in a hurry to have his supper, and in a short time he would get out of the house, to be with a girl, to go back to work at the poolroom. He was most conscious of time when he was near Bobbie; everywhere else he moved slowly, spoke deliberately, answered hesitantly. But after the move to Fair Grounds he spent more time in the house, with the children, with Bobbie. He would sit in the front room, doing paper work from the plant, while Bobbie sewed. At the Tavern he would say to Bobbie: "It's time we were getting home." He no longer darted in and out of the house and ate his meals rapidly and in silence.

He had a new girl. Martha—"Martie"—Klinger was a typist at the plant, a Fair Grounds woman whose husband was in the Coast Guard at Lewes, Delaware. She was Bobbie's age and likewise had two children. She retained a young prettiness in the now round face and her figure had not quite reached the stage of plumpness. Sometimes when she moved an arm the flesh of her breast seemed to go all the way up to her neckline, and she had been one of the inspirations for a plant memo to women employees, suggesting that tight sweaters and tight slacks were out of place in wartime industry. Pete brought her to the Tavern one day after work, and she never took her eyes off Bobbie. She looked up and down, up and down, with her mouth half open as though she were listening to Bobbie through her lips. She showed no animosity of a defensive nature and was not openly possessive of Pete, but Bobbie knew on sight that she was Pete's new girl. After several sessions at the Tavern Bobbie could tell which of the men had already slept with Martie and which of them were likely to again. It was impossible to be jealous of Martie, but it was just as impossible not to feel superior to her. Pete, the somewhat changed Pete, kept up the absurd pretense that Martie was just a girl from the plant whom he happened to bring along for a drink, and there was no unpleasantness until one evening Martie said: "Jesus, I gotta go or I won't get any supper."

"Come on back to our house and have supper with us," said Pete. "That's okay by you, isn't it, Bobbie?"

"No, it isn't," said Bobbie.

"Rudy'll give us a steak and we can cook it at home," said Pete.

"I said no," said Bobbie, and offered no explanation.

"I'll see you all tomorrow," said Martie. "Goodnight, people."

"Why wouldn't you let her come home with us? I could have got a steak from Rudy. And Martie's a hell of a good cook."

"When we can afford a cook I may hire her," said Bobbie.

"Oh, that's what it is. The old snob department."

"That's exactly what it is."

"We're not in any position—"

"*You're* not."

"*We're* not. If I can't have my friends to my house," he said, but did not know how to finish.

"It's funny that she's the first one you ever asked. Don't forget what I told you about having boarders, and fifty cents a shirt. You keep your damn Marties out of my house. If you don't, I'll get a job and you'll be just another boarder yourself."

"Oh, why are you making such a stink about Martie?"

"Come *off* it, Pete, for heaven's *sake.*"

The next statement, he knew, would have to be a stupidly transparent lie or an admission, so he made no statement. If there had to be a showdown he preferred to avert it until the woman in question was someone more entertaining than Martie Klinger. And he liked the status quo.

They both liked the status quo. They had hated each other, their house, the dinginess of their existence on Mill Street. When the fire whistle blew it was within the hearing of Mill Street and of Lantenengo Street; rain from the same shower fell on Mill Street and Lantenengo Street; Mill Street and Lantenengo Street read the same Gibbsville newspaper at the same time every evening. And the items of their proximity only made the nearness worse, the remoteness of Mill Street from Lantenengo more vexatious. But Fair Grounds was a new town, where they had gone knowing literally nobody. They had spending money, a desirable house, the respectability of a white-collar job, and the restored confidence in a superiority to their neighbors that they had not allowed themselves to feel on Mill

Street. In the Dan Patch Tavern they would let things slip out that would have been meaningless on Mill Street, where their neighbors' daily concern was a loaf of bread and a bottle of milk. "Pete, did you know Jimmy Stewart, the movie actor?" "No, he was several classes behind me, but he was in my club." "Bobbie, what's it like on one of them yachts?" "I've only been on one, but it was fun while it lasted." They could talk now about past pleasures and luxuries without being contradicted by their surroundings, and their new friends at the Tavern had no knowledge of the decade of dinginess that lay between that past and this present. If their new friends also guessed that Pete McCrea was carrying on with Martie Klinger, that very fact made Bobbie more credibly and genuinely the woman who had once cruised in a yacht. They would have approved Bobbie's reason for not wanting Martie Klinger as a guest at supper, as they would have fiercely resented Pete's reference to Bobbie as the Queen of the Klondike. Unintentionally they were creating a symbol of order that they wanted in their lives as much as Bobbie needed admiration, and if the symbol and the admiration were slightly ersatz, what, in war years, was not?

There was no one among the Tavern friends whom Bobbie desired to make love with. "I'd give a week's pay to get in bed with you, Bobbie," said one of them.

"Fifty-two weeks' pay, did you say?" said Bobbie.

"No dame is worth fifty-two weeks' pay," said the man, a foreman named Dick Hartenstein.

"Oh, I don't know. In fifty-two weeks you make what?"

"A little over nine thousand. Nine gees, about."

"A lot of women can get that, Dick. I've heard of women getting a diamond necklace for just one night, and they cost a lot more than nine thousand dollars."

"Well, I tell you, Bobbie, if I ever hit the crap game for nine gees I'd seriously consider it, but not a year's pay that I worked for."

"You're not romantic enough for me. Sorry."

"Supposing I did hit the crap game and put nine gees on the table in front of you? Would you and me go to bed?"

"No."

"No, I guess not. If I asked you a question would you give me a truthful answer? No. You wouldn't."

"Why should I?"

"Yeah, why should you? I was gonna ask you, what does it take to get you in bed with a guy?"

"I'm a married woman."

"I skipped all that part, Bobbie. You'd go, if it was the right guy."

"You could get to be an awful nuisance, Dick. You're not far from it right this minute."

"I apologize."

"In fact, why don't you take your drink and stand at the bar?"

"What are you sore at? You get propositioned all the time."

"Yes, but you're too persistent, and you're a bore. The others don't keep asking questions when I tell them no. Go on, now, or I'll tell Rudy to keep you out of here."

"You know what you are?"

"Rudy! Will you come here, please?" she called. "All right, Dick. What am I? Say it in front of Rudy."

Rudy Schau made his way around from the bar. "What can I do for you, Bobbie?"

"I think Dick is getting ready to call me a nasty name."

"He won't," said Rudy Schau. He had the build of a man who had handled beer kegs all his life and he was now ready to squeeze the wind out of Hartenstein. "Apolochise to Bobbie and get the hell outa my place. And don't forget you got a forty-dollar tab here. You won't get a drink nowheres else in tahn."

"I'll pay my God damn tab," said Hartenstein.

"That you owe me. Bobbie you owe an apolochy."

"I apologize," said Hartenstein. He was immediately clipped behind the ear, and sunk to the floor.

"I never like that son of a bitch," said Rudy Schau. He looked down at the unconscious Hartenstein and very deliberately kicked him in the ribs.

"Oh, *don't*, Rudy," said Bobbie. "*Please* don't."

Others in the bar, which was now half filled, stood waiting for Rudy's next kick, and some of them looked at each other and then at Rudy, and they were already to rush him. Bobbie stood up quickly. "Don't, Rudy," she said.

"All right. I learned him. Joe, throw the son of a bitch out," said Rudy. Then suddenly he wheeled and grabbed a man by the belt and lifted him off the floor, holding him tight against his body with one hand and making a hammer of his other hand. "You, you son of a bitch, you was gonna go after me, you was, yeah? Well, go ahead. Let's see you, you son of a bitch. You son of a bitch, I break you in pieces." He let go and the man retreated out of range of Rudy's fist. "Pay your bill and don't come back. Don't ever show your face in my place again. And any other son of a bitch was gonna gang me. You gonna gang Rudy, hey? I kill any two of you." Two of the men picked Hartenstein off the floor before the bartender got to him. "Them two, they paid up, Joe?"

"In the clear, Rudy," said the bartender.

"You two. Don't come back," said Rudy.

"Don't worry. We won't," they said.

Rudy stood at Bobbie's table. "Okay if I sit down with you, Bobbie?"

"Of course," said Bobbie.

"Joe, a beer, please, hey? Bobbie, you ready?"

"Not yet, thanks," she said.

Rudy mopped his forehead with a handkerchief. "You don't have to take it from these bums," said Rudy. "Any time any of them get fresh, you tell me. You're what keeps this place decent, Bobbie. I know. As soon as you go home it's a pigpen. I get sick of hearing them, some of the women as bad as the men. Draft-dotchers. Essengial industry! Draft-dotchers. A bunch of 4-F draft-dotchers. I like to hear what your Daddy would say about them."

"Did you know him, my father?"

"Know him? I was in his platoon. Second platoon, C Company. I went over with him and come back with him. Phil Hammersmith."

"I never knew that."

Rudy chuckled. "Sure. Some of these 4-F draft-dotchers from outa town, they think I'm a Nazi because I never learn to speak good English, but my Daddy didn't speak no English at all and he was born out in the Walley. My old woman says put my dischartch papers up over the back-bar. I say what for? So's to make the good impression on a bunch of draft-dotchers? Corporal Rudolph W. Schau. Your Daddy was a good man and a good soldier."

"Why didn't you ever tell me you knew him?"

"Oh, I don't know, Bobbie. I wasn't gonna tell you now, but I did. It don't pay to be a talker in my business. A listener, not a talker."

"You didn't approve of me, did you?"

"I'm a saloonkeeper. A person comes to my—"

"You didn't approve of me. Don't dodge the issue."

"Well, your Daddy wouldn't of liked you coming to a saloon that often. But times change, and you're better off here than the other joints."

"I hope you don't *mind* my coming here."

"Listen, you come here as much as you want."

"Try and stop me," she said, smiling.

Pete joined them. "What happened to Dick Hartenstein?" he said.

"The same as will happen to anybody gets fresh with your wife," said Rudy, and got up and left them.

"There could be a hell of a stink about this. Rudy could lose his license if the Company wanted to press the point."

"Well, you just see that he doesn't," said Bobbie.

"Maybe it isn't such a good idea, your coming here so often."

"Maybe. On the other hand, maybe it's a wonderful idea. I happen to think it's a wonderful idea, so I'm going to keep on coming. If *you* want to go to one of the other places, that's all right. But I like Rudy's. I like it better than ever, now."

No action was taken against Rudy Schau, and Bobbie visited the Tavern as frequently as ever. Hartenstein was an unpopular foreman and the women said he got what had been coming to him for a long time. Bobbie's friends were pleased that their new symbol had such a forthright defender. It was even said that Bobbie had saved Hartenstein from a worse beating, a rumor that added to the respect she was given by the men and the women.

The McCrea children were not being brought up according to Lantenengo Street standards. On the three or four afternoons a week that Bobbie went to the

Tavern she would take her son and daughter to a neighbor's yard. On the other afternoons the neighbors' children would play in her yard. During bad weather and the worst of the winter the McCreas' house was in more frequent service as a nursery, since some of the neighbors were living in one- or two-room apartments. But none of the children, the McCreas' or the neighbors', had individual supervision. Children who had learned to walk were separated from those who were still crawling, on the proven theory that the crawling children were still defenseless against the whimsical cruelties of the older ones. Otherwise there was no distinction, and all the children were toughened early in life, as most of their parents had been. "I guess it's all right," Pete once said to Bobbie. "But I hate to think what they'll be like when they get older. Little gangsters."

"Well, that was never your trouble, God knows," said Bobbie. "And I'm no shining example of having a nannie take care of me. Do you remember my nannie?"

"Vaguely."

" 'Let's go and see the horsies,' she'd say. And we'd go to Mr. Duncan's stable and I'd come home covered with scratches from the stable cat. And I guess Patrick was covered with scratches from my nannie. Affectionate scratches, of course. Do you remember Mr. Duncan's Patrick?"

"Sure."

"He must have been quite a man. Phyllis used to go there with her nannie, too. But the cat liked Phyllis."

"I'm not suggesting that we have a nannie."

"No. You're suggesting that I stay away from the Tavern."

"In the afternoon."

"The afternoon is the only time the mothers will watch each other's children, except in rare cases. Our kids are all right. I'm with them all day most of the time, and we're home every evening, seven nights a week."

"What else is there to do?"

"Well, for instance once a month we could go to a movie."

"Where? Gibbsville?"

"Yes. Two gallons of gas at the most."

"Are you getting the itch to move back to Gibbsville?"

"Not at all. Are you?"

"Hell, no."

"We could get some high school kid to watch the children. I'd just like to have a change once in a while."

"All right. The next time there's something good at the Globe."

Their first trip to the Globe was their last. They saw no one they knew in the theatre or in the bar of the John Gibb Hotel, and when they came home the high school kid was naked in bed with a man Pete recognized from the plant. "Get out of here," said Pete.

"Is she your kid, McCrea?"

"No, she's not my kid. But did you ever hear of statutory rape?"

"Rape? This kid? I had to wait downstairs, for God's sake. She took on three other guys tonight. Ten bucks a crack."

The girl put on her clothes in sullen silence. She never spoke except to say to the man: "Do you have a room some place?"

"Well," said Pete, when they had gone. "Where did you get her from? The Junior League?"

"If you'd stared at her any more you'd have had to pay ten dollars too."

"For sixteen she had quite a shape."

"She won't have it much longer."

"You got an eyeful, too, don't pretend you didn't."

"Well, at least she won't get pregnant that way. And she *will* get *rich*," said Bobbie.

Pete laughed. "It was really quite funny. Where *did* you get her?"

"If you want her name and telephone number, I have it downstairs. I got her through one of the neighbors. She certainly got the word around quickly enough, where she'd be. There's the doorbell. Another customer?"

Pete went downstairs and informed the stranger at the door that he had the wrong address.

"Another customer, and I think he had two guys with him in the car. Seventy dollars she was going to make tonight. I guess I'm supposed to report this at the plant. We have a sort of a V-D file of known prostitutes. We sic the law on them before they infect the whole outfit, and I'll bet this little character—"

"Good heavens, yes. I must burn everything. Bed linen. Towels. Why the little bitch. Now I'm getting sore." She collected the linen and took it downstairs and to the trash burner in the yard. When she returned Pete was in bed, staring at the ceiling. "I'm going to sleep in the other room," she said.

"What's the matter?"

"I didn't like that tonight. I don't want to sleep with you."

"Oh, all right then, go to hell," said Pete.

She made up one of the beds in the adjoining room. He came and sat on the edge of her bed in the dark. "Go away, Pete," she said.

"Why?"

"Oh, all right, I'll *tell* you why. Tonight made me think of the time you wanted to exchange with Mary and Frank. That's all I've been able to think of."

"That's all passed, Bobbie. I'm not like that any more."

"You would have got in bed with that girl. I saw you."

"Then I'll tell you something. You would have got in bed with that man. I saw you, too. You were excited."

"How could I help being excited, to suddenly come upon something like that. But I was disgusted, too. And still am. Please go away and let me try to get some sleep."

She did not sleep until first light, and when the alarm clock sounded she prepared his and the children's breakfasts. She was tired and nervous throughout the day. She could not go to the Tavern because it was her turn to watch neighbors' children, and Pete telephoned and said bluntly that he would not be home for supper, offering no excuse. He got home after eleven that night, slightly drunk and with lipstick on his neck.

"Who was it? Martie?" said Bobbie.

"What difference does it make who it was? I've been trying to give up other women, but you're no help."

"I have no patience with that kind of excuse. It's easy enough to blame me. Remember, Pete, I can pick up a man as easily as you can make a date with Martie."

"I know you can, and you probably will."

It was the last year of the war, and she had remained faithful to Pete throughout the life of their son Angus. A week later she resumed her affair with Bill Charney. "You never forgot me," he said. "I never forgot you, either, Bobbie. I heard about you and Pete living in Fair Grounds. You know a couple times I took my car and dro' past your house to see which one it was. I didn't know, maybe you'd be sitting out on the front porch and if you saw me, you know. Maybe we just say hello and pass the time of day. But I didn't think no such thing, to tell you the God's honest truth. I got nothing against my wife, only she makes me weary. The house and the kids, she got me going to Mass every Sunday, all like that. But I ain't built that way, Bobbie. I'm the next thing to a hood, and you got that side of you, too. I'll make you any price you say, the other jerks you slept with, they never saw that side of you. You know, you hear a lot about love, Bobbie, but I guess I came closer to it with you than any other woman I ever knew. I never forgot you any more than you ever forgot me. It's what they call a mutual attraction. Like you know one person has it for another person."

"I know."

"I don't see how we stood it as long as we did. Be honest, now, didn't you often wish it was me instead of some other guy?"

"Yes."

"All right, I'll be honest with you. Many's the time in bed with my wife I used to say to myself, 'Peggy, you oughta take lessons from Bobbie McCrea.' But who can give lessons, huh? If you don't have the mutual attraction, you're nothin'. How do you think I look?" He slapped his belly. "You know I weigh the same as I used to weigh? You look good. You put on a little. What? Maybe six pounds?"

"Seven or eight."

"But you got it distributed. In another year Peggy's gonna weigh a hundred and fifty pounds, and I told her, I said either she took some of that off or I'd get another girl. Her heighth, you know. She can't get away with that much weight. I eat everything, but I do a lot of walking and standing. I guess I use up a lot of excess energy. Feel them muscles. Punch me in the belly. I got no fat on me anywhere, Bobbie. For my age I'm a perfect physical specimen. I could get any amount of insurance if I got out of The Numbers. But nobody's gonna knock me off so why do I want insurance? I may even give up The Numbers one of these days. I got a couple of things lined up, strictly, strictly legitimate, and when my kids are ready to go away to school, I may just give up The Numbers. For a price, naturally."

"That brings up a point."

"You need money? How much do you want? It's yours. I *mean* like ten, fifteen gees."

"No, no money. But everybody knows you now. Where can we meet?"

"What's the matter with here? I told you, I own this hotel."

"But I can't just come and go. People know me, too. I have an idea, though."

"What?"

"Buy a motel."

"Buy a motel. You know, that thought crossed me a year ago, but you know what I found out? They don't make money. You'd think they would, but those that come out ahead, you be surprised how little they make."

"There's one near Swedish Haven. It's only about a mile from my house."

"We want a big bed, not them twin beds. I tell you what I could do. I could rent one of the units by the month and move my own furniture in. How would that suit you?"

"I'd like it better if you owned the place."

"Blackmail? Is that what you're thinking about? Who'd blackmail me, Bobbie? Or my girl? I'm still a hood in the eyes of some people."

There was no set arrangement for their meetings. Bill Charney postponed the purchase of the motel until she understood he had no intention of buying it or of making any other arrangement that implied permanence. At first she resented his procrastination, but she discovered that she preferred his way; he would telephone her, she would telephone him whenever desire became urgent, and sometimes they would be together within an hour of the telephone call. They spaced out their meetings so that each one produced novelty and excitement, and a year passed and another and Bobbie passed the afternoon of her fortieth birthday with him.

It was characteristic of their relationship that she did not tell him it was her birthday. He always spoke of his wife and children and his business enterprises, but he did not notice that she never spoke of her home life. He was a completely egocentric man, equally admiring of his star sapphire ring on his strong short-fingered hand and of her slender waist, which in his egocentricity became his possession. Inevitably, because of the nature of his businesses, he had a reputation for being closemouthed, but alone with Bobbie he talked freely. "You know, Bobbie, I laid a friend of yours?"

"Was it fun?"

"Aren't you gonna ask me who?"

"You'll tell me."

"At least I guess she's a friend of yours. Mary Lander."

"She used to be a friend of mine. I haven't seen her in years."

"Yeah. While her husband was in the service. Frank."

"You're so busy, with all your women."

"There's seven days in the week, honey, and it don't take up too much of your time. This didn't last very long, anyway. Five, maybe six times I slept with her. I took her to New York twice, that is I met her there. The other times in her house. You know, she's a neighbor of mine."

"And very neighborly."

"Yeah, that's how it started. She come to my house to collect for something, some war drive, and Peggy said I took care of all them things so when I got home I made out a cheque and took it over to the Landers' and inside of fifteen minutes—less than that—we were necking all over the parlor. Hell, I knew the minute she opened the door—"

"One of those mutual attractions?"

"Yeah, sure. I gave her the cheque and she said, 'I don't know how to thank you,' and I said if she had a couple minutes I'd show her how. 'Oh, Mr. Charney,' but she didn't even tell me to get out, so I knew I was in."

"What ever broke up this romance?"

"Her. She had some guy in Washington, D.C., she was thinking of marrying, and when I finally got it out of her who the guy was, I powdered out. Joe Whipple. I gotta do business with Joe. We got a home-loan proposition that we're ready to go with any day, and this was three years ago when Joe and I were just talking about it, what they call the talking stage."

"So you're the one that broke it off, not Mary."

"If a guy's looking at you across a desk and thinking you're laying his girl, you stand to get a screwing from that guy. Not that I don't trust Joe, because I do."

"Do you trust Mary?"

"I wondered about that, if she'd blab to Joe. A dame like Mary Lander, is she gonna tell the guy she's thinking of marrying that she's been laying a hood like me? No. By the way, she's queer. She told me she'd go for a girl."

"I'm surprised she hasn't already."

"Maybe she has. I couldn't find out. I always try to find out."

"You never asked me."

"I knew you wouldn't. But a dame like Mary, as soon as she opened the door I knew I was in, but then the next thing is you find out what else she'll go for. In her case, the works, as long as it isn't gonna get around. I guess I always figured her right. I have to figure all angles, men *and* women. That's where my brother Ed was stupid. I used to say to him, find out what kind of a broad a guy goes for before you declare him in. Ed used to say all he had to do was play a game of cards with a guy. But according to my theory, everybody goes into a card game prepared. Both eyes open. But not a guy going after a broad. You find out more from broads, like take for instance Mary. Now I know Frank is married to a dame that is screwing his best friend, laid a hood like me, and will go for a girl. You think I'd ever depend on Frank Lander? No. And Joe Whipple. Married to a lush, and sleeping with his best friend's wife, Mary."

"Then you wouldn't depend on Joe, either?"

"Yes, I would. Women don't bother him. He don't care if his wife is a lush, he'll get his nooky from his best friend's wife, he *isn't* going to marry her because that was three-four years ago, and he's tough about everybody. His wife, his dame, his best friend, *and* the United States government. Because I tell you something, if we ever get going on the home-loan proposition, don't think Joe didn't use his job in Washington every chance he got. The partnership is gonna be me and Joe Whipple, because he's just as tough as I am. And one fine day he'll fall over dead from not taking care of himself, and I'll be the main guy. You know the only thing I don't like about you, Bobbie, is the booze. If you'd lay off the sauce for a year I'd get rid of Peggy, and you and I could get married. But booze is women's weakness like women are men's weakness."

"Men are women's weakness."

"No, you're wrong. Men don't make women talk, men don't make women lose their looks, and women can give up men for a hell of a long time, but a female lush is the worst kind of lush."

"Am I a lush?"

"You have a couple drinks every day, don't you?"

"Yes."

"Then you're on the way. Maybe you only take three-four drinks a day now, but five years from now three or four drinks will get you stewed, so you'll be stewed every day. That's a lush. Peggy eats like a God damn pig, but if she ever started drinking, I'd kick her out. Fortunately her old man died with the D.T.'s, so she's afraid of it."

"Would you mind getting me a nice double Scotch with a little water?"

"Why should I mind?" He grinned from back molar to back molar. "When you got a little load on, you forget home and mother." He got her the drink, she took it in her right hand and slowly poured it down his furry chest. He jumped when the icy drink touched him.

"Thank you so much," she said. "Been a very pleasant afternoon, but the party's over."

"You sore at me?"

"Yes, I am. I don't like being called a lush, and I certainly don't like you to think I'd make a good substitute for Peggy."

"You *are* sore."

"Yes."

The children did not know it was her birthday, but when Pete came home he handed her two parcels. "For me?" she said.

451

"Not very much imagination, but I didn't have a chance to go to Gibbsville," he said.

One package contained half a dozen nylons, the other a bottle of Channel Number 5. "Thank you. Just what I wanted. I really did."

He suddenly began to cry, and rushed out of the room.

"Why is Daddy crying?" said their daughter.

"Because it's my birthday and he did a very sweet thing."

"Why should he cry?" said their son. He was nine years old, the daughter eleven.

"Because he's sentimental," said the daughter.

"And it's a very nice thing to be," said Bobbie.

"Aren't you going to go to him?"

"Not quite yet. In a minute. Angus, will you go down to the drug store and get a quart of ice cream? Here's a dollar, and you and your sister may keep the change, divided."

"What flavor?" said the boy.

"Vanilla and strawberry, or whatever else they have."

Pete returned. "Kids gone to bed?"

"I sent them for some ice cream."

"Did they see me bawling?"

"Yes, and I think it did them good. Marjorie understood it. Angus was a little mystified. But it was good for both of them."

"Marjorie understood it? Did you?"

"She said it was because you were sentimental."

He shook his head. "I don't know if you'd call it sentimental. I just couldn't help thinking you were forty years old. Forty. You forty. Bobbie Hammersmith. And all we've been through, and what I've done to you. I know why you married me, Bobbie, but why did you stick it out?"

"Because I married you."

"Yes. Because you married Ichabod. You know, I wasn't in love with you when we were first married. You thought I was, but I wasn't. It was wonderful, being in bed with you and watching you walking around without any clothes on. Taking a bath. But it was too much for me and that's what started me making passes at everybody. And underneath it all I knew damn well why you married me and I hated you. You were making a fool of me and I kept waiting for you to say this farce was over. If you had, I'd have killed you."

"And I guess rightly."

"And all the later stuff. Running a poolroom and living on Mill Street. I blamed all of that on you. But things are better now since we moved here. Aren't they?"

"Yes, much better, as far as the way we live—"

"That's all I meant. If we didn't have Lantenengo Street and Princeton and those things to look back on, this wouldn't be a bad life for two ordinary people."

"It's not bad," she said.

"It's still pretty bad, but that's because we once had it better. Here's what I want to say. Any time you want to walk out on me, I won't make any fuss. You can have the children, and I won't fight about it. That's my birthday present to you, before it's too late. And I have no plans for myself. I'm not trying to get out of this marriage, but you're forty now and you're entitled to whatever is left."

"Thank you, Pete. I have nobody that wants to marry me."

"Well, maybe not. But you may have, sometime. I love you now, Bobbie, and I never used to. I guess you can't love anybody else while you have no self-respect. When the war was over I was sure I'd get the bounce at the plant, but they like me there, they've kept me on, and that one promotion. We'll never be back on Lantenengo Street, but I think I can count on a job here maybe the rest of my life. In a couple of years we can move to a nicer house."

"I'd rather buy this and fix it up a little. It's a better-built house than the ones they're putting up over on Fair Grounds Heights."

"Well, I'm glad you like it too," he said. "The other thing, that we hardly ever talk about. In fact never talk about. Only fight about sometimes. I'll try, Bobbie. I've been trying."

"I know you have."

"Well—how about you trying, too?"

"I did."

"But not lately. I'm not going to ask you who or when or any of that, but why is it you're faithful to me while I'm chasing after other women, and then when I'm faithful to you, you have somebody else? You're forty now and I'm forty-four. Let's see how long we can go without cheating?"

"You don't mean put a time limit on it, or put up a trophy, like an endurance contest? That's the way it sounds. We both have bad habits, Pete."

"Yes, and I'm the worst. But break if off, Bobbie, whoever it is. Will you please? If it's somebody you're not going to marry, and that's what you said, I've—well, it's a long time since I've cheated, and I like it much better this way. Will you stop seeing this other guy?"

"All right. As a matter of fact I *have* stopped, but don't ask me how long ago."

"I won't ask you anything. And if you fall in love with somebody and want to marry him—"

"And he wants to marry me."

"And he wants to marry you, I'll bow out." He leaned down and kissed her cheek. "I know you better than you think I do, Bobbie."

"That's an irritating statement to make to any woman."

"I guess it is, but not the way I meant it."

Now that is as far as I need go in the story of Pete and Bobbie McCrea. I promised a happy ending, which I shall come to in a moment. We have left Pete and Bobbie in 1947, on Bobbie's fortieth birthday. During the next thirteen years I saw them twice. On one occasion my wife and I spent the night with them in their house in Fair Grounds, which was painted, scrubbed and dusted like the Fair Grounds houses of old. My wife went to bed early, and Pete and Bobbie and I talked until past midnight, and then Pete retired and Bobbie and I continued our conversation until three in the morning. Twice she emptied our ash trays of cigarette butts, and we drank a drip-flask of coffee. It seemed to me that she was so thorough in her description of their life because she felt that the dinginess would vanish if she once succeeded in exposing it. But as we were leaving in the morning I was not so sure that it had vanished. My wife said to me: "Did she get it all out of her system?"

"Get what out of her system?"

"I don't know, but I don't think she did, entirely."

"That would be asking too much," I said. "But I guess she's happy."

"Content, but not happy," said my wife. "But the children are what interested me. The girl is going to be attractive in a few more years, but that boy! You didn't talk to him, but do you know about him? He's fourteen, and he's already passed his senior mathematics. He's *finished* the work that the high school seniors are supposed to be taking. The principal is trying to arrange correspondence courses for him. He's the brightest student they ever had in Fair Grounds High School, ever, and all the scientific men at the aluminum plant know about him. And he's a good-looking boy, too."

"Bobbie didn't tell me any of this."

"And I'll bet I know why. He's their future. With you she wanted to get rid of the past. She adores this boy, adores him. That part's almost terrifying."

"Not to me," I said. "It's the best thing that could have happened to her, and to Pete. The only thing that's terrifying is that they could have ruined it. And believe me, they could have."

In 1960, then, I saw Pete and Bobbie again. They invited me, of all their old friends, to go with them to the Princeton commencement. Angus McCrea, Junior, led his class, was awarded the mathematics prize, the physics prize, the Eubank Prize for scholarship, and some other honors that I am sure are listed in the program. I could not read the program because I was crying most of the time. Pete would lean forward in his chair, listening to the things that were being said about his son, but in an attitude that would have been more suitable to a man who was listening to a pronouncement of sentence. Bobbie sat erect and smiling, but every once in a while I could hear her whisper, "Oh, God. Oh, God."

There, I guess, is our happy ending.

KATHERINE ANNE PORTER
(1890–1980)

KATHERINE ANNE PORTER was born in Indian Creek, Texas, and educated in Texas convent schools. Her mother died when she was two; she was raised by a strong-willed grandmother and by her father; both, in different ways, seem to have been remote in their affections. As an adult, from the twenties to the late thirties, Katherine Anne Porter lived in New York, Europe, and Mexico. In the introduction to her *Collected Stories* (1965), she called Mexico her "much-loved second country"; it is the setting for a number of her stories. She did a stint as a newspaper reporter and editor, published translations of Spanish, Latin American, and French fiction, and wrote a study of the arts and crafts of Mexico. Her career as a writer of fiction spanned five decades—from the twenties to the sixties. Her first published story, "María Concepción," appeared in 1922 in *Century Magazine,* under the editorship of the critic Carl Van Doren, an early, influential admirer of her work. Among her many awards and honors were two Guggenheim Fellowships, the National Book Award, the Pulitzer Prize for fiction, and the National Academy and National Institute of Arts and Letters Gold Medal for fiction, as well as numerous honorary degrees. She held writer-in-residence posts at Stanford University, the University of Chicago, and the University of Michigan.

Porter had a passionate, extravagant nature, and an accompanying tendency to embellish some of the facts of her life and to obscure others, such as her birthdate and the number of her marriages (four). Whatever facts may be in dispute, what is indisputable is that Katherine Anne Porter was an exemplary artist. In her relation to the truth of her stories, she was exacting. She was not prolific; her output consists chiefly of some twenty-seven short works—stories and short novels. Her only long work was the novel *Ship of Fools,* published in 1962, some twenty years in the making. But what was sustained, in her shorter work certainly, was quality. Her art and her craft were of the highest order, with language, structure, and meaning wholly integrated in their fidelity to the story.

In the space of a few pages, "Rope" (1930) depicts a childless marriage, where each partner works, with an adultery having occurred in the recent past. The husband brings home a rope from the store; his wife's request for coffee just slipped his mind. She asks: Where is my coffee? Why a rope? He doesn't exactly know, except to indicate a rope has its uses. Its uses are left to our inference: the tie that binds? at the end of one's rope? In the course of the story, the rope and the argument it triggers reveal, layer by layer, the marriage's multiple meanings as well as its facts. All are condensed here, to a rare perfection.

Rope

On the third day after they moved to the country he came walking back from the village carrying a basket of groceries and a twenty-four-yard coil of rope. She came out to meet him, wiping her hands on her green smock. Her hair was tumbled, her nose was scarlet with sunburn; he told her that already she looked like a born country woman. His gray flannel shirt stuck to him, his heavy shoes were dusty. She assured him he looked like a rural character in a play.

Had he brought the coffee? She had been waiting all day long for coffee. They had forgot it when they ordered at the store the first day.

Gosh, no, he hadn't. Lord, now he'd have to go back. Yes, he would if it killed him. He thought, though, he had everything else. She reminded him it was only because he didn't drink coffee himself. If he did he would remember it quick enough. Suppose they ran out of cigarettes? Then she saw the rope. What was that for? Well, he thought it might do to hang clothes on, or something. Naturally she asked him if he thought they were going to run a laundry? They already had a fifty-foot line hanging right before his eyes? Why, hadn't he noticed it, really? It was a blot on the landscape to her.

He thought there were a lot of things a rope might come in handy for. She wanted to know what, for instance. He thought a few seconds, but nothing occurred. They could wait and see, couldn't they? You need all sorts of strange odds and ends around a place in the country. She said, yes, that was so; but she thought just at that time when every penny counted, it seemed funny to buy more rope. That was all. She hadn't meant anything else. She hadn't just seen, not at first, why he felt it was necessary.

Well, thunder, he had bought it because he wanted to, and that was all there was to it. She thought that was reason enough, and couldn't understand why he hadn't said so, at first. Undoubtedly it would be useful, twenty-four yards of rope, there were hundreds of things, she couldn't think of any at the moment, but it would come in. Of course. As he had said, things always did in the country.

But she was a little disappointed about the coffee, and oh, look, look, look at the eggs! Oh, my, they're all running! What had he put on top of them? Hadn't he known eggs mustn't be squeezed? Squeezed, who had squeezed them, he wanted to know. What a silly thing to say. He had simply brought them along in the basket with the other things. If they got broke it was the grocer's fault. He should know better than to put heavy things on top of eggs.

She believed it was the rope. That was the heaviest thing in the pack, she saw him plainly when he came in from the road, the rope was a big package on top of everything. He desired the whole wide world to witness that this was not a fact. He had carried the rope in one hand and the basket in the other, and what was the use of her having eyes if that was the best they could do for her?

Well, anyhow, she could see one thing plain: no eggs for breakfast. They'd have to scramble them now, for supper. It was too damned bad. She had planned to have steak for supper. No ice, meat wouldn't keep. He wanted to know why she couldn't finish breaking the eggs in a bowl and set them in a cool place.

Cool place! if he could find one for her, she'd be glad to set them there. Well, then, it seemed to him they might very well cook the meat at the same time they cooked the eggs and then warm up the meat for tomorrow. The idea simply choked her. Warmed-over meat, when they might as well have had it fresh. Second best and scraps and makeshifts, even to the meat! He rubbed her shoulder a little. It doesn't really matter so much, does it, darling? Sometimes when they were playful, he would rub her shoulder and she would arch and purr. This time she hissed and almost clawed. He was getting ready to say that they could surely manage somehow when she turned on him and said, if he told her they could manage somehow she would certainly slap his face.

He swallowed the words red hot, his face burned. He picked up the rope and started to put it on the top shelf. She would not have it on the top shelf, the jars and tins belonged there; positively she would not have the top shelf cluttered up with a lot of rope. She had borne all the clutter she meant to bear in the flat in town, there was space here at least and she meant to keep things in order.

Well, in that case, he wanted to know what the hammer and nails were doing up there? And why had she put them there when she knew very well he needed that hammer and those nails upstairs to fix the window sashes? She simply slowed down everything and made double work on the place with her insane habit of changing things around and hiding them.

She was sure she begged his pardon, and if she had had any reason to believe he was going to fix the sashes this summer she would have left the hammer and nails right where he put them; in the middle of the bedroom floor where they could step on them in the dark. And now if he didn't clear the whole mess out of there she would throw them down the well.

Oh, all right, all right—could he put them in the closet? Naturally not, there were brooms and mops and dustpans in the closet, and why couldn't he find a place for his rope outside her kitchen? Had he stopped to consider there were seven God-forsaken rooms in the house, and only one kitchen?

He wanted to know what of it? And did she realize she was making a complete fool of herself? And what did she take him for, a three-year-old idiot? The whole trouble with her was she needed something weaker than she was to heckle and tyrannize over. He wished to God now they had a couple of children she could take it out on. Maybe he'd get some rest.

Her face changed at this, she reminded him he had forgot the coffee and had bought a worthless piece of rope. And when she thought of all the things they actually needed to make the place even decently fit to live in, well, she could cry, that was all. She looked so forlorn, so lost and despairing he couldn't believe it was only a piece of rope that was causing all the racket. What *was* the matter, for God's sake?

Oh, would he please hush and go away, and *stay* away, if he could, for five minutes? By all means, yes, he would. He'd stay away indefinitely if she wished. Lord, yes, there was nothing he'd like better than to clear out and never come back. She couldn't for the life of her see what was holding him, then. It was a swell time. Here she was, stuck, miles from a railroad, with a half-empty house on her hands, and not a penny in her pocket, and everything on earth to do; it seemed the God-sent moment for him to get out from under. She was surprised he hadn't stayed in town as it was until she had come out and done the work and got things straightened out. It was his usual trick.

It appeared to him that this was going a little far. Just a touch out of bounds, if she didn't mind his saying so. Why the hell had he stayed in town the summer before? To do a half-dozen extra jobs to get the money he had sent her. That was it. She knew perfectly well they couldn't have done it otherwise. She had agreed with him at the time. And that was the only time so help him he had ever left her to do anything by herself.

Oh, he could tell that to his great-grandmother. She had her notion of what had kept him in town. Considerably more than a notion, if he wanted to know. So, she was going to bring all that up again, was she? Well, she could just think what she pleased. He was tired of explaining. It may have looked funny but he had simply got hooked in, and what could he do? It was impossible to believe that she was going to take it seriously. Yes, yes, she knew how it was with a man: if he was left by himself a minute, some woman was certain to kidnap him. And naturally he couldn't hurt her feelings by refusing!

Well, what was she raving about? Did she forget she had told him those two weeks alone in the country were the happiest she had known for four years? And how long had they been married when she said that? All right, shut up! If she thought that hadn't stuck in his craw.

She hadn't meant she was happy because she was away from him. She meant she was happy getting the devilish house nice and ready for him. That was what she had meant, and now look! Bringing up something she had said a year ago simply to justify himself for forgetting her coffee and breaking the eggs and buying a wretched piece of rope they couldn't afford. She really thought it was time to drop the subject, and now she wanted only two things in the world. She wanted him to get that rope from underfoot, and go back to the village and get her coffee, and if he could remember it, he might bring a metal mitt for the skillets, and two more curtain rods, and if there were any rubber gloves in the village, her hands were simply raw, and a bottle of milk of magnesia from the drugstore.

He looked out at the dark blue afternoon sweltering on the slopes, and mopped his forehead and sighed heavily and said, if only she could wait a minute for *anything*, he was going back. He had said so, hadn't he, the very instant they found he had overlooked it?

Oh, yes, well . . . run along. She was going to wash windows. The country was so beautiful! She doubted they'd have a moment to enjoy it. He meant to go, but he could not until he had said that if she wasn't such a hopeless melancholiac she might see that this was only for a few days. Couldn't she remember anything pleasant about the other summers? Hadn't they ever had any fun? She hadn't time to talk about it, and now would he please not leave that rope lying around for her to trip on? He picked it up, somehow it had toppled off the table, and walked out with it under his arm.

Was he going this minute? He certainly was. She thought so. Sometimes it seemed to her he had second sight about the precisely perfect moment to leave her ditched. She had meant to put the mattresses out to sun, if they put them out this minute they would get at least three hours, he must have heard her say that morning she meant to put them out. So of course he would walk off and leave her to it. She supposed he thought the exercise would do her good.

Well, he was merely going to get her coffee. A four-mile walk for two pounds of coffee was ridiculous, but he was perfectly willing to do it. The habit was making a wreck of her, but if she wanted to wreck herself there was nothing he could do about it. If he thought it was coffee that was making a wreck of her, she congratulated him: he must have a damned easy conscience.

Conscience or no conscience, he didn't see why the mattresses couldn't very well wait until tomorrow. And anyhow, for God's sake, were they living *in* the house, or were they going to let the house ride them to death? She paled at this, her face grew livid about the mouth, she looked quite dangerous, and reminded him that housekeeping was no more her work than it was his: she had other work to do as well, and when did he think she was going to find time to do it at this rate?

Was she going to start on that again? She knew as well as he did that his work brought in the regular money, hers was only occasional, if they depended on what *she* made—and she might as well get straight on this question once for all!

That was positively not the point. The question was, when both of them were working on their own time, was there going to be a division of the housework, or wasn't there? She merely wanted to know, she had to make her plans. Why, he thought that was all arranged. It was understood that he was to help. Hadn't he always, in summers?

Hadn't he, though? Oh, just hadn't he? And when, and where, and doing what? Lord, what an uproarious joke!

It was such a very uproarious joke that her face turned slightly purple, and she screamed with laughter. She laughed so hard she had to sit down, and finally a rush of tears spurted from her eyes and poured down into the lifted corners of her mouth. He dashed towards her and dragged her up to her feet and tried to pour water on her head. The dipper hung by a string on a nail and he broke it loose. Then he tried to pump water with one hand while she struggled in the other. So he gave it up and shook her instead.

She wrenched away, crying out for him to take his rope and go to hell, she had simply given him up: and ran. He heard her high-heeled bedroom slippers clattering and stumbling on the stairs.

He went out around the house and into the lane; he suddenly realized he had a blister on his heel and his shirt felt as if it were on fire. Things broke so suddenly you didn't know where you were. She could work herself into a fury about simply nothing. She was terrible, damn it: not an ounce of reason. You might as well talk to a sieve as that woman when she got going. Damned if he'd spend his life humoring her! Well, what to do now? He would take back the rope and exchange it for something else. Things accumulated, things were mountainous, you couldn't move them or sort them out or get rid of them. They just lay and rotted around. He'd take it back. Hell, why should he? He wanted it. What was it anyhow? A piece of rope. Imagine anybody caring more about a piece of rope than about a man's feelings. What earthly right had she to say a word about it? He remembered all the useless, meaningless things she bought for herself: Why? because I wanted it, that's why! He stopped and selected a large stone by the road. He would put the rope behind it. He would put it in the tool-box when he got back. He'd heard enough about it to last him a life-time.

When he came back she was leaning against the post box beside the road waiting. It was pretty late, the smell of broiled steak floated nose high in the cooling air. Her face was young and smooth and fresh-looking. Her unmanageable funny black hair was all on end. She waved to him from a distance, and he speeded up. She called out that supper was ready and waiting, was he starved?

You bet he was starved. Here was the coffee. He waved it at her. She looked at his other hand. What was that he had there?

Well, it was the rope again. He stopped short. He had meant to exchange it but forgot. She wanted to know why he should exchange it, if it was something he really wanted. Wasn't the air sweet now, and wasn't it fine to be here?

She walked beside him with one hand hooked into his leather belt. She pulled and jostled him a little as he walked, and leaned against him. He put his arm clear around her and patted her stomach. They exchanged wary smiles. Coffee, coffee for the Ootsum-Wootsums! He felt as if he were bringing her a beautiful present.

He was a love, she firmly believed, and if she had had her coffee in the morning, she wouldn't have behaved so funny . . . There was a whippoorwill still coming back, imagine, clear out of season, sitting in the crab-apple tree calling all by himself. Maybe his girl stood him up. Maybe she did. She hoped to hear him once more, she loved whippoorwills . . . He knew how she was, didn't he?

Sure, he knew how she was.

V. S. PRITCHETT

(1900–)

V. S. PRITCHETT, essayist, novelist, and short-story writer, was born Victor Sawdon Pritchett in Ipswich, England. He married Dorothy Rudge Roberts in 1936; they have two children. Early on, Pritchett worked in the leather trade, and later as a commercial traveler and shop assistant. From 1921 to 1928, as a free-lance journalist, he traveled to France, Ireland, Spain, Morocco, and the United States. Turning subsequently to literary criticism, Pritchett wrote for the *New Statesman* and *Nation,* and became a frequent contributor to such American publications as the *New York Times Book Review.* His writings include several books of literary criticism, as well as memoirs, biographies (of Balzac, Turgenev, and Chekhov), travel books, novels, and numerous volumes of short stories, including the *Complete Collected Stories* (1991), which features more than eighty stories. Pritchett has lectured and taught at Smith College, Princeton University, the University of California at Berkeley, Brandeis University, Columbia University, and Cambridge University. His awards include the Royal Society of Literature Award and the Heinemann and PEN awards for nonfiction; he is an honorary foreign member of the American Academy of Arts and Sciences and the American Academy of Arts and Letters. In 1975 he was knighted.

Pritchett is considered one of the preeminent writers of our time, distinguished in all of the forms to which he has contributed. Still, if one of these is to be given an edge, the critical consensus seems to be that it goes to his masterly short stories; Pritchett himself has been said to prize them most.

"Blind Love" (1969) is a characteristically deft and deep performance in which the story line remains consistently in the foreground. The narrative tautness relaxes at startling intervals to allow room for the complications of plot and character. The story elements, having to do with the alchemy of love, are all orchestrated with superb control. When Mrs. Johnson takes a job as housekeeper to the blind Mr. Armitage, she finds his household intricately organized under a system he has devised, designed to serve as a foolproof way for him to get around. Part of Mrs. Johnson's job is to help maintain this system. The structure of the household, for the story, is life as it was. But it does get disturbed, for Mrs. Johnson has brought her own unhappy history with her. Just as Mr. Armitage is marked by his blindness, her body is disfigured by a "stain" she has been at pains to conceal. But this badge of her shame could not be noted by a blind man. Or could it? The story may be using the motif of the lovers' dovetailing handicaps as metaphors for the hurdles to intimacy that people themselves create.

Blind Love

"I'm beginning to be worried about Mr. 'Wolverhampton' Smith," said Mr. Armitage to Mrs. Johnson, who was sitting in his study with her notebook on her knee and glancing from time to time at the window. She was watching the gardener's dog rooting in a flower bed. "Would you read his letter again: the second paragraph about the question of a partnership?"

Since Mr. Armitage was blind it was one of Mrs. Johnson's duties to read his correspondence.

"He had the money—that is certain; but I can't make out on what conditions," he said.

"I'd say he helped himself. He didn't put it into the business at Ealing—he used it to pay off the arrears on the place at Wolverhampton," she said in her cheerful manner.

"I'm afraid you're right. It's his character I'm worried about," said Mr. Armitage.

"There isn't a single full stop in his letter—a full page on both sides. None. And all his words are joined together. It's like one word two pages long," said Mrs. Johnson.

"Is that so?" said Mr. Armitage. "I'm afraid he has an unpunctuated moral sense."

Coming from a blind man whose open eyes and face had the fixed gleam of expression you might have seen on a piece of rock, the word "unpunctuated" had a sarcasm unlike an ordinary sarcasm. It seemed, quite delusively, to come from a clearer knowledge than any available to the sighted.

"I think I'll go and smell out what he's like. Where is Leverton Grove? Isn't it on the way to the station? I'll drop in when I go up to London tomorrow morning," said Mr. Armitage.

The next morning he was driven in his Rolls-Royce to Mr. Smith's house, one of two or three little villas that were part of a building speculation that had come to nothing fifty years before. The yellow-brick place was darkened by the firs that were thick in this district. Mrs. Johnson, who had been brought up in London houses like this, winced at the sight of them. (Afterwards she said to Mr. Armitage, "It brings it back." They were talking about her earlier life.) The chauffeur opened the car door, Mrs. Johnson got out, saying "No kerb," but Armitage waving her aside, stepped out unhelped and stood stiff with the sainted upward gaze of the blind; then, like an Army detail, the party made a sharp right turn, walked two paces, then a sharp left to the wooden gate, which the chauffeur opened, and went forward in step.

"Daffodils," said Mrs. Johnson, noting a flower bed. She was wearing blue to match her bold, practical eyes, and led the way up the short path to the door. It was opened before she rang by an elderly, sick-looking woman with swollen knuckles who half hid behind the door as she held it, to expose Smith standing with his grey jacket open, his hands in his pockets—the whole man an arrangement of soft smiles from his snowball head to his waistcoat, from his fly to his knees, sixteen stone of modest welcome with nothing to hide.

"It is good of you to come," he said. He had a reverent voice.

"On my way to the station," said Armitage.

Smith was not quite so welcoming to Mrs. Johnson. He gave her a dismissive frown and glanced peremptorily at his wife.

"In here?" said Mrs. Johnson, briskly taking Armitage's arm in the narrow hall.

"Yes," he said.

They all stood just inside the doorway of the front room. A fir tree darkened it. It had, Mrs. Johnson recorded at once, two fenders in the fireplace, and two sets of fire-irons; then she saw two of everything—two clocks on the fireplace, two small sofas, a dining table folded up, even two carpets on the floor, for underneath the red one, there was the fringe of a worn yellow one.

Mr. Smith saw that she noted this and, raising a grand chin and now unsmiling, said, "We're sharing the 'ouse, the house, until we get into something bigger."

And at this, Mrs. Smith looked with the searching look of an agony in her eyes, begging Mrs. Johnson for a word.

"Bigger," echoed Mrs. Smith and watched to see the word sink in. And then, putting her fingers over her face, she said, "Much bigger," and laughed.

"Perhaps," said Mr. Smith, who did not care for his wife's laugh, "while we talk—er . . ."

"I'll wait outside in the car," said the decisive Mrs. Johnson, and when she was in the car she saw Mrs. Smith's gaze of appeal from the step.

A half an hour later, the door opened and Mrs. Johnson went to fetch Mr. Armitage.

"At this time of the year the daffodils are wonderful round here," said Armitage as he shook hands with Smith, to show that if he could not see there were a lot of things he knew. Mr. Smith took the point and replaced his smiling voice with one of sportive yet friendly rebuke, putting Mr. Armitage in his place.

"There is only one eye," he stated as if reading aloud. "The eye of God."

Softly the Rolls drove off, with Mrs. Smith looking at it fearfully from the edge of the window curtain.

"Very rum fellow," said Armitage in the car. "I'm afraid he's in a mess. The Inland Revenue are after him as well. He's quite happy because there's nothing to be got out of him. Remarkable. I'm afraid his friends have lost their money."

Mrs. Johnson was indignant.

"What's he going to do down here? He can't open up again."

"He's come here," Armitage said, "because of the chalk in London water. The chalk, he says, gets into the system with the result that the whole of London is riddled with arthritis and nervous diseases. Or rather the whole of London is riddled with arthritis and nervous diseases because it believes in the reality of chalk. Now, chalk has no reality. We are not living on chalk or even on gravel: we dwell in God. Mr. Smith explains that God led him to manage a chemist's shop in Wolverhampton, and to open one of his own in Ealing without capital. He now realizes that he was following his own will, not the will of God. He is now doing God's work. Yesterday he had a cable from California. He showed it to me. 'Mary's cancer cured gratitude cheque follows.' He's a faith healer."

"He ought to be in jail," said Mrs. Johnson.

"Oh, no. He's in heaven," said Armitage. "I'm glad I went to see him. I didn't know about his religion, but it's perfect: you get witnesses like him in court every day, always moving on to higher things."

The Rolls arrived at the station and Mr. Armitage picked up his white stick.

"Cancer today. Why not blindness tomorrow? Eh?" he said. Armitage gave one low laugh from a wide mouth. And though she enjoyed his dryness, his rare laugh gave a dangerous animal expression to a face that was usually closed. He got out of the car and she watched him walk into the booking hall and saw knots of people divide to make way for him on the platform.

In the damp town at the bottom of the hills, in the shops, at the railway station where twice a week the Rolls waited for him to come back from London, it was agreed that Armitage was a wonder. A gentleman, of course, they said; he's well-off, that helps. And there is that secretary-housekeeper, Mrs. Johnson. That's how he can keep up his legal business. He takes his stick to London, but down here he never uses it. In London he has his lunch in his office or in his club, and can manage the club stairs which worry some of the members when they come out of the bar. He knows what's in the papers—ever had an argument with him?—of course Mrs. Johnson reads them to him.

All true. His house stood, with a sudden flash of Edwardian prosperity, between two larch coppices on a hill five miles out and he could walk out on to the brick terrace and smell the lavender in its season and the grass of the lawns that went steeply down to his rose garden and the blue tiles of his swimming pool boxed in by yew.

"Fabian Tudor. Bernard Shaw used to come here—before our time, of course," he would say, disparaging the high, panelled hall. He was really referring to his wife, who had left him when he was going blind twenty-two years ago. She had chosen and furnished the house. She liked leaded windows, brass, plain velvet curtains, Persian carpets, brick fireplaces and the expensive smell of wood smoke.

"All fake," he would say, "like me."

You could see that pride made him like to embarrass. He seemed to know the effect of jokes from a dead face. But, in fact, if he had no animation—Mrs. Johnson had soon perceived in her commonsensical way—this was because he was not affected, as people are, by the movements on other faces. Our faces, she had learned from Armitage, threw their lives away every minute. He stored his. She knew this because she stored hers. She did not put it like this, in fact what she said appeared to contradict it. She liked a joke.

"It's no good brooding. As Mother used to say, as long as you've got your legs you can give yourself an airing."

Mrs. Johnson had done this. She had fair hair, a good figure, and active legs, but usually turned her head aside when she was talking, as if to an imaginary friend. Mrs. Johnson had needed an airing very badly when she came to work for Mr. Armitage.

At their first interview—he met her in the panelled hall: "You do realize, don't you, that I am totally blind. I have been blind for more than twenty years," he said.

"Yes," she said. "I was told by Dr. James." She had been working for a doctor in London.

He held out his hand and she did not take it at once. It was not her habit to shake hands with people; now, as always, when she gave in she turned her head away. He held her hand for a long time and she knew he was feeling the bones. She had heard that the blind do this, and she took a breath as if to prevent her bones or her skin passing any knowledge of herself to him. But she could feel her dry hand coming to life and she drew it away. She was surprised that, at the touch, her nervousness had gone.

To her, Armitage's house was a wonderful place. The space, the light made friendly by the small panes of the tall leaded windows, charmed her.

"Not a bit like Peckham," she said cheerfully.

Mr. Armitage took her through the long sitting-room, where there were yellow roses in a bowl, into his study. He had been playing a record and put it off.

"Do you like music?" he said. "That was Mozart."

"I like a bit of a singsong," she said. "I can't honestly say I like the classical stuff."

He took her round the house, stopped to point to a picture or two and, once more down in the long room, took her to a window and said, "This is a bad day for it. The haze hasn't lifted. On a clear day you can see Sevenham Cathedral. It's twelve miles away. Do you like the country?"

"Frankly I've never tried it."

"Are you a widow, Mrs. Johnson?"

"No. I changed my name from Thompson to Johnson and not for the better. I divorced my husband," said Mrs. Johnson crisply.

"Will you read something to me—out of the paper?" he said. "A court case."

She read and read.

"Go on," he said. "Pick out something livelier."

"Lonely monkeys at the zoo?"

"That will do."

She read again and she laughed.

"Good," he said.

"As Father used to say, 'Speak up . . .' " she began, but stopped. Mr. Armitage did not want to hear what Father said.

"Will you allow me," Armitage said, getting up from his desk, "would you allow me to touch your face?"

Mrs. Johnson had forgotten that the blind sometimes asked this.

She did not answer at once. She had been piqued from the beginning because he could not see her. She had been to the hairdresser's. She had bought a blouse with a high frilled neck which was meant to set off the look of boyish impudence and frankness of her face. She had forgotten about touch. She feared he would have a pleading look, but she saw that the wish was part of an exercise for him. He clearly expected her to make no difficulty about it.

"All right," she said, but she meant him to notice the pause, "if you want to."

She faced him and did not flinch as his hand lightly touched her brow and cheek and chin. He was, she thought, "after her bones," not her skin, and that, though she stiffened with resistance, was "O.K. by her." But when, for a second, the hand seemed about to rest on her jaw, she turned her head.

"I weigh eight stone," she said in her bright way.

"I would have thought less," he said. That was the nearest he came to a compliment. "It was the first time," she said afterwards to her friend Marge in the town, "that I ever heard of a secretary being bought by weight."

She had been his secretary and housekeeper for a long time now. She had understood him at once. The saintly look was nonsense. He was neither a saint nor a martyr. He was very vain; especially he was vain of never being deceived, though in fact his earlier secretaries had not been a success. There had been three or four before her. One of them—the cook told her—imagined him to be a martyr because she had a taste for martyrdom and drank to gratify it; another yearned to offer the compassion he hated, and muddled everything. One reckoning widow lasted only a month. Blatantly she had added up his property and wanted to marry him. The last, a "lady," helped herself to the household money, behind a screen of wheezing grandeur and name-dropping.

Remembering the widow, the people who came to visit Mr. Armitage when he gave a party were relieved after their meeting with Mrs. Johnson.

"A good honest-to-God Cockney" or "Such a cheery soul." "Down to earth," they said. She said she had "knocked about a bit." "Yes, sounds as if she had": they supposed they were denigrating. She was obviously not the kind of woman who would have any dangerous appeal to an injured man. And she, for her part, would go to the pictures when she had time off or simply flop down in a chair at the house of her friend Marge and say, "Whew, Marge. His nibs has gone to London. Give me a strong cuppa. Let's relax."

"You're too conscientious."

"Oh, I don't mind the work. I like it. It occupies your mind. He has interesting cases. But sometimes I get keyed up."

Mrs. Johnson could not herself describe what "keyed her up"—perhaps being on the watch? Her mind was stretched. She found herself translating the world to him and it took her time to realize that it did not matter that she was not "educated up to it." He obviously liked her version of the world, but it was a strain having versions. In the mornings she had to read his letters. This bothered her. She was very moral about privacy. She had to invent an impersonal, uninterested voice. His lack of privacy irked her; she liked gossip and news as much as any woman, but here it lacked the salt of the secret, the whispered, the found out. It was all information and statement. Armitage's life was an abstraction for him. He had to know what he could not see. What she liked best was reading legal documents to him.

He dressed very well and it was her duty to see that his clothes were right. For an orderly, practical mind like hers, the order in which he lived was a new pleasure. They lived under fixed laws: no chair or table, even no ashtray must be moved. Everything must be in its place. There must be no hazards. This was understandable: the ease with which he moved without accident in the house or garden depended on it. She did not believe when he said, "I can hear things before I get to them. A wall can shout, you know." When visitors came she noticed he stood in a fixed spot: he did not turn his head when people spoke to him and among all the head-turning and gesturing he was the still figure, the lawgiver. But he was very cunning. If someone described a film they had seen, he was soon talking as if he had been there. Mrs. Johnson, who had duties when he had visitors, would smile to herself, at the surprise on the faces of people who had not noticed the quickness with which he collected every image or scene or character described. Sometimes, a lady would say to her, "I do think he's absolutely marvellous," and, if he overheard this—and his hearing was acute—Mrs. Johnson would notice a look of ugly boredom on his face. He was, she noted, particularly vain of his care of money and accounts. This pleased Mrs. Johnson because she was quick to understand that here a blind man who had servants might be swindled. She was indignant about the delinquency of her predecessor. He must have known he was being swindled.

Once a month Mrs. Johnson would go through the accounts with him. She would make out the cheques and take them to his study and put them on his desk.

The scene that followed always impressed her. She really admired him for this. How efficient and devious he was! He placed the cheque at a known point on his blotter. The blunt fingers of his hairless hands had the art of gliding and never groping, knowing the inches of distance; and then, as accurately as a geometrician, he signed. There might be a pause as the fingers secretly measured, a pause alarming to her in the early days, but now no longer alarming; sometimes she detected a shade of cruelty in this pause. He was listening for a small gasp of anxiety as she watched.

There was one experience which was decisive for her. It occurred in the first month of her employment and had the lasting stamp of a revelation. (Later on, she thought he had staged the incident in order to show her what his life was like and to fix in her mind the nature of his peculiar authority.) She came into the sitting-room one evening in the winter to find a newspaper and heard sharp, unbelievable sounds coming from his study. The door was open and the room was in darkness. She went to it, switched on the light, and saw he was sitting there typing in the darkness. Well, she could have done that if she had been put to it—but now she *saw* that for him there was no difference between darkness and light.

"Overtime, I see," she said, careful not to show surprise.

This was when she saw that his mind was a store of maps and measured things; a store of sounds and touches and smells that became an enormous translated paraphernalia.

"You'd feel sorry for a man like that," her friend Marge said.

"He'd half kill you if you showed you were sorry," Mrs. Johnson said. "I don't feel sorry. I really don't."

"Does he ever talk about his wife?"

"No."

"A terrible thing to do to leave a man because he's blind."

"She had a right to her life, hadn't she?" said Mrs. Johnson flatly. "Who would want to marry a blind man?"

"You are hard," Marge said.

"It's not my business," said Mrs. Johnson. "If you start pitying people you end up by hating them. I've seen it. I've been married, don't forget."

"I just wish you had a more normal life, dear."

"It suits me," said Mrs. Johnson.

"He ought to be very grateful to you."

"Why should he be? I do my job. Gratitude doesn't come into it. Let's go and play tennis."

The two women went out and played tennis in the park and Mrs. Johnson kept her friend running from court to court.

"I smell tennis balls and grass," said Mr. Armitage when she returned.

In the March of her third year a bad thing happened. The winter was late. There was a long spell of hard frost and you could see the cathedral tower clearly over the low-lying woods on most days. The frost coppered the lawns and scarcely faded in the middle of the day. The hedges were spiked and white. She had moved her typing table into the sitting-room close to the window to be near a radiator and when she changed a page she would glance out at the garden. Mr. Armitage was out there somewhere and she had got into the habit of being on the watch. Now she saw him walk down the three lawns and find the brick steps that led to the swimming pool. It was enclosed by a yew hedge and was frozen over. She could see Armitage at the far side of it pulling at a small fallen branch that had been caught by the ice. His foot had struck it. On the other side of the hedge, the gardener was cutting cabbage in the kitchen garden and his dog was snuffling about. Suddenly a rabbit ran out, ears down, and the dog was yelping after it. The rabbit ran through the hedge and almost over Armitage's feet with the dog nearly on it. The gardener shouted. The next moment Armitage, who was squatting, had the dog under his legs, lost his balance, and fell full length through the ice into the pool. Mrs. Johnson saw this. She saw the gardener drop his knife and run to the gap in the hedge to help Armitage out. He was clambering over the side. She saw him wave the gardener's hand away and shout at him and the gardener step away as Armitage got out. He stood clawing weed off his face, out of his hair, wringing his sleeves and brushing ice off his shirt as he marched back fast up the garden. He banged the garden door in a rage as he came in.

"That bloody man. I'll have that dog shot," shouted Armitage. She hurried to meet him. He had pulled off his jacket and thrown it on a chair. Water ran off his trousers and sucked in his shoes. Mrs. Johnson was appalled.

"Go and change your things quickly," she said. And she easily raced him to the stairs to the landing and to his room. By the time he got there she had opened several drawers, looking for underclothes, and had pulled out a suit from his cupboard. Which suit? She pulled out another. He came squelching after her into the room.

"Towel," she cried. "Get it all off. You'll get pneumonia."

"Get out. Leave me alone," shouted Armitage, who had been tugging his shirt over his head as he came upstairs.

She saw then that she had done a terrible thing. By opening drawers and putting clothes on the bed, she had destroyed one of his systems. She saw him grope. She had never seen him do this before. His bare white arms stretched out in a helpless way and his brown hands pitiably closed on air. The action was slow and his fingers frightened her.

"I told you to leave me alone," he shouted.

She saw she had humiliated him. She had broken one of the laws. For the first time she had been incompetent.

Mrs. Johnson went out and quietly shut the door. She walked across the landing to the passage in the wing where her own room was, looking at the wet marks of his muddy shoes on the carpet, each one accusing her. She sat down on the edge of her bed. How could she have been such a fool! How could she have forgotten his rule? Half naked to the waist, hairy on the chest and arms, he shocked because the rage seemed to be not in his mind but in his body like an animal's. The rage had the pathos of an animal's. Perhaps when he was alone he often groped; perhaps the drilled man she was used to, who came out of his bedroom or his study, was the expert survival of a dozen concealed disasters?

Mrs. Johnson sat on her bed listening. She had never known Armitage to be angry; he was a monotonously considerate man. The shout abashed her and there was a strange pleasure in being abashed; but her mistake was not a mere mistake. She saw that it struck at the foundation of his life and was so gross that the surface of her own confidence was cracked. She was a woman who could reckon on herself, but now her mind was scattered. Useless to say to herself, "What a fuss about nothing," or "Keep calm." Or, about him, "Nasty temper." His shout, "Get out. I told you to leave me alone," had, without reason (except that a trivial shame is a spark that sets fire to a long string of greater shames), burned out all the security of her present life.

She had heard those words, almost exactly those words, before. Her husband had said them. A week after their wedding.

Well, *he* had had something to shout about, poor devil. She admitted it. Something a lot more serious than falling into a pool and having someone commit the crime of being kind to you and hurting your silly little pride.

She got up from the bed and turned on the tap of the washbasin to cool down her hot face and wash her hands of the dirt of the jacket she had brought upstairs. She took off her blouse and as she sluiced her face she looked through the water at herself in the mirror. There was a small birthmark the size of a red leaf which many people noticed and which, as it showed over the neck of the high blouses she usually wore, had the enticement of some signal or fancy of the blood; but under it, and invisible to them, were two smaller ones and then a great spreading ragged liver-coloured island of skin which spread under the tape of her slip and crossed her breast and seemed to end in a curdle of skin below it. She was stamped with an ineradicable bloody insult. It might have been an attempt to impose another woman on her. She was used to seeing it, but she carried it about with her under her clothes, hiding it and yet vaunting.

Now she was reaching for a towel and inside the towel, as she dried herself, she was talking to Armitage.

"If you want to know what shame and pride are, what about marrying a man who goes plain sick at the sight of your body and who says 'You deceived me. You didn't tell me.' "

She finished drying her face and put the towel on the warm rail and went to her dressing table. The hairbrush she picked up had been a wedding present and at each hard stroke of the brush on her lively fair hair, her face put up a fight, but it exhausted her. She brushed the image of Armitage away and she was left staring at the half-forgotten but never-forgotten self she had been.

How could she have been such a fool as to deceive her husband? It was not through wickedness. She had been blinded too—blinded by love; in a way, love had made her so full of herself that perhaps she had never seen *him*. And her deceptions: she could not stop herself smiling at them, but they were really pitiable because she was so afraid of losing him and to lose him would be to lose this new beautifully deluded self. She ought to have told him. There were chances. For example, in his flat with the grey sofa with the spring that bit your bottom going clang, clang at every kiss, when he used to carry on about her wearing dresses that a man couldn't get a hand into. He knew very well she had had affairs with men, but why, when they were both "worked up," wouldn't she undress and go to the bedroom? The sofa was too short. She remembered how shocked his face looked when she pulled up her skirts and lay on the floor. She said she believed in sex before marriage, but she thought some things ought to wait: it would be wrong for him to see her naked before their wedding day. And to show him she was no prude—there was that time they pretended to be looking out of the window at a cricket match; or Fridays in his office when the staff was gone and the cleaners were only at the end of the passage.

"You've got a mole on your neck," he said one day.

"Mother went mad with wanting plums when she was carrying me. It's a birthmark."

"It's pretty," he said and kissed it.

He kissed it. He kissed it. She clung to that when after the wedding they got to the hotel and she hid her face in his shoulder and let him pull down the zip of her dress. She stepped away, and pretending to be shy, she undressed under her slip. At last the slip came off over her head. They both looked at each other, she with brazen fear and he—she couldn't forget the shocked blank disgust on his face. From the neck over the left shoulder down to the breast and below, and spreading like a red tongue to the back was this ugly blob—dark as blood, like a ragged liver on a butcher's window, or some obscene island with ragged edges. It was as if a bucket of paint had been thrown over her.

"You didn't tell me," he said. If only she had told him, but how could she have done? She knew she had been cursed.

"That's why you wouldn't undress, you little hypocrite."

He himself was in his underpants with his trousers on the bed and with his cuff links in his hand, which made his words absurd and awful. His ridiculous look made him tragic and his hatred frightening. It was terrible that for two hours while they talked he did not undress and worse that he gave her a dressing gown to cover herself. She heard him going through the catalogue of her tricks.

"When . . ." he began in a pathetic voice. And then she screamed at him.

"What do you think? Do you think I got it done, that I got myself tattooed in the Waterloo Road? I was born like it."

"Ssh," he said. "You'll wake the people in the next room."

"Let them hear. I'll go and show them," she screamed. It was kind of him to put his arm around her. When she had recovered, she put on her fatal, sporty manner. "Some men like it," she said.

He hit her across the face. It was not then but in the following weeks when pity followed and pity turned to cruelty he had said, "Get out. Leave me alone."

Mrs. Johnson went to her drawer and got out a clean blouse.

Her bedroom in Armitage's house was a pretty one, far prettier than any she had ever had. Up till now she had been used to bed sitters since her marriage. But was it really the luxury of the house and the power she would have in it that had weighed with her when she had decided to take on this strange job? She understood now something else had moved her in the low state she had been in when she came. As a punished and self-hating person she was drawn to work with a punished man. It was a return to her girlhood: injury had led her to injury.

She looked out of the window at the garden. The diamond panes chopped up the sight of the frozen lawns and the firs that were frost-whiskered. She was used to the view. It was a view of the real world; that, after all, was her world, not his. She saw that gradually in three years she had drifted out of it and had taken to living in Armitage's filed memory. If he said, for example, "That rambler is getting wild. It must be cut back," because a thorn caught his jacket, or if he made his famous remark about seeing the cathedral on a clear day, the landscape limited itself to these things and in general reduced itself to the imposed topographical sketch in his mind. She had allowed him, as a matter of abnegation and duty, to impose his world on hers. Now this shock brought back a lost sense of the right to her own landscape; and then to the protest that this country was not hers at all. The country bored her. The fir trees bored her. The lanes bored her. The view from this window or the tame protected view of the country from the Rolls-Royce window bored her. She wanted to go back to London, to the streets, the buses and the crowds, to crowds of people with eyes in their heads. And—her spirits rising—"To hell with it, I want people who can *see* me."

She went downstairs to give orders for the carpet to be brushed.

In the sitting-room she saw the top of Armitage's dark head. She had not heard him go down. He was sitting in what she called the cathedral chair facing the window and she was forced to smile when she saw a bit of green weed sticking to his hair. She also saw a heavy glass ashtray had fallen off the table beside him. "Clumsy," she said. She picked it up and lightly pulled off the piece of weed from his hair. He did not notice this.

"Mr. Armitage," she said in her decisive manner, "I lost my head. I'm sorry."

He was silent.

"I understand how you feel," she said. For this (she had decided in her room) was the time for honesty and for having things out. The impersonality could not go on, as it had done for three years.

"I want to go back to London," she said.

"Don't be a damn fool," he said.

Well, she was not going to be sworn at. "I'm not a damn fool," she said. "I understand your situation." And then, before she could stop herself, her voice shaking and loud, she broke out with: "I know what humiliation is."

"Who is humiliated?" said Armitage. "Sit down."

"I am not speaking about you," she said stiffly.

That surprised him, she saw, for he turned his head.

"I'm sorry, I lost my temper," he said. "But that stupid fellow and his dog . . ."

"I am speaking about myself," she said. "We have our pride, too."

"Who is *we?*" he said, without curiosity.

"Women," she said.

He got up from his chair, and she stepped back. He did not move and she saw that he really had not recovered from the fall in the pool, for he was uncertain. He was not sure where the table was.

"Here," he said roughly, putting out a hand. "Give me a hand out of this."

She obediently took him by the arm and stood him clear of the table.

"Listen to me. You couldn't help what happened and neither could I. There's nothing to apologize for. You're not leaving. We get on very well. Take my advice. Don't be hard on yourself."

"It is better to be hard," she said. "Where would you have been if you had not been hard? I'm not a girl. I'm thirty-nine." He moved towards her and put his hand on her right shoulder and she quickly turned her head. He laughed and said, "You've brushed your hair back." He knew. He always knew.

She watched him make for his study and saw him take the wrong course, brush against the sofa by the fireplace, and then a yard or two further, he shouldered the wall.

"Damn," he said.

At dinner, conversation was difficult. He offered her a glass of wine which she refused. He poured himself a second glass and as he sat down he grimaced with pain.

"Did you hurt your back this afternoon?" she asked.

"No," he said. "I was thinking about my wife."

Mrs. Johnson blushed. He had scarcely ever mentioned his wife. She knew only what Marge Brook had told her of the town gossip: how his wife could not stand his blindness and had gone off with someone and that he had given her a lot of money. Someone said, ten thousand pounds. What madness! In the dining-room Mrs. Johnson often thought of all those notes flying about over the table and out of the window. He was too rich. Ten thousand pounds of hatred and rage, or love, or madness. In the first place, she wouldn't have touched it.

"She made me build the pool," he said.

"A good idea," she said.

"I don't know why. I never thought of throwing her into it," he said.

Mrs. Johnson said, "Shall I read the paper?" She did not want to hear more about his wife.

Mrs. Johnson went off to bed early. Switching on the radio in her room and then switching it off because it was playing classical music, she said to herself, "Well, funny things bring things back. What a day!" and stepped yawning out of her skirt. Soon she was in bed and asleep.

An hour later she woke up, hearing her name.

"Mrs. Johnson. The water got into my watch, would you set it for me?" He was standing there in his dressing gown.

"Yes," she said. She was a woman who woke up alert and clear-headed.

"I'm sorry. I thought you were listening to a program. I didn't know you were in bed," he said. He was holding the watch to his ear.

"Would you set it for me and put my alarm right?" He had the habit of giving orders. They were orders spoken into space—and she was the space, nonexistent. He gave her the watch and went off. She put on her dressing gown and followed him to his room. He had switched on the light for her. She went to the bedside table and bent down to wind the clock. Suddenly she felt his arms around her, pulling her upright, and he was kissing her head. The alarm went off suddenly and she dropped the clock. It went on screeching on the floor at her feet.

"Mr. Armitage," she said in a low angry voice, but not struggling. He turned her round and he was trying to kiss her on the lips. At this she did struggle. She twisted her head this way and that to stop him, so that it was her head rather than her body that was resisting him. Her blue eyes fought with all their light, but his eyes were dead as stone.

"Really, Mr. Armitage. Stop it," she managed to mutter. "The door is open. Cook will hear."

She was angry at being kissed by a man who could not see her face, but she felt the shamed insulted woman in her, that blotched inhabitant, blaze up in her skin.

The bell of the alarm clock was weakening and then choked to a stop and in her pettish struggle she stepped on it; her slipper had come off.

"I've hurt my foot." Distracted by the pain she stopped struggling, and Armitage took his opportunity and kissed her on the lips. She looked with pain into his sightless eyes. There was no help there. She was terrified of being drawn into the dark where he lived. And then the kiss seemed to go down her throat and spread into her shoulders, into her breasts and branch into all the veins and arteries of her body and it was the tongue of the shamed woman who had sprung up in her that touched his.

"What are you doing?" she was trying to say, but could only groan the words. When he touched the stained breast she struck back violently, saying, "No, no."

"Come to bed with me," he said.

"Please let me go. I've hurt my foot."

The surprising thing was that he did let her go, and as she sat panting and white in the face on the bed to look at her foot, she looked mockingly at him. She forgot that he could not see her mockery. He sat beside her but did not touch her and he was silent. There was no scratch on her foot. She picked up the clock and put it back on the table.

Mrs. Johnson was proud of the adroitness with which she had kept men away from her since her marriage. It was a war with the inhabitant of the ragged island on her body. That creature craved for the furtive, for the hand that slipped under a skirt, for the scuffle in the back seat of a car, for a five-minute disappearance into a locked office.

But the other Mrs. Johnson, the cheerful one, was virtuous. She took advantage of his silence and got quickly up to get away; she dodged past him, but he was quick too. He was at the closed door. For a moment she was wily. It would be easy for her to dodge him in the room. And then she saw once more the sight she could not bear that melted her more certainly than the kisses which had filled her mouth and throat: she saw his hands begin to open and search and grope in the air as he came towards the sound of her breathing. She could not move. His hand caught her. The woman inside her seemed to shout, "Why not? You're all right. He cannot see." In her struggle she had not thought of that. In three years he had made her forget that blindness meant not seeing.

"All right," she said, and the virtue in Mrs. Johnson pouted. She gently tapped his chest with her fingers and said with the sullenness of desire, "I'll be back in a minute."

It was a revenge: that was the pleasure.

"Dick," she called to her husband, "look at this," when the man was on top of her. Revenge was the only pleasure and his excitement was soon over. To please him she patted him on the head as he lay beside her and said, "You've got long legs." And she nearly said, "You are a naughty boy" and "Do you feel better?" but she stopped herself and her mind went off on to what she had to do in the morning; she listened and wondered how long it would be before he would fall asleep and she could stealthily get away. Revenge astonished by its quickness.

She slyly moved. He knew at once and held her. She waited. She wondered where Dick was now. She wished she could tell him. But presently this blind man in the bed leaned up and put both his hands on her face and head and carefully followed the round of her forehead, the line of her brow, her nose and lips and chin, to the line of her throat and then to her nape and shoulders. She trembled, for after his hands had passed, what had been touched seemed to be new. She winced as his hand passed over the stained shoulder and breast and he paused, knowing that she winced, and she gave a groan of pleasure to deceive him; but he went on, as if he were modelling her, feeling the pit under the arms, the space of ribs and belly and the waist of which she was proud, measuring them, feeling their depth, the roundness of her legs, the bone in her knees until, throwing all clothes back, he was holding her ankle, the arch of her foot, and her toes. Her skin and her bones became alive. His hands knew her body as she had never known it. In her brief love affairs, which had excited her because of the risk of being caught, the first touch of a man stirred her at once and afterwards left her looking demurely at him; but she had let no one know her with a pedantry like his. She suddenly sat up and put her arms round him, and now she went wild. It was not a revenge now; it was a triumph. She lifted the sad breast to his lips. And when they lay back she kissed his chest and then—with daring—she kissed his eyes.

It was six o'clock before she left him, and when she got to her room the stained woman seemed to bloom like a flower. It was only after she had slept and saw her room in daylight again that she realized that once more she had deceived a man.

It was late. She looked out of the window and saw Armitage in his city clothes talking to the chauffeur in the garden. She watched them walk to the garage.

"O.K.," she said dryly to defend herself. "It was a rape." During the day there would be moments when she could feel his hands moving over her skin. Her legs tingled. She posed as if she were a new-made statue. But as the day went on she hardened and instead of waiting for him to return she went into the town to see Marge.

"You've put your hair up," Marge said.

"Do you like it?"

"I don't know. It's different. It makes you look severe. No, not severe. Something. Restless."

"I am not going back to dinner this evening," she said. "I want a change. Leonard's gone to London."

"Leonard!" said Marge.

Mrs. Johnson wanted to confide in Marge, but Marge bored her. They ate a meal together and she ate fast. To Marge's astonishment she said, "I must fly."

"You *are* in a mood," Marge said.

Mrs. Johnson was unable to control a longing to see Armitage. When she got back to the house and saw him sitting by the fire she wanted him to get up and at least put his arms round her; but he did not move, he was listening to music. It was always the signal that he wanted to be alone.

"It is just ending," said Armitage.

The music ended in a roll of drums.

"Do you want something, Helen?" he said.

She tried to be mocking, but her voice could not mock and she said seriously, "About last night. It must not happen again. I don't want to be in a false position. I could not go on living in the house."

She did not intend to say this; her voice, between rebuke and tenderness, betrayed this.

"Sit down."

She did not move.

"I have been very happy here," she said. "I don't want to spoil it."

"You are angry," he said.

"No, I'm not," she said.

"Yes, you are; that is why you were not here when I got back," he said.

"You did not wait for me this morning," she said. "I was glad you didn't. I don't want it to go on."

He came nearer to her and put his hand on her hair.

"I like the way your hair shows your ears," he said. And he kissed them.

"Now, please," she said.

"I love you," he said and kissed her on the forehead and she did not turn her head.

"Do you? I'm glad you said that. I don't think you do. When something has been good, don't spoil it. I don't like love affairs," she said.

And then she changed. "It was a party. Good night."

"You made me happy," he said, holding on to her hand.

"Were you thinking about it a long time?" she said in another voice, lingering for one more word.

"Yes," he said.

"It is very nice of you to say that. It is what you ought to say. But I mean what I said. Now, really, good night. And," giving a pat to his arm, she said, "keep your watch wound up."

Two nights later he called to her loudly and curtly from the stairs: "Mrs. Johnson, where are you?" and when she came into the hall he said quietly, "Helen."

She liked that. They slept together again. They did not talk.

Their life went on as if nothing had happened. She began to be vain of the stain on her body and could not resist silently displaying, almost taunting him, when she undressed, with what he could not see. She liked the play of deceiving him like this; she was paying him out for not being able to see her; and when she was ashamed of doing this the shame itself would rouse her desire: two women uniting in her. And fear roused her too; she was afraid of his blindness. Sometimes the fear was that the blind can see into the mind. It often terrified her at the height of her pleasure that she was being carried into the dark where he lived. She knew she was not but she could not resist the excitement of imagining it. Afterwards she would turn her back to him, ashamed of her fancies, and as his finger followed the bow of her spine she would drive away the cynical thought that he was just filing this affair away in one of the systems of his memory.

Yet she liked these doubts. How dead her life had been in its practical certainties. She liked the tenderness and violence of sexual love, the simple kindness of the skin. She once said to him, "My skin is your skin." But she stuck to it that she did not love him and that he did not love her. She wanted to be simply a body: a woman like Marge who was always talking about love seemed to her a fool. She liked it that she and Armitage were linked to each other only by signs. And she became vain of her disfigurement, and looking at it, even thought of it as the lure.

I know what would happen to me if I got drunk, she thought at one of Armitage's cocktail parties, I'm the sort of woman who would start taking her clothes off. When she was a young woman she had once started doing so, and someone, thank God, stopped her.

But these fancies were bravado.

They were intended to stop her from telling him.

On Sundays Mrs. Johnson went to church in the village near the house. She had made a habit of it from the beginning, because she thought it the proper thing to do: to go to church had made her feel she need not reproach herself for impropriety in living in the same house as a man. It was a practical matter: before her love affair the tragic words of the service had spoken to her evil. If God had done this to her, He must put up with the sight of her in His house. She was not a religious woman; going to church was an assertion that she had as much right to fair play as anyone else. It also stopped her from being "such a fool" as to fall to the temptation of destroying her new wholeness by telling him. It was "normal" to go to church and normality had been her craving ever since her girlhood. She had always taken her body, not her mind, to church.

Armitage teased her about her churchgoing when she first came to work for him; but lately his teasing became sharper: "Going to listen to Dearly Beloved Brethren?" he would say.

"Oh, leave him alone," she said.

He had made up a tale about her being in love with the vicar; at first it was a joke, but now there was a sharp edge to it. "A very respectable man," he said.

When the church bells rang on Sunday evening he said, "He's calling to you." She began to see that this joke had the grit of jealousy in it; not of the vicar, of course, but a jealousy of many things in her life.

"Why do you go there? I'd like to understand, seriously," he said.

"I like to get out," she said.

She saw pain on his face. There was never much movement in it beyond the deepening of two lines at the corners of his mouth; but when his face went really dead, it was as sullen as earth in the garden. In her sense, she knew, he never went out. He lived in a system of tunnels. She had to admit that when she saw the grey church she was glad, because it was not his house. She knew from gossip that neither he nor his wife had ever been to it.

There was something else in this new life; now he had freed her they were both more watchful of each other. One Sunday in April she saw his jealousy in the open. She had come in from church and she was telling him about the people who were there. She was sitting on the sofa beside him.

"How many lovers have you had?" he said. "That doctor you worked for, now?"

"Indeed not," she said. "I was married."

"I know you were married. But when you were working for those people in Manchester? And in Canada after the war?"

"No one else. That was just a trip."

"I don't believe you."

"Honestly, it's true."

"In court I never believe a witness who says 'Honestly.' "

She blushed, for she had had three or four lovers, but she was defending herself. They were no business of his.

The subject became darker.

"Your husband," he said. "He saw you. They all saw you."

She knew what he meant, and this scared her.

"My husband. Of course he saw me. Only my husband."

"Ah, so there were others."

"Only my husband saw me," she said. "I told you about it. How he walked out of the hotel after a week."

This was a moment when she could have told him, but to see his jealousy destroy the happiness he had restored to her made her indignant.

"He couldn't bear the sight of me. He had wanted," she invented, "to marry another woman. He told me on the first night of our marriage. In the hotel. Please don't talk about it."

"Which hotel was this?" he said.

The triviality of the question confused her. "In Kensington."

"What was the name?"

"Oh, I forget, the something Royal . . ."

"You don't forget."

"I do honestly . . ."

"Honestly!" he said.

He was in a rage of jealousy. He kept questioning her about the hotel, the length of their marriage. He pestered for addresses, for dates, and tried to confuse her by putting his questions again and again.

"So he didn't leave you at the hotel!" he said.

"Look," she said. "I can't stand jealous men and I'm not going to be questioned like one of your clients."

He did not move or shout. Her husband had shouted and paced up and down, waving his arms. This man sat bolt upright and still, and spoke in a dry, exacting voice.

"I'm sorry," he said.

She took his hand, the hand that groped like a helpless tentacle and that had modelled her; it was the most disturbing and living thing about him.

"Are you still in love with your husband?"

"Certainly not."

"He saw you and I have never seen you." He circled again to his obsession.

"It is just as well. I'm not a beautiful woman," she laughed. "My legs are too short, my bottom is too big. You be grateful—my husband couldn't stand the sight of me."

"You have a skin like an apple," he said.

She pushed his hand away and said, "Your hands know too much."

"*He* had hands. And he had eyes," he said in a voice grinding with violence.

"I'm very tired. I am going to bed," she said. "Good night."

"You see," he said. "There is no answer."

He picked up a braille book and his hand moved fast over the sheets.

She went to her room and kicked off her shoes and stepped out of her dress.

I've been living in a dream, she thought. Just like Marge, who always thinks her husband's coming back every time the gate goes. It is a mistake, she thought, living in the same house.

The jealous fit seemed to pass. It was a fire, she understood, that flared up just as her shame used to flare, but two Sundays later the fit came on again. He must hate God, she thought, and pitied him. Perhaps the music that usually consoled him had tormented him. At any rate, he stopped it when she came in and put her prayer book on the table. There was a red begonia, which came from the greenhouse, on the table beside the sofa where he was sitting very upright, as if he had been waiting impatiently for her to come back.

"Come and sit down," he said and began kindly enough. "What was church like? Did they tell you what to do?"

"I was nearly asleep," she said. "After last night. Do you know what time it was?" She took his hand and laughed.

He thought about this for a while. Then he said, "Give me your hands. No. Both of them. That's right. Now spit on them."

"Spit!"

"Yes, that is what the church tells you."

"What *are* you talking about?" she said, trying to get her hands away.

"Spit on them." And he forced her hands, though not roughly, to her lips.

"What are you doing?" She laughed nervously and spat on her fingers.

"Now—rub the spittle on my eyes."

"Oh, no," she said.

He let go of her wrist.

"Do as I tell you. It's what your Jesus Christ did when he cured the blind man."

He sat there waiting and she waited.

"He put dust or earth or something on them," he said. "Get some."

"No," she said.

"There's some here. Put your fingers in it," he said shortly. She was frightened of him.

"In the pot," he insisted as he held one of her wrists so that she could not get away. She dabbed her wet fingers in the earth of the begonia pot.

"Put it on my eyes."

"I can't do that. I really can't," she said.

"Put it on my eyes," he said.

"It will hurt them."

"They are hurt already," he said. "Do as I tell you." She bent to him and, with disgust, she put her dirty fingers on the wet eyeballs. The sensation was horrible, and when she saw the dirty patches on his eyes, like two filthy smudges, she thought he looked like an ape.

"That is what you are supposed to do," he said. Jealousy had made him mad.

I can't stay with a mad man, she thought. He's malicious. She did not know what to do, but he solved that for her. He reached for his braille book. She got up and left him there. The next day he went to London.

His habits changed. He went several times into the nearby town on his own and she was relieved that he came back in a silent mood which seemed happy. The horrible scene went out of her mind. She had gone so far as to lock her bedroom door for several nights after that scene, but now she unlocked it. He had brought her a bracelet from London; she drifted into unguarded happiness. She knew so well how torment comes and goes.

It was full undreaming June, the leaves in the garden still undarkened, and for several days people were surprised when day after day the sun was up and hot and unclouded. Mrs. Johnson went down to the pool. Armitage and his guests often tried to persuade her to go in but she always refused.

"They once tried to get me to go down to Peckham Baths when I was a kid, but I screamed," she said.

The guests left her alone. They were snobbish about Peckham Baths.

But Mrs. Johnson decided to become a secret bather. One afternoon when Armitage was in London and the cook and gardener had their day off, she went down with the gardener's dog. She wore a black bathing suit that covered her body and lowered herself by the steps into the water. Then she splashed at the shallow end of the pool and hung on to the rail while the dog barked at her. He stopped barking when she got out and sniffed round the hedge where she pulled down her bathing dress to her waist and lay down to get sun-drunk on her towel.

She was displaying herself to the sun, the sky and the trees. The air was like hands that played on her as Armitage did and she lay listening to the snuffles of the dog and the humming of the bees in the yew hedge. She had been there an hour when the dog barked at the hedge. She quickly picked up a towel and covered herself and called to the dog: "What is it?"

He went on barking and then gave up and came to her. She sat down. Suddenly the dog barked again. Mrs. Johnson stood up and tried to look through one of the thinner places in the hedge. A man who must have been close to the pool and who must have passed along the footpath from the lane, a path used only by the gardener, was walking up the lawns towards the house carrying a trilby hat in his hand. He was not the gardener. He stopped twice to get his breath and turned to look at the view. She recognized the smiling grey suit, the wide figure and snowball head: it was "Wolverhampton" Smith. She waited and saw him go on to the house and ring a bell. Then he disappeared round the corner and went to the front of the house. Mrs. Johnson quickly dressed. Presently he came back to look into the windows of the sitting-room. He found the door and for a minute or two went into the house and then came out.

"The cheek," she said. She finished dressing and went up the lawn to him.

"Ah, there you are," he said. "What a sweet place this is. I was looking for Mr. Armitage."

"He's in London."

"I thought he might be in the pool," he said. Mr. Smith looked rich with arch, smiling insinuation.

"When will he be back?"

"About six. Is there anything I can do?"

"No, no, no," said Mr. Smith in a variety of genial notes, waving a hand. "I was out for a walk."

"A long walk—seven miles."

"I came," said Mr. Smith, modestly lowering his eyes in financial confession, "by bus."

"The best way. Can I give you a drink?"

"I never touch it," Mr. Smith said, putting up an austere hand. "Well, a glass of water perhaps. As the Americans say, 'I'm mighty thirsty.' My wife and I came down here for the water, you know. London water is chalky. It was very bad for my wife's arthritis. It's bad for everyone, really. There's a significant increase in neuralgia, neuritis, arthritis in a city like London. The chalky water does it. People don't realize it"—and here Mr. Smith stopped smiling and put on a stern excommunicating air—"If you believe that man's life is ruled by water. I personally don't."

"Not by water only, anyway," said Mrs. Johnson.

"I mean," said Mr. Smith gravely, "if you believe that the material body exists." And when he said this, the whole sixteen stone of him looked scornfully at the landscape which, no doubt, concealed thousands of people who believed they had bodies. He expanded: he seemed to threaten to vanish.

Mrs. Johnson fetched a glass of water. "I'm glad to see you're still there," she laughed when she came back.

Mr. Smith was resting on the garden seat. "I was just thinking—thank you—there's a lot of upkeep in a place like this," he said.

"There is."

"And yet—what is upkeep? Money—so it seems. And if we believe in the body, we believe in money, we believe in upkeep, and so it goes on," said Mr. Smith sunnily, waving his glass at the garden. And then sharply and loftily, free of this evil: "It gives employment." Firmly telling her she was employed. "But," he added, in warm contemplation, putting down his glass and opening his arms, gathering in the landscape, "but there is only one employer."

"There are a hell of a lot of employers."

Mr. Smith raised an eyebrow at the word "hell" and said, "Let me correct you there. I happen to believe that God is the only employer."

"I'm employed by Mr. Armitage," she said. "Mr. Armitage loves this place. You don't have to see to love a garden."

"It's a sweet place," said Mr. Smith. He got up and took a deep breath. "Pine trees. Wonderful. The smell! My wife doesn't like pine trees. She is depressed by them. It's all in the mind," said Mr. Smith. "As Shakespeare says. By the way, I suppose the water's warming up in the pool? June—it would be. That's what I should like—a swim."

He *did* see me! thought Mrs. Johnson.

"You should ask Mr. Armitage," she said coldly.

"Oh, no, no," said Mr. Smith. "I just *feel* that to swim and have a sunbathe would be the right idea. I should like a place with a swimming pool. And a view like this. I feel it would suit me. And, by the way," he became stern again, "don't let me hear you say again that Mr. Armitage enjoys this place although he doesn't see it. Don't tie his blindness on him. You'll hold him back. He *does* see it. He reflects all-seeing God. I told him so on Wednesday."

"On Wednesday?"

"Yes," he said. "When he came for treatment. I managed to fit him in. Good godfathers, look at the time! I've to get the bus back. I'm sorry to miss Mr. Armitage. Just tell him I called. I just had a thought to give him, that's all. He'll appreciate it."

"And now," Mr. Smith said sportively, "I must try and avoid taking a dive into that pool as I go by, mustn't I?"

She watched his stout marching figure go off down the path.

For treatment! What on earth did Mr. Smith mean? She knew the rest when Armitage came home.

"He came for his cheque," he said. "Would you make out a cheque for a hundred and twenty pounds—"

"A hundred and twenty pounds!" she exclaimed.

"For Mr. Smith," he repeated. "He is treating my eyes."

"Your eyes! He's not an ophthalmic surgeon."

"No," said Armitage coldly. "I have tried those."

"You're not going to a faith healer!"

"I am."

And so they moved into their second quarrel. It was baffling to quarrel with Armitage. He could hear the firm ring of your voice but he could not see your eyes blooming wider and bluer with obstinacy; for her, her eyes were herself. It was like quarrelling with a man who had no self, or perhaps with one that was always hidden.

"Your church goes in for it," he said.

"Proper faith healing," she said.

"What is proper?" he said.

She had a strong belief in propriety.

"A hundred and twenty pounds! You told me yourself Smith is a fraud. I mean, you refused his case. How can you go to a fraud?"

"I don't think I said fraud," he said.

"You didn't like the way he got five thousand pounds out of that silly young man."

"Two thousand," he said.

"He's after your money," she said. "He's a swindler."

In her heart, having been brought up poor, she thought it was a scandal that Armitage was well-off; it was even more scandalous to throw money away.

"Probably. At the end of his tether," he said. He was conveying, she knew, that he was at the end of his tether too.

"And you fall for that? You can't possibly believe the nonsense he talks."

"Don't you think God was a crook? When you think of what He's done?"

"No, I don't." (But in fact the stained woman thought He was.)

"What did Smith talk about?"

"I was in the pool. I think he was spying on me. I forget what he was talking about—water, chalky water, was it?"

"He's odd about chalk!" Armitage laughed. Then he became grim again: "You see—even Smith can see *you*. You see people, you see Smith, everyone sees everything, and so they can afford to throw away what they see and forget. But I have to remember everything. You know what it is like trying to remember a dream. Smith is right, I'm dreaming a dream," Armitage added sardonically. "He says that I'm only dreaming I cannot see."

She could not make out whether Armitage was serious.

"All right. I don't understand, but all right. What happens next?"

"You can wake up."

Mr. Armitage gave one of his cruel smiles. "I told you. When I used to go to the courts I often listened to witnesses like Smith. They were always bringing 'God is my witness' into it. I never knew a more religious lot of men than dishonest witnesses. They were always bringing in a higher power. Perhaps they were in contact with it."

"You don't mean that. You are making fun of me," she said. And then vehemently: "I hate to see you going to an ignorant man like that. I thought you were too proud. What has happened to you?"

She had never spoken her mind so forcibly to him before.

"If a man can't see," he said, "if *you* couldn't see, humiliation is what you'd fear most. I thought I ought to accept it."

He had never been so open with her.

"You couldn't go lower than Mr. Smith," she said.

"We're proud. That is our vice," he said. "Proud in the dark. Everyone else has to put up with humiliation. You said you knew what it was—I always remember that. Millions of people are humiliated: perhaps it makes them stronger because they forget it. I want to join them."

"No, you don't," she said.

They were lying in bed and leaning over him she put her breast to his lips, but he lay lifeless. She could not bear it that he had changed her and that she had stirred this profound wretchedness in him. She hated confession: to her it was the male weakness—self-love. She got out of bed.

"Come to that," she said. "It's you who are humiliating me. You are going to this quack man because we've slept together. I don't like the compliment."

"And you say you don't love me," he said.

"I admire you," she said. She dreaded the word "love." She picked up her clothes and left the room. She hadn't the courage to say she hadn't the courage. She stuck to what she had felt since she was a child: that she was a body. He had healed it with his body.

Once more she thought, I shall have to go. I ought to have stuck to it and gone before. If I'd been living in the town and just been coming up for the day it would have been O.K. Living in the house was your mistake, my girl. You'll have to go and get another job. But of course when she calmed down, she realized that all this was self-deception: she was afraid to tell him. She brusquely drove off the thought, and her mind went to the practical.

That hundred and twenty pounds! She was determined not to see him swindled. She went with him to Mr. Smith's next time. The roof of the Rolls-Royce gleamed over the shrubbery of the uncut hedge of Mr. Smith's house. A cat was sitting on the window sill. Waiting on the doorstep was the little man, wide-waisted and with his hands in his optimistic pockets, and changing his smile of welcome to a reminder of secret knowledge when he saw her. Behind the undressing smile of Mr. Smith stood the kind, cringing figure of his wife, looking as they all walked into the narrow hall.

"Straight through?" said Mrs. Johnson in her managing voice. "And leave them to themselves, I suppose?"

"The back gets the sun. At the front it's all these trees," said Mrs. Smith, encouraged by Mrs. Johnson's presence to speak out in a weak voice, as if it was all she did get. "I was a London girl."

"So am I," said Mrs. Johnson.

"But you've got a beautiful place up there. Have you got these pine trees too?"

"A few."

"They give me the pip," said Mrs. Smith. "Coffee? Shall I take your coat? My husband said you'd got pines."

"No, thank you, I'll keep it," said Mrs. Johnson. "Yes, we've got pines. I can't say they're my favourite trees. I like to see leaves come off. And I like a bit of traffic myself. I like to see a shop."

"Oh, you would," said Mrs. Smith.

The two women looked with the shrewd London look at each other.

"I'm so busy up there I couldn't come before. I don't like Mr. Armitage coming alone. I like to keep an eye on him," said Mrs. Johnson, set for attack.

"Oh, yes, an eye."

"Frankly, I didn't know he was coming to see Mr. Smith."

But Mrs. Johnson got nothing out of Mrs. Smith. They were both half listening to the rumble of men's voices next door. Then the meeting was over and they went out to meet the men. In his jolly way Mr. Smith said to Mrs. Johnson as they left, "Don't forget about that swim!"

Ostentatiously to show her command and to annoy Armitage, she armed him down the path.

"I hope you haven't invited that man to swim in the pool," said Mrs. Johnson to Mr. Armitage on the way home.

"You've made an impression on Smith," said Armitage.

"No, *I* haven't."

"Poor Mrs. Smith," said Mrs. Johnson.

Otherwise they were silent.

She went a second, then a third time to the Smiths' house. She sat each time in the kitchen talking and listening to the men's voices in the next room. Sometimes there were long silences.

"Is Mr. Smith praying?" Mrs. Johnson asked.

"I expect so," said Mrs. Smith. "Or reading."

"Because it *is* prayer, isn't it?" said Mrs. Johnson.

Mrs. Smith was afraid of this healthy downright woman and it was an effort for her to make a stand on what evidently for most of her married life had been poor ground.

"I suppose it is. Prayer, yes, that is what it would be. Dad . . ."—she changed her mind—"my husband has always had faith." And with this, Mrs. Smith looked nervously at being able loyally to put forward the incomprehensible.

"But what does he actually *do?* I thought he had a chemist's shop," pursued Mrs. Johnson.

Mrs. Smith was a timid woman who wavered now between the relics of dignity and a secretive craving to impart.

"He has retired," said Mrs. Smith. "When we closed the shop he took this up." She said this, hoping to clutch a certainty.

Mrs. Johnson gave a bustling laugh. "No, you misunderstand me. What I mean is, what does he actually *do?* What is the treatment?"

Mrs. Smith was lost. She nodded, as it were, to nothingness several times.

"Yes," she said. "I suppose you'd call it prayer. I don't really understand it."

"Nor do I," said Mrs. Johnson. "I expect you've got enough to do keeping house. I have my work cut out too."

They still heard the men talking. Mrs. Johnson nodded to the wall.

"Still at it," said Mrs. Johnson. "I'll be frank with you, Mrs. Smith. I am sure your husband does whatever he does do for the best . . ."

"Oh, yes, for the best," nodded Mrs. Smith. "It's saved us. He had a writ out against him when Mr. Armitage's cheque came in. I know he's grateful."

"But I believe in being open . . ."

"Open," nodded Mrs. Smith.

"I've told him and I've told Mr. Armitage that I just don't believe a man who has been blind for twenty-two years—"

"Terrible," said Mrs. Smith.

"—can be cured. Certainly not by—whatever this is. Do you believe it, Mrs. Smith?"

Mrs. Smith was cornered.

"Our Lord did it," she said desperately. "That is what my husband says . . ."

"I was a nurse during the war and I have worked for doctors," said Mrs. Johnson. "I am sure it is impossible. I've knocked about a lot. You're a sensible woman, Mrs. Smith. I don't want to offend you, but you don't believe it yourself, do you?"

Mrs. Johnson's eyes grew larger and Mrs. Smith's older eyes were helpless and small. She longed for a friend. She was hypnotized by Mrs. Johnson, whose face and pretty neck grew firmly out of her frilled and high-necked blouse.

"I try to have faith . . ." said Mrs. Smith, rallying to her husband. "He says I hold him back. I don't know."

"Some men need to be held back," said Mrs. Johnson, and she gave a fighting shake to her healthy head. All Mrs. Smith could do in her panic was to watch every move of Mrs. Johnson's, study her expensive shoes and stockings, her capable skirt, her painted nails. Now, at the shake of Mrs. Johnson's head, she saw on the right side of the neck the small petal of the birthmark just above the frill of the collar.

"None of us are perfect," said Mrs. Smith slyly.

"I have been with Mr. Armitage four years," Mrs. Johnson said.

"It is a lovely place up there," said Mrs. Smith, eager to change the subject. "It must be terrible to live in such a lovely place and never see it . . ."

"Don't you believe it," said Mrs. Johnson. "He knows that place better than any of us, better than me."

"No," groaned Mrs. Smith. "We had a blind dog when I was a girl. It used to nip hold of my dress to hold me back if it heard a car coming when I was going to cross the road. It belonged to my aunt and she said 'That dog can see. It's a miracle.' "

"He heard the car coming," said Mrs. Johnson. "It's common sense."

The words struck Mrs. Smith.

"Yes, it is, really," she said. "If you come to think of it."

She got up and went to the gas stove to make more coffee and new courage came to her. We know why she doesn't want Mr. Armitage to see again! She was thinking: the frightening Mrs. Johnson was really weak. Housekeeper and secretary to a rich man, sitting very pretty up there, the best of everything. Plenty of money, staff, cook, gardener, chauffeur, Rolls-Royce—if he was cured where would her job be? Oh, she looks full of herself now, but she is afraid. I expect she's got round him to leave her a bit.

The coffee began to bubble up in the pot and that urgent noise put excitement into her and her old skin blushed.

"Up there with a man alone. As I said to Dad, a woman can tell! Where would she get another man with that spot spreading all over? She's artful. She's picked the right one." She was telling the tale to herself.

The coffee boiled over and hissed on the stove and a sudden forgotten jealousy hissed up in Mrs. Smith's uncertain mind. She took the pot to the table and poured out a boiling-hot cup and, as the steam clouded up from it, screening her daring stare at the figure of Mrs. Johnson, Mrs. Smith wanted to say: "Lying there stark naked by that swimming pool right in the face of my husband. What was he doing up there anyway?"

She could not say it. There was not much pleasure in Mrs. Smith's life; jealousy was the only one that enlivened her years with Mr. Smith. She had flown at him when he came home and had told her that God had guided him, that prayer always uncovered evil and brought it to the surface; it had revealed to him that the Devil had put his mark on Mrs. Johnson, and that he wouldn't be surprised if that was what was holding up the healing of Mr. Armitage.

"What were you doing," she screamed at him, "looking at a woman?"

The steam cleared and Mrs. Smith's nervousness returned as she saw that composed face. She was frightened now of her own imagination and of her husband's. She knew him. He was always up to something.

"Don't you dare say anything to Mr. Armitage about this!" she had shouted at him.

But now she fell back on admiring Mrs. Johnson again.

Settled for life, she sighed. She's young. She is only fighting for her own. She's a woman.

And Mrs. Smith's pride was stirred. Her courage was fitful and weakened by what she had lived through. She had heard Mrs. Johnson was divorced and it gave Mrs. Smith strength as a woman who had "stuck to her husband." She had not gone round taking up with men as she guessed Mrs. Johnson might have done. She was a respectable married woman.

Her voice trembled at first but became stronger.

"Dad wanted to be a doctor when he was a boy," Mrs. Smith was saying, "but there wasn't the money so he worked in a chemist's but it was always church on Sundays. I wasn't much of a one for church myself. But you must have capital and being just behind the counter doesn't lead anywhere. Of course I tried to egg him on to get his diploma and he got the papers—but I used to watch him. He'd start his studying and then he'd get impatient. He's a very impatient man and he'd say 'Amy, I'll try the ministry'—he's got a good voice—'church people have money.' "

"And did he?"

"No, he always wanted to, but he couldn't seem to settle to a church—I mean a religion. I'll say this for him, he's a fighter. Nixon, his first guv'nor, thought the world of him: quick with the sales. Nixon's Cough Mixture—well, he didn't invent it, but he changed the bottles and the labels, made it look—fashionable, dear—you know? A lot of Wesleyans took it."

Mrs. Smith spread her hands over her face and laughed through her fingers.

"When Nixon died someone in the church put up some money, a very religious, good man. One day Dad said to me—I always remember it—'It's not medicine. It's faith does it.' He's got faith. Faith is—well, faith."

"In himself?" suggested Mrs. Johnson.

"That's it! That's it!" cried Mrs. Smith with excitement. Then she quietened and dabbed a tear from her cheek. "I begged him not to come down here. But this Mrs. Rogers, the lady who owns the house, she's deaf and on her own, he knew her. She believes in him. She calls him Daniel. He's treating her for deafness, she can't hear a word, so we brought our things down after we closed up in Ealing, that's why it's so crowded, two of everything, I have to laugh."

"So you don't own the house?"

"Oh, no, dear—oh, no," Mrs. Smith said, frightened of the idea. "He wants something bigger. He wants space for his work."

Mrs. Smith hesitated and looked at the wall through which the sound of Mr. Smith's voice was coming. And then, fearing she had been disloyal, she said, "She's much better. She's very funny. She came down yesterday calling him. 'Daniel. Daniel. I hear the cuckoo.' Of course I didn't say anything: it was the man calling out "Coal." But she is better. She wouldn't have heard him at all when we came here."

They were both silent.

"You can't live your life from A to Z," Mrs. Smith said, waking up. "We all make mistakes. We've been married for forty-two years. I expect you have your troubles too, even in that lovely place."

After the hour Mr. Smith came into the kitchen to get Mrs. Johnson.

"What a chatter!" he said to her. "I never heard such a tittle-tattle in my life."

"Yes, we had a fine chat, didn't we?"

"Oh, yes," said Mrs. Smith boldly.

"How is it going on?" said Mrs. Johnson.

"Now, now," Mr. Smith corrected her. "These cases seemingly take time. You have to get to the bottom of it. We don't intend to, but we keep people back by the thoughts we hold over them."

And then, in direct attack on her—"I don't want you to hold no wrong thoughts over me. You have no power over divine love." And he turned to his wife to silence her.

"And how would I do that?" said Mrs. Johnson.

"Cast the mote out of thine own eye," said Smith. "Heal yourself. We all have to." He smiled broadly at her.

"I don't know what all this talk about divine love is," said Mrs. Johnson. "But I love Mr. Armitage as he is."

Smith did not answer.

Armitage had found his way to the door of the kitchen. He listened and said, "Good-bye, Mrs. Smith." And to Mr. Smith: "Send me your bill. I'm having the footpath closed."

They drove away.

"I love Mr. Armitage as he is." The words had been forced out of her by the detestable man. She hated that she had said to him what she could not say to Armitage. They surprised her. She hoped Armitage had not heard them.

He was silent in the car. He did not answer any of her questions.

"I'm having that path closed," he repeated.

I know! she thought. Smith has said something about me. Surely not about "it"!

When they got out of the car at the house he said to the chauffeur, "Did you see Mr. Smith when he came up here three weeks ago? It was a Thursday. Were you down at the pool?"

"It's my afternoon off, sir."

"I know that. I asked whether you were anywhere near the pool. Or in the garden?"

"No, sir."

Oh, God, Mrs. Johnson groaned. Now he's turned on Jim.

"Jim went off on his motorbike. I saw him," said Mrs. Johnson.

They went into the house.

"You don't know who you can trust," Armitage said and went across to the stairs and started up. But instead of putting his hand to the rail which was on the right, he put it out to the left, and not finding it, stood bewildered. Mrs. Johnson quietly went to that side of him and nudged him in the right direction.

When he came down to lunch he sat in silence before the cutlets on his plate.

"After all these years! I know the rail is on the right and I put out my left hand."

"You just forgot," she said. "Why don't you try forgetting a few more things?"

She was cross about the questioning of the chauffeur.

"Say, one thing a day," she said.

He listened and this was one of those days when he cruelly paused a long time before replying. A minute went by and she started to eat.

"Like this?" he said, and he deliberately knocked his glass of water over. The water spread over the cloth towards her plate.

"What's this silly temper?" she said, and lifting her plate away, she lifted the cloth and started mopping with her table napkin and picked up the glass.

"I'm fed up with you blind people," she said angrily. "All jealousy and malice, just childish. You're so clever, aren't you? What happened? Didn't that good Mr. Smith do the magic trick? I don't wonder your wife walked out on you. Pity the poor blind! What about other people? I've had enough. You have an easy life; you sail down in your Rolls and think you can buy God from Mr. Smith just because—I don't know why—but if he's a fraud you're a fraud." Suddenly the wronged inhabitant inside her started to shout: "I'll tell you something about that Peeping Jesus: he saw the lot. Oh, yes, I hadn't a stitch on. The lot!" she was shouting. And then she started to unzip her dress and pull it down over her shoulder and drag her arm out of it. "You can't see it, you silly fool. The whole bloody Hebrides, the whole plate of liver."

And she went to his place, got him by the shoulder and rubbed her stained shoulder and breast against his face.

"Do you want to see more?" she shouted. "It made my husband sick. That's what you've been sleeping with. And"—she got away as he tried to grip her and laughed—"you didn't know! *He* did."

She sat down and cried hysterically with her head and arms on the table.

Armitage stumbled in the direction of her crying and put his hand on her bare shoulder.

"Don't touch me! I hate your hands." And she got up, dodged round him to the door and ran out sobbing; slower than she was, he was too late to hear her steps. He found his way back to the serving hatch and called to the cook.

"Go up to Mrs. Johnson. She's in her room. She's ill," he said.

He stood in the hall waiting; the cook came downstairs and went into the sitting-room.

"She's not there. She must have gone into the garden." And then she said at the window, "She's down by the pool."

"Go and talk to her," he said.

The cook went out of the garden door and on to the terrace. She was a thin round-shouldered woman. She saw Mrs. Johnson move back to the near side of the pool; she seemed to be staring at something in the water. Then the cook stopped and came shouting back to the house.

"She's fallen in. With all her clothes on. She can't swim. I know she can't swim." And then the cook called out, "Jim! Jim!" and ran down the lawns.

Armitage stood helpless.

"Where's the door?" he called. There was no one there.

491

Armitage made an effort to recover his system, but it was lost. He found himself blocked by a chair, but he had forgotten which chair. He waited to sense the movement of air in order to detect where the door was, but a window was half open and he found himself against glass. He made his way feeling along the wall, but he was travelling away from the door. He stood still again, and smelling a kitchen smell he made his way back across the centre of the long room and at last found the first door and then the door to the garden. He stepped out, but he was exhausted and his will had gone. He could only stand in the breeze, the disorderly scent of the flowers and the grass mocking him. A jeering bird flew up. He heard the gardener's dog barking below and a voice, the gardener's voice, shouting "Quiet!" Then he heard voices coming slowly nearer up the lawn.

"Helen," called Armitage, but they pushed past him. He felt her wet dress brush his hand and her foot struck his leg; the gardener was carrying her.

"Marge," Armitage heard her voice as she choked and was sick.

"Upstairs. I'll get her clothes off," said the cook.

"No," said Armitage.

"Be quiet," said the cook.

"In my room," said Armitage.

"What an idea!" said the cook. "Stay where you are. Mind you don't slip on all this wet."

He stood, left behind in the hall, listening, helpless. Only when the doctor came did he go up.

She was sitting up in bed and Armitage held her hand.

"I'm sorry," she said. "You'd better fill that pool up. It hasn't brought you any luck."

Armitage and Mrs. Johnson are in Italy now; for how long it is hard to say. They themselves don't know. Some people call her Mrs. Armitage, some call her Mrs. Johnson; this uncertainty pleases her. She has always had a secret and she is too old, she says, to give up the habit now. It still pleases Armitage to baffle people. It is impossible for her to deny that she loves Armitage, because he heard what she said to Smith; she has had to give in about that. And she does love him because his system has broken down completely in Italy. "You are my eyes," he says. "Everything sounds different here." "I like a bit of noise," she says.

Pictures in churches and galleries he is mad about and he likes listening to her descriptions of them and often laughs at some of her remarks, and she is beginning, she says, to get "a kick out of the classical stuff" herself.

There was an awkward moment before they set off for Italy when he made her write out a cheque for Smith and she tried to stop him.

"No," he said. "He got it out of you. I owe you to him."

She was fighting the humiliating suspicion that in his nasty prying way Smith had told Armitage about her before *she* had told him. But Armitage said, "I knew all the time. From the beginning. I knew everything about you."

She still does not know whether to believe him or not. When she does believe, she is more awed than shamed; when she does not believe she feels carelessly happy. He depends on her entirely here. One afternoon, standing at the window of their room and looking at the people walking in the lemonish light across the square, she suddenly said, "I love you. I feel gaudy!" She notices that the only thing he doesn't like is to hear a man talk to her.

ISAAC BASHEVIS SINGER

(1904–1991)

ISAAC BASHEVIS SINGER was born in Poland; his father and grandfathers were rabbis, and he was educated at the Warsaw Rabbinical Seminary. In 1935 he emigrated to the United States, following his older brother, the writer I. J. Singer. He made his home in New York City, and became an American citizen in 1943. He worked as a journalist for many years, writing in Yiddish for the *Jewish Daily Forward,* where he published most of his stories. Though his work has long been translated into English, throughout his writing life Yiddish was the language in which he composed. His output was formidable, consisting, in addition to his novels and stories, of books for children, essays, memoirs, and plays. The settings of his works vary; many of his stories and novels have an American locale. But a key and characteristic setting is the shtetl, the Eastern European Jewish ghetto, where "Short Friday" (tr. 1964) takes place. Singer's novels include *The Family Moskat* (the first work to be translated into English, in 1950), *Enemies* (tr. 1972), and *The Penitent* (tr. 1983). Among his short-story collections are *Gimpel the Fool and Other Stories* (tr. 1961), *The Spinoza of Market Street and Other Stories* (tr. 1961), and *The Death of Methuselah* (tr. 1985). His *Collected Stories* appeared in 1982. His numerous awards include the 1974 National Book Award for fiction for *A Crown of Feathers and Other Stories* (1973), Newbery medals and a National Book Award honoring various children's books, and the 1989 American Academy and Institute of Arts and Letters Gold Medal for fiction. In 1978 he received the Nobel Prize for literature, the first to be awarded to a Yiddish-language writer.

Singer's work is imbued not only with the Jewish tradition—including its mystical elements—in which he was steeped, but also with his own sense of life's magic and mystery. When he was asked, in a 1987 PBS profile "Isaac in America: A Journey with Isaac Bashevis Singer," why he wrote in Yiddish, after all a dying language, he replied: "Ghosts love Yiddish. They all speak it."

"Short Friday" is the story of the "great love" of the clumsy and unprepossessing tailor, Shmul-Leibele, and his "jewel of a wife," Shoshe. Only in his honesty, piety, and infinite capacity for love is Shmul-Leibele without flaw. The story takes place in the village of Lapschitz, on the shortest Friday of the year: "The stars on this Friday seemed larger and sharper, and Shmul-Leibele's hut, which was situated not far from the synagogue, now hung suspended in space." In this Chagall-like village, where even gravity seems to be defied, the couple together make the traditional meticulous preparations for the Sabbath. They share this ritual as they share everything.

Short Friday

I

In the village of Lapschitz lived a tailor named Shmul-Leibele with his wife, Shoshe. Shmul-Leibele was half tailor, half furrier, and a complete pauper. He had never mastered his trade. When filling an order for a jacket or a gaberdine, he inevitably made the garment either too short or too tight. The belt in the back would hang either too high or too low, the lapels never matched, the vent was off center. It was said that he had once sewn a pair of trousers with the fly off to one side. Shmul-Leibele could not count the wealthy citizens among his customers. Common people brought him their shabby garments to have patched and turned, and the peasants gave him their old pelts to reverse. As is usual with bunglers, he was also slow. He would dawdle over a garment for weeks at a time. Yet, despite his shortcomings, it must be said that Shmul-Leibele was an honorable man. He used only strong thread and none of his seams ever gave. If one ordered a lining from Shmul-Leibele, even one of common sackcloth or cotton, he bought only the very best material, and thus lost most of his profit. Unlike other tailors who hoarded every last bit of remaining cloth, he returned all scraps to his customers.

Had it not been for his competent wife, Shmul-Leibele would certainly have starved to death. Shoshe helped him in whatever way she could. On Thursdays she hired herself out to wealthy families to knead dough, and on summer days went off to the forest to gather berries and mushrooms, as well as pinecones and twigs for the stove. In winter she plucked down for brides' featherbeds. She was also a better tailor than her husband, and when he began to sigh, or dally and mumble to himself, an indication that he could no longer muddle through, she would take the chalk from his hand and show him how to continue. Shoshe had no children, but it was common knowledge that it wasn't she who was barren, but rather her husband who was sterile, since all of her sisters had borne children, while his only brother was likewise childless. The townswomen repeatedly urged Shoshe to divorce him, but she turned a deaf ear, for the couple loved one another with a great love.

Shmul-Leibele was small and clumsy. His hands and feet were too large for his body, and his forehead bulged on either side as is common in simpletons. His cheeks, red as apples, were bare of whiskers, and but a few hairs sprouted from his chin. He had scarcely any neck at all; his head sat upon his shoulders like a snowman's. When he walked, he scraped his shoes along the ground so that every step could be heard far away. He hummed continuously and there was always an amiable smile on his face. Both winter and summer he wore the same caftan and sheepskin cap and earlaps. Whenever there was any need for a messenger, it was always Shmul-Leibele who was pressed into service, and however far away he was sent, he always went willingly. The wags saddled him with a variety of nicknames and made him the butt of all sorts of pranks, but he never took offense. When others scolded his tormentors, he would merely observe: "What do I care? Let them have their fun. They're only children, after all . . ."

Sometimes he would present one or another of the mischief makers with a piece of candy or a nut. This he did without any ulterior motive, but simply out of good-heartedness.

Shoshe towered over him by a head. In her younger days she had been considered a beauty, and in the households where she worked as a servant they spoke highly of her honesty and diligence. Many young men had vied for her hand, but she had selected Shmul-Leibele because he was quiet and because he never joined the other town boys who gathered on the Lublin road at noon Saturdays to flirt with the girls. His piety and retiring nature pleased her. Even as a girl Shoshe had taken pleasure in studying the Pentateuch, in nursing the infirm at the alms-house, in listening to the tales of the old women who sat before their houses darning stockings. She would fast on the last day of each month, the Minor Day of Atonement, and often attended the services at the women's synagogue. The other servant girls mocked her and thought her old-fashioned. Immediately following her wedding she shaved her head and fastened a kerchief firmly over her ears, never permitting a stray strand of hair from her matron's wig to show as did some of the other young women. The bath attendant praised her because she never frolicked at the ritual bath, but performed her ablutions according to the laws. She purchased only indisputably kosher meat, though it was a half-cent more per pound, and when she was in doubt about the dietary laws she sought out the rabbi's advice. More than once she had not hesitated to throw out all the food and even to smash the earthen crockery. In short, she was a capable, God-fearing woman, and more than one man envied Shmul-Leibele his jewel of a wife.

Above all of life's blessings the couple revered the Sabbath. Every Friday noon Shmul-Leibele would lay aside his tools and cease all work. He was always among the first at the ritual bath, and he immersed himself in the water four times for the four letters of the Holy Name. He also helped the beadle set the candles in the chandeliers and the candelabra. Shoshe scrimped throughout the week, but on the Sabbath she was lavish. Into the heated oven went cakes, cookies and the Sabbath loaf. In winter, she prepared puddings made of chicken's neck stuffed with dough and rendered fat. In summer she made puddings with rice or noodles, greased with chicken fat and sprinkled with sugar or cinnamon. The main dish consisted of potatoes and buckwheat, or pearl barley with beans, in the midst of which she never failed to set a marrow bone. To insure that the dish would be well cooked, she sealed the oven with loose dough. Shmul-Leibele treasured every mouthful, and at every Sabbath meal he would remark: "Ah, Shoshe love, it's food fit for a king! Nothing less than a taste of Paradise!" to which Shoshe replied, "Eat hearty. May it bring you good health."

Although Shmul-Leibele was a poor scholar, unable to memorize a chapter of the Mishnah, he was well versed in all the laws. He and his wife frequently studied *The Good Heart* in Yiddish. On half-holidays, holidays, and on each free day, he studied the Bible in Yiddish. He never missed a sermon, and though a pauper, he bought from peddlers all sorts of books of moral instructions and religious tales, which he then read together with his wife. He never wearied of reciting sacred phrases. As soon as he arose in the morning he washed his hands and began to mouth the preamble to the prayers. Then he would walk over to the study house and worship as one of the quorum. Every day he recited a few chapters of the Psalms, as well as those prayers which the less serious tended to skip over. From his father he had inherited a thick prayer book with wooden covers, which contained the rites and laws pertaining to each day of the year. Shmul-Leibele and his wife heeded each and every one of these. Often he would observe to his wife: "I shall surely end up in Gehenna, since there'll be no one on earth to say Kaddish over me." "Bite your tongue, Shmul-Leibele," she would counter. "For one, everything is possible under God. Secondly, you'll live until the Messiah comes. Thirdly, it's just possible that I will die before you and you will marry a young woman who'll bear you a dozen children." When Shoshe said this, Shmul-Leibele would shout: "God forbid! You must remain in good health. I'd rather rot in Gehenna!"

Although Shmul-Leibele and Shoshe relished every Sabbath, their greatest satisfaction came from the Sabbaths in wintertime. Since the day before the Sabbath evening was a short one, and since Shoshe was busy until late Thursday at her work, the couple usually stayed up all of Thursday night. Shoshe kneaded dough in the trough, covering it with cloth and a pillow so that it might ferment. She heated the oven with kindling wood and dry twigs. The shutters in the room were kept closed, the door shut. The bed and bench-bed remained unmade, for at day-break the couple would take a nap. As long as it was dark Shoshe prepared the Sabbath meal by the light of a candle. She plucked a chicken or a goose (if she had managed to come by one cheaply), soaked it, salted it and scraped the fat from it. She roasted a liver for Shmul-Leibele over the glowing coals and baked a small Sabbath loaf for him. Occasionally she would inscribe her name upon the loaf with letters of dough, and then Shmul-Leibele would tease her: "Shoshe, I am eating you up. Shoshe, I have already swallowed you." Shmul-Liebele loved warmth, and he would climb up on the oven and from there look down as his spouse cooked, baked, washed, rinsed, pounded and carved. The Sabbath loaf would turn out round and brown. Shoshe braided the loaf so swiftly that it seemed to dance before Shmul-Leibele's eyes. She bustled about efficiently with spatulas, pokers, ladles and goosewing dusters, and at times even snatched up a live coal with her bare fingers. The pots perked and bubbled. Occasionally a drop of soup would spill and the hot tin would hiss and squeal. And all the while the cricket continued its chirping. Although Shmul-Leibele had finished his supper by this time, his appetite would be whetted afresh, and Shoshe would throw him a knish, a chicken gizzard, a cookie, a plum from the plum stew or a chunk of the pot roast. At the same time she would chide him, saying that he was a glutton. When he attempted to defend himself she would cry: "Oh, the sin is upon me, I have allowed you to starve . . ."

At dawn they would both lie down in utter exhaustion. But because of their efforts Shoshe would not have to run herself ragged the following day, and she could make the benediction over the candles a quarter of an hour before sunset.

The Friday on which this story took place was the shortest Friday of the year. Outside, the snow had been falling all night and had blanketed the house up to the windows and barricaded the door. As usual, the couple had stayed up until morning, then had lain down to sleep. They had arisen later than usual, for they hadn't heard the rooster's crow, and since the windows were covered with snow and frost, the day seemed as dark as night. After whispering, "I thank Thee," Shmul-Leibele went outside with a broom and shovel to clear a path, after which he took a bucket and fetched water from the well. Then, as he had no pressing work, he decided to lay off for the whole day. He went to the study house for the morning prayers, and after breakfast wended his way to the bathhouse. Because of the cold outside, the patrons kept up an eternal plaint: "A bucket! A bucket!" and the bath attendant poured more and more water over the glowing stones so that the steam grew constantly denser. Shmul-Leibele located a scraggly willow-broom, mounted to the highest bench and whipped himself until his skin glowed red. From the bathhouse, he hurried over to the study house where the beadle had already swept and sprinkled the floor with sand. Shmul-Leibele set the candles and helped spread the tablecloths over the tables. Then he went home again and changed into his Sabbath clothes. His boots, resoled but a few days before, no longer let the wet through. Shoshe had done her washing for the week, and had given him a fresh shirt, underdrawers, a fringed garment, even a clean pair of stockings. She had already performed the benediction over the candles, and the spirit of the Sabbath emanated from every corner of the room. She was wearing her silk kerchief with the silver spangles, a yellow and gray dress, and shoes with gleaming, pointed tips. On her throat hung the chain that Shmul-Leibele's mother, peace be with her, had given her to celebrate the signing of the wedding contract. The marriage band sparkled on her index finger. The candlelight reflected in the windowpanes, and Shmul-Leibele fancied that there was a duplicate of this room outside and that another Shoshe was out there lighting the Sabbath candles. He yearned to tell his wife how full of grace she was, but there was no time for it, since it is specifically stated in the prayer book that it is fitting and proper to be among the first ten worshippers at the synagogue; as it so happened, going off to prayers he was the tenth man to arrive. After the congregation had intoned the Song of Songs, the cantor sang, "Give thanks," and "O come, let us exult." Shmul-Leibele prayed with fervor. The words were sweet upon his tongue, they seemed to fall from his lips with a life of their own, and he felt that they soared to the eastern wall, rose above the embroidered curtain of the Holy Ark, the gilded lions, and the tablets, and floated up to the ceiling with its painting of the twelve constellations. From there, the prayers surely ascended to the Throne of Glory.

II

The cantor chanted, "Come, my beloved," and Shmul-Leibele trumpeted along in accompaniment. Then came the prayers, and the men recited, "It is our duty to praise . . ." to which Shmul-Leibele added a "Lord of the Universe." Afterwards, he wished everyone a good Sabbath: the rabbi, the ritual slaughterer, the head of the community, the assistant rabbi, everyone present. The cheder lads shouted, "Good Sabbath, Shmul-Leibele," while they mocked him with gestures and grimaces, but Shmul-Leibele answered them all with a smile, even occasionally pinched a boy's cheek affectionately. Then he was off for home. The snow was piled high so that one could barely make out the contours of the roofs, as if the entire settlement had been immersed in white. The sky, which had hung low and overcast all day, now grew clear. From among white clouds a full moon peered down, casting a day-like brilliance over the snow. In the west, the edge of a cloud still held the glint of sunset. The stars on this Friday seemed larger and sharper, and through some miracle Lapschitz seemed to have blended with the sky. Shmul-Leibele's hut, which was situated not far from the synagogue, now hung suspended in space, as it is written: "He suspendeth the earth on nothingness." Shmul-Leibele walked slowly since, according to law, one must not hurry when coming from a holy place. Yet he longed to be home. "Who knows?" he thought. "Perhaps Shoshe has become ill? Maybe she's gone to fetch water and, God forbid, has fallen into the well? Heaven save us, what a lot of troubles can befall a man."

On the threshold he stamped his feet to shake off the snow, then opened the door and saw Shoshe. The room made him think of Paradise. The oven had been freshly whitewashed, the candles in the brass candelabras cast a Sabbath glow. The aromas coming from the sealed oven blended with the scents of the Sabbath supper. Shoshe sat on the bench-bed apparently awaiting him, her cheeks shining with the freshness of a young girl's. Shmul-Leibele wished her a happy Sabbath and she in turn wished him a good year. He began to hum, "Peace upon ye ministering angels . . ." and after he had said his farewells to the invisible angels that accompany each Jew leaving the synagogue, he recited: "The worthy woman." How well he understood the meaning of these words, for he had read them often in Yiddish, and each time reflected anew on how aptly they seemed to fit Shoshe.

Shoshe was aware that these holy sentences were being said in her honor, and thought to herself, "Here am I, a simple woman, an orphan, and yet God has chosen to bless me with a devoted husband who praises me in the holy tongue."

Both of them had eaten sparingly during the day so that they would have an appetite for the Sabbath meal. Shmul-Leibele said the benediction over the raisin wine and gave Shoshe the cup so that she might drink. Afterwards, he rinsed his fingers from a tin dipper, then she washed hers, and they both dried their hands with a single towel, each at either end. Shmul-Leibele lifted the Sabbath loaf and cut it with the bread knife, a slice for himself and one for his wife.

He immediately informed her that the loaf was just right, and she countered: "Go on, you say that every Sabbath."

"But it happens to be the truth," he replied.

Although it was hard to obtain fish during the cold weather, Shoshe had purchased three-fourths of a pound of pike from the fishmonger. She had chopped it with onions, added an egg, salt and pepper, and cooked it with carrots and parsley. It took Shmul-Leibele's breath away, and after it he had to drink a tumbler of whiskey. When he began the table chants, Shoshe accompanied him quietly. Then came the chicken soup with noodles and tiny circlets of fat which glowed on the surface like golden ducats. Between the soup and the main course, Shmul-Leibele again sang Sabbath hymns. Since goose was cheap at this time of year, Shoshe gave Shmul-Leibele an extra leg for good measure. After the dessert, Shmul-Leibele washed for the last time and made a benediction. When he came to the words: "Let us not be in need either of the gifts of flesh and blood nor of their loans," he rolled his eyes upward and brandished his fists. He never stopped praying that he be allowed to continue to earn his own livelihood and not, God forbid, become an object of charity.

After grace, he said yet another chapter of the Mishnah, and all sorts of other prayers which were found in his large prayer book. Then he sat down to read the weekly portion of the Pentateuch twice in Hebrew and once in Aramaic. He enunciated every word and took care to make no mistake in the difficult Aramaic paragraphs of the Onkelos. When he reached the last section, he began to yawn and tears gathered in his eyes. Utter exhaustion overcame him. He could barely keep his eyes open and between one passage and the next he dozed off for a second or two. When Shoshe noticed this, she made up the bench-bed for him and prepared her own featherbed with clean sheets. Shmul-Leibele barely managed to say the retiring prayers and began to undress. When he was already lying on his bench-bed he said: "A good Sabbath, my pious wife. I am very tired . . ." and turning to the wall, he promptly began to snore.

Shoshe sat a while longer gazing at the Sabbath candles which had already begun to smoke and flicker. Before getting into bed, she placed a pitcher of water and a basin at Shmul-Leibele's bedstead so that he would not rise the following morning without water to wash with. Then she, too, lay down and fell asleep.

They had slept an hour or two or possibly three—what does it matter, actually?—when suddenly Shoshe heard Shmul-Leibele's voice. He waked her and whispered her name. She opened one eye and asked, "What is it?"

"Are you clean?" he mumbled.

She thought for a moment and replied, "Yes."

He rose and came to her. Presently he was in bed with her. A desire for her flesh had roused him. His heart pounded rapidly, the blood coursed in his veins.

He felt a pressure in his loins. His urge was to mate with her immediately, but he remembered the Law, which admonished a man not to copulate with a woman until he had first spoken affectionately to her, and he now began to speak of his love for her and how this mating could possibly result in a male-child.

"And a girl you wouldn't accept?" Shoshe chided him, and he replied, "Whatever God deigns to bestow would be welcome."

"I fear this privilege isn't mine any more," she said with a sigh.

"Why not?" he demanded. "Our mother Sarah was far older than you."

"How can one compare oneself to Sarah? Far better you divorce me and marry another."

He interrupted her, stopping her mouth with his hand. "Were I sure that I could sire the twelve tribes of Israel with another, I still would not leave you. I cannot even imagine myself with another woman. You are the jewel of my crown."

"And what if I were to die?" she asked.

"God forbid! I would simply perish from sorrow. They would bury us both on the same day."

"Don't speak blasphemy. May you outlive my bones. You are a man. You would find somebody else. But what would I do without you?"

He wanted to answer her, but she sealed his lips with a kiss. He went to her then. He loved her body. Each time she gave herself to him, the wonder of it astonished him anew. How was it possible, he would think, that he, Shmul-Leibele, should have such a treasure all to himself? He knew the law, one dared not surrender to lust for pleasure. But somewhere in a sacred book he had read that it was permissible to kiss and embrace a wife to whom one had been wed according to the laws of Moses and Israel, and he now caressed her face, her throat and her breasts. She warned him that this was frivolity. He replied, "So I'll lie on the torture rack. The great saints also loved their wives." Nevertheless, he promised himself to attend the ritual bath the following morning, to intone psalms and to pledge a sum to charity. Since she loved him also and enjoyed his caresses, she let him do his will.

After he had satiated his desire, he wanted to return to his own bed, but a heavy sleepiness came over him. He felt a pain in his temples. Shoshe's head ached as well. She suddenly said, "I'm afraid something is burning in the oven. Maybe I should open the flue?"

"Go on, you're imagining it," he replied. "It'll become too cold in here."

And so complete was his weariness that he fell asleep, as did she.

That night Shmul-Leibele suffered an eerie dream. He imagined that he had passed away. The Burial Society brethren came by, picked him up, lit candles by his head, opened the windows, intoned the prayer to justify God's ordainment. Afterwards, they washed him on the ablution board, carried him on a stretcher to the cemetery. There they buried him as the gravedigger said Kaddish over his body.

"That's odd," he thought. "I hear nothing of Shoshe lamenting or begging forgiveness. Is it possible that she would so quickly grow unfaithful? Or has she, God forbid, been overcome by grief?"

He wanted to call her name, but he was unable to. He tried to tear free of the grave, but his limbs were powerless. All of a sudden he awoke.

"What a horrible nightmare!" he thought. "I hope I come out of it all right."

At that moment Shoshe also awoke. When he related his dream to her, she did not speak for a while. Then she said, "Woe is me. I had the very same dream."

"Really? You too?" asked Shmul-Leibele, now frightened. "This I don't like."

He tried to sit up, but he could not. It was as if he had been shorn of all his strength. He looked toward the window to see if it were day already, but there was no window visible, nor any windowpane. Darkness loomed everywhere. He cocked his ears. Usually he would be able to hear the chirping of a cricket, the scurrying of a mouse, but this time only a dead silence prevailed. He wanted to reach out to Shoshe, but his hand seemed lifeless.

"Shoshe," he said quietly, "I've grown paralyzed."

"Woe is me, so have I," she said. "I cannot move a limb."

They lay there for a long while, silently, feeling their numbness. Then Shoshe spoke: "I fear that we are already in our graves for good."

"I'm afraid you're right," Shmul-Leibele replied in a voice that was not of the living.

"Pity me, when did it happen? How?" Shoshe asked. "After all, we went to sleep hale and hearty."

"We must have been asphyxiated by the fumes from the stove," Shmul-Leibele said.

"But I said I wanted to open the flue."

"Well, it's too late for that now."

"God have mercy upon us, what do we do now? We were still young people . . ."

"It's no use. Apparently it was fated."

"Why? We arranged a proper Sabbath. I prepared such a tasty meal. An entire chicken neck and tripe."

"We have no further need of food."

Shoshe did not immediately reply. She was trying to sense her own entrails. No, she felt no appetite. Not even for a chicken neck and tripe. She wanted to weep, but she could not.

"Shmul-Leibele, they've buried us already. It's all over."

"Yes, Shoshe, praised be the true Judge! We are in God's hands."

"Will you be able to recite the passage attributed to your name before the Angel Dumah?"

"Yes."

"It's good that we are lying side by side," she muttered.

"Yes, Shoshe," he said, recalling a verse: *Lovely and pleasant in their lives, and in their death they were not divided.*

"And what will become of our hut? You did not even leave a will."

"It will undoubtedly go to your sister."

Shoshe wished to ask something else, but she was ashamed. She was curious about the Sabbath meal. Had it been removed from the oven? Who had eaten it? But she felt that such a query would not be fitting of a corpse. She was no longer Shoshe the dough-kneader, but a pure, shrouded corpse with shards covering her eyes, a cowl over her head, and myrtle twigs between her fingers. The Angel Dumah would appear at any moment with his fiery staff, and she would have to be ready to give an account of herself.

Yes, the brief years of turmoil and temptation had come to an end. Shmul-Leibele and Shoshe had reached the true world. Man and wife grew silent. In the stillness they heard the flapping of wings, a quiet singing. An angel of God had come to guide Shmul-Leibele the tailor and his wife, Shoshe, into Paradise.

WILLIAM TREVOR
(1928–   )

WILLIAM TREVOR was born in Mitchelstown, County Cork, Ireland, where he was educated. From 1942 to 1946 he attended St. Columba's College in Dublin and received a B.A. from Dublin's Trinity College in 1950. In 1952 he married Jane Ryan; they have two sons. Between 1951 and 1964 he taught history in Northern Ireland and art in Rugby, England; he worked as a sculptor, and in London as an advertising copywriter. He makes his home in England.

Trevor is considered one of the masters of the short story written in the English language. Graham Greene likened the accomplishment of Trevor's fourth collection, *Angels at the Ritz (1975),* to Joyce's *Dubliners.* Trevor's *Collected Stories* appeared in 1992. He has also written several novels. *Two Lives,* published in 1991, consists of two novellas, *Reading Turgenev* (shortlisted for the Booker Prize) and *My House in Umbria* (shortlisted for the *Sunday Express* Prize). He has been the recipient of numerous other awards, including two Giles Cooper Awards for radio plays, the British Academy Award for a television play, two Irish Community prizes, the 1964 *Transatlantic Review* prize, the Hawthornden Prize in 1965, and, in 1976, both the Heinemann and Whitbread Awards.

"Lovers of Their Time" (1978) a deceptively simple story spanning the sixties, is told with what seems, for Trevor, unusual lightheartedness. Norman Britt, a travel agent on his lunch hour, stops into the chemist's and meets Marie, who works there. A flirtation fans into a love affair, progressing from lunches to lovemaking in the great, grand bathtub of an otherwise unused bathroom in a hotel nearby. There they can lock the door and forget such impediments to their love as Norman's wife, Marie's mother. Years pass, as this fevered love, denied the comfort of a bed, continues to spend itself in a bathtub and other equally cramped quarters. The vivid preposterousness of the sixties—its fashion, its music, its James Bond, all its artful evasions—merges with the account of Norman and Marie's love. Their story doesn't merely parallel their time; it ramifies, like the decade itself, into ours.

Lovers of Their Time

Looking back on it, it seemed to have to do with that particular decade in London. Could it have happened, he wondered, at any other time except the 1960s?

That feeling was intensified, perhaps, because the whole thing had begun on New Year's Day, 1963, long before that day became a bank holiday in England. 'That'll be two and nine,' she'd said, smiling at him across her counter, handing him toothpaste and emery boards in a bag. 'Colgate's, remember,' his wife had called out as he was leaving the flat. 'The last stuff we had tasted awful.'

His name was Norman Britt. It said so on a small plastic name-plate in front of his position in the travel agency where he worked, Travel-Wide as it was called. *Marie* a badge on her light-blue shop-coat announced. His wife, who worked at home, assembling jewellery for a firm that paid her on a production basis, was called Hilda.

Green's the Chemist's and Travel-Wide were in Vincent Street, a street that was equidistant from Paddington station and Edgware Road. The flat where Hilda worked all day was in Putney. Marie lived in Reading with her mother and her mother's friend Mrs Druk, both of them widows. She caught the 8.05 every morning to Paddington and usually the 6.30 back.

He was forty in 1963, as Hilda was; Marie was twenty-eight. He was tall and thin, with a David Niven moustache. Hilda was thin also, her dark hair beginning to grey, her sharply-featured face pale. Marie was well-covered, carefully made up, her reddish hair dyed blond. She smiled a lot, a slack half-crooked smile that made her eyes screw up and twinkle; she exuded laziness and generosity. She and her friend Mavis went dancing a lot in Reading and had a sizeable collection of men friends. 'Fellas' they called them.

Buying things from her now and again in Green's the Chemist's Norman had come to the conclusion that she was of a tartish disposition, and imagined that if ever he sat with her over a drink in the nearby Drummer Boy the occasion could easily lead to a hug on the street afterwards. He imagined her coral-coloured lips, like two tiny sausages, only softer, pressed upon his moustache and his abbreviated mouth. He imagined the warmth of her hand in his. For all that, she was a little outside reality: she was there to desire, to glow erotically in the heady atmosphere of the Drummer Boy, to light cigarettes for in a dream.

'Isn't it cold?' he said as she handed him the emery boards and the toothpaste.

'Shocking,' she agreed, and hesitated, clearly wanting to say something else. 'You're in that Travel-Wide,' she added in the end. 'Me and my friend want to go to Spain this year.'

'It's very popular. The Costa Brava?'

'That's right.' She handed him threepence change. 'In May.'

'Not too hot on the Costa in May. If you need any help—'

'Just the bookings.'

'I'd be happy to make them for you. Look in any time. Britt the name is. I'm on the counter.'

'If I may, Mr Britt. I could slip out maybe at four, or roundabout.'

'Today, you mean?'

'We want to fix it up.'

505

'Naturally. I'll keep an eye out for you.'

It was hard not to call her madam or miss, the way he'd normally do. He'd heard himself saying that he'd be happy to make the bookings for her, knowing that that was business jargon, knowing that the unfussy voice he'd used was a business one also. Her friend was a man, he supposed, some snazzy tough in a car. 'See you later then,' he said, but already she was serving another customer, advising about lipstick refills.

She didn't appear in Travel-Wide at four o'clock; she hadn't come when the doors closed at five-thirty. He was aware of a sense of disappointment, combined with one of anticipation: for if she'd come at four, he reflected as he left the travel agency, their bit of business would be in the past rather than the future. She'd look in some other time and he'd just have to trust to luck that if he happened to be busy with another customer she'd be able to wait. There'd be a further occasion, when she called to collect the tickets themselves.

'Ever so sorry,' she said on the street, her voice coming from behind him. 'Couldn't get away, Mr Britt.'

He turned and smiled at her, feeling the movement of his moustache as he parted his lips. He knew only too well, he said. 'Some other time then?'

'Maybe tomorrow. Maybe lunchtime.'

'I'm off myself from twelve to one. Look, you wouldn't fancy a drink? I could advise you just as easily over a drink.'

'Oh, you wouldn't have the time. No, I mustn't take advantage—'

'You're not at all. If you've got ten minutes?'

'Well, it's awfully good of you, Mr Britt. But I really feel I'm taking advantage, I really do.'

'A New Year's drink.'

He pushed open the doors of the saloon bar of the Drummer Boy, a place he didn't often enter except for office drinks at Christmas or when someone leaving the agency was being given a send-off. Ron Stocks and Mr Blackstaffe were usually there in the evenings: he hoped they'd be there now to see him in the company of the girl from Green's the Chemist's. 'What would you like?' he asked her.

'Gin and peppermint's my poison, only honestly I should pay. No, let me ask you—'

'I wouldn't dream of it. We can sit over there, look.'

The Drummer Boy, so early in the evening, wasn't full. By six o'clock the advertising executives from the firm of Dalton, Dure and Higgins, just round the corner, would have arrived, and the architects from Frine and Knight. Now there was only Mrs Gregan, old and alcoholic, known to everyone, and a red-fleshed man called Bert, with his poodle, Jimmy. It was disappointing that Ron Stocks and Mr Blackstaffe weren't there.

'You were here lunchtime Christmas Eve,' she said.

'Yes, I was.' He paused, placing her gin and peppermint on a cardboard mat that advertised Guinness. 'I saw you too.'

He drank some of his Double Diamond and carefully wiped the traces of foam from his moustache. He realized now that it would, of course, be quite impossible to give her a hug on the street outside. That had been just imagination, wishful thinking as his mother would have said. And yet he knew that when he arrived home twenty-five or so minutes late he would not tell Hilda that he'd been advising an assistant from Green's the Chemist's about a holiday on the Costa Brava. He wouldn't even say he'd been in the Drummer Boy. He'd say Blackstaffe had kept everyone late, going through the new package that Eurotours were offering in Germany and Luxembourg this summer. Hilda wouldn't in a million years suspect that he'd been sitting in a public house with a younger woman who was quite an eyeful. As a kind of joke, she quite regularly suggested that his sexual drive left something to be desired.

'We were thinking about the last two weeks in May,' Marie said. 'It's when Mavis can get off too.'

'Mavis?'

'My friend, Mr Britt.'

Hilda was watching Z-*Cars* in the sitting-room, drinking V.P. wine. His stuff was in the oven, she told him. 'Thanks,' he said.

Sometimes she was out when he returned in the evenings. She went round to friends, a Mr and Mrs Fowler, with whom she drank V.P. and played bridge. On other occasions she went to the Club, which was a place with a licence, for card-players and billiard-players. She quite liked her social life, but always said beforehand when she'd be out and always made arrangements about leaving food in the oven. Often in the daytime she'd go and make jewellery with Violet Parkes, who also went in for this occupation; and often Violet Parkes spent the day with Hilda. The jewellery-making consisted for the most part of threading plastic beads on to a string or arranging plastic pieces in the settings provided. Hilda was quick at it and earned more than she would have if she went out every day, saving the fares for a start. She was better at it than Violet Parkes.

'All right then?' she said as he carried his tray of food into the sitting-room and sat down in front of the television set. 'Want some V.P., eh?'

Her eyes continued to watch the figures on the screen as she spoke. He knew she'd prefer to be in the Fowlers' house or at the Club, although now that they'd acquired a TV set the evenings passed easier when they were alone together.

'No, thanks,' he said in reply to her offer of wine and he began to eat something that appeared to be a rissole. There were two of them, round and brown in a tin-foil container that also contained gravy. He hoped she wasn't going to be demanding in their bedroom. He eyed her, for sometimes he could tell.

'Hi,' she said, noticing the glance. 'Feeling fruity, dear?' She laughed and winked, her suggestive voice seeming odd as it issued from her thin, rather dried-up face. She was always saying things like that, for no reason that Norman could see, always talking about feeling fruity or saying she could see he was keen when he wasn't in the least. Norman considered that she was unduly demanding and often wondered what it would be like to be married to someone who was not. Now and again, fatigued after the intensity of her love-making, he lay staring at the darkness, wondering if her bedroom appetites were related in some way to the fact that she was unable to bear children, if her abandon reflected a maternal frustration. Earlier in their married life she'd gone out every day to an office where she'd been a filing clerk; in the evenings they'd often gone to the cinema.

He lay that night, after she'd gone to sleep, listening to her heavy breathing, thinking of the girl in Green's the Chemist's. He went through the whole day in his mind, seeing himself leaving the flat in Putney, hearing Hilda calling out about the emery boards and the toothpaste, seeing himself reading the *Daily Telegraph* in the Tube. Slowly he went through the morning, deliciously anticipating the moment when she handed him his change. With her smile mistily hovering, he recalled the enquiries and demands of a number of the morning's customers. 'Fix us up Newcastle and back?' a couple enquired. 'Mid-week's cheaper, is it?' A man with a squashed-up face wanted a week in Holland for himself and his sister and his sister's husband. A woman asked about Greece, another about cruises on the Nile, a third about the Scilly Isles. Then he placed the Closed sign in front of his position at the counter and went out to have lunch in Bette's Sandwiches off the Edgware Road. 'Packet of emery boards,' he said again in Green's the Chemist's, 'and a small Colgate's.' After that there was the conversation they'd had, and then the afternoon with her smile still mistily hovering, as in fact it had, and then her presence beside him in the Drummer Boy. Endlessly she lifted the glass of gin and peppermint to her lips, endlessly she smiled. When he slept he dreamed of her. They were walking in Hyde Park and her shoe fell off. 'I could tell you were a deep one,' she said, and the next thing was Hilda was having one of her early-morning appetites.

'I don't know what it is about that chap,' Marie confided to Mavis. 'Something though.'

'Married, is he?'

'Oh, he would be, chap like that.'

'Now, you be careful, girl.'

'He has Sinatra's eyes. That blue, you know.'

'Now, Marie—'

'I like an older fella. He's got a nice moustache.'

'So's that fella in the International.'

'Wet behind the ears. And my God, his dandruff!'

They left the train together and parted on the platform, Marie making for the Underground, Mavis hurrying for a bus. It was quite convenient, really, living in Reading and travelling to Paddington every day. It was only half an hour and chatting on the journey passed the time. They didn't travel back together in the evenings because Mavis nearly always did an hour's overtime. She was a computer programmer.

'I talked to Mavis. It's O.K. about the insurance,' Marie said in Travel-Wide at half-past eleven that morning, having slipped out when the shop seemed slack. There'd been some details about insurance which he'd raised the evening before. He always advised insurance, but he'd quite understood when she'd made the point that she'd better discuss the matter with her friend before committing herself to the extra expenditure.

'So I'll go ahead and book you,' he said. 'There'll just be the deposit.'

'Mavis wrote the cheque.' She pushed the pink slip across the counter to him. 'Payable to Travel-Wide.'

'That's quite correct.' He glanced at it and wrote her a receipt. He said:

'I looked out another brochure or two. I'd quite like to go through them with you. So you can explain what's what to your friend.'

'Oh, that's very nice, Mr Britt. But I got to get back. I mean, I shouldn't be out in the middle of the morning.'

'Any chance of lunchtime?'

His suavity astounded him. He thought of Hilda, deftly working at her jewellery, stringing orange and yellow beads, listening to the Jimmy Young programme.

'Lunchtime, Mr Britt?'

'We'd maybe talk about the brochures.'

He fancied her, she said to herself. He was making a pass, talking about brochures and lunchtime. Well, she wasn't disagreeable. She'd meant what she'd said to Mavis: she liked an older fella and she liked his moustache, so smooth it looked as if he put something on it. She liked the name Norman.

'All right then,' she said.

He couldn't suggest Bette's Sandwiches because you stood up at a shelf on the wall and ate the sandwiches off a cardboard plate.

'We could go to the Drummer Boy,' he suggested instead. 'I'm off at twelve-fifteen.'

'Say half-past, Mr Britt.'

'I'll be there with the brochures.'

Again he thought of Hilda. He thought of her wiry, pasty limbs and the way she had of snorting. Sometimes when they were watching the television she'd suddenly want to sit on his knee. She'd get worse as she grew older; she'd get scrawnier; her hair, already coarse, would get dry and grey. He enjoyed the evenings when she went out to the Club or to her friends the Fowlers. And yet he wasn't being fair because in very many ways she did her best. It was just that you didn't always feel like having someone on your knee after a day's work.

'Same?' he said in the Drummer Boy.

'Yes please, Mr Britt.' She'd meant to say that the drinks were definitely on her, after all he'd spent last night. But in her flurry she forgot. She picked up the brochures he'd left on the seat beside her. She pretended to read one, but all the time she was watching him as he stood by the bar. He smiled as he turned and came back with their drinks. He said something about it being a nice way to do business. He was drinking gin and peppermint himself.

'I meant to pay for the drinks. I meant to say I would. I'm sorry, Mr Britt.'

'Norman, my name is.' He surprised himself again by the ease with which he was managing the situation. They'd have their drinks and then he'd suggest some of the shepherd's pie, or a ham-and-salad roll if she'd prefer it. He'd buy her another gin and peppermint to get her going. Eighteen years ago he used to buy Hilda further glasses of V.P. wine with the same thought in mind.

They finished with the brochures. She told him she lived in Reading; she talked about the town. She mentioned her mother and her mother's friend Mrs Druk, who lived with them, and Mavis. She told him a lot about Mavis. No man was mentioned, no boyfriend or fiancé.

'Honestly,' she said, 'I'm not hungry.' She couldn't have touched a thing. She just wanted to go on drinking gin with him. She wanted to get slightly drunk, a thing she'd never done before in the middle of the day. She wanted to put her arm through his.

'It's been nice meeting you,' he said.

'A bit of luck.'

'I think so too, Marie.' He ran his forefinger between the bones on the back of her hand, so gently that it made her want to shiver. She didn't take her hand away, and when she continued not to he took her hand in his.

After that they had lunch together every day, always in the Drummer Boy. People saw them, Ron Stocks and Mr Blackstaffe from Travel-Wide, Mr Fineman, the pharmacist from Green's the Chemist's. Other people from the travel agency and from the chemist's saw them walking about the streets, usually hand in hand. They would look together into the shop windows of Edgware Road, drawn particularly to an antique shop full of brass. In the evenings he would walk with her to Paddington station and have a drink in one of the bars. They'd embrace on the platform, as other people did.

Mavis continued to disapprove; Marie's mother and Mrs Druk remained ignorant of the affair. The holiday on the Costa Brava that June was not a success because all the time Marie kept wishing Norman Britt was with her. Occasionally, while Mavis read magazines on the beach, Marie wept and Mavis pretended not to notice. She was furious because Marie's low spirits meant that it was impossible for them to get to know fellas. For months they'd been looking forward to the holiday and now, just because of a clerk in a travel agency, it was a flop. 'I'm sorry, dear,' Marie kept saying, trying to smile; but when they returned to London the friendship declined. 'You're making a fool of yourself,' Mavis pronounced harshly, 'and it's dead boring having to hear about it.' After that they ceased to travel together in the mornings.

The affair remained unconsummated. In the hour and a quarter allotted to each of them for lunch there was nowhere they might have gone to let their passion for one another run its course. Everywhere was public: Travel-Wide and the chemist's shop, the Drummer Boy, the streets they walked. Neither could easily spend a night away from home. Her mother and Mrs Druk would guess that something untoward was in the air; Hilda, deprived of her bedroom mating, would no longer be nonchalant in front of the TV. It would all come out if they were rash, and they sensed some danger in that.

'Oh, darling,' she whispered one October evening at Paddington, huddling herself against him. It was foggy and cold. The fog was in her pale hair, tiny droplets that only he, being close to her, could see. People hurried through the lit-up station, weary faces anxious to be home.

'I know,' he said, feeling as inadequate as he always did at the station.

'I lie awake and think of you,' she whispered.

'You've made me live,' he whispered back.

'And you me. Oh, God, and you me.' She was gone before she finished speaking, swinging into the train as it moved away, her bulky red handbag the last thing he saw. It would be eighteen hours before they'd meet again.

He turned his back on her train and slowly made his way through the crowds, his reluctance to start the journey back to the flat in Putney seeming physical, like a pain, inside him. 'Oh, for God's sake!' a woman cried angrily at him, for he had been in her way and had moved in the same direction as she had in seeking to avoid her, causing a second collision. She dropped magazines on to the platform and he helped her to pick them up, vainly apologizing.

It was then, walking away from this woman, that he saw the sign . . . *Hotel Entrance* it said in red neon letters, beyond the station's main bookstall. It was the back of the Great Western Royal, a short cut to its comforts for train travellers at the end of their journey. If only, he thought, they could share a room there. If only for one single night they were granted the privilege of being man and wife. People passed through the swing-doors beneath the glowing red sign, people hurrying, with newspapers or suitcases. Without quite knowing why, he passed through the swing-doors himself.

He walked up two brief flights of steps, through another set of doors, and paused in the enormous hall of the Great Western Royal Hotel. Ahead of him, to the left, was the long, curved reception counter and, to the right, the porter's desk. Small tables and armchairs were everywhere; it was carpeted underfoot. There were signs to lifts and to the bar and the restaurant. The stairway, gently rising to his left, was gracious, carpeted also.

They would sit for a moment in this hall, he imagined, as other people were sitting now, a few with drinks, others with pots of tea and plates half empty of assorted biscuits. He stood for a moment, watching these people, and then, as though he possessed a room in the hotel, he mounted the stairs, saying to himself that it must somehow be possible, that surely they could share a single night in the splendour of this place. There was a landing, made into a lounge, with arm-chairs and tables, as in the hall below. People conversed quietly; a foreign waiter, elderly and limping, collected silver-plated tea-pots; a Pekinese dog slept on a woman's lap.

The floor above was different. It was a long, wide corridor with bedroom doors on either side of it. Other corridors, exactly similar, led off it. Chambermaids passed him with lowered eyes; someone gently laughed in a room marked *Staff Only*; a waiter wheeled a trolley containing covered dishes, and a bottle of wine wrapped in a napkin. *Bathroom* a sign said, and he looked in, just to see what a bathroom in the Great Western Royal Hotel would be like. 'My God!' he whis-pered, possessed immediately with the idea that was, for him, to make the decade of the 1960s different. Looking back on it, he was for ever after unable to recall the first moment he beheld the bathroom on the second floor without experienc-ing the shiver of pleasure he'd experienced at the time. Slowly he entered. He locked the door and slowly sat down on the edge of the bath. The place was huge, as the bath itself was, like somewhere in a palace. The walls were marble, white veined delicately with grey. Two monstrous brass taps, the biggest bath taps he'd ever in his life seen, seemed to know already that he and Marie would come to the bathroom. They seemed almost to wink an invitation to him, to tell him that the bathroom was a comfortable place and not often in use since private bath-rooms were now attached to most of the bedrooms. Sitting in his mackintosh coat on the edge of the bath, he wondered what Hilda would say if she could see him now.

He suggested it to Marie in the Drummer Boy. He led up to it slowly, describing the interior of the Great Western Royal Hotel and how he had wandered about it because he hadn't wanted to go home. 'Actually,' he said, 'I ended up in a bathroom.'

'You mean the toilet, dear? Taken short—'

'No, not the toilet. A bathroom on the second floor. Done out in marble, as a matter of fact.'

She replied that honestly he was a one, to go into a bathroom like that when he wasn't even staying in the place! He said:

'What I mean, Marie, it's somewhere we could go.'

'Go, dear?'

'It's empty half the time. Nearly all the time it must be. I mean, we could be there now. This minute if we wanted to.'

'But we're having our lunch, Norman.'

'That's what I mean. We could even be having it there.'

From the saloon bar's juke-box a lugubrious voice pleaded for a hand to be held. 'Take my hand,' sang Elvis Presley, 'take my whole life too.' The advertising executives from Dalton, Dure and Higgins were loudly talking about their hopes of gaining the Canadian Pacific account. Less noisily the architects from Frine and Knight complained about local planning regulations.

'In a bathroom, Norman? But we couldn't just go into a bathroom.'

'Why not?'

'Well, we couldn't. I mean, we *couldn't.*'

'What I'm saying is we could.'

'I want to marry you, Norman. I want us to be together. I don't want just going to a bathroom in some hotel.'

'I know; I want to marry you too. But we've got to work it out. You know we've got to work it out, Marie—getting married.'

'Yes, I know.'

It was a familiar topic of conversation between them. They took it for granted that one day, somehow, they would be married. They had talked about Hilda. He'd described Hilda to her, he'd drawn a picture in Marie's mind of Hilda bent over her jewellery-making in a Putney flat, or going out to drink V.P. with the Fowlers or at the Club. He hadn't presented a flattering picture of his wife, and when Marie had quite timidly said that she didn't much care for the sound of her he had agreed that naturally she wouldn't. The only aspect of Hilda he didn't touch upon was her bedroom appetite, night starvation as he privately dubbed it. He didn't mention it because he guessed it might be upsetting.

What they had to work out where Hilda was concerned were the economics of the matter. He would never, at Travel-Wide or anywhere else, earn a great deal of money. Familiar with Hilda's nature, he knew that as soon as a divorce was mooted she'd set out to claim as much alimony as she possibly could, which by law he would have to pay. She would state that she only made jewellery for pin-money and increasingly found it difficult to do so due to a developing tendency towards chilblains or arthritis, anything she could think of. She would hate him for rejecting her, for depriving her of a tame companion. Her own resentment at not being able to have children would somehow latch on to his unfaithfulness: she would see a pattern which wasn't really there, bitterness would come into her eyes.

Marie had said that she wanted to give him the children he had never had. She wanted to have children at once and she knew she could. He knew it too: having children was part of her, you'd only to look at her. Yet that would mean she'd have to give up her job, which she wanted to do when she married anyway, which in turn would mean that all three of them would have to subsist on his meagre salary. And not just all three, the children also.

It was a riddle that mocked him: he could find no answer, and yet he believed that the more he and Marie were together, the more they talked to one another and continued to be in love, the more chance there was of suddenly hitting upon a solution. Not that Marie always listened when he went on about it. She agreed they had to solve their problem, but now and again just pretended it wasn't there.

She liked to forget about the existence of Hilda. For an hour or so when she was with him she liked to assume that quite soon, in July or even June, they'd be married. He always brought her back to earth.

'Look, let's just have a drink in the hotel,' he urged. 'Tonight, before the train. Instead of having one in the buffet.'

'But it's a hotel, Norman. I mean, it's for people to stay in—'

'Anyone can go into a hotel for a drink.'

That evening, after their drink in the hotel bar, he led her to the first-floor landing that was also a lounge. It was warm in the hotel. She said she'd like to sink down into one of the armchairs and fall asleep. He laughed at that; he didn't suggest an excursion to the bathroom, sensing that he shouldn't rush things. He saw her on to her train, abandoning her to her mother and Mrs Druk and Mavis. He knew that all during the journey she would be mulling over the splendours of the Great Western Royal.

December came. It was no longer foggy, but the weather was colder, with an icy wind. Every evening, before her train, they had their drink in the hotel. 'I'd love to show you that bathroom,' he said once. 'Just for fun.' He hadn't been pressing it in the least; it was the first time he'd mentioned the bathroom since he'd mentioned it originally. She giggled and said he was terrible. She said she'd miss her train if she went looking at bathrooms, but he said there'd easily be time. 'Gosh!' she whispered, standing in the doorway, looking in. He put his arm around her shoulders and drew her inside, fearful in case a chambermaid should see them loitering there. He locked the door and kissed her. In almost twelve months it was their first embrace in private.

They went to the bathroom during the lunch hour on New Year's Day, and he felt it was right that they should celebrate in this way the anniversary of their first real meeting. His early impression of her, that she was of a tartish disposition, had long since been dispelled. Voluptuous she might seem to the eye, but beneath that misleading surface she was prim and proper. It was odd that Hilda, who looked dried-up and wholly uninterested in the sensual life, should also belie her appearance. 'I've never done it before,' Marie confessed in the bathroom, and he loved her the more for that. He loved her simplicity in this matter, her desire to remain a virgin until her wedding. But since she repeatedly swore that she could marry no one else, their anticipating of their wedding night did not matter. 'Oh, God, I love you,' she whispered, naked for the first time in the bathroom. 'Oh, Norman, you're so good to me.'

After that it became a regular thing. He would saunter from the hotel bar, across the huge entrance lounge, and take a lift to the second floor. Five minutes later she would follow, with a towel brought specially from Reading in her hand-bag. In the bathroom they always whispered, and would sit together in a warm bath after their love-making, still murmuring about the future, holding hands beneath the surface of the water. No one ever rapped on the door to ask what was going on in there. No one ever questioned them as they returned, separately, to the bar, with the towel they'd shared damping her compact and her handkerchief.

Years instead of months began to go by. On the juke-box in the Drummer Boy the voice of Elvis Presley was no longer heard. *Why she had to go I don't know,* sang the Beatles, *she didn't say . . . I believe in yesterday.* And Eleanor Rigby entered people's lives, and Sergeant Pepper with her. The fantasies of secret agents, more fantastic than ever before, filled the screens of London's cinemas. Carnaby Street, like a jolly trash-can, overflowed with noise and colour. And in the bathroom of the Great Western Royal Hotel the love affair of Norman Britt and Marie was touched with the same preposterousness. They ate sandwiches in the bathroom; they drank wine. He whispered to her of the faraway places he knew about but had never been to: the Bahamas, Brazil, Peru, Seville at Easter, the Greek islands, the Nile, Shiraz, Persepolis, the Rocky Mountains. They should have been saving their money, not spending it on gin and peppermint in the bar of the hotel and in the Drummer Boy. They should have been racking their brains to find a solution to the problem of Hilda, but it was nicer to pretend that one day they would walk together in Venice or Tuscany. It was all so different from the activities that began with Hilda's bedroom appetites, and it was different from the coarseness that invariably surfaced when Mr Blackstaffe got going in the Drummer Boy on an evening when a Travel-Wide employee was being given a send-off. Mr Blackstaffe's great joke on such occasions was that he liked to have sexual intercourse with his wife at night and that she preferred the conjunction in the mornings. He was always going on about how difficult it was in the mornings, what with the children liable to interrupt you, and he usually went into details about certain other, more intimate preferences of his wife's. He had a powerful, waxy guffaw, which he brought regularly into play when he was engaged in this kind of conversation, allying it with a nudging motion of the elbow. Once his wife actually turned up in the Drummer Boy and Norman found it embarrassing even to look at her, knowing as he did so much about her private life. She was a stout middle-aged woman with decorated spectacles: her appearance, too, apparently belied much.

In the bathroom all such considerations, disliked equally by Norman Britt and Marie, were left behind. Romance ruled their brief sojourns, and love sanctified— or so they believed—the passion of their physical intimacy. Love excused their eccentricity, for only love could have found in them a willingness to engage in the deception of a hotel and the courage that went with it: that they believed most of all.

But afterwards, selling tickets to other people or putting Marie on her evening train, Norman sometimes felt depressed. And then gradually as more time passed, the depression increased and intensified. 'I'm so sad,' he whispered in the bathroom once, 'when I'm not with you. I don't think I can stand it.' She dried herself on the towel brought specially from Reading in her large red handbag. 'You'll have to tell her,' she said, with an edge in her voice that hadn't ever been there before. 'I don't want to leave having babies too late.' She wasn't twenty-eight any more; she was thirty-one. 'I mean, it isn't fair on me,' she said.

He knew it wasn't fair on her, but going over the whole thing yet again in Travel-Wide that afternoon he also knew that poverty would destroy them. He'd never earn much more than he earned now. The babies Marie wanted, and which he wanted too, would soak up what there was like blotting paper; they'd probably have to look for council accommodation. It made him weary to think about it, it gave him a headache. But he knew she was right: they couldn't go on for ever, living off a passing idyll, in the bathroom of a hotel. He even thought, quite seriously for a moment, of causing Hilda's death.

Instead he told her the truth, one Thursday evening after she'd been watching *The Avengers* on television. He just told her he'd met someone, a girl called Marie, he said, whom he had fallen in love with and wished to marry. 'I was hoping we could have a divorce,' he said.

Hilda turned the sound on the television set down without in any way dimming the picture, which she continued to watch. Her face did not register the hatred he had imagined in it when he rejected her; nor did bitterness suddenly enter her eyes. Instead she shook her head at him, and poured herself some more V.P. She said:

'You've gone barmy, Norman.'

'You can think that if you like.'

'Wherever'd you meet a girl, for God's sake?'

'At work. She's there in Vincent Street. In a shop.'

'And what's she think of you, may I ask?'

'She's in love with me, Hilda.'

She laughed. She told him to pull the other one, adding that it had bells on it.

'Hilda, I'm not making this up. I'm telling you the truth.'

She smiled into her V.P. She watched the screen for a moment, then she said:

'And how long's this charming stuff been going on, may I enquire?'

He didn't want to say for years. Vaguely, he said it had been going on for just a while.

'You're out of your tiny, Norman. Just because you fancy some piece in a shop doesn't mean you go getting hot under the collar. You're no tomcat, you know, old boy.'

'I didn't say I was.'

'You're no sexual mechanic.'

'Hilda—'

'All chaps fancy things in shops: didn't your mother tell you that? D'you think I haven't fancied stuff myself, the chap who came to do the blinds, that randy little postman with his rugby songs?'

'I'm telling you I want a divorce, Hilda.'

She laughed. She drank more V.P. wine. 'You're up a gum-tree,' she said, and laughed again.

'Hilda—'

'Oh, for God's sake!' All of a sudden she was angry, but more, he felt, because he was going on, not because of what he was actually demanding. She thought him ridiculous and said so. And then she added all the things he'd thought himself: that people like them didn't get divorces, that unless his girlfriend was well-heeled the whole thing would be a sheer bloody nonsense, with bloody solicitors the only ones to benefit. 'They'll send you to the cleaners, your bloody solicitors will,' she loudly pointed out, anger still trembling in her voice. 'You'd be paying them back for years.'

'I don't care,' he began, although he did. 'I don't care about anything except—'

'Of course you do, you damn fool.'

'Hilda—'

'Look, get over her. Take her into a park after dark or something. It'll make no odds to you and me.'

She turned the sound on the television up and quite quickly finished the V.P. wine. Afterwards, in their bedroom, she turned to him with an excitement that was greater than usual. 'God, that switched me on,' she whispered in the darkness, gripping him with her limbs. 'The stuff we were talking about, that girl.' When she'd finished her love-making she said, 'I had it with that postman, you know. Swear to God. In the kitchen. And since we're on the subject, Fowler looks in here the odd time.'

He lay beside her in silence, not knowing whether or not to believe what she was saying. It seemed at first that she was keeping her end up because he'd mentioned Marie, but then he wasn't so sure. 'We had a foursome once,' she said, 'the Fowlers and me and a chap that used to be in the Club.'

She began to stroke his face with her fingers, the way he hated. She always seemed to think that if she stroked his face it would excite him. She said, 'Tell me more about this piece you fancy.'

He told her to keep her quiet and to make her stop stroking his face. It didn't seem to matter now if he told her how long it had been going on, not since she'd made her revelations about Fowler and the postman. He even enjoyed telling her, about the New Year's Day when he'd bought the emery boards and the Colgate's, and how he'd got to know Marie because she and Mavis were booking a holiday on the Costa Brava.

'But you've never actually?'

'Yes, we have.'

'For God's sake where? Doorways or something? In the park?'

'We go to a hotel.'

'You old devil!'

'Listen, Hilda—'

'For God's sake go on, love. Tell me about it.'

He told her about the bathroom and she kept asking him questions, making him tell her details, asking him to describe Marie to her. Dawn was breaking when they finished talking.

'Forget about the divorce stuff,' she said quite casually at breakfast. 'I wouldn't want to hear no more of that. I wouldn't want you ruined for my sake, dear.'

He didn't want to see Marie that day, although he had to because it was arranged. In any case she knew he'd been going to tell his wife the night before; she'd want to hear the outcome.

'Well?' she said in the Drummer Boy.

He shrugged. He shook his head. He said:

'I told her.'

'And what'd she say, Norman? What'd Hilda say?'

'She said I was barmy to be talking about divorce. She said what I said to you: that we wouldn't manage with the alimony.'

They sat in silence. Eventually Marie said:

'Then can't you leave her? Can't you just not go back? We could get a flat somewhere. We could put off kiddies, darling. Just walk out, couldn't you?'

'They'd find us. They'd make me pay.'

'We could try it. If I keep on working you could pay what they want.'

'It'll never pan out, Marie.'

'Oh, darling, just walk away from her.'

Which is what, to Hilda's astonishment, he did. One evening when she was at the Club he packed his clothes and went to two rooms in Kilburn that he and Marie had found. He didn't tell Hilda where he was going. He just left a note to say he wouldn't be back.

They lived as man and wife in Kilburn, sharing a lavatory and a bathroom with fifteen other people. In time he received a court summons, and in court was informed that he had behaved meanly and despicably to the woman he'd married. He agreed to pay regular maintenance.

The two rooms in Kilburn were dirty and uncomfortable, and life in them was rather different from the life they had known together in the Drummer Boy and the Great Western Royal Hotel. They planned to find somewhere better, but at a reasonable price that wasn't easy to find. A certain melancholy descended on them, for although they were together they seemed as far away as ever from their own small house, their children, and their ordinary contentment.

'We could go to Reading,' Marie suggested.

'Reading?'

'To my mum's.'

'But your mum's nearly disowned you. Your mum's livid, you said yourself she was.'

'People come round.'

She was right. One Sunday afternoon they made the journey to Reading to have tea with Marie's mother and her friend Mrs Druk. Neither of these women addressed Norman, and once when he and Marie were in the kitchen he heard Mrs Druk saying it disgusted her, that he was old enough to be Marie's father. 'Don't think much of him,' Marie's mother replied. 'Pipsqueak really.'

Nevertheless, Marie's mother had missed her daughter's contribution to the household finances and before they returned to London that evening it was arranged that Norman and Marie should move in within a month, on the firm understanding that the very second it was feasible their marriage would take place. 'He's a boarder, mind,' Marie's mother warned. 'Nothing only a boarder in this house.' There were neighbours, Mrs Druk added, to be thought of.

Reading was worse than the two rooms in Kilburn. Marie's mother continued to make disparaging remarks about Norman, about the way he left the lavatory, or the thump of his feet on the staircarpet, or his fingermarks around the light-switches. Marie would deny these accusations and then there'd be a row, with Mrs Druk joining in because she loved a row, and Marie's mother weeping and then Marie weeping. Norman had been to see a solicitor about divorcing Hilda, quoting her unfaithfulness with a postman and with Fowler. 'You have your evidence, Mr Britt?' the solicitor enquired, and pursed his lips when Norman said he hadn't.

He knew it was all going to be too difficult. He knew his instinct had been right: he shouldn't have told Hilda, he shouldn't have just walked out. The whole thing had always been unfair on Marie; it had to be when a girl got mixed up with a married man. 'Should think of things like that,' her mother had a way of saying loudly when he was passing an open door. 'Selfish type he is,' Mrs Druk would loudly add.

Marie argued when he said none of it was going to work. But she wasn't as broken-hearted as she might have been a year or so ago, for the strain had told on Marie too, especially the strain in Reading. She naturally wept when Norman said they'd been defeated, and so for a moment did he. He asked for a transfer to another branch of Travel-Wide and was sent to Ealing, far away from the Great Western Royal Hotel.

Eighteen months later Marie married a man in a brewery. Hilda, hearing on some grapevine that Norman was on his own, wrote to him and suggested that bygones should be allowed to be bygones. Lonely in a bed-sitting-room in Ealing, he agreed to talk the situation over with her and after that he agreed to return to their flat. 'No hard feelings,' Hilda said, and no deception: there's been a chap from the Club in here, the Woolworth's manager.' No hard feelings, he agreed.

For Norman Britt, as the decade of the 1960s passed, it trailed behind it the marvels of his love affair with Marie. Hilda's scorn when he had confessed had not devalued them, nor had the two dirty rooms in Kilburn, nor the equally unpleasant experience in Reading. Their walk to the Great Western Royal, the drinks they could not afford in the hotel bar, their studied nonchalance as they made their way separately upstairs, seemed to Norman to be a fantasy that had miraculously become real. The second-floor bathroom belonged in it perfectly, the bathroom full of whispers and caressing, where the faraway places of his daily work acquired a hint of magic when he spoke of them to a girl as voluptuous as any of James Bond's. Sometimes on the Tube he would close his eyes and with the greatest pleasure that remained to him he would recall the delicately veined marble and the great brass taps, and the bath that was big enough for two. And now and again he heard what appeared to be the strum of distant music, and the voices of the Beatles celebrating a bathroom love, as they had celebrated Eleanor Rigby and other people of that time.

JOHN UPDIKE
(1932–)

JOHN UPDIKE was born in Shillington, Pennsylvania, and educated at Harvard University. After graduating in 1954, he spent a year studying drawing at the Ruskin School of Drawing and Fine Arts in Oxford, England. From 1955 until 1957 he worked on the staff of *The New Yorker*, and since then has been a frequent contributor to its pages.

Updike is among the most protean of contemporary American writers, having produced a substantial body of work in a variety of forms—the novel, short story, essay, and poetry. He is also the author of a play, *Buchanan Dying* (1974). His best-known work may be the four novels comprising the *Rabbit* series, detailing the life and other misfortunes of one Harry Angstrom: *Rabbit, Run* (1961), *Rabbit Redux* (1971), *Rabbit Is Rich* (1981), and *Rabbit at Rest* (1990). His other novels include *The Poorhouse Fair* (1959), *The Centaur* (1962), *Couples* (1968), *A Month of Sundays* (1975), *Marry Me: A Romance* (1976), *The Coup* (1978), *The Witches of Eastwick* (1984), and *Brazil* (1994). Among his short-story collections are *Pigeon Feathers* (1962) and *Trust Me* (1987). *Problems and Other Stories* (1957) contains the linked accounts of marital travail of the Maples, including "Separating." Updike's awards include two Pulitzer Prizes (for *Rabbit Is Rich* and *Rabbit at Rest*), the National Book Award for *The Centaur*, the 1981 MacDowell Medal, the 1989 National Medal of Arts, and the 1990 National Book Critics Circle Award. He is a member of the American Academy of Arts and Letters and the American Academy of Arts.

Much of Updike's fiction is devoted to exploring the contrariness of romantic and sexual experience, in and outside of marriage. His materials are marvelously served by a lithe prose that dazzles at the same time that it dissects; he can move seamlessly from passages of sensuous richness nearly formal in their elegance, to remorseless, undercutting insight, colloquially couched. His sinuous language seems a perfectly designed instrument for investigating the nuances of ambivalence—in Updike's fictive world, perhaps the most abiding concomitant of love. He is faithful to his often faithless characters, a troubadour of the divided heart.

Separation for Richard and Joan Maples is portrayed as an integral phase of their marriage, as momentous as any other. On the night they have set aside to tell their children, the rituals they have devised for the occasion come into play—to be carried out with the same tenderness and delicacy with which marriages are put together. Their script is both followed and not followed; a constant undertow puts Richard at odds even with his own intentions. "Guiltily, he realized he did not feel separated."

Separating

The day was fair. Brilliant. All that June the weather had mocked the Maples' internal misery with solid sunlight—golden shafts and cascades of green in which their conversations had wormed unseeing, their sad murmuring selves the only stain in Nature. Usually by this time of the year they had acquired tans; but when they met their elder daughter's plane on her return from a year in England they were almost as pale as she, though Judith was too dazzled by the sunny opulent jumble of her native land to notice. They did not spoil her homecoming by telling her immediately. Wait a few days, let her recover from jet lag, had been one of their formulations, in that string of gray dialogues—over coffee, over cocktails, over Cointreau—that had shaped the strategy of their dissolution, while the earth performed its annual stunt of renewal unnoticed beyond their closed windows. Richard had thought to leave at Easter; Joan had insisted they wait until the four children were at last assembled, with all exams passed and ceremonies attended, and the bauble of summer to console them. So he had drudged away, in love, in dread, repairing screens, getting the mowers sharpened, rolling and patching their new tennis court.

The court, clay, had come through its first winter pitted and windswept bare of redcoat. Years ago the Maples had observed how often, among their friends, divorce followed a dramatic home improvement, as if the marriage were making one last effort to live; their own worst crisis had come amid the plaster dust and exposed plumbing of a kitchen renovation. Yet, a summer ago, as canary-yellow bulldozers gaily churned a grassy, daisy-dotted knoll into a muddy plateau, and a crew of pigtailed young men raked and tamped clay into a plane, this transformation did not strike them as ominous, but festive in its impudence; their marriage could rend the earth for fun. The next spring, waking each day at dawn to a sliding sensation as if the bed were being tipped, Richard found the barren tennis court—its net and tapes still rolled in the barn—an environment congruous with his mood of purposeful desolation, and the crumbling of handfuls of clay into cracks and holes (dogs had frolicked on the court in a thaw; rivulets had eroded trenches) an activity suitably elemental and interminable. In his sealed heart he hoped the day would never come.

Now it was here. A Friday. Judith was re-acclimated; all four children were assembled, before jobs and camps and visits again scattered them. Joan thought they should be told one by one. Richard was for making an announcement at the table. She said, "I think just making an announcement is a cop-out. They'll start quarrelling and playing to each other instead of focusing. They're each individuals, you know, not just some corporate obstacle to your freedom."

"O.K., O.K. I agree." Joan's plan was exact. That evening, they were giving Judith a belated welcome-home dinner, of lobster and champagne. Then, the party over, they, the two of them, who nineteen years before would push her in a baby carriage along Fifth Avenue to Washington Square, were to walk her out of the house, to the bridge across the salt creek, and tell her, swearing her to secrecy. Then Richard Jr., who was going directly from work to a rock concert in Boston, would be told, either late when he returned on the train or early Saturday morning before he went off to his job; he was seventeen and employed as one of a golf-course maintenance crew. Then the two younger children, John and Margaret, could, as the morning wore on, be informed.

"Mopped up, as it were," Richard said.

"Do you have any better plan? That leaves you the rest of Saturday to answer any questions, pack, and make your wonderful departure."

"No," he said, meaning he had no better plan, and agreed to hers, though to him it showed an edge of false order, a hidden plea for control, like Joan's long chore lists and financial accountings and, in the days when he first knew her, her too-copious lecture notes. Her plan turned one hurdle for him into four—four knife-sharp walls, each with a sheer blind drop on the other side.

All spring he had moved through a world of insides and outsides, of barriers and partitions. He and Joan stood as a thin barrier between the children and the truth. Each moment was a partition, with the past on one side and the future on the other, a future containing this unthinkable *now*. Beyond four knifelike walls a new life for him waited vaguely. His skull cupped a secret, a white face, a face both frightened and soothing, both strange and known, that he wanted to shield from tears, which he felt all about him, solid as the sunlight. So haunted, he had become obsessed with battening down the house against his absence, replacing screens and sash cords, hinges and latches—a Houdini making things snug before his escape.

The lock. He had still to replace a lock on one of the doors of the screened porch. The task, like most such, proved more difficult than he had imagined. The old lock, aluminum frozen by corrosion, had been deliberately rendered obsolete by manufacturers. Three hardware stores had nothing that even approximately matched the mortised hole its removal (surprisingly easy) left. Another hole had to be gouged, with bits too small and saws too big, and the old hole fitted with a block of wood—the chisels dull, the saw rusty, his fingers thick with lack of sleep. The sun poured down, beyond the porch, on a world of neglect. The bushes already needed pruning, the windward side of the house was shedding flakes of paint, rain would get in when he was gone, insects, rot, death. His family, all those he would lose, filtered through the edges of his awareness as he struggled with screw holes, splinters, opaque instructions, minutiae of metal.

Judith sat on the porch, a princess returned from exile. She regaled them with stories of fuel shortages, of bomb scares in the Underground, of Pakistani workmen loudly lusting after her as she walked past on her way to dance school. Joan came and went, in and out of the house, calmer than she should have been, praising his struggles with the lock as if this were one more and not the last of their long succession of shared chores. The younger of his sons for a few minutes held the rickety screen door while his father clumsily hammered and chiseled, each blow a kind of sob in Richard's ears. His younger daughter, having been at a slumber party, slept on the porch hammock through all the noise—heavy and pink, trusting and forsaken. Time, like the sunlight, continued relentlessly; the sunlight slowly slanted. Today was one of the longest days. The lock clicked, worked. He was through. He had a drink; he drank it on the porch, listening to his daughter. "It was so sweet," she was saying, "during the worst of it, how all the butchers and bakery shops kept open by candlelight. They're all so plucky and cute. From the papers, things sounded so much worse here—people shooting people in gas lines, and everybody freezing."

Richard asked her, "Do you still want to live in England forever?" *Forever:* the concept, now a reality upon him, pressed and scratched at the back of his throat.

"No," Judith confessed, turning her oval face to him, its eyes still childishly far apart, but the lips set as over something succulent and satisfactory. "I was anxious to come home. I'm an American." She was a woman. They had raised her; he and Joan had endured together to raise her, alone of the four. The others had still some raising left in them. Yet it was the thought of telling Judith—the image of her, their first baby, walking between them arm in arm to the bridge— that broke him. The partition between his face and the tears broke. Richard sat down to the celebratory meal with the back of his throat aching; the champagne, the lobster seemed phases of sunshine; he saw them and tasted them through tears. He blinked, swallowed, croakily joked about hay fever. The tears would not stop leaking through; they came not through a hole that could be plugged but through a permeable spot in a membrane, steadily, purely, endlessly, fruitfully. They became, his tears, a shield for himself against these others—their faces, the fact of their assembly, a last time as innocents, at a table where he sat the last time as head. Tears dropped from his nose as he broke the lobster's back; salt flavored his champagne as he sipped it; the raw clench at the back of his throat was delicious. He could not help himself.

His children tried to ignore his tears. Judith, on his right, lit a cigarette, gazed upward in the direction of her too energetic, too sophisticated exhalation; on her other side, John earnestly bent his face to the extraction of the last morsels—legs, tail segments—from the scarlet corpse. Joan, at the opposite end of the table, glanced at him surprised, her reproach displaced by a quick grimace, of forgiveness, or of salute to his superior gift of strategy. Between them, Margaret, no longer called Bean, thirteen and large for her age, gazed from the other side of his pane of tears as if into a shopwindow at something she coveted—at her father, a crystalline heap of splinters and memories. It was not she, however, but John who, in the kitchen, as they cleared the plates and carapaces away, asked Joan the question: *"Why is Daddy crying?"*

Richard heard the question but not the murmured answer. Then he heard

Bean cry, "Oh, no-oh!"—the faintly dramatized exclamation of one who had long expected it.

John returned to the table carrying a bowl of salad. He nodded tersely at his father and his lips shaped the conspiratorial words "She told."

"Told what?" Richard asked aloud, insanely.

The boy sat down as if to rebuke his father's distraction with the example of his own good manners. He said quietly, "The separation."

Joan and Margaret returned; the child, in Richard's twisted vision, seemed diminished in size, and relieved, relieved to have had the bogieman at last proved real. He called out to her—the distances at the table had grown immense—"You knew, you always knew," but the clenching at the back of his throat prevented him from making sense of it. From afar he heard Joan talking, levelly, sensibly, reciting what they had prepared: it was a separation for the summer, an experiment. She and Daddy both agreed it would be good for them; they needed space and time to think; they liked each other but did not make each other happy enough, somehow.

Judith, imitating her mother's factual tone, but in her youth off-key, too cool, said, "I think it's silly. You should either live together or get divorced."

Richard's crying, like a wave that has crested and crashed, had become tumultuous; but it was overtopped by another tumult, for John, who had been so reserved, now grew larger and larger at the table. Perhaps his younger sister's being credited with knowing set him off. "Why didn't you *tell* us?" he asked, in a large round voice quite unlike his own. "You should have *told* us you weren't getting along."

Richard was startled into attempting to force words through his tears. "We *do* get along, that's the trouble, so it doesn't show even to us—" *That we do not love each other* was the rest of the sentence; he couldn't finish it.

Joan finished for him, in her style. "And we've always, *especially*, loved our children."

John was not mollified. "What do you care about *us?*" he boomed. "We're just little things you *had*." His sisters' laughing forced a laugh from him, which he turned hard and parodistic: "Ha ha *ha*." Richard and Joan realized simultaneously that the child was drunk, on Judith's homecoming champagne. Feeling bound to keep the center of the stage, John took a cigarette from Judith's pack, poked it into his mouth, let it hang from his lower lip, and squinted like a gangster.

"You're not little things we had," Richard called to him. "You're the whole point. But you're grown. Or almost."

The boy was lighting matches. Instead of holding them to his cigarette (for they had never seen him smoke; being "good" had been his way of setting himself apart), he held them to his mother's face, closer and closer, for her to blow out. Then he lit the whole folder—a hiss and then a torch, held against his mother's face. Prismed by tears, the flame filled Richard's vision; he didn't know how it was extinguished. He heard Margaret say, "Oh stop showing off," and saw John, in response, break the cigarette in two and put the halves entirely into his mouth and chew, sticking out his tongue to display the shreds to his sister.

Joan talked to him, reasoning—a fountain of reason, unintelligible. "Talked about it for years . . . our children must help us . . . Daddy and I both want . . ." As the boy listened, he carefully wadded a paper napkin into the leaves of his salad, fashioned a ball of paper and lettuce, and popped it into his mouth, looking around the table for the expected laughter. None came. Judith said, "Be mature," and dismissed a plume of smoke.

Richard got up from this stifling table and led the boy outside. Though the house was in twilight, the outdoors still brimmed with light, the lovely waste light of high summer. Both laughing, he supervised John's spitting out the lettuce and paper and tobacco into the pachysandra. He took him by the hand—a square gritty hand, but for its softness a man's. Yet, it held on. They ran together up into the field, past the tennis court. The raw banking left by the bulldozers was dotted with daisies. Past the court and a flat stretch where they used to play family baseball stood a soft green rise glorious in the sun, each weed and species of grass distinct as illumination on parchment. "I'm sorry, so sorry," Richard cried. "You were the only one who ever tried to help me with all the goddam jobs around this place."

Sobbing, safe within his tears and the champagne, John explained, "It's not just the separation, it's the whole crummy year, I *hate* that school, you can't make any friends, the history teacher's a scud."

They sat on the crest of the rise, shaking and warm from their tears but easier in their voices, and Richard tried to focus on the child's sad year—the weekdays long with homework, the weekends spent in his room with model airplanes, while his parents murmured down below, nursing their separation. How selfish, how blind, Richard thought; his eyes felt scoured. He told his son, "We'll think about getting you transferred. Life's too short to be miserable."

They had said what they could, but did not want the moment to heal, and talked on, about the school, about the tennis court, whether it would ever again be as good as it had been that first summer. They walked to inspect it and pressed a few more tapes more firmly down. A little stiltedly, perhaps trying now to make too much of the moment, Richard led the boy to the spot in the field where the view was best, of the metallic blue river, the emerald marsh, the scattered islands velvety with shadow in the low light, the white bits of beach far away. "See," he said. "It goes on being beautiful. It'll be here tomorrow."

"I know," John answered, impatiently. The moment had closed.

Back in the house, the others had opened some white wine, the champagne being drunk, and still sat at the table, the three females, gossiping. Where Joan sat had become the head. She turned, showing him a tearless face, and asked, "All right?"

"We're fine," he said, resenting it, though relieved, that the party went on without him.

In bed she explained, "I couldn't cry I guess because I cried so much all spring. It really wasn't fair. It's your idea, and you made it look as though I was kicking you out."

"I'm sorry," he said. "I couldn't stop. I wanted to but couldn't."

"You *didn't* want to. You loved it. You were having your way, making a general announcement."

"I love having it over," he admitted. "God, those kids were great. So brave and funny." John, returned to the house, had settled to a model airplane in his room, and kept shouting down to them, "I'm O.K. No sweat." "And the way," Richard went on, cozy in his relief, "they never questioned the reasons we gave. No thought of a third person. Not even Judith."

"That *was* touching," Joan said.

He gave her a hug. "You were great too. Very reassuring to everybody. Thank you." Guiltily, he realized he did not feel separated.

"You still have Dickie to do," she told him. These words set before him a black mountain in the darkness; its cold breath, its near weight affected his chest. Of the four children, his elder son was most nearly his conscience. Joan did not need to add, "That's one piece of your dirty work I won't do for you."

"I know. I'll do it. You go to sleep."

Within minutes, her breathing slowed, became oblivious and deep. It was quarter to midnight. Dickie's train from the concert would come in at one-fourteen. Richard set the alarm for one. He had slept atrociously for weeks. But whenever he closed his lids some glimpse of the last hours scorched them—Judith exhaling toward the ceiling in a kind of aversion, Bean's mute staring, the sun-struck growth in the field where he and John had rested. The mountain before him moved closer, moved within him; he was huge, momentous. The ache at the back of his throat felt stale. His wife slept as if slain beside him. When, exasperated by his hot lids, his crowded heart, he rose from bed and dressed, she awoke enough to turn over. He told her then, "Joan, if I could undo it all, I would."

"Where would you begin?" she asked. There was no place. Giving him courage, she was always giving him courage. He put on shoes without socks in the dark. The children were breathing in their rooms, the downstairs was hollow. In their confusion they had left lights burning. He turned off all but one, the kitchen overhead. The car started. He had hoped it wouldn't. He met only moonlight on the road; it seemed a diaphanous companion, flickering in the leaves along the roadside, haunting his rearview mirror like a pursuer, melting under his headlights. The center of town, not quite deserted, was eerie at this hour. A young cop in uniform kept company with a gang of T-shirted kids on the steps of the bank. Across from the railroad station, several bars kept open. Customers, mostly young, passed in and out of the warm night, savoring summer's novelty. Voices shouted from cars as they passed; an immense conversation seemed in progress. Richard parked and in his weariness put his head on the passenger seat, out of the commotion and wheeling lights. It was as when, in the movies, an assassin grimly carries his mission through the jostle of a carnival—except the movies cannot show the precipitous, palpable slope you cling to within. You cannot climb back down; you can only fall. The synthetic fabric of the car seat, warmed by his cheek, confided to him an ancient, distant scent of vanilla.

A train whistle caused him to lift his head. It was on time; he had hoped it would be late. The slender draw-gates descended. The bell of approach tingled happily. The great metal body, horizontally fluted, rocked to a stop, and sleepy teen-agers disembarked, his son among them. Dickie did not show surprise that his father was meeting him at this terrible hour. He sauntered to the car with two friends, both taller than he. He said "Hi" to his father and took the passenger's seat with an exhausted promptness that expressed gratitude. The friends got in the back, and Richard was grateful; a few more minutes' postponement would be won by driving them home.

He asked, "How was the concert?"

"Groovy," one boy said from the back seat.

"It bit," the other said.

"It was O.K.," Dickie said, moderate by nature, so reasonable that in his childhood the unreason of the world had given him headaches, stomach aches, nausea. When the second friend had been dropped off at his dark house, the boy blurted, "Dad, my eyes are killing me with hay fever! I'm out there cutting that mothering grass all day!"

"Do we still have those drops?"

"They didn't do any good last summer."

"They might this." Richard swung a U-turn on the empty street. The drive home took a few minutes. The mountain was here, in his throat. "Richard," he said, and felt the boy, slumped and rubbing his eyes, go tense at his tone, "I didn't come to meet you just to make your life easier. I came because your mother and I have some news for you, and you're a hard man to get ahold of these days. It's sad news."

"That's O.K." The reassurance came out soft, but quick, as if released from the tip of a spring.

Richard had feared that his tears would return and choke him, but the boy's manliness set an example, and his voice issued forth steady and dry. "It's sad news, but it needn't be tragic news, at least for you. It should have no practical effect on your life, though it's bound to have an emotional effect. You'll work at your job, and go back to school in September. Your mother and I are really proud of what you're making of your life; we don't want that to change at all."

"Yeah," the boy said lightly, on the intake of his breath, holding himself up.

They turned the corner; the church they went to loomed like a gutted fort. The home of the woman Richard hoped to marry stood across the green. Her bedroom light burned.

"Your mother and I," he said, "have decided to separate. For the summer. Nothing legal, no divorce yet. We want to see how it feels. For some years now, we haven't been doing enough for each other, making each other as happy as we should be. Have you sensed that?"

"No," the boy said. It was an honest, unemotional answer: true or false in a quiz.

Glad for the factual basis, Richard pursued, even garrulously, the details. His apartment across town, his utter accessibility, the split vacation arrangements, the advantages to the children, the added mobility and variety of the summer. Dickie listened, absorbing. "Do the others know?"

"Yes."

"How did they take it?"

"The girls pretty calmly. John flipped out; he shouted and ate a cigarette and made a salad out of his napkin and told us how much he hated school."

His brother chuckled. "He did?"

"Yeah. The school issue was more upsetting for him than Mom and me. He seemed to feel better for having exploded."

"He did?" The repetition was the first sign that he was stunned.

"Yes. Dickie, I want to tell you something. This last hour, waiting for your train to get in, has been about the worst of my life. I hate this. *Hate* it. My father would have died before doing it to me." He felt immensely lighter, saying this. He had dumped the mountain on the boy. They were home. Moving swiftly as a shadow, Dickie was out of the car, through the bright kitchen. Richard called after him, "Want a glass of milk or anything?"

"No thanks."

"Want us to call the course tomorrow and say you're too sick to work?"

"No, that's all right." The answer was faint, delivered at the door to his room; Richard listened for the slam that went with a tantrum. The door closed normally, gently. The sound was sickening.

Joan had sunk into that first deep trough of sleep and was slow to awake. Richard had to repeat, "I told him."

"What did he say?"

"Nothing much. Could you go say goodnight to him? Please."

She left their room, without putting on a bathrobe. He sluggishly changed back into his pajamas and walked down the hall. Dickie was already in bed, Joan was sitting beside him, and the boy's bedside clock radio was murmuring music. When she stood, an inexplicable light—the moon?—outlined her body through the nightie. Richard sat on the warm place she had indented on the child's narrow mattress. He asked him, "Do you want the radio on like that?"

"It always is."

"Doesn't it keep you awake? It would me."

"No."

"Are you sleepy?"

"Yeah."

"Good. Sure you want to get up and go to work? You've had a big night."

"I want to."

Away at school this winter he had learned for the first time that you can go short of sleep and live. As an infant he had slept with an immobile, sweating intensity that had alarmed his babysitters. In adolescence he had often been the first of the four children to go to bed. Even now, he would go slack in the middle of a television show, his sprawled legs hairy and brown. "O.K. Good boy. Dickie, listen. I love you so much, I never knew how much until now. No matter how this works out, I'll always be with you. Really."

Richard bent to kiss an averted face but his son, sinewy, turned and with wet cheeks embraced him and gave him a kiss, on the lips, passionate as a woman's. In his father's ear he moaned one word, the crucial, intelligent word: "*Why?*"

Why. It was a whistle of wind in a crack, a knife thrust, a window thrown open on emptiness. The white face was gone, the darkness was featureless. Richard had forgotten why.

GIOVANNI VERGA

(1840–1922)

GIOVANNI VERGA was born in Catania, Sicily, to a family owning land in rural Sicily. He turned from the study of law to literature. He was the author of novels, plays, and short stories dealing with both the Sicilian middle class and its peasantry. Verga, along with his fellow native Sicilian writer, Luigi Capuana, was considered the founder of the school of Italian literary realism, called *verismo*, which reflected the influence of Gustave Flaubert's work and later that of Émile Zola with whom Verga's work has been compared. In his later writing particularly, he sought in his style and technique to reproduce an Italian idiom and syntax that, while generally correct, was elastic enough to represent faithfully the unaffected speech and natural behaviors of his characters; as a further aim, traces of the authorial presence were to be erased as much as possible, so as to let the materials speak for themselves.

His novels include *I Malavoglia* (1881) and *Mastro-don Gesualdo* (1889). His story, *Cavalleria rusticana* (1880), subsequently adapted for the stage, was produced in 1884 and also became the libretto for the opera by Pietro Mascagni. D. H. Lawrence translated many of Verga's stories as well as *Mastro-don Gesualdo*, which—under the title *Master don Gesualdo*—appeared in 1928.

Verga died where he was born, in Catania, in his eighty-second year. It was only toward the end of his life that his peers accorded him the recognition he justly felt was his due.

In "The Wolf" (1880) Verga makes his protagonist the embodiment of a relentless and predatory passion. Human as she is, the universality of her implacable need gives her virtually mythic stature. Heedless of taboo, let alone of propriety, she advances toward the object of her desire, in a story in which ferocity becomes indistinguishable from lust.

The Wolf

She was tall and slim, and though no longer young, had the strong firm breasts of the dark-haired woman. She was pale, as if she suffered permanently from malaria, and out of that pallor her cool red lips and her large eyes devoured you.

In the village they called her 'The Wolf', because she could never be sated. The women would cross themselves when they saw her passing, with the cautiously ambling pace of a hungry wolf, alone like an ill-tempered bitch. She could deprive them of their sons and husbands in the twinkling of an eye, with those red lips of hers, and one look from her devilish eyes could make them run after her skirts, from the altar of Saint Agrippina herself. It was a good thing the Wolf never came to church, even at Easter or Christmas, either for mass or for confession. Father Angiolino of the Church of Saint Mary of Jesus, a true servant of the Lord, had lost his soul on her account.

Poor Maricchia, a good and decent girl, cried secretly, because she was the Wolf's daughter and no one would marry her, though she had finery enough in her bottom drawer, and as good a piece of sunny land as any girl in the village.

One day the Wolf fell in love with a good-looking lad just back from the army, who was cutting hay with her in the notary's field. She was so much in love that she felt her flesh burning under the cotton of her vest, and when she looked into his eyes her throat felt as parched as on a June day down in the hottest part of the valley. But the young lad went on mowing quietly, his face turned towards the cut grass. 'What's up with you, Mother Pina?' he said to her. In the immense fields where the crackle of flying cicadas was the only sound under that sun that beat down from straight overhead, the Wolf bundled up handful after handful, sheaf after sheaf, without tiring, without straightening up for a moment or putting her lips to the flask, just to be able to keep behind Nanni, who mowed and mowed, and kept asking her: 'What do you want, Mother Pina?'

One night she told him. While the men, tired from the long day's work, were drowsing on the threshing ground, and the dogs howled in the vast darkness of the countryside, she said: 'I want *you*. You're as lovely as the sun, and as sweet as honey, and I want you!'

'And *I* want that young daughter of yours!' replied Nanni with a smile.

The Wolf put her hands in her hair and, scratching her head silently, walked away; she didn't come to the threshing ground any more. She saw Nanni again in October, when the olives were being pressed; he was working close to her house, and the screeching of the oil-press kept her awake all night.

She said to her daughter: 'Take the sack of olives and come with me.'

Nanni was busy shovelling the olives under the millstone, shouting 'Ohee!' at the mule to keep him moving.

'Do you want my daughter Maricchia?' asked Mother Pina.

'What are you giving with your daughter Maricchia?' replied Nanni.

'She has everything her father left, and on top of that I'll give her my house. I'll be happy if you leave me a corner of the kitchen where I can spread my mattress.'

'If that's it, we can settle it at Christmas,' said Nanni.

Nanni was all greasy and grimy with oil and half-fermented olives, and Maricchia wouldn't have him on any terms; but her mother seized her by the hair, in front of the fire-place, and said to her through clenched teeth: 'If you don't take him I'll kill you!'

The Wolf looked ill, and people were saying the devil turns hermit in old age. No longer was she seen about, or sitting in front of her door peering out of her mad eyes. When she looked into her son-in-law's face those eyes of hers made him laugh, then fumble for the shred of the Virgin Mary's dress that he carried as an amulet, and cross himself with it. Maricchia stayed at home feeding the children, and her mother went out to the fields, working with the men like a man, weeding, hoeing, feeding the animals, pruning the vineyards, in the north-east winds of January and in the sirocco of August, when the mules drooped their heads and the men slept face downwards under a north-facing wall. During those hours of 'midday sun and afternoon's heat when no decent woman's on her feet', Mother Pina was the only living soul to be seen in the countryside, walking over the blazing stones of the bridle-paths, across the scorched stubble of the vast fields which faded into the heat-haze far, far away towards cloud-covered Etna, where the sky lay heavy on the horizon.

'Wake up!' said the Wolf to Nanni, who was asleep in the ditch under the dusty hedge, his head between his arms. 'Wake up! I've brought you some wine to freshen your throat.'

Nanni opened his eyes wide in astonishment and stared sleepily at her as she stood facing him, pale, her breasts erect and her eyes black as coal, and he involuntarily raised his hands.

'No! No decent woman's on her feet between midday sun and afternoon's heat!' sobbed Nanni, and with his fingers in his hair he pressed his face against the dry grass at the bottom of the ditch. 'Go away, go away! Don't come to the threshing ground!'

And the Wolf went away, re-fastening her proud tresses, looking straight in front of her feet with her eyes black as coal as she stepped over the hot stubble.

But she came back to the threshing stead, time and again, and Nanni did not object. And if she was late in coming, in those hours between midday sun and afternoon's heat, he would go with sweat on his brow to the top of the deserted white path to await her; and each time afterwards he would bury his hands in his hair and repeat: 'Go away, go away! Don't come to the threshing ground again!'

Maricchia wept day and night, and every time she saw her mother coming back pale and silent from the fields, she pierced her with eyes that burned with tears and jealousy, herself like a wolf cub.

'Wicked creature!' she spat. 'You wicked mother!'

'Hold your tongue!'

'Thief! Thief!'

'Hold your tongue!'

'I'll go to the police, I will!'

'All right, go!'

And Maricchia did go, carrying her children, dry-eyed and fearless, like a madwoman, because now she loved the husband they had forced on her, greasy and grimy with oil and half-fermented olives.

The police sergeant sent for Nanni; he threatened him with jail and gallows. Nanni sobbed and tore his hair, but he denied nothing and made no excuses.

'It's temptation!' he said. 'It's the temptation of hell!'

He threw himself at the sergeant's feet and begged to be sent to prison.

'For mercy's sake, sergeant, take me away from this hell! Have me hanged or send me to prison, but don't let me see her again, ever again!'

'No,' said the Wolf to the sergeant. 'When I gave him the house as a dowry, I kept a corner of the kitchen for myself. The house is mine, and I won't leave it!'

Not long afterwards Nanni was kicked in the chest by his mule, and looked near death, but the priest refused to come with the Holy Sacrament unless the Wolf left the house. The Wolf went, and Nanni prepared to go too, as a good Christian should; he confessed and took communion with such clear signs of repentance that all the neighbours, and many curious, came to weep at the sick man's bedside. And it would have been better for Nanni had he died that day, before the devil could come back to tempt him and enter his body and soul, after he recovered.

'Leave me alone,' Nanni begged the Wolf. 'For mercy's sake, leave me in peace! I have seen death staring me in the face. Poor Maricchia is in despair. Everyone knows now! It will be better for you and for me if I never see you again.'

He would willingly have torn out his own eyes to avoid seeing those of the Wolf, those eyes that had made him lose body and soul when they stared into his. He no longer knew how to free himself from her spell. He paid for masses to be said for the souls in purgatory, and asked the priest and the sergeant for help. At Easter he went to confession, and publicly crawled over the forecourt of the church and licked six hand's-breadths of cobblestones in penance. When the Wolf came to tempt him again, he said:

'Listen: don't come back to the threshing ground, because if you come after me again, as sure as God exists, I'll kill you.'

'Kill me,' replied the Wolf. 'It doesn't matter to me: I don't want to live without you.'

When he saw her in the distance coming across the field of green corn he stopped hoeing in the vineyard, and went to pull his axe out of the elm tree. The Wolf saw him coming towards her, pale and wild-eyed, with the axe gleaming in the sun, and did not retreat a single step, did not lower her eyes, but continued to walk towards him, with her hands full of red poppies, devouring him with her black eyes.

'Your soul be cursed!' choked Nanni.

ALICE WALKER

(1944–   )

Alice Walker was born in Eatonton, Georgia, the daughter of sharecroppers. She received a B.A. from Sarah Lawrence College in 1966; her honorary degrees include a Ph.D. from Russell Sage University (1972) and a D.H.L. from the University of Massachussetts (1983). Her many publications include novels, volumes of poetry, and essays. Among her novels are *The Third Life of Grange Copeland* (1970), *Meridian* (1976), and *The Color Purple* (1982), for which Walker won the 1983 Pulitzer Prize in fiction, and *Possessing the Secret of Joy* (1992). Her poetry includes the 1991 volume *Her Blue Body Everything We Know: Earthling Poems (1965–90)*. *In Love and Trouble: Stories of Black Women* (1967) and *You Can't Keep A Good Woman Down* (1981) represent her short story collections. "To Hell with Dying" first appeared among the stories collected in *In Love and Trouble* and was published as a book for children in 1988. Walker's awards include the Rosenthal Award of the National Institute of Arts and Letters (1973), a Guggenheim Foundation award (1979) and, along with the Pulitzer Prize, an American Book Award for *The Color Purple* in 1983.

In the sixties, Walker worked for the New York City Welfare Department, in the Civil Rights movement, and in the Head Start program. Alice Walker's literary voice and social activism have been expressed notably on behalf of black women, their heroism, and the saving power of their love.

The narrator of "To Hell with Dying" is a little girl when we first encounter her and when she first meets Mr. Sweet. A lined and grizzled black man who likes his booze, he is a friend to her whole family, a person of infinite playfulness and kindness. She becomes the main actor in a tradition the family has with Mr. Sweet; when he comes close to dying, as he regularly does, the children surround him. There is not a syllable of didacticism in the story when the narrator is finally able to give her long-standing tender feeling for him a name.

To Hell with Dying

"To hell with dying," my father would say, "these children want Mr. Sweet!"

Mr. Sweet was a diabetic and an alcoholic and a guitar player and lived down the road from us on a neglected cotton farm. My older brothers and sisters got the most benefit from Mr. Sweet, for when they were growing up he had quite a few years ahead of him and so was capable of being called back from the brink of death any number of times—whenever the voice of my father reached him as he lay expiring. . . . "To hell with dying, man," my father would say, pushing the wife away from the bedside (in tears although she knew the death was not necessarily the last one unless Mr. Sweet really wanted it to be), "the children want Mr. Sweet!" And they did want him, for at a signal from Father they would come crowding around the bed and throw themselves on the covers and whoever was the smallest at the time would kiss him all over his wrinkled brown face and begin to tickle him so that he would laugh all down in his stomach, and his moustache which was long and sort of straggly, would shake like Spanish moss and was also that color.

Mr. Sweet had been ambitious as a boy, wanted to be a doctor or lawyer or sailor, only to find that black men fare better if they are not. Since he could be none of those things he turned to fishing as his only earnest career and playing the guitar as his only claim to doing anything extraordinarily well. His son, the only one that he and his wife, Miss Mary, had, was shiftless as the day is long and spent money as if he were trying to see the bottom of the mint, which Mr. Sweet would tell him was the clean brown palm of his hand. Miss Mary loved her "baby," however, and worked hard to get him the "li'l necessaries" of life, which turned out mostly to be women.

Mr. Sweet was a tall, thinnish man with thick kinky hair going dead white. He was dark brown, his eyes were very squinty and sort of bluish, and he chewed Brown Mule tobacco. He was constantly on the verge of being blind drunk, for he brewed his own liquor and was not in the least a stingy sort of man, and was always very melancholy and sad, though frequently when he was "feelin' good" he'd dance around the yard with us, usually keeling over just as my mother came to see what the commotion was.

Toward all of us children he was very kind, and had the grace to be shy with us, which is unusual in grown-ups. He had great respect for my mother for she never held his drunkenness against him and would let us play with him even when he was about to fall in the fireplace from drink. Although Mr. Sweet would sometimes lose complete or nearly complete control of his head and neck so that he would loll in his chair, his mind remained strangely acute and his speech not too affected. His ability to be drunk and sober at the same time made him an ideal playmate, for he was as weak as we were and we could usually best him in wrestling, all the while keeping a fairly coherent conversation going.

We never felt anything of Mr. Sweet's age when we played with him. We loved his wrinkles and would draw some on our brows to be like him, and his white hair was my special treasure and he knew it and would never come to visit us just after he had had his hair cut off at the barbershop. Once he came to our house for something, probably to see my father about fertilizer for his crops, for although he never paid the slightest attention to his crops he liked to know what things would be best to use on them if he ever did. Anyhow, he had not come with his hair since he had just had it shaved off at the barbershop. He wore a huge straw hat to keep off the sun and also to keep his head away from me. But as soon as I saw him I ran up and demanded that he take me up and kiss me, with his funny beard which smelled so strongly of tobacco. Looking forward to burying my small fingers into his woolly hair I threw away his hat only to find he had done something to his hair, that it was no longer there! I let out a squall which made my mother think that Mr. Sweet had finally dropped me in the well or something and from that day I've been wary of men in hats. However, not long after, Mr. Sweet showed up with his hair grown out and just as white and kinky and impenetrable as it ever was.

Mr. Sweet used to call me his princess, and I believed it. He made me feel pretty at five and six, and simply outrageously devastating at the blazing age of eight and a half. When he came to our house with his guitar the whole family would stop whatever they were doing to sit around him and listen to him play. He liked to play "Sweet Georgia Brown," that was what he called me sometimes, and also he liked to play "Caldonia" and all sorts of sweet, sad, wonderful songs which he sometimes made up. It was from one of these songs that I learned that he had had to marry Miss Mary when he had in fact loved somebody else (now living in Chi'-ca-go, or De-stroy, Michigan). He was not sure that Joe Lee, her "baby," was also his baby. Sometimes he would cry and that was an indication that he was about to die again. And so we would all get prepared, for we were sure to be called upon.

I was seven the first time I remember actually participating in one of Mr. Sweet's "revivals"—my parents told me I had participated before, I had been the one chosen to kiss him and tickle him long before I knew the rite of Mr. Sweet's rehabilitation. He had come to our house, it was a few years after his wife's death, and he was very sad, and also, typically, very drunk. He sat on the floor next to me and my older brother, the rest of the children were grown-up and lived else-where, and began to play his guitar and cry. I held his woolly head in my arms and wished I could have been old enough to have been the woman he loved so much and that I had not been lost years and years ago.

When he was leaving my mother said to us that we'd better sleep light that night for we'd probably have to go over to Mr. Sweet's before daylight. And we did. For soon after we had gone to bed one of the neighbors knocked on our door and called my father and said that Mr. Sweet was sinking fast and if he wanted to get in a word before the crossover he'd better shake a leg and get over to Mr. Sweet's house. All the neighbors knew to come to our house if something was wrong with Mr. Sweet, but they did not know how we always managed to make him well, or at least stop him from dying, when he was often so near death. As soon as we heard the cry we got up, my brother and I and my mother and father, and put on our clothes. We hurried out of the house and down the road for we were always afraid that we might someday be too late and Mr. Sweet would get tired of dallying.

When we got to the house, a very poor shack really, we found the front room full of neighbors and relatives and someone met us at the door and said that it was all very sad that old Mr. Sweet Little (for Little was his family name although we mostly ignored it) was about to kick the bucket. My parents were advised not to take my brother and me into the "death-room" seeing we were so young and all, but we were so much more accustomed to the death-room than he that we ignored him and dashed in without giving his warning a second thought. I was almost in tears, for these deaths upset me fearfully, and the thought of how much depended on me and my brother (who was such a ham most of the time) made me very nervous.

The doctor was bending over the bed and turned back to tell us for at least the tenth time in the history of my family that alas, old Mr. Sweet Little was dying and that the children had best not see the face of implacable death (I didn't know what "implacable" was, but whatever it was, Mr. Sweet was not!). My father pushed him rather abruptly out of the way saying as he always did and very loudly for he was saying it to Mr. Sweet, "To hell with dying, man, these children want Mr. Sweet!" which was my cue to throw myself upon the bed and kiss Mr. Sweet all around the whiskers and under the eyes and around the collar of his nightshirt where he smelled so strongly of all sorts of things, mostly liniment.

I was very good at bringing him around, for as soon as I saw that he was struggling to open his eyes I knew he was going to be all right and so could finish my revival sure of success. As soon as his eyes were open he would begin to smile and that way I knew that I had surely won. Once though I got a tremendous scare for he could not open his eyes and later I learned that he had had a stroke and that one side of his face was stiff and hard to get into motion. When he began to smile I could tickle him in earnest for I was sure that nothing would get in the way of his laughter, although once he began to cough so hard that he almost threw me off his stomach, but that was when I was very small, little more than a baby, and my bushy hair had gotten in his nose.

When we were sure he would listen to us we would ask him why he was in bed and when he was coming to see us again and could we play with his guitar which more than likely would be leaning against the bed. His eyes would get all misty and he would sometimes cry out loud, but we never let it embarrass us for he knew that we loved him and that we sometimes cried too for no reason. My parents would leave the room to just the three of us; Mr. Sweet, by that time, would be propped up in bed with a number of pillows behind his head and with me sitting and lying on his shoulder and along his chest. Even when he had trouble breathing he would not ask me to get down. Looking into my eyes he would shake his white head and run a scratchy old finger all around my hairline, which was rather low down nearly to my eyebrows and for which some people said I looked like a baby monkey.

My brother was very generous in all this, he let me do all the revivaling—he had done it for years before I was born and so was glad to be able to pass it on to someone new. What he would do while I talked to Mr. Sweet was pretend to play the guitar, in fact pretend that he was a young version of Mr. Sweet, and it always made Mr. Sweet glad to think that someone wanted to be like him—of course we did not know this then, we played the thing by ear, and whatever he seemed to like, we did. We were desperately afraid that he was just going to take off one day and leave us.

It did not occur to us that we were doing anything special; we had not learned that death was final when it did come. We thought nothing of triumphing over it so many times, and in fact became a trifle contemptuous of people who let themselves be carried away. It did not occur to us that if our own father had been dying we could not have stopped it, that Mr. Sweet was the only person over whom we had power.

When Mr. Sweet was in his eighties I was a young lady studying away in a university many miles from home. I saw him whenever I went home, but he was never on the verge of dying that I could tell and I began to feel that my anxiety for his health and psychological well-being was unnecessary. By this time he not only had a moustache but a long flowing snow-white beard which I loved and combed and braided for hours. He was still a very heavy drinker and was like an old Chinese opium-user, very peaceful, fragile, gentle, and the only jarring note about him was his old steel guitar which he still played in the old sad, sweet, downhome blues way.

On Mr. Sweet's ninetieth birthday I was finishing my doctorate in Massachusetts and had been making arrangements to go home for several weeks' rest. That morning I got a telegram telling me that Mr. Sweet was dying again and could I please drop everything and come home. Of course I could. My dissertation could wait and my teachers would understand when I explained to them when I got back. I ran to the phone, called the airport, and within four hours I was speeding along the dusty road to Mr. Sweet's.

The house was more dilapidated than when I was last there, barely a shack, but it was overgrown with yellow roses which my family had planted many years ago. The air was heavy and sweet and very peaceful. I felt strange walking through the gate and up the old rickety steps. But the strangeness left me as I caught sight of the long white beard I loved so well flowing down the thin body over the familiar quilt coverlet. Mr. Sweet!

His eyes were closed tight and his hands, crossed over his stomach, were thin and delicate, no longer rough and scratchy. I remembered how always before I had run and jumped up on him just anywhere; now I knew he would not be able to support my weight. I looked around at my parents, and was surprised to see that my father and mother also looked old and frail. My father, his own hair very gray, leaned over the quietly sleeping old man who, incidentally, smelled still of wine and tobacco, and said as he'd done so many times, "To hell with dying, man! My daughter is home to see Mr. Sweet!" My brother had not been able to come as he was in the war in Asia. I bent down and gently stroked the closed eyes and gradually they began to open. The closed, wine-stained lips twitched a little, then parted in a warm, slightly embarrassed smile. Mr. Sweet could see me and he recognized me and his eyes looked very spry and twinkly for a moment. I put my head down on the pillow next to his and we just looked at each other for a long time. Then he began to trace my peculiar hairline with a thin, smooth finger. I closed my eyes when his finger halted above my ear (he used to rejoice at the dirt in my ears when I was little), his hand stayed cupped around my cheek. When I opened my eyes, sure I had reached him in time, his were closed.

Even at twenty-four how could I believe that I had failed? that Mr. Sweet was really gone? He had never gone before. But when I looked up at my parents I saw that they were holding back tears. They had loved him dearly. He was like a piece of rare and delicate china which was always being saved from breaking and which finally fell. I looked long at the old face, the wrinkled forehead, the red lips, the hands that still reached out to me. Soon I felt my father pushing something cool into my hands. It was Mr. Sweet's guitar. He had asked them months before to give it to me, he had known that even if I came next time he would not be able to respond in the old way. He did not want me to feel that my trip had been for nothing.

The old guitar! I plucked the strings, hummed "Sweet Georgia Brown." The magic of Mr. Sweet lingered still in the cool steel box. Through the window I could catch the fragrant delicate scent of tender yellow roses. The man on the high old-fashioned bed with the quilt coverlet and the flowing white beard had been my first love.

EUDORA WELTY

(1909–)

EUDORA WELTY, the oldest of three children, was born where she now lives, in Jackson, Mississippi. She went to school in Jackson, and attended Mississippi State College for Women for two years before transferring in her junior year to the University of Wisconsin. In 1929, after graduating from Wisconsin, she went to New York, where she attended the Columbia University School of Business.

By Welty's own account—notably in her memoir, *One Writer's Beginnings* (Harvard University Press, Cambridge, Mass: 1984)—hers was a happy childhood. Her father, Christian Welty, an insurance salesman, and her mother, Chestina, seemed to have fashioned a home where love flowed freely between husband and wife, between parents and children; the atmosphere seems also to have been permeated with a love of books. Welty's father furnished the home with dictionaries and illustrated encyclopedias; her mother, according to *One Writer's Beginnings*, "read secondarily for information; she sank as a hedonist into novels. She read Dickens in the spirit in which she would have eloped with him." Even before Welty learned to read, she seems to have brought the same impeccable powers of observation to the world around her— from the hum of her parents' conversations to the rhythmic ticking of a clock.

Her several volumes of short stories are included in *The Collected Stories* (Harcourt Brace Jovanovich, NY: 1980); her novels include *Delta Wedding* (1946), *The Ponder Heart* (1954), and *The Optimist's Daughter* (1972), for which she won the 1973 Pulitzer Prize. Her essays are collected in the 1979 volume *The Eye of the Story*. Among other tributes, she is a recipient of the Howells Medal for fiction (1955) from the American Academy of Arts and Letters and the Gold Medal (1972) for the novel from the National Institute of Arts and Letters. Among those who encouraged her early on were Cleanth Brooks, Robert Penn Warren, and Katherine Anne Porter.

In her preface to the *Collected Stories*, Welty writes (p. xi): "What I do in writing of any character is to try to enter into the mind, heart and skin of a human being who is not myself." In "The Wide Net" (1942) Welty's generous and wise entry is into the characters of William Wallace Jamieson and his young, pregnant wife Hazel. In a fit of masculine contrariness, William stays out all night with a drinking buddy. Returning home, he finds a note from Hazel telling him she's going to drown herself in the river. The wide net that drags the river seems to drag up the flotsam and jetsam of existence itself while William imagines how he would cope without the love that is at the center of his own existence.

The Wide Net

This story is for John Fraiser Robinson

William Wallace Jamieson's wife Hazel was going to have a baby. But this was October, and it was six months away, and she acted exactly as though it would be tomorrow. When he came in the room she would not speak to him, but would look as straight at nothing as she could, with her eyes glowing. If he only touched her she stuck out her tongue or ran around the table. So one night he went out with two of the boys down the road and stayed out all night. But that was the worst thing yet, because when he came home in the early morning Hazel had vanished. He went through the house not believing his eyes, balancing with both hands out, his yellow cowlick rising on end, and then he turned the kitchen inside out looking for her, but it did no good. Then when he got back to the front room he saw she had left him a little letter, in an envelope. That was doing something behind someone's back. He took out the letter, pushed it open, held it out at a distance from his eyes. . . . After one look he was scared to read the exact words, and he crushed the whole thing in his hand instantly, but what it had said was that she would not put up with him after that and was going to the river to drown herself.

"Drown herself . . . But she's in mortal fear of the water!"

He ran out front, his face red like the red plums hanging on the bushes there, and down in the road he gave a loud shout for Virgil Thomas, who was just going in his own house, to come out again. He could just see the edge of Virgil, he had almost got in, he had one foot inside the door.

They met half-way between the farms, under the shade-tree.

"Haven't you had enough of the night?" asked Virgil. There they were, their pants all covered with dust and dew, and they had had to carry the third man home flat between them.

"I've lost Hazel, she's vanished, she went to drown herself."

"Why, that ain't like Hazel," said Virgil.

William Wallace reached out and shook him. "You heard me. Don't you know we have to drag the river?"

"Right this minute?"

"You ain't got nothing to do till spring."

"Let me go set foot inside the house and speak to my mother and tell her a story, and I'll come back."

"This will take the wide net," said William Wallace. His eyebrows gathered, and he was talking to himself.

"How come Hazel to go and do that way?" asked Virgil as they started out.

William Wallace said, "I reckon she got lonesome."

"That don't argue—drown herself for getting lonesome. My mother gets lonesome."

"Well," said William Wallace. "It argues for Hazel."

"How long is it now since you and her was married?"

"Why, it's been a year."

"It don't seem that long to me. A year!"

"It was this time last year. It seems longer," said William Wallace, breaking a stick off a tree in surprise. They walked along, kicking at the flowers on the road's edge. "I remember the day I seen her first, and that seems a long time ago. She was coming along the road holding a little frying-size chicken from her grandma, under her arm, and she had it real quiet. I spoke to her with nice manners. We knowed each other's names, being bound to, just didn't know each other to speak to. I says, 'Where are you taking the fryer?' and she says, 'Mind your manners,' and I kept on till after while she says, 'If you want to walk me home, take littler steps.' So I didn't lose time. It was just four miles across the field and full of blackberries, and from the top of the hill there was Dover below, looking sizeable-like and clean, spread out between the two churches like that. When we got down, I says to her, 'What kind of water's in this well?' and she says, 'The best water in the world.' So I drew a bucket and took out a dipper and she drank and I drank. I didn't think it was that remarkable, but I didn't tell her."

"What happened that night?" asked Virgil.

"We ate the chicken," said William Wallace, "and it was tender. Of course that wasn't all they had. The night I was trying their table out, it sure had good things to eat from one end to the other. Her mama and papa sat at the head and foot and we was face to face with each other across it, with I remember a pat of butter between. They had real sweet butter, with a tree drawed down it, elegant-like. Her mama eats like a man. I had brought her a whole hatful of berries and she didn't even pass them to her husband. Hazel, she would leap up and take a pitcher of new milk and fill up the glasses. I had heard how they couldn't have a singing at the church without a fight over her."

"Oh, she's a pretty girl, all right," said Virgil. "It's a pity for the ones like her to grow old, and get like their mothers."

"Another thing will be that her mother will get wind of this and come after me," said William Wallace.

"Her mother will eat you alive," said Virgil.

"She's just been watching her chance," said William Wallace. "Why did I think I could stay out all night."

"Just something come over you."

"First it was just a carnival at Carthage, and I had to let them guess my weight . . . and after that . . ."

"It was nice to be sitting on your neck in a ditch singing," prompted Virgil, "in the moonlight. And playing on the harmonica like you can play."

"Even if Hazel did sit home knowing I was drunk, that wouldn't kill her," said

William Wallace. "What she knows ain't ever killed her yet. . . . She's smart, too, for a girl," he said.

"She's a lot smarter than her cousins in Beulah," said Virgil. "And especially Edna Earle, that never did get to be what you'd call a heavy thinker. Edna Earle could sit and ponder all day on how the little tail of the 'C' got through the 'L' in a Coca-Cola sign."

"Hazel *is* smart," said William Wallace. They walked on. "You ought to see her pantry shelf, it looks like a hundred jars when you open the door. I don't see how she could turn around and jump in the river."

"It's a woman's trick."

"I always behaved before. Till the one night—last night."

"Yes, but the one night," said Virgil. "And she was waiting to take advantage."

"She jumped in the river because she was scared to death of the water and that was to make it worse," he said. "She remembered how I used to have to pick her up and carry her over the oak-log bridge, how she'd shut her eyes and make a dead-weight and hold me round the neck, just for a little creek. I don't see how she brought herself to jump."

"Jumped backwards," said Virgil. "Didn't look."

When they turned off, it was still early in the pink and green fields. The fumes of morning, sweet and bitter, sprang up where they walked. The insects ticked softly, their strength in reserve; butterflies chopped the air, going to the east, and the birds flew carelessly and sang by fits and starts, not the way they did in the evening in sustained and drowsy songs.

"It's a pretty *day* for sure," said William Wallace. "It's a pretty *day* for it."

"I don't see a sign of her ever going along here," said Virgil.

"Well," said William Wallace. "She wouldn't have dropped anything. I never saw a girl to leave less signs of where she's been."

"Not even a plum seed," said Virgil, kicking the grass.

In the grove it was so quiet that once William Wallace gave a jump, as if he could almost hear a sound of himself wondering where she had gone. A descent of energy came down on him in the thick of the woods and he ran at a rabbit and caught it in his hands.

"Rabbit . . . Rabbit . . ." He acted as if he wanted to take it off to himself and hold it up and talk to it. He laid a palm against its pushing heart. "Now . . . There now . . ."

"Let her go, William Wallace, let her go." Virgil, chewing on an elderberry whistle he had just made, stood at his shoulder: "What do you want with a live rabbit?"

William Wallace squatted down and set the rabbit on the ground but held it under his hand. It was a little, old, brown rabbit. It did not try to move. "See there?"

"Let her go."

"She can go if she wants to, but she don't want to."

Gently he lifted his hand. The round eye was shining at him sideways in the green gloom.

"Anybody can freeze a *rabbit*, that wants to," said Virgil. Suddenly he gave a far-reaching blast on the whistle, and the rabbit went in a streak. "Was you out catching cotton-tails, or was you out catching your wife?" he said, taking the turn to the open fields. "I come along to keep you on the track."

"Who'll we get, now?" They stood on top of a hill and William Wallace looked critically over the countryside. "Any of the Malones?"

"I was always scared of the Malones," said Virgil. "Too many *of* them."

"This is my day with the net, and they would have to watch out," said William Wallace. "I reckon some Malones, and the Doyles, will be enough. The six Doyles and their dogs, and you and me, and two little nigger boys is enough, with just a few Malones."

"That ought to be enough," said Virgil, "no matter what."

"I'll bring the Malones, and you bring the Doyles," said William Wallace, and they separated at the spring.

When William Wallace came back, with a string of Malones just showing behind him on the hilltop, he found Virgil with the two little Rippen boys waiting behind him, solemn little towheads. As soon as he walked up, Grady, the one in front, lifted his hand to signal silence and caution to his brother Brucie, who began panting merrily and untrustworthily behind him.

Brucie bent readily under William Wallace's hand-pat, and gave him a dreamy look out of the tops of his round eyes, which were pure green-and-white like clover tops. William Wallace gave him a nickel. Grady hung his head; his white hair lay in a little tail in the nape of his neck.

"Let's let them come," said Virgil.

"Well, they can come then, but if we keep letting everybody come it is going to be too many," said William Wallace.

"They'll appreciate it, those little-old boys," said Virgil. Brucie held up at arm's length a long red thread with a bent pin tied on the end; and a look of helpless and intense interest gathered Grady's face like a drawstring—his eyes, one bright with a sty, shone pleadingly under his white bangs, and he snapped his jaw and tried to speak. . . . "Their papa was drowned in the Pearl River," said Virgil.

There was a shout from the gully.

"Here come all the Malones," cried William Wallace. "I asked four of them would they come, but the rest of the family invited themselves."

"Did you ever see a time when they didn't," said Virgil. "And yonder from the other direction comes the Doyles, still with biscuit crumbs on their cheeks, I bet, now it's nothing to do but eat as their mother said."

"If two little niggers would come along now, or one big nigger," said William Wallace. And the words were hardly out of his mouth when two little Negro boys came along, going somewhere, one behind the other, stepping high and gay in their overalls, as though they waded in honeydew to the waist.

"Come here, boys. What's your names?"

"Sam and Robbie Bell."

"Come along with us, we're going to drag the river."

"You hear that, Robbie Bell?" said Sam.

They smiled.

The Doyles came noiselessly, their dogs made all the fuss. The Malones, eight giants with great long black eyelashes, were already stamping the ground and pawing each other, ready to go. Everybody went up together to see Doc.

Old Doc owned the wide net. He had a house on top of the hill and he sat and looked out from a rocker on the front porch.

"Climb the hill and come in!" he began to intone across the valley. "Harvest's over . . . slipped up on everybody . . . corn's all in, hogs gettin' ripe . . . hay cut . . . molasses made around here. . . . Big explosion's over, supervisors elected, some pleased, some not. . . . We're hearing talk of war!"

When they got closer, he was saying, "Many's been saved at revival, twenty-two last Sunday including a Doyle, ought to counted two. Hope they'll be a blessing to Dover community besides a shining star in Heaven. Now what?" he asked, for they had arrived and stood gathered in front of the steps.

"If nobody is using your wide net, could we use it?" asked William Wallace.

"You just used it a month ago," said Doc. "It ain't your turn."

Virgil jogged William Wallace's arm and cleared his throat. "This time is kind of special," he said. "We got reason to think William Wallace's wife Hazel is in the river, drowned."

"What reason have you got to think she's in the river drowned?" asked Doc. He took out his old pipe. "I'm asking the husband."

"Because she's not in the house," said William Wallace.

"Vanished?" and he knocked out the pipe.

"Plum vanished."

"Of course a thousand things could have happened to her," said Doc, and he lighted the pipe.

"Hand him up the letter, William Wallace," said Virgil. "We can't wait around till Doomsday for the net while Doc sits back thinkin'."

"I tore it up, right at the first," said William Wallace. "But I know it by heart. It said she was going to jump straight in the Pearl River and that I'd be sorry."

"Where do you come in, Virgil?" asked Doc.

"I was in the same place William Wallace sat on his neck in, all night, and done as much as he done, and come home the same time."

"You-all were out cuttin' up, so Lady Hazel has to jump in the river, is that it? Cause and effect? Anybody want to argue with me? Where do these others come in, Doyles, Malones, and what not?"

"Doc is the smartest man around," said William Wallace, turning to the solidly waiting Doyles, "but it sure takes time."

"These are the ones that's collected to drag the river for her," said Virgil.

"Of course I am not going on record to say so soon that *I* think she's drowned," Doc said, blowing out blue smoke.

"Do you think . . ." William Wallace mounted a step, and his hands both went into fists. "Do you think she was *carried off?*"

"Now that's the way to argue, see it from all sides," said Doc promptly. "But who by?"

Some Malone whistled, but not so you could tell which one.

"There's no booger around the Dover section that goes around carrying off young girls that's married," stated Doc.

"She was always scared of the Gypsies." William Wallace turned scarlet. "She'd sure turn her ring around on her finger if she passed one, and look in the other direction so they couldn't see she was pretty and carry her off. They come in the end of summer."

"Yes, there are the Gypsies, kidnappers since the world began. But was it to be you that would pay the grand ransom?" asked Doc. He pointed his finger. They all laughed then at how clever old Doc was and clapped William Wallace on the back. But that turned into a scuffle and they fell to the ground.

"Stop it, or you can't have the net," said Doc. "You're scaring my wife's chickens."

"It's time we was gone," said William Wallace.

The big barking dogs jumped to lean their front paws on the men's chests.

"My advice remains, Let well enough alone," said Doc. "Whatever this mysterious event will turn out to be, it has kept one woman from talking a while. However, Lady Hazel is the prettiest girl in Mississippi, you've never seen a prettier one and you never will. A golden-haired girl." He got to his feet with the nimbleness that was always his surprise, and said, "I'll come along with you."

The path they always followed was the Old Natchez Trace. It took them through the deep woods and led them out down below on the Pearl River, where they could begin dragging it upstream to a point near Dover. They walked in silence around William Wallace, not letting him carry anything, but the net dragged heavily and the buckets were full of clatter in a place so dim and still.

Once they went through a forest of cucumber trees and came up on a high ridge. Grady and Brucie, who were running ahead all the way, stopped in their tracks; a whistle had blown and far down and far away a long freight train was passing. It seemed like a little festival procession, moving with the slowness of ignorance or a dream, from distance to distance, the tiny pink and gray cars like secret boxes. Grady was counting the cars to himself, as if he could certainly see each one clearly, and Brucie watched his lips, hushed and cautious, the way he would watch a bird drinking. Tears suddenly came to Grady's eyes, but it could only be because a tiny man walked along the top of the train, walking and moving on top of the moving train.

They went down again and soon the smell of the river spread over the woods, cool and secret. Every step they took among the great walls of vines and among the passion-flowers started up a little life, a little flight.

"We're walking along in the changing-time," said Doc. "Any day now the change will come. It's going to turn from hot to cold, and we can kill the hog that's ripe and have fresh meat to eat. Come one of these nights and we can wander down here and tree a nice possum. Old Jack Frost will be pinching things up. Old Mr. Winter will be standing in the door. Hickory tree there will be yellow. Sweet-gum red, hickory yellow, dogwood red, sycamore yellow." He went along rapping the tree trunks with his knuckle. "Magnolia and live-oak never die. Remember that. Persimmons will all get fit to eat, and the nuts will be dropping like rain all through the woods here. And run, little quail, run, for we'll be after you too."

They went on and suddenly the woods opened upon light, and they had reached the river. Everyone stopped, but Doc talked on ahead as though nothing had happened. "Only today," he said, "today, in October sun, it's all gold—sky and tree and water. Everything just before it changes looks to be made of gold."

William Wallace looked down, as though he thought of Hazel with the shining eyes, sitting at home and looking straight before her, like a piece of pure gold, too precious to touch.

Below them the river was glimmering, narrow, soft, and skin-colored, and slowed nearly to stillness. The shining willow trees hung round them. The net that was being drawn out, so old and so long-used, it too looked golden, strung and tied with golden threads.

Standing still on the bank, all of a sudden William Wallace, on whose word they were waiting, spoke up in a voice of surprise. "What is the name of this river?"

They looked at him as if he were crazy not to know the name of the river he had fished in all his life. But a deep frown was on his forehead, as if he were compelled to wonder what people had come to call this river, or to think there was a mystery in the name of a river they all knew so well, the same as if it were some great far torrent of waves that dashed through the mountains somewhere, and almost as if it were a river in some dream, for they could not give him the name of that.

"Everybody knows Pearl River is named the Pearl River," said Doc.

A bird note suddenly bold was like a stone thrown into the water to sound it.

"It's deep here," said Virgil, and jogged William Wallace. "Remember?"

William Wallace stood looking down at the river as if it were still a mystery to him. There under his feet, which hung over the bank, it was transparent and yellow like an old bottle lying in the sun, filling with light.

Doc clattered all his paraphernalia.

Then all of a sudden all the Malones scattered jumping and tumbling down the bank. They gave their loud shout. Little Brucie started after them, and looked back.

"Do you think she jumped?" Virgil asked William Wallace.

II

Since the net was so wide, when it was all stretched it reached from bank to bank of the Pearl River, and the weights would hold it all the way to the bottom. Jug-like sounds filled the air, splashes lifted in the sun, and the party began to move upstream. The Malones with great groans swam and pulled near the shore, the Doyles swam and pushed from behind with Virgil to tell them how to do it best; Grady and Brucie with his thread and pin trotted along the sandbars hauling buckets and lines. Sam and Robbie Bell, naked and bright, guided the old oarless rowboat that always drifted at the shore, and in it, sitting up tall with his hat on, was Doc—he went along without ever touching water and without ever taking his eyes off the net. William Wallace himself did everything but most of the time he was out of sight, swimming about under water or diving, and he had nothing to say any more.

The dogs chased up and down, in and out of the water, and in and out of the woods.

"Don't let her get too heavy, boys," Doc intoned regularly, every few minutes, "and she won't let nothing through."

"She won't let nothing through, she won't let nothing through," chanted Sam and Robbie Bell, one at his front and one at his back.

The sandbars were pink or violet drifts ahead. Where the light fell on the river, in a wandering from shore to shore, it was leaf-shaped spangles that trembled softly, while the dark of the river was calm. The willow trees leaned overhead under muscadine vines, and their trailing leaves hung like waterfalls in the morning air. The thing that seemed like silence must have been the endless cry of all the crickets and locusts in the world, rising and falling.

Every time William Wallace took hold of a big eel that slipped the net, the Malones all yelled, "Rassle with him, son!"

"Don't let her get too heavy, boys," said Doc.

"This is hard on catfish," William Wallace said once.

There were big and little fishes, dark and bright, that they caught, good ones and bad ones, the same old fish.

"This is more shoes than I ever saw got together in any store," said Virgil when they emptied the net to the bottom. "Get going!" he shouted in the next breath.

The little Rippens who had stayed ahead in the woods stayed ahead on the river. Brucie, leading them all, made small jumps and hops as he went, sometimes on one foot, sometimes on the other.

The winding river looked old sometimes, when it ran wrinkled and deep under high banks where the roots of trees hung down, and sometimes it seemed to be only a young creek, shining with the colors of wildflowers. Sometimes sandbars in the shapes of fishes lay nose to nose across, without the track of even a bird.

"Here comes some alligators," said Virgil. "Let's let them by."

They drew out on the shady side of the water, and three big alligators and four middle-sized ones went by, taking their own time.

"Look at their great big old teeth!" called a shrill voice. It was Grady making his only outcry, and the alligators were not showing their teeth at all.

"The better to eat folks with," said Doc from his boat, looking at him severely.

"Doc, you are bound to declare all you know," said Virgil. "Get going!"

When they started off again the first thing they caught in the net was the baby alligator.

"That's just what we wanted!" cried the Malones.

They set the little alligator down on a sandbar and he squatted perfectly still; they could hardly tell when it was he started to move. They watched with set faces his incredible mechanics, while the dogs after one bark stood off in inquisitive humility, until he winked.

"He's ours!" shouted all the Malones. "We're taking him home with us!"

"He ain't nothing but a little-old baby," said William Wallace.

The Malones only scoffed, as if he might be only a baby but he looked like the oldest and worst lizard.

"What are you going to do with him?" asked Virgil.

"Keep him."

"I'd be more careful what I took out of this net," said Doc.

"Tie him up and throw him in the bucket," the Malones were saying to each other, while Doc was saying, "Don't come running to me and ask me what to do when he gets big."

They kept catching more and more fish, as if there was no end in sight.

"Look, a string of lady's beads," said Virgil. "Here, Sam and Robbie Bell."

Sam wore them around his head, with a knot over his forehead and loops around his ears, and Robbie Bell walked behind and stared at them.

In a shadowy place something white flew up. It was a heron, and it went away over the dark treetops. William Wallace followed it with his eyes and Brucie clapped his hands, but Virgil gave a sigh, as if he knew that when you go looking for what is lost, everything is a sign.

An eel slid out of the net.

"Rassle with him, son!" yelled the Malones. They swam like fiends.

"The Malones are in it for the fish," said Virgil.

It was about noon that there was a little rustle on the bank.

"Who is that yonder?" asked Virgil, and he pointed to a little undersized man with short legs and a little straw hat with a band around it, who was following along on the other side of the river.

"Never saw him and don't know his brother," said Doc.

Nobody had ever seen him before.

"Who invited you?" cried Virgil hotly. "Hi . . . !" and he made signs for the little undersized man to look at him, but he would not.

"Looks like a crazy man, from here," said the Malones.

"Just don't pay any attention to him and maybe he'll go away," advised Doc.

But Virgil had already swum across and was up on the other bank. He and the stranger could be seen exchanging a word apiece and then Virgil put out his hand the way he would pat a child and patted the stranger to the ground. The little man got up again just as quickly, lifted his shoulders, turned around, and walked away with his hat tilted over his eyes.

When Virgil came back he said, "Little-old man claimed he was harmless as a baby. I told him to just try horning in on this river and anything in it."

"What did he look like up close?" asked Doc.

"I wasn't studying how he looked," said Virgil. "But I don't like anybody to come looking at me that I am not familiar with." And he shouted, "Get going!"

"Things are moving in too great a rush," said Doc.

Brucie darted ahead and ran looking into all the bushes, lifting up their branches and looking underneath.

"Not one of the Doyles has spoke a word," said Virgil.

"That's because they're not talkers," said Doc.

All day William Wallace kept diving to the bottom. Once he dived down and down into the dark water, where it was so still that nothing stirred, not even a fish, and so dark that it was no longer the muddy world of the upper river but the dark clear world of deepness, and he must have believed this was the deepest place in the whole Pearl River, and if she was not here she would not be anywhere. He was gone such a long time that the others stared hard at the surface of the water, through which the bubbles came from below. So far down and all alone, had he found Hazel? Had he suspected down there, like some secret, the real, the true trouble that Hazel had fallen into, about which words in a letter could not speak . . . how (who knew?) she had been filled to the brim with that elation that they all remembered, like their own secret, the elation that comes of great hopes and changes, sometimes simply of the harvest time, that comes with a little course of its own like a tune to run in the head, and there was nothing she could do about it—they knew—and so it had turned into this? It could be nothing but the old trouble that William Wallace was finding out, reaching and turning in the gloom of such depths.

"Look down yonder," said Grady softly to Brucie.

He pointed to the surface, where their reflections lay colorless and still side by side. He touched his brother gently as though to impress him.

"That's you and me," he said.

Brucie swayed precariously over the edge, and Grady caught him by the seat of his overalls. Brucie looked, but showed no recognition. Instead, he backed away, and seemed all at once unconcerned and spiritless, and pressed the nickel

William Wallace had given him into his palm, rubbing it into his skin. Grady's inflamed eyes rested on the brown water. Without warning he saw something . . . perhaps the image in the river seemed to be his father, the drowned man— with arms open, eyes open, mouth open. . . . Grady stared and blinked, again something wrinkled up his face.

And when William Wallace came up it was in an agony from submersion, which seemed an agony of the blood and of the very heart, so woeful he looked. He was staring and glaring around in astonishment, as if a long time had gone by, away from the pale world where the brown light of the sun and the river and the little party watching him trembled before his eyes.

"What did you bring up?" somebody called—was it Virgil?

One of his hands was holding fast to a little green ribbon of plant, root and all. He was surprised, and let it go.

It was afternoon. The trees spread softly, the clouds hung wet and tinted. A buzzard turned a few slow wheels in the sky, and drifted upwards. The dogs promenaded the banks.

"It's time we ate fish," said Virgil.

On a wide sandbar on which seashells lay they dragged up the haul and built a fire.

Then for a long time among clouds of odors and smoke, all half-naked except Doc, they cooked and ate catfish. They ate until the Malones groaned and all the Doyles stretched out on their faces, though for long after, Sam and Robbie Bell sat up to their own little table on a cypress stump and ate on and on. Then they all were silent and still, and one by one fell asleep.

"There ain't a thing better than fish," muttered William Wallace. He lay stretched on his back in the glimmer and shade of trampled sand. His sunburned forehead and cheeks seemed to glow with fire. His eyelids fell. The shadow of a willow branch dipped and moved over him. "There is nothing in the world as good as . . . fish. The fish of Pearl River." Then slowly he smiled. He was asleep.

But it seemed almost at once that he was leaping up, and one by one up sat the others in their ring and looked at him, for it was impossible to stop and sleep by the river.

"You're feeling as good as you felt last night," said Virgil, setting his head on one side.

"The excursion is the same when you go looking for your sorrow as when you go looking for your joy," said Doc.

But William Wallace answered none of them anything, for he was leaping all over the place and all, over them and the feast and the bones of the feast, trampling the sand, up and down, and doing a dance so crazy that he would die next. He took a big catfish and hooked it to his belt buckle and went up and down so that they all hollered, and the tears of laughter streaming down his cheeks made him put his hand up, and the two days' growth of beard began to jump out, bright red.

But all of a sudden there was an even louder cry, something almost like a cheer, from everybody at once, and all pointed fingers moved from William Wallace to the river. In the center of three light-gold rings across the water was lifted first an old hoary head ("It has whiskers!" a voice cried) and then in an undulation loop after loop and hump after hump of a long dark body, until there were a dozen rings of ripples, one behind the other, stretching all across the river, like a necklace.

"The King of the Snakes!" cried all the Malones at once, in high tenor voices and leaning together.

"The King of the Snakes," intoned old Doc in his profound bass.

"He looked you in the eye."

William Wallace stared back at the King of the Snakes with all his might.

It was Brucie that darted forward, dangling his little thread with the pin tied to it, going toward the water.

"That's the King of the Snakes!" cried Grady, who always looked after him.

Then the snake went down.

The little boy stopped with one leg in the air, spun around on the other, and sank to the ground.

"Git up," Grady whispered. "It was just the King of the Snakes. He went off whistling. Git up. It wasn't a thing but the King of the Snakes."

Brucie's green eyes opened, his tongue darted out, and he sprang up; his feet were heavy, his head light, and he rose like a bubble coming to the surface.

Then thunder like a stone loosened and rolled down the bank.

They all stood unwilling on the sandbar, holding to the net. In the eastern sky were the familiar castles and the round towers to which they were used, gray, pink, and blue, growing darker and filling with thunder. Lightning flickered in the sun along their thick walls. But in the west the sun shone with such a violence that in an illumination like a long-prolonged glare of lightning the heavens looked black and white; all color left the world, the goldenness of everything was like a memory, and only heat, a kind of glamor and oppression, lay on their heads. The thick heavy trees on the other side of the river were brushed with mile-long streaks of silver, and a wind touched each man on the forehead. At the same time there was a long roll of thunder that began behind them, came up and down mountains and valleys of air, passed over their heads, and left them listening still. With a small, near noise a mockingbird followed it, the little white bars of its body flashing over the willow trees.

"We are here for a storm now," Virgil said. "We will have to stay till it's over."

They retreated a little, and hard drops fell in the leathery leaves at their shoulders and about their heads.

"Magnolia's the loudest tree there is in a storm," said Doc.

Then the light changed the water, until all about them the woods in the rising wind seemed to grow taller and blow inward together and suddenly turn dark. The rain struck heavily. A huge tail seemed to lash through the air and the river broke in a wound of silver. In silence the party crouched and stooped beside the trunk of the great tree, which in the push of the storm rose full of a fragrance and unyielding weight. Where they all stared, past their tree, was another tree, and beyond that another and another, all the way down the bank of the river, all towering and darkened in the storm.

"The outside world is full of endurance," said Doc. "Full of endurance."

Robbie Bell and Sam squatted down low and embraced each other from the start.

"Runs in our family to get struck by lightnin'," said Robbie Bell. "Lightnin' drawed a pitchfork right on our grandpappy's cheek, stayed till he died. Pappy got struck by some bolts of lightnin' and was dead three days, dead as that-there axe."

There was a succession of glares and crashes.

"This'n's goin' to be either me or you," said Sam. "Here come a little bug. If he go to the left, be me, and to the right, be you."

But at the next flare a big tree on the hill seemed to turn into fire before their eyes, every branch, twig, and leaf, and a purple cloud hung over it.

"Did you hear that crack?" asked Robbie Bell. "That were its bones."

"Why do you little niggers talk so much!" said Doc. "Nobody's profiting by this information."

"We always talks this much," said Sam, "but now everybody so quiet, they hears us."

The great tree, split and on fire, fell roaring to earth. Just at its moment of falling, a tree like it on the opposite bank split wide open and fell in two parts.

"Hope they ain't goin' to be no balls of fire come rollin' over the water and fry all the fishes with they scales on," said Robbie Bell.

The water in the river had turned purple and was filled with sudden currents and whirlpools. The little willow trees bent almost to its surface, bowing one after another down the bank and almost breaking under the storm. A great curtain of wet leaves was borne along before a blast of wind, and every human being was covered.

"Now us got scales," wailed Sam. "Us is the fishes."

"Hush up, little-old colored children," said Virgil. "This isn't the way to act when somebody takes you out to drag a river."

"Poor lady's-ghost, I bet it is scareder than us," said Sam.

"All I hoping is, us don't find her!" screamed Robbie Bell.

William Wallace bent down and knocked their heads together. After that they clung silently in each other's arms, the two black heads resting, with wind-filled cheeks and tight-closed eyes, one upon the other until the storm was over.

"Right over yonder is Dover," said Virgil. "We've come all the way. William Wallace, you have walked on a sharp rock and cut your foot open."

III

In Dover it had rained, and the town looked somehow like new. The wavy heat of late afternoon came down from the watertank and fell over everything like shiny mosquito-netting. At the wide place where the road was paved and patched with tar, it seemed newly embedded with Coca-Cola tops. The old circus posters on the store were nearly gone, only bits, the snowflakes of white horses, clinging to its side. Morning-glory vines started almost visibly to grow over the roofs and cling round the ties of the railroad track, where bluejays lighted on the rails, and umbrella chinaberry trees hung heavily over the whole town, dripping intermittently upon the tin roofs.

Each with his counted fish on a string, the members of the river-dragging party walked through the town. They went toward the town well, and there was Hazel's mother's house, but no sign of her yet coming out. They all drank a dipper of the water, and still there was not a soul on the street. Even the bench in front of the store was empty, except for a little corn-shuck doll.

But something told them somebody had come, for after one moment people began to look out of the store and out of the post office. All the bird dogs woke up to see the Doyle dogs and such a large number of men and boys materialize suddenly with such a big catch of fish, and they ran out barking. The Doyle dogs joyously barked back. The blue-jays flashed up and screeched above the town, whipping through their tunnels in the chinaberry trees. In the café a nickel clattered inside a music box and a love song began to play. The whole town of Dover began to throb in its wood and tin, like an old tired heart, when the men walked through once more, coming around again and going down the street carrying the fish, so drenched, exhausted, and muddy that no one could help but admire them.

William Wallace walked through the town as though he did not see anybody or hear anything. Yet he carried his great string of fish held high where it could be seen by all. Virgil came next, imitating William Wallace exactly, then the modest Doyles crowded by the Malones, who were holding up their alligator, tossing it in the air, even, like a father tossing his child. Following behind and pointing authoritatively at the ones in front strolled Doc, with Sam and Robbie Bell still chanting in his wake. In and out of the whole little line Grady and Brucie jerked about. Grady, with his head ducked, and stiff as a rod, walked with a springy limp; it made him look forever angry and unapproachable. Under his breath he was whispering, "Sty, sty, git out of my eye, and git on somebody passin' by." He traveled on with narrowed shoulders, and kept his eye unerringly upon his little brother, wary and at the same time proud, as though he held a flying June-bug on a string. Brucie, making a twanging noise with his lips, had shot forth again, and he was darting rapidly everywhere at once, delighted and tantalized, running in circles around William Wallace, pointing to his fish. A frown of pleasure like the print of a bird's foot was stamped between his faint brows, and he trotted in some unknown realm of delight.

"Did you ever see so many fish?" said the people in Dover.

"How much are your fish, mister?"

"Would you sell your fish?"

"Is that all the fish in Pearl River?"

"How much you sell them all for? Everybody's?"

"Take 'em free," said William Wallace suddenly and loud. The Malones were upon him and shouting, but it was too late. "I don't want no more of 'em. I want my wife!" he yelled, just at the moment when Hazel's mother walked out of her front door.

"You can't head her mother off," said Virgil. "Here she comes in full bloom."

"What have you done with my child?" Hazel's mother shouted.

But William Wallace turned his back on her, that was all, and on everybody, for that matter, and that was the breaking-up of the party.

Just as the sun went down, Doc climbed his back steps, sat in his chair on the back porch where he sat in the evenings, and lighted his pipe. William Wallace hung out the net and came back and Virgil was waiting for him, so they could say good evening to Doc.

"All in all," said Doc, when they came up, "I've never been on a better river-dragging, or seen better behavior. If it took catching catfish to move the Rock of Gibraltar, I believe this outfit could move it."

"Well, we didn't catch Hazel," said Virgil.

"What did you say?" asked Doc.

"He don't really pay attention," said Virgil. "I said, 'We didn't catch Hazel.' "

"Who says Hazel was to be caught?" asked Doc. "She wasn't in there. Girls don't like the water—remember that. Girls don't just haul off and go jumping in the river to get back at their husbands. They got other ways."

"Didn't you ever think she was in there?" asked William Wallace. "The whole time?"

"Nary once," said Doc.

"He's just smart," said Virgil, putting his hand on William Wallace's arm. "It's only because we didn't find her that he wasn't looking for her."

"I'm beholden to you for the net, anyway," said William Wallace.

"You're welcome to borry it again," said Doc.

On the way home Virgil kept saying, "Calm down, calm down, William Wallace."

"If he wasn't such an old skinny man I'd have wrung his neck for him," said William Wallace. "He had no business coming."

"He's too big for his britches," said Virgil. "Don't nobody know everything. And just because it's his net. Why does it have to be his net?"

"If it wasn't for being polite to old men, I'd have skinned him alive," said William Wallace.

"I guess he don't really know nothing about wives at all, his wife's so deaf," said Virgil.

"He don't know Hazel," said William Wallace. "I'm the only man alive knows Hazel: would she jump in the river or not, and I say she would. She jumped in because I was sitting on the back of my neck in a ditch singing, and that's just what she ought to done. Doc ain't got no right to say one word about it."

"Calm down, calm down, William Wallace," said Virgil.

"If it had been you that talked like that, I'd have broke every bone in your body," said William Wallace. "Just let you talk like that. You're my age and size."

"But I ain't going to talk like that," said Virgil. "What have I done the whole time but keep this river-dragging going straight and running even, without no hitches? You couldn't have drug the river a foot without me."

"What are you talking about! Without who!" cried William Wallace. "This wasn't your river-dragging! It wasn't your wife!" He jumped on Virgil and they began to fight.

"Let me up." Virgil was breathing heavily.

"Say it was my wife. Say it was my river-dragging."

"Yours!" Virgil was on the ground with William Wallace's hand putting dirt in his mouth.

"Say it was my net."

"Your net!"

"Get up then."

They walked along getting their breath, and smelling the honeysuckle in the evening. On a hill William Wallace looked down, and at the same time there went drifting by the sweet sounds of music outdoors. They were having the Sacred Harp Sing on the grounds of an old white church glimmering there at the crossroads, far below. He stared away as if he saw it minutely, as if he could see a lady in white take a flowered cover off the organ, which was set on a little slant in the shade, dust the keys, and start to pump and play. . . . He smiled faintly, as he would at his mother, and at Hazel, and at the singing women in his life, now all one young girl standing up to sing under the trees the oldest and longest ballads there were.

Virgil told him good night and went into his own house and the door shut on him.

When he got to his own house, William Wallace saw to his surprise that it had not rained at all. But there, curved over the roof, was something he had never seen before as long as he could remember, a rainbow at night. In the light of the moon, which had risen again, it looked small and of gauzy material, like a lady's summer dress, a faint veil through which the stars showed.

He went up on the porch and in at the door, and all exhausted he had walked through the front room and through the kitchen when he heard his name called. After a moment, he smiled, as if no matter what he might have hoped for in his wildest heart, it was better than that to hear his name called out in the house. The voice came out of the bedroom.

"What do you want?" he yelled, standing stock-still.

Then she opened the bedroom door with the old complaining creak, and there she stood. She was not changed a bit.

"How do you feel?" he said.

"I feel pretty good. Not too good," Hazel said, looking mysterious.

"I cut my foot," said William Wallace, taking his shoe off so she could see the blood.

"How in the world did you do that?" she cried, with a step back.

"Dragging the river. But it don't hurt any longer."

"You ought to have been more careful," she said. "Supper's ready and I wondered if you would ever come home, or if it would be last night all over again. Go and make yourself fit to be seen," she said, and ran away from him.

After supper they sat on the front steps a while.

"Where were you this morning when I came in?" asked William Wallace when they were ready to go in the house.

"I was hiding," she said. "I was still writing on the letter. And then you tore it up."

"Did you watch me when I was reading it?"

"Yes, and you could have put out your hand and touched me. I was so close."

But he bit his lip, and gave her a little tap and slap, and then turned her up and spanked her.

"Do you think you will do it again?" he asked.

"I'll tell my mother on you for this!"

"Will you do it again?"

"No!" she cried.

"Then pick yourself up off my knee."

It was just as if he had chased her and captured her again. She lay smiling in the crook of his arm. It was the same as any other chase in the end.

"I will do it again if I get ready," she said. "Next time will be different, too."

Then she was ready to go in, and rose up and looked out from the top step, out across their yard where the China tree was and beyond, into the dark fields where the lightning-bugs flickered away. He climbed to his feet too and stood beside her, with the frown on his face, trying to look where she looked. And after a few minutes she took him by the hand and led him into the house, smiling as if she were smiling down on him.

EDITH WHARTON

(1862–1937)

EDITH WHARTON was born Edith Newbold Jones in New York City, to a socially prominent family. She was educated privately by governesses while the family divided its time between New York, Newport, Rhode Island, and Europe. In 1885 Edith married Edward Wharton, a native of Boston who was a friend of her brother's; but the marriage, as shaky as it was socially appropriate, ended in divorce in 1913, after Edith had made her home in France.

Her first published work was poetry; her mother arranged for private publication in 1878 of a collection, *Verses,* written while Edith was still in her teens. Other poems appeared subsequently in *Scribner's Magazine.* Her early stories appeared in three collections: *The Greater Inclination* (1899), *Crucial Instances* (1901), and *The Descent of Man* (1904). Her novels include *The House of Mirth* (1905), *Ethan Frome* (1911), *The Custom of the Country* (1913), and *The Age of Innocence,* for which she won the 1920 Pulitzer Prize. She was the author of essays and travel books, as well as an autobiography, *A Backward Glance* (1934). She became the first woman to receive the honorary degree of Doctor of Letters from Yale University and the Gold Medal of the National Institute of Arts and Letters. In 1915 the French government, in recognition of her relief work during World War I, awarded her the Cross of the Legion of Honor. Her long and distinguished literary career was paralleled by a rich social life; of the many notable figures she counted as friends, Henry James, also a key literary influence, was perhaps the closest. Others included Henry Adams, Bernard Berenson, and Theodore Roosevelt.

Her work is notable for its keen powers of social observation, particularly of the upper-class, convention-bound milieu in which she was raised. Her stories and novels depict the tension between the forces of social propriety and individual person's own needs.

In "Roman Fever," when Mrs. Ansley and Mrs. Slade, both middle-aged widows, reconvene in Rome—the locale of their youthful courtships—they summon up the past in a conversation driven by one-upmanship and braided with ironies. As the two women talk, the alloy emotions of love—such as envy—disclose themselves. Rome, where the past is as alive as the present, is a fitting setting for this story, which renders love as a fever that never breaks.

Roman Fever

I.

From the table at which they had been lunching two American ladies of ripe but well-cared-for middle age moved across the lofty terrace of the Roman restaurant and, leaning on its parapet, looked first at each other, and then down on the outspread glories of the Palatine and the Forum, with the same expression of vague but benevolent approval.

As they leaned there a girlish voice echoed up gaily from the stairs leading to the court below. "Well, come along, then," it cried, not to them but to an invisible companion, "and let's leave the young things to their knitting"; and a voice as fresh laughed back: "Oh, look here, Babs, not actually knitting—" "Well, I mean figuratively," rejoined the first. "After all, we haven't left our poor parents much else to do . . ." and at that point the turn of the stairs engulfed the dialogue.

The two ladies looked at each other again, this time with a tinge of smiling embarrassment, and the smaller and paler one shook her head and coloured slightly.

"Barbara!" she murmured, sending an unheard rebuke after the mocking voice in the stairway.

The other lady, who was fuller, and higher in colour, with a small determined nose supported by vigorous black eyebrows, gave a good-humoured laugh. "That's what our daughters think of us!"

Her companion replied by a deprecating gesture. "Not of us individually. We must remember that. It's just the collective modern idea of Mothers. And you see—" Half guiltily she drew from her handsomely mounted black hand-bag a twist of crimson silk run through by two fine knitting needles. "One never knows," she murmured. "The new system has certainly given us a good deal of time to kill; and sometimes I get tired just looking—even at this." Her gesture was now addressed to the stupendous scene at their feet.

The dark lady laughed again, and they both relapsed upon the view, contemplating it in silence, with a sort of diffused serenity which might have been borrowed from the spring effulgence of the Roman skies. The luncheon-hour was long past, and the two had their end of the vast terrace to themselves. At its opposite extremity a few groups, detained by a lingering look at the outspread city, were gathering up guide-books and fumbling for tips. The last of them scattered, and the two ladies were alone on the air-washed height.

"Well, I don't see why we shouldn't just stay here," said Mrs. Slade, the lady of the high colour and energetic brows. Two derelict basketchairs stood near, and she pushed them into the angle of the parapet, and settled herself in one, her gaze upon the Palatine. "After all, it's still the most beautiful view in the world."

"It always will be, to me," assented her friend Mrs. Ansley, with so slight a stress on the "me" that Mrs. Slade, though she noticed it, wondered if it were not merely accidental, like the random underlinings of old-fashioned letter-writers.

"Grace Ansley was always old-fashioned," she thought; and added aloud, with a retrospective smile: "It's a view we've both been familiar with for a good many years. When we first met here we were younger than our girls are now. You remember?"

"Oh, yes, I remember," murmured Mrs. Ansley, with the same undefinable stress.—"There's that head-waiter wondering," she interpolated. She was evidently far less sure than her companion of herself and of her rights in the world.

"I'll cure him of wondering," said Mrs. Slade, stretching her hand toward a bag as discreetly opulent-looking as Mrs. Ansley's. Signing to the head-waiter, she explained that she and her friend were old lovers of Rome, and would like to spend the end of the afternoon looking down on the view—that is, if it did not disturb the service? The head-waiter, bowing over her gratuity, assured her that the ladies were most welcome, and would be still more so if they would condescend to remain for dinner. A full moon night, they would remember . . .

Mrs. Slade's black brows drew together, as though references to the moon were out-of-place and even unwelcome. But she smiled away her frown as the head-waiter retreated. "Well, why not? We might do worse. There's no knowing, I suppose, when the girls will be back. Do you even know back from *where?* I don't!"

Mrs. Ansley again coloured slightly. "I think those young Italian aviators we met at the Embassy invited them to fly to Tarquinia for tea. I suppose they'll want to wait and fly back by moonlight."

"Moonlight—moonlight! What a part it still plays. Do you suppose they're as sentimental as we were?"

"I've come to the conclusion that I don't in the least know what they are," said Mrs. Ansley. "And perhaps we didn't know much more about each other."

"No; perhaps we didn't."

Her friend gave her a shy glance. "I never should have supposed you were sentimental, Alida."

"Well, perhaps I wasn't." Mrs. Slade drew her lids together in retrospect; and for a few moments the two ladies, who had been intimate since childhood, reflected how little they knew each other. Each one, of course, had a label ready to attach to the other's name; Mrs. Delphin Slade, for instance, would have told herself, or any one who asked her, that Mrs. Horace Ansley, twenty-five years ago, had been exquisitely lovely—no, you wouldn't believe it, would you? . . . though, of course, still charming, distinguished . . . Well, as a girl she had been exquisite; far more beautiful than her daughter Barbara, though certainly Babs, according to the new standards at any rate, was more effective—had more *edge*, as they say. Funny where she got it, with those two nullities as parents. Yes; Horace Ansley was—well, just the duplicate of his wife. Museum specimens of old New York. Good-looking, irreproachable, exemplary. Mrs. Slade and Mrs.

Ansley had lived opposite each other—actually as well as figuratively—for years. When the drawing-room curtains in No. 20 East 73rd Street were renewed, No. 23, across the way, was always aware of it. And of all the movings, buyings, travels, anniversaries, illnesses—the tame chronicle of an estimable pair. Little of it escaped Mrs. Slade. But she had grown bored with it by the time her husband made his big *coup* in Wall Street, and when they bought in upper Park Avenue had already begun to think: "I'd rather live opposite a speak-easy for a change; at least one might see it raided." The idea of seeing Grace raided was so amusing that (before the move) she launched it at a woman's lunch. It made a hit, and went the rounds—she sometimes wondered if it had crossed the street, and reached Mrs. Ansley. She hoped not, but didn't much mind. Those were the days when respectability was at a discount, and it did the irreproachable no harm to laugh at them a little.

A few years later, and not many months apart, both ladies lost their husbands. There was an appropriate exchange of wreaths and condolences, and a brief renewal of intimacy in the half-shadow of their mourning; and now, after another interval, they had run across each other in Rome, at the same hotel, each of them the modest appendage of a salient daughter. The similarity of their lot had again drawn them together, lending itself to mild jokes, and the mutual confession that, if in old days it must have been tiring to "keep up" with daughters, it was now, at times, a little dull not to.

No doubt, Mrs. Slade reflected, she felt her unemployment more than poor Grace ever would. It was a big drop from being the wife of Delphin Slade to being his widow. She had always regarded herself (with a certain conjugal pride) as his equal in social gifts, as contributing her full share to the making of the exceptional couple they were: but the difference after his death was irremediable. As the wife of the famous corporation lawyer, always with an international case or two on hand, every day brought its exciting and unexpected obligation: the impromptu entertaining of eminent colleagues from abroad, the hurried dashes on legal business to London, Paris or Rome, where the entertaining was so handsomely reciprocated; the amusement of hearing in her wake: "What, that handsome woman with the good clothes and the eyes is Mrs. Slade—*the* Slade's wife? Really? Generally the wives of celebrities are such frumps."

Yes; being *the* Slade's widow was a dullish business after that. In living up to such a husband all her faculties had been engaged; now she had only her daughter to live up to, for the son who seemed to have inherited his father's gifts had died suddenly in boyhood. She had fought through that agony because her husband was there, to be helped and to help; now, after the father's death, the thought of the boy had become unbearable. There was nothing left but to mother her daughter; and dear Jenny was such a perfect daughter that she needed no excessive mothering. "Now with Babs Ansley I don't know that I *should* be so quiet," Mrs. Slade sometimes half-enviously reflected; but Jenny, who was younger than her brilliant friend, was that rare accident, an extremely pretty girl who somehow made youth and prettiness seem as safe as their absence. It was all perplexing—and to Mrs. Slade a little boring. She wished that Jenny would fall in love—with the wrong man, even; that she might have to be watched, out-manoeuvred, rescued. And instead, it was Jenny who watched her mother, kept her out of draughts, made sure that she had taken her tonic . . .

Mrs. Ansley was much less articulate than her friend, and her mental portrait of Mrs. Slade was slighter, and drawn with fainter touches. "Alida Slade's awfully brilliant; but not as brilliant as she thinks," would have summed it up; though she would have added, for the enlightenment of strangers, that Mrs. Slade had been an extremely dashing girl; much more so than her daughter, who was pretty, of course, and clever in a way, but had none of her mother's—well, "vividness," some one had once called it. Mrs. Ansley would take up current words like this, and cite them in quotation marks, as unheard-of audacities. No; Jenny was not like her mother. Sometimes Mrs. Ansley thought Alida Slade was disappointed; on the whole she had had a sad life. Full of failures and mistakes; Mrs. Ansley had always been rather sorry for her . . .

So these two ladies visualized each other, each through the wrong end of her little telescope.

II.

For a long time they continued to sit side by side without speaking. It seemed as though, to both, there was a relief in laying down their somewhat futile activities in the presence of the vast Memento Mori which faced them. Mrs. Slade sat quite still, her eyes fixed on the golden slope of the Palace of the Caesars, and after a while Mrs. Ansley ceased to fidget with her bag, and she too sank into meditation. Like many intimate friends, the two ladies had never before had occasion to be silent together, and Mrs. Ansley was slightly embarrassed by what seemed, after so many years, a new stage in their intimacy, and one with which she did not yet know how to deal.

Suddenly the air was full of that deep clangour of bells which periodically covers Rome with a roof of silver. Mrs. Slade glanced at her wrist-watch. "Five o'clock already," she said, as though surprised.

Mrs. Ansley suggested interrogatively: "There's bridge at the Embassy at five." For a long time Mrs. Slade did not answer. She appeared to be lost in contemplation, and Mrs. Ansley thought the remark had escaped her. But after a while she said, as if speaking out of a dream: "Bridge, did you say? Not unless you want to . . . But I don't think I will, you know."

"Oh, no," Mrs. Ansley hastened to assure her. "I don't care to at all. It's so lovely here; and so full of old memories, as you say." She settled herself in her chair, and almost furtively drew forth her knitting. Mrs. Slade took sideway note of this activity, but her own beautifully cared-for hands remained motionless on her knee.

"I was just thinking," she said slowly, "what different things Rome stands for to

each generation of travellers. To our grandmothers, Roman fever; to our mothers,
sentimental dangers—how we used to be guarded!—to our daughters, no more
dangers than the middle of Main Street. They don't know it—but how much
they're missing!"

The long golden light was beginning to pale, and Mrs. Ansley lifted her knitting a little closer to her eyes. "Yes; how we were guarded!"

"I always used to think," Mrs. Slade continued, "that our mothers had a much
more difficult job than our grandmothers. When Roman fever stalked the streets
it must have been comparatively easy to gather in the girls at the danger hour; but
when you and I were young, with such beauty calling us, and the spice of disobe-
dience thrown in, and no worse risk than catching cold during the cool hour after
sunset, the mothers used to be put to it to keep us in—didn't they?"

She turned again toward Mrs. Ansley, but the latter had reached a delicate
point in her knitting. "One, two, three—slip two; yes, they must have been," she
assented, without looking up.

Mrs. Slade's eyes rested on her with a deepened attention. "She can knit—in
the face of *this!* How like her . . ."

Mrs. Slade leaned back, brooding, her eyes ranging from the ruins which
faced her to the long green hollow of the Forum, the fading glow of the church
fronts beyond it, and the outlying immensity of the Colosseum. Suddenly she
thought: "It's all very well to say that our girls have done away with sentiment and
moonlight. But if Babs Ansley isn't out to catch that young aviator—the one who's
a Marchese—then I don't know anything. And Jenny has no chance beside her.
I know that too. I wonder if that's why Grace Ansley likes the two girls to go
everywhere together? My poor Jenny as a foil—!" Mrs. Slade gave a hardly audible
laugh, and at the sound Mrs. Ansley dropped her knitting.

"Yes—?"

"I—oh, nothing. I was only thinking how your Babs carries everything before
her. That Campolieri boy is one of the best matches in Rome. Don't look so
innocent, my dear—you know he is. And I was wondering, ever so respectfully,
you understand . . . wondering how two such exemplary characters as you and
Horace had managed to produce anything quite so dynamic." Mrs. Slade laughed
again, with a touch of asperity.

Mrs. Ansley's hands lay inert across her needles. She looked straight out at the
great accumulated wreckage of passion and splendour at her feet. But her small
profile was almost expressionless. At length she said: "I think you overrate Babs,
my dear."

Mrs. Slade's tone grew easier. "No; I don't. I appreciate her. And perhaps
envy you. Oh, my girl's perfect; if I were a chronic invalid I'd—well, I think
I'd rather be in Jenny's hands. There must be times . . . but there! I always
wanted a brilliant daughter . . . and never quite understood why I got an angel
instead."

Mrs. Ansley echoed her laugh in a faint murmur. "Babs is an angel too."

"Of course—of course! But she's got rainbow wings. Well; they're wandering by the sea with their young men; and here we sit . . . and it all brings back the past a little too acutely."

Mrs. Ansley had resumed her knitting. One might almost have imagined (if one had known her less well, Mrs. Slade reflected) that, for her also, too many memories rose from the lengthening shadows of those august ruins. But no; she was simply absorbed in her work. What was there for her to worry about? She knew that Babs would almost certainly come back engaged to the extremely eligible Campolieri. "And she'll sell the New York house, and settle down near them in Rome, and never be in their way . . . she's much too tactful. But she'll have an excellent cook, and just the right people in for bridge and cocktails . . . and a perfectly peaceful old age among her grandchildren."

Mrs. Slade broke off this prophetic flight with a recoil of self-disgust. There was no one of whom she had less right to think unkindly than of Grace Ansley. Would she never cure herself of envying her? Perhaps she had begun too long ago.

She stood up and leaned against the parapet, filling her troubled eyes with the tranquillizing magic of the hour. But instead of tranquillizing her the sight seemed to increase her exasperation. Her gaze turned toward the Colosseum. Already its golden flank was drowned in purple shadow, and above it the sky curved crystal clear, without light or colour. It was the moment when afternoon and evening hang balanced in mid-heaven.

Mrs. Slade turned back and laid her hand on her friend's arm. The gesture was so abrupt that Mrs. Ansley looked up, startled.

"The sun's set. You're not afraid, my dear?"

"Afraid—"

"Of Roman fever or penumonia? I remember how ill you were that winter. As a girl you had a very delicate throat, hadn't you?"

"Oh, we're all right up here. Down below, in the Forum, it does get deathly cold, all of a sudden . . . but not here."

"Ah, of course you know because you had to be so careful." Mrs. Slade turned back to the parapet. She thought: "I must make one more effort not to hate her." Aloud she said: "Whenever I look at the Forum from up here, I remember that story about a great-aunt of yours, wasn't she? A dreadfully wicked great-aunt?"

"Oh, yes; Great-aunt Harriet. The one who was supposed to have sent her young sister out to the Forum after sunset to gather a night-blooming flower for her album. All our great-aunts and grand-mothers used to have albums of dried flowers."

Mrs. Slade nodded. "But she really sent her because they were in love with the same man—"

"Well, that was the family tradition. They said Aunt Harriet confessed it years afterward. At any rate, the poor little sister caught the fever and died. Mother used to frighten us with the story when we were children."

"And you frightened *me* with it, that winter when you and I were here as girls. The winter I was engaged to Delphin."

Mrs. Ansley gave a faint laugh. "Oh, did I? Really frightened you? I don't believe you're easily frightened."

"Not often; but I was then. I was easily frightened because I was too happy. I wonder if you know what that means?"

"I—yes . . ." Mrs. Ansley faltered.

"Well, I suppose that was why the story of your wicked aunt made such an impression on me. And I thought: 'There's no more Roman fever, but the Forum is deathly cold after sunset—especially after a hot day. And the Colosseum's even colder and damper.' "

"The Colosseum—?"

"Yes. It wasn't easy to get in, after the gates were locked for the night. Far from easy. Still, in those days it could be managed; it *was* managed, often. Lovers met there who couldn't meet elsewhere. You knew that?"

"I—I daresay. I don't remember."

"You don't remember? You don't remember going to visit some ruins or other one evening, just after dark, and catching a bad chill? You were supposed to have gone to see the moon rise. People always said that expedition was what caused your illness."

There was a moment's silence; then Mrs. Ansley rejoined: "Did they? It was all so long ago."

"Yes. And you got well again—so it didn't matter. But I suppose it struck your friends—the reason given for your illness, I mean—because everybody knew you were so prudent on account of your throat, and your mother took such care of you . . . You *had* been out late sight-seeing, hadn't you, that night?"

"Perhaps I had. The most prudent girls aren't always prudent. What made you think of it now?"

Mrs. Slade seemed to have no answer ready. But after a moment she broke out: "Because I simply can't bear it any longer—!"

Mrs. Ansley lifted her head quickly. Her eyes were wide and very pale. "Can't bear what?"

"Why—your not knowing that I've always known why you went."

"Why I went—?"

"Yes. You think I'm bluffing, don't you? Well, you went to meet the man I was engaged to—and I can repeat every word of the letter that took you there."

While Mrs. Slade spoke Mrs. Ansley had risen unsteadily to her feet. Her bag, her knitting and gloves, slid in a panic-stricken heap to the ground. She looked at Mrs. Slade as though she were looking at a ghost.

"No, no—don't," she faltered out.

"Why not? Listen, if you don't believe me. 'My one darling, things can't go on like this. I must see you alone. Come to the Colosseum immediately after dark tomorrow. There will be somebody to let you in. No one whom you need fear will suspect'—but perhaps you've forgotten what the letter said?"

Mrs. Ansley met the challenge with an unexpected composure. Steadying herself against the chair she looked at her friend, and replied: "No; I know it by heart too."

"And the signature? 'Only *your* D.S.' Was that it? I'm right, am I? That was the letter that took you out that evening after dark?"

Mrs. Ansley was still looking at her. It seemed to Mrs. Slade that a slow struggle was going on behind the voluntarily controlled mask of her small quiet face. "I shouldn't have thought she had herself so well in hand," Mrs. Slade reflected, almost resentfully. But at this moment Mrs. Ansley spoke. "I don't know how you knew. I burnt that letter at once."

"Yes; you would, naturally—you're so prudent!" The sneer was open now. "And if you burnt the letter you're wondering how on earth I know what was in it. That's it, isn't it?"

Mrs. Slade waited, but Mrs. Ansley did not speak.

"Well, my dear, I know what was in that letter because I wrote it!"

"You wrote it?"

"Yes."

The two women stood for a minute staring at each other in the last golden light. Then Mrs. Ansley dropped back into her chair. "Oh," she murmured, and covered her face with her hands.

Mrs. Slade waited nervously for another word or movement. None came, and at length she broke out: "I horrify you."

Mrs. Ansley's hands dropped to her knee. The face they uncovered was streaked with tears. "I wasn't thinking of you. I was thinking—it was the only letter I ever had from him!"

"And I wrote it. Yes; I wrote it! But I was the girl he was engaged to. Did you happen to remember that?"

Mrs. Ansley's head drooped again. "I'm not trying to excuse myself . . . I remembered . . ."

"And still you went?"

"Still I went."

Mrs. Slade stood looking down on the small bowed figure at her side. The flame of her wrath had already sunk, and she wondered why she had ever thought there would be any satisfaction in inflicting so purposeless a wound on her friend. But she had to justify herself.

"You do understand? I'd found out—and I hated you, hated you. I knew you were in love with Delphin—and I was afraid; afraid of you, of your quiet ways, your sweetness . . . your . . . well, I wanted you out of the way, that's all. Just for a few weeks; just till I was sure of him. So in a blind fury I wrote that letter . . . I don't know why I'm telling you now."

"I suppose," said Mrs. Ansley slowly, "it's because you've always gone on hating me."

"Perhaps. Or because I wanted to get the whole thing off my mind." She paused. "I'm glad you destroyed the letter. Of course I never thought you'd die."

Mrs. Ansley relapsed into silence, and Mrs. Slade, leaning above her, was conscious of a strange sense of isolation, of being cut off from the warm current of human communion. "You think me a monster!"

"I don't know . . . It was the only letter I had, and you say he didn't write it?"

"Ah, how you care for him still!"

"I cared for that memory," said Mrs. Ansley.

Mrs. Slade continued to look down on her. She seemed physically reduced by the blow—as if, when she got up, the wind might scatter her like a puff of dust. Mrs. Slade's jealousy suddenly leapt up again at the sight. All these years the woman had been living on that letter. How she must have loved him, to treasure the mere memory of its ashes! The letter of the man her friend was engaged to. Wasn't it she who was the monster?

"You tried your best to get him away from me, didn't you? But you failed; and I kept him. That's all."

"Yes. That's all."

"I wish now I hadn't told you. I'd no idea you'd feel about it as you do; I thought you'd be amused. It all happened so long ago, as you say; and you must do me the justice to remember that I had no reason to think you'd ever taken it seriously. How could I, when you were married•to Horace Ansley two months afterward? As soon as you could get out of bed your mother rushed you off to Florence and married you. People were rather surprised—they wondered at its being done so quickly; but I thought I knew. I had an idea you did it out of *pique*—to be able to say you'd got ahead of Delphin and me. Girls have such silly reasons for doing the most serious things. And your marrying so soon convinced me that you'd never really cared."

"Yes. I suppose it would," Mrs. Ansley assented.

The clear heaven overhead was emptied of all its gold. Dusk spread over it, abruptly darkening the Seven Hills. Here and there lights began to twinkle through the foliage at their feet. Steps were coming and going on the deserted terrace—waiters looking out of the doorway at the head of the stairs, then reappearing with trays and napkins and flasks of wine. Tables were moved, chairs straightened. A feeble string of electric lights flickered out. Some vases of faded flowers were carried away, and brought back replenished. A stout lady in a dustcoat suddenly appeared, asking in broken Italian if any one had seen the elastic band which held together her tattered Baedeker. She poked with her stick under the table at which she had lunched, the waiters assisting.

The corner where Mrs. Slade and Mrs. Ansley sat was still shadowy and deserted. For a long time neither of them spoke. At length Mrs. Slade began again: "I suppose I did it as a sort of joke—"

"A joke?"

"Well, girls are ferocious sometimes, you know. Girls in love especially. And I remember laughing to myself all that evening at the idea that you were waiting around there in the dark, dodging out of sight, listening for every sound, trying to get in—. Of course I was upset when I heard you were so ill afterward."

Mrs. Ansley had not moved for a long time. But now she turned slowly toward her companion. "But I didn't wait. He'd arranged everything. He was there. We were let in at once," she said.

Mrs. Slade sprang up from her leaning position. "Delphin there? They let you in?—Ah, now you're lying!" She burst out with violence.

Mrs. Ansley's voice grew clearer, and full of surprise. "But of course he was there. Naturally he came—"

"Came? How did he know he'd find you there? You must be raving!"

Mrs. Ansley hesitated, as though reflecting. "But I answered the letter. I told him. I'd be there. So he came."

Mrs. Slade flung her hands up to her face. "Oh, God—you answered! I never thought of your answering . . ."

"It's odd you never thought of it, if you wrote the letter."

"Yes. I was blind with rage."

Mrs. Ansley rose, and drew her fur scarf about her. "It is cold here. We'd better go . . . I'm sorry for you," she said, as she clasped the fur about her throat.

The unexpected words sent a pang through Mrs. Slade. "Yes; we'd better go." She gathered up her bag and cloak. "I don't know why you should be sorry for me," she muttered.

Mrs. Ansley stood looking away from her toward the dusky secret mass of the Colosseum. "Well—because I didn't have to wait that night."

Mrs. Slade gave an unquiet laugh. "Yes; I was beaten there. But I oughtn't to begrudge it to you, I suppose. At the end of all these years. After all, I had everything; I had him for twenty-five years. And you had nothing but that one letter that he didn't write."

Mrs. Ansley was again silent. At length she turned toward the door of the terrace. She took a step, and turned back, facing her companion.

"I had Barbara," she said, and began to move ahead of Mrs. Slade toward the stairway.

Epilogue
JAMES JOYCE
(1882–1941)

JAMES JOYCE was born in Dublin; he was the oldest of ten children. He was educated at Jesuit schools, and at University College in Dublin. In 1902, after receiving his degree from the Royal University, he left Dublin for Paris. On the death of his mother in 1904, he returned briefly to Ireland, where he met Nora Barnacle, whom he eventually married and with whom he was to spend the rest of his life. They had a son and a daughter. The couple lived for some years in Trieste, then Zurich, settling after World War I in Paris. *Chamber Music* (1907), a book of verse, was his first published work, followed by his collection of stories, *Dubliners*, in 1914. *Dubliners'* publication was beset with difficulties and delays, having to do with publishers' fears of prosecution on grounds of the stories' possible violation of obscenity and libel laws; such difficulties, in fact, attended the publication of virtually all of Joyce's work. An appreciative review of *Dubliners* by Ezra Pound provided his career with a needed boost. The friendships of Pound, William Butler Yeats, and others were ongoing sources of support. *A Portrait of the Artist as a Young Man* appeared first in serial form; its book publication took place in 1916. The publication of *Ulysses,* which Joyce worked on from 1914 to 1921, also encountered opposition; as a result, sections from the book appeared first in periodicals. In 1922 Sylvia Beach, the American owner of the Paris bookstore Shakespeare & Co., published it in book form. The ban on the novel's American publication, based on its supposed defiance of obscenity laws, was not lifted until 1933. *Finnegans Wake,* Joyce's last work, appeared in 1939.

An indisputable genius who knew some eighteen languages, including Greek and Sanskrit, Joyce was perhaps the century's most prodigious literary innovator. One of his revolutionary contributions was stream-of-consciousness or interior monologue, in which the characters' (or narrator's) minds track associatively, rather than in rational or logically governed sequence. This technique—allusive, idiosyncratic, filled with puns, coinages, and other wordplay—was employed with increasing intricacy, even to the point of obscurity, in *Portrait of the Artist, Ulysses,* and *Finnegans Wake.*

Ulysses, which the Molly Bloom soliloquy concludes, reproduces a day—June 16, 1904, the date of Joyce's first walk with Nora—in the life of advertising-space salesman Leopold Bloom. Bloom's Dublin wanderings recapitulate episodes of Homer's *Odyssey,* with each chapter, among other things, paralleling one of Odysseus's adventures. Bloom, like his Homeric counterpart, at last is drawn home. Home is Molly's mind and consciousness, her equally expansive bed, her feminine essence.

From the Molly Bloom Soliloquy, Ulysses

. . . the sun shines for you he said the day we were lying among the rhododen-
drons on Howth head in the grey tweed suit and his straw hat the day I got him
to propose to me yes first I gave him the bit of seedcake out of my mouth and it
was leapyear like now yes 16 years ago my God after that long kiss I near lost my
breath yes he said I was a flower of the mountain yes so we are flowers all a
womans body yes that was one true thing he said in his life and the sun shines
for you today yes that was why I liked him because I saw he understood or felt
what a woman is and I knew I could always get round him and I gave him all the
pleasure I could leading him on till he asked me to say yes and I wouldnt answer
first only looked out over the sea and the sky I was thinking of so many things he
didnt know of Mulvey and Mr Stanhope and Hester and father and old captain
Groves and the sailors playing all birds fly and I say stoop and washing up dishes
they called it on the pier and the sentry in front of the governors house with the
thing round his white helmet poor devil half roasted and the Spanish girls laughing in their shawls and their tall combs and the auctions in the morning the
Greeks and the jews and the Arabs and the devil knows who else from all the ends
of Europe and Duke street and the fowl market all clucking outside Larby Sharons
and the poor donkeys slipping half asleep and the vague fellows in the cloaks
asleep in the shade on the steps and the big wheels of the carts of the bulls and
the old castle thousands of years old yes and those handsome Moors all in white
and turbans like kings asking you to sit down in their little bit of a shop and
Ronda with the old windows of the posadas 2 glancing eyes a lattice hid for her
lover to kiss the iron and the wineshops half open at night and the castanets and
the night we missed the boat at Algeciras the watchman going about serene with
his lamp and O that awful deepdown torrent O and the sea the sea crimson
sometimes like fire and the glorious sunsets and the figtrees in the Alameda gardens yes and all the queer little streets and the pink and blue and yellow houses
and the rosegardens and the jessamine and geraniums and cactuses and Gibraltar
as a girl where I was a Flower of the mountain yes when I put the rose in my
hair like the Andalusian girls used or shall I wear a red yes and how he kissed me
under the Moorish wall and I thought well as well him as another and then I
asked him with my eyes to ask again yes and then he asked me would I yes to say
yes my mountain flower and first I put my arms around him yes and drew him
down to me so he could feel my breasts all perfume yes and his heart was going
like mad and yes I said yes I will Yes.

Acknowledgments

I AM GRATEFUL TO CLIFTON FADIMAN, who invited this book into Book-of-the-Month Club's *World Treasury* series, and whose uncommon literary knowledge was a wonderful resource and inspiration. Al Silverman and Maron Waxman were important early advocates of the project. I am more appreciative than I can say of Alice Van Straalen's efforts on the book's behalf. My heartfelt thanks to Linda Morse and Susan Hannan of Oxford University Press for their kind and professional support. Leslie Pockell helped see the book through its final stages. Margaret Gorenstein's assistance was indispensable. Anna P. Wiese, Gita Enders, and Dalia Sofer were exemplary research assistants. Wendy Weil, with the able assistance of Claire Needell has, as always, my gratitude. Larry Shapiro, Josephine Hendin, David Willis McCullough, Francine Klagsbrun, Louis S. Peterson, and Vinni Marie D'Ambrosio offered the kind of help that only wise friends can. I will always be grateful to the late Professor Robert F. Haugh of the University of Michigan.

Grateful acknowledgment is made to the following for permission to reprint copyrighted material:

Alice Adams: "Sintra" from *Return Trips* by Alice Adams. Copyright © 1984 by Alice Adams. Reprinted by permission of Alfred A. Knopf, Inc. and International Creative Management, Inc.

Book of Ruth: From *The New English Bible*. Copyright © The Delegates of the Oxford University Press and The Syndics of the Cambridge University Press, 1961, 1970. Reprinted by permission.

Italo Calvino: "The Adventure of a Soldier" from *Difficult Loves* by Italo Calvino, translated by William Weaver. Copyright 1949 by Giulio Einaudi editore, Torino; copyright © 1958 by Giulio Einaudi editore, s.p.a., Torino; English translation copyright © 1984 by Harcourt Brace Jovanovich, Inc. Reprinted by permission of Harcourt Brace Jovanovich, Inc., Wylie Aitken & Stone, Inc., and Martin Secker and Warburg Ltd.

Raymond Carver: "Fever" from *Cathedral* by Raymond Carver. Copyright © 1983 by Tess Gallagher. Reprinted by permission of Alfred A. Knopf, Inc. and Tess Gallagher via International Creative Management, Inc.

John Cheever: "The Country Husband" from *The Stories of John Cheever* by John Cheever. Copyright © 1954 by John Cheever. Reprinted by permission of Alfred A. Knopf, Inc. and Wylie Aitken & Stone, Inc.

Acknowledgments

Nadine Gordimer: "A Find" from *Jump and Other Stories* by Nadine Gordimer. Copyright © 1991 by Felix Licensing, B.V. Reprinted by permission of the publishers Farrar, Straus and Giroux, Inc., Penguin Books Canada Ltd., and Bloomsbury Publishing Ltd., London.

Yasunari Kawabata: "The Moon on the Water" by Yasunari Kawabata, translated by George Saito, from *Modern Japanese Stories: An Anthology*, edited by Ivan Morris. Copyright © 1962 by Charles E. Tuttle Co., Inc. Used by permission of Charles E. Tuttle Co., Inc. All rights reserved.

Heinrich von Kleist: "The Marquise of O" from *The Marquise of O and Other Stories* by Heinrich von Kleist, translated by Martin Greenberg. Introductions and English translation of the stories copyright © 1960 by Martin Greenberg. Reprinted by permission of HarperCollins Publishers Inc.

Milan Kundera: "The Hitchhiking Game" from *Laughable Loves* by Milan Kundera, translated by S. Rappaport. Copyright © 1974 by Alfred A. Knopf, Inc. Reprinted by permission of Alfred A. Knopf, Inc. and John Murray (Publishers) Ltd.

D. H. Lawrence: "The Horse Dealer's Daughter" by D. H. Lawrence from *Complete Short Stories of D. H. Lawrence*. Copyright 1922 by Thomas B. Seltzer, Inc., renewed 1950 by Frieda Lawrence. Used by permission of Viking Penguin, a division of Penguin Books USA Inc.

David Leavitt: "Territory" from *Family Dancing* by David Leavitt. Copyright © 1983, 1984 by David Leavitt. Originally published in *The New Yorker* in slightly different form. Reprinted by permission of Alfred A. Knopf, Inc. and Wylie Aitken & Stone, Inc.

Doris Lessing: "One off the Short List" from *A Man and Two Women* by Doris Lessing. Copyright © 1963 Doris Lessing. Reprinted by permission of Jonathan Clowes Ltd., London, on behalf of Doris Lessing.

Yukio Mishima: "Patriotism" from *Death in Midsummer and Other Stories* by Yukio Mishima, translated by Geoffrey W. Sargent. Copyright © 1966 by New Directions Publishing Corporation. Published in the United Kingdom by Martin Secker & Warburg, Ltd. Reprinted by permission of New Directions Publishing Corp. and Laurence Pollinger Limited.

Vladimir Nabokov: "First Love" from *Nabokov's Dozen* by Vladimir Nabokov. Copyright © 1958 by Vladimir Nabokov. Originally published in *The New Yorker*. Reprinted by permission of Vintage Books, a division of Random House, Inc.

John O'Hara: *Imagine Kissing Pete* by John O'Hara from *The Collected Stories of John O'Hara* edited with an introduction by Frank MacShane. Copyright © 1984 by Frank MacShane. Reprinted by permission of Random House, Inc.

Katherine Anne Porter: "Rope" from *Flowering Judas and Other Stories* by Katherine Anne Porter. Copyright 1930 and renewed 1958 by Katherine Anne Porter. Reprinted by permission of the publishers Harcourt Brace Jovanovich, Inc. and Jonathan Cape Ltd. on behalf of the author's Estate.

V. S. Pritchett: "Blind Love" from *Collected Stories* by V. S. Pritchett. Copyright © 1969 by V. S. Pritchett. Reprinted by permission of Random House, Inc. and the Peters Fraser & Dunlop Group Ltd.

Isaac Bashevis Singer: "Short Friday" from *Short Friday* by Isaac Bashevis Singer, translated by Joseph Singer and Roger Klein. Copyright © 1964 by Isaac Bashevis Singer. Copyright renewed 1992 by Alma Singer. Reprinted by permission of Farrar, Straus & Giroux, Inc.

William Trevor: "Lovers of Their Time" from *Lovers of Their Time* by William Trevor. Copyright © 1978 by William Trevor. Reprinted by permission of Viking Penguin, a division of Penguin Books USA Inc. and Peters Fraser & Dunlop Group Ltd.

John Updike: "Separating" from *Problems and Other Stories* by John Updike. Copyright © 1957 by John Updike. Reprinted by permission of Alfred A. Knopf, Inc. and Hamish Hamilton Ltd.

Jean Valentine: Lines from the poem "The Summer Was Not Long Enough" by Jean Valentine. Originally published in *The New Yorker* and later in *The River at Wolf* by Jean Valentine, published by Alicejamesbooks, 1992. Reprinted by permission of the author.

Giovanni Verga: "The Wolf" by Giovanni Verga, translated by Alfred Alexander, from *Stories of Sicily* edited by Alfred Alexander. Originally published by Paul Elek. Reprinted by permission of Grafton Books, an imprint of HarperCollins Publishers Limited.

Alice Walker: "To Hell with Dying" from *In Love & Trouble: Stories of Black Women* by Alice Walker. Copyright © 1967 by Alice Walker. Published in the United Kingdom by The Women's Press. Reprinted by permission of Harcourt Brace & Company and David Higham Associates Limited.

Eudora Welty: "The Wide Net" from *The Wide Net and Other Stories* by Eudora Welty. Copyright 1942 and renewed 1970 by Eudora Welty. Reprinted by permission of Harcourt Brace Jovanovich, Inc. and Russell and Volkening, Inc. as agent for the author.

Edith Wharton: "Roman Fever" from *Roman Fever and Other Stories* by Edith Wharton. Copyright 1934 Liberty Magazine, renewed © 1962 by William R. Tyler. Reprinted with the permission of Charles Scribner's Sons, an imprint of Macmillan Publishing Company.

Epilogue, from "The Molly Bloom Soliloquy" from *Ulysses* by James Joyce. Copyright 1934 and renewed 1962 by Lucia and George Joyce. Reprinted by permission of Random House, Inc.

Index